Evaluation in Education

CURRENT APPLICATIONS

Edited by

W. James Popham

University of California,
Los Angeles

McCutchan Publishing Corporation
2526 Grove Street
Berkeley, California 94704

This work was developed under a grant from the U.S. Office of Education,
Department of Health, Education, and Welfare. However, the opinions
and other content do not necessarily reflect the position or policy of the
Agency, and no official endorsement should be inferred.

Introduction

Exciting may be too strong a term to characterize the field of education these days, but perhaps not. For a variety of reasons, such as legislative mandates, public dissatisfaction with schools, and the influence of responsible educators, we find that educational evaluations are being carried out not only with increasing frequency, but also with increasing excellence. Many first-rate scholars are turning their attention to the study of educational evaluation as a field of disciplined inquiry. Many able people are choosing educational evaluation as their area of professional specialization. Many books and articles specifically addressed to the topic of educational evaluation are now being published. Many people, including legislators, lay citizens, and all sorts of educators, are beginning to believe that the conscientious application of evaluative procedures will actually enhance the quality of American schooling. And all of this sometimes furious activity has taken place in less than a decade. No, perhaps it is not too lavish to depict the current status of educational evaluation as being genuinely exciting.

Consistent with a mood of excitement, this book contains nine thought-provoking chapters, each written by an individual who has specialized in a theoretical or technical field impinging on the work

of today's educational evaluator. An examination of the table of contents will reveal a set of high-import topics that might indeed constitute a liturgical litany for any evaluator inclined to chant morning or evening prayers. For example, what respectable itemization of significant evaluation concerns would be without such ingredients as sampling, data-gathering designs, measurement, data analysis, and costs? Because each of the chapters was written by a recognized scholar on the topic under consideration, the reader will benefit from the perspectives of authors truly at the leading edges of their specializations.

Some of the ideas presented in the following pages are literally brand new, having been designed especially for inclusion in this volume. For those who have followed the writings of such well-known evaluation theorists as Scriven and Stufflebeam, their chapters will provide some refreshing insights and some intriguing theoretical modifications in their approaches to evaluation. The chapter by Sax on the role of norm-referenced measures in educational evaluation is in sharp contrast to the chapter by Millman, which deals with the more recent criterion-referenced approaches to measurement. These two measurement chapters, as well as a number of other chapters, make it clear that no effort was made to present a single one-party line in the volume. The attentive reader will note more than one disagreement among the contributors.

Sirotnik's chapter on matrix sampling represents one of the first attempts to provide evaluators with a readable account of this important sampling technique. Baker's chapter on formative evaluation procedures synthesizes her considerable experience in ameliorating sickly instructional sequences. Airasian's chapter on data-gathering models covers a range of technical and interpersonal factors to be considered by those who must plan evaluation studies. And, after the data gathering, Wolf's chapter on data analysis and reporting offers sound advice regarding how to treat and report such information. One of the volume's several unique contributions is the chapter on costing procedures in which Haller examines a number of heretofore overlooked techniques to help evaluators approach the important task of cost determination with more sophistication.

Several of the chapters are replete with well-specified objectives, plus practice exercises to help the reader accomplish those objectives. In general, the writers were responsive to a directive that they make their chapters *training* vehicles rather than discursive essays. While

surely not exhaustive, for other topics might have been included, the nine chapters comprising this volume represent a set of required readings for those who would keep abreast of developments in the field of educational evaluation.

Books such as this do not spring forth from the publisher's presses without a history, sometimes an interesting history. Because the background of a volume featuring multiple contributors can often help the reader understand the book's sometimes differing viewpoints, a brief account will be provided of how the volume came into existence.

The group that initiated the project was the Standing Committee on Research Training of the American Educational Research Association (AERA). In the spring of 1973 that committee was in the midst of supervising a research training investigation under provisions of a contract with the National Institute of Education. One phase of the project called for the creation of instructional materials suitable for the training of educational research personnel. The committee agreed that there was an urgent need for training materials in the field of educational evaluation, both for individuals just beginning their preparation as educational evaluators as well as for those who had been pressed into service as evaluators, perhaps without sufficient training. Accordingly, it was concluded that a series of instructional monographs that would deal with important skills needed by evaluators should be assembled. These booklets, it was hoped, would be made available both as a single complete volume and as separate booklets, thereby increasing the flexibility with which they could be used in diverse instructional settings.

The time line was short. The contract was drawing to a close in six months. The committee had to identify appropriate topics and high-quality contributors, then persuade the contributors to produce an original manuscript containing at last seventy-five double-spaced, typed pages in a four-month period. The committee came up with a list of names plus topics, then directed the committee chairman (the editor) to contact the potential contributors. Of the twelve writers contacted, ten agreed to take on the rather substantial writing task. Two others had prior commitments that precluded acceptance of the committee's invitation.

With some initial guidance from the committee chairman regarding topic limits, the desired instructional focus, and permissible

ingredients (such as practice exercises), the contributors undertook their assignments. All essays were transmitted to the chairman who supplied an initial editorial review. The manuscripts received were judged to be excellent. Some were returned with suggestions for modification, but most were considered basically acceptable as they arrived. One contributor was unable to complete the writing task on schedule, leaving the nine chapters contained herein.

In an effort to obtain additional reactions to the chapters, external reviews were solicited, most of which proved quite helpful to the contributors. Meanwhile, because of the apparent timeliness of the materials, it was decided to release them as soon as possible through a commercial publisher according to the shared-royalty copyright arrangements of the National Institute of Education. This decision interrupted the completion of the AERA Publication Committee's normal procedures for reviewing such publications, so no official AERA endorsement of this volume should be inferred.

A formal request for proposals to publish the materials had been issued by AERA to interested publishers. The proposal of the McCutchan Publishing Corporation was judged to be the best of those submitted, and that firm was awarded the contract to publish the book in both single-copy form and as separate booklets.

All royalties emerging from sale of the book will be divided equally between AERA (to be used for additional training activities) and the federal government, the original sponsoring agency. The chapter contributors, having received honoraria as a consequence of the original training contract, receive no royalties; nor does the editor.

McCutchan Publishing Corporation and its president, John McCutchan, are to be commended on several counts. First, in order to increase the potential utility of these materials they agreed to produce these training materials in two forms, both as separates and as a single volume when, frankly, it would have been commercially advantageous to bring out only one bound volume. Second, the McCutchan editor assigned to this project, M. Rita Howe, worked with amazing alacrity and excellent editorial insight. Her stylistic criticisms and coordination of the chapters strenthened the book immeasurably. Finally, McCutchan has moved the book from receipt of manuscripts to published volume in only five months, a nontrivial publishing feat by anyone's standards. This constituted a particularly important accomplishment since the field of educational evaluation is so badly

in need of instructional materials such as those contained in the following pages.

The editor is indebted to Dr. William C. Russell, Executive Officer of AERA, who deftly coordinated the administrative and financial aspects of the project from the Association's central office. Most importantly, of course, the nine writers whose chapters constitute the volume are due special credit for getting out their chapters—on time and on target.

W. James Popham
Los Angeles, California
July 1974

Contents

Figures

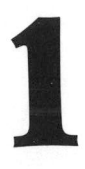

Evaluation Perspectives and Procedures

Michael Scriven
University of California, Berkeley

Evaluation Perspectives
and Procedures

Michael Scriven

QUALITATIVE AND QUANTITATIVE RESEARCH
AND EVALUATION

Many evaluations, but not all of them, involve a quantitative component, in which statistical or data-reduction skills and conceptualizations are central. But in all evaluations another component takes precedence over the quantitative: namely, concern for the general features of the evaluation design and the broad justification of the framework, which might require much detailed quantitative fine structuring. Often there is important interaction between the two. Training in statistics and measurement covers many design considerations I consider to be qualitative, but it is notably deficient when the time comes to incorporate value elements. Nobody reading the usual experimental method texts would learn what a needs assessment is or when it has to be done, what the relative utility and evidence requirements are for comparative evaluations in contrast with "absolute" ones (of the kind Lee Cronbach prefers), or how to handle considerations about the justice of certain classroom procedures. Nor are these axiological considerations all that qualitative evaluation is concerned with; evaluation is unlike typical research in the extent to which the designs have to take account of role and threat problems, in the extent to which credibility is an additional concern beyond reliability, and in the extent to which audiences (in Bob Stake's sense) control

the format of reports, to give but three examples. The following studies, then, are studies in the area of qualitative evaluation.

Evaluation is emerging as a discipline in its own right, and, as we look back on the very earliest attempts to grapple with or eliminate the distinction between evaluation and research or between "straight" research and evaluation research, we realize that we have come a long way toward understanding evaluation. The distinction is not simply, mainly, or always one of generalizability, policy implications, or decision servicing. These factors permeate and affect some of the methods of evaluation research, but the basic distinction seems to be that evaluation research must produce as a conclusion exactly the kind of statement that social scientists have for years been taught is illegitimate: a judgment of value, worth, or merit. That is the great scientific and philosophical significance of evaluation research.

It may well be that the emergence of evaluation as a discipline will ultimately have its greatest specific impact on one of its parents, educational psychology. I like the idea that, for example, Ph.D. proposals should be evaluated in the full sense and not just technically. Serious efforts should be made to weigh their potential contributions to knowledge and society before there is a huge commitment of effort and resources, and I think this could best be done before an audience of faculty and students. To the average academic, that smacks of political control of scientific research. Once I would have had the same reaction. Now I think that it is the failure to do what I am suggesting that leads to political control. Continued neglect of the social implications of research leads to backlash, as it did in the Jensen-Shockley case, and it is a powerful factor in the left-wing take-overs of universities such as the University of Berlin. In turn, excesses of the totally political approach to research produce the Lysenkoist kind of absurdity and the counterrevolutionary take-overs that occur in South America. The only escape from this pendulum-swinging sequence of excesses appears to lie in a reasonable incorporation of the valid arguments of both sides into a standard procedure wherein research proposals are evaluated in terms of probable costs and benefits (for example, social consequences, use of scarce resources) rather than their technical validity. I am not suggesting that "pure" research is never justified in this larger evaluation framework; I think almost all research in pure mathematics could be justified on social payoff

grounds alone. Good evaluation looks at the record of results rather than at the motivation of the researcher. Nor am I suggesting an evaluation scheme that includes *only* social payoff (at least in the usual crude sense). Knowledge and understanding are legitimate values.

Research, whether proposed or completed, ought to be evaluated for what it is: not an ivory tower five-finger exercise, but a private and public expenditure with high opportunity costs and often high direct costs as well. Present practices seem irresponsible to me. Whether or not this procedure would defuse radical criticisms of academic amorality if a strong case could be made for it in its own right and if no better alternative is suggested, it might well be given serious trial in some departments just to gather experience for better assessment.

Such a suggestion only identifies one of many possible ways in which evaluation might come to affect traditional research, and there would probably be little consensus concerning it among evaluators at this point. It is, however, scarcely idle speculation in view of the stakes and present trends. At the moment we are struggling with related problems in the area of "informed consent," which is interpreted as requiring description of possible effects on the reputation of subjects' groups. This is one of the moves toward (or beyond) social responsibility in the area of research, and it reflects a concern present in the qualitative evaluation of any experiment. It is easy to see that this goes beyond the quantitative element and the quantitative tradition in evaluation. Whether it goes too far can only be answered by systematic investigation and consideration of alternatives. Academic research interests have had as little practice in this area as they have in the evaluation of teaching, and they very quickly reveal their incompetence in either area when a discussion starts. Thus I believe that concern with and training in evaluation, in the broad sense used here, has considerable significance even for the "pure" researcher and certainly for those with a heavy commitment to social utility, such as educational psychologists.

As for the kind of training that is required, it is reasonable to suppose that in this work the more elementary issues of design are unnecessary. And constraints of length mean that only a fraction of the remaining topics can be covered. I have chosen to concentrate on areas involving something relatively novel, often somewhat controversial, thinking along Ausubel's lines that the best way to produce

sharp improvements in cognitive skills in a short time usually involves destruction of roadblocks (rigidities) rather than the laying of new roadbed. I have used dialogue format on occasion and included one background article with criticisms by others to introduce a new discussion. I have, regretfully, excluded discussion of half the topics that appeared on my first list of possibilities.

CHECKLIST FOR THE EVALUATION OF PRODUCTS, PRODUCERS, AND PROPOSALS

The following checklist can be used to evaluate almost any product to which the language refers. In the educational field, it can be used as an instrument for evaluating *products* and as an instrument for evaluating *producers* in the payoff dimension without considering such matters as personnel policy, community impacts, potentiality, and so forth. It can also be used as an instrument for weighing *evaluation proposals* focused on products or producers, as an instrument for evaluating production proposals (since a competent producer should incorporate plans for achieving each of these standards and for establishing that these standards have been achieved), and as an instrument for evaluating *evaluators* of products, producers, and so forth since it is argued that competent evaluation must cover each of these points. The checklist, if sound, thus provides an extremely versatile instrument for determining the quality of all kinds of educational activities and products, the more so because the concept of "product," as here used, is very broad, covering processes and institutions as well as technical devices.

This covers applicability in theory, but what about applicability in practice? Few educational products have ever been produced that met all these standards prior to production, although that is exactly when they should be met in order to justify production. (The early programmed texts put out by the *Encyclopaedia Britannica* and the later Sullivan ones published by Behavioral Research Labs would probably have scored well.) Few educational products have met enough of the standards to justify even retrospective confidence in the merit of the product, but enough have—the better correspondence courses in technical subjects, for example—to make clear that the standards are not unrealistic. To justify producing a new course, now, in such areas, is naturally harder since it has to outperform existing ones by a margin that would justify its marginal cost.

Satisfactory achievement of all of these standards is not, of course, the only criterion for funding a project. Exploratory, research, or realistic field trial projects are defensible, even when there is little chance of meeting all of the standards, but they should be seen as no more than temporary projects, funded as such, and moved into the production phase when all standards, or enough of them to make a

very convincing case, are met. The application of this hard line would not only greatly reduce the costs of educational research and development (R&D) activity, which should only be a short-term effect, but it would transform the conception of satisfactory performance in education. The long-term positive results of such an altered conception would be far more significant and beneficial than dropping a few substandard projects now.

Since use of this checklist can be extremely lethal, potential users should know something about its validity and utility. First, and most significantly, every checkpoint on the checklist has a clear a priori rationale, in most cases so obvious that elaboration would be otiose. That is, a straightforward argument can be constructed that failure to meet any one of the checkpoints immediately leaves open a serious doubt that the product is simply not of good quality. Second, medical and industrial products—your car, your aspirin, your food—routinely pass, and are often required to pass, every checkpoint. Despite the real problems of still-emerging undesirable side effects that beset all of them, they at least avoid the far worse results that would be likely to arise if the checkpoints on this list were not met. I can see no way to argue that the effects of bad education are less significant than the effects of bad food, drugs, and cars. Third, the checklist has been developed out of the most intensive systematic and large-scale product evaluation activities with which I am familiar—the Product Review Panels of 1971-72 and 1972-73 done for the National Center for Educational Communication, on subcontract to the Educational Testing Service. Fifteen experienced evaluators and educators worked to provide the raw material in the detailed assessment procedures from which I extracted the first eight versions of this checklist. It has been further refined as a result of interaction with other groups, notably the Educational Products Information Exchange (EPIE) in New York City (Item 13 was suggested by Ken Komoski), and my assistants Michael Barger and Howard Levine.

Fourth, the checklist has also been reviewed, at my request, by some of the most experienced developers in the country. Their reaction has not been impressive. The general criticism has been to claim excessive perfectionism, which is possible indeed, but the support for the claim has been extremely weak. It consists either of saying that nothing has ever been produced anywhere that met these standards (counterexamples have been given above), that the cost of meeting

them would be prohibitive, or that they may be appropriate for summative but certainly not for formative evaluation. I have examined the cost complaint very carefully, and it is not generally true. For example, the Center for the Study of Evaluation (CSE) handbooks of all tests available for secondary students, products which rated well with the Product Review Panels, can be evaluated rather easily and inexpensively in order to meet the standards. (As presented, too much guessing was required.) The cost is going to be large when we start looking at huge curriculum projects, which reflects not only the huge costs of development but also the great difficulty in justifying such projects. Where raw gains are likely to be marginal, as in most of these projects, one has to develop ingenious instruments and use large groups to identify benefits. I think the checklist correctly reflects these facts, and of course it indirectly suggests the marginal merit of most such projects.

The second reason I find the reactions of producers unimpressive (to date) is that the checklist could easily have been extracted from the writings or conversation of these same people when they were extolling the merits of the R&D approach. That approach begins with needs assessment and goes on through a series of field trials toward dissemination. The checklist refers to these areas and uses the same criteria that identify the superiority of a properly developed product. None of the checkpoints are alien intruders in the context of justification (of an R&D project). They begin to look threatening only in the context of evaluation. The same factors must, however, be present in each context.

To claim that the checklist is inappropriate for formative evaluation is methodologically precarious since good formative evaluation normally involves giving the best possible simulation of a summative evaluation. The latent point could, I think, be made. The checklist refers to some data that cannot be gathered the instant a project is conceived or even in its early days. The sixth checkpoint, for example, refers to long-term or follow-up data. It is a grievous error to conclude from this that the checklist, or even that particular checkpoint, is not relevant for formative evaluation since one of the tasks of formative evaluation is to set up the process and instruments for collecting that data, and then to collect it, at least on early versions of the product. Formative evaluation is what goes on during the pre-production, improvement-oriented phase of development, and any-

one who wants to produce a worthwhile product will want to get follow-up data from throughout the period during which significant changes of effects can reasonably be expected to occur. This may well mean extending the developmental time line somewhat; it certainly cannot legitimately be taken to mean that follow-up data is not relevant to formative evaluation.

The "follow-up checkpoint" is the extreme case, the item that might seem most remote from formative concerns. Even if the argument of the preceding paragraph were unsound, one could scarcely argue that the checklist as a whole was irrelevant to formative evaluation since almost every remaining item is obviously relevant.

A related complaint that deserves attention concerns the fifth checkpoint, which requires comparative performance data from competitive or possibly competitive products. Understanding the issues in this case, however, is considerably facilitated by reading the general rationale of that checkpoint in the ensuing section; discussion of the complaint will, therefore, be postponed.

My final item of evidence about utility concerns use of the checklist by several hundred school administrators in the Nova Ed.D. program and by students in the evaluation training seminar at the University of California, Berkeley. They frequently state that it is of more value to them in doing actual evaluations than any other document in the literature. They do not frequently state that it is not helpful or that other documents prove as helpful. Their response is undoubtedly contaminated by my attitudes and personal elaborations, but it is difficult to disregard entirely. I suspect that the search for "models" of evaluation, although possibly more appropriate than the search for theories of learning is for experimental or educational psychology, does not pay off either conceptually or pedagogically as much as do the more mundane approaches of the checklist and the trouble-shooting chart.

I therefore believe that the validity of the checklist as a conceptual design has been established and is based on a proper rather than a superficial use of the R&D iterative cycle, a consideration which alone would make it superior to most products currently available. (Of course, it is much easier to do a decent R&D job on a two-page checklist than on a K-12 mathematics program.)

As an educational product, the checklist is of course self-referent, and a study of this introduction with the checklist in mind will show

that there are still substantial gaps in the direct empirical evidence that the present version is worthwhile, as is to be expected with any newly revised product. Some of these gaps will be closed if every reader and particularly every user of the checklist will accept part of the responsibility for the improvement of educational quality that I believe we all share and will send me criticisms and alternatives. They will be acknowledged and incorporated as appropriate. For my part, I believe that I have a responsibility to convince evaluators, developers, and funding organizations, including legislatures, of the crucial importance of using this checklist. Since I have already had some success with this, it is particularly important that errors or shortcomings be identified as soon as possible. I have every confidence in the R&D process, and consequently believe that such errors exist, even in this thirteenth iteration. Most obviously, the scoring sheets will need improvement; they are a recent addition.

A note on the status of the checkpoints themselves: Rod Stephens, one of the most brilliant yacht designers of the twentieth century, recently published a hundred-item checklist to be used in the evaluation of racing and cruising yachts. The status of every item in that checklist can be expressed by saying that each is desirable. But the items in the following checklist are not, except perhaps in the one case noted, *desiderata*; they are *necessitata*. One or two of them are, by definition, not relevant to certain very special products; those are neither desiderata nor necessitata for other such products, but they are necessitata and not desiderata for all types of products to which they apply. So, unless there are deficiencies in the argument, each of these conditions must be met in order to provide a firm basis for a conclusion of merit when considering an educational product.

There are often occasions when a decision must be made where nothing meets all these standards. For example, a course may be planned, and the arrangements are such that it must be given; hence, *some* materials must be selected for it. We may not be able to determine whether the materials selected are really good, but it would be desirable to know that the ones selected were the best available. In such a case, the checklist provides an opportunity for comparative assessment. Quite often, too, it is acceptable to speculate about two or three of the items on which there is no direct evidence, especially when evaluation funds are minimal. Remember, however, that the opportunity cost of time spent on materials of dubious value is very

high; it is nearly always possible to rearrange a curriculum, training institute, or some other program so that something of proven value in the appropriate area can be used. After all, French courses do teach some French, and calculus courses do teach some calculus. There is no possibility that these subjects are being acquired in some other way—by the vast majority of students, at least. These are special cases where a product can be defensibly used without all the checkpoints being met, but the reader should generally treat each item in the list as a claimed necessity. With that challenge in mind, errors are more likely to be discovered.

The general structure of the checklist is as follows: Checkpoints 1 and 2 (need and market) are the preconditions, without which nothing will have any value. If they are met, at least tentatively, we can then proceed to develop (or investigate further) a new product. Checkpoints 3-10 tell you the kind of information you must establish (or look for). They only refer to categories of information, not the quality of the product's performance in each category. To put it another way, in checking items 3-10, you are only finding out whether the car has wheels, not whether they are round. For designing or evaluating an evaluation, that is all you need. If you are evaluating a product, you may go one stage further. If the product passes this preliminary inspection, you then ask how *well* it did on items 3-10, rated against the need and market considerations of items 1 and 2. (Are the wheels perfectly round? Square? In-between?) A synthesis of items 1-10 then provides the score for checkpoint 11 (educational significance), which is a big payoff checkpoint. When you look at cost and combine it with item 11 to give cost-effectiveness, you have arrived at checkpoint 12 (the other major indicator). And, finally, you look ahead to the mere desideratum of checkpoint 13, post-marketing support.

It is suggested that the following items be marked on a five-point scale, 0-4. "Meeting a checkpoint" is then defined as scoring 2 or better. The numbers are expanded verbally (on the full form that follows), as illustrated here for the first checkpoint.

1. Need (Justification)

We are concerned here to determine whether the product satisfies a *genuine need* or is at least a *defensible want*, which is a weaker alternative. This is not covered by market research data showing that

the product is salable; so is snake oil. True needs assessments involve establishing that the product actually facilitates survival, health, or some other defensible need that is not now adequately serviced; it may involve moral, social, or environmental impact considerations. Thus it normally involves assessment of the adequacy of the performance of other products serving the same need(s). For our present purposes, however, we will use this checkpoint to indicate the importance of the need being served, whether or not it is already well served by existing products. Then we will pick up on the question of redundancy at a later point, when we look at comparative performance.

This item is listed first because most proposed products fail to pass even this requirement. The usual data under "needs assessment" refers to deficiencies on norm-referenced tests, which tells you nothing about need at all without further data. No one has a need for an average score on a test without external justification.

The five-point scale for need might look like this:

Maximum priority, a desperate need	4
Great importance	3
Probably significant need	2
Possibly significant need	1
No good evidence of significant need	0

In scoring need, the following should be taken into account: the number of people involved, social significance (compensatory justice or some other factor), urgency, possible multiplicative effects (for example, the need for tool skills is not just a function of immediate utility but also of how much other accomplishments depend on them). Cost level may or may not be part of the need specifications; it should be, but, if it is not, it is picked up at a later checkpoint.

It is undesirable to use "selected expert" judgments to establish need if there is any chance that another selection would deny it. (Many important innovative projects can, however, do no better.) Quoting actual statistics on, say, functional illiteracy in the population that this product services is a much better approach.

2. Market (Disseminability)

Many needed products, especially educational ones, are unsalable by ordinary methods (for example, safety belts). It is only possible to argue for developing such products if there is a special, preferably

tested, plan for getting them used (for example, subsidy, legislation, agents), if there probably will be such a plan, or if they have high standby value (for example, civil defense pamphlets). For this reason, dissemination plans should antedate detailed product development plans. Checkpoint 2 requires that there be dissemination plans that ensure a market; it is scored on the size and importance of the demonstrably reachable market, which is quite different from the size of the group that needs the product. It is, if you like, the pragmatic aspect of need. Such a plan (or procedure, if already operative) has to be clear and feasible in terms of available resources, expert and ingenious in its use of those resources, and keyed to the need(s).

3. Performance—True Field Trials

The first of several "performance criteria"—actually criteria for evidence about performance—stresses the necessity for field trial data that refer (*a*) to the final version and (*b*) to typical users who are (*c*) operating without producer (or other special) assistance, in (*d*) a typical setting-time frame. It is very tempting to think one can extrapolate from field trials with volunteer schools who get the materials and a phone—consultant free—or from the penultimate edition of the materials, but this has frequently proved unsound. The research, development, diffusion, and evaluation (RDD&E) model makes this point quite clear, but, in actual practice, deadlines, overcommitment, and underfinancing combine to render almost all products deficient on this checkpoint. Sometimes it is possible to make a reasonable guess, but producers tend to make optimistic guesses instead, which is one argument for outside evaluation.

4. Performance—True Consumer

The concept of "the consumer" is a free variable in the RDD&E model, and it tends to be interpreted differently by different participants. In-service teacher training materials, for example, will be "consumed" by superintendents or assistant superintendents in charge of staff development programs, teacher trainers, teachers, students, and taxpayers. To decide on the data needs with regard to each of these groups requires a very clear sense of the function of evaluation itself: which audiences it is addressed to, commissioned by, and—regardless of these two considerations—responsible to. The result of such considerations indicts a great deal of evaluation. In the case just mentioned, for example, it is common to run the tests on teachers. This

would be entirely adequate if we had the research base to connect specific changes in teacher behavior with increased learning, joy, or some other reaction on the part of the students. We have almost no such connections, and, consequently, we can scarcely ever justify heavy expenditures aimed at changing teacher behavior. Perhaps some modest costs for a project responsive to teachers' requests could be tossed in as a fringe benefit, or for some "trouble-shooting" training, but, otherwise, we are simply doing idle experiments with public money.

Quite often there will be several groups of consumers of a given product, each interested in different aspects of it. Data should be gathered on all aspects, scored separately, and only then combined. Failure to provide data on any of the important relevant groups may constitute a fatal defect in the evaluation data or it may just be a weakness.

5. Performance—Crucial Comparisons

Few if any useful evaluations avoid the necessity to present data on the comparative performance of critically competitive products. All too often the data refers to some pre-established standards of merit, and the reader has no idea whether one can do better for less, or twice as well for 5 percent more, which is the kind of information a consumer wants. Where comparisons are done, the results are sometimes useless because the competitor is chosen so as to give a false impression. The worst example of this is the use of a single "no treatment" or "last year's treatment" control group. It is not too thrilling to discover that an injection of $100,000 worth of computer-assisted instruction (CAI) can improve the math performance of a school by 15 percent if there is a possibility that $1,500 worth of programmed texts would do as well or better. There are few points where good evaluators distinguish themselves more clearly than in their choice of critical competitors. Sometimes they must be created, for example, by converting the program from the CAI memory into a programmed text, which may yield a competitor at 10 percent of the cost and with the same content plus the advantages of portability and simultaneous multiple usability. The most important critical competitor for most audiovisual products, to give another example, is the blackboard; for professors, the book.

6. Performance—Long-term

A follow-up is almost always desirable and often crucial since certain undesirable side effects may take quite a while to surface, and good results fade fast. Often, too, the *only* really valuable outcome will be a (or the) long-lasting ones.

7. Performance—Side Effects

There must be a systematic, skilled, independent search for side effects during, at the end of, and after the "treatment." Project staff are peculiarly handicapped in such a search by goal-oriented tunnel vision. This is where the outside evaluator, operating in the goal-free mode (see the next section), is particularly helpful. It is tempting to view this checkpoint as icing on the cake, but the history of educational innovation makes it clear that the risk of doing so is too high to be conscionable.

8. Performance—Process

Process observation is necessary even though the payoff emphasis is of primary importance. It may substantiate or invalidate (*a*) certain descriptions of the product, (*b*) the causal claims involved in evaluation (that the gains were due to this treatment), or (*c*) it may bear on moral questions that have pre-emptive force in any social interaction such as education. Since (*c*) is always possible, this checkpoint is always necessary. In many cases (*a*) or (*b*) also make this checkpoint necessary, but this is not true in all cases. For example, a product called an inquiry skills kit may not deserve the title either because of its content or because of the way it is or is not implemented in the classroom. (In extreme cases one is not actually evaluating the product at all, but the teachers.) Again, the dimensions of injustice, unhappiness, cruelty—and their opposites—should be independently observed. (They are not side effects since they may be part of the treatment rather than a result of it.)

9. Performance—Causation

One way or another, it must be shown that the effects reported could not reasonably be attributed to something other than the treatment or product. No way of doing this compares well with the fully controlled experiment, and ingenuity can expand its use into most situations. There are sometimes reasonably good alternatives (as well as bad ones), and the best possible ones must be used—in fact, the

best possible combination since modus operandi checks (see the third part of this chapter) should be done in most designs as insurance. (It is for picking up modus operandi data that the process observation is sometimes useful in checking causation.)

10. Performance—Statistical Significance

This requires no great sophistication, and it is frequently the only mark of sophistication in an evaluation design. It is worthless without, but rarely accompanied by, the next item, for which it is merely one of ten preconditions—the single necessarily quantitative one.

11. Performance—Educational Significance

Now we need to look at actual achievement on items 3-10, not just whether there is *some* data corresponding to each checkpoint. Checkpoint 11 represents a synthesis of items 1-10. Statistical significance is a necessity, but it is all too easily obtained without the results having any educational significance, especially (*a*) by using the magnifying power of a large *n,* (*b*) by using instruments that test mere vocabulary gains, or (*c*) by measuring nongeneralizable gains (where they should be generalizable). The evaluator needs to look at raw score gains, displayed by item; then he or she must make or get an independent, expert judgment that gains of that size on those items represent an educationally significant result. The raw scores need not be reported in the evaluation, but the grounds for thinking them important must be reported. Usually this involves referring back to the needs assessment, typically somewhat amplified in detail. For example, an English-as-second-language (ESL) course for the Portuguese minority in New Bedford might show very significant statistical gains on the tests. To rule out possibilities (*a*) and (*b*), above, one would normally use the judgment of independent experts on English who are native to Portugal, speak Portuguese, and are at the appropriate age level. Such experts would, of course, have to look at raw scores and item analyses, which they need not report. But an explicit congruence check with the needs assessment would still have to be given, at some level, to ensure that their judgment of educational significance relates to the ESL need and not, for example, to an alleged need for cultural identity or nationalistic pride that such a minority group might experience in the United States. If the latter is the main basis for the judgment of gain (or an important element in it), then we do not have evidence that the need we have carefully validated at

the first checkpoint is being met. It may be possible also to validate the (generally acknowledged) need to which the side effect does speak, but this should be done separately, and the evaluation is in limbo until we succeed. There should be no suggestion that late-discovered dimensions of educational significance are illicit; any development process must search for them and hope for them, but they require a review of the needs assessment.

The illustration just given concerns a very simple and incomplete case where the difference between statistical significance and educational significance is judged against needs by experts, looking at instrument validity and the item analysis. The evaluator has to go beyond the subject matter experts' reports, for the evaluator has to combine this with results from checkpoints 3-10 in order to achieve an overall rating of educational significance. If there is some doubt, for example, whether the results were due to the treatment or whether the side effects offset the main effect, then the merit of materials must be judged less positively, even if the needs congruence leads to a very favorable rating of the test scores by the experts.

In a perfectly planned, successful program, the producer would have converted needs into measurable objectives and achieved exactly those results. Backtracking from results to needs would then be greatly simplified. Of course, the evaluator still has to do it, with the help, perhaps, of subject matter experts, because the perfect program has to be identified. It is more usual that the evaluator plays a slightly different game where he tries to solve the equation so as to be able to express the achievements (not the aims) in terms of some needs (not necessarily those at which the producer aimed), rather than to solve it for a method, given the needs. Thus:

Role	Given	Derives	Must discover
Producer (P)	$Needs_p$	$Goals_p$; $objectives_p$	Device (product) to achieve $objectives_p$
Consumer (C)	$Needs_c$	$Objectives_c$	Device to achieve $objectives_c$
Evaluator (E)	Effects on C of using device (preferably under controlled conditions)	Effects of device (product) on C by contrast with natural changes	$Needs_c$, if any, which these effects meet

It is obvious from this table that good matching will coalesce all of the subscripts, so that the producer is satisfying the consumer and the evaluator can see it.

In practice it is thus suggested that (after checking items 1 and 2) one first check for the presence of items 3-10 to eliminate the hopeless situations (the product may not be hopeless, but any attempt at evaluating it will be unless these data are available). If the data can support some kind of evaluation, then it is possible to consider the extent to which the needs and market are met by the actual results (rather than the type of data) on items 3-10. This is where we look below the surface requirement of statistical significance to the deep requirement that the actual gains (on *these* items, on *this* instrument) match significant needs. Or, again, here is where we check not just that there was a side-effects search but the nature of any effects that were found. And here is where we decide how tolerant we can reasonably be about minor shortcomings in items 3-10; the configural properties of these preclude the use of any across-the-board compensatory factor.

It is obvious that, for all the breaking out of the components in the evaluative judgment that we do in the checklist, checkpoint 11 will often require a pretty substantial synthesizing performance. Exactly what kind of reliability can we get? The key to high figures here is the use of a "calibration" procedure—mutual discussion of a carefully chosen set of examples to resolve ambiguities and variations in base line and weightings. (Paul Diderich's unpublished research on essay grading led to unforced correlations in the 80's.) The evidence from the product review panels was that we achieved very good agreement with a much less coherent instrument. But this is where we sorely need field trial data (to turn checkpoints 3 and 4 on themselves). It is pathetic that educational and scientific agencies should act as if their evaluation procedures (especially their present ones) are somehow immune to validation, although everything those products are used to evaluate (proposals, personnel, instruments, results, hiring practices, and so forth) is, in its turn, supposed to supply evaluation data to support its claims to knowledge. This apparent hangover from the idea that evaluations are not cognitive assertions (or from the failure to see the practice of science as a form of science) does considerable harm. There is indeed a proper place for the a priori in evaluation—for example, the argument for including a causa-

tion checkpoint is a priori contrasted with the argument for a follow-up, which is based on knowledge about the dependence of learning on time. But no a priori argument will tell you whether the decision to fund a certain proposal would have been duplicated by a second panel of comparably expert judges, and it is surely of some interest to science to adopt procedures that yield the most objective judgment possible within the given cost constraints.

12. Costs and Cost-Effectiveness

Cost data must be:

(a) Comprehensive. That means covering maintenance as well as capital costs, psychic as well as dollar costs, "weaning" costs and costs of in-service updating of needed helpers as well as direct costs, and so forth. There should be some consideration of opportunity costs other than those covered previously that were concerned with critical competitors. (What else could the district or the state have done with the funds?) A qualitative cost-effectiveness analysis should be attempted where possible, and, if it is impossible, then cost-benefit analysis should be done as systematically as possible.

(b) Verified. Cost estimates and real costs, on a project of any size, should be verified independently. It is not satisfactory to treat cost data as if they were immune to bias. Performance data should also have some independent certification, and the procedures outlined above involve this at several points. The cost data require this for reasons that have not so far been so generally recognized. Costing is an extremely difficult business, requiring technical skills that at the moment are no part of the training of evaluators. As a matter of fact, many certified public accountants are quite incompetent at estimating the costs of educational products of a nonstandard kind. Nevertheless, the advice of one or more CPA's is certainly required in costing large projects. One might also get advice from experienced businessmen who have a background of work in a Small-Business Investment Corporation (SBIC). The function of an SBIC is to invest funds that are partly provided through federal sources in struggling small businesses. A successful SBIC graduate is used to looking at a wide variety of relatively young business entities, and that description fits most producers of educational materials quite well. Here, as in other aspects of evaluation, there are advantages to employing more than one consultant, working independently, as a check on reliability.

(This is what Stake thinks of as "desirable redundancy"; it might be less controversially described as "reliability estimation.")

(c) Separated. Costs must of course be provided for the critical competitors, something which would be covered by the admonition to include opportunity costs, given under *(a)*, above. But it might perhaps be worth independently stressing the need to provide rather careful cost estimates for artificial competitors that the ingenious evaluator creates as part of an analysis. Strictly speaking, both should be part of a decent opportunity cost analysis, but I believe this has not been traditional. Hence, this is a separate itemization.[1]

13. Extended Support

This item can at the moment be regarded as desirable rather than necessary, but it is to be hoped that this state of affairs will change in the near future. In the educational field, unlike, for example, the pharmaceutical or automobile field, the responsibility for the product is all too frequently supposed to terminate upon the commencement of production. If it should subsequently transpire that important improvements could or should be made in the product, they may or may not get made, depending upon commercial considerations. This is scarcely a service to the consumer. It should, therefore, be regarded as a strong plus for a product (or a proposal to produce a product) if there is or will be a systematic procedure for updating and upgrading it in the light of postmarketing field experience. Of course, this implies the necessity for a systematic continuing procedure for collecting field data. One type of data that ought to be collected is data on new critical competitors, and one decision that should remain open is the decision to cease production, even if it is commercially profitable to continue, when the evidence clearly indicates the existence of a superior product that can reasonably be expected to take over a free market. Federal agencies thus have followup responsibilities for their offspring. An important kind of "improvement" that is covered by this checkpoint might be described as extensions of the use of the product into new circumstances or in

---

1. The preceding considerations bear on the quality of the cost data. But this checkpoint is not treated as merely methodological. Since one already has the judgment of educational significance and since the cost data includes the cost of comparable products, one can here score cost-effectiveness as being, roughly, the justifiability of the expenditure.

conjunction with new auxiliary products. These require new evaluation and explanations of use. Providing for the training of users, itself subject to progressive cycles of improvement, should be assessed as a desideratum. Possible procedures for cost reduction by means of format change or implementation "tricks" are other items that ultimately deserve to be recognized and treated as reasonable expectations by responsible producers. Above all, this checkpoint refers to the use of long-term, follow-up data to guide postissuance improvement.

The Upgrading Phase

Given that few products meet these requirements, and few products meet even half of them, what can reasonably be done at the moment?

It should be stressed that appropriate interim policy is not to treat those products that meet the largest number of these requirements as deserving of full support. No product that fails to meet checkpoints 1-13 deserves full support, for we do not have good grounds for supposing that such a product is really worthwhile. Nevertheless, we may well have grounds that justify further investigation in order to fill the gaps in the evaluation checklist. And, as mentioned before, we may indeed have enough grounds to support the tentative use of such a product pending further investigation.

I would like to conclude by describing what I believe is a realistic and responsible policy for producer certification. Available funding should, according to this plan, be allocated in the following way: It should be made rather easy to obtain small production grants, suitable for producing a module of curriculum materials or a small product, when there is some rather persuasive empirical or a priori evidence to support the possibility that the product will provide a substantial breakthrough. Producers that succeed in establishing, by use of the preceding checklist (or improved successors), that their miniproject has really been successful would then be the only ones eligible for major product development grants. A producer could receive several sequential minigrants, even without scoring real successes, up to the point where the selection panel thinks they have evidence of his incompetence, because these, like most experiments in education, are very long shots. But nobody gets even a single maxigrant without success with a minigrant. (The required management skills would also

have to be exhibited by management performance under a minigrant subsidy, if not otherwise.) A cost of this approach is that it rules out synergistic payoff unless it can be approached stepwise, which may not be possible in some important cases. At the present stage of our experience, however, I believe that such a cost is trivial compared to the cost of funding large, poor-quality enterprises.

Summary Version of Product Checklist

Notice that the scales are sometimes hybrid crosses of methodological and substantive merit. Top scores require good evidence of good performance; the bottom score implies that *either* good evidence *or* good performance is lacking. (It does not require, for example, that there is good evidence of bad performance, for otherwise products which turned in no data would do better than those that were known to fare badly.) It is helpful not only to indicate ratings but also to circle relevant terms, such as "no good evidence," if feedback and not just a yes or no decision is to result from the evaluation.

The list of considerations should affect the rater's decision either as to adequacy of evidence or merit. By check marking (or adding) the salient factors affecting the rater's judgment (using X's to express deficiencies, if there is any possibility of ambiguity), the form can provide a quite detailed explanation as well as an evaluation, be useful for formative as well as summative purposes, and help improve the form itself. A double check mark (or double X to indicate deficiency) can be used to indicate considerations that were felt to be more important than those receiving a single check mark.

The scales are often interactive. For example, the need rating is a factor in the market rating since the greater the need that is met, the more important the market is. It is diagnostically valuable to have the separate scales at this point, but sometimes this interdependency requires reassessment of an earlier rating.

Most of the scales can sometimes be used twice, once simply as quality-of-*data* or "methodological" scales (such as a side-effects check), and these are marked with a dagger. They represent necessities, but a high score does not show intrinsic merit of the product, only of the data or the design. They will be crucial in this form when the checklist is used to evaluate evaluations or proposals. When evaluating products, the situation is that any score less than 3 on one of

these will weaken the rating on educational significance (a score under 2 would destroy it), however high the need or market scores. When rating educational significance (item 11), one goes back over these, especially 5, 6, 7, and 8, to get a merit rating. Of course, the wording associated with the 0-4 scale in its first role (as given in the following pages) will then be inappropriate, and one would simply read 0-4 as corresponding to the grades F-A ("unacceptable, marginally acceptable, acceptable, meritorious, excellent" is a translation that avoids reference to averages).

1. NEED

Consider*

_____ Number affected
_____ Social significance
_____ Absence of substitutes
_____ Multiplicative effects
_____ Other

Comments:

Rate**

4 Maximum priority, a desperate need
3 Great importance
2 Probably significant need
1 Possibly significant need
0 No good evidence of significant need

2. MARKET

Consider*

_____ Dissemination plan: clarity, feasibility, ingenuity, economy
_____ Size
_____ Importance
_____ Other

Comments:

Rate**

4 Very large and/or very important market will be reached
3 Large and/or important market will be reached
2 Significant market will probably be reached
1 Possible, but not probable, that a significant market will be reached
0 Inadequate evidence to suggest that a significant market will be reached

---

* Also place single (or double) check next to factors that you felt were particularly (or overwhelmingly) significant in this case. Use X's where you wish to indicate deficiencies rather than strengths.
**Also circle relevant terms.

3. PERFORMANCE—TRUE FIELD TRIALS[†]

Consider*	*Rate***
____ Final version?	4 Perfectly typical
____ Typical user?	3 Minor differences
____ Typical aid?	2 Reasonable bet for generalization
____ Typical setting?	1 Serious weakness
____ Typical time frame?	0 Relevance unclear

Comments:

4. PERFORMANCE—TRUE CONSUMER[†]

Consider*	*Rate***
____ Congress?	4 Full data on all relevant "consumers"
____ Federal agency?	3 Fair data on all relevant "consumers"
____ State Department?	2 Good data on the most important "consumers"
____ District?	
____ Principal?	1 Weak data on the most important "consumers"
____ Teacher?	
____ Student?	0 Only speculation about the most important "consumers"
____ Taxpayer?	
____ Other	

Comments:

5. PERFORMANCE—CRITICAL COMPARISONS[†]

Consider*	*Rate***
____ No treatment group	4 Good data on all important competitors
____ Existing competitors	3 Good data on the most important competitor(s)
____ Projected competitors	
____ Created competitors	2 Fair data on the most important competitor(s)
____ Hypothesized competitors	1 Lacking data on some of the more important competitors
	0 Little or no useful comparative data

Comments:

---

* Also place single (or double) check next to factors that you felt were particularly (or overwhelmingly) significant in this case. Use X's where you wish to indicate deficiencies rather than strengths.

**Also circle relevant terms.

[†] Can be used as quality-of-data or merit scale.

6. PERFORMANCE—LONG-TERM[†]

Consider*

____ Week to month later
____ Month to year later
____ Year to few years later
____ Many years later
____ On-the-job or life-space
         sample

Rate**

4 Good direct evidence about the effects at
     times needed
3 Some direct evidence about the effects at
     times needed
2 Follow-up gives reasonable support to a con-
     clusion about effects when needed
1 Follow-up or other data suggests a conclu-
     sion about effects when needed
0 Useless or no follow-up; no other grounds
     for inferring long-term effects

Comments:

7. PERFORMANCE—SIDE EFFECTS[†]

Consider*

____ Comprehensive search?
____ Skilled?
____ Independent?
____ Goal-free?
____ During/end/later?

Rate**

4 Meets all requirements well
3 Generally good
2 Barely acceptable
1 Some study made, but incomplete
0 No worthwhile study

Comments:

8. PERFORMANCE—PROCESS[†]

Consider*

____ Descriptive congruence
         check?
____ Causal clues check?
____ Instrument validity?
____ Judge-observer
         reliability?
____ Justice and joy?

Rate**

4 Passes with flying colors
3 Appears satisfactory
2 Reasonable risk
1 Significant omission(s)
0 Inadequate

Comments:

* Also place single (or double) check next to factors that you felt were particu-
     larly (or overwhelmingly) significant in this case. Use X's where you wish to
     indicate deficiencies rather than strengths.
**Also circle relevant terms.
[†] Can be used as quality-of-data or merit scale.

9. PERFORMANCE—CAUSATION[†]

Consider*	*Rate***
____ Randomized experimental design?	4 Impeccable
	3 Good bet
____ Quasi-experimental design?	2 Plausible bet
____ Ex post facto?	1 Weak bet
____ MO method?	0 Hopeless bet
____ A priori interpretation of correlational data?	

Comments:

10. PERFORMANCE—STATISTICAL SIGNIFICANCE[†]

Consider*	*Rate***
____ Appropriate analysis?	4 Flawless analysis, astronomical significance
____ Appropriate significance level?	3 High significance, well-tested
	2 Reasonably significant
	1 Marginal significance
	0 Not shown to be significant

Comments:

11. PERFORMANCE—EDUCATIONAL SIGNIFICANCE

Consider*	*Rate***
____ Independent judgment?	4 Very high significance demonstrated
____ Expert judgment?	3 High significance demonstrated
____ Judgment based on item analysis?	2 Moderate significance demonstrated
	1 Slight or rather uncertain significance
____ Judgment based on raw scores?	0 Neglible or unknown significance
____ Teaching to the tests?	
____ Testing to the teaching?	
____ Congruence with needs?	
____ Side effects taken into account?[‡]	

* Also place single (or double) check next to factors that you felt were particularly (or overwhelmingly) significant in this case. Use X's where you wish to indicate deficiencies rather than strengths.

** Also circle relevant terms.

[†] Can be used as quality-of-data or merit scale.

[‡] It will be especially helpful here to use either checks or 0-4 scores or A-F grades alongside these factors to indicate the basis for the overall rating.

11. PERFORMANCE—EDUCATIONAL SIGNIFICANCE (Continued)

Consider* (Continued)

_____ Long-term effects taken
        into account?‡
_____ Comparative gains taken
        into account?‡
_____ Multiple consumer goups
        served?‡
_____ Process significance taken
        into account?‡

Comments:

12. COST-EFFECTIVENESS

Consider*

_____ Comprehensive cost
        analysis?
_____ Expert judgment of
        costs?
_____ Independent judgment of
        costs?
_____ Costs for all competitors?

Rate**

4 Breakthrough for comparable products
3 Significantly lower than comparable products
2 Reasonable for comparable products
1 Probably high for comparable products, or
  somewhat incomplete data
0 Apparently excessive for comparable products, or data inadequate

Comments:

13. EXTENDED SUPPORT

Consider*

_____ Postmarketing data
        collection?
_____ Postmarketing system
        for improvement?
_____ In-service training?
_____ Updating of aids?
_____ New uses and user data?

Rate**

4 Excellent and comprehensive
3 Good and fairly comprehensive
2 Minimally acceptable
1 Weak—less than adequate
0 Neglible—apparently none

Comments:

* Also place single (or double) check next to factors that you felt were particularly (or overwhelmingly) significant in this case. Use X's where you wish to
indicate deficiencies rather than strengths.
**Also circle relevant terms.
† Can be used as quality-of-data or merit scale.
‡ It will be especially helpful here to use either checks or 0-4 scores or A-F
grades alongside these factors to indicate the basis for the overall rating.

Product Evaluation Profile (PEP)

Clear presentation is an essential part of good evaluation, and the attached profile is better for this than the filled-out checklist (which one can refer back to for amplification of profile features of interest). Minor notes follow.

One can make sense of intermediate scores (3.5, etc.) although it is doubtful whether that degree of refinement (±12 percent accuracy) could be validated. After some practice using the actual verbal equivalents of the numerical scores, the evaluator gets to the point where he can score onto the profile form directly, which is useful when evaluating a large number of products.

There is a cumulative dependence of the payoff ratings (educational significance and cost-effectiveness) on the quality-of-data ratings as well as on the need and market ratings. Serious flaws in the data automatically drop the later scores. (See the example of application of the PEP.)

I deliberately use the technique of fading to develop short cue word titles for the various dimensions on the profile form, but it should be understood that these are only abbreviations for the fuller titles on the checklist and the sometimes still fuller titles in earlier explanations. The sequence of the thirteen scales seems fairly natural. Perhaps they should be grouped by color or lines if there is a later version of the form.

1. Need	Where it all begins—justification of product development.
2. Market	If you had a product that in principle meets the need, could you actually meet the need?
3-10. Data	What you have to know about the product in order to draw a conclusion as to whether in principle it meets the need(s).
11. Performance— Educational significance	Does it meet the need?
12. Cost-Effectiveness	Is it worth it?
13. Extended support	If checkpoints 1-12 are passed, here is an important further desideratum that bears on continued production.

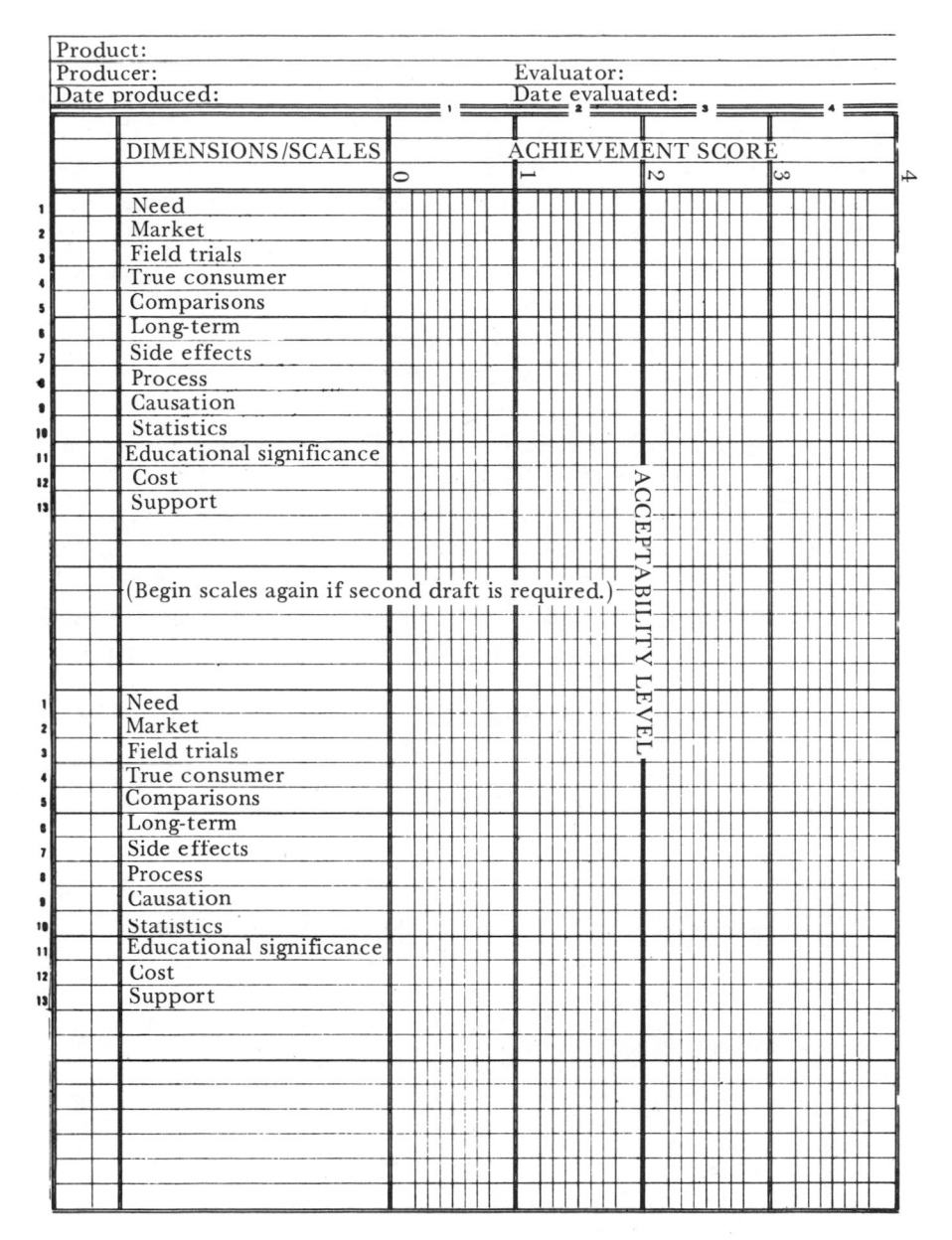

Figure 1-1
Form for product evaluation profile

The profile form on the preceding page uses commercially available accounting paper and produces a "sideways profile." The example on this page uses graph (quadrant or squared) paper and yields the more usual "cross-sectional profile" or "block diagram."

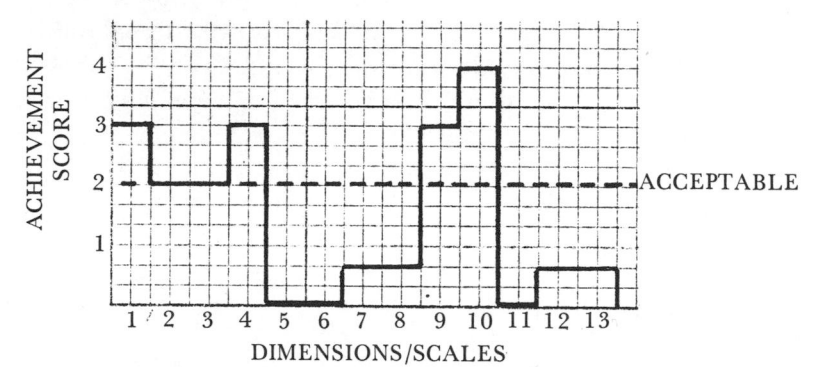

Comments on dimensions/scales:

5: No data on the critical competitors, namely other expensive math innovations

6: No follow-up; can disregard if only requesting funding for further field trials

7: Casual side-effects study

8: No observation of student interaction with terminal at all; justice not relevant, however

11: Significance unknown because of comment 5, above

12: Cost is so high that there are almost certainly competitors that would outperform for less

13: Apparently very limited

Figure 1-2
Example of the use of the product evaluation profile for a
CAI math program in New York City

Second Example of Use of PEP

Product evaluation profile:

This checklist could be evaluated as an educational device for training evaluators to think evaluatively, as a device for evaluating products to be used by professionals, as a device for evaluating products to be used by amateurs, as something for which development and evaluation funds are being requested, as something for which dissemination funds are being requested, and so forth. Some scores will be significantly affected by the classification used; for example, there is

field test data on some of the suggested uses, but none on others. Independently, funding priority would be much affected by the classification. A better case can be made for developing over disseminating, and for disseminating over agency adoption. Again, where dissemination is going to be done with one's own funds (by mail, for example) or with the nonspecific funding of professional publication, one only needs grounds for supposing it to be worth discussing and peer reviews would be the best judge of that. To make it look as bad as possible, rate it as a proposed standard for federal funding (new or continuing) of R&D projects. I will rate it as an advocate.

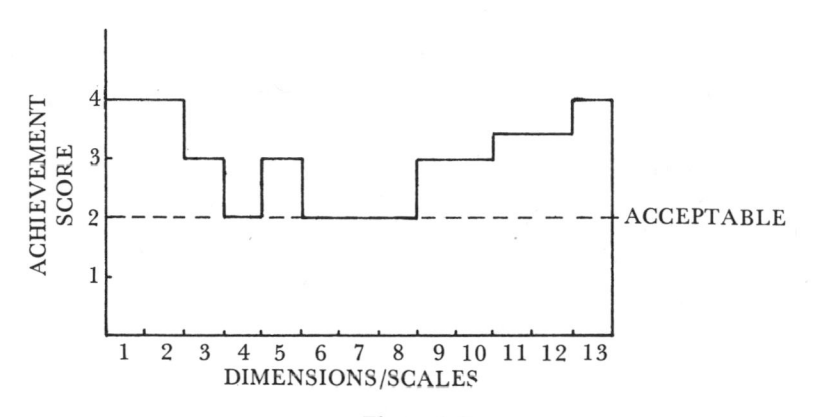

Figure 1-3
Second example of a product evaluation profile

Argument as follows (parts only):
1. Need to improve evaluation materials themselves is documented by most careful evaluations of the new curricula, national assessment, international studies, and cost figures.
2. Market is large and guaranteed if adopted as official guidelines.
3. Field trials have been of earlier versions.
4. Trials have involved the main types of consumer, including administrators and evaluators, but records are informal and samples not adequate in size.
5. The two critical competitors, both recent developments, have been carefully analyzed and appear much weaker, but we still need comparative field trials.
6. Results of agency evaluation decisions usually stick, so main long-

term effects are very similar to short-term ones although no direct long-term study (in which new side effects might turn up) has been done on latest version, and it has been three years since the original one was used. A fairly good informal feedback system has been maintained through NIE and the Association of Lab and Center Evaluators.

7. Side effects of earlier version were informally surveyed by agencies.
8. Not a crucial issue here.
9. A fully controlled study would be an improvement but pre-post comparisons make causal connection (between use of PEP and improved evaluation) indisputable.
10. Naked eye.
11. Appears to meet the need well—evidence not complete.
12. Probably the lowest-cost product ever evaluated.
13. Developer's track record of continual spontaneous revision is good.

PROSE AND CONS ABOUT GOAL-FREE EVALUATION

In the winter of 1970-71, the National Center for Educational Communications (NCEC) of the United States Office of Education (USOE) asked the Educational Testing Service (ETS) to evaluate the disseminable products of the regional labs and R&D centers. The reward for success was to be substantial grants to assist dissemination. ETS set up an external committee to do the evaluation, under the chairmanship of David Krathwohl, and provided very extensive and excellent staff support for what had to be a rather rapid review. In order to standardize the practice as well as the products of the committee (on which I served) I began to develop a standard form to serve as a checklist for us and, when filled out, as a summary for ETS and NCEC. There were originally about seventy entries in what became known as the Product Evaluation Pool, and they ranged from toys for preschoolers through publications on teacher training and bilingual curricula to vast new systems for managing schools. On these we had varying amounts of data about field trials, mostly very thin, we had the write-ups by the producing staff and other observers, and we had the products themselves. Other input was the list of current USOE priorities in education.

It seemed very natural to start off the evaluation form with a rating of goals of the project and to go on with a rating of the effectiveness in meeting them, costs, etc. By the sixth draft of the form, another item had become very prominent, namely side-effects. Naturally, these had also to be rated, and in one case a product finished up in the "Top Ten" in spite of zero results with respect to its intended outcomes because it did so well on an unanticipated effect.

Intended and Unintended Effects—Why Distinguish?

Reflecting on this experience later, I became increasingly uneasy about the separation of goals and side effects. After all, we weren't there to evaluate goals as such—that would be an important part of an evaluation of a *proposal,* but not (I began to think) of a product. All that should be concerning us, surely, was determining exactly

This article by Michael Scriven and the comments that follow are reprinted from *Evaluation Comment,* III (No. 4, December 1972), 1-8. The replies, all by Michael Scriven, appear here for the first time.

what effects this product had (or most likely had), and evaluating those, whether or not they were intended.

In fact, it was obvious that the rhetoric of the original proposal, which had led to a particular product, was frequently put forward as if it somehow constituted supporting evidence for the excellence of the product. This rhetoric was often couched in terms of the "in" phrases of five-year-old educational fads, sometimes given a swift updating with references to the current jargons or lists of educational priorities. That is, the rhetoric of intent was being used as a substitute for evidence of success. Was it affecting us? It would be hard to prove it didn't. And it contributed nothing since we were not supposed to be rewarding good intentions.

Furthermore, the whole language of "side effect" or "secondary effect" or even "unanticipated effect" (the terms were then used as approximate synonyms) tended to be a put-down of what might well be the crucial achievement, especially in terms of new priorities. Worse, it tended to make one look less hard for such effects in the data and to demand less evidence about them, which is extremely unsatisfactory with respect to the many potentially very harmful side effects that have turned up over the years.

It seemed to me, in short, that consideration and evaluation of goals was an unnecessary but also a possibly contaminating step. I began to work on an alternative approach—simply, the evaluation of actual effects against (typically) a profile of demonstrated needs in this region of education. (This is close to what Consumers' Union actually does.) I call this goal-free evaluation (GFE).

Goal-free Formative Evaluation

At first, it seemed that the proper place for GFE was in the summative role, like the NCEC activity. In the formative situation, the evaluator's principal task must surely be telling the producer whether the project's goals were being met.

But the matter is not so simple. A crucial function of good formative evaluation is to give the producer a preview of the summative evaluation. Of course, a producer has made the bet that, if the goals of the project are achieved, the summative evaluation will be or should be favorable. But one can scarcely guarantee the nonoccurrence of undesirable side effects, and one should not overlook the possibility of desirable ones that can be cultivated with some care

and attention in later developmental cycles. Now, who is going to give the producer a sneak preview of summative results? The staff evaluator will try, and often can do a very good job. But that role is not conducive to objectivity. Not only is it dependent on the payroll (and hence one where criticism can produce resentments with which the evaluator will have to live), but it is also very quickly tied in to the production activity. Typically, the staff evaluators are the actual authors of most of the tests in curriculum products, and responsible for some of the form and content of much of the rest. Finally, the staff person is likely to have occupational tunnel vision with respect to the effects of the materials (or methods, etc.), that is, a tendency to look mainly in the direction of the announced goals.

Hence, it now seems to me that a producer or staff evaluator who wants good formative evaluation has got to use some external evaluators to get it. Using them does not render the staff evaluator redundant; on the contrary, implementation or correction of the external evaluation depends in large part on the staff person. Psychologically, the staff evaluator may find it priceless to have support from an external source for some personal, and previously unshared, worries or complaints. Now, what I have said so far supports a practice of many producers in using external evaluators. But what I have said also implies, because it springs from the hunt for objectivity independence, the desirability of arranging goal-free conditions for the external evaluator.

As summative evaluation becomes increasingly goal-free, and I believe it will, the formative evaluation must do so to preserve the simulation. But forget that point; the same conclusion is forced on us by interest in picking up what are for the producer "side effects." The less the external evaluator hears about the goals of the project, the less tunnel vision will develop, the more attention will be paid to *looking* for actual effects (rather than *checking* on alleged effects).

Other Favorable Considerations

Look at the effects of considering goals on those who formulate them. It is likely to seem to them that it will pay better to err in the direction of grandiose goals rather than modest ones, as one can see from experience in reading proposals requesting funds where it is entirely appropriate to evaluate goals. This strategy assumes that a gallant try at Everest will be perceived more favorably than successful

mounting of molehills. That may or may not be so, but it is an unnecessary noise source for the evaluator.

The alleged goals are often very different from the real goals. Why should the evaluator get into the messy job of trying to disentangle that knot?

The goals are often stated so vaguely as to cover both desirable and undesirable activities by almost anyone's standards. Why try to find out what was really intended, if anything? (Similarly, the stated goals often conflict. Why try to decide which one should supervene?)

A trickier point: The identification of "side effects" with "unanticipated effects" is a mistake. Goals are only a subset of anticipated effects; they are the ones of special importance, or the ones distinctive of this project. (For example, the goals of a new math curriculum project do not usually include "employing a secretary to type up corrected copy," but of course that effect is anticipated.) Hence, "side effects" includes more phenomena than "unanticipated effects," and some of the ones it alone includes may be important. In short, evaluation with respect to goals does not even include all the anticipated effects and gives much too limited a profile of the project. Why get into the business of trying to make distinctions like this?

Since almost all projects either fall short of their goals or overachieve them, why waste time rating the goals; which usually *are not* what is achieved?

GFE is unaffected by, and hence does not legislate against, the shifting of goals midway in a project. Given the amount of resentment caused by evaluation designs that require rigidity of the treatment throughout, this is an important benefit. But it's a real advantage only to the extent that the project remains within the much larger but still finite ballpark the GFE has carved out of the jungle of possible effects.

Unfavorable Considerations—Methodological and Practical

These are usually an amalgam of criticisms from various sources, sometimes real quotes.

"The GFE'r simply substitutes his own goals for those of the project." No. The GFE may use USOE's goals, or what the best evidence identifies as the needs of the nation, as standards, but simply to use his (or her) own personal preferences would obviously be to invali-

date the evaluation. One needs standards of merit for an evaluation, indeed; the error is to think these have to be the goals of the evaluator or the evaluated. Another commonly connected error is to think that all standards of merit are arbitrary or subjective. There is nothing subjective about the claim that we need a cure for cancer more than a new brand of soap. The fact that some people have the opposite preference (if true) doesn't even weakly undermine the claim about which of these alternatives the nation needs most. So the GFE may use needs and not goals, or the goals of the consumer or the funding agency. Which of these is appropriate depends on the case. But in no case is it proper to use anyone's goals as the standard unless they can be shown to be the appropriate ones and morally defensible.

"Great idea—but hopelessly impractical. You can never keep the evaluator from inferring the goals of the project." This is certainly false. I and others have done evaluations where only the feeblest guesses would be possible, and of no great interest. If you control the data going to the evaluator, you can obviously reduce it to the point where goals are not inferable. And interesting, not exhaustive, evaluations are still possible. An evaluator with considerable experience in goal-based evaluation does indeed find it tempting, in fact almost neurotically necessary, to reach for the security blanket of goals. But once one learns to do without it, then, like riding a bicycle or swimming without the aids one uses at first, there is a remarkable sense of freedom, of liberation.

"Why use an evaluator who only gets part of the data—you simply increase the chance that some of the most important effects (which happen to have been intended) will be missed?" Yes, this is the trade-off. The value of GFE does not lie in picking up what everyone already "knows," but in noticing something that everyone else has overlooked, or in producing a novel overall perspective. Of course, when summative time comes around, the intended effects had better be large enough to be obvious to the unaided (but expert) eye or, in general, they are not worth very much. (The same is therefore true to a lesser extent for formative evaluation.)

"Attacking the emphasis on careful goal formulation approaches can only lead to poor planning, a catch-as-catch-can approach, and general carelessness—which you are giving intellectual sanction." Planning and production require goals, and formulating them in test-

able terms is absolutely necessary for the manager as well as the internal evaluator who keeps the manager informed. That has nothing to do with the question of whether the external evaluator needs or should be given any account of the project's goals.

"I still can't see how GFE is supposed to work in practice. You can't test for all possible effects, and it is surely absurd to think you should not even *bother* with testing the real goals." The external evaluator is not there to test goals, but rather to evaluate achievement which turns out to be conceptually distinct—and often different in practice, too. As to the idea that GFE requires testing for every possible effect, the best reply is to say that any evaluator worth hiring has to look for side effects, and there is no limitation on where or in what form they crop up. So even the goal-based evaluator (GBE'r) has to do this allegedly impossible task. (And so, for that matter, does any applied scientist searching for the effects of a new drug, or the scientist looking for unknown causes of an important effect, e.g., death or cancer—except he searches for every possible cause, not effect.) The GFE'r looks at the treatment and/or curricular materials, after all, and can immediately formulate some hypothesis about probable effects based on previous experience and knowledge of the research literature. Often, too, the GFE'r can look at the results of quizzes etc., though it's desirable to do that after formulating the hypothesis just mentioned, to avoid premature fixation on the variables of concern to the project.

"I'm afraid that GFE is going to be seen as a threat by many producers, perhaps enough to prevent its use." It's true that even GBE was and is so threatening that its introduction has been prevented or rendered useless on many projects. But it has gradually become increasingly a requirement, and the standards for it are creeping upward. The same is likely to be true of GFE. Now it is important to see why GFE is more of a threat. Primarily this is because the GFE'r is less under the control of management; not only are the main variables no longer specified by management, but they may not even include those that management has been advertising. The reactions by management to GFE have really brought out the extent to which evaluation has become or has come to seem a controllable item, an unhealthy situation. The idea of an evaluator who will not even talk to you for fear of contamination can hardly be expected to make the producer rest easy. It's probably very important, psychologically, to

talk to your judge, to feel you have got across a sense of your mission, the difficulties, etc. We all have some faith in "tout comprendre c'est tout pardonner." But the evaluator is not our judge, just the judge of something we have produced. Even if it is not much good, there is a long way to go before blame can be laid at the producer's door. If a producer really cares about quality control, it will not do to insist that the project's definition of quality must be used.

Methodological Analogies of GFE (in Other Fields)

The Intentional Fallacy. In the field of aesthetics it has been widely but not universally accepted that it is fallacious for a critic to consider the intentions of the artist in assessing the work of art. If the "meaning" does not show, it does not (or should not) count. I am inclined to think this is a perverse view, a purist limit that goes beyond the bounds of sense. The titles of paintings, the locale of photographers, program notes at the symphony, the period of a building, even the biographies of Russian novelists, "cast new light on" the art object itself and are interesting in themselves. The fallacy is to suppose that the only legitimate framework in which to see a work of art is as an autonomous entity. Art can enlighten, it can give pleasure, it can communicate feeling, and so on—and there's nothing in there that says the background and context of the art work cannot contribute. It is really a case where the consumer can choose. One may say that assessing the artist legitimately brings in these considerations, but assessing the art work does not, but the slight attraction of this "tidying-up" move scarcely amounts to a compelling argument for any reasonable man.

In the educational materials production situation, on the other hand, as in the consumer field in general, we can usually establish that the intentions of the producer are of negligible concern to the consumer by comparison with satisfactory performance on the criterion dimensions (e.g., gains in reading scores). Not only *is* this so, but there seems to be little reason why it should not be so. When the history of educational R&D is written (if ever historians can be found to stoop to such a low-status task which happens to be socially valuable) then the intentions of producers will be of great interest. For the future producer, a study of these may be far more valuable than a study of the products.

So the "intentional fallacy" is not, in my view, a fallacy in the area where the term was introduced, but it would be one in the evaluation of consumer goods.

Motives and Morality. A tremendous tension has long existed in philosophical ethics between those who believe that the morality of acts is principally determined by their motivation ("He meant well") and those who would assess acts in terms of their consequences alone ("Write that on his gravestone; first, he should be shot"). Current pop ethics is on the conscience trip—the "pragmatist" is seen as the opposition.

The special feature of this case is that the act involves the motive in a much more intimate way than the product involves the producer's intent. It has been argued that the same physical motions performed with different intentions are definitionally a different act; the distinctions between manslaughter and murder, between borrowing and theft, erring and lying, for example, are said to be distinctions between different acts. One cannot argue that a programmed text supposed to teach economics better than the competition but which actually teaches reading better (and economics the same) is crucially different for the consumer from one in which the side effect was the primary aim of the producer. And it is for just this reason I prefer the role of the GFE'r for summative evaluation.

On the philosophical issue, I prefer to say that neither exclusive position is defensible, that the issue is resolved one way or the other in particular cases where the point of the evaluation becomes clear.

Double-Blind Designs. A correspondent writes, "The so-called 'double-blind' medical experiment is not blind in terms of goal or purpose. A treatment is being tested for its effect on a specific disease. The 'blind' is strictly in terms of S's or E's knowledge of who is getting what treatment. Thus I think your use of the analogy is inappropriate." The analogy is not intended to be an identity. The point of the analogy is to remind one that medical research, until the scurvy study, ignored the error due to the agent and evaluator knowing that the treatment being given to a particular patient was a dummy. Not only did this affect the agent's behavior in giving it, but it affected the evaluator's care in assessing the effects. After all, how could one seriously look for therapeutic results from a sugar-pill? "Blinding" the assessor made the search equally careful in both cases.

Analogously, "blinding" the educational evaluator ensures (to the maximum possible extent?) equal care in looking for effects that happen not to have been goals. Now it is true that the GFE'r may make it the first order of business to infer the goals of the producer. In fact, that is what happened in the second GFE study of which I have received details. (But in the medical case this is often possible, too. In 1958 or so I spent a great deal of time refining placebo-effect research designs; the problems of matching for the taste and side effects of the experimental drug, amongst other difficulties, are typically not solvable.) All one can do is to make it as hard as possible. In particular, one can try to cut out cues which allow inference of intent other than via noticing success. It's not disastrous if the medical researcher infers from the results that treatment B must have been the new medication; treatment A, the placebo. The inference may or may not be correct; it can only be damaging if it is made during the experiment and hence might influence the later procedures. But even that possibility can usually be handled by splitting the role of recorder from that of agent. By analogy, we cannot get too worried about an evaluator who, seeing massive gain scores on an addition-of-integers test, infers that a major goal of the materials was to improve addition of integers. On the other hand, we must try to avoid having the evaluator come to this conclusion by reading the introduction to the materials because that is likely to corrupt his later perceptions. When the evaluator devises special instruments for assessing inventory on a parameter that has not previously been tested, we can isolate the role of the agent doing the testing from the role of the scorer, and we can arrange that the scorer does not know the pretests from the posttests, or the experimental group's tests from the control group's tests.

In the early GFE just mentioned, where the evaluator worked diligently to reconstruct the goals, he was doing this by observing various effects which seemed desirable. He concluded that these were probably intended. But the step of inferring goals was totally unnecessary; he could just as well have left the matter by noting the desirable results. Similarly, where he inferred failure (e.g., at teaching the inquiry approach) he could just as well have made no comment, or noted lack of performance in this desirable dimension, from which the developer can conclude failure.

Finally, although it is typical of the medical situation that a major parameter is identified in advance, no evaluation of drugs today can avoid the search for side effects from the most remote area of the symptom spectrum. Nor is this obligation restricted to federal checks; the formative evaluation of drugs requires that the manufacturer run studies that are both double-blind and side-effect sensitive. It would not be difficult to run these evaluations goal free, but it has little point; given only the characteristics of the patients to be treated, the goal of the treatment would be fairly obvious. In education, the situation is different, more like preventive medicine.

In sum, I think there's an illuminating analogy between the move to double-blind methodology and the (further) move to GFE. The gains from double-blind were not significant in the physical sciences; it was an innovation of great value to medicine. The gains from GFE are not great for medicine, but it is an innovation that may pay off for education.

COMMENT BY DANIEL L. STUFFLEBEAM: SHOULD OR CAN EVALUATION BE GOAL-FREE?

> Evaluation is . . . a methodological activity which . . . consists simply in the gathering and combining of performance data with a weighted set of goal scales to yield either comparative or numerical ratings, and in the justification of (a) the data-gathering instruments, (b) the weightings, and (c) the selection of goals.
>
> (Michael Scriven, *The methodology of evaluation,* AERA Monograph Series on Curriculum Evaluation, Book 1 [Chicago: Rand McNally & Company, 1967], pp. 39ff.)

In setting forth the above definition of evaluation, Michael Scriven emphasized that evaluators must evaluate goals. The following is a critique of his more recent position that evaluators should pay no attention to goals. In this regard, I will list and respond to four questions that I believe to be important in assessing the merit of goal-free evaluation.

Question: Should GFE be considered as a possible alternative to existing models of evaluation?

Answer: No. GFE has been proposed as one methodological strategy that can be used to supplement others, including goal-based evaluation (GBE) and the evaluation of goals. This is consistent with

Scriven's past practice of analyzing evaluation in order to identify and describe the many kinds of evaluation that evaluators need to be able to perform. In addition to GFE he has proposed formative, summative, intrinsic, payoff, meta, fact-free (with tongue in cheek, I hope), and pathway evaluation. Scriven has not offered any one of these evaluation types, nor all of them collectively, as a theory or model of evaluation. Thus, we should consider GFE in its proper perspective as one strategy that can be used in conjunction with others in evaluation work.

Question: What is the essence of GFE?

Answer: It is to identify effects accurately and determine their importance and quality. That Scriven believes this can best be accomplished by preventing the evaluator from seeing goal statements seems to me both a secondary issue and an empirical question. Perhaps evaluators can be trained not to develop tunnel vision upon seeing a set of goal statements but to use them as clues for identifying important outcome variables. The main concern is how best to ensure that evaluators will identify and properly judge actual results, whether planned or not.

Question: How should GFE be conducted?

Answer: This presently is the rub. Which variables, instruments, extant data, and standards should the evaluator use? When should he gather his data? And how can program people be protected against the potentially arbitrary actions of an inept or unscrupulous goal-free evaluator, especially when he is employed by an external funding agent that may be a bureaucracy with neither a conscience nor a memory?

Presently Dr. Scriven's response seems to be that two goal-free evaluators should operate independently, beginning about midway in a project and continuing to a point after its completion. While this does not guarantee good quality and fair evaluation, it at least provides an opportunity to estimate the "error term" involved in GFE.

The problems of gathering data seem far from solution. There are thousands of potentially relevant attainment variables and associated measuring devices, and GFE methodology does not provide much guidance for choosing among them. Goal statements at least provide hypotheses as to what some (*not all*) of the variables are. It would seem that system analyses would be helpful, but these also are goal based.

As to how to judge the GFE results, we encounter a conceptual problem. Scriven suggests that they should be compared with the results of prior needs assessments. This is sound advice if prior needs assessments were done. But if needs assessment is the comparison of the real with an ideal and if the ideal amounts to a prior statement of macrogoals, then needs take on their meaning as a function of the discrepancy between an actual situation and prior goal statements. Hence, needs assessments are goal based and the use of needs assessment data to determine the value meanings of GFE observations is also goal based. In this respect, the methodological suggestion seems sound, but it raises a question whether GFE can be goal-free. Further, based on Scriven's 1967 definition, evaluation should not be goal-free. The essence of evaluation is value judgments; these are made in relation to standards, and the standards almost always are goals.

Question: Taken in its essential meaning of accurately identifying and properly judging effects, how much can GFE contribute within a broad evaluation framework?

Answer: A great deal. This type of GFE is the essence of identifying and judging needs, opportunities, and problems to serve as a foundation for determining goals. It is also applicable for identifying and judging alternative program strategies; solution strategies need to be assessed for their power with respect to a wide range of potential desirable impacts, not just those associated with stated goals. Also, through a comprehensive GFE of alternative program strategies one can get a fix on the tractability of each of a range of problems and needs, not just the ones associated with the stated goals. GFE is further useful for identifying and judging a project's effects. Scriven is absolutely correct that it is unnecessary in identifying outcomes to focus on the stated project objectives. This will be done directly by the goal-based evaluators, and they probably won't have time to search out side effects.

On the other side of the ledger, GFE will not suffice for meeting accountability requirements. Sponsors pay money so that certain priority needs (goals, if you will) can be met. These needs must be evaluated, and those responsible for meeting them must be judged in terms of their attempts and their achievements and failures. In some cases it is appropriate to penalize one for failing to produce what was needed and what he agreed to produce, especially if the evaluation

revealed that the responsible agent did not try to live up to his agree-ment but instead worked on something more satisfying to him. Such determinations require the use of GBE, although this does not dimin-ish the desirability of GFE.

Within this brief piece I have commented on Michael Scriven's GFE methodological contribution. It fits in with his pattern of ana-lyzing various methodological aspects of evaluation. GFE is not an alternative model of evaluation; rather it is one evaluation strategy. The essence of the strategy should not be to prevent evaluators from seeing goal statements, but to insure that all relevant effects will be accurately identified and properly judged. Conceptually, based on Scriven's own definition and arguments, it is questionable that GFE can or should be goal-free. The strategy is potentially useful, but far from operational and replicable. Because of its promise, I believe that Scriven and others should further develop it, test it, and report back to the profession on the effects of GFE, whatever they turn out to be.

Reply to the Comments by Stufflebeam

Stufflebeam begins with a quotation that, if consistency is the mark of a narrow mind, shows that I am broad-minded. Excellent! What I should have said, of course, was "criterion scales" not "goal scales."

Evaluators and goals: Stufflebeam describes my present position as "that evaluators should pay no attention to goals." Now I do not want to say this at all—only that certain evaluators, those in certain roles in the complex evaluation processes associated with almost any responsible production or review activity, can probably do better goal-free. I stress that they may do worse; to find out, one must also have goal-based evaluators. I stress that there have to be staff evalua-tors who work in the GBE mode; I am only saying that it is desirable to do some formative and some or possibly all summative evaluation in the GFE mode.[2] Stufflebeam gives essentially this interpretation

2. Where the summative evaluation is being done for the funding agency, it could be entirely GFE if the project director gets a chance to append his or her reactions to it. Normally the agency expects a summative evaluation from the producer and also commissions an external review, both being GBE's. What I recommend in such a case is making the external review GFE. I would also say that the producer doing a summative evaluation, where the agency is not going to commission an external GFE, should get one done as an input or supplement for the summative evaluation.

of my view in responding to the first question he sets himself, and I endorse that interpretation. (Oddly enough, however, he appears to reject it in his answer to the third question.)

The issue between GFE and GBE: He stresses that the issue is empirical, and I agree (except for a slight qualification discussed below). I was delighted when the National Science Foundation (NSF) decided to run an experiment using Stufflebeam and me as heads of teams visiting the same sites, but operating respectively in the goal-based and goal-free mode. (Unfortunately, special features of the situation contraindicated an evaluation experiment.[3]) It will take only a few such experiments (some with our trainees doing it instead of ourselves, to better isolate some of our own individual differences) to give us a good picture of GFE. I think its value will be demonstrated if it sometimes picks up something significant at a cost that makes the discovery worthwhile. Its purpose is only to improve GBE in certain sites, not to replace it, just as double-blind methodology only improves and does not replace unblinded clinical experimentation. Thorough evaluation in educational or medical contexts will, I believe, call for both methodologies.

Tunnel vision: He speculates that we may be able to train evaluators to avoid this. Even if we can, which would in my view be unlikely in view of the research on contextual influence ("set") on perception, there is still the credibility constraint on the evaluation to be met, in contrast with the reliability constraint. That is, as long as an influential audience is likely to think that the result may have been spuriously generated by subliminal cueing, even if we have good research evidence that shows these particular highly trained evaluators are (or have been) highly immune to it, the evaluation is not going to be satisfactory to them. To some extent, the function of evaluation is analogous to that of justice. One might say: "It is not enough that good evaluation be done, it is necessary that it be seen that good evaluation is done." The situation would be different if evaluation (or the administration of justice) were just research. Evaluation involves research, but it often goes beyond that. It is sometimes a certification process, and, in fulfilling that function, it has to be beyond

3. E.g., funding essentially guaranteed regardless of evaluation; no evaluation requirement in proposal, hence, any evaluation viewed as an imposition (let alone two of them); extremely diffuse projects (both state-wide), hence, large teams; much traveling and interaction necessary, hence, leakage to GFE team too probable and dilution of method effects too great.

reproach. If a judge tells us that his attitude toward a trial was in no way affected when an interested party approached him and discussed at length the offer of a prestigious position, this is unlikely. But even if he were in no way affected, the judge still acted improperly in allowing the discussion to continue because the mere suggestion of bias, the *possibility* of which can hardly be denied, makes the judicial process suspect, weakening it and, thus, the expectation of loyalty to it. (Hence, of course, those who thus approach a judge subvert the law.) Similarly, once the source of bias involved in the visiting fireman treatment accorded external evaluators, in the sweet rhetoric about laudable goals, and in selective presentation by the staff has been identified as a threat to objectivity, it is not realistic to suppose that evaluators are naturally or by training immune. If it can also be shown that there is another way to do the same evaluation, then continued, exclusive use of the old procedures is improper. And it will always be improper for accountability purposes even if it can be shown experimentally that future evaluators can be inoculated against the effects with good success.

"GFE threat": "How can program people be protected against the potentially arbitrary actions of an inept or unscrupulous goal-free evaluator, especially when he is employed by an external funding agency that may be a bureaucracy with neither a conscience nor a memory?"

Now why should one suppose this risk is any different for the goal-free as opposed to the goal-based evaluator? Stufflebeam's response here closely parallels that of several project or unit directors who have written to me about GFE. Is it possibly because of the bond of loyalty—friendship—co-option that rather frequently and quickly develops between the producer and even the external evaluator? That is a somewhat cynical suggestion, but I put it forward only because I can think of no other. I cannot myself see any respect at all in which the actions of goal-free evaluators can be more arbitrary or unscrupulous than those of the goal-based evaluator. And a monstrously powerful reason why they tend to be less "inept and unscrupulous" is that their professional reputation is on the line to a much larger extent.

Stufflebeam's reaction would make more sense if evaluations were simply letter grades without supporting arguments and if agency monitors ever decide on the basis of a single evaluation with no opportunity for rebuttal. But Stufflebeam knows that such condi-

tions essentially never occur separately, let alone together. Nor should they ever occur since the interjudge reliability of evaluators is known, but it is almost certainly not close to 1 on most program judgments. Since I am arguing for GFE as only part of the total evaluation battery,[4] the second condition never applies to the process I am supporting. As a second standard procedure, I suggest that the project director automatically have the opportunity for rebuttal. (I normally try to get this anyway, before turning in a final draft; so, usually, do all agencies I have worked for.) In the cases where the GFE should be part of an internally commissioned evaluation, where it is done as a service to the project or unit, it could obviously not be a threat in the sense he has in mind, so one should be careful about adopting Stufflebeam's characterization here as if it even could apply to all GFE. Of course, the main problem with evaluations is not that they tend to be mere letter grades, but that they tend to be far too long. Hence, the test of internal coherence, of logic, is always applied. Does the evaluation give good grounds for the evaluative conclusion? Of course, this is just as true of GBE as of GFE—no more, no less. The difference is that ineptitude will show up far more clearly in a GFE. That is why I say GFE puts the professional reputation on the line far more acutely than GBE, providing extra protection against the "inept or unscrupulous." I am not sure, for example, whether I am a good enough evaluator to make the best test case for GFE. I do know—I should have thought it obvious—that the risks involved for me are far greater than in other evaluations I have done: GFE is not a comfortable role. These risks to reputation are the best insurance the project people have, and such risks have been most successful in other areas; for example, the tissue committee in a hospital checks the patient's pathology, not the surgeon's intent.

Have we covered the basis for GFE threat? Presumably, the fear is that a goal-free evaluator will come in, attack the project for not having done what it was never intended to do, overlook what it did that was valuable, and leave, to be replaced by the hatchet men. But irrelevant criticism and overlooking merit is a demonstrable error and, since projects normally have considerably more power than the evaluators (look at the economics and ego-involvement of the situation),

4. Since Stufflebeam recognizes this in the response to the first question, his response here is puzzling.

the project would have no difficulty in nailing the evaluator. All of this is based on special assumptions without which the goal-free evaluator could not conceivably be a threat in that it is an externally originated review.

GFE procedure: Is there a practical way to do GFE? "There are thousands of potentially relevant attainment variables and associated measuring devices, and GFE methodology does not provide much guidance for choosing amongst them." It provides none at all, in fact, which is exactly the situation with GBE, except that a few variables are there identified as "goals." There is just no way around the fact that every evaluator has to face those "thousands of possibly relevant variables" and decide which ones to check in order to determine side effects. Having three or four or ten identified for you is scarcely a drop in the bucket. Yet evaluations can be and are done rather thoroughly. How? By relying on the huge pool of background knowledge we possess about what treatments tend to have what effects. The GFE, just like the GBE, looks very carefully at treatments in order to get ideas about possible effects, and then checks for them.

I have working charts from which I can read off the best sequence to follow in doing a GFE of common types of products. For example, one wants to watch a class before talking to teachers using the materials. One wants to read the materials that are read by the students before looking at their test results. One wholly avoids reading the introduction to the text materials, talking to the writers, or other activities that might yield goals explicitly. It is preferable to use someone trained in GFE as liaison at the site, through whom information can be filtered, and that person is normally disqualified from contributing to the evaluation. Untrained liaisons too readily let something slip. The least "contaminating" goal data concerns target population descriptors such as grade level since the tests for that are obvious and necessary. It is hard for people thinking about GFE for the first time not to worry about the goal-free evaluator's "cheating." Once one understands the point of GFE, however, it becomes clear that one's hopes of doing something useful are dependent on avoiding contamination; hence, the goal-free evaluator lacks motivation to cheat unless he is extremely insecure. In that case a minimax strategy would counsel one to avoid the worst possible outcome (of missing the most important variable) by "cheating"; but a goal-free evaluator will scarcely advance the cause of GFE or of himself or of

the client by imperfectly duplicating the GBE component of the evaluation.

Exactly what can be done depends heavily on the point at which the evaluator is brought in. If it is for a snapshot summative evaluation, there is no chance to broaden the spectrum of pre-post tests or needs assessment, even if they appear necessary. One may, however, still be able to point out crucial omissions in the evaluation data (and to say why they are crucial), which of course radically affects the evaluation conclusions that can be drawn.

Ultimate standards of value: Here, Stufflebeam is worried because it looks as if the way I suggest doing GFE—via matching against needs—reintroduces goals. Now GFE is not standards-free, and any standard may be (and usually is) *someone's* goal. The goals of which GFE is free are the goals of the producer (or the teacher or any other person involved), which are the goals previously used as the usual criteria for evaluation. Often GFE will be using standards that are quite similar to the goals of the *consumer* (or at least some consumers), or of the funding agency, or even, de facto, of the producer. The point is that the basic standards of merit used are constructed in the absence of knowledge about (more precisely, without reference to) the known goals of anybody involved in the project.

The one possible exception is that sometimes one will use the consumers' goals as secondary indicators of merit because in special cases needs assessment collapses into wants assessment. Never, however, does one use the producer's goals as such. It is true that, when a consumer wants to evaluate something himself, the standards used are the individual's own desiderata, which can reasonably be called goals. It was years of work on formalizing that process that lulled me into the definition Stufflebeam quotes from a 1967 paper of mine. But it is not possible to apply the reasonable, though sloppy, position that evaluation requires standards that are *someone's justified* goals (as my 1967 definition states), to the practice of evaluating products in terms of the *producer's uncriticized* goals. Someone reading the Phi Delta Kappa volume on evaluation (Stufflebeam *et al., Educational Evaluation and Decision Making,* 1972) would probably take the latter to be their recommendation, although this is not Stufflebeam's present view and perhaps was not his view then. It has certainly characterized a great deal, perhaps nearly all, educational evaluation.

Evaluating the producer: Surely in this case we at least need to

look at program goals when trying to evaluate the performance or achievement of the producer. For example, is it not important in such evaluations to check whether the agent "did not try to live up to his agreement but instead worked on something more satisfying to him"? It seems to me that the best possible way to establish this is a diligent GFE which turns up whatever was done and fails to turn up what was supposed to have been done. It is not clear to me that producers cannot con evaluators rather easily by putting on suitable circuses and sideshows at site-visit time; the grapevine groans with anecdotes about brilliant performances of this kind. The goal-free evaluator is considerably better insulated against such distractions and better able to focus on the results. So I do not really agree with Stufflebeam that "such determinations absolutely require the use of GBE." Evaluation of producers is, however, globally rather less important than evaluation of their products. If I had to concede some ground, therefore, I would do it here.

In sum, then, I much appreciate Stufflebeam's correct emphasis on the "one more tool, but not a different model" interpretation of GFE, and his general effort to approach it sympathetically. I hope the preceding reactions clarify the notion and possibly justify staking out a larger claim for it.

COMMENT BY MARVIN C. ALKIN: WIDER CONTEXT GOALS AND GOAL-BASED EVALUATORS

. . . Scriven makes some interesting and important points in defense of what he calls the "goal-free evaluator"—the GFE. This term, GFE, is not to be taken literally. The GFE does recognize goals (and not just idiosyncratic ones), but they are to be wider-context goals rather than the specific objectives[5] of a program. (USOE goals are mentioned as an example.)

In addition to this broader frame of reference, the GFE is to be characterized by a scrupulous concern for objectivity. Not only should he refuse to read the program objectives to avoid contamination by the "rhetoric of intent," but he should even decline to talk to the project director.

5. The GFE should perhaps be called an OFE (objective-free evaluator), but the unfortunate auditory association with oaf might lead one to think of him as someone who just sits around with no particular purpose in mind.

Insofar as GFE's bring perspective, objectivity, and independence to evaluations they are indeed "a good thing." Manifestly, however, they are not one of the best things in life since they are not free. Evaluation costs money; it removes money from program management and implementation funds. Thus, before programs start hiring GFE's we need to discuss what roles are to be played by an internal evaluator (whom Scriven always assumes to exist) and an external evaluator (including the GFE). How does the presence of one affect the activities and responsibilities of the other and to what purpose is each employed?

First, let me point out that, in understanding the nature of the evaluation to be performed, the "internal-external" distinction is not nearly as critical as the designation of the decision context to be served by each evaluator. That is, the ultimate purpose of an evaluation is to provide information upon which present or potential decisions are to be made, and it is this crucial factor that distinguishes evaluation from research. The nature of the evaluation that will be performed, framed as it is by a particular decision context, will be dependent upon such factors as who hired the evaluator, who receives the evaluation reports, and the nature of the evaluation decision that is to be made (formative, refunding, adoption, etc.). Thus, when Scriven talks about an "internal evaluator," I presume that he is referring to an evaluator hired by the project director primarily to provide formative information for program modification purposes and whose reports will be directed primarily toward the project director (and perhaps secondarily to the sponsoring agency). In addition to this internal evaluator there should perhaps be an evaluator *hired by* the superintendent of schools to report on the project; perhaps the sponsoring agency should also hire an external GBE to report to them. There are many decision contexts requiring evaluation information, and ·it is necessary to establish priorities on these various evaluation requirements.

By "goal-free" Scriven simply means that the evaluator is free to choose a wider context of goals. By his description he implies that a goal-free evaluation is always free of the goals of the specific program and sometimes free of the goals of the program sponsor. In reality, then, goal-free evaluation is not really goal-free at all, but is simply directed at a different and usually wider decision audience. The typical goal-free evaluator must surely think (especially if he rejects the

goals of the sponsoring agency) that his evaluation will extend at least to the level of "national policy formulators." The question is whether this decision audience is of the highest priority in our present concerns for improving evaluation.

The high priority that Scriven attaches to the goal-free evaluator seems to be based primarily upon his experience in considering the evaluation of packaged instructional products designed to be used widely and in a variety of contexts. Scriven's major examples come from product evaluations performed at only a limited number of centers, laboratories, and other organizations that produce validated instructional materials. Each of these organizations has an internal evaluation staff. But the materials they are concerned with represent merely the tip of a giant iceberg of instructional products, most of which undergo little or no evaluation—neither formative nor summative nor goal-based of any kind. Moreover, when one considers problems related to the evaluation of instructional programs (such as the Title programs—I, III, VII, VIII) and the evaluation of teachers (such as that mandated by the Stull Bill in California), then the iceberg of instructional product evaluation pales in importance compared to the Arctic Sea of evaluation problems. Thus, while it is difficult to dispute Scriven's point that there is a role for a person called a goal-free evaluator, one can certainly question his judgment as to the areas of greatest "demonstrated need" in evaluation at this time. And if one can question a goal-free evaluator on how well he interprets "demonstrated need," what else is left?

And so, what are the alternatives to a goal-free evaluator? Scriven comes to see the need for goal-free evaluators because he questions the goals (or objectives) specified by project personnel as potentially not being expressions of "demonstrated need" or as being ambiguously stated. If this is the case, then why must the evaluator wait for the program to become fully implemented before providing evaluative feedback on the rightness of goals. In part, this lack of foresight attributed to a goal-based evaluator (GBE) by Scriven is related to his rather limited definition of the role of the evaluator. Scriven thinks of the evaluator as participating in formative and summative evaluation, in essence limiting the evaluative engagement to the period following the adoption of the educational program. This oversight is corrected in the evaluation model of the Center for the Study of Evaluation in which we conceive of the evaluative responsibility be-

ginning with "needs assessment." In the needs assessment stage the evaluator assists in providing explicit data as to the relevance of stated goals to real and demonstrated needs. Scriven's goal-free evaluation is in essence a retrospective (and nonexplicit) needs assessment. This would be all right, but for the fact that performing this function retrospectively raises the cost enormously, not only of the evaluation but of a program that may have gone astray and [that] could have been brought back on course at an earlier time.

If the goals that are alleged are not the "real" ones or the "right" ones then let the GBE establish a procedure, an explicit procedure, for determining the goals. If mere rhetoric constituted the supporting evidence, then let the GBE do a better job in assessing the goals. Condemning the GBE procedure because of inadequacies in its execution does not solve the problem. Performing a better job of GBE does offer some hope.

Reply to the Comments by Alkin

Is GFE literally goal-free? Alkin says no; I say yes. Goals are not the point, not relevant, and no data about them is necessary for any external (and some internal) evaluation, at least not for GFE. It is irrelevant that some of the criteria happen to be someone's goals. Evaluation has to use standards of merit, and in an enlightened society one hopes that people's goals coincide with standards of merit. Whether they do or do not, however, does not matter to the evaluator, per se; his obligation is to the standards. (This is further elaborated where I discuss ultimate standards of value in reply to Stufflebeam.) An evaluation of a medicine proceeds in terms of harmful, as well as beneficial, effects. This is necessary in order to be objective, even if the target population were unloved orphan infants below the age where they could be said to have goals and the producer's only real goal were to make money. The same applies to commercial kindergarten packages. The evaluator does not in general need any data about the goals of any party affected. To see that what is used (standards of merit) may happen to be someone's goals is irrelevant; remember that they will also often be someone else's anathema, which scarcely shows that all evaluation is based on loathing.

Do we need GFE? Alkin questions my judgment as to the areas of greatest "demonstrated need in evaluation at this time." In particular, he does not think GFE is such an area. I never said it was. To

dismiss my imagined position, he refers to all the many problems related to the federal title programs and the evaluation of teachers. GFE could, in my view, significantly improve evaluation performance in all these areas, but I would not argue that it takes priority. Apparently he thinks that the evaluation project that first led me to formulate the GFE approach (a product evaluation job) is the limit of its applicability. Let me stress that it is a device for improving both formative and summative evaluation wherever they are done. I also work in the other areas he mentions, and it obviously applies to each of them. Is it the most important improvement we could make there? Is corn the most important thing a starving man needs? No, but it would surely help.

When should an evaluator work? Alkin then discusses some further imaginary positions of mine, the limitations of which he contrasts with his own model of evaluation. First, he says that I limit "the evaluative engagement" so as to exclude needs assessment advice to a project. Since I said "a crucial function of good formative evaluation is to give the producer a preview of the summative evaluation" and since, as Alkin points out, I take summative evaluation to involve needs assessment, it is a little implausible to argue that I exclude it from formative evaluation. He also says, "Scriven's goal-free evaluation is in essence a retrospective (and nonexplicit) needs assessment." This comment happens to contradict the first criticism, but let that pass. Intrinsically, it is about as plausible as the claim that Alkin is his foot. Obviously, GFE is an evaluation, one part of which involves explicit[6] needs assessment. An evaluation involves, but goes on from, a needs assessment, and I cannot see that anything I have said would suggest GFE involves less interest in drawing conclusions than GBE.

Having thus characterized GFE as retrospective, implicit needs assessment, Alkin goes on to say: "This would be alright but for the fact that performing this function retrospectively raises the cost enormously, not only of the evaluation but of a program that may have gone astray and [that] could have been brought back on course at an earlier time." The moral, as he sees it, is to pre-empt GFE by doing good advisory work for the project. It's touching that Alkin should think that summative evaluation of a project on which he

6. MA quotes my reference to "demonstrated needs"; how would they be demonstrated without a demonstration? This would surely mean that one had an explicit needs assessment.

helped the staff with the original needs assessment will be unnecessary, but it is somewhat unrealistic in either a suspicious or a scientific world. The facts of life and good evaluation are that external summative evaluation is partly a check on and, hence, a *replication* of, the internal formative evaluation; his internal needs assessment role scarcely provides one of the "alternatives to a goal-free evaluator," as he labels it. Both are part of good[7] evaluation. In any event, since I have a whole section on GFE in the *formative* role, it's surely a touch bizarre for Alkin to define GFE as *retrospective* implicit needs assessment and then to claim that the proper alternative to it is something I am excluding, namely, prospective evaluation. Since there is a perfectly good prospective version of GFE, it follows that the only error is in his definition, and he is just playing straw man games.

Concluding sentences: "Condemning the GBE procedure because of inadequacies in its execution does not solve the problem . . . Performing a better job of GBE does offer some hope." I trust that by now it is clear that I do not condemn GBE since I argue for continuing to use it. In particular, I do not *just* condemn it, but I offer what could be construed as an explicit procedure to "solve the problem" with it. Improving GBE, devoutly to be desired, indeed, is about as likely to close the loophole we are talking about as making a judge swear on his scout's honor that a dangled bribe had no influence on him.

COMMENT BY W. JAMES POPHAM:
RESULTS RATHER THAN RHETORIC

Whether Michael Scriven ever uttered the phrase "results rather than rhetoric," I am not certain. I came away from a conference many months ago in Colorado thinking that he had. It was there that Michael was testing an early conception of his goal-free evaluation position. If he didn't use that particular phrase, he will probably not be too displeased if I attribute it to him. After all, not only is the phrase alluringly alliterative, but it conveys a commitment to empirical evidence and a dismissal of mere word wizardry. And Michael

---

7. The summative evaluator can hardly assume either that the earlier evaluation advice was infallible or that the needs situation has not changed since the early days of the project. Either possibility eliminates Alkin's suggestion as an "alternative."

Scriven has a strong allegiance to empirical methods and a special flair for walloping word wizards. I do not think he would mind the attribution at all.

But beyond questions of its ancestry, the idea of results rather than rhetoric, as embodied in Scriven's goal-free evaluation writings, provides a useful caution to those educators who have recently become so enamored of instructional objectives that they think the mere act of articulating their goals precisely is not only the beginning but the end of the instructional ball game. And as you can learn from any baseball pitcher who has set out in the first inning to pitch a shutout, the game's final score is the thing that counts, not good intentions. Goal-based evaluation has offered educators a way of counteracting the heavy emphasis on instructional process which has been so fashionable in our country for years. GBE made it easier to describe intended instructional effects, then see if they were actually produced. But, as Professor Scriven's goal-free evaluation paper reminds us, GBE has often led to a tunneling of vision so that important results of instruction were overlooked. If GFE does nothing more than remind educators to appraise an educational undertaking on the basis of all its important effects, not just those which were described beforehand (even in flawlessly fashioned behavioral objectives), then GFE will have been a useful contribution.

But while the logic of Scriven's GFE stance is commendable, there are a few implementation operations which currently vex me. It is so early in the GFE game that Professor Scriven has not had time to wrestle with all of them. He undoubtedly will in time.

First, there was a clear implication in several of his early essays on GFE that the GFE'r could derive special raptures from spotting the educational catastrophes that a goal-blinded evaluator would not discern. Scriven spent a fair amount of time describing how the GFE'r would "set snares" to pick up a program's effects. While discovering all important effects is the proper province of the GFE'r, one has the distinct impression that his real kicks come from isolating an undiagnosed malignancy. We will have to see whether goal-free evaluators can be trained so that they develop a balanced search for the beneficial as well as the harmful results of an instructional program.

Second, there is a practical difficulty which the GFE'r will have trouble resolving, particularly in a formative context. If it is true, as Scriven contends, that actual effects must be evaluated against "a

profile of demonstrated needs," then clearly the GFE'r will either have to conduct some sort of an independent needs assessment or must rely on an existing effort to demonstrate needs. Relying on an existing needs assessment operation, particularly if carried out by the staff of the project being evaluated, carries with it the same deficits as GBE; that is, there may be subtle project staff biases operating which distort the validity of the assessment. But conducting an independent needs assessment is costly business and may not be considered cost-effective by the project's management. These problems may be more easily resolved in the summative context because the stakes are often perceived as higher and a summative evaluator may therefore more readily be able to demand the resources needed to secure an unbiased needs profile. But for a formative evaluator, I think this is a sticky problem. We want to foster as much independence for our GFE'r as possible, yet a totally independent needs assessment seems uneconomical.

A third problem stems from the degree to which a GFE'r can remain insulated from the instructional designer's goal preferences when it comes to devising the measures required to assess program impact on learners. In the abstract it is easy for a GFE'r to turn off the instructional designer who is about to spout goal talk. In constructing tests, observation scales, unobtrusive measures, etc., the GFE'r needs to have some kind of clues regarding what results the instruction is apt to yield. But as the requisite inferences are made from instructional procedures, materials, etc., there will be a strong likelihood that the project goals will insinuate themselves in the perceptions of the GFE'r. I suspect, therefore, that the possibility of keeping GFE completely uncontaminated by goal preferences is unrealistic. We must make it as goal-free as we can.

A final problem with GFE is that many educators, terrorized by the possible repercussions of goal-based evaluation, will use GFE as a philosopher-approved excuse for chucking out goals altogether. Yet Scriven makes it very clear that goals are required for planning, production, and internal evaluation. We must guard against those who will try to use GFE as an intellectually respectable cover for not thinking rigorously about their educational intentions.

Goal-free evaluation is destined to become very popular among educational folk. It is new. It was sired by an eminent academic philosopher who, all blessings abound, speaks with an educated British

accent. I can see future evaluators clamoring for specially designed GFE blinders to protect them from the taint of project goals. Short courses in snare setting will be conducted jointly by university departments of education and state game commissions. GFE will be IN.

But, because I have been persuaded by an eminent academic philosopher who speaks with an educated British accent, I will have to wait until all this GFE stuff has been tried out in a good number of real educational evaluations. You see, I have recently become somewhat committed to results rather than rhetoric.

Reply to the Comments by Popham

Popham believes that even GBE is a big step forward compared to the typical process evaluations of an earlier phase. I agree. As far as I am concerned, it will be a long time before we can compensate for the overemphasis on transaction studies, input analyses, and academic content criteria that persists.

Is GBE biased against programs? Popham fears that looking for bad side effects may be more attractive to me than looking for good ones. I think we would find more bad ones through GFE than we did through GBE for two reasons. First, I think goal-based evaluators tend to be influenced by the enthusiasm of the project staff, which encourages "false positives." Second, if you compare the summative terminal evaluations of educational innovations, such as curricular innovations, of the 1950's and 1960's with the present best judgment of their significance, you would have to say that the summatives were nearly always too optimistic. These examples tend to be of negative side-effect discoveries, in all honesty, but, in the case of the Toy Library, which was evaluated by the Product Review Panel, a huge favorable side effect converted an "unsuccessful" project into a winner. Quite possibly the instructive nervousness of producers toward GFE is based on their judgment that it will tend to discover hitherto unnoticed drawbacks. To the extent that this is the reason for their opposition, it is understandable but not justifiable.

It may be worth remembering that Popham and I both work pretty hard as producers, not just as evaluators. I have no doubt that GFE will improve my products, and I plan to include it in my next materials development proposal.

Is it economically feasible for the goal-free evaluator to do another needs assessment? The needs assessments I have seen range from in-

credibly overpriced to off-the-top-of-the-head, and the funds available for evaluation on the project where I currently have a major role in evaluation, for example, run from $1,000 to $5,000,000. No general answer is possible. Even if goal-free evaluators never obtained such funds, their utility would by no means be eliminated. Operating in the goal-free role at a site, I can formulate (and write out) a hypothesis about what needs data are required to justify the activity I am observing. Then I can call for the project's needs assessment and see whether it fits my specifications. If not, and if I can make my case stick, we have learned something very important about the existing evaluation, namely, that it is seriously deficient. Whether the funds can be found to do it right is up to project and sponsor. My view is that there is no justification for estimating or spending an evaluation budget that has no margin for an outcome such as that described. On a well-planned project, funds would be available. The other possibility (on balance somewhat, and more likely given the relative resource allocation assumed) is that the needs assessment will show that I was wrong, in which case the project evaluation staff is to be congratulated, and the project is spared an illegitimate criticism.

The general tenor of Popham's remarks here suggests a system response that I prefer to the rather specific comments just made. Most of the data on which a needs assessment is based, for most cases, should be publicly and readily available, say in the Educational Resources Information Center (ERIC), and, hence, very cheaply identifiable. To do this, we clearly "need" much more needs data, and I think that should be a priority for NIE. But something like that is already possible with regard to many types of projects, for example, a new math curriculum.

Can we really avoid contaminating the goal-free evaluator? I think the answer is yes, with regard to the quickie formative or summative evaluation (the site visit), which may be the most common kind of external evaluation. For long-term planned evaluation, the leakage Popham describes is increasingly a risk, but the later it comes the less harm it does. The crucial time to insulate the goal-free evaluator is, fortunately, that time when it is easiest, namely, when forming the overall picture and preliminary hypotheses and questions that emerge as the evaluation design. What I am really saying is that, even if we cannot eliminate contamination, we can often control it long enough

to obtain some useful results. The nice thing about GFE is that, at worst, it only deteriorates into GBE, whereas GBE is an irreversible condition. You cannot forget the goals once you have heard them. Experiments with GFE versus GBE could produce some immensely valuable and sorely needed data about the interjudge reliability of GBE.

If you are interested in GFE, you can easily try it on your next quick evaluation by allowing an hour or so on-site to write up a few notes on the GFE appearance of the project—then calling in the project staff to hear about goals and so forth. Both you and the project staff can then determine whether you have gained. As far as undupli-cated quick evaluations are concerned (formative or summative), I do not recommend pure GFE, only the GFE-GBE "doublecheck." Why not eat your cake and have it too?

Is GFE a threat to the use of goals? The evaluator may not need to know the producer's (teacher or other) goals, but the producer or teacher surely does. Pointless activity is not going to sprout better effects when looked at through the GFE-scope unless by an act of God. GFE has two great advantages for projects, including innovative teaching, that should help offset any perceived threat. First, GFE is extremely nondisruptive. We have all heard the complaints about the amount of time the project staff must spend in scheduling, preparing for, and participating in site visits. The amount of time can be enor-mously reduced when the site team does not expect to be enter-tained, briefed, or attended. At most, one person would be around for liaison, that is, collection of products, schedules, or other mate-rials. This feature of GFE increases the chance of getting a true sam-ple of the process, too, if that is crucial. Second, GFE is not tied to the original goals of the projects since it is not tied to goals at all; it is tolerant of change in direction, and it is oriented toward final results, not original rhetoric.

I still like that slogan, and Popham's recall of it sets the right note. I support the idea that GFE is an addition to the evaluator's reper-toire that will sometimes pay off. The purpose of this discussion is simply to clarify what the proposal is so it will get a *fair* trial and to encourage people to think it has some chance of success so it will get *a* trial.

COMMENT BY GEORGE F. KNELLER:
GOAL-FULL EVALUATION

Professor Scriven advocates goal-free evaluation as a remedy for certain weaknesses in contemporary research design. The remedy, however, is unnecessary, since, as I shall point out, these weaknesses can be corrected more efficiently by modifying either the design itself, or the training of evaluators, or both.

Scriven's most substantial argument in favor of goal-free evaluation is that, the more an evaluator concerns himself with the goals of a project, the less likely he is to notice the project's side effects. This tendency, however, may be corrected in two ways without resort to GFE: first, by training evaluators to observe *both* goals (and outcomes) *and* side effects; second, by the researcher's specifying as many likely side effects as possible within the original research design. Thus the researcher himself gathers many of the relevant data while conducting his own project.

Scriven also argues that the use of GFE makes it harder for an evaluator to persuade himself that the goals of a project have been achieved simply because they have been set. But bias in favor of goals is only one of many biases to which evaluators are subject, and little is gained by seeking to eliminate this form of subjectivity while leaving other forms untouched. The wisest course is not to rely on GFE to eliminate one form of subjectivity but to train evaluators in advance to be objective judges in as many respects as possible.

Scriven's other arguments in favor of GFE carry little weight:

—He maintains that research projects often are designed to attain grandiose goals which distract the evaluator's attention from the project's actual achievements. I reply that (*a*) evaluators should be trained to spot and to criticize grandiose goals, and (*b*) researchers should be trained to set realistic goals.

—Similarly Scriven asserts that the alleged goals of a project often differ from the real ones. Once again, however, proper training should (*a*) correct this sort of misunderstanding in the researcher, and (*b*) improve the evaluator's ability to recognize the discrepancy when it occurs.

—Scriven also claims that the goals of many research designs are too vague. Indeed, they may be. But the way to eliminate the fault is

not to introduce GFE after the event but to educate researchers to
draw up their designs more carefully at the outset.

—Scriven calls for GFE on the grounds that projects often fail to
achieve their goals. But unless we take these goals into account, we
shall never know which projects have succeeded in their aims and
which have not.

The frailties which Scriven correctly criticizes in research designers
may also be found in evaluators, goal-free or otherwise. These are
human frailties, and they may come into play anywhere in the course
of a project from its preliminary drafting to its completion. It is not
enough, therefore, to provide one particular safeguard by introducing
GFE after the project is finished. Instead, safeguards should be built
into the design at many points.

Also, Scriven makes no provision for the defense of researchers
against the bias of his breed of evaluators. In my view, researchers are
fully entitled to object to evaluators who are not concerned to find
out what the goals are of the projects they are examining. I am not
arguing for a balance of power between researchers and evaluators,
but I am saying that evaluators, too, can become irrational and im-
moderate.

Scriven's metaphors and analogies are bright and amusing, but
they do not make for tight logical argument. Moreover, some of
them are ill-conceived. The goal-free evaluator, he says, once having
learned to be free of a security blanket of goals, "like riding a bicycle
or swimming without the aids one uses at first, (experiences) a remarkable sense of freedom, of liberation." In fact, (*a*) aids are not in
the same class as goals, and (*b*) security blankets may save the lives of
those who feel so free that they outswim (lose control of) themselves.

If I had to make a choice, I would reject GFE, not only in consequence of the counterarguments I draw above but also because of my
gestaltist tendency to see things in more or less complete patterns,
hence to take the goals of enterprises into consideration. In any case,
I do not see the issue as theoretical but as one appealing to taste,
about which there can be no dispute. One simply makes a choice
and, if called upon to justify the choice, can offer only personal
opinions.

Scriven's essay is not without nuggets of wisdom. For example, he
points out: "But in no case is it proper to use anyone's goals as the

standard unless they can be shown to be the appropriate ones and morally defensible." This remark should be taken seriously not only by researchers and evaluators but by people in every walk of life.

Reply to the Comment by Kneller

The problem of bias. Kneller has a brilliant solution, namely, train evaluators to be unbiased. That would certainly render GFE unnecessary. From the day that he succeeds in implementing his solution, I promise never to mention GFE again. Until that time, however, lesser mortals working in the fields of law, medicine, and education have to worry about such things, and they will probably continue to use devices like professional codes on the conflicts of interest that arise, double-blind designs, and randomization.

Kneller generalizes this solution in other directions. It is no argument against GBE, he says, that goals are usually incomprehensible, incomplete, inconsistent, outdated, and so forth. Why not, he says, just train evaluators to avoid or correct such deficiencies? This is an admirable, indeed, it is an inspiring, goal. I have even been inspired to try it myself. However, I suppose there is something to be said for an approach that does not depend on making people perfect (at least in these dimensions).

The choice between GFE and GBE. Is this merely a matter of taste? Kneller thinks so, but he is wrong. Whether the addition of GFE to the repertoire leads to enough significant extra insight (objectively validated) to offset any extra costs it involves is an empirical matter. In the small number of cases where it has so far been tried, it has always produced such insights, which is not a bad record for a new procedure. It need only produce them occasionally to earn its keep, especially since its keep might be immediately paid for by the insights if they should lead to cost reductions or quality gains.

Bias of GFE evaluators. "Scriven makes no provision for the defense of researchers against the bias of his breed of evaluators." (For a while there, I guess, it was a one-man breed, which at least makes genetic history.) Kneller continues: "In my view, researchers are fully entitled to object to evaluators who are not concerned to find out what the goals are of the project they are examining." I am not quite sure how we got onto the subject of researchers, but evaluation of them does provide an interesting topic. I had always thought that serendipitous discoveries produced Nobel Prizes. If so, that would be

one reason for concluding that meritorious achievement in research is not based on goal attainment. Another would be provided by looking at all of the insignificant stuff published in journals of educational research, most of which consists of investigations that achieved exactly what they set out to do. What really counts is what you do, not what you meant to do, and good evaluation should properly often focus on the former. There are other roles for evaluation that bring in the latter, and my "breed" of evaluator (speaking for myself, at least) spends most of his time on projects that involve both. It seems a pity that one cannot suggest a new tool without the implication being drawn that one never uses anything else.

Conclusion and Proposal

Although GFE could be evaluated in the GFE mode, it certainly could not be done by me, I am glad to say. ("My poor baby—and those *heartless* men.") Here are some possible evaluation models of the conventional kind, drawn up when contemplating the NSF trial, which would have compared GBE and GFE.[8]
(a) Stufflebeam's team and Scriven's team would each evaluate the same two sites: Stufflebeam would use GBE, and Scriven would use GFE (the NSF suggestion). Possible drawbacks:
    i. Stufflebeam knows he is competing against GFE and, hence, does better than he might do otherwise. The differences are, therefore, atypical.
    ii. The same applies for Scriven.
    iii. Differences between skills (for the particular sites) of Scriven's team and those of Stufflebeam's team might account for all variance.
    iv. Sequence effects at sites offer the remote possibility of a counterexplanation.
(b) Stufflebeam uses GBE; Scriven uses GFE-GBE. More realistic since the "double-check" approach is the best candidate politically and looks better methodologically (since GFE and GBE have complementary sources of error). This design partially controls for differences between Scriven and Stufflebeam. Possible drawbacks:

---

8. Al Buccino at NSF deserves great credit for this attempt to break up the long-established tradition of regarding evaluation as something about which it is improper to do research.

i. Scriven and team may not work hard in GFE mode since they know they will get the news eventually. (This may be a general drawback of the double-check procedure.)

ii. Project staffs may not provide same briefing to both teams, perhaps because of learning effects, fatigue, or bias.

(c) Both teams use double-check procedure. This controls for Scriven-Stufflebeam differences by allowing the order of site visits to be switched. (It also controls somewhat for learning effects, although the n is too small.) It reduces application of any anti-GFE bias, involves important experiment in "transportability" of GFE to other evaluators, allows Stufflebeam to make his own judgment of utility, and so on. The main drawback is (b)i, above, which applies to both teams.

(d) An interesting possibility would be to have Scriven do GFE and Stufflebeam do a double check. Main gain is to partially correct for the (b)i problem without making everything depend on guessing about the extent to which Scriven-Stufflebeam differences account for the result, and we still pick up some transportability experience. Interpretation of results is tricky in this respect. My position would be that Stufflebeam would do better so my motivation might be submaximal.

However, the outcome of such experiments—you will be amazed to learn—is not crucial. GFE has an extraordinarily powerful side effect that is clearly so beneficial we really do not need to see how it works in practice. The side effect is that it stimulates discussion among lethargic evaluators, which proves to be most revealing about their conceptualization (or misconceptualization) of the most basic notions in their field, and is thereby extremely educational. It also proves to have similar effects on students of evaluation, as Stufflebeam and I found out when running the AERA road show on evaluation in 1972-73. So, if all else fails, behold GFE as part of the Adult Toy Library!

MAXIMIZING THE POWER OF CAUSAL INVESTIGATIONS: THE MODUS OPERANDI METHOD

Granted that control-group studies (including possibly self-controls) are the method of choice for studies of social intervention (Campbell, Tatsuoka, Mosteller, Meehl), we must frequently face the need to do the best we can with nonexperimental data. I want to present a sketch of what is sometimes the best methodology for this, reconstructed from the procedures of the historian, the detective, the anthropologist, and the engineering troubleshooter. This methodology has been completely neglected in evaluation theory, though not completely ignored in practice since anthropologists and historians have occasionally been used as evaluators. I believe that a reasonable account of these methods would make them accessible to the more traditionally trained and oriented evaluator, especially as a substitute for the usually more desirable experimental and quasi-experimental approaches when these approaches are impossible. And, in almost every investigation, they would serve as a supplementary device to increase the reliability of conclusions reached by the more common designs.

It is not adequate to increase the use of this approach by using more historians and anthropologists (or clinicians) in evaluation teams, although this is not a bad idea. What is more important is that the method itself become an explicitly formulated and understood tool in the repertoire of every investigator, for in most evaluations there are no resources for auxiliary personnel. Moreover, scholars whose field requires them to depend on the modus operandi (MO) approach often cannot articulate it well and, hence, do not interact too well with scholars to whom the approach is strange. (For general background, see the discussions in P. L. Gardiner, ed., *Theories of History* (New York: Free Press) and in William Dray, ed., *Philosophical Analysis and History* (New York: Harper and Row).

The procedures outlined here involve more than a formalization of MO analysis; they represent a set of causal inference patterns of which MO analysis is probably the most distinctive. Full conversion of the modus operandi method into quantitative techniques may or

An earlier version of this section was commissioned by, and presented orally at, the Battelle Institute in Seattle, Washington.

may not be possible, but some suggestions as to procedure follow. Some conversion may already have been done in as-yet-unpublished developments of path analysis, from the Wisconsin conference or elsewhere. But I have been so struck by the excessive crudity and impracticality of early work in path analysis, and by the continued neglect of MO methodology by sophisticated investigators, that I felt it would be worth spending some time trying to do the job in my own way. I would be most grateful for criticism including references to earlier methodological discussions of this approach. It is, of course, related to John Platt's "strong inference" and to Gilbert Harman's "inference to the best explanation," though it antedates both.

Statement of the Problem

Assume the general form of the problem is to identify the cause or causes of phenomenon X. Of particular interest is factor A, which represents an earlier intervention that it is our task to evaluate. Factor A will be deemed successful (or unsuccessful) to some degree if A caused X (and certain other conditions are met), not otherwise. X is thus some effect which is demonstrably meritorious (or undesirable) such as learning gains (or increased vandalism). X may of course be a change in the value of a variable, or, atypically, the absence of such a change; or the appearance of a new variable or configuration of variables. It should be noted that the identification of causes is of crucial importance not only for intervention studies (planning social change), but for "pure understanding," which is often the historian's concern. We are thus searching for the cause of X (general problem) or testing the hypothesis that A was the cause (special case).

Now cause hunting, like lion hunting, is only likely to be successful if we have a considerable amount of relevant background knowledge. The most general proposition in this stock of background knowledge, the most general presupposition of our search, must be a claim of weak local determinism, which means that we must have grounds for supposing that X's (or X's in these circumstances, C) are usually caused. Such an assumption fails for many phenomena in the realm of elementary particles. It is well supported in much of the social domain, but it fails even there with respect to certain decision behaviors (by analogy with the argument in my "An Essential Unpredictability in Human Behavior," in *Scientific Psychology,* ed. Benjamin Wolman and Ernest Nagel [New York: Basic Books, 1965]).

Note that we do not require absolute (that is, exceptionless) as opposed to limited or statistical determinism since all we can hope for anyway, given limitations of measurement, is a probable conclusion and we can get that from the statistical ("weak") version of determinism. Methodologically, as long as X is *probably* caused, we have to act as if it *is* caused, on minimax grounds (consider also the optimal betting strategy for a coin known to have slight bias toward a known side). And we only require local determinism (limited to X-like entities, possibly only in specified circumstances, C) as opposed to general or universal determinism (that is, a determinism of all sociological phenomena or all phenomena).

Now most automobile mechanics (and many historians) are not interested in abstract determinism; instead, they need something more specific. They rely, although they may not realize it, on a claim that entails the one just mentioned, namely: Most X's (in C) are caused by A, A', A'', . . . , A^n. Let us call this a *quasi-exhaustive causal list*. The sense in which they need this does not imply that they can state it, but it is easy to prove that they know it without relying on verbalization (a distinction overlooked by the Educational Testing Service [ETS] in constructing the national auto mechanics test first used this year), and only a little less easy to show that they need it, as we will see. What is interesting about these lists is that they are rather modest claims by contrast with "determinism," that is, strong general determinism, which is usually said to be a required assumption for scientific investigation. As a matter of fact, something can still be done even if we only know some of the entries in such a list.

Causal List Inference

Given the preceding background data, we can sometimes determine the cause of X very simply, by means of the "presence check." We merely check for the presence of each of the A's, and hope that only one is present. The inference is then easy. (See note at bottom of page 84 concerning this inference.)

> Almost all A's are caused by A, A', A'', . . . , A^n.
> X has occurred.
> A did occur.
> A', A'', . . . , A^n did not occur.
> _____
> (Probably) A caused X on this occasion.

The probability can be very high if the causal list covers nearly all cases with few causes, and we can often give such lists.

If no A from the list occurred, we strive to discover the cause of this particular X by applying causal lists about analogous phenomena; and, if we do so, we are able to add an extra A to the list for X and increase our confidence in its completeness. If we do not discover the cause of X after such an investigation, and such cases recur, we have to reduce our confidence in the list's completeness. Since the third premise is not necessary, checking it provides some confirmation of the conclusion or increases the probability of the conclusion. This is an important source of internal confirmation and can be cast in classical predictive form if we leave the check for A's presence till the end. The absence of the other possible causes then generates the prediction of A's presence which is then confirmed.

Modus Operandi Inference

If more than one A occurs, we move to the modus operandi check. Since it always provides some further confirmation (probability increment), it is good practice to use this check anyway. Suppose that both A and A' were present. There are four possibilities of interest: A was the (sole) cause, A' was the (sole) cause; A and A' were co-causes; neither was a cause. We now move toward discrimination among these alternatives.

The MO of a particular cause is an associated configuration of events, processes, or properties, usually in time sequence, which can often be described as the *characteristic causal chain* (or certain distinctive features of this chain) connecting the cause with the effect. In its most common usage, in criminalistics, the term refers to such characteristics as the method of entry used by a burglar, the kind of weapon and occasion used by a hit man, the communications procedure used by kidnappers. In the autopsy context (X=death), to go one step further, the MO's for drowning, poisons, and heart failure are well known; the art or science of differential diagnosis for the toxicologist partly consists of MO analysis. It is not the only technique, however, although the line of demarcation is not sharp. If the detective notices the smell of bitter almonds (one of the few experiences which, apparently, everyone can be said to recognize without having any memory of it), he is not using MO analysis; if he notices the characteristic facial rictus, he is. The first is a property of the poison; the second is one of its effects.

In cases where the cause occurred substantially earlier than the effect, MO analysis is easily distinguished from identification of the presence of the cause in that it refers to processes occupying the temporal gap between cause and effect. But we are often not so fortunate as to have such an interval.

The basic truism for MO analysis is that only real, that is, operative, causes fulfill their MO "contracts." Even if A and A′ are both present, which we may determine directly or by inference from certain MO cues, one may not have completed the causal connection to the effect. The victim was poisoned and shot, but it was the shot that killed him because we do not find the knotted muscles that would be associated with death caused by an alkaloid from this group, although we do find that poison in the stomach and some of the early symptoms of its ingestion such as crossed eyes. We will often use "MO" to refer to the whole causal chain, rather than just to the most distinctive features of it.

The general nature of our task is thus one of pattern recognition or, in the language of educational psychology, configural scoring. In general terms, this part of the investigation focuses on discovering how many *complete* MO's are present. Thus, the total sequence of tasks, inferences being of course probabilistic, is as follows:

(i) Check for the presence of each A. If only one, that is the cause.

(ii) If more than one is present, check for complete MO's. If none, then none of those A's was a cause.

(iii) If only one MO is complete, the A with which that MO is associated is the cause.

(iv) If more than one complete MO is present, the associated factors are co-causes.

Pattern-recognition computer programs rely heavily on the fact that they only have to discriminate between a finite set of possibilities, and this makes cause hunting feasible (just as it made possible Mosteller's brilliant solution to the problem of determining authorship of the Federalist Papers, a typical MO approach). Hence, the reliability of the MO methodology depends upon the reliability of the causal list since it provides the candidates. Anyone who has worked from a trouble-shooting chart knows that very high reliability, even without an exhaustive causal list, can be attained in the mechanical-electrical-medical domain. The same is true of criminalistics. What about the

educational-clinical-social context? And what about looking for the causes of desirable effects, as opposed to trouble? I would say the situation is closely comparable, although this fact is greatly obscured by the tendency to think that gross differences in predictive power between these groups of disciplines has a bearing on the explanatory situation. The fact remains that causes are, by their nature, explanatory and not predictive factors although we are sometimes lucky enough to get the predictive power as a bonus. It is not hard to list, and it is easier still to recognize, most and often nearly all of the likely causes of a given, substantial, and highly specified social phenomenon, be it recession, depression, regression, or delectation, in particular forms and circumstances.

Even where that is impossible, there is a reserve position. Partial causal lists are still useful, even though they will not support a definite eliminative analysis from mere presence checks, as does the quasi-exhaustive list. Both lists support a highly probable conclusion if the MO check is both complex and successful. The antecedent likelihood that an unknown factor will have the same MO is, in general, very low. Thus:

(i) A and A' can sometimes cause X.
(ii) Nothing else is known to cause X.
(iii) A but not A' was present.
(iv) The MO of A, which is highly distinctive, was present.

A probably caused X.

Again, the third premise can be omitted, but, with this weaker inference, its presence is valuable. The sense of "highly distinctive" that is needed for validity here refers to unknown other possible causes of X. Since they are unknown, the safest inferences will be those where the MO configuration is very complex.

A hybrid case, which reflects a good deal of acute implicit reasoning, involves a first premise that lists known possible causes and also hypothetical or speculative possible causes that have never actually been demonstrated as such. The combination might conceivably yield a quasi-exhaustive list, but it is more likely simply to improve the reliability of the conclusion, just as it would if the extra causes were known to be capable of producing X. There is often some prob-

lem in deciding what "this phenomenon" is, when trying to give a list of all possible causes of it. After all, there may be something special about this occurrence of "it," which, if known, would preclude the possibility that one of our candidates could have done it. The argument just given, which shows that the inference is still possible even with entirely speculative candidates, entails that there is no need to agonize over such a question. One should simply include any possible cause, in any pragmatic sense of "possible," with either weak theoretical (or analogical) or direct empirical support for its candidacy. The cost of extra length in the causal list is minor, and the gains may be large.

We are thus able to get plausible conclusions from incredibly weak and commonly available premises. Does this have practical applications for the design and support of evaluations? I believe it does. I believe that the main thrust of efforts towards sophistication should now turn from the quasi-experimental toward the modus operandi approach.

Consequences for Research Design and Ideology

One direct consequence of making MO inference patterns explicit is the suggestion that our experimental designs should incorporate what one might call "signature arrangements," "tracers," or "tell-tales," which will expose distinctive characteristics of the causal candidates of interest. Another is that more attention needs to be given to externalizing the implicit knowledge of causal lists and MO's possessed by many specialists, be they master teachers or union leaders. In fact, these points connect with and mutually reinforce a larger perspective. I think the time has come to change our orientation in the development of social science away from the goal of abstract, quantitative, predictive theories toward specific, qualitative, explanatory checklists and trouble-shooting charts. I think that such a large-scale change is quite closely related to the simple models of argument discussed above, for the ideology of competing methodologies is usually expressible in very simple formal models (think of the Hypothetico-Deductive Model, Covering Law Model, and others). It is not that evaluators, social psychologists, sociologists, and others have never done this kind of fine-structure analysis. Rather, they have done it, rarely and unsystematically, as a work of supererogation or with a degree of informality that leaves it in the category of anec-

dotal evidence, and it has been done with little or no assistance from the statisticians whereas it should have been a major focus of attention and development.

There are many complications and implications of this account that need careful consideration. Most notably, there are three species of overdetermination that lead to refinements of the MO procedure, and there is the fundamental problem of the origin of the causal lists, their relation to more conventional laws, and the alleged ultimate connections of causation with prediction manipulation and determinism. I have discussed some aspects of these, and other related issues, in "The Logic of Cause" (*Theory and Decision*, II [No. 1, October 1971, 49-66]).

Application to Evaluation Design

Suppose we wish to evaluate the performance of a small-scale bureau we set up on a campus to improve undergraduate and other teaching. We cannot count on the interrupted time-series approach because there are too many novel, powerful, and erratic external influences on the dependent variables at this time, among them, pressure from professional associations and legislatures to improve teaching. We cannot run a proper control group because of moral considerations (we should not withhold help in this area) and contamination. We could try ex post facto matching, but the main problems are the need for a large sample, which is certainly too expensive and may be impossible on a small campus, and the essential bias of an ex post facto study, which is likely to have serious substantive significance.

If the MO approach is used, we first set up a signature or tracer system, trying to arrange things so that the procedures recommended by the bureau are distinguishable from those coming from other sources at least in minor, nonfundamental ways. Where the procedures are novel, this presents no difficulty. If another source has the best available solution, for example, to the problem of designing a student evaluation questionnaire, insignificant changes can be made in the wording on copies distributed by the bureau, and they can be distributed without cost to facilitate getting the tracer into the bloodstream. We try to ensure, and here the intrusiveness may be a small trade-off cost, that verbal counseling is accompanied by written materials with tracers in them or that the verbalized content itself uses a novel, preferably useful, term or two. Monitoring the blood-

stream of information through the university later, we can detect the passage of "signed" material and assess deterioriation, implementation, and so forth.

Focusing on MO in another way, we identify a sample of information couriers or influence peddlers, people using bureau services and exhibiting some evangelical zeal; they are interviewed on a regular schedule to catch diffusion effects, and the hypotheses generated by the interviews are followed up. They (or others) may be encouraged to keep logs of dissemination transactions. (Here we find a useful reinforcement between evaluation procedures and improving diffusion strategies.)

Working backward from any detectable gains in the quality of undergraduate teaching, perhaps showing up in percentage acceptances at graduate schools, on Law School Acceptance Tests (LSAT) or other tests, on student ratings of courses and faculty, or on departmental examinations, we bring to bear the whole apparatus of MO analysis. We carefully examine causal lists, using enemies of the bureau as a vital source of alternative explanations (causes); we develop the most elaborate possible formulation of MO's for each of these candidates and then go after straight presence and MO completion checks; we set out explicitly the elements that discriminate between the members of this set of MO's, and set forth the evidence that we believe excludes the rejected candidates. We look with care at the span of the induction that is used to bring experience elsewhere or at other times to bear on this experiment, that is, at many of the inferences that generate our causal list. We check for co-causation and overdetermination. We use a goal-free or social process expert consultant to seek undesirable side effects in the academic jungle. We track down the sources of rumors and advice that are reported to have had significant effects, using journalists and historians as aides rather than educational psychologists and anthropologists; perhaps even a clinician could be helpful in digging into motives and memories to establish causal connections. We perform microexperiments to check the minipredictions that sometimes emerge from MO hypotheses. We may schedule a program of random (or random within the most probably influenced group) snapshots of the teaching process, looking for tracers or configural MO signatures. We should ultimately be able to develop a picture of the spreading influence of the bureau, in spite of its external and internal competitors, that is beyond the pos-

sibility of reasonable doubt. And perhaps we shall have narrowed the gap between respectable and anecdotal evaluation so that evaluation will seem a little less threatening to our humanistic friends because it is a little more familiar. Of course we have not handled all the problems for the evaluator. It must be realized that discovering:

A did cause X, where X is desirable,

does not always guarantee that A is desirable, although it justifies a prima facie inference to this conclusion. Of the many difficulties with this inference, some of which involve side effects, perhaps the strongest is the possibility that X could have been (or perhaps even would have been) achieved by a B that costs half as much as A. The second caution is also for the methodologist. The usual definitions of cause—explicit and implicit—are erroneous in a crucial respect, one where the MO method is not in error. Typical experimental designs for the investigation of psychotherapy success, for example, involve the assumption that parity of results between the experimental group and a no-treatment control group demonstrates that the psychotherapy is having no effect. This is an error because the controls may be engaged in autotherapeutic activities that simply have the same, significant-sized effect as psychotherapy. For an evaluator looking at interventions that might deserve federal support, this shows the psychotherapy to have zero cost-effectiveness, but it does not show zero effectiveness in the "scientific" sense. Either a second (pseudotherapy) control or MO analysis is required to distinguish this case from or identify it with a situation in which the effects of auto- and psychotherapy are both zero. Suppose those effects are not zero, only equal. Even though psychotherapy must be evaluated as a poor intervention strategy, there is a different framework in terms of which the evaluator would come to a different conclusion. Suppose the evaluator is looking at the options open to a neurotic patient. He or she will then rate (typically) the autotherapy and the psychotherapy as quite effective, and the latter as less cost-effective than the former. (Since the latter has a somewhat different MO from the former, including reduction of anxiety earlier and possibly serious withdrawal symptoms later, a time integration of the benefits may show some advantages for one or the other.) The question of "effectiveness" thus involves implicit reference to a base line, to a context of inquiry. This is more likely to occur to an evaluator, but it is true

even for the scientist, who is less likely to accept the idea of relativity of effects.

One might argue that, for purposes of evaluation, one should always use the cruder notion of causation, which involves the axiom that the absence of the cause entails the absence of the effect, and hence the lemma that, if the absence of a putative cause leads to no difference in outcome compared to a group lacking the alleged cause, the "cause" has no effect, that is, it is not a cause. But the "insight function" of causal analysis is obviously blunted by such a usage, and, therefore, I reject the claim that it is mandatory.

Applying this point to the teaching bureau example, we have to realize that the discovery of many significant and desirable effects that really are due to its activities does not show that these effects would not have occurred if the bureau had never existed, perhaps with less cost. Causal power is not the same as utility or value; it is just a necessary condition for the latter.

Must MO methodology always be supported by control-group methodology? It depends on the question of interest. Is the question: Did the bureau really have a significant effect—or almost no effect? If so, then MO is appropriate. Or is the question one that is not usually distinguished from the first: Did the bureau bring about results that would not have occurred anyway? If this is the question, then you do supplementary work involving the usual controls or you simply have to make a bet based on intuition or trend analysis.

Don Campbell has suggested, in conversation, a neat way to set up the control group for this study if one gets in at the start of the intervention. One might ask the bureau to focus on the A-M faculty and use N-Z as control. But there are still real difficulties over the rejection of requests for help from the controls and leakage of the treatment. (It is always unfortunate to use an evaluation design where a real-world desirable effect has to be regarded as experimentally undesirable.) Once the system is off and running, there is no way to apply this design in retrospect. The MO approach can also be incorporated in the planning phase, as suggested, with decided advantages as far as getting a picture of the evaluee's total contribution is concerned. (For this reason, it is not just a subspecies of ex post facto design.) Although it will still work well as the study progresses, it will not tell you conclusively what would have happened if the treatment were not there. I think the evaluator or administrator must assume (an MO

assumption) that external causes cannot be relied on to produce the desired effect either in regard to degree or to speed. The way to find out whether you have pulled the right lever is MO analysis.

The case we have been discussing involves a bureau that is given a strong interventionist charge (mission). Suppose it is given or adopts a low profile and simply responds to requests for help based on mere notification of its existence. Good results are somewhat more likely to be its very own and somewhat less likely to have been achieved by other factors in its absence. (On the other hand, it is less likely to achieve significant results in the absence of an aggressive campaign.) There is also a powerful credibility advantage if serious holistic evaluation is not done or if one's activities have all been based on requests for service and one can show MO evidence of services rendered in response to such requests. MO analysis of this sort can often show that the kind of assistance rendered simply was not available elsewhere, either when required or later. Nor would it have been available in the absence of the bureau because it would have required expertise and time only a central office could supply.

Campbell points out (in correspondence) some traps that bear on any serious classical evaluation of this kind of intervention. For example, in a controlled study one might find a highly significant correlation between treatment and *below*-average teaching performance, but this may be due to self-selection of treatment by the worst teachers. Or, if one looked at pretest-posttest gains, one might be seduced into thinking the treatment is highly successful with the low scorers on the pretest whereas the correlation with treatment is simply a consequence of a test-retest correlation. Of course there are analytical tools for protection against such misinterpretations (for example, using regressed pretest scores as the base line for gains in the second case). I am inclined to think that MO methodology is rather less liable to fall into such traps across the board. But we should examine more dangerous examples, where traps must be carefully avoided by the MO analyst.

Another context where this approach is called for is the accountability context: we need to know whether what was supposed to be done was done, and by the agency funded, but not necessarily whether it was done in the best possible way. Yet another context is the exploratory one in which we are investigating to see whether this independent variable can actually produce this effect, intending to

do further studies if it can but to work elsewhere if it cannot. In areas where such studies are very costly in time, dollars, or skills, the MO approach provides a valuable early screening procedure.

Of great importance, it seems to me, is the fact that MO analysis does not violate the social-political taboos that sometimes render full experimental treatment impossible. It can be relatively unobtrusive.

One hope I have for this methodology is that it can help with Aptitude-Treatment-Interaction (ATI) problems. As is generally recognized, the confidence that significant ATI discoveries would emerge from the study of teaching styles and student characteristics such as cognitive style has so far been matched only by the barrenness of the results. An example that is of particular concern to me at the moment concerns role playing since I am evaluating a teacher-training package aimed at that goal. In defending it to me, the producer said that it did not really need any defense since he knew it worked "for some kids." (We could also take an example of large-scale social interventions like Head Start where the possibility exists that it worked very well at some sites.) I shall try to explain what I think the MO approach can do to test such hunches, which I believe are closely related to the *verstehen* intuitions of the historian and should not be dismissed as casually as is common.

The crudest approach to the evaluation of teaching role playing would perhaps consist in looking at the gain in the mean score on some appropriate instrument. It would be less crude to look at the distribution of individual gains. But this will not distinguish between two competing explanations of individual cases. Take a case like that Dave Berliner may have had in mind when speaking to me so favorably of role playing. The pre-post gain for a certain student has been very large, not only by comparison with other students in this class but also by "absolute" standards, that is, it is judged to represent a highly significant and difficult-to-achieve educational gain. We might throw in the fact that the child has greatly enjoyed the learning experience.

Now it is possible that this gain is simply a regression artifact, or it may be due to an educationally important matching of the treatment to the student characteristics. If we apply regression corrections to the scores, as Don Campbell was suggesting, we achieve the best statistically possible guide to the "genuineness" of the effect. But to do so will sometimes wrongly mask what is a real effect. Try to look at

the situation with MO techniques in mind. Here is a student (or a school) with unusually low pretest scores. The specific meaning of "statistical artifact" here—or, I should say, the particular kind with which I am concerned at the moment and which seems to provide the most threatening competing explanation—is that the test items were an "unlucky" choice for this individual. There is a direct way of testing this, a retest, but it is not available after the treatment begins. It is also very costly, and there are hazards about its interpretation. One alternative explanation is that the individual's prior knowledge is really very limited. Now, are there differences in the way in which these two "causes" operate to produce their common effect, the low score? Both of them operate through the head of the subject, and that is where we should look for MO differentiae. Was it really the emptiness of the head that caused the low score? One obvious detector would be a tack-on question of a yes-no kind, which simply asks the student to rate his or her answers to this test as a fair indication of their present knowledge about the topic. In spite of the unreliability of such self-ratings, I am willing to bet there are populations of sufficient sophistication to make this a better indicator of "statistical artifact low-scorers" than anything else we have. (Remember, the students gain nothing by asserting that the test did not tap their knowledge. Their answer to this question can be deleted from their papers before correction to avoid contamination of the grader.)

Going a step further, can we design the test itself to discriminate between these causes? Of course, other things being equal, doubling its length is probably the best simple bet, but let us assume that is impossible. In any case, it is not optimal. Increasing the amount of choice of questions allowed the subject *is* desirable. Comparability of marking is thereby seriously weakened, but that is not usually fatal or we would not use item sampling. A good compromise, I have found, is a batch of compulsory items and then one or two open-ended, or almost open-ended, items like: "Discuss any other topic (or two topics) from this area or from the following list with which you are familiar." Even the use of multiple-choice questions in which any number of options, including zero, may be correct reveals a great deal more about the causes of a certain performance than the present ones.

It was a considerable step forward in testing to introduce item sampling, and it came about from rethinking the purpose of testing,

realizing there is more than one, and seeing that the purposes would be best served by different kinds of tests. What I am suggesting is that MO analysis (and, indirectly, education) will be facilitated by certain types of tests currently in disfavor for the quite good but not conclusive reasons of lower scoring validity and more cumbersome processing.

Another MO check for ATI, perhaps more relevant for the role-playing example, would involve some process observations on each individual. These are expensive, but they are often desirable for other reasons. Look for *consonance,* for example, between (*a*) teacher's reports of quick learning or "surprising" lack of knowledge at an early stage and outstanding performance later, and (*b*) the pre's and the post's. We're looking for the MO signature of a highly effective teaching device, which will be absent if the effect is due to test unreliability.

In which of these cases should we use regressed pretest scores instead of raw scores? My instincts suggest looking at it both ways rather than standardizing on that correction. Experts may well know better, and I hope they will set the matter straight.

MO Corroboration

It was argued earlier that MO is not just a type of ex post facto design. Another reason for this view is the importance of combining MO checks with classical and semiclassical design. A nice example of where this would have helped was suggested in correspondence by Gene Glass after reading an earlier draft of this study. In *Pygmalion in the Classroom,* by R. Rosenthal and L. Jacobson (New York: Holt, Rinehart, and Winston, 1968), evidence is given from a classical design that teachers' beliefs about the potentialities of their students affect their estimates of the quality of work. Now the MO here is, of course, a causal chain involving the teachers' beliefs in the existence of differences between students that in some cases did not exist (since the teachers had been deliberately misinformed that some students were latently outstanding). An MO check would involve, inter alia, checking for the presence of each key cognitive component at the time when it was supposed to be functioning. Interestingly enough, there was a check on one such item, namely, the teachers' memory of which students were, according to their information, latent high performers. It turned out that the teachers could not re-

member to any significant degree which students were in this category. This automatically makes the study's overall conclusion very implausible; psychological causes cannot operate across time without intervening links. One must explore the possibility of unconscious retention, but it is here extremely implausible. Hence, one is not surprised to find that the statistics, which led to the apparent significance of the results, were faulty. (See Rosenthal and Jacobson, *Pygmalion in the Classroom*; the best summary of critiques appears in *Second Handbook of Research on Teaching,* ed. R. M. W. Travers [Chicago: Rand McNally, 1973], especially T. X. Barber, "Pitfalls in Research," on pages 393-398.)

In designing any classical study, it generally seems worthwhile to devote a little time to the questions: What is the means whereby the putative cause is supposed by bringing about the effect? What are the links in the causal chain between them? Can we look for these links or arrange that they will be easy to look for? Can we use their occurrence to distinguish between the alternative causal hypotheses? How?

Further Directions

There are a number of directions in which I would like to expand this discussion if I had space, time, and talent. Let me conclude by mentioning them briefly in the hope that they will start others thinking or talking or even both.

1. I would like to show how MO technique applies in the field of economic analysis, especially economic case studies, for in that field control groups are essentially impossible and MO technique is correspondingly important.

2. I would like to show how "microexperiments" to test MO hypotheses are often possible where full experimental studies (of the whole treatment) are impossible.

3. I would like to discuss the various species of overdeterminism, some of which can only be "resolved" by MO analysis.

4. I would like to point out the fallacy inherent in the statistician's incorrect use of the term "explained" when referring to distributing the variance amongst various factors; MO analysis clarifies it.

5. And, finally, I would like to explore the quantitative dimension of MO analysis, the ways in which we could convert it into pattern-recognition computer programs and make it amenable to covariance analysis.

Common sense leads us to develop the science of using control groups and randomization, and, when this fails, it leads us to quasi-experiments. Even when these are impossible, we have not exhausted the resources of common sense. MO methodology can be used both as an alternative to, and a strengthening of, the other approaches. It gives us greater robustness and better defenses against the assaults of attrition and artifacts.

Note: The inference drawn on pages 69-71 is not deductively valid, only mnemonically useful. It needs one—or a set—of other premises to yield a strong probability inference; *which* ones we can use depends on the particular kind of phenomenon. For example, it is typically the case that the set A_i includes all the "big" candidates; formally this means that, if the unknown causes are B_j, then the relative frequency of any A_i in the class of X's is much greater than that of any B_j (roughly because we would have identified any big B_j). Hence, if the only big candidate that is present is A, its only competitors are low-frequency events, and A is thus *the most likely* of all the possible causes, i.e., max $P(A_i$ caused X) = $P(A$ caused X). For it to be *most likely the cause*, i.e., for $P(A$ caused X) $>.5$, we need a further condition, for example, that the frequency of A's (in the class of X-occurrences) is greater than the sum of the frequencies of all B_j. This is the relevant sense of "almost all." This condition is more easily met the more evenly the A_i divide the spoils, the smaller the number of big candidates is, and the smaller the proportion of unexplained cases. For example, if three, four, five, . . ., up to nine known causes account for 91 percent of X's, then (as long as each of them accounts for at least 10 percent of X's) the inference pattern works. But if only four causes are known to account for only 80 percent of X's, we cannot pull off the inference to any of them as a better-than-even chance. Still—often importantly—we can get the "modal" conclusion (that A is the best bet to be the cause) as long as the weaker assumption holds (that no B_j is as often successful as any A_i). (Many thanks to Frederick Mosteller for identifying and forcing me to bridge the logical gap here.)

COST ANALYSIS IN EVALUATION AND THE DOCTRINE OF COST-FREE EVALUATION

Costs are shadowy figures hovering in the background of evaluation, specters that come to haunt those who try to ignore them, Janus-faced figures more elusive than the most ghostly of the mental entities to which the hard-nosed empiricist objects in the scientific context, and yet the very substance of the hard-nosed empiricist's position in the management area.

I wish to set out some of the conceptual and practical difficulties that currently concern me in the hope that others more expert than I—economists or accountants, perhaps—can provide answers. For the evaluator, such answers are badly needed, indeed; where I have ventured one, it is with a strong sense of my own limitations in this kind of analysis and mainly in the hope that providing a target to shoot at may improve the aim of the expert. It is less easy to simply take the advice of experts in this area than it is in many areas for two reasons. First, the way that experts use the notion of cost is often highly technical and, although the advantages of such an approach are probably considerable in the expert's special field, for example, cost accounting, it is not at all obvious that the educator, author, federal agency, legislator, or evaluator will gain from adopting the technical use. Second, the interjudge reliability of the experts in the crunch is not impressive, as Abraham Briloff (*Unaccountable Accounting* [New York: Harper and Row, 1972]) so ably documents. There may be some value in starting afresh to work out the conceptual points for oneself. I begin with a few elementary facts and examples in order to lay the ground for others. Even these examples suggest that the usual level of consideration is pretty superficial.

Direct and Indirect Costs

You tell your secretary to order a book through the mail, sending along a check with the order. The book "costs" $7.50. To whom? Not to you. Its cost to you is $7.50 plus the cost of your time spent dictating the order plus the direct cost of your secretary's time transcribing, typing, filing, checkwriting, folding, stamping, and mailing (better than $2.50 on the usual estimates), plus postage, plus proportional amortization of office equipment and capital and maintenance costs, plus a slice of rent, heating, cleaning, mortgage interest, insur-

ance, accounting and legal fees, and taxes on the office (or two offices), plus fringe benefits, plus supplies.[9] For many academics who use college-provided departmental staff for such chores, most of these costs are essentially unrecognized fringe benefits. For those of us who pay our own office expenses, "unrecognized" is not applicable. Even evaluators who work in a large unit have very little sense of indirect or overhead costs. They occasionally receive memos from the business manager imploring them to go easy on the long-distance phone calls, or not to shred scratch paper, and so forth, but this is usually a remote voice, often perceived as a faint echo of the voice of oppression. Such memos stimulate natural touchiness more often than they promote conservation-mindedness. It is all too possible that individualizing overhead costs as deductions against a larger basic salary would increase the cost-effectiveness of large-scale educational research and development more than individualizing the curricular output does.

The Generalizability of Proposed Remedies

It is tempting to react to the discovery that your book cost you perhaps $10.75 instead of $7.50 by deciding to do your own book ordering. After all, you think, it will just take a moment to scribble a memo and a check. But this remedy, though it should be considered, is not generalizable. If the same argument is applied to evaluating what your secretary does, it leads to the usually erroneous conclusion that the secretary is dispensable. It is useful where an extra secretarial position, or a part-time position, could be avoided. The justification for a secretary is that labor can be divided. Unless you have time to spare or lack of money to hire a secretary, it is considerably more effective for your secretary to do the ordering, both absolutely

9. I here avoid the convenient practice of "spreading" all indirect costs across all the work done in the office. For example, suppose there are telephone charges of $250 per month. Refined accounting would not allot any of that to the task of ordering a book, which does not involve telephoning. Crude accounting would spread it across all office work, e.g., on a job-time basis. The crude accounting procedure often turns out to be closer to the truth of the matter, however; for if the main commodity marketed from the office is your skill and knowledge, and if the book contributes to that, and if the telephone bill refers partly to marketing that skill, the book ordering should bear some of the phone cost since it is an (indirect) income-producing activity, and it should carry its load of the general overhead.

and cost-effectively, except where there are inelasticities in the situation: the secretary is overworked and your action can avoid either a resignation, excess strain, or the hiring of an extra secretary. In such cases, your time buys more than the dollar saving on each order.

Of course, the most elementary error of all, still atractive enough to be implicit in the practice of most academics, is to act as if it is not necessary to put a slice of the overhead on top of the direct costs of each secretarial task, or even to treat secretaries as fixed costs. The practice of requesting the departmental office to type a final draft of class notes from a slightly corrected but legible original that could be copied as is shows complete oblivion to real costs; a more extreme case is the practice of dictating brief replies to letters instead of typing or writing on the original (filing a Xerox of the result only if a copy is needed). Note that (*a*) typing, even addresses on envelopes done by the hunt-and-peck method, is much faster than writing, (*b*) even if you have to rent your own personal Xerox, the per copy cost will normally run below $0.15 as opposed to approximately $2.75 for each letter typed by a secretary, (*c*) this solution does not contradict the caution of the previous paragraph (provided that you stick with very short replies) because the trade-off between skills and time (qualified by consideration of error costs and probabilities), offers a larger saving here that is more likely to produce significant savings in terms of total secretarial cost. If we are talking in the context of a departmental or group office, the generalization argument works the other way, too. That is, a general agreement to use these "photo replies" will produce a large saving of secretarial load that can decrease turn-around time or be used for other, more valuable purposes.

Now, is the remedy proposed at the end of the last section really generalizable, that is, providing an overhead allowance to each professor and making an appropriate deduction? One would have to look at the systematic costs of running individual cost-budgets coordinated with salary-incentive-penalty arrangements, and then discover whether real net savings materialized in field trials. In general, a major risk would be to encourage wasteful use of faculty time since they would in effect be paid more for doing secretarial work. The administration's visible costs would drop, but students would suffer. It would be better to reward efficiency in use, rather than nonuse, of secretarial services. The absence of serious thought about costs by administrations, analogous to the examples of faculty insensitivity to

costs just mentioned, can be seen in their approach to parking, housing, and transportation on and around a campus.

It should be clear from these examples that the costing of simple activities and alternatives is not simple. When one turns to closed circuit television (CCTV) or CAI, the problem is even more difficult. The "classic" issue of whether carpeting is ultimately cheaper than vinyl for school floor covering illustrates the extraordinary difficulty of serious cost analysis; it has not yet been satisfactorily resolved.

The Relativity of Costs

Suppose that the book you are ordering is the *Handbook of Qualitative Educational Evaluation,* which I recently produced under a Model Training Program grant from USOE/NIE. If I undertake to make it available "at cost" in order to fulfill the agency's desire to disseminate useful products, what does "at cost" mean? For a publisher that would normally have to cover the development cost of the materials (talent scouts, advances, and so forth), copyright payments, editing, printing, binding, selling, and general overhead. When development is federally funded, cost, one might suppose, would refer only to printing, or, more exactly, to what publishers call "manufacturing," that is, materials, printing, and binding. But that is superficial. There are also warehousing and distribution costs, shipments to the post office, wrapping, order processing, and other steps. If successful dissemination is the aim, some modest effort at direct-mail advertising or a small advertisement in *Educational Researcher* could also be justified as part of the costs. The total effort requires planning, coordination, and immediate supervision, but by whom? Suppose it is handled by the author who wants to avoid the gigantic markup that occurs in commercial distribution. This markup greatly limits the possible market and hence the effectiveness of dissemination, so for this and other reasons the AIR study of optimal dissemination of federally funded materials recommends against it. "Cost," then, will have to include a reasonable charge for managerial time, but, since it does not promise any royalty to the author or profit and safety margin to the publisher, the cost should still be well below the commercial level since alleged "economies of scale" in large businesses get swallowed up by inefficiency and profit taking. Some "insurance" contingencies still remain: If the price does not adequately reflect "costs," the true cost to the author will be very high in terms

of unreimbursed time or outlay. Should that risk be regarded as a cost? If distribution is incompetently handled, this also cuts into effectiveness. Here, being able to average risks across many publications becomes very important. This, in addition to other potential economies of scale, including division of labor in a large organization, *might* make it possible for the commercial publisher to undercut the individual author-publisher. It is probably the arteriosclerosis of established industry that has taken the heaviest toll in publishing, as it has in the railroads, with featherbedding, looting by speculators, and quasi-monopolistic practices combining to render them relatively inefficient. The independent producer must take risks that might make "at cost" publishing of a single (or a few) books a matter of luck. The government's reluctance to use such methods, which are almost sure to amount either to exploitation of the individual, or to subsidy, is understandable, but this reluctance is weakening with the realization that the hidden costs of the commercial establishments, including lost sales because of extreme prices, more than offset such considerations.

Note the different cost frameworks that have been identified. First, there is cost to the consumer-user. So far we have stressed indirect costs of the more obvious kind, but the associated opportunity cost considerations implied in that argument are also important. For example, by spending time on book orders, the consumer decreases marginal earnings (in psychological or intellectual currency), and by spending cash resources on books the purchaser loses the pleasures available from alternative purchases. Second, there are development and manufacturing costs for the publisher, the author, or the agency. Third, there are distribution costs for whoever does that. These in turn may have both a manifest and a latent form; the latent form will be whatever it really costs whoever does it. There are other frameworks that are of considerable importance on occasion: The secretary's cost framework may involve variable psychic costs of different types of work, the "overhead" of special clothing, cleaning of clothes and hands, travel time, rebates to employment agencies, opportunity costs of foregone advanced training, purchased advantages for spouse, and intellectual or financial gains from on-the-job training, among others. Then there is the taxpayer's framework, which is sometimes matched by the framework of the legislator as the taxpayer's representative. From that point of view, the cost of the subsi-

dized handbook includes the cost of development; marketing it "at cost" would mean huge costs for the purchasing consumer ("prices"). A good argument can be made that most evaluation should involve some, perhaps principal, reference to this cost, but it is rarely discussed seriously. Even an obviously public cost, such as a fire in a national forest, is rarely costed out in a comprehensive way. Costs are nearly always expressed from a certain point of view, that is, with regard to a particular framework. Usually this framework is just as much subject to evaluation as, for example, the framework set by the goals of a project.

Negative Costs—Profits and Gains

Suppose you order the book mentioned, by mail, and you then incur the further immense investment involved in reading it, after which the book has to be housed, dusted, insured, possibly repaired and cataloged. Eventually it represents a cost in the hundreds of dollars region, and the cost continues to mount as long as you keep the book. Even getting rid of it adds to the cost. Of course, there is another side to the ledger. You may simply derive psychic gains from the book, or you may generate increased income from it, but one way or another there is some chance of profit from it. You may profit from the book with or without reading it, as collectors well know. You may profit now or later from buying it now, regardless of when you read it. Having it (and not having to order it when actually needed) may make it possible to accept or reject a later job offer or speaking engagement within the response time available with consequent very great advantage (perhaps by avoiding a disastrous commitment). But let us focus on a very specific and, I think, quite important case. Suppose that the book you order contains advice that you apply in making an important management decision. If the book is a book of advice on real estate speculation, the decision might be against a particular investment with your own savings. If it is Briloff's book, the decision might be to employ a different accounting firm because of revelations about your present firm in that book. If the book concerns evaluation, it may suggest a novel procedure for reviewing a project you are managing or evaluating. In each case, it is possible that the effect of reading the book will be a very large profit (or the avoidance of a very large loss), or the opposite. If the outcome is favorable, it is clear that the net cost to you of the book

should be regarded as negative. In the case of books which yield no immediate payoff, there may be cumulative long-run payoffs, whether intellectual, social, or fiscal, and one should offset their costs against those gains. This is the generalization argument again, where, as with evaluating curriculum materials, one must look for obvious traceable (for example, vocational) gains but also for lifelong gains or expectations of gains.

Price versus Costs of Evaluation

Evaluation is normally provided as a service rather than as a product like a book, but the same approach should apply. One should be able to determine whether the net cost is positive or negative. I wish here to propose the view that evaluation should in general involve no net (positive) cost to the producer, the taxpayer, or the evaluator. This, then, is the doctrine of cost-free evaluation (CFE),[10] and it applies both to formative and, less obviously, to summative evaluation. Of course, like the book, it has a *price*; it will appear as an expense for whoever pays to have the project evaluated. But, as with the book, that is hardly the end of the matter. Evaluation may—and in general should be so designed that it is likely to—have cost-saving or effectiveness-increasing consequences. Part of the cost saving, since a substantial part of formative evaluation involves educating project staff toward a more analytic and critical approach to their work, should consist of indirect effects showing up in the cost or quality of other work by these people later on, even when no external evaluation is involved.

The CFE doctrine does not assert that evaluation always pays off. Evaluation will not improve a perfect project. Nor will evaluation of a long-dead institution done for historical purposes save money. Evaluation of work done by college students is tremendously expensive. It may run a thousand dollars a grade in terms of its one framework, and the result is often of little benefit. Nevertheless, the normative doctrine of cost-free evaluation sets a realistic standard, for the criticisms just mentioned are, respectively, nonexistent, rare, and correctable. Evaluation has often not been cost-free in the past, and a major reason has been the lack of self-reference in the evaluation tradition. It does seem appropriate that evaluators should look at their own

10. The label is due to Dan Stufflebeam.

work with an extremely critical eye before complaining about motes in others' eyes. And cost-quality considerations are surely the point at which to start.

The most obvious way in which evaluation can save money is by killing off worthless enterprises. This represents a savings from the taxpayer's (or, in general, the consumer's) point of view, but it also represents a savings to the producer on the assumption that something better can be done with the released time or resources. It may not represent a savings for dismissed employees or discontinued suppliers, but evaluation can also make more constructive suggestions than termination, for example, ways to improve quality without increased cost or ways to improve quality when this is highly desirable or essential to survival and attainable at easily manageable cost. This kind of suggestion will seem to some to intrude on the management domain, but, if it is assumed that all useful evaluation is comparative, then this is an inescapable consequence of good evaluation. The evaluator should constantly be looking for, or if necessary inventing, "critical competitors" against which to compare the performance of the evaluator. When these competitors do better, it is sometimes appropriate for the project to switch horses in midstream. In those cases where the evaluation is supposed to include diagnosis, such as identification of particular features or components that are producing the good or bad effects, it is obvious that recommendations for improvement will often result.

From the point of view of the "ultimate consumer" of education, whether we take that to be student, teacher, administrator, employer, or taxpayer, educational evaluation should serve as a reliable guide for selecting options and provide immediate gains in quality or savings. From the point of view of the evaluation client, a prospective evaluation should show clear expectations of being a worthwhile activity in the broadest sense before it is undertaken. I believe that conscience requires that the CFE standard should be met. Evaluation should offer a good chance of producing cost-savings greater than its own cost, or quality gains that are "worth" the price of the evaluation. This self-appraisal stance has produced many changes in my own procedure.

One change has been an attempt to draft a rough profit-and-loss picture for the client and other relevant populations while negotiating the contract; this is repeated in more detail in the final report. An-

other change has been heightened concern to avoid disruptive evaluation, one example of which is working around existing staff schedules instead of requesting them to work around mine. I also budget for the evaluation of my own evaluation by a client-credible external authority. Other changes include treating the evaluation report as a product itself, getting feedback on early drafts from those assessed; arranging seminars and not just mailing for dissemination; using client facilities very cautiously and cost-consciously; returning unused funds even if contractually entitled to them; offering some (free) follow-up service; producing documents, such as checklists, that can serve the client beyond the confines of the particular evaluation; and metaevaluation (the evaluation of evaluations), which is a special type of evaluation and not to every evaluator's taste. Self-critical metaevaluation is one subspecialty that every evaluator should, however, practice.

The most notable effect of these changes has been higher client satisfaction, but sometimes the reverse occurs when concern for the ultimate consumer or the product has led me to make ego-disruptive recommendations to the client. The doctrine of CFE is proposed as a criterion that should be used by both the evaluator in self-assessment and the client in evaluator-assessment.

2

Alternative Approaches to Educational Evaluation: A Self-Study Guide for Educators

Daniel L. Stufflebeam
Western Michigan University

Alternative Approaches to Educational Evaluation: A Self-Study Guide for Educators

Daniel L. Stufflebeam

Evaluators need appropriate conceptual frameworks to assist in determining and communicating about evaluation objectives and procedures and to provide grounds for judging evaluation designs and reports. There are several alternative frameworks, the oldest and best known being that proposed by Ralph Tyler (1942). Since then, newer approaches have been proposed by Michael Scriven (1967), Robert Stake (1967), Robert Hammond (1967), Malcolm Provus (1969), and myself (1967). These and other approaches were described in a recent book by Blaine Worthen and James Sanders (1973). Their book is the best single source to support this instructional manual approach.

This manual includes self-instructional modules relating to the evaluation efforts of Michael Scriven and myself. I plan to develop additional and more complete modules covering the work of other evaluators if these first two prove useful to teachers and students of evaluation. This manual is in a formative stage of development, and it has not yet been field tested.

MODULE I: EVALUATION ACCORDING TO MICHAEL SCRIVEN

Michael Scriven is a philosopher of science who has contributed extensively to the growth of evaluation theory. Three of his main evaluation contributions are: formative-summative evaluation, goal-free evaluation, and the Pathway Comparison Model. You can develop a basic understanding of these conceptualizations by working through this module. Study the objectives for the module so that you have a clear understanding of what you are to achieve; study the written material that summarizes Scriven's ideas; complete the knowledge test over the Scriven assignment, checking your answers against the keyed ones; and complete the provided application exercises, comparing your responses with the keyed ones.

The objectives of the module are:

1. to develop an understanding of the "formative-summative" conceptualization by
   a. defining formative, summative, intrinsic, and payoff evaluation;
   b. noting Scriven's distinction between role and goal related to evaluation;
   c. determining Scriven's definition of evaluation;
   d. identifying Scriven's position concerning the role of judgment in evaluation;
   e. explaining the formative-summative conceptualization;
   f. evaluating the Tylerian rationale for evaluation based on Scriven's formative-summative scheme;
   g. explaining Scriven's position concerning the desirability of employing professional versus amateur evaluators in formative evaluation work.
2. to develop an understanding of "goal-free evaluation" by
   a. distinguishing between goal-free and goal-based evaluation;
   b. correctly identifying the rationale for using goal-free evaluation;
   c. explaining the meaning of side effects in the context of goal-free evaluation.
3. to develop an understanding of the Pathway Comparison Model (PCM) by
   a. identifying the correct rationale for the PCM;
   b. listing the steps in the PCM;

    c. explaining how the formative-summative conception relates
      to the PCM;

    d. explaining how the goal-free conception relates to PCM.

These objectives may be achieved by reading only the material in this document. To enrich your understanding of Scriven's ideas, however, you should study Chapter 1 in this volume and his original works, especially those listed at the end of this chapter. When I prepared this chapter, nothing had been published on the Pathway Comparison Model. My information about PCM was based on several lectures presented by Scriven.

Formative-Summative Evaluation

In a classic paper Scriven (1967) stated that evaluators must judge both goals and results. He charged that the Tylerian definition of evaluation—determining whether objectives have been achieved—is too narrow since such determinations are uninteresting or misleading if the objectives are not meritorious. Hence, evaluators who follow Scriven's advice will assess results of programs, judge the program's goals, and arrive at conclusions about the overall merit of the programs.

Formally Scriven defined evaluation as a methodological activity that "consists simply in the gathering and combining of performance data with a weighted set of criterial scales to yield either comparative or numerical ratings, and in the justification of (*a*) the data-gathering instruments, (*b*) the weightings, and (*c*) the selection of criteria." In presenting and explicating this definition, Scriven asserted that evaluators should not merely present information for program people to use in formulating judgments, but the evaluators should arrive at and publicly report their independent judgments. According to Scriven, the evaluator's main responsibility is to make judgments.

In this respect Scriven noted that the goal of evaluation is always the same—to judge. But he also noted that the roles of evaluation are enormously varied. They may "form part of a teacher-training activity, of the process of curriculum development, of a field experiment connected with the improvement of learning theory, of an investigation preliminary to a decision about purchase or rejection of materials . . . ," and so forth. He reasoned that the failure to distinguish between evaluation's goal (to judge the merit of something) and its roles (constructive uses of evaluative data) has led to the dilution of

what is called evaluation so that it no longer achieves its goal of assessing worth. In other words, he said that evaluators too often try to help educators improve their programs and fail to judge the merit of the programs. Thus, a hard-hitting independent, objective assessment of merit is, for Scriven, the sine qua non of evaluation.

With the paramount importance of the goal of evaluation firmly established, Scriven proceeded to analyze the roles of evaluation. He noted that there are two main evaluation roles: formative, to assist in developing curricula; and summative, to assess the merit of curricula once they have been developed and placed on the market.

Formative evaluation is part of the curriculum development process. It provides continual feedback to assist in the development of a product, and it addresses questions about content validity, vocabulary level, usability, appropriateness of media, durability of materials, efficiency, and other matters. Overall formative evaluation is internal evaluation that serves to improve the product being developed.

In the summative role, evaluation "may serve to enable administrators to decide whether the entire finished curriculum, refined by use of the evaluation process in its first (formative) role, represents a sufficiently significant advance on the available alternatives to justify the expense of adoption by a school system." Summative evaluation probably should be performed by an external evaluator and certainly should be reported outside the production agency. This type of evaluation addresses questions about whether the product is more cost-effective than the competition. Overall summative evaluation serves consumers by providing them with independent assessments of the merit of marketed products.

In the early stages of curriculum development Scriven prefers "amateur evaluation" (self-evaluation) to "professional evaluation." Curriculum developers, when they serve as their own amateur evaluators, are supportive, nonthreatening, dedicated to producing a success, and tolerant of ambiguity of objectives and curriculum development procedures; hence, they are unlikely to stifle creativity in the early stages of curriculum work. Professional evaluators, if involved too early, may "dampen the creative fires of a productive group," slow down the development process by urging that objectives be clarified, or lose their independence, among other considerations. They are, however, needed to perform both formative and summative evaluation during the later stages of curriculum development.

Both types of evaluation require high-level technical skills and objectivity seldom possessed by nonprofessional evaluators. Scriven recommends that a professional evaluator be included on the curriculum construction staff, and he would probably advise that external professional evaluators be employed to conduct summative evaluations.

Scriven also distinguishes between intrinsic and payoff evaluation. Intrinsic evaluation appraises the qualities of a teaching instrument, regardless of its effects, by assessing such factors as content, goals, grading procedures, materials, and teacher attitude. Payoff evaluation is concerned not with the nature of the teaching instrument but, rather, with its effects on students. Scriven acknowledges the importance of intrinsic evaluation, but emphasizes that one must also determine and judge the effects of the teaching instrument. He explains that both can serve either formative or summative roles.

Goal-Free Evaluation

Scriven subsequently introduced and described the concept of goal-free evaluation, where the evaluator purposely remains ignorant of a program's written goals and searches for all effects of a program regardless of any rhetoric concerning what the program was intended to produce. There are no side effects to examine since data about all effects, whatever the intent of the program, are equally admissible. The claimed advantage for goal-free evaluation is that the goal-free evaluator may discover unanticipated important effects that the goal-based evaluator would miss because of his preoccupation with stated goals. He claims that goal-free evaluation is more objective than goal-based evaluation since the goal-free evaluator does not allow the program staff to orient him concerning the program's intent. Overall, Scriven has proposed goal-free evaluation as a powerful supplement to goal-based evaluation.

The Pathway Comparison Model

The Pathway Comparison Model extends Scriven's earlier ideas. Essentially, he presents it as a checklist containing nine steps that evaluators should follow in evaluating programs. The nine steps include:
1. characterizing the nature of the program to be evaluated;
2. clarifying the nature of the conclusion wanted from the evaluation;

3. assessing evidence about cause-and-effect relationships between independent and dependent variables in the program;
4. comprehensively checking for all consequences of the program;
5. determining and assessing the criteria of merit and the philosophical arguments pertaining to the program;
6. assessing various kinds of program costs;
7. identifying and assessing the program's critical competitors;
8. identifying the program's constituents and performing a needs assessment to determine the program's potential impact;
9. forming a conclusion about the merit of the program.

These steps are not intended to be performed in any particular sequence, but all of them must be completed before the Pathway Model has been properly implemented. Also, an evaluator may cycle through the model several times during the evaluation of a program. Early cycles are formative evaluation; the last cycle is what Scriven terms summative evaluation.

The rationale for the Pathway Comparison Model is that evaluation essentially is a data reduction process that obtains and assesses large amounts of data and then synthesizes them into an overall judgment of merit. In describing this data reduction process, Scriven suggests that his first six steps characterize a program or product and his last three steps testify as to its validity.

This is just a brief summary of some of Michael Scriven's main ideas about evaluation. He has developed these ideas over the past ten years, and they have significantly influenced evaluation practice. Serious students of evaluation should study his original writings and keep abreast of future contributions as he continues his study of evaluation.

KNOWLEDGE TEST OVER THE SCRIVEN ASSIGNMENT

This section contains objective questions and correct and incorrect responses to the questions that will help you determine whether you have achieved the knowledge objectives for the Scriven module. A broken line separates the questions from the responses. You can self-administer the test, responding to the questions by circling the letter preceding what you consider to be the best response. Compare your answer with the responses that follow each of the questions. After

you have completed all of the questions, you will be directed to score your performance.

Question 1. Formative evaluation is used to:
        a. formulate judgments about the overall worth of a new textbook.
        b. assign credit or blame for the results of a completed project.
        c. assess the early stages of a project.
        d. determine the payoff of a prior investment.

- -

Correct response

You should have circled "c": *Formative evaluation is used to assess the early stages of a project.* This is correct because formative evaluation assists program personnel to carry through developmental efforts.

Incorrect responses

a—incorrect because the textbook has already been published, and formative evaluation of it would have to occur during its development.

b—incorrect for a similar reason.

c—incorrect because the investment process has already been completed.

Question 2. Summative evaluation is best described as:
        a. assessing the early forms of a new product.
        b. appraising a product already on the market.
        c. improving a product while it is still fluid.
        d. bridging the gap between intrinsic and payoff evaluation.

- -

Correct response

The best response is "b": *Summative evaluation is best described as appraising a product already on the market.* This is correct because summative evaluation involves judging a developmental effort after the development work has been completed.

Incorrect responses

a—incorrect because it denotes an instance of formative evaluation.

c—incorrect for the same reason.

d—incorrect because it refers to a methodological as opposed to a role problem in evaluation. The problem in bridging intrinsic and payoff evaluation is how to make the causal link between independent and dependent variables, not whether the evaluation aids development or judges its finished products.

Question 3. Intrinsic evaluation can briefly be defined as an appraisal of:

    a. change in students' attitudes.

    b. the design of an instructional program.

    c. the degree and intensity of student motivation.

    d. effects of the teaching instrument on students' knowledge.

- -

Correct response

You should have circled "b": *Intrinsic evaluation can briefly be defined as an appraisal of the design of an instructional program.* This is correct because intrinsic evaluation is the evaluation of qualities inherent in a treatment as opposed to results achieved by administering the treatment.

Incorrect responses

a—incorrect because "change in student attitude" is an effect produced by a program, as opposed to a quality, such as "the inquiry orientation," of the program that produced the change.

c—incorrect for a similar reason. The "degree and intensity of student motivation" is an effect, not a characteristic, of an instructional program.

d—incorrect because of its emphasis on effects on students.

Question 4. According to Scriven, the pure payoff approach to evaluation is characterized by concern for:

    a. results of the curriculum but not its goals.

    b. the goals of the curriculum but not its results.

    c. both the goals and the results of the curriculum.

    d. neither the goals nor the results of the curriculum.

- -

Correct response

You should have circled "a": *According to Scriven, the pure pay-off approach to evaluation is characterized by concern for results of the curriculum but not its goals.* While it determines whether goals have been achieved, its main limitation is said by Scriven to be that it does not judge whether the goals are worth achieving.

Incorrect responses

b—wrong on both counts. Payoff evaluation does not assess goals, but it does assess results.

c—wrong since payoff evaluation does not assess goals.

d—wrong because payoff evaluation does assess results.

Question 5. Which of the following best illustrates Scriven's differentiation between role and goal relating to evaluation?

    a. The goal of evaluation may vary enormously since any study may address a wide range of questions; the role of evaluation is always, however, the same: to facilitate decision making.

    b. By stressing the constructive part that evaluation can play in nonthreatening activities (roles), we neglect the fact that its goals always include estimation of value.

    c. The goals of any evaluation study should be tempered according to the relative sensitivity of roles to be served by the study.

    d. The goal of any evaluative study is summative, while its role is usually formative.

Correct response

You should have circled "b": *By stressing the constructive part that evaluation can play in nonthreatening activities (roles), we neglect the fact that its goals always include estimation of value.* While evaluation may serve many roles (both constructive and destructive), its goal is always the same: to judge merit. This has been Scriven's main argument, and it has led him to insist that evaluators render judgments.

Incorrect responses

a—wrong because Scriven sees only one goal for evaluation (judgments of merit), but many roles (public relations, record keeping, and so forth) that serve decision making.

c—the opposite of Scriven's position. He believes that evaluators shirk their responsibility when they do not formulate and report judgments about the programs they evaluate.

d—wrong because formative and summative evaluation are both roles to be served by evaluation.

Question 6. According to Scriven, evaluation is:

a. the process of determining the extent to which valued goals have been achieved.

b. the process of delineating, obtaining, and providing useful information for judging decision making.

c. the process of determining discrepancies between performance and given standards.

d. the assessment of merit

- -

Correct response

You should have circled "d": *According to Scriven, evaluation is the assessment of merit.* He noted this in his AERA tape, and it is consistent with the formal definition of evaluation that he presented in "The Methodology of Evaluation." ("Evaluation is . . . a methodological activity which . . . consists simply in the gathering of and combining of performance data with a weighted set of goal scales to yield either comparative or numerical ratings, and in the justification of [a] the data gathering instruments, [b] the weightings, and [c] the selection of goals.)

Incorrect responses

a—incorrect because Scriven believes that evaluation guided by a given set of goals may miss important effects, and he also believes that goals also must be evaluated.

b—incorrect because it emphasizes that the evaluator should provide information for decision making but not actually make the decision, while Scriven believes that the evaluator must judge program options and thus make decisions about the program he is evaluating.

c—incorrect because it is a variant of "a." Scriven would not accept as sufficient a definition of evaluation that only determined discrepancies between given standards and performance. He would insist that the standards should be assessed and not be the sole basis for assessing performance.

Question 7. With which of the following statements would Scriven most likely agree?
- a. Evaluators should decide to judge or not to judge educational practices in accord with the role an evaluation study is to serve.
- b. Evaluators should obviate the need for subjective judgment by employing designs with high degrees of internal and external validity and with preset decision rules.
- c. Evaluators should judge the merits of the educational practices they evaluate.
- d. Evaluators should describe educational practices fully, but they should avoid passing judgments on the practices.

- -

Correct response

You should have circled "c": *Evaluators should judge the merits of the educational practices they evaluate.* Scriven has asserted that evaluators must formulate and report their judgments of whatever they evaluate.

Incorrect responses

a—incorrect because Scriven has stated that evaluators must make judgments in formative as well as summative evaluation.

b—incorrect because Scriven has noted that the evaluator usually must operate in ambiguous, uncontrolled situations. He notes that evaluators should expect this and not shy away from such assignments. Hence, evaluators cannot depend on preset decision rules or complete information. Therefore, they must generally perform the most professional of all evaluative functions: formulating and publicizing judgments in the face of inadequate and insufficient information. Scriven has offered the consolation that, even though the judgments of evaluators will often be wrong, they will be right more often than those of any other group.

d—incorrect because Scriven has noted that evaluators who fail to make judgments are failing to meet their full responsibilities as evaluators.

Question 8. Which of the following statements most correctly distinguishes between goal-free and goal-based evaluation?
   a. Goal-free evaluation is intrinsic evaluation, while goal-based evaluation is the same as payoff evaluation.
   b. Goal-free evaluation is subjective, while goal-based evaluation is data-based evaluation.
   c. Goal-free evaluations assess all effects irrespective of stated goals, while goal-based evaluations search for effects that pertain to stated goals.
   d. Goal-free evaluation assesses outcomes, side effects, costs, feasibility, and other nongoal attributes of a teaching instrument, while goal-based evaluation assesses the morality, clarity, and importance of goals.

- -

Correct response
   You should have circled "c": *Goal-free evaluations assess all effects irrespective of stated goals, while goal-based evaluations search for effects that pertain to stated goals.* According to Scriven, the rhetoric of goals should not dictate and constrain the search for results.

Incorrect responses
a—incorrect because instrinsic and payoff evaluations differentiate between variables that relate to the qualities of a treatment and its effects; knowledge of intrinsic and payoff evaluation concepts does not assist in distinguishing between goal-free and goal-based evaluation.
b—incorrect because both goal-free and goal-based evaluation are data based, and both involve the development of subjective conclusions.
d—incorrect because both goal-free and goal-based evaluations assess outcomes.

Question 9. Which of the following is *not* a part of Scriven's rationale for using goal-free evaluation?
   a. Goal-based evaluations have consistently failed to produce sound and useful evaluative findings and must be replaced by a more effective evaluation strategy.
   b. Goal-free evaluators likely will discover significant

  outcomes that usually are missed by goal-based evaluators.

 c. So long as evaluations determine the positive and negative outcomes of a project, it is not necessary to assess particularly whether stated goals have been achieved.

 d. In developing a mindset to check on the achievement of stated objectives, evaluators are likely to be insensitive to significant effects that do not relate to the stated objectives.

- -

Correct response

 You should have circled "a": *Goal-based evaluations have consistently failed to produce sound and useful evaluative findings and must be replaced by a more effective evaluation strategy.* The rationale for goal-free evaluations is not that they should replace goal-based evaluations. On the contrary, Scriven sees a continued need for goal-based evaluations. But he believes that findings from goal-free evaluations will add useful and unique information to that produced by goal-based evaluations.

Incorrect responses

b—a part of Scriven's rationale for goal-free evaluation is that goal-free evaluation supplements the data provided by goal-based evaluation.

c—another part of the rationale for goal-free evaluation is that not knowing program goals is not a handicap so long as the evaluator systematically searches for all important effects of a program.

d—also a part of the rationale for goal-free evaluation because Scriven has argued that knowing a program's goals can be a handicap insofar as this knowledge causes an evaluator to concentrate his attention on results related to objectives to the exclusion of other results.

Question 10. Which of the following best explains the meaning of side effects in the context of goal-free evaluation?

 a. In goal-free evaluation side effects are the primary concern since goal-based evaluation will provide a thorough analysis of the main effects.

b. Goal-free evaluations are not concerned with side effects since these are intrinsic qualities of the teaching instrument and not the proper concern of evaluations designed to identify and assess outcomes.

c. In goal-free evaluation side effects are the effects that evaluative feedback has on the behavior of the audiences for the evaluation findings.

d. In goal-free evaluation there are no side effects since all effects, not just those related to stated goals, are of primary concern.

- -

Correct response

You should have circled "d": *In goal-free evaluation there are no side effects since all effects, not just those related to stated goals, are of primary concern.* There is no concern for assessing side effects since, from the outset of the evaluation, all outcome variables, not just those related to the stated goals, are equally important.

Incorrect responses

a—incorrect because in goal-free evaluation there is no distinction between side effects and main effects.

b—incorrect because it contains an incorrect definition of side effects.

c—incorrect because it also is based on an improper definition of side effects.

Question 11. Which of the following is the best rationale for the Pathway Comparison Model?

a. Evaluation is the process of formulating and executing a sequence of critical comparative experiments that lead to knowledge of certain phenomena such that outcomes of specified actions are predictable.

b. Evaluation is a data reduction process that involves characterizing a project and synthesizing a judgment concerning the project's overall merit.

c. Evaluation guides a project through five developmental stages by assessing and reporting discrep-

ancies between performance and standards at each of
the stages.
d. Evaluation involves the progressive comparison of a
program's intended and actual antecedents, transactions, and outcomes.

- -

Correct response

You should have circled "b": *Evaluation is a data reduction process that involves characterizing a project and synthesizing a judgment concerning the project's overall merit.* Scriven sees evaluation as a systematic process involving the characterizing and assessing of a project. Essentially evaluators gather and analyze large sets of data and then synthesize the data so an overall judgment of merit can be rendered.

Incorrect responses

a—incorrect because it refers to the rationale for programmatic experimentation and not to the rationale for the Pathway Comparison Model.

c—incorrect because it is more the rationale for Provus' Discrepancy Evaluation Model than for the Pathway Comparison Model.

d—incorrect because it references Stake's Countenance Evaluation Model and does not present a valid rationale for the Pathway Comparison Model.

Question 12. Which of the following best explains the relationship between Scriven's formative-summative conception of evaluation and his Pathway Comparison Model?
a. The nine steps in the Pathway Comparison Model are both formative and summative.
b. The first five steps—the characterizing steps—are formative; the last four validating steps are summative evaluation.
c. The Pathway Comparison Model is a summative evaluation model.
d. The Pathway Comparison Model is basically a formative evaluation model.

- -

Correct response
  You should have circled "a": *The nine steps in the Pathway Comparison Model are both formative and summative.* The last cycle through the nine steps is summative evaluation, while prior cycles constitute formative evaluation.

Incorrect responses
b—incorrect because Scriven has not equated the characterizing and validating stages with formative and summative evaluations.
c and d—incorrect because the Pathway Comparison Model is both formative and summative.

Question 13. Which of the following best explains the relationship between Scriven's goal-free evaluation conception and his Pathway Comparison Model?
  a. Goal-free evaluation and the Pathway Comparison Model are two different but complementary evaluation strategies.
  b. The Pathway Comparison Model explicates the steps that one follows in conducting a goal-free evaluation.
  c. The Pathway Comparison Model is a model of the development process, while goal-free evaluation is a model of the evaluation process.
  d. Goal-free evaluation is an appropriate methodological strategy to be employed in the comprehensive check of program consequences.

- -

Correct response
  You should have circled "d": *Goal-free evaluation is an appropriate methodological strategy to be employed in the comprehensive check of program consequences.* This explanation of the relationship between goal-free evaluation and the Pathway Comparison Model is correct because goal-free evaluation is a methodological strategy that checks for all program consequences and because step four of the Pathway Comparison Model calls for a comprehensive check of consequences.

Incorrect responses
a—incorrect because the Pathway Comparison Model is an overall approach to evaluation that subsumes strategies such as goal-free evaluation.

b—incorrect because the Pathway Comparison Model is not an explication of goal-free evaluation.

c—incorrect because the Pathway Comparison Model models evaluation and not development, and because goal-free evaluation is not an evaluation model but a particular methodological strategy.

Scoring of the Knowledge Test

You have now completed the knowledge test over the Scriven assignment. Total the number of correct responses you had and write the number on the line below.

Number of correct responses _____

If your score was 10 or above, you have demonstrated an adequate knowledge of Scriven's evaluation philosophy and concepts. Thus you are ready to proceed to the application exercises in the next section. If your score was 5 to 9, you have shown some grasp of Scriven's ideas, but probably could benefit by a review of the prior material. If your score was lower than 5 and if you still do not understand why, before proceeding to the next section you should again work through the material in this section.

APPLICATION EXERCISES

This section contains four essay exercises to demonstrate whether you understand the basic premises and concepts in Scriven's formative-summative evaluation approach. Answer the questions on separate sheets of paper. Following each exercise is a list of points that should have been included in your response, and reviewing them will help you assess your response. Complete the first exercise before proceeding to the second. Refer as often as needed to the assigned reading and the keys contained in the preceding knowledge test.

Exercise 1

Introduce and define Scriven's evaluation conceptualization by responding, as you think he would, to the following questions:
a. What is evaluation?
b. What is it for?
c. What is the difference between the role and goal of evaluation?
d. What are the different kinds of evaluation?
e. Illustrate the difference between payoff and intrinsic evaluation.

- -

Responses to Exercise 1 should present and develop the following points:
   a. Evaluation is the assessment of merit.
   b. Basically it serves two roles called formative and summative evaluation.
   c. Roles of evaluation are purposes that it serves, e.g., guiding projects, ranking textbooks, and public relations, and these may vary widely. However, the goal of evaluation is always to make judgments of merit.
   d. Scriven, in analyzing evaluation, has identified many different kinds of evaluation: formative, summative, payoff, intrinsic, meta, mediated, and pathway.
   e. The illustration should show payoff evaluation as concerned with effects related to dependent variables. It should show intrinsic evaluation as concerned with qualities that are inherent in some independent variable.

Exercise 2

Explain how you think Scriven would respond to the following statement: "The purpose of evaluation is to determine the extent to which program objectives are achieved."

- -

Responses to Exercise 2 should present and develop the following points:
   a. Scriven would disagree with the statement.
   b. He would note that evaluation should judge the merit of a program irrespective of the rhetoric of program goals.
   c. In the past he has noted that program goals themselves should be judged.
   d. He would note that confining one's attention to stated goals can result in evaluations that miss important effects not related to goals.
   e. Recently he has noted that goal-free evaluators can assess all important effects without paying any attention to program goals.

Exercise 3

Explain what Scriven means in the following quotation: "formative evaluation is a necessary part of any rational approach to producing good results on the summative evaluation, but the question of whether and how professional evaluators should be employed depends very much upon whether they do more harm than good."

- -

Responses to Exercise 3 should present and develop the following points:
   a. Success in developmental efforts depends on feedback from ongoing formative evaluation.
   b. Summative evaluations, in judging the success of completed developmental

efforts, reflect whether formative evaluation existed and guided the effort to a successful conclusion.
c. Generally professional evaluators are needed to conduct effective formative evaluation.
d. However, professional evaluators, when introduced very early in developmental efforts, can stifle creativity and lose their objectivity.
e. Hence, professional evaluators are needed to conduct formative evaluations, but, since they may do more harm than good in the early stages of projects, it is best to do one's own formative evaluation early in a project and to employ a professional evaluator to take over this role after the project has developed a modicum of stability.

Exercise 4

Suppose you are going to evaluate a team-teaching program using the Pathway Comparison Model. Summarize the steps you would follow.

- -

Responses to Exercise 4 should include the following:
   a. Characterizing the nature of the team-teaching program to be evaluated.
   b. Clarifying the nature of the conclusion wanted regarding the program.
   c. Assessing evidence about cause and effect relationships between team teaching and educational outcomes.
   d. Comprehensively checking for all effects of the program.
   e. Determining and assessing the criteria of merit and the philosophical arguments pertaining to the team-teaching program.
   f. Assessing the various financial, psychological, and other costs of the team-teaching program.
   g. Identifying and assessing critical competitors to team teaching.
   h. Identifying the program's constituents and performing a needs assessment to determine the potential impacts of team teaching on the needs of the group to be served.
   i. Forming a conclusion about the merit of the team-teaching program.

The responses should also note that the evaluator would have to cycle through these steps several times in the process of evaluating the program.

CONCLUDING STATEMENT

This concludes Module I over the work of Michael Scriven. If you have worked through the module, you should understand Scriven's basic concepts concerning evaluation and you should have some ability to apply them. Generally, you should have a good foundation for examining and utilizing Scriven's newer and future contributions to the field of evaluation.

MODULE II: EVALUATION ACCORDING TO
DANIEL L. STUFFLEBEAM

As an educational researcher, I have worked on the development of evaluation theory since 1965. From 1968 through 1970 I was privileged to chair the Phi Delta Kappa (PDK) National Study Committee on Evaluation. The members of that committee—Egon G. Guba, Robert Hammond, Walter Foley, William Gephart, Howard O. Merriman, and Malcolm Provus—have significantly influenced my work, and our joint contribution appeared as a book, *Educational Evaluation and Decision Making* (Stufflebeam *et al.,* 1971).

This module stems from a critical analysis of classical evaluation theory and the development of the CIPP (Context, Input, Process, Product) Evaluation Model. The PDK committee contributed greatly to the critical analysis, and Egon Guba helped significantly in the development of the CIPP Model through his criticism of the initial conceptualization and his expert assistance in refining and extending it. In working through the module, study its objectives so that you have a basic understanding of what you are to achieve; study the assigned reading; complete the knowledge test over the reading material, checking your answers against the keyed ones; and complete the provided application exercises, comparing your responses with the keyed ones.

The objectives of this module are:

1. to develop an understanding of the PDK committee's critique of classical evaluation theory by
   a. assessing the consequences of equating evaluation to measurement, to experimental design, or to professional judgment;
   b. defining the levels problem;
   c. evaluating the Tylerian rationale for evaluation based on CIPP ideas.
2. to develop an understanding of the CIPP Model by
   a. determining the most unique characteristic of the CIPP Evaluation Model;
   b. describing the CIPP conception of the evaluation process;
   c. identifying and applying the criteria prescribed by CIPP for judging evaluation designs and reports;
   d. identifying planning, structuring, implementing, and recycling decisions;

e. defining context, input, process, and product evaluation;
f. illustrating the use of CIPP for accountability;
g. using the CIPP Model to respond to a request for evaluation service;
h. analyzing the relationship of the CIPP and the formative-summative conceptions of evaluation;
i. analyzing a project to identify the decisions to be served and the pertinent types of evaluation.

These objectives may be achieved by reading the descriptive material and working through the problems in this module. For supplementary work, however, it is suggested that you study earlier works that are listed at the end of this chapter.

The CIPP Evaluation Model

This module concerns why the CIPP Evaluation Model was developed and what it is. Based on evaluation experiences with school districts and critical analysis of classic approaches to evaluation, the model was initially designed to assist school personnel in planning and successfully implementing evaluations of federal projects. Serving decision making in change efforts was and is the most unique characteristic of the model. It has been extended recently, however, to provide information both for decision making and accountability in change efforts.

The particular stimulus for development of the CIPP Model was the evaluation requirement in the Elementary and Secondary Education Act (ESEA) of 1965. This act provided billions of dollars to assist schools in improving education. But the act contained an evaluation requirement that created a crisis since schools were neither accustomed to, nor equipped for, evaluating projects.

Moreover, available conceptions of evaluation were not responsive to the unique evaluation problems of ESEA. The position espoused by the developers of the CIPP Model was that evaluation must not be equated to measurement, to professional judgment, nor to experimental design. While each of these approaches was acknowledged to provide certain advantages for use in evaluation, each approach was also judged to have serious limitations. The advantages and limitations of these three approaches are summarized in Table 2-1, which is taken from the PDK book (Stufflebeam *et al.,* 1971).

As shown in the table, the measurement approach provides rigor

Table 2-1

Advantages and disadvantages accruing from different traditional approaches to evaluation (from Stufflebeam *et al.*, 1971, p. 15)

Approach	Advantages	Disadvantages
Evaluation is identical to measurement	Builds directly on scientific measurement movement Objective Reliable Data are mathematically manipulatable Norms and standards emerge	Narrow instrumental focus Inflexibility because of time and cost to produce new instruments Judgments and the criteria for making them are obscured Variables currently considered not measurable are eliminated, or labeled unimportant
Evaluation is identical to professional judgment	Easy to implement Brings all variables into consideration Takes experience and expertise into account No time lag while waiting for data analysis	Dictated mainly because of ignorance or lack of sophistication Questionable reliability Questionable objectivity Not susceptible to ordinary scientific prudential measures Both data and criteria are ambiguous Generalization very difficult
Evaluation is identical to experimental design	High degree of integration with the instructional process Data available on both student and curriculum Possibility of feedback Objective referent and built-in criteria Possibility of process and product data	Places evaluator in technical role Focuses narrowly on objectives Elevates behavior as the ultimate criterion of *every* educational action Focuses on evaluation as a terminal process

and efficiency in evaluation, but it is too narrow and inflexible to meet the wide range of information requirements in evaluation. Equating evaluation to measurement was not found to be a useful paradigm for evaluating ESEA projects since existing tests were not adequate to measure many key variables in the projects and since following standard test development practices would have prohibited the feedback of timely information needed to guide the projects. Thus testing was judged to offer useful but limited contributions to a comprehensive program evaluation scheme.

In contrast to the measurement approach, Table 2-1 shows that equating evaluation to professional judgment does provide for assessing all relevant variables, but it is seriously lacking in rigor. This approach, which relies on the use of highly respected judges in accreditation-type visits, is high in credibility and is relatively easy to use. The problem is that independent judgments yielded by judges are notoriously unreliable. Hence, the professional judgment approach focuses on all potentially relevant variables, but lacks technical adequacy in measuring these variables and in arriving at defensible judgments.

Of the three approaches considered in Table 2-1, experimental design is shown to provide the greatest amount of rigor but it is the most expensive approach and the most highly restricted in terms of the questions it can address. Equating evaluation to experimental research was a poor approach to evaluating ESEA projects since random assignment of students to ESEA projects was neither feasible nor morally acceptable. Also, experimental research designs offered only terminal data, and they did not assist in determining students' needs or in developing and carrying through innovative ESEA projects. Thus experimental design, while it is the most rigorous of the available approaches to evaluation, was judged inapplicable and virtually useless for evaluating ESEA projects.

Closely associated with the experimental design approach is the evaluation rationale developed by Ralph Tyler (1942), which asserts that evaluation is the process of determining whether objectives have been achieved. This definition, widely recognized in the field of education, does provide guidance for clarifying project objectives and relating outcomes to the objectives, but it is weak in responding to the problem of evaluating ESEA projects since it does not assess the efficacy of objectives, it provides only data related to stated objectives,

and it yields findings only at the end of a project. On balance, the Tylerian approach provided some guidance for evaluating ESEA projects, but it was too limited in its offerings.

While all of the classic approaches to evaluation (measurement, professional judgment, experimental design, and the Tylerian rationale) have desirable qualities, none was adequate to respond to the evaluation requirements of ESEA. A new and better conceptualization of evaluation was needed that would overcome the weaknesses of the available approaches.

The PDK committee defined five problems that needed to be addressed in improving conceptualizations of evaluation. The problems were:

1. *Definition*—Existing definitions that equate evaluation to measurement, to experimental research, and to professional judgment are not adequate; therefore, a new definition is needed to prescribe comprehensive, technically adequate, and useful evaluative activities.

2. *Decision making*—Evaluation should guide change efforts, but the decisions to be served in change efforts are unknown and no process exists to guide evaluators in projecting decision problems and associated information requirements.

3. *Values*—Measurements must be based on criteria that reflect some value system(s), and evaluators have no proven means of determining what value system(s) would best serve as the basis for their data-gathering activities.

4. *Levels*—Different audiences at different organizational levels have different information requirements. An evaluation designed to meet the requirements of a particular audience, for example, a school project staff, would not be likely to meet the requirements of other audiences, for example, the U. S. Office of Education. Therefore, a process of designing evaluation studies is needed that will guide evaluators in identifying audiences and assessing their unique and common information needs.

5. *Research design*—Research and evaluation have different purposes that require different procedures, and research and evaluation designs should be judged by different standards. Serious problems were encountered in ESEA evaluations when classic research designs, intended to develop generalizable truth, were used to evaluate innovative projects, where the need was not for generalizable knowledge but for timely guidance to serve particular decision problems.

The PDK Study Committee on Evaluation chose the CIPP Model as a framework for responding to the problems identified above. I had developed the initial version of this model based on my attempts to evaluate ESEA projects. The PDK committee further developed this model to provide a viable alternative evaluation approach for school persons to use in evaluating innovative programs.

The definition that provided the unifying theme for the CIPP Model is:

> *Evaluation is the process of delineating, obtaining,* ✓
> *and providing useful information for judging*
> *decision alternatives.*

This definition emphasizes that evaluation is a continuing process, that the process includes the three steps—delineating, obtaining, and providing information—and that the information obtained should meet criteria of utility and should guide decision making.

Given that evaluation supplies information for decision making, the decisions to be served must be known. The CIPP Model divides decisions into four classes: planning, structuring, implementing, and recycling. In planning decisions there are choices of objectives. Structuring decisions are made when designing projects to achieve given objectives. Operationalizing and executing a project design require implementing decisions. Judgment of, and reaction to, project results can be termed recycling decisions.

Since there are four kinds of decisions, the model includes four kinds of evaluation: Context evaluation serves planning decisions by identifying unmet needs, unused opportunities, and underlying problems. Input evaluation serves structuring decisions by projecting and analyzing alternative procedural designs. Process evaluation serves implementing decisions by monitoring project operations. Product evaluation serves recycling decisions by identifying and assessing project results.

In addition to serving decision making, CIPP provides a basis for accountability. Context evaluation provides a record of objectives chosen, those rejected, and the relation of chosen and rejected objectives to information about needs, opportunities, and problems. Input evaluation provides a record of chosen and rejected procedural designs and data concerning the strengths and weaknesses of alternative designs. Process evaluation provides a record of the actual implementation process. Product evaluation records project attainments and

decisions concerning the continuation, modification, or termination of the project. Overall, through recording CIPP information and the decisions influenced by the information, program managers can maintain a strong basis for accountability.

One way to summarize the CIPP Model is to develop a framework that relates its four evaluation types to their two uses. Figure 2-1 shows that context, input, process, and product evaluation serve both decision making and accountability. By equating evaluation for decision making to formative evaluation and evaluation for accountability to summative evaluation, one can see the relationship between the Scriven and the CIPP conceptualizations of evaluation. The four kinds of evaluation are formative if they are conducted proactively to serve decision making. They are summative if they are conducted retroactively to serve accountability.

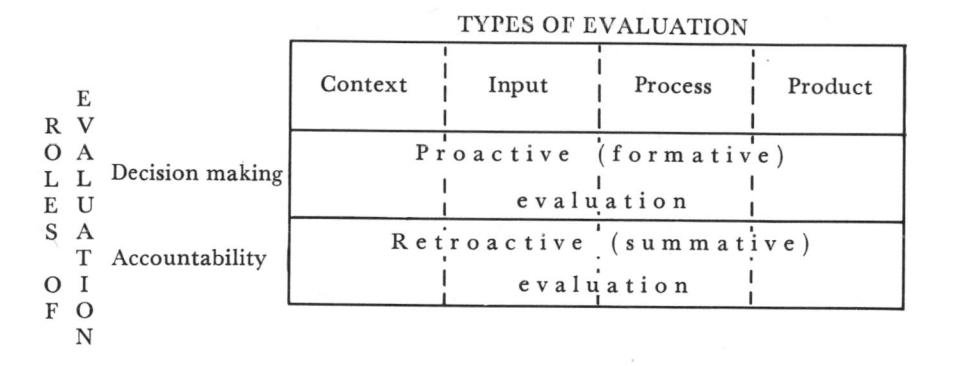

Figure 2-1
A framework that relates CIPP to the formative-summative
conception of evaluation

The CIPP evaluation process includes the three main steps of delineating, obtaining, and providing. Delineating the questions to be answered and providing information for decision makers are interface activities requiring collaboration between evaluator and decision maker. The obtaining of information is a technical activity, involving measurement, data processing, and statistics, that is executed mainly by the evaluator. The delineating, obtaining, and providing steps provide the basis for the CIPP methodology of evaluation. (Students who want in-depth knowledge of the methodology of the CIPP Model should study Stufflebeam *et al.* (1971, chapters 6, 7).

Figure 2-2 is a framework for designing CIPP evaluation studies. It includes the dimensions of types of evaluation, the uses of evaluation, and the steps in the evaluation process. To use this framework, one should first determine what types of evaluation will be conducted and then, for each selected type, determine whether decision making, accountability, or both are to be served. Then the delineating, obtaining, and providing steps should be defined for each of the chosen columns in the matrix. Using the framework in this way provides a set of evaluation designs to be implemented, and such designs generally specify what questions will be addressed, how the needed information will be obtained, and how the information will be reported to the designated audiences.

TYPES OF EVALUATION

		Context Role		Input Role		Process Role		Product Role	
		Decision making	Account-ability	Decision making	Account-ability	Decision making	Account-ability	Decision making	Account-ability
E V S A T L E U P A S T I I N O N	Delineating			(What questions will be addressed?)					
	Obtaining			(How will the needed information be obtained?)					
	Providing			(How will the obtained information be reported?)					

Figure 2-2
A framework for designing CIPP evaluation studies

According to CIPP, evaluation designs and reports should be judged in terms of three standards: technical adequacy concerns validity, reliability, and objectivity; utility involves the relevance, scope, timeliness, importance, pervasiveness, and credibility of the evaluation; cost-effectiveness constitutes the final standard.

This concludes my brief summary of the so-called CIPP Model of evaluation, which has been developing and changing for some time and will continue to do so. The basis for such change has been, and will continue to be, field testing and theoretical development.

KNOWLEDGE TEST OVER THE STUFFLEBEAM ASSIGNMENT

This section contains objective questions and correct and incorrect responses to the questions that will help you determine whether you have achieved the knowledge objectives for the Stufflebeam module. Once again, a broken line separates the questions from the responses. You can self-administer the test, responding to the questions by circling the letter preceding what you consider to be the best response. Compare your answer with the responses that follow each of the questions. After you have completed all of the questions, you will be directed to score your performance.

Question 1. Which of the following is the most unique characteristic of the CIPP Model?
   a. It focuses on providing information for the major types of educational decisions.
   b. It considers the unmet needs of the school system.
   c. It evaluates outcomes in terms of their behaviorally stated objectives.
   d. It emphasizes the role of the evaluator as decision maker.

- -

Correct response
   You should have circled "a": *It focuses on providing information for the major types of educational decisions.* This is the most unique characteristic of the CIPP Model because the CIPP's main departure from classical evaluation theory was to require that evaluation provide timely information for decision making.

Incorrect responses
b—not the best response because it focuses on only one type of information that is gathered through use of the CIPP Model.
c—incorrect because it denotes the main feature of the Tylerian approach, which does not focus on decision making.
d—incorrect because CIPP distinguishes sharply between the roles of evaluator and decision maker.

Question 2. Which of the following is *not* a potential advantage of equating evaluation to measurement?

a. In the measurement approach, evaluation reports are based upon objective data.
b. Data obtained under the measurement approach to evaluation usually meet the assumptions required for interval and ordinal scales.
c. Under the measurement approach, most variables of interest can be considered in the evaluation.
d. The task of developing objective bases for judging program or pupil performance is quite feasible.

- -

Correct response

You should have chosen "c": *Under the measurement approach, most variables of interest can be considered in the evaluation.* It is *not* a main advantage of the measurement approach because this approach directs educators to use available tests that have been carefully validated. By following this advice, the evaluator cannot consider many variables for which tests have not been developed.

Incorrect responses

a—an advantage of equating evaluation to measurement because the measurement approach offers sound procedures for objectivity in administering and scoring tests.

b—an advantage because the measurement approach is based on methods that strive toward meeting the requirements of ordinal and interval scales.

d—an advantage because objective tests have been used widely to provide information for judging both pupil and program performance.

Question 3. Which of the following is a likely consequence of equating evaluation to experimental design?
a. Projects being evaluated will be modified and refined frequently, based on continual feedback from the evaluation.
b. Evaluation will provide explicitly for the assessment of project goals.
c. Evaluation will provide in-depth case study findings concerning the operation of a single project design.
d. Evaluation will provide relatively unequivocal findings

concerning the relative performance of competing project designs.

- -

Correct response

You should have responded "d": *Evaluation will provide relatively unequivocal findings concerning the relative performance of competing project designs.*

Incorrect responses

a—incorrect because experimental design requires that treatments be held constant during the period of the experiment and because experiments provide findings only at the end of the study.

b—incorrect because experimental design does not provide for performing needs assessment or in any other way judging goals.

c—incorrect because experimental design focuses on more than one treatment and assesses product as opposed to process.

Question 4. Which of the following best illustrates the difficulties associated with equating evaluation to professional judgment?

    a. In this approach evaluators are not restricted in the variables they may consider in assessing the merit of a program, and they may consider variables for which no valid measuring devices exist.

    b. This approach provides only a flimsy data base for the professional judgments that are rendered, and these are notoriously unreliable.

    c. This approach lacks independence since the evaluators who make the professional judgments usually are the persons who are in charge of the programs being evaluated.

    d. This approach is excessively expensive in terms of both time and money.

- -

Correct response

You should have circled "b": *The professional judgment approach to evaluation provides only a flimsy data base for the professional judgments that are rendered, and these are notoriously unreliable.* This had been borne out in many studies of the interjudge reliability of project review panels and doctoral examination committees.

Incorrect responses

a—incorrect because not being restricted to variables for which valid measures exist potentially enhances the validity of the study since all relevant variables may be considered in arriving at judgments.

c—incorrect because the professional judgment approach does utilize outside, independent judges.

d—incorrect because the professional judgment approach actually is cheaper and less time consuming than most other evaluation approaches.

Question 5. Which of the following best characterizes the levels problem?

    a. Evaluators do not properly aggregate data gathered at a system's microlevel so that these same data can be applied to assist decision making at the macrolevel of the system.

    b. Evaluators do not determine what information is needed at each level of the system before designing their data gathering and analysis activities.

    c. Evaluators do not control their evaluation reports for appropriate levels of readability.

    d. Evaluators do not properly disaggregate data gathered at a system's macrolevel so that these same data can be used to answer specific questions at microlevels of the same system.

- -

Correct response

You should have responded "b": *The levels problem is that evaluators do not determine what information is needed at each level of the system before designing their data gathering and analysis activities.* Since information requirements vary significantly across system levels, evaluations designed to serve one level will not likely meet the needs of other levels.

Incorrect responses

a—incorrect because it assumes incorrectly that data gathered to serve the needs of the microlevel of a system, if properly aggregated, will be sufficient to serve the needs of higher levels of the same system.

c—incorrect because it denotes a different problem from what has been termed the levels problem.

d—incorrect for two reasons. It assumes incorrectly that data gathered to serve one level of questions can be disaggregated to serve more specific questions. It also assumes incorrectly that the information requirements of a macrolevel encompass those of lower levels of the system.

Question 6. Which of the following best represents the CIPP conception of the evaluation *process?*

a. Determine the operationally defined objectives, gather relevant outcome data, and compare outcomes with objectives.

b. Determine the questions to be answered, collect relevant information, process and interpret the information, and report the results.

c. Describe the antecedents, monitor the transactions, measure the outcomes, and interpret the full set of information.

d. Focus the study, obtain appropriate information, evaluate the information, and select the best action alternative.

- -

Correct response

You should have answered "b": *Determine the questions to be answered, collect relevant information, process and interpret the information, and report the results.* These are the steps that best illustrate the CIPP process of delineating, obtaining, and providing information.

Incorrect responses

a—incorrect because it illustrates the process that is recommended in the Tylerian approach.

c—incorrect because it illustrates not CIPP, but some of the steps that are recommended by Stake in his Countenance Model.

d—incorrect because it emphasizes Scriven's point that evaluators should decide what actions should be taken based on their evaluations.

Question 7. Using the CIPP criteria cited for judging the worth of an evaluation study, which of the following statements *best* describes an adequate evaluation study?
  a. It provides data that are unequivocal and that possess a high degree of generalizability.
  b. It is generalizable to a specified set of conditions and a specified population of subjects.
  c. It provides a relevant rationale for action choices that is timely, rigorous, and provided at reasonable cost.
  d. It provides information that is free from effects due to history, maturation of subjects, instrumentation, laboratory arrangements, and initial differences between comparison groups.

- -

Correct response
  You should have answered "c": *An adequate evaluation study provides a relevant rationale for action choices that is timely, rigorous, and provided at reasonable cost.* This is the best response because it denotes the need for sound evaluation studies to provide information that is technically adequate, useful, and cost-effective. These are the three main standards that CIPP prescribes for sound evaluation designs and reports.

Incorrect responses
a—incorrect because it is incomplete. It requires that evaluations be technically adequate, but does not mention utility and cost-effectiveness.
b—incorrect because it is also incomplete. It requires only that evaluations be externally valid. It does not mention internal validity, utility, or cost-effectiveness.
d—incorrect because it deals only with the internal validity portion of technical adequacy, and does not mention utility and cost-effectiveness.

_____

Question 8. According to the PDK book (Stufflebeam *et al.,* 1971), decisions which specify procedure, personnel, facilities, budget, and time requirements are:
  a. planning decisions.

b. structuring decisions.

c. implementing decisions.

d. recycling decisions.

- -

Correct response

You should have answered "b": *Decisions which specify proce-dures, personnel, facilities, budget, and time requirements are structuring decisions.* This is consistent with the CIPP position that structuring decisions are those that specify what procedural design should be implemented to achieve given objectives.

Incorrect responses

a—incorrect because planning decisions specify not designs but objec-tives.

c—incorrect because implementing decisions are those for carrying out chosen procedural designs.

d—incorrect because recycling decisions are those based on the re-sults of trying a given design and then deciding whether, and if so how, to continue using the design.

Question 9. Decisions that result in continuation of a project beyond its initial funding period are:

a. planning decisions.

b. recycling decisions.

c. structuring decisions.

d. implementing decisions.

- -

Correct response

You should have answered "b": *Decisions that result in continua-tion, modification, or termination of projects beyond their initial funding periods are called recycling decisions.*

Incorrect responses

a—incorrect because planning decisions spell out the initial objectives of special projects and not the decisions that determine whether to terminate, modify, or continue the project after its implemen-tation.

c—incorrect; a structuring decision determines the procedural design to be followed in addressing selected objectives.

d—incorrect because implementing decisions do not determine

whether a project will be phased out or repeated. Instead implementing decisions concern how a project design is to be carried out.

Question 10. According to CIPP evaluation theory, what decisions are designed to answer any combination of the following questions: Should the project staff be retrained? Should new procedures be instituted? Should the project schedule be modified?
a. Structuring decisions.
b. Planning decisions.
c. Recycling decisions.
d. Implementing decisions.

- -

Correct response
You should have answered "d": *Decisions that involve the retraining of project staff, the instituting of new project procedures, and the modification of project schedules, according to the CIPP Model, are implementing decisions.*

Incorrect responses
a—incorrect because structuring decisions specify initial project designs, whereas implementing decisions concern how the designs should be carried out.
b—incorrect because planning decisions spell out objectives and are not directly concerned with what procedures will be used to achieve the objectives.
c—incorrect because recycling decisions concern whether a project will be repeated or institutionalized, not how the project design is to be operationalized.

Question 11. Based on a study of student needs, a school board decides to assign its highest priority to improving school services for children with learning disabilities, which is:
a. a planning decision.
b. a structuring decision.
c. an implementing decision.
d. a recycling decision.

- -

Correct response

You should have answered "a": *Decisions that determine goals, objectives, priorities, ends, and so forth are planning decisions.* Ideally, planning decisions are based on context evaluations that reveal important needs.

Incorrect responses

b—incorrect because structuring decisions determine not what objectives should be served but *how* given objectives should be achieved.

c—incorrect because implementing decisions concern how to carry out a given project design to achieve given objectives.

d—incorrect because recycling decisions concern not what objectives should be pursued but whether a special project already instituted to achieve given objectives should be canceled or continued.

Question 12. The board of education of a large city school district requests assistance in determining the causes of the high dropout rate in their district. The most appropriate type of evaluation would be:
a. context evaluation.
b. input evaluation.
c. process evaluation.
d. product evaluation.

- -

Correct response

You should have answered "a": *Identifying needs and diagnosing their underlying causes are main functions of context evaluation.* Hence, context evaluation would be the appropriate way to determine the causes of a district's high dropout rate.

Incorrect responses

b—incorrect because input evaluation assesses alternative responses to problems once they have been determined through context evaluation.

c—incorrect because process evaluation assesses the implementation of a given strategy (identified through input evaluation) for solving given problems (diagnosed through context evaluation).

d—incorrect because product evaluation assesses the results of a process that has been designed to solve certain problems. Hence, prod-

uct evaluation in this case would assess the results of a special effort to reduce the dropout rate.

Question 13. A school superintendent requests help in finding out whether a new language laboratory is being used in accordance with the specifications for its use. The type of evaluation that best responds to the superintendent's requests is:

a. context evaluation.
b. input evaluation.
c. process evaluation.
d. product evaluation.

- -

Correct response

You should have responded "c": *Process evaluation assesses the extent to which designs actually are being carried out.* In this case process evaluation would assist the superintendent to identify any discrepancies between his district's actual and planned use of the language laboratory.

Incorrect responses

a—incorrect because a context evaluation fundamentally is concerned with student needs and not one particular response, such as a language laboratory.

b—incorrect because input evaluations assess alternative procedural designs for serving given objectives; they do not assess the ongoing operation of a chosen procedural design.

d—incorrect because product evaluations monitor results, not procedures.

Question 14. If a curriculum committee wishes to determine whether a special tutorial project is aiding in the reduction of the school's dropout rate as it was supposed to do, the most appropriate type of evaluation would be:

a. context evaluation.
b. input evaluation.
c. process evaluation.
d. product evaluation.

- -

Correct response
  You should have responded "d": *Product evaluations describe and judge project outcomes.* Thus, determining whether a tutorial project is aiding in reducing a school's dropout problem calls for a product evaluation.

Incorrect responses
a—incorrect because context evaluations focus on system needs, problems, and opportunities, as opposed to the attainments of special projects.
b—incorrect because input evaluations assess procedural plans as opposed to project results.
c—incorrect because process evaluations assess whether designs are being implemented as opposed to what results are being achieved.

Question 15. When a school curriculum committee identifies and assesses the relative merits of several available curricula for high school physics, this involves:
        a. context evaluation.
        b. input evaluation.
        c. process evaluation.
        d. product evaluation.

- -

Correct response
  You should have responded "b": *Input evaluations identify and assess the relative merits of competing strategies and designs.* Thus, an input evaluation would be involved in identifying and assessing alternative curricula for high school physics.

Incorrect responses
a—incorrect because context evaluation assesses system needs, problems, and opportunities as opposed to assessing alternative strategies and designs for responding to targeted needs, problems, and opportunities.
c—incorrect because process evaluation describes and judges the implementation of a given design as opposed to assisting in its initial selection.
d—incorrect because product evaluation does not assist in choosing a procedural design, but assesses its results once it has been chosen and implemented.

Question 16. The CIPP Model can be used for decision making and accountability. Which of the following statements illustrates its use for accountability?

    a. The model provides information on the needs, problems, and opportunities of a system from which goals and objectives can be derived.

    b. The model provides a record of the objectives chosen and the bases for their choice.

    c. The model provides information on whether to terminate, continue, or modify a program.

    d. The model provides for the monitoring of project activities so that the program can be improved as it is implemented.

- -

Correct response

You should have responded "b": *The model provides a record of the objectives chosen and the bases for their choice.* Accountability is the ability to describe and defend past decisions and actions. Hence, providing a record of what objectives were chosen, which were rejected, and why is a use of context evaluation to serve accountability.

Incorrect responses

a—incorrect because it denotes not an instance of accountability but a use of context evaluation to assist in choosing objectives.

c—incorrect because it denotes a use of product evaluation to serve a recycling decision as opposed to serving an accountability need.

d—incorrect because it denotes a use of process evaluation to assist in implementing a design instead of to assist in retrospectively describing and judging the completed process.

Scoring of the Knowledge Test

You have now completed the knowledge test over the Stufflebeam assignment. Total the number of correct responses you had and write the number on the line below.

Number of correct responses _____

If your score was 12 or above, you have responded adequately and

you are ready to proceed to the application exercises in the next section. If your score was 5 to 11, you should refer to the reading assignment to clarify your understanding of those questions you missed. If your score was lower than 5, you should repeat the reading assignment and exercises before working on the application questions.

APPLICATION EXERCISES

This section includes four essay exercises to demonstrate whether you understand the basic premises and concepts of the CIPP Model. Answer the questions on separate sheets of paper. Following each exercise is a list of points that should have been included in your response, and reviewing these will help you assess your response. Complete the first exercise before proceeding to the second. Refer as often as needed to the assigned reading and the keys contained in the knowledge test.

Exercise 1

The CIPP conceptualization of evaluation identified four types of evaluation and four types of decisions. Below is a brief description of a hypothetical project. Analyze this example to identify what instances of context, input, process, and product evaluation are involved in supporting instances of planning, structuring, implementing, and recycling decisions.

A school district obtained funds to upgrade the teaching of instrumental music for disadvantaged children.

It had been ascertained that poor children rarely received opportunities to develop their musical interests and abilities. This led to a decision to improve the music education opportunities available to these children. Further assessment revealed that the district was especially weak in the area of instrumental music offerings, so the district officials decided to concentrate on improving their instrumental music offerings for disadvantaged students.

A decision-making committee was formed and charged to develop a proposal for external funding of an instrumental music project. They identified (and employed external consultants to judge) several possible strategies for improving the district's instrumental music offerings for the disadvantaged. Finally they decided on (and got funds for) a plan to buy musical instruments for use by poor children, to employ five new instrumental music teachers, and institute a volunteer program for talented musicians in the community to assist in the program.

In carrying through the program, it was decided that only four new music teachers would be hired, and that the additional money would be used to buy

more instruments. This decision was served by evaluation indicating that four new teachers could handle the teaching but that insufficient money was available to buy all the needed instruments.

At the end of the project, evaluation indicated that the project had effectively served the instrumental music needs of disadvantaged children. The district board therefore appropriated regular funds to institutionalize the project.

- -

Responses to Exercise 1 should include the following:

a. Context evaluation was involved in determining that poor children rarely received opportunities to develop their musical interests and abilities. More context evaluation was involved in discovering that the district was especially weak in the area of instrumental music offerings.

b. Planning decisions were, first, the decision to improve music education opportunities available to poor children and, second, the decision to concentrate on improving the instrumental music offerings.

c. Input evaluation was used to identify and assess several possible strategies for improving the district's instrumental music offerings for the disadvantaged.

d. Structuring decisions determined that instruments would be purchased, five teachers would be hired, a volunteer program would be instituted, and sufficient funds would be provided to carry out these activities.

e. Process evaluation was useful in determining that four instead of five new teachers could carry out the project and that more money than originally allocated was needed to purchase instruments.

f. Implementing decisions were involved in the decisions to hire only four new music teachers and to use the savings to buy more instruments.

g. Product evaluation indicated that the project had effectively served the instrumental music needs of disadvantaged children.

h. A recycling decision was made when the board decided to appropriate regular funds for institutionalizing the project.

Exercise 2

Assume that you direct an evaluation service agency that conducts evaluations based on the CIPP Model. Develop a brief evaluation proposal in response to the following letter.

J & L Evaluation Agency
112—12th Street
Waverly, Iowa

Dear Mr. McJudge:

Presently, Justice Family Foundation is implementing a three-phased program to assist private or independent colleges in our region. The program pri-

marily attempts to assist colleges in the field of improving their enrollment and retention rate, the efficiency of the teaching-learning process, and the exploitation of an area unfamiliar to most colleges at this time deferred giving. It is assumed that the Foundation will designate several million dollars to participant colleges to apply some of the innovative programs to their own situations for the specific reasons of increasing college revenue, decreasing the rate of expenditure, increasing and maintaining the quality of the educational product.

Given this brief summary of the Foundation's program, I would like to indicate to you that we are deeply interested in developing an evaluation program that will tell us, rather precisely, how effective our grants have been. If you feel that your center could be of some service, I would encourage you to explain your ideas and outline a specific proposal explaining how you might tackle this very challenging problem-opportunity.

Sincerely,

R. B. Johnson

Responses to Exercise 2 should present and develop the following points:
a. The approach we recommend serves both decision making and accountability.
b. The approach called CIPP includes four kinds of evaluation.
c. The CIPP model should be described.
d. Illustrations should be provided concerning how the CIPP Model applies to the request for assistance.
e. Specific suggestions should be given concerning how your service agency would respond to the request for service.

Sample Response for Exercise 2
Mr. R. B. Johnson
Justice Family Foundation
St. Louis, MO

Dear Mr. Johnson:

Thank you very much for your letter of September 10. My staff and I were pleased to learn that the administration of the Justice Family Foundation is planning to fund significant programs for the improvement of education and operations in private and independent colleges in the Midwest. We were also very much interested in your statement that the Foundation is seeking to design and operate a sound evaluation system for the overall Foundation program and in the possibility that our Agency might work with your Foundation to develop and implement a sound evaluation system for your program.

The evaluation approach that we follow calls for conducting evaluation to serve both decision making and accountability; thus, we believe that a sound evaluation procedure provides information before the fact to people in projects to assist them in making their decisions, and records decisions made in the program, along with the evaluative bases for those decisions.

We believe that such evaluation should focus on four classes of information. The first concerns the merit of alternative goals that might be sought. The judgment of alternative goals should be in relation to unmet needs, special opportunities that might be used to improve a system, and specific problems that need to be solved before needs can be met. The second class of information pertains to the merit of competing plans or designs for achieving given objectives. Too often educational groups focus in too early on only one proposed approach for serving their objectives when, in fact, they ought to seek out alternative plans and evaluate them for their power to achieve given objectives. The third class of information concerns the adequacy of the actual process. Here we are concerned with a continuing discrepancy analysis of the extent to which the chosen procedural design is actually being carried out. Such an ongoing evaluation of the process can enable project managers to implement their projects in accordance with their project designs; it can also assist in identifying where their projects are weak and need to be altered. The fourth kind of information concerns results. Traditionally, evaluation has been concerned only with this category of information. We believe it is necessary, but not sufficient, for the conduct of evaluation. An assessment of results should consider all effects of a project, not just those associated with the originally stated objectives. For projects may have both positive and negative side effects that in some cases are more important than the main effects. In summary, our approach to evaluation asks: "What is the problem?" "What can be done about it?" "Is it being done adequately?" "Are valuable results being achieved?"

By collecting the four kinds of information in an ongoing evaluation, it should be possible to assist decision makers in choosing better goals, better designs, better ways of carrying out the designs, and determining whether the project is worth institutionalizing or should be phased out. By maintaining a record of such evaluative information and resulting decisions, an institution has a good base for being accountable to funding agents, the public, and other constituencies. Hence, implementation of the above process should allow a college to present information to your Foundation at the conclusion of the college's project to indicate which goals were chosen, which were rejected, and why. The college also would be able to identify the plan of operation that was chosen, those that were rejected, and the information that was available to indicate the relative costs and potential benefits of alternative approaches. A college that would implement this process would further be able to indicate, after the fact, the extent to which they actually carried out the procedural plan they had adopted. Finally, implementation of this approach to evaluation would enable the college to report to your Foundation all of the results that were achieved from the effort, along with their positive and negative attributes. So, we are proposing for your consideration an approach to evaluation that provides information for both decision making and accountability, and that provides information about the merit of goals, designs, processes, and results.

If this approach seems sound to you and your Foundation associates, I would be glad to work further with you to spell out exactly how it could be

applied to your program. Among the activities that we might pursue with you are the development of evaluation guidelines that could be sent to persons interested in writing proposals to your Foundation. This would increase the probability that people from the colleges would specify sound evaluation designs within their proposals. If you desired, we could assist you in evaluating proposals. Another possible activity would be to provide in-service training in evaluation for personnel from colleges who are to receive funds from your Foundation. This would be a further step toward helping college personnel further refine and then carry out their evaluation plans. Another possibility is that our Agency could carry out for your Foundation audits of the evaluations being conducted in the colleges, so that these institutions could be helped to detect flaws in their evaluation work early enough to correct such problems and increasingly improve their evaluation work. Finally, if there are general questions that should be addressed across a number of colleges, our Agency could conduct an overall external evaluation of the projects. These are some of the activities that our Agency might pursue with your Foundation to ensure that your funded programs will include sound evaluations.

I would need to know more of the specific questions that you have concerning these programs before I could be definitive about the evaluation guidelines that might be developed for your "requests for proposals." However, I do have some initial thoughts based on your letter of September 10. All of these, at this point, pertain to formative evaluations for decision making that would be conducted by the colleges.

Regarding the selection of goals and objectives, each college might conduct a needs assessment to provide a basis for stating objectives. In their needs assessments, representatives of the colleges might specify what they consider to be the ideal enrollments for their institution, the acceptable retention rate, appropriate per student expenditures, minimum annual college revenue, qualitative characteristics of graduates, and targeted impacts on given populations of institutions. They would then assess the actual situation in their institution in relation to each of these variables. They might also project situations five years from now concerning their ideals and their expected situations. Such information would then be used by the colleges to focus the particular objectives for which they would like assistance from your Foundation.

Next, the colleges might set up teams to focus on their chosen objectives and to develop competing innovative plans for achieving the objectives. The development of these plans would be followed by evaluations of them to determine their relative costs and potential impacts on the chosen objectives. This evaluative work would provide a basis for the college to make a rational choice of the plan that they want to have funded.

Next, the college could employ a special evaluation person to serve their project and assign this person to monitor the extent to which the chosen design is actually being carried. Both oral and written reports, on at least a monthly basis, concerning this evaluation of process could help college personnel carry out their design and determine when the design is in need of modification.

Every year the college evaluator and project staff could assess the extent to which objectives were being achieved and they could search for negative and positive side effects of the project. This evaluation of results would be used by persons inside the college to determine whether the project should be continued, whether it ought to be institutionalized, whether it ought be modified in some way. Of course, this information would be of use to the Foundation also in its recycling decisions at the end of each funding period.

The above is an initial attempt to describe some of the evaluative activities that might be conducted by colleges that your Foundation will fund. I've tried to show that such evaluation activities would be designed to help the personnel of the colleges to plan important projects and to carry them out successfully. It is also to be noted that, by recording the evaluative information collected and the decisions made in response to the information, the colleges would be in a good position to provide comprehensive accountability reports to your Foundation so that you could track a project from its initial work in focusing on objectives through its design, implementation, and actual results.

Members of our Agency have had considerable experience in implementing the above approach. We believe it is one that promises to assist not only in judging educational work, but in improving the quality of educational processes. We recommend it strongly to your Foundation for consideration in the program that you are mounting. If you are interested in having members of my staff and me work further with you, please contact me. If I can provide any additional information, I will be pleased to do so.

Sincerely,

John McJudge
J & L Evaluation Agency

Exercise 3

From the perspective of the CIPP Evaluation Model, evaluate the Tylerian rationale for evaluation.

- -

Responses to Exercise 3 should include the following points:
a. The Tylerian rationale for evaluation is that evaluation should determine whether objectives have been achieved.
b. The Tylerian rationale is the same as product evaluation in the CIPP Model.
c. Thus, the CIPP Model provides a much more comprehensive approach to evaluation than that provided by the Tyler Model.
d. A serious limitation of the Tyler Model is that it does not evaluate the efficacy of goals.
e. Also, the Tyler Model is not designed to facilitate decision making.

f. The strongest feature of the Tyler Model is that it serves accountability by providing information about project results.

Exercise 4

Analyze the relationship between the CIPP and formative-summative conceptions of evaluation.

- -

Response to Exercise 4 should include the following points:
   a. The emphasis in the formative-summative conceptualization is on the assessment of merit whereas the CIPP Model concentrates on serving decision making. '
   b. In the CIPP Model, serving decision making is much like formative evaluation whereas serving accountability is similar to summative evaluation.
   c. Context, input, process, and product evaluations may be either formative or summative.
   d. A good way to summarize the relationship is a two-by-four matrix (see Figure 2-1).

CONCLUDING STATEMENT

This concludes Module II over the CIPP Evaluation Model. If you have worked through the module, you should understand why it was developed and recognize CIPP concepts concerning evaluation. You should have some ability to apply the model, and you should be able to evaluate it. Generally, you should have a good foundation for examining and utilizing future developments related to the CIPP Evaluation Model.

REFERENCES

Hammond, Robert L., 1967. "Evaluation at the local level," address to the Miller Committee for the National Study of ESEA Title III.

Provus, Malcolm (principal investigator), 1969. *Discrepancy evaluation model.* Pittsburgh, Pa.: Pittsburgh Public Schools.

Scriven, Michael, 1967. "The methodology of evaluation," in *Perspectives on curriculum evaluation.* AERA Monograph Series on Curriculum Evaluation, No. 1. Chicago: Rand McNally and Co.

———— , tape. "Evaluation skills." AERA Tape Series on Educational Research, Audiotape 6B. Washington, D. C.: American Educational Research Association.

_____ , 1972. "Prose and cons about goal-free evaluation." *Evaluation Comment*, 3.4(December):1-8; reprinted in Chapter 1 of this volume.

Stake, Robert E., 1967. "The countenance of educational evaluation." *Teachers College Record*, 68:523-540.

Stufflebeam, Daniel L., 1967. "The use and abuse of evaluation in Title III." *Theory into Practice*, 6(June):126-133.

_____ , 1971a. "The relevance of the CIPP evaluation model for educational accountability," *Journal of Research and Development in Education*, 5.1(Fall).

_____ , 1971b. "The use of experimental design in educational evaluation." *Journal of Educational Measurement*, 8.4(Winter):267-274.

_____ , 1973. "A conceptualization of evaluation." AERA Tape Series on Educational Research, Audiotape. Washington, D. C.: American Educational Research Association.

Stufflebeam, Daniel L., *et al.*, 1971. *Educational evaluation and decision making.* Itasca, Ill.: F. E. Peacock Publishers, Inc., esp. chs. 1, 2, 3, 7.

Tyler, Ralph W., 1942. "General statement on evaluation." *Journal of Educational Research*, 35:492-501.

Worthen, Blaine R., and Sanders, James R., 1973. *Educational evaluation: Theory and practice.* Worthington, Ohio: Charles A. Jones Publishing Company.

3

Designing Summative Evaluation Studies at the Local Level

Peter W. Airasian
Boston College

Designing Summative Evaluation Studies at the Local Level

Peter W. Airasian

Evaluation, the judgment of merit or worth, is a pervasive feature of all schools. School personnel continually are called upon to make both overt and covert judgments about individuals, programs, and policies. Teachers evaluate student learning; principals evaluate teacher competence; school boards evaluate administrative efficiency. Apart from the evaluation of people, the school setting calls for the evaluation of new curricula, programs, policies, schedules, and practices. The impact of a Title I summer session, a media center, team teaching, the open campus, flexible scheduling, a new science textbook, or an occupational education program are but a few examples of innovations and practices that require evaluation in school settings. Evaluative decisions are needed at all levels of school organization, and they affect personnel and practices at each level.

To help sort out and systematize the multiplicity of roles evaluation can play in educational decision making, numerous conceptual models outlining various types and functions of evaluation have been advanced (see, for example, Airasian and Madaus, 1972; Cronbach,

The organization and substance of this manuscript have benefited greatly from the reactions of several colleagues, particularly Edward F. Iwanicki, George F. Madaus, and Julian M. Shlager.

1963; Provus, 1971; Scriven, 1967; Stake, 1967; Stufflebeam, 1969). The aim of such models is to identify crucial decision-making points within the educational process. It is important to note that evaluation models themselves are not blueprints for conducting an evaluation study. Instead, they identify the informational or decision-making needs to be considered in planning an evaluation. Once a particular model is selected as a guide, the evaluator is faced with such practical problems as identifying appropriate data-gathering instruments, selecting samples, and analyzing data. In sum, the many evaluation models advanced in recent years suggest what decisions need to be made but not how they should be made (Iwanicki, 1973).

Certainly many criteria are available to aid in making judgments about people, programs, or policies, and it is fair to say that at one time or another, in every school or school district, diverse criteria serve as the basis for evaluative decisions. Some decisions are made on the basis of authority, exemplified by the practice of basing action upon the solicited opinions of experts or specialists. Other decisions are made on the basis of tradition, exemplified by the practice of "letting well enough alone" or adopting the policies of some model school system. Still other decisions are made on the basis of logical deduction, exemplified by the practice of arriving at a course of action by a chain of deductive reasoning starting from certain premises or assumptions. Finally, there are decisions based on empirical evidence, exemplified by the practice of arriving at solutions on the basis of collected data.

While each of these approaches to educational decision making warrants extensive examination and explication, this chapter is concerned principally with evaluative decisions derived from empirical evidence. More particularly, it is about the ways and the conditions under which appropriate evidence can be gathered to facilitate decision making, and it is concerned with the design of evaluation studies. The focus, then, is practical, dealing with the question of how data are to be gathered rather than what types of decisions need to be made. In a sense, this approach represents an operationalizing of many of the concerns and issues raised in many evaluation models.

Given the multiplicity of evaluative decisions required by the educational process and the many levels and individuals at which evaluation can be aimed, it is necessary to limit the scope of the evaluation designs being considered. There are at least three such limitations.

First, attention is focused upon the design of evaluation studies at the local school or school district level. Large-scale regional, state, or national evaluation studies are not a major concern although some of the methodologies discussed, if generalized, might apply to large-scale studies. Second, concern is centered upon the evaluation of programs, policies, or practices rather than upon the evaluation of students, teachers, or administrators per se. Third, the emphasis is upon summative, product evaluation designs and not upon formative, ongoing evaluation designs. Survey, needs assessment, or diagnostic designs, while important in the school setting, are not the focus here. How effective was my new ninth-grade science program? Did our Title I program change attitudes toward learning? Did team teaching result in improved reading competency? Are the results engendered by the work-study program better than the traditional vocational education program? These are the types of questions that are of concern. Summative designs are not only important in their own right; they also set many of the parameters for formative evaluation designs.

The general task of designing an evaluation study to answer questions similar to those posed above can be divided into a number of substeps including: defining the objectives of the program or practice of interest, operationalizing potential program activities, structuring the setting so that outcomes can be observed and measured, selecting dependent variables, gathering evidence, and analyzing data (Rieken, 1972). While proper concern for each of these substeps is important to a design which engenders interpretable, unambiguous data for decision making, this chapter is concentrated largely upon the problem related to the conditions under which valid data are gathered, rather than upon the important, and more widely discussed, problems of defining objectives, selecting dependent measures, implementing a program, or analyzing data. It is assumed that any innovation being evaluated has intended aims or goals and that these can and should be made explicit. It is further assumed that dependent measures can be identified to assess whether the intended outcomes are manifested. Finally, it is assumed that data gathering in the context of an evaluation study can be summarized and analyzed in a number of appropriate ways. This chapter is concerned principally with the problem of how to arrange the conditions under which data are gathered to ensure obtaining the most valid data possible for judging the

adequacy of the innovation or the program being studied. More specifically, the aim is to present various schemata or designs for gathering unambiguous data concerning the impact of a particular program, policy, or practice. Such designs control for a variety of factors that often invalidate the results of evaluation studies performed at the local level. When particular issues related to the definition of objectives, the selection of dependent measures, and the analysis of data have bearing upon the problem of the validity of data gathered, these aspects are identified and discussed, but these areas are not the primary focus of this study.

There is a distinction between evaluation and design. Evaluation is concerned with judgments of merit or worth, and design is concerned with the conditions under which data are gathered. A premise of this study is that valid, empirical data should provide some input for evaluative decisions. It must be noted, however, that data, in and of themselves, do not result in judgments or decisions. There is, in essence, an important difference between the process of gathering data to aid in decision making and the decisions that result. Perhaps the clearest way to illustrate this point is to consider a typical classroom situation. Suppose a class is given a test and evidences a six-month achievement gain over some prior test administration. The average class gain represents the teacher's datum; it does not, in and of itself, indicate anything about the quality of the class's performance. Only after the average gain (that is, the datum) is compared to some standard can a judgment of merit or worth be made. The teacher must compare the average class gain to some criterion of worth to arrive at an evaluation of the class's performance. So it is with the design of evaluation studies to judge programs, policies, or practices. Data collection is not evaluation. Evaluation occurs only when data are compared to some standard and a judgment of worth is made. Hence, when we talk about designing evaluative studies, the emphasis is upon providing data that can aid in decision making, regardless of the standards that will be applied in arriving at the decision.

This chapter, in addition to providing a number of specific evaluation designs useful for conducting local-level summative evaluation studies, should also enable the reader to identify motivational, organizational and attitudinal constraints on the conduct of local-level evaluations; select treatment conditions and dependent variables so as to overcome common pitfalls often encountered in local evalua-

tion studies; recognize the basic threats to the interpretability of evaluation studies; cite general strategies for overcoming common threats to interpretability; explain how various evaluation designs and strategies control for specific threats to interpretability.

Now that the direction of the study has been established, the setting in which an evaluation study is likely to be developed—the local school or school district—must be examined.

CONTEXT OF LOCAL-LEVEL EVALUATION STUDIES

While a central premise of this chapter is that empirically derived evidence is a necessary prerequisite to summative, product evaluation and evaluation studies can be designed to supply valid empirical data, it would be naive to assume that such data are the only relevant input for educational decision making. Factual evidence does not represent the sole criterion, or even the only "rational" criterion, for making school-related decisions. Politics, authority, tradition, deductive reasoning, and other factors are influential (Lortie, 1967). It is important, therefore, to consider the place of designed evaluation studies in the context of decision-making realities at the local level.

Most school settings are not now, nor are they likely to be in the immediate future, readily tailored to accommodate all the methodological needs of adequately designed summative evaluation studies. Attitudinal objections, policy restrictions, time constraints, and bureaucratic reluctance face many local school evaluators and impede their activities. Given the current nature and practices of some American schools, evaluation studies represent an imposition on many teachers, administrators, and students. Whether schools should be constituted in another manner, one which facilitates and encourages empirical evaluation, must be argued elsewhere. Here we are considering the current context of most schools and classrooms and attempting to tailor design techniques to these realities. In any discussion of the design of summative evaluation studies at the local level, cause-effect relationships, the unambiguous data, and "proof" of goodness or merit may have to be replaced by less ambitious goals. The designer of local evaluation studies may often have to be contented with designing studies that simply "reduce ambiguity."

To understand more clearly the constraints that often hamper the design of local evaluation studies, it is important to review the many

attitudes toward and motives surrounding evaluation studies at the local level. Such attitudes and motives color the receptivity of many administrators and teachers to evaluation and, as a consequence, either expand or inhibit the flexibility allowed the evaluator in constructing an evaluation design.

Demand for Evaluation

At the local level, the demand for summative evaluation studies to assess the outcome of programs, policies, or practices arises from many sources. In cases where governmental funding provides the basis of support, the granting of funds is often contingent upon evaluation. When resources are in short supply and allocation or reallocation of limited funds, materials, or personnel is required, an evaluation study is often undertaken to determine where the resources should go. When a teacher or administrator wishes to delay action, as, for example, in dealing with the demands of a group of irate parents, he is likely to respond to the situation by saying: "That problem is currently being evaluated and when the data are in we shall be in a better position to make a decision." When an individual or a group attempts to prove a point or criticize a person, program, or practice, evaluation often proves to be the basis for criticism or defense. Evaluation studies at the local level are also often conducted to provide a type of public or political validity to a new undertaking: a school board may require evaluation of a new program for which they recommend funding, less because they are particularly interested in the results of the evaluation than because the banner of evaluation and demonstrated results lends public credence to their commitment to rational educational change. Finally, in contrast to many of the motives cited above, there are instances when a school board, administrator, or teacher engages in an evaluation study because there is a genuine interest in conserving something perceived as good, in building upon strategies which appear to work, or in learning about and improving school practices.

Many of the above motives admittedly appear to be rather cynical, which is somewhat unfair to those administrators and teachers who use evaluation to learn about and improve practice. Formal evaluation studies do not yet, however, play a central role in aiding educational decision making. Instead, such studies are generally ordered after a problem is perceived and has reached a crisis state. Many prin-

cipals and school boards avoid formal evaluation of their high school English program until a group of parents registers a complaint that mean verbal CEEB scores have dropped over the last two years. An alternative, open school arrangement at a local elementary school might go unevaluated in any formal sense until a group of concerned parents or teachers complains about the activities and anticipated outcomes of the program. School boards often find no need to evaluate the effectiveness and impact of curriculum specialists when the budget permits addition of such specialists to the staff. Not until money becomes tight and requires the elimination of staff does evaluation of the specialists become a priority item. Formal evaluation is more often an ex post facto phenomenon than an inherent consideration in most schools.

Evaluation is, in many situations, a political activity (House, 1973), and it is not viewed as requisite to rational decision making in many local school systems. Decisions are more often made on the basis of authority, tradition, or deduction, and evidence gathering, in the form of formal evaluation studies, is resorted to only in the face of parental pressure, budgetary tightness, or another such factor. We can lament the political, ax-grinding motivation behind so many evaluation studies, but the local-level evaluator must at least recognize the many motives, admirable and less than admirable, that prompt the call for evaluation studies.

Procedural Constraints

In addition to recognizing the inherent motives for much local-level evaluation, the evaluator must also be aware of difficulties he will encounter in attempting to implement an evaluation study. Many factors can confound efforts to arrange conditions for the collection of unambiguous evidence about the program, policy, or practice under study. First, the cooperation and understanding of classroom teachers are needed since it is their programs and their activities that will most often be evaluated. A prevalent dichotomy exists between the interest and needs of the evaluator and the interest and needs of most classroom teachers. Evaluation emphasizes goals, objectives, and outcomes. It emphasizes the need for formal statements of outcomes and plans data gathering around such intended outcomes. While most evaluators recognize the need to gather evidence about unintended or unanticipated program outcomes, these, by definition,

are often difficult to define and, as a consequence, the evaluator usually places primary emphasis upon defined outcomes. Moreover, the defined outcomes, from the evaluator's viewpoint, must be specific and behavioral so that appropriate evidence-gathering instruments and procedures can be identified. In essence, the evaluator is concerned with observable changes in modes of thought, feeling, or acting.

Classroom teachers have a similar orientation, but they are more intimately concerned with the instructional process itself and not with formally stated objectives or formally evaluated outcomes (Jackson, 1968; Good and Brophy, 1973). While the evaluator emphasizes formal evidence, teachers may emphasize and rely upon informal evidence such as student interest, attention, questioning, or some other student response to determine whether practice is successful. Also, the evaluator, by the very nature of his task, questions the innovation or program being evaluated; the teacher, as practitioner, believes in what he is doing.

Many teachers, as well as administrators, view formal evaluation and evaluators as being unnecessary, counterproductive, and alien. Formal evaluation studies are often perceived to be threatening, and they are unwelcome, which makes it difficult to obtain cooperation and assistance from either teachers or administrators.

An evaluator will frequently be called upon to evaluate a program, policy, or practice about which administrators or teachers have already made judgments. Most impetus for school change stems from some individual or group noticing a school regulation, practice, or program that is considered undesirable (or the absence of a regulation, practice, or program considered desirable). The individual or group then lobbies for change in the desired direction. There are, therefore, those who believe in the innovation, propagandize it to others, and work to establish it within the school setting. Their enthusiasm often leads them to assume that the innovation will be successful, making formal evaluation appear superfluous.

There is often a tendency for administrators or teachers at the local level to be program-oriented instead of problem-oriented. They stake their prestige upon a particular approach to a problem, advocate that approach as if it were certain to be successful, and defend it against those who advocate other approaches to the problem. Emphasis is upon the open school, structured classrooms, team teaching,

programmed instruction, mastery learning, or other techniques rather than upon the problems these and competing approaches are advanced to solve.

The ego involvement of school personnel in their own particular pet program or policy of practice has two related implications. First, advocates have already performed an implicit evaluation and "their" innovation has been certified as desirable or successful. The result of this implicit evaluation, in turn, often negates, in the mind of the advocates, the need for formal evaluation. In fact, advocates often perceive formal evaluation of the outcomes of the innovation as threatening, and either they refuse to participate in the evaluation or they endeavor to sabotage it. Second, even after an evaluation is accomplished, negative results are refuted or disbelieved by these advocates (Carter, 1971).

A further difficulty the summative evaluator can encounter in his attempt to implement a designed evaluation study is more a consequence of the methodology he employs than a consequence of the attitudes or prejudgments of school personnel. As indicated previously, the evaluation studies discussed in this chapter are based upon a planned, data-based approach to decision making. Designing and implementing an evaluation study, analyzing data, and reporting on the evidence gathered are time-consuming activities. Inherent in formal evaluation studies, then, is the notion of gradual, data-based decision making. Often conditions that facilitate the conduct of an evaluation study shift during the study. Pressures brought to bear on administrators or teachers, which cause them to alter or change the context or program under study, can destroy a complex design. The gradualness inherent in formal evaluation studies can, in many cases, work against the rational, evidence-based approach such studies are intended to foster. Frequently, situations at the local level will shift so that it will be impossible for local administrators to wait until the study is completed to make their evaluative decisions.

Numerous other factors can hamper the conduct of evaluation studies at the local level. Funds for carrying out evaluation typically are limited. Maintaining diffuse and ambiguous goals is in the interest of control and privacy. Change in school practices is as often tied to boredom with previous activities as it is to notions of improving education per se. Any such factor is likely to influence the evaluator's attempt to define an appropriate design for the conduct of an evaluation study.

Reception Granted Evaluation Results

Given these difficulties and the fact that evaluation is a subjective activity, the evaluator must be prepared for a litany of objections to his findings. When the results of the study run counter to the expectations of administrators, teachers, or parents, the evaluator will often be taken to task for one or more of the following reasons: the outcomes of the program were too subtle to measure; the presence of outsiders, in the form of the evaluator himself, disturbed the normal conduct of the program; despite the fact that the evaluation could identify no visible effects, participants are better human beings for having participated; the "real" effects of the program or policy are long range, and failure to identify immediate or intermediate outcomes is a verification of this fact; the program or practice is an appropriate one, but it is just not for these particular individuals; the program is an appropriate one, but it just was not implemented extensively enough; the program or practice is justified if it "saved" just one student. There are, in fact, very few replies that the evaluator can make to such objections because they arise less from the methodology of the study than they do from biases, prejudgments, and preconceptions that objectors hold toward the program, practice, or policy evaluated. Such objections are warranted in some situations, but in other situations they represent a conflict between the empirical, evidence-oriented approach to making decisions and alternative approaches that rely upon authority, tradition, or deduction. Adversary evaluation (Owens, 1973) may be one method for resolving such conflicts. Such an approach represents, in essence, a jury trial for an evaluation report, with the evaluator acting as defendant, some party opposed to the report as prosecutor, and the decision maker as judge. To return, however, to the context that surrounds most evaluations at the local level, it must be made clear that, while the rather pessimistic portrait painted thus far does not apply in all situations, local-level evaluators must contend with such attitudes and handicaps. The culture of most American schools offers no explicit rewards for examining and evaluating one's practices or effects.

Overcoming Contextual Constraints

Certain of the criticisms and problems which the local-level evaluator is likely to encounter cannot be overcome by increased method-

ological rigor. If teachers oppose gathering formal evidence, the most rigorously designed evaluation study can do little to alter such attitudes. If people make prejudgments about the efficacy of their programs, policies, and practices on the basis of authority, tradition, or deduction, hard evaluative evidence may be insufficient to alter these prejudgments although a tradition of adequate, useful, formal evaluation may, in part, soften attitudes. If individuals cannot accept the gradualness inherent in carefully designed product evaluation studies, more careful attention to methodology is likely to exacerbate, not alleviate, this feeling.

Thus, the evaluator often is faced with two types of problems in his attempt to implement local-level evaluation. On the one hand, he may be faced with attitudes, opinions, fears, prejudgments, and interests that are antithetical to an evidence-based, formal evaluation approach. On the other hand, he may be faced with the practical problem of arranging conditions for data gathering so that he can produce the most valid evidence about the program, policy, or practice under investigation. The first problem is largely attitudinal, while the second is largely methodological. While the two problems can be related to some extent, as when fear of results engenders reluctance to participate in an evaluation study or refusal to permit data gathering at the time dictated by the evaluation design, the inherent issues are basically distinct.

In most local contexts it will be possible to carry out some type of formal evaluation study, if only because evaluation is, as we have seen, a motivated activity. As a consequence, it will receive support from those individuals at the local level who seek the evidence evaluation provides. Regardless of whether all concerned individuals at the local level appreciate the need for formal evaluation or accept the results of such evaluations, the process will be carried out. In spite of the inevitability of evaluation studies, there should be some attempt to overcome the attitudinal reservations of teachers and administrators by informing them of the activities, aims, expected benefits (to them and their school), and results of such a study. Although attitudinal reservation toward or rejection of evaluation will not disappear overnight and mutual trust between teachers and evaluators cannot be built in a short time, it is at the interpersonal, interactive level that feelings against evaluation must first be attacked.

I have concentrated upon the attitudinal and motivational context

in which evaluation designs usually will be implemented to illustrate the dichotomy that often exists between the perceptions of the evaluator regarding the activities he engages in and the perceptions of many school personnel regarding these same activities. The realities of the evaluator and school personnel are often different and antithetical, and the evaluator must comprehend, balance, and work within these realities to accomplish his task. The difficulty is not between what can be considered a "right" set of attitudes and a "wrong" set.

The needs, interests, concerns, and goals of many school teachers and administrators at present are not concomitant with the needs, interests, concerns, and goals of most evaluators. To be fearful of how evidence will be used, to place emphasis on the individual child and not a program or practice, to weigh the success of a program in terms of its effect upon one child rather than its effect upon a group, to trust perceptions made in day-to-day contact rather than formal evidence, or to be reluctant to give up a belief in the face of evidence considered irrelevant is neither wrong nor bad. These traits are simply different from those emphasized by most evaluators. The evaluator should respect such views, but strive to clarify how his activities add a different, but relevant, dimension to such concerns.

In sum, the local-level evaluator must strive to perform his task as best he can, attempting to overcome attitudinal fear and resistance when possible. At the very least, however, the evaluator should seek to design rigorous studies—always within the methodological constraints he will face—and to provide the least ambiguous evidence possible to aid in decision making. The evaluator cannot control either the motives or the attitudes of school personnel; nor can he control the extent to which the results of his efforts will influence ultimate decision making. He can, however, seek to apply his methodological knowledge to implement the best possible design and to provide the least ambiguous evidence. It may be difficult for the evaluator to do more, but it is wrong for him to do less. It is with these thoughts in mind that we approach the more practical problems of designing evaluation studies to evaluate the outcomes of school programs, practices, and policies.

OVERVIEW OF EVALUATION DESIGN

Design relates to the conditions and procedures that guide data collection. The purpose of an evaluation design is to facilitate gather-

ing data, thereby making possible valid statements about the effects or outcomes of the program, practice, or policy under study. Intuitive reasonableness and impressionistic worth are rejected as the primary bases for decision making, and valid, empirical data are considered necessary inputs for the evaluation process.

Consider a plan for gathering data to assess the impact of a new fifth-grade science unit on the environment. Let us assume that the data-gathering plan consists of the following features: a teacher who expressed interest in the new unit was selected to implement it in his classroom; an achievement test consisting of items concerned with environmental facts and processes was administered to the class as a pretest at the beginning of instruction on the unit; the same achievement test was administered to the class at the conclusion of the unit. Let us also assume that the class average increased between pre- and posttesting. Similar data-gathering plans are in common use in many local school systems.

To assess the adequacy of any design, the basic question asked is: How unambiguous are the data in indicating that the observed outcomes can be attributed to the program and not to extraneous confounding factors? In our example, we can ask whether the data are sufficiently unambiguous to warrant the claim that increases in student learning can be attributed to the new science unit. We can seek to identify rival hypotheses which represent other, plausible explanations for the increase in student learning. On reflection, it is apparent that there are a number of factors, quite apart from the new unit, to which increased learning can be attributed. There is, first, the effect of testing, that is, the extent to which the pretesting sensitized students to items or processes that were retested again on the posttest. Typically, the more unusual or esoteric the items and format of the pretest, the more likely it is to sensitize students or draw their attention to important learning and, hence, the more likely the pretest is to influence the results of the posttest. Alternatively, the increase from pre- to posttest performance could be attributed to history, or the occurrence of some specific event between the two testings that influenced learning or interest but was independent of the new unit. For example, suppose that Earth Week was celebrated, a strict antipollution bill was passed, or automobile antipollution requirements were rescinded during teaching of the unit. It is quite likely that such events would both increase the students' interest in the environment and

teach them salient facts about their environment. Intervening events independent of the science unit might, as a consequence, be a rival explanation for the increase in student learning. Selection factors, in this case related more to the teacher than to the students, might also explain observed differences between pre- and posttests. The teacher selected to try out the new unit in his classroom was selected on the basis of expressed interest in the unit. Given the data collection plan, it is not possible to tell whether the teacher's interest carried over into preparing students for the posttest, emphasizing tested facts and processes, or some other aid. Selection biases constitute another potential rival hypothesis for observed learning.

Two facts concerning the data collection plan of the study just described are important. First, the plan does not provide unambiguous data that permit one to say with a degree of certitude that the new environmental unit, in and of itself, resulted in improved student learning. The plan is, therefore, weak. Second, the possibility that testing, history, selection, or some other factor represents a plausible alternative explanation to the observed results does not mean that these factors were, in fact, operating. It is conceivable that the observed pre-post test differences were the result of the new unit. The mere existence of plausible rival explanations, explanations which may or may not be valid but which cannot be eliminated from consideration given the data collection plan, suffice, however, to render data ambiguous and conclusions tentative. In this light, it should be evident that what an evaluator is striving to attain when he designs an evaluation study for a school program is accurate evidence that the observed outcomes are, in fact, a consequence of the program under investigation. The designer of evaluation studies should seek to arrange the conditions of the study in such a way that, at its conclusion, cause-effect relationships between the program and its observed outcomes can be made.

Internal and External Validity

Causality implies at least three conditions. The first concerns the temporal precedence of the causative factor to the observed result. That is, it is necessary to demonstrate that the presumed cause of some outcome did in fact precede the observed effect and that the effect was not present before the causative factor was applied. The second factor concerns covariation or the existence of a statistical

relationship between the presumed cause and the anticipated effect, and the third is that causality is based upon the demonstration of a one-to-one relationship between the observed outcome and the purported cause of that outcome. In the preceding example of the study concerned with assessing the impact of a new environmental unit, a number of rival hypotheses were advanced to explain the observed increase in student learning. To the extent that such alternative explanations cannot be negated or dismissed from consideration, a cause-effect relationship between the unit and resulting learning cannot be made. In addition to temporal concerns and covariance, cause-effect relationships are predicated upon the absence of rival explanations for the effect.

The temporal problem of cause preceding effect may plague the designer of evaluation studies to some extent, especially when new school programs or practices are tied to "hot" topics in the society in general. For example, a recent evaluation conducted at my university sought to determine whether a program aimed at sensitizing students' attitudes toward environmental protection was successful. A pretest revealed that students in the school as a whole already possessed such positive attitudes toward environmental protection that the planned program was not really necessary. Had no pretest been given and a posttest revealed positive student attitudes toward the environment, it is likely that the program would have been claimed as the major causative factor when, in reality, the effect was present before the "cause." Similarly, at times it may be difficult to demonstrate a clear and significant relationship between a program and its effects. The most pressing problem encountered in the design of local-level evaluation studies will, however, involve ruling out competing alternative explanations for observed effects. The most important aspect of the design of evaluation studies is, then, the attempt to eliminate or control competing explanations for the effects of the program of interest. In essence, a design will be successful when the observed effects of a program can unequivocally be attributed to that program, that is, when the design permits one to conclude that the manipulation of concern can be said to be the only plausible explanation for the observed outcomes.

Arranging data collection procedures to arrive at unambiguous conclusions is a problem of internal validity (Campbell and Stanley, 1963). Internal validity, the determination that the program, policy,

or practice under investigation did engender the results observed, is the basic minimum prerequisite for the design of interpretable evaluation studies. In addition to concern about internal validity, the designer of evaluation studies may also have to contend with problems of external validity. External validity relates to the problem of the generalizability of the results of the study: to what groups, settings, schools, and so forth can the observed effect be generalized (Campbell and Stanley, 1963)?

The emphasis of evaluation studies at the local level typically will be upon pragmatic, situation-bound results. Rarely will the results of evaluation studies be generalized across school district boundaries, and, in many situations, results will not be generalized across schools within a district. Evaluation studies at the local level will most often emphasize utility and action and not study relationships and nuances related to substantive contributions to an area of knowledge. Practical, not theoretical, issues will be at stake in local-level evaluations. Results are much more likely to be applied in situ than they are to be exported to other schools or locales. Hence, while external validity may have some relevance for the design of local-level evaluation studies, it is secondary in relation to internal validity.

Threats to Internal Validity

Many factors threaten the internal validity of evaluation studies. Much of the preceding discussion and much of what follows is drawn from the work of Donald Campbell, who has produced numerous major works on the problems of the design of evaluation studies and the problems of design validity (Campbell, 1957; Campbell and Stanley, 1963; Campbell, 1969; Campbell and Erlebacher, 1971; Cook and Campbell, in preparation).

The most prevalent threats to the internal validity of an evaluation study are:
1. History—events external to the program, policy, or practice under investigation which occur between pre- and posttesting.
2. Maturation—natural biological, psychological, or sociological development of subjects occurring between pre- and posttesting.
3. Instability—unreliability of measures, which causes fluctuation in scores independent of the program, policy, or practice under investigation.

4. Testing—the effect of taking a test at one point in time upon taking the same test at a subsequent point in time.
5. Instrumentation—the effect of changes in the measuring instrument between pre- and posttests so that observed effects are a result of the instrument change and not the program, policy, or practice.
6. Selection—biases resulting from differences between types of individuals recruited for comparison groups.
7. Mortality—differential loss of subjects from comparison groups.
8. Statistical regression—the effect of selecting individuals on the basis of their extremely high or extremely low scores on a measuring instrument. Scores at extreme ends of a distribution are unreliable and retesting tends to result in either extremely high scorers scoring relatively lower and hence "regressing" downward in test scores or extremely low scorers scoring relatively higher and hence "regressing" upward in test scores. Unreliability of test scores at extreme ends of the distribution, in and of itself, results in changes in scores upon retesting.

Each of the above threats to internal validity can pose a plausible rival hypothesis for the observed outcomes of an evaluation study. Each of these threats should, therefore, be accounted for and eliminated as plausible explanations if the results of evaluation studies are to be considered valid. Thus the primary aim of design is to plan evaluation studies so that unwanted, potentially confounding sources of variation are controlled or eliminated.

GENERAL PROCEDURES FOR OVERCOMING THREATS TO INTERNAL VALIDITY

In laboratory research, where the confounding effects of the environment are more easily manipulated, two basic techniques are used to control extraneous factors and to make research internally valid. The first of these techniques, the identification of a control or comparison group, is implemented to overcome the effects of uncontrolled events external to the subjects in the evaluation study. The second technique, random assignment of subjects to participating groups, is implemented to overcome selection biases or systematic differences between comparison groups. In addition to these two methods of ensuring internal validity, there are other, less formal

circumstances that permit the definition of internally valid evaluation designs.

Control Groups

Instead of implementing a program with a single group, two groups can be identified: one, which participates in the program of interest, is generally called the "treatment" group; the other, which serves as a control or comparison group, is not exposed to the program. As a result of having two groups, one to serve as a comparison for the other, such internal validity threats as history, testing, and instrumentation are negated. Assuming that the only difference between the groups is the presence or absence of the program, policy, or practice under study, the effects of history, testing, regression, instrumentation, maturation, and mortality should be manifested equally in both groups. Thus, if history represents the primary reason for an increase in posttest scores, the scores of the two groups should be similar. If the group utilizing the new program is superior in posttest achievement to the comparison group, the program, and not history, can be considered the cause of the superiority. Similarly, if two groups are equivalent in all respects save the presence or absence of the treatment under study, it can be expected that the effect of maturation, mortality, regression, and the like will be manifested equally in the two groups, thereby eliminating these factors as potential rival explanations for observed group differences. Hence, the existence of a control or comparison group is one aid for designing interpretable evaluation studies.

Randomization

The second procedure used in laboratory research to strengthen internal validity is randomization. Rather than assigning students or subjects to a particular program or practice in a purposive manner, based on teacher preference, student preference, or some other factor, subjects are placed in either the treatment group or the control group by a chance or random process. The process itself may consist of flipping a coin for each subject, assigning "heads" to the treatment group and "tails" to the control group, rolling a die with odd-numbered sides representing assignment to one group and even-numbered sides to the other group, or assigning each subject a number and using a table of random numbers to constitute the two groups.

The aim of the randomization process is to ensure that every subject to be assigned has an equal chance of appearing in the treatment group, thus negating pre-existing differences between groups. In essence, conditions are arranged so that the only determiner of whether a subject is in the treatment or control group is a chance or random event such as flipping a coin or rolling a die. Randomization is the primary means used to ensure that the two groups are equivalent, insofar as randomization ensures that any inequalities between subjects will have an equal opportunity to show up in all groups (Fisher, 1951; Cox, 1958).

In discussing the use of a control group in the preceding section, it was stated that control groups eliminate the threats of history, instrumentation, and testing, "assuming the only difference between the groups is the presence or absence of the program, policy, or practice under study." Randomization is the basic technique utilized to assure that the treatment and comparison groups are equivalent in all respects save presence or absence of the treatment.

Randomization is the optimum method of assuring group equality. It is superior to and more powerful than so-called matching techniques, in which subjects or groups are equated on one or more variables. The basic problem with matching, or covariance analysis, which is a special case of matching, is that groups equated on one or more variables will inevitably differ on other, nonmatched variables. Random assignment serves to equate groups on all possible variables (Cronbach and Furby, 1970).

The two primary means of eliminating threats to internal validity, control groups and randomization, are, therefore, related. The existence of a control group, in and of itself, is a necessary, but not a sufficient, requisite for eliminating all internal validity threats. It is possible, for example, for the control and treatment groups to be nonequivalent to begin with so that final differences between groups could be attributed to initial differences and not to the program under investigation. Randomization is also a necessary, but not a sufficient, condition to render inoperative all threats to internal validity. A design incorporating a randomly selected treatment group but no comparison group is subject to threats such as testing, regression, instrumentation, and history. In designed studies which eliminate the major threats to internal validity, comparison groups and randomization function hand in hand. Comparison groups afford a standard

against which to judge the impact of the program of interest. Randomization helps ensure that the comparison and treatment groups are equivalent at the start of the study. The consequence of utilizing these concomitant procedures is the elimination of the threats to internal validity as plausible rival explanations of observed differences between groups.

Other Circumstances in Which Threats to Internal Validity Are Controlled

Randomization and the use of comparison groups are powerful aids for defining tight, valid designs. When studies are conducted in a laboratory setting, where the researcher can arrange conditions pretty much as needed and where he is free from many of the confounding influences present when designs are implemented in functioning social systems, it is relatively easy to construct and put into practice designs that control or eliminate threats to internal validity. The evaluator at the local level, however, is often forced to operate within the patterns of organizational roles, policies, duties, and interpersonal relationships of the functioning social system. He may not be able to separate the program being investigated from the institution that is the school in order to put it into an "ideal" setting. He may find, for example, that he cannot randomly assign students to treatment and control groups because the computer has already assigned students to intact classes on the basis of their course schedules. Teacher preferences regarding what programs or practices they can accept and feel comfortable with may preclude random assignment of teachers to treatment and comparison groups. Administrators who have a vested interest in the success of a policy or practice may require that only a particular teacher or group of teachers be permitted to adopt the innovation under study. Even when it is possible to select intact classrooms at random, instead of students, the local-level evaluator is likely to find that there are only two or three classrooms available for selection. Further, the use of a control group implies withholding a treatment from some individuals or classrooms. The extent to which prejudgments about the new program, policy, or practice can be held in abeyance, and a "wait-and-see" attitude adopted concerning the merits of the innovation, is the extent to which it will be possible, both practically and ethically, to withhold treatment from some students or classes. There is always a temptation to equate new-

ness with goodness and to advocate total adoption of an innovation, arguing that it would be improper to deny all students the anticipated benefits. Conversely, but equally confounding from the point of view of establishing a viable and reasonable comparison group, are those instances when a program such as an alternative school is established and parents, students, and teachers are allowed to self-select themselves into either the alternative school or a traditional arrangement. Differences in attitudes and preferences manifested in self-selection opportunities can confound interpretation of evaluation results.

In order for systematically designed evaluation studies to be feasible, it is necessary for some individuals at the local level to accept the possibility that the program to be implemented might be a failure. Further, it is necessary that such individuals give priority to evaluation in the sense that they afford both moral and substantive support to facilitate the conditions required by the evaluation design. Because tradition, political realities, established organizational policies, prejudgments, interpersonal relationships, and a host of other factors are powerful determinants of practice in many school systems, it is unlikely that conditions in some local systems will permit the evaluator to incorporate both randomization and comparison groups in his design. Although it is possible for individuals within the local school system who have the authority to dictate to subordinates that the conditions required for a design which controls all internal validity threats be met, such authorities rightfully are reluctant to do so because of the resentment and ramifications that might ensue.

While randomization and control groups represent the optimum methods of accounting for various threats to internal validity and should be used when possible, it is important to remember that these techniques are means to an end, not ends in themselves. The end sought when randomization and control groups are utilized is internal validity, and, under certain conditions, various threats to internal validity can be accounted for without resorting to either technique. For example, when the treatment is of short duration, lasting perhaps an hour or a day, the threat posed by history and maturation can, for all intents and purposes, be eliminated without the presence of a control group. Similarly, when unobtrusive or nonreactive measures represent the sole mode of data collection, no control group is needed to eliminate the threat posed by testing. When the treatment

group can be insulated or placed in a controlled environment, when participation is mandatory, or when subjects are from the middle ranges of the distribution on the measuring instrument, history, mortality, and regression, respectively, can be discounted as plausible rival explanations for observed outcomes regardless of whether or not a control group exists. Finally, in situations where the treatment is aimed at all members of a small specific group of subjects who exhibit strongly maladaptive behaviors and where remission of systems is the desired outcome, selection biases can be discounted as a plausible rival hypothesis.

In point of fact, then, randomization and control groups, while they are the most powerful methods of controlling threats to internal validity, are not the only methods useful in local-level evaluation studies. Very often particular threats to internal validity are controlled by the nature of the treatment, its intended clientele, its duration, or the conditions under which it is applied. In such situations, random assignment and a control group may not be necessary to ensure valid data.

PREDESIGN CONCERNS

Thus far, it has been implied that, if an evaluation study is designed properly, that is, with controls for the various threats to internal validity, an "effect" or observable difference between treatment and control groups will be manifested. Evaluators and school personnel who have had even passing experience with evaluation in school settings know that the results of summative evaluation studies do not always yield differences between programs under investigation. More often than not, the observed outcomes indicate no effect or significant difference between the treatment and some comparison group. Although lack of demonstrable differences between alternative approaches is often attributable to faulty design, other factors are related to and often are the cause of "no effect" conclusions in evaluation studies.

First, and most obviously, the program of concern may actually be ineffective or no better than alternative or traditional approaches. If we could be certain in advance that every innovation or change in school practice would result in increased learning, better efficiency, more positive attitudes, or some other improvement, there would be

no need for evaluation studies. As was indicated previously, the acceptance of potential failure represents a prime justification for carefully designed evaluation studies. Underlying all attempted change in school settings are the assumptions that man can change his social or educational environment, that he knows the relevant variables to manipulate in order to engender such change, and that change is good for someone's perspective. Some of the recent work of Forrester (1971) has, however, indicated that social, and, by implication, educational, change is not as easily managed or implemented as might be first imagined. Forrester has argued persuasively that social systems tend to draw our attention to those facets which, if selected as the variables to manipulate in seeking to bring about change, most often doom intervention to failure. For example, in recent years the plight of the high school dropout has been recognized and attacked through various early identification and incentive programs. The success of these programs in keeping students in schools has drastically reduced the opportunities for nongraduates to obtain even the most menial form of work. Further, since a high school diploma no longer suffices to sort candidates on the basis of employability, a college education is becoming the new sorting criterion. This phenomenon serves to diminish the value of the high school diploma. In essence, social or educational change is not particularly easy to implement, and it is to be expected that many courses of action intended to produce change will be unsuccessful.

Besides studies that accurately conclude that a program or practice had no effect when one was not present, there are numerous other studies that result in a conclusion of no effect for reasons other than improper design or true lack of effect. A number of relevant features of an evaluation study can account for incorrect or misleading "no effect" findings. The features of interest here relate not specifically to the design of the evaluation study as defined earlier, but to characteristics of studies upon which design is predicated. These characteristics provide the basis for selecting an appropriate design and influence the types and conditions of data gathering. In any discussion about the design of evaluation studies at the local level, therefore, it is important to consider factors related to the data-gathering plan and procedures. Earlier discussion centered on the attitudinal context (prejudgments, motives for evaluation, objections to conclusions) that often surrounds the conduct of evaluation studies at the

local level. Present concern, however, is with factors more closely
aligned to implementing the design itself.

Specifically, concern is focused upon two areas: what the data are
gathered about, that is, the characteristics and properties of the treatment; and the instruments selected to gather data, that is, the dependent variable or variables. Decisions made about these areas prior
to and during the conduct of an evaluation study can affect the observed outcomes greatly. The best-designed evaluation study can result in nonobservable effects, even when such effects are present, if
proper consideration is not given to specification of treatment and
identification of dependent variables. In this light it is useful to explore issues related to each of these areas.

Treatment Considerations

Concern over treatment specification and implementation is focused in two areas. First and foremost is the basic design problem of
not confounding the treatment variable with other contextual variables. This problem is essentially related to establishing the internal
validity of the observed data and will be considered in greater detail
in succeeding sections. Second is the problem related to the fact that
the observed outcomes of the treatment are dependent upon the
manner in which the treatment is conceived and the outcomes which
are anticipated from the treatment. The method in which the treatment is defined and implemented can greatly affect the outcomes of
the most appropriately designed study.

Changes in educational programs, policies, and practices over the
past forty years have alleviated many basic problems in education:
literacy is a reality for the vast majority of the American public;
schools provide opportunities for various types of vocational as well
as academic programs; most students complete high school; and so
on through the many achievements of the educational system. In
some respects, it can be argued that many of the "easy" problems,
the problems that are likely to evidence massive, readily observable
effects when successful, have been attacked and at least partially
solved. Many of the problems currently identified are more difficult
to overcome and may require greater resources, more trained personnel, and longer periods of time to alleviate than some of the problems tackled thirty or forty years ago. Groups once shunned or allowed to drop by the educational wayside are now the targets of

varied compensatory programs. Changes in societal values have expanded expectations for school-related outcomes. Students who complete public education are called upon to possess many more skills than the three R's. In light of increased demands upon education, it may be that the educational sphere is a weak or wrong arena in which to attack present-day problems such as aesthetics, morality, honesty, attitudes, job training, and citizenship.

Innovations and programs at the local level should set aims and expectations in terms of reasonably attainable outcomes. Smaller steps that are likely to pay off are better than giant steps where the likelihood of payoff is risky at best. I am reminded of a student in one of my research design courses. In all seriousness and with the noblest of intentions, the student suggested that the solution to all the educational, physical, psychological, and sociological difficulties of urban, disadvantaged youngsters rested in three-week summer sessions in which such youngsters were taught sailing. I am not suggesting that sailing lessons would not benefit disadvantaged youngsters; nor am I impugning the motives of the student who made this suggestion. It is unlikely, however, that three weeks of anything could overcome all the educational, physical, psychological, or sociological problems of any youngster. In essence, and at the risk of belaboring a somewhat extreme example, it is clear that the expected outcome, total remission of all symptoms, was unrealistic in light of the proposed treatment—three weeks of sailing lessons. However extreme the preceding example might be, one might question the reasonableness of expecting completely changed attitudes toward school, teachers, or education as a result of a four-week summer session, or the reasonableness of remedying deficiencies in academic subjects in a twenty-hour summer session.

Programs, policies, or practices instituted to bring about educational change should be realistic in terms of expectations of what is possible given the personnel, students, material, and time available. To attempt to develop creativity, critical thinking skills, positive attitudes, and the like through a three-month program consisting of activities for one hour per week is likely to result in no visible end effect, regardless of how appropriately an evaluation study is designed, because one hour per week, divorced from other reinforcing and complimentary activities, is probably insufficient to alter such characteristics as creativity, critical thinking, and attitudes in any visible way.

A general axiom, not necessarily applicable in all situations but certainly applicable more often than not, is that, given fixed resources, there is an inverse relationship between the impact and the coverage of a program. The greater the number of people serviced with fixed resources, the less likely the impact. Outcomes are the result of inputs, and it is rare in education today when low initial investment in time, money, or personnel reaps substantial outcomes. The specification of new programs, policies, or practices at the local level and the expectations held for these should be realistic in light of the resources and time available. To expect miracles from shoddy or ill-conceived treatments is one way to ensure "no effect" findings, regardless of the rigor of the evaluation design.

One way to avoid this pitfall is to consider precisely what is "new" about a program, policy, or practice. A tendency prevalent among many educators is to be satisfied with "brand name" descriptions of innovations. Team teaching, individualized instruction, open classrooms, programmed instruction, and the like are often accepted and discussed as though their meanings were universally understood and as though their implementation were uniform across all teachers, schools, or districts. Obviously neither meaning nor implementation are accorded such unanimity in practice. Upon close inspection of such innovations one often finds that a few relatively minor aspects of prior instruction or policy have been changed and that the change is labeled individualized instruction, discovery approach, or the like. When the processes and the actual activities involved in the new program are considered, there is relatively little that is different from what went on before under a different name. The terms lecture method and discussion method appear, on the surface, to be polar opposites. However, when discussion method in practice means that teachers ask students highly structured questions and students respond with short, precise, structured answers, how different is this approach from the lecture method? When the processes, the actual activities involved in a new program, policy, or practice, are at wide variance to the activities embodied in the older or comparison approach, one can hope to find differences in outcomes. Expectations for treatments should be based upon the activities involved, and not upon the brand name given the activities. If what is really "new" can be identified, it will be possible to postulate the size of the effect with some degree of confidence.

Another approach to avoid building in "no effect" outcomes by improper definition of treatments or their realistic outcomes is to consider what is already known about similar programs, policies, and practices. For example, many research studies have supported the finding that a slight decrease in class size or a slight increase in per pupil expenditure is unlikely to evidence visible effects on learning. Similarly, other studies have shown that, when a particular topic is the source of community or national interest, media coverage, and discussion, programs aimed at fostering student interest in the topic are likely to result in no effect because students manifest an initially high interest at the start of the program. Consideration of such facts can result in postponing or altering programs or practices with little hope of success as initially conceived.

At the implementation level, that is, at the point when the planned program is ready to be used and after it has been screened and amended in terms of the above suggestions, it is important, when possible, to avoid contamination of the treatment group with the control group. At the local school level, contamination usually results from two practices: assigning a single teacher to use both the treatment and comparison condition or permitting two teachers in the same school each to use one of the two approaches under study. In the former case, it is not unusual for the single teacher to confound the two programs by carrying over what appears successful in one group and utilizing it with the other group and vice versa. Instead of having two distinct programs to compare, there is a single hybrid of both, resulting in the strong likelihood of no differences between the groups. In the latter case the same type of confounding is possible, except with two teachers it is more likely to result from one teacher communicating the successes of his approach to the other, who then borrows the techniques, units, and exercises. The result, again, is loss of uniqueness between the two programs being compared, often leaving no observed differences between programs. In both situations two essentially distinct approaches become, over time, more similar in techniques, emphases, and aims.

As we have seen, the manner in which a program is conceived, specified, and implemented at the local level can have an important bearing upon the outcome of a study which compares the new treatment to another, different program. Randomization of subjects, the existence of control groups, and other methods used to ensure inter-

nal validity in evaluation studies can easily be rendered useless if treatments are not realistic, clearly defined in terms of important processes, and implemented to avoid contamination with comparison groups.

Dependent Variables

The measurement instruments or procedures used to gather evidence about the results of an innovation or program at the local level are important to consider from the viewpoint of evaluation design. Whatever dependent measures are used explicitly define the important outcomes of the program under investigation. Planners may talk at length about what the "real" outcomes of a treatment are expected to be, but it is the evidence-gathering measures that certify reality. If a program is designed to improve attitudes toward school or some particular content area and the dependent variable selected to assess the outcomes of the program is a cognitive achievement test, then the important aims of the program were cognitive, not attitudinal. It would not be unusual to find no cognitive learning effects if the aim of the program were affective. Yet, on the basis of the evidence collected, one would most likely conclude that the program was ineffective. It is important, therefore, that the dependent variable or variables measured be in line with the aims of the program. Clearly, the more specifically the goals or aims of a program or practice are stated, the more likely that appropriate dependent variables can be identified and agreed upon.

It is relatively rare that a completely irrelevant dependent variable is utilized to assess an educational program at the local level, but this can happen. Rather than the use of irrelevant dependent variables, the most likely problem encountered at the local level is that of using dependent variables that are either too specific or too gross to record the intended effects of a program. The basic problem concerns the precision of the dependent measures and the matching of measures of appropriate precision to likely program outcomes. It should be clear that, if the measuring instruments are too specific or too detailed to record a relatively general effect, or too gross to record a relatively small effect, the results of the evaluation will show no program effects, regardless of whether or not the program actually had an effect.

   With regard to the dependent variables in many local-level evaluations, there is a tendency either to use a scalpel when a chain saw would be more appropriate or to use a chain saw in lieu of the more appropriate scalpel. In general, the less likely the anticipated effects of a program, the more refined and precise the dependent variable should be. This observation has obvious relevance to the argument advanced in the preceding section on treatments, concerning the necessity of keeping expectations in line with the reality of the treatment itself. As an example, consider a local school summer program which is concerned principally with altering students' negative attitudes toward school. Assume the program is to last four weeks, with activities related to the desired outcomes planned for two hours per day, discounting time for recesses, assemblies, "play periods," lunch breaks, and other such activities. Assume also that the students are fifth and sixth graders and that the teachers are essentially the same ones the students are exposed to during the school year (a somewhat common occurrence). Finally, assume that the program seeks to provide the students with reinforcing experiences concerning their learning of academic subjects and the value of schooling for future occupational plans. In viewing such a program, one is struck by a number of facts: the students have already had at least four years of previous schooling in which to form attitudes; the total immersion time in the program is about forty hours; the teachers are the same ones the students are used to seeing; the teaching of academic subjects in a "different," reinforcing manner is the crux of the program; the program is conducted during the summer, thereby being divorced in some sense from "school" as defined by the regular ten-month session. One wonders, in light of these facts, whether a general attitudinal questionnaire—devoted to such questions as, "Do you like school?" "Is learning important to you?"—is appropriate to pick up the changes likely to occur in student attitudes. One wonders whether dependent measures which assess attendance, completion of assignments, books taken out of the library, and similar factors are not of more appropriate sensitivity in gathering evidence about likely changes brought about by the summer program.

   Alternatively, consider a design that endeavors to compare a new reading method to the one traditionally used in the school. Suppose that treatment and control groups were established by randomly

assigning first graders to one or the other group. At the end of the year, a standardized reading achievement test was given to both groups. Standardized tests are favorite measures for assessing program outcomes, particularly in federally funded programs. Standardized intelligence tests (which in general do not appear to be particularly relevant measures for programs designed to alter achievement, but which are, nonetheless, widely used), ability tests, and achievement tests are often mandated or strongly recommended as the dependent variable in state or federally funded projects. The reason for such a mandate or recommendation is that the federal or state government seeks some way to ensure the ability to assess the comparability of programs conducted in numerous locales. The norms provided by standardized tests provide one way of obtaining such comparability. Although, from the point of view of personnel at the local level, standardized measures may not be the optimum means of measuring program outcomes, mandates from sponsors will probably require continuation of such measures.

Returning to the example of the study of two first-grade reading programs, consider some of the difficulties in using a standardized reading test as a dependent variable. First, it is important that the content of the test reflect about equally the content of the two programs. Otherwise, one program will have a built-in advantage over the other that is quite unrelated to the treatment itself. Assuming that the test is actually "fair" to both programs, a second relevant problem then arises. Most standardized tests are indirect measures of educational achievements that have been developed to measure correlates of learning (generally, prediction of later learning) rather than learning itself (Stake, 1972). The resulting items often tend to depend heavily upon a "g," a general intellective factor. Moreover, items chosen for inclusion on standardized tests go through a screening process which tends to make test scores relatively immune to instructional programs or practices (Madaus, 1973). First, the items must discriminate between individuals. Second, the domain from which items are chosen is diffuse. Third, items are tried out in various school systems, and the test is standardized across systems. As a consequence, the items and norms for standardized tests have a built-in control that minimizes differences in instructional programs and emphases that may prevail across classrooms and systems. The surviving items are more general and more or less immune to instructional

or program differences. Hence, it takes a radical departure in curricular emphasis or instruction before effects are evidenced in standardized test scores. In essence the use of standardized tests as dependent variables in comparative evaluation studies can be summarized as the process of using insensitive, individually discriminating measures to identify differences between groups.

The point here is not to indict standardized testing and the many useful functions served by such testing. Rather, the attempt is to emphasize that the precision or sensitivity of dependent variables selected for use in an evaluation design must be considered in light of the anticipated outcomes of the study. Choice of overly sensitive or insensitive dependent variables can hide actual program effects and differences, regardless of the design of the study. At the local level, it will probably be useful to supplement mandated, standardized test performance dependent variables with other measures more appropriate to local questions and concerns.

Given that new school programs are not introduced into a hermetically sealed environment, but, rather, into an operative and complicated social system, it is reasonable to expect that many of the outcomes of an innovation will be manifested beyond the immediate context where it was introduced. Many of the outcomes of a new math program are manifested in the manner in which students approach physics or chemistry. If the results of an English program emphasizing paragraph-writing skills are positive, the effect should be seen on essays written in history class. The impact of a program is not likely to be discrete and confined to a particular class or time of day. Its outcomes are likely to be manifested in many contexts. It is appropriate, therefore, to conceive of the dependent variables in local evaluation studies as consisting of multiple imperfect measures (Campbell, 1969), measures which do not singly tap all effects but which, when taken in combination, tap numerous, widespread outcomes. Nonreactive measures ought to be among these multiple imperfect variables (Webb *et al.,* 1966) since it is inconvenient to flood a school or a group of students with large numbers of paper-and-pencil techniques. These measures are usually gathered from data occurring naturally or in a manner that precludes the subjects' knowing that their behavior is being observed. As a consequence, such measures are not as susceptible as reactive measures to respondents' cheating or "psyching out" correct or anticipated responses. The

frequency with which an event is practiced, attendance for events, or wear on materials or apparatus are general examples of nonreactive variables (Webb *et al.,* 1966). Outcomes of an English or math program might be judged by comparing the College Board scores of the treatment group with the scores of the comparison group. The number of students selecting particular courses, their attendance in classes, the number electing to take the College Boards in various areas—all are readily available, nonobtrusive measures that can be used to assess, in part, the outcomes of local school programs. Nonreactive measures in and of themselves may not be sufficiently strong evidence to claim treatment effects, but, in combination with other, more formal, reactive data-gathering measures, they may provide a useful web of evidence for assessing treatment effects.

EVALUATION DESIGNS

Treatment definition and implementation and the selection of dependent variables are predesign considerations. It has been shown that, if proper concern and attention are not directed toward these facets of evaluation studies, the true impact of programs being investigated can be masked, regardless of how appropriately the study is designed. Having discussed these predesign concerns, we can now consider various evaluation designs for local-level summative evaluation studies.

As has been noted, random assignment of subjects and the existence of a control or comparison group are the usual methods for controlling the many threats to the internal validity of evaluation studies. The extent to which an evaluator is unable to implement these methodologies is usually, though not exclusively, the extent to which observed differences can be attributed to plausible rival explanations. Designs where there is treatment in the form of active manipulation, where something is done to or for subjects, where there is at least one comparison group in addition to the treatment group, and where subjects are assigned to treatment or comparison groups by means of random procedures are called true experimental designs. Such designs are the most powerful for establishing cause-effect relationships because they eliminate all potential threats to internal validity. From the point of view of valid, unambiguous evaluation study results, true experimental designs represent the desired optimum.

As has been stated, however, it is unlikely that most evaluation studies conducted at the local level can approach the rigor inherent in true experimental designs. It is often impossible for the evaluator to randomly assign students or teachers to treatment and control groups. Further, control or comparison groups equivalent to, or even resembling, the treatment group may not be available because the program or practice of interest is aimed at a limited number of specially qualified students or because, as often happens, prejudgment about the goodness of the program or practice leads to its implementation throughout a school or district.

The evaluator, usually because he does not have the opportunity to implement true experimental designs in the local school setting, has to contend with problems such as preestablished groupings, self-selection, erosion of control subjects, nonequivalent or nonexistent control groups and a host of other factors that confound and make more difficult the design of summative evaluation studies. As a consequence, the evaluation designs most likely to be practical at the local level may be unable to control all threats to internal validity. Alternative designs, formally called quasi-experimental designs, are often more useful at the local level than true experimental designs, given present constraints on, and attitudes toward, evaluation.

Extensive examples of useful quasi-experimental designs have been presented by Donald Campbell and his coworkers (Campbell, 1969; Cook and Campbell, in process; Campbell and Stanley, 1963; Campbell and Erlebacher, 1970). This chapter does not consider all possible quasi-experimental designs; instead, a limited number of such designs which both exemplify typical designs and illustrate basic design issues likely to occur at the local level are included. An attempt will be made to discuss practicable designs and the situations in which such designs can be utilized. Construction of appropriate evaluation designs at the local level, where conditions usually do not approximate conditions present in laboratory research, calls for a certain amount of creativity on the part of the study designer.

The remaining discussion of evaluation designs is divided into three sections, each setting forth a particular set of conditions at the local level that calls for different approaches to design. The discussion begins with a consideration of the designs possible under the most favorable conditions, and it concludes with designs possible under the least favorable conditions likely to be encountered. The threats to internal validity controlled by each design will also be noted and discussed.

The conventions utilized by Campbell and Stanley (1963) will be adopted to represent symbolically the discussed designs: O represents an observation or measurement; R, the random assignment of subjects to groups; X, the presence of the program, practice, or policy under investigation. For example, a design represented by

$$R \quad O \qquad X \qquad O$$
$$R \quad O \qquad \qquad O$$

includes the random assignment of a pool of subjects to two groups —one, the group implementing the program, practice, or policy of interest (X); the other, a control group—and the administration of a pretest and posttest to each group.

Situations Where Randomization Is Possible

Although it is not likely that the evaluator at the local level will be able to assign subjects to treatment and control groups at random, a number of situations that do not impose on people, schedules, or plans are conducive to randomization. It is possible, of course, that the evaluator may encounter an administrator or group of teachers willing to tailor their school or classrooms to accommodate random sampling, but it is not likely. The evaluator, if he wishes to make use of the rigor afforded by randomization, will probably have to rely upon situations that occur naturally but that permit random assignment.

Very often the demand for a new program or practice outstrips supply. Programs or practices that must limit clientele are advantageous, from a design point of view, in that they provide a justification for randomization. When supply is more in line with demand, administrators or teachers may be reluctant to withhold the program or practice from individuals who might benefit from it. Even if no reluctance is manifest, client demands and pressures will probably abort attempts to establish a "no treatment" or control group. When demand exceeds supply, however, randomization is a viable and fair method for assigning individuals to treatment and control groups. Thus, when more students want admittance to a course than can be accommodated, when preschool or summer programs can serve only a limited number of individuals, when released-time vocational training programs are oversubscribed, or when only a few teachers or administrators can be allocated aids, random assignment of subjects to treatment and comparison groups is possible.

Occasionally a program, policy, or practice cannot be implemented in all classrooms or schools simultaneously. The intent may be to realize total implementation, but resources or other constraints may necessitate staged implementation. In such situations it is possible to assign the program, policy, or practice at random to classrooms or schools and to use those units which must wait for sufficient resources to receive the treatment as comparison groups.

Situations in which demand for a program or practice exceeds the supply or when resource limitations necessitate staged intervention are often present in schools and school systems, but, for a variety of reasons, go unused or unnoticed. A part of the reason why such situations are not used can undoubtedly be attributed to the attitudes and pressures on local-level decision makers urging purposive rather than random selection of subjects, teachers, or schools. Another part is due to the lack of emphasis on formal evaluation studies as potential and relevant decision-making inputs. Whatever the reasons, there are natural occurrences within local school systems that, if used, permit the definition of true experimental designs based on randomization and control groups. The emphasis is upon *natural* occurrences since after-the-fact or artificial use of randomization is not generally feasible at the local level.

Often, when resources and attitudes permit, random assignment to treatment and control groups can be implemented by using intact units. Rather than assigning individual students to either a treatment or a control group, it may be possible to assign intact classrooms in lieu of students (Wiley and Bock, 1967). Such an approach does not require disturbing classroom assignments made on the basis of student ability, class schedule, or teacher preference. If teachers lack interest or enthusiasm for the program or its comparison activities, the feasibility of randomization may still be limited. Even if the problem of teacher preference and acceptance of a program assigned to them on the basis of chance can be overcome, another problem presents itself. Randomization utilizing intact classrooms requires that a sufficiently large number of classes be available to permit replication of the treatment and comparison conditions. Strictly speaking, in an evaluation study, one piece of data is generated by each randomly assigned unit. Thus, when individuals are randomly assigned to treatment and control conditions, each individual's score on the dependent variable measure is a data point to be used in the data analysis. When an intact unit comprised of a number of individuals is random-

ly assigned, however, only a single data point (usually the class mean) is generated for analysis. Thirty intact classrooms would need to be randomly assigned to equal the data generated by randomly assigning thirty individuals. To ensure some consistency of data, a number of intact classrooms are needed, and, hence, large schools or school districts are required. Random assignment of intact classrooms is an alternative when individuals cannot be randomly assigned, but it is impractical and difficult to implement.

When randomization is possible at the local level, regardless of whether individuals or intact groups are randomly assigned, the evaluator is in a position to construct true experimental designs. In such designs, given consideration of the factors related to treatments and dependent variables, all threats to internal validity are accounted for and cause-effect conclusions are possible. Two basic true experimental designs commonly used in comparative product evaluation studies follow. Design 1 is identical to the example used earlier to introduce symbols used in representing design parameters.

$$R \quad O \quad X \quad O$$
$$R \quad O \qquad \quad O$$

Design 1

In Design 1, a group of subjects is randomly divided between participation in the treatment group and participation in the control group. A pretest is given to each group, primarily to establish base-rate data. All conditions, save the presence or absence of the treatment, are kept the same for both groups. At the conclusion of the study, both groups are given a posttest, and differences are compared to ascertain whether the treatment group performed better.

Consideration of the facets of this design reveals that the threats to internal validity posed by differences in maturation rates, statistical regression, selection biases, and mortality are controlled, given no pretest differences, by the random assignment of individuals to either the treatment or the comparison group. Randomization is the optimum method of equalizing the groups on the basis of selection threats, and it thereby eliminates such threats as plausible rival explanations for observed effects. The presence of the control group itself eliminates the threats posed by history, testing, instrumentation and the like, since the effects of any or all of these phenomena should be similarly manifested in each group. The design, therefore,

controls or eliminates the major threats to internal validity and thereby permits cause-effect interpretations to be made.

Design 2 is called the "posttest only control group design" by Campbell and Stanley (1963). It is identical to Design 1 in all respects save that no pretest is administered. The design is used when

R X O
R   O

Design 2

the evaluator for one reason or another does not want, or cannot use, a pretest because it may be reactive, inconvenient, or simply unavailable. In effect, randomization represents the optimum method to equate groups prior to the start of a study. In this sense, a pretest may be redundant, although it is often difficult for the evaluator to refrain from this additional check on the initial equivalence of the treatment and control groups. Note also that, because no pretest data are collected, the threats posed by testing and regression are not manifested. This fact illustrates the previously made point that certain threats to internal validity are often controlled without the use of randomization or control groups. For all intents and purposes, however, Design 2 is as adequate as Design 1 for controlling threats to internal validity. Randomization and the control group account for or eliminate all the internal validity threats in Design 2 in the same manner as they do in Design 1.

The designs just discussed are the most basic ones that include control of all relevant internal validity threats. If the evaluator at the local level is able to implement either of these designs, he can make strong cause-effect conclusions from his data with little concern about the existence or reasonability of alternative explanations for the observed outcomes. Many more complex experimental designs could be provided but they are beyond the intended purpose and scope of this study. The reader is referred to Campbell and Stanley (1963) for discussion of other designs. Suffice it to say that these more complex designs utilize the control inherent in randomization and comparison groups in basically the same manner as the designs given here.

Two final notes are needed concerning the designs just discussed and designs yet to be presented. For clarity, all designs shown include, where applicable, only the treatment and the control groups. If multiple treatments are under investigation, a situation uncommon

but not unknown at the local level, the designs shown can be extended using the same reasoning used for the two-group example. Thus, if two different treatments and a control group were under investigation, Design 1 would be amended so that X_1 would represent one of the treatments and X_2, the other. Individuals would be as-

$$
\begin{array}{lll}
R & O & X_1 & O \\
R & O & X_2 & O \\
R & O & & O
\end{array}
$$

signed at random to three groups instead of two, but that change would not affect the strength of the conclusions or the interpretations. The basic minimum required for true experimental designs is two randomly assigned groups undergoing different experiences. Three or more randomly assigned groups can be incorporated into the design at will, according to the concerns of the evaluation study. At the local level it is probably better to concentrate on designs which compare the outcomes of a single strong, well-developed treatment to those of a comparison treatment, than on designs incorporating multiple treatment conditions. Second, none of the designs to be presented discusses the technique of stratifying treatment and control groups on the basis of such factors as sex or socioeconomic status. The reason for the omission of stratified designs is that the reality at the local level most often precludes utilization of results which compare the effects of a program for different sexes or socioeconomic classes. Regardless of whether a treatment is shown to be superior for one sex or social class, it is usually not feasible for local school officials to segregate students on these bases in order to capitalize on the benefits of a program. Most school programs must be offered students regardless of sex or socioeconomic class and, hence, unstratified designs are the focus here.

Situations Where Randomization Is Impossible, but Control Groups Are Available

Although random assignment of individuals or intact units to treatment and comparison groups may not be a readily accessible methodology to the local-level evaluator, he can usually expect to identify or establish some comparison or control group against which to compare the effects of the program or practice of interest. In most cases, however, such comparison groups will be preselected and orga-

nized according to some instructional or administrative policy. As a consequence, the local-level evaluator will not have the assurances of group equivalence provided when random assignment is possible. This limitation, in turn, leads to difficulty in establishing the internal validity of the evaluation results. Designs in which comparison groups are selected on the basis of availability or opportunity, rather than on the basis of random assignment are, in general, weaker designs. Nonrandomly assigned control groups can be considered in terms of a continuum running from groups approximately equivalent to the treatment group to groups definitely nonequivalent. Clearly, the greater the initial divergence between the treatment and control groups, the greater the ambiguity in the observed results.

In some schools students are distributed across classes in a more or less random manner, with occasional parent or teacher preferences interfering with the random process. If two fifth-grade classes assigned in this manner form the treatment and comparison groups, the evaluator is in a relatively stronger position to assume equivalence than if students were assigned on the basis of the prior year's achievement test scores or on the basis of teacher preference. In the high school, where differences in major course of study, level within major course of study, or subject matter schedule often dictate the basis for selection of classes, it may be difficult to find approximately equivalent comparison groups. Just as classes at a particular grade level in a school can range from approximate equivalence to nonequivalence, so, too, can classes at the same grade level in various schools within the same system vary. It is not uncommon, particularly in large towns or cities, to find wide variations across schools in terms of socioeconomic background, achievement, or ability. The designer of evaluation studies should strive to select groups that are as equivalent as possible to avoid confounding his results with initial differences between nonrandomly selected individuals or classes. In many cases, however, he may have to settle upon a design which compares the effects of a treatment and its comparison activities on decidedly nonequivalent groups.

In this light, two points concerning design are relevant. First, given nonrandomly assigned groups, it is better in most cases to have a control group, regardless of its relative equivalence or nonequivalence to the treatment group. The power of a nonrandomly assigned control group to eliminate or account for possible rival hypotheses is a func-

tion of the similarity of the control group to the treatment group. The more initially equivalent the two groups are, the better the design accounts for plausible rival hypotheses. However, a control group dissimilar to a treatment group on one variable, achievement, for example, may still be useful to control such threats to internal validity as maturation or history. Second, in order to assess initial group equivalence when groups are selected on a nonrandom basis, it is essential to pretest the two groups to note pre-existing differences on the dependent variable measures. Pretesting empirically verifies relative equivalence or nonequivalence and provides a context within which to interpret posttest results.

Design 3 is the basic design used when nonrandomly assigned treatment and control groups are utilized in a study. Note that Design 3 differs from Design 1 in that Design 1 incorporates random assignment of subjects to treatment or control groups while Design 3 docs not. Both designs have pretests and posttests administered to the two groups.

O X O
O   O

Design 3

To the extent that recruitment criteria and pretesting indicate similarity between the groups, the threats to internal validity posed by the effects of history, maturation, testing, and instrumentation are accounted for because observed differences in pre- and posttest scores for the treatment group cannot be explained by the effects of these threats. Such threats would be expected to affect the control group similarly. The threat posed by mortality, the differential loss of subjects from one of the groups, is rarely a problem in educational designs except when treatment or control conditions are voluntary. In most instances, the program, policy, or practice under investigation will be nonvoluntary, students or teachers will be more or less a captive sample, and mortality will not be a major threat to interpretation. Although selection biases introduced in designs employing nonrandom groups will always be a potential threat to the validity of an evaluation study, it will often be possible to gather data of a descriptive nature to assess the likely impact of selection factors. When participation in the program, policy, or practice is both voluntary

and nonrandom, selection will represent a major threat to the validity of Design 3.

The final two threats to validity, statistical regression and instrumentation, become more powerful potential rival explanations for observed results as the similarities between treatment and control groups diminish. Statistical regression represents the tendency for scores of students selected for their extreme (either high or low) standing on some trait, characteristic, or measure to score more closely to the overall group mean on retesting. Thus, subjects selected for their extremely low scores on, say, a vocabulary achievement test will tend to have their scores regress upward toward the group mean on retesting. The regression phenomenon works in reverse for students selected on the basis of their extremely high scores. The main point is that changes in scores of extreme groups on retesting is a statistical artifact and independent of treatment effects. Note here that, unlike Design 2, which did not include a pretest and therefore inherently controlled for the regression threat, Design 3 requires a pretest because groups are not assigned to treatment and control conditions by a random procedure. Instrumentation is concerned with stability or reliability of the measuring instrument. The more homogeneous a group, in general, the less reliability or stability a measuring instrument possesses. When extreme groups are selected either to undergo the program, policy, or practice of concern or to serve as a control group, the stability of the measure used to assess outcomes becomes suspect. Thus, when there are differences between the initial status of the treatment and control groups, and particularly when one group's pretest scores are very low or very high relative to the other group's, statistical regression and instrumentation are viable rival explanations which are neither controlled nor eliminated in Design 3. Of course, when both groups score extremely high or low on the pretest, these factors are largely controlled.

Thus, Design 3 is a useful alternative to Design 1 when random assignment of individuals to treatment or control groups is not possible. The greater the initial difference between groups evidenced on the pretest, the less powerful Design 3 is in controlling a number of threats to internal validity.

A second design that is useful for comparing the effects of a program or practice on a nonrandomly selected comparison group is

called the control time series design (Campbell and Stanley, 1963), and it is diagramed below. As can be seen, the design incorporates

$$O_1 \quad O_2 \quad O_3 \quad O_4 \quad O_5 \quad X \quad O_6 \quad O_7 \quad O_8 \quad O_9 \quad O_{10}$$
$$O_1 \quad O_2 \quad O_3 \quad O_4 \quad O_5 \qquad O_6 \quad O_7 \quad O_8 \quad O_9 \quad O_{10}$$

Design 4

nonrandomly selected treatment and control groups. Instead of a single pretest and posttest, however, Design 4 includes a number of measurements made at different times prior to instituting the treatment and a number of measurements made at different times after the conclusion of the treatment. This design is an appropriate one to study both the immediate and longer-range impact of a treatment. For example, the effects of a new administrative policy could be studied using Design 4 by selecting two schools, obtaining a series of base line measurements on each school over time, instituting the treatment, and then obtaining, again over a period of time, a series of posttest measures. Administrative policies or practices, instructional programs which have general cognitive or affective outcomes, and remedial summer programs that are intended to have an impact during the regular school year are examples of treatments amenable to Design 4. In each case the impact is expected to be long range, and Design 4 permits charting of the impact over time. The evaluator who utilizes Design 4 is in a position to determine the extent to which the effects of a program are accumulative or extinguishable over time. One problem with implementing this design is the large number of measurements involved. The evaluator should seek a series of equivalent measures, preferably nonreactive, for retesting. Records maintained in the normal course of administrative or classroom routine can often be utilized in time series designs, obviating the need to collect an additional set of measurements. Another problem with time series designs is analysis, although progress is being made on significance tests for time series designs (Glass, Willson, and Gottman, 1972). Also, given the number of measurements involved and the fact that the evaluator is concerned with comparison of a treatment and control group, the number of potential outcomes or patterns is huge. An explication of some of these patterns and their interpretation is found in Campbell (1969) and Ross, Campbell, and Glass (1970).

Design 4 includes Design 3, but extends it to control additional threats to internal validity. In a sense, the observed effect of a program is doubly evidenced, first in comparison to the control group and second in comparison to its own pretreatment scores. Because a series of preimplementation measures is included, the effects of selection, instrumentation, and statistical regression can be accounted for or observed prior to instituting the treatment. That is, such effects can be expected to reveal themselves in the various pretestings, and, if they do not, there is little likelihood that they will suddenly appear on the testing immediately preceding the start of the treatment. Design 4 is, therefore, one of the more powerful evaluation designs in that it provides a control for most major threats to internal validity.

Designs 3 and 4 represent two basic approaches to obtaining the least ambiguous data from an evaluation study when nonrandom, potentially nonequivalent treatment and control groups must be used. It is important to re-emphasize the need of pretest data for designs implemented under this condition. Without the information provided by the pretest, resultant data will be all but uninterpretable.

The features inherent in Designs 3 and 4 can be embellished to permit a variety of somewhat more complicated designs. For example, Design 4 could be altered so that the treatment conditions were applied to each group, but at different times (Cook and Campbell, in process). In Design 5, one has the basic features of Design 4, with

$$O_1 \; O_2 \; O_3 \; X \; O_4 \; O_5 \; O_6 \; O_7 \; O_8 \; O_9 \; O_{10} \; O_{11}$$
$$O_1 \; O_2 \; O_3 \quad O_4 \; O_5 \; O_6 \; O_7 \; O_8 \; X \; O_9 \; O_{10} \; O_{11}$$

Design 5

the added feature that at different times each group receives the treatment condition. As a consequence, the generalizability of observed effects is enhanced. Ideally, if the treatment had its maximum impact and manifested no remission over time, a graph of the results of study conducted utilizing Design 5 would appear as illustrated in Figure 3-1. Various other possibilities indicating greater or lesser treatment impact or retention can also be envisioned. Design 5 is useful in situations where staged implementation without randomization is required. The lines drawn in Figure 3-1 are straight lines used to illustrate the ideal outcome of a study. In practice, however, time-series measurements will not yield straight lines, but, instead, will

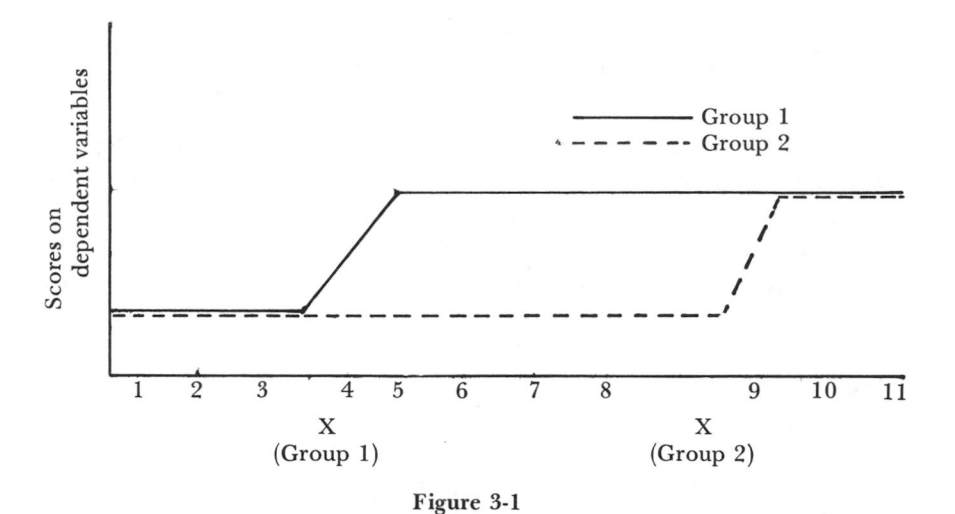

Figure 3-1
Outcome of crossing treatment time series design

yield a series of peaks and valleys due to measurement error. It is because time-series measurements rarely engender straight-line graphs that analysis is a problem.

A final design useful when randomization of subjects to treatment and control groups is not possible is based upon the existence of repeated institutional cycles. School settings, where a particular practice may be cyclical and continually being used with new groups of students, are ideal contexts for such a design.

$$X \quad O_1$$
$$O_2 \quad X \quad O_3$$

Design 6

In Design 6, a treatment, say a new ninth-grade English program, is given to a class and at the end of the year a posttest (O_1) is administered. At the same time, the same instrument is administered as a pretest (O_2) to eighth-grade students who will participate in the program at some later time. When the current eighth graders finally take part in the new English program, a posttest (O_3) will be administered to them at the conclusion. Two kinds of comparisons can be made: O_1 can be compared to O_2, and O_2 can be compared to O_3. While neither of these comparisons alone provides particularly valid data,

when taken in combination they control many threats to internal validity.

Note, however, that Design 6 is predicated upon the assumption that the nature of the ninth-grade students being exposed to the English program in succeeding years is relatively constant. Also, two cycles of the program are required to obtain evaluative evidence.

The major weaknesses of this design are its failure to control for the threats of maturation and regression. Thus, in the O_1-O_2 comparison, groups of different ages are being compared, and the effect of differential maturation rates is, therefore, a plausible explanation for observed group differences. Similarly, because the O_2-O_3 comparison does not include a control group, differences manifested between O_2 and O_3 could also reasonably be attributed to maturation. If the results attained by students on O_2 serve as a basis for selection into the treatment condition, then the threat of the regression effect is a viable alternative explanation for observed differences between O_2 and O_3. Further, since no control group is available for the O_2-O_3 comparison, history and testing represent threats to the internal validity of this design. While Design 6 is weaker than the previously discussed designs and is heavily dependent upon the assumption of similarity between groups of students in succeeding treatment cycles, it does control many of the threats to internal validity, and it is more readily implemented in the school setting than some of the other designs presented.

The most important point illustrated in this section is that judicious concern for the conditions under which data are gathered, even when randomization of subjects to treatment and control groups is not feasible, can result in evaluation designs that provide highly interpretable data. Campbell discusses other relevant designs that are beyond the scope of this presentation.

Situations Where No Control Group Can Be Identified

Every individual who designs evaluation studies at the local level sooner or later encounters a situation where it is impossible or impractical to identify a control group for the evaluation study. It may happen that all students or teachers receive the program or innovation of interest. Or it may happen that the new treatment (speech therapy for stutterers or a special curriculum for handicapped, emotionally disturbed children) is aimed at a group so vastly different

from other available control groups that it is impractical to identify a reasonable comparison group. Teachers or administrators might also refuse to participate or permit more than a single group in the school to be tested or studied. Whatever the cause, however, situations which prohibit the use of a control group are not uncommon in lo-cal-level evaluation studies (Guba, 1965).

There are four basic approaches to handling design problems when no control group can be used: remission of symptoms models, time series designs, replication, and utilization of salutary treatment or testing parameters. The basic aim in both the remission of symptoms approach and the time series design is to utilize a single group as its own control. Replication involves repeating the entire study with a different group at a different time and seeking to accumulate evidence of program effects over a number of trials. Salutary treatment or testing parameters occur when the conditions surrounding implementation of the treatment and evidence gathering are of such a nature that most threats to internal validity are inherently controlled. Each of these general approaches will be considered in turn.

Often the symptoms a program is intended to alter are particularly overt and observable. Symptoms which are the consequence of physical difficulties (for example, stuttering, lisping, bad posture) or social-emotional maladjustment (hyperactivity, extreme immaturity) are readily observed as to their presence or absence. Such behavioral manifestations are more observable than most cognitive or affective learning. Given the overtness of many physical or social-emotional symptoms, it is often possible to consider a program successful if, at its conclusion, the initial symptoms are remitted. The very overtness of such symptoms often removes the need for a control group (Rossi, 1972). Note the question posed in such studies is not, "Did students learn more or feel differently than other students?" Rather, it is, "Are observable behavior symptoms remitted at the conclusion of the treatment?" Hence, such an approach is usually more applicable in special education contexts than in normal classrooms.

Success in such programs is determined by student change in the direction of some absolute standard of goodness, usually the eradication of symptoms deemed undesirable. Comparisons are made between students' behavior on entering and their behavior on leaving, rather than between students in a treatment group and students in a control group. In essence, the remission of symptoms approach relies upon absolute rather than relative criteria of success (Popham, 1971).

Such factors as maturation and selection can, however, present viable rival explanations for the observed successes of some programs designed to correct physical or emotional symptoms. Statistical regression, however, is not usually a threat to internal validity in remission of symptoms studies, despite the fact that extreme groups are usually treated, for the regression phenomenon usually applies to test scores while remission of symptoms studies most often utilize observational data-gathering techniques.

A second design applicable when no control group is available is the time series design (Campbell, 1969). This design is diagramed below, and it is similar to Design 4, except that no control group is

$$O_1 \ O_2 \ O_3 \ X \ O_4 \ O_5 \ O_6$$
Design 7

present. The basic feature of Design 7 is that a single group is assessed at numerous different times prior to the introduction of the treatment and these measurements serve as the standard against which posttreatment effects will be studied. The design is similar to a one-group longitudinal study. Design 7 controls most of the threats to internal validity present in evaluation studies except history, which could be eliminated as a plausible rival hypothesis through the presence of a control group. Maturation threats are largely ruled out because the numerous pretestings provide a base line indication of maturational progress, although it is possible that maturation may not be a smooth or regular process. Testing likewise seems implausible as an explanation for a change from O_3 to O_4, given previous instances when a testing threat could be manifested. Barring changes in calibration or scoring of the measuring instrument, instrumentation is ruled out as a threat to internal validity. Selection is not a threat because only one group is being studied. Nor is statistical regression a reasonable alternative explanation to observed results in the light of numerous pretestings. Finally, mortality is not a viable threat because of the time span involved and the use of a single group. Overall, then, the one-group time series design is a powerful design in terms of the threats to internal validity it either eliminates or controls. However, as pointed out in the discussion of Designs 4 and 5, analysis presents a problem with time series designs.

To further illustrate the power of the time series, consider a one-group single pretest, single posttest design as diagramed below. In general, the lack of a series of pretreatment assessments leads to the

plausibility of history, maturation, testing, and instrumentation as rival explanations for observed results. Except in rare instances which

O X O

Design 8

will be discussed below, one-shot, one-group pre-post testing rarely can remove the plausibility that observed changes from pre- to post-testing are due to maturation, testing, or some other factor. Time series designs do control these threats.

Confidence in the results of an evaluation study which does not have a control group also can be attained through replication. Replication is not a design per se, but rather a strategy basic to all scientific investigation. In this sense, the following comments are applicable to all designs discussed previously as well as to situations where there is no control group. The notion inherent in replication is simply described as attaining confidence in observed results when numerous independent, imperfect studies, using various students, teachers, schools, and so forth converge in their findings. In essence, if one repeats the same study a number of times and attains similar results, one begins to have confidence that the treatment is, in fact, the cause of the results. For example, the one-group time series design cannot control the effects of history as a plausible rival explanation for observed results. If, however, the design were implemented three different times with three different groups and the observed results were similar each time, one would be more likely to dismiss history as a plausible rival explanation. The aim of replication is simply put: repeating the evaluation study with a different group or at a different time is a useful method of determining the validity of the observed results. If the program, policy, or practice is successful with one group or teacher but not successful when replicated with other groups or teachers, the plausibility of history, selection, instrumentation, regression, and the like as explanations for the one successful implementation is increased.

At the local-school level, replication of evaluation studies is important because of the effects particular teachers can have on the observed outcomes of a treatment. Even in well-designed studies at the local level, it will often be difficult to separate effects attributable to the program or practice activities from those attributable to teacher style, interest, warmth, and the like. That is, in many cases the teach-

er can be considered as part of the treatment and not merely its implementer. Effects observed for one teacher's implementation of a program may be different from effects observed from another teacher's implementation of the program because of differences between the teachers. Practically, the only manner of disentangling program from teacher effects—save by simultaneously incorporating many teachers in the treatment and control groups—is by means of replication. It is not always essential to separate teacher and program effects at the local level, but, when system-wide implementation depends upon the results of the evaluation study, it may be useful to obtain evidence about the relative influence of teacher versus program effects.

All of the designs and strategies discussed thus far, with the exception of the remission of symptoms approach which is basically a one-group pre-post test design with an absolute rather than a relative determination of success, control for threats to internal validity by externally manipulating the conditions under which the treatment is conducted and data is collected. Thus, each design relies upon randomization, control groups, or time series measurements to overcome various threats to internal validity. While the use of such techniques represents the most widely discussed and practiced approach to designing evaluation studies—principally because such techniques are derived from more rigorous laboratory, experimental research—it is important to note that very often the nature of the treatment being studied and the way it is studied present the evaluator with a situation in which many of the most viable threats to validity are inherently controlled. That is, valid, interpretable results can sometimes be derived from the study of a single group without need of randomization, control groups, or time series techniques.

For example, consider the problem of determining the impact a visit to the local planetarium would have on student interest in a science unit on astronomy. Let us assume that all ninth-grade students enrolled in the science course are to be taken on the field trip and that, prior to the trip, science teachers completed a behavioral checklist indicating class interest in astronomy. In essence, such a design is the one-group pre-post test design that was discussed somewhat disparagingly above. In this example, however, the fact that all students are to be included in the field trip, and the use of an unobtrusive dependent variable control for all threats to internal validity save

instability. The treatment is of short duration, lasting no more than two or three hours, thereby all but negating the plausibility of history and maturation threats. Since all students are to be included in the field trip, the threats posed by selection, regression, and mortality are controlled. Finally, testing and instrumentation threats are controlled by the use of the nonreactive behavioral checklist as the dependent measure. Only instability, the potential unreliability of teachers in completing the checklist, is a threat, and estimates of reliability are easily obtained to investigate the plausibility of this threat.

There are numerous contexts within which one or more threats to internal validity are controlled inherently and where the need to resort to external controls such as randomization is unnecessary. Duration of the treatment and the unobtrusiveness of dependent measures have already been cited as influencing the reasonableness of history, maturation, testing, and regression as viable alternative explanations for observed outcomes. If a school institutes a new program which is voluntary and if all volunteers can be accommodated, selection biases are not relevant. The reactivity of paper and pencil tests is dependent upon the initial competence of students, so that when students are quite naive concerning the material on the pretest, the reactive nature of testing may not be a viable threat.

There are numerous instances in the evaluation of local-level programs when other threats to the internal validity of an evaluation study are inherently controlled. The evaluator should be aware of such situations and capitalize upon them when applicable. In many cases, a control group, random assignment, or time series techniques will be required to ensure valid results. The primary function of design is, however, to control for plausible rival explanations for the evaluation results, and the evaluator should not automatically institute external controls before determining whether adequate control is already inherent in the nature of the treatment, its implementation, and measurement.

CONCLUSION

The aim of this chapter has been to present a number of problems related to designing local-level summative evaluation studies and to suggest solutions to these problems. Three general areas have been

covered. First, many of the motivational, organizational, and attitudinal constraints likely to face the local-level evaluator have been discussed. Second, various threats to the interpretability of evaluation results have been explained, and general strategies for overcoming these threats have been considered. Finally, a series of designs applicable to implementing formal evaluation studies in the face of a variety of contextual parameters have been identified and related to threats to data interpretability.

In this overview of the issues, problems, and methodologies associated with designing summative evaluation studies at the local school or school district level, space limitations have precluded discussion of such additional relevant topics as data analysis, preparation and dissemination of results, and the ethical aspects of data collection and maintenance. In spite of the fact that this is not an in-depth treatment of all aspects of evaluation design, many important concepts have been presented, and the reader should consider them carefully, especially those concerned with the basic threats to internal validity and methods for controlling these threats.

The designs discussed should not be treated as cookbook solutions to be followed slavishly when designing local-level evaluations. Although the sample designs presented here are viable in some settings, they will rarely be implemented without some modification to suit local conditions.

There usually is no single, correct design for an evaluation study. All evaluation design represents a compromise between the search for methodological rigor and the realities imposed by situational constraints. The nature of the subject under investigation and contextual restrictions placed on the study designer will often require a creative implementation of basic designs and strategies. Most often, hypotheses can be studied and questions answered by means of different designs emphasizing different methods. Hence, although the sample designs discussed in this chapter are viable in some settings, they may have to be modified somewhat to suit local conditions. Given these facts, it is the concepts and goals of evaluation design that the reader should focus upon, and not the specific designs.

REFERENCES

Airasian, P. W., and Madaus, G. F., 1972. "Functional types of student evaluation." *Measurement and Evaluation in Guidance,* 4.4:221-233.

Campbell, D. T., 1969. "Reforms as experiments." *American Psychologist*, 24.4:409-429.

――――, and Erlebacher, A. E., 1970. "How regression artifacts in quasi-experimental evaluations can mistakenly make compensatory education look harmful," in J. Hellmuth (ed.), *Disadvantaged child.* Volume 3, *Compensatory education: A national debate.* New York: Bruner Mazel.

――――, and Stanley, J. C., 1963. "Experimental and quasi-experimental designs for research on teaching," in N. Gage (ed.), *Handbook of research on teaching.* Chicago: Rand-McNally, pp. 171-246.

Carter, R. K., 1971. "Clients' resistance to negative findings." *The American Sociologist*, 6:118-124.

Cook, T. D., and Campbell, D. T., in process. "The design and conduct of quasi-experiments and true experiments in field settings," in M. D. Dunnette (ed.), "Handbook of industrial and organizational research."

Cox, D. R., 1958. *Planning of experiments.* New York: Wiley.

Cronbach, L. J., 1963. "Course improvement through evaluation." *Teachers College Record*, 64:672-683.

――――, and Furby, L., 1970. "How we should measure 'change'—Or should we?" *Psychological Bulletin*, 74:68-80.

Fisher, R. A., 1951. *The design of experiments.* New York: Hafner.

Forrester, J. W., 1971. "Counterintuitive behavior of social systems." *Technology Review*, 73.3:1-16.

Glass, G. V., Willson, V. L., and Gottman, J. M., 1972. *Design and analysis of time-series experiments.* Boulder, Colo.: Laboratory of Educational Research, University of Colorado.

Good, T. L., and Brophy, J. E., 1973. *Looking in classrooms.* New York: Harper and Row.

Guba, E. G., 1965. "Methodological strategies for educational change." Paper presented to the conference on Strategies for Educational Change, Washington, D. C., November 1965.

House, E. R. (ed.), 1973. *School evaluation, the politics and process.* Berkeley, Calif.: McCutchan Publishing Corp.

Iwanicki, E. F., 1973. "Perspectives on some of the problems associated with the evaluation of federally funded educational programs." Invited address to the seminar on Evaluating School Effectiveness, Harvard University, July 1973 (mimeo).

Jackson, P. W., 1968. *Life in classrooms.* New York: Holt, Rinehart, and Winston.

Lortie, D. C., 1967. "Rational decision making: Is it possible today?" *EPIE Forum*, 1:6-9.

Madaus, G. F., 1973. "Memorandum to the joint committee on *Test Standards* revision, on the need for a companion volume dealing with standards for the use of tests in program evaluation, 1973" (mimeo).

Owens, T. R., 1973. "Educational evaluation by adversary proceedings," in E. R. House (ed.), *School evaluation.* Berkeley, Calif.: McCutchan Publishing Corp., pp. 295-305.

Popham, W. J. (ed.), 1971. *Criterion-referenced measurement.* Englewood Cliffs, N. J.: Educational Technology Publications.

Provus, M., 1971. *Discrepancy evaluation.* Berkeley, Calif.: McCutchan Publishing Corp.

Reiken, H. W., 1972. "Memorandum on program evaluation," in C. Weiss (ed.), *Evaluating action programs.* Boston: Allyn and Bacon, pp. 85-104.

Ross, H. L., Campbell, D. T., and Glass, G. V., 1970. "Determining the social effects of a legal reform: The British 'breathalyser' crackdown of 1967." *American Behavioral Scientist,* 13:493-509.

Rossi, P. H., 1972. "Boobytraps and pitfalls in the evaluation of social action programs," in C. Weiss (ed.), *Evaluating action programs.* Boston: Allyn and Bacon, pp. 224-235.

Scriven, M., 1967. "The methodology of evaluation," in R. Stake (ed.), *Perspectives of curriculum evaluation.* American Educational Research Association Monograph Series on Curriculum Evaluation, No. 1. Chicago: Rand-McNally, pp. 39-83.

Stake, R. E., 1967. "The countenance of educational evaluation." *Teachers College Record,* 68:523-540.

————— , 1972. "Measuring what learners learn (with a special look at performance contracting)." Urbana, Ill.: Center for Instructional Research and Curriculum Evaluation, University of Illinois (mimeo).

Stufflebeam, D. I., 1969. "Evaluation as enlightenment for decision making," in W. H. Beatty (ed.), *Improving educational assessment and an inventory of measures of affective behavior.* Washington, D. C.: Association for Supervision and Curriculum Development, pp. 41-73.

Webb, E. J., *et al.,* 1966. *Unobtrusive measures: Non-reactive research in the social sciences.* Chicago: Rand-McNally.

Wiley, D. E., and Bock, R. D., 1967. "Quasi-experimentation in educational settings: Comment." *The School Review,* Winter:353-366.

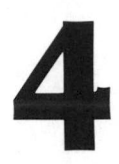

Data Analysis and Reporting Considerations in Evaluation

Richard M. Wolf
Teachers College, Columbia University

Data Analysis and Reporting Considerations in Evaluation

Richard M. Wolf

After one has planned and conducted an evaluation study, the resulting information has to be treated and analyzed in ways that are appropriate for obtaining answers to evaluation questions. This, of course, is easier said than done. The path from a collection of observations and measurements to a set of warranted conclusions and interpretations is fraught with hazards that can perplex even a seasoned investigator. This chapter describes the path and offers some guidance on how to negotiate it; it also discusses presenting results in a way that can be understood by nontechnically trained persons. It should enable the reader to better identify and classify each variable in a study in terms of its status and scale of measurement; acquire information about the data to be analyzed; identify the stages of treatment of data; select an appropriate statistical procedure; and present the results of a statistical analysis in a way that can be understood by nontechnically trained persons (teachers, administrators, school board members, and parents).

Before one hastily concludes that this study will make one an expert on matters statistical, let me quickly add that this is not a detailed how-to-do-it booklet on statistics. A great many statistical texts are available, and existing presentations need not be repeated

here. Statistical procedures do not compensate for poor planning and execution of evaluation studies. The view that statistics provides a magical set of procedures that can overcome defects of design is completely false. If an evaluation enterprise has used inappropriate, unreliable, or invalid measuring instruments, no amount of statistical manipulation can solve the problem of obtaining accurate answers to evaluation questions.

The collection of information in an evaluation study is a time-consuming, burdensome chore. The general term used to refer to such an aggregation of information is *data,* from the Latin word meaning "given." In evaluation and research studies, especially in a school setting, it has been suggested that the word *capta* be used instead. *Capta* comes from the Latin word meaning "taken" and reflects the fact that one's information often has to be wrested from an unwilling clientele. The administrative arrangements needed to gather one's information are sometimes the slickest and most sophisticated aspect of such a study.

The resulting aggregation of information typically consists of variables present in a number of individuals or groups. A variable is a characteristic that can take on a number of values. Arithmetic test scores, reading comprehension test scores, and scholastic ability test scores are just a few examples of such variables. In each case, the scores vary from some low value to some high value—the amount of variation depending to a large extent on the nature of the measure, the age of the students, their background, and other school and non-school-related factors. Test scores are not the only variables one deals with in evaluation studies. Membership in a group is another variable, but the range of values in this variable is, of course, highly limited compared to the range of values in test scores. In the case of membership in one group or another, there are only two values—innovative or conventional—but there may be three or four different groups. In analyzing the data from a study, one routinely sorts students into the groups to which they belong and performs some computations on the various test scores. One should not overlook the fact that group membership is a variable, often a highly crucial one. In studies where one seeks to demonstrate that a particular program promotes certain kinds of student performance, group membership is the treatment variable—the presumed cause of student performance.

IDENTIFICATION AND CLASSIFICATION OF VARIABLES

The first task for an evaluator who has collected information in connection with an evaluation study is to identify and classify each variable in terms of its status and scale of measurement. The evaluator is then encouraged to list each of the variables in the study. Outcome variables that are readily identifiable include scores on tests and results from such affective measures as attitude scales, opinionnaires, and ratings, whether supplied by teachers, peers, parents, or others. Group membership is somewhat less apparent, but it must also be included. One other variable—a control variable—should also be included if it is available. Information about student performance is often routinely collected as part of a school testing program. Inspection of a school's testing program schedule or the cumulative record folders of students involved in a program reveals whether achievement or school ability test scores were obtained shortly (within about six months) before a new program was introduced.[1] Such information can be of considerable value in improving the precision of one's analysis, and checking on its availability is well worth the effort. If it is available, it is usually easy to obtain, requiring only transcription from cumulative folders or master records. Neither students nor teachers need be involved in this aspect of information gathering.

Once the complete list of variables has been compiled, the evaluator's first task is to classify them. Each fits into one of four mutually exclusive categories: independent, dependent, control, and supplemental.

An independent variable, sometimes referred to as a treatment variable, is the presumed cause in any educational endeavor. An inno-

---

1. It is important that scores be obtained *before* a program is initiated. Scholastic ability test scores obtained after the program is started may provide useful descriptive information about the students involved, but they cannot be used in any formal analyses. This well-taken point has been made with considerable vigor in technical journals in the past few years. Technically, the issue involved is the possible confounding of the control variable, the test scores, and the treatment variable or program. If the test scores are obtained after the program is initiated, they will be affected by the program, and their use as a control variable will be invalid. Timing is crucial. Test scores must be gathered before a program is initiated so that they are not affected by the program. While this point seems perfectly clear, a number of recent articles have noted a surprising number of occasions when this principle was violated.

vative program, a teaching method, or instructional material are examples of independent or treatment variables. They represent the efforts of educators to help students grow and develop in ways that are considered desirable.

A dependent variable measure represents an outcome or objective. Scores on achievement tests, attitude scale scores, and ratings by teachers, peers, and others are examples of dependent variables. They are presumed to depend on the effect of the independent or treatment variable.

A control variable is an item of information about a student that was obtained before the student entered the program. Scholastic ability or IQ scores, previous achievement test scores, and ratings by former teachers are examples of control variables. The crucial consideration in determining whether a variable is a control variable is whether it was obtained prior to the introduction of the independent or treatment variable. Thus, if one's list of variables contains two reading test scores, one obtained at the end of the third grade and one at the end of the fourth grade as part of the evaluation of an innovative fourth-grade reading program, the third-grade reading score would be classified as a control variable while the fourth-grade reading score would be classified as a dependent variable.

A supplemental variable, simply stated, is a variable that does not fit into any of the three categories previously mentioned. If, in the above example, the school testing program had called for testing the reading and arithmetic achievement of fourth-grade students in the autumn of fourth grade, the resulting information would have supplemental status. One could not regard these variables as control variables since they were obtained after the program had started. Nor would it be wise to consider them dependent variables since they were not obtained at the conclusion of the program and they do not, consequently, constitute a fair measure of the effectiveness of a program. Premature measurement of the effect of a program is to be avoided at all costs. While administrators continually press evaluators for information on program effectiveness to assist them in carrying out their responsibilities for planning, it is important to resist such pressure since premature measurement often reveals no special benefits accruing from a new program. This may be the conclusion one eventually reaches, but not until the program has been in operation for its intended duration.

It is a desirable practice to maintain a list of all the variables in a study with the status of each variable noted after each variable. The sample studies that follow should help in applying the ideas and principles presented here.

Study 1: Reading Program Study

The Franklin Pierce Elementary School contains one hundred fourth-grade students in four self-contained classrooms. The principal wanted to initiate a new reading program to help fourth graders in the transition from the primary school reading program to the upper elementary program. The details of the new program were developed by the school district's reading consultant and a committee of teachers. Two of the four fourth-grade teachers, selected at random, were asked to use the program, and they agreed to do so. In the meantime, students were assigned to class groups by third-grade teachers on the basis of the school's policy of heterogeneous grouping. Once this was done, the school psychologist, at the principal's request, randomly assigned the four class groups to the four teachers.

Inspection of the cumulative files revealed that the students had been given a scholastic ability test in the spring of their third-grade year and the Gates Reading Comprehension Test at the end of the same year. The students will be given the Metropolitan Reading Test when they finish the fourth grade.

The program is to be initiated in September 1974.

Exercise 1
Classifying variables according to status

From the above description, list all variables included in the preceding study and indicate whether each variable is independent, dependent, control, or supplemental.

- -

The correct answers are presented below. It is not necessary to have listed the variables in the order shown; inclusion and correct classification are sufficient.

Variable	*Status*
1. Reading program (new or old)	Independent
2. Scholastic ability	Control
3. Gates Reading Comprehension	Control
4. Metropolitan Reading	Dependent

The type of reading program used is the independent variable since it is what is presumed to bring about changes in the reading performance of students. In fact, if the program developers did not feel that the new program was better than the old one, there would be no reason for instituting it.

The performance of students on the Metropolitan Reading Test is the dependent variable in the study. It is the presumed effect of the type of reading program used. In the present example it is easy to identify the dependent variable since it is the only one obtained at the conclusion of the program. While dependent variable measures are usually obtained at the end of a program, this is not always so. Some dependent variable measures may be obtained at the conclusion of a part of a program. For example, an arithmetic skills program may require proficiency of a particular skill at an intermediate point in the program rather than at the end. Thus, one must ask whether a particular variable is considered to be an outcome or an effect of the program in order to determine whether or not it is a dependent variable.

It is not always easy to make such a determination. A test might be administered at the end of a program, but it might be difficult to decide whether the variable represents an intended outcome or effect of the program. The variable might have no apparent logical connection to the aims of the program. One could argue that obtaining a measure at the conclusion of a program does not automatically give it status as a dependent variable and that it must pass a test of logical relevance in order to be considered as one. Until then, such a variable might be considered supplemental. This point of view is not universally held, however. Cronbach (1963) suggests that outcomes beyond those which have been set for a given course or curriculum might well be accorded dependent variable status.

In course evaluation, we need not be much concerned about making measuring instruments fit the curriculum. However startling this declaration may seem, and however contrary to the principles of evaluation for other purposes, this must be our position if we want to know what changes a course produces in the pupil. An ideal evaluation would include measures of all the types of proficiency that might reasonably be desired in the area in question, not just the selected outcomes to which *this* curriculum directs substantial attention. If you wish only to know how well a curriculum is achieving *its* objectives, you fit the test to the curriculum; but if you wish to know how well the curriculum is serving the national interest, you measure all outcomes that might be worth striving for. One

of the new mathematics courses might disavow any attempt to teach numerical trigonometry, and indeed, might discard nearly all computational work. It is still perfectly reasonable to ask how well graduates of the course can compute and can solve right triangles. Even if the course developers went so far as to contend that computational skill is no proper objective of secondary instruction, they will encounter educators and laymen who do not share their view. If it can be shown that students who come through the new course are fairly proficient in computation despite the lack of direct teaching, the doubters will be reassured. If not, the evidence makes clear how much is being sacrificed [p. 680].

While Cronbach is directing his discussion toward large national curriculum projects, his comments have relevance for even the most modest locally developed programs. To severely restrict the variables which will have status as dependent variables might result in an unfortunate amount of parochialism. On the other hand, inclusion of a large number of dependent variables might make a program liable for effects that were never intended by its developers. One must find some way out of the dilemma. Certainly, the assignment of all variables that could reasonably be classified as dependent variables to that status is justified. The classification of other variables obtained at the end of the program or along the way to supplemental status with the expectation that they will be analyzed separately, as if they were dependent variables, is probably a reasonable compromise. If this were done, it would be possible to investigate for unintended outcomes or side effects of programs, an issue that evaluators have been rather sensitive about recently.

The remaining variables in the study, scholastic ability and Gates Reading Comprehension, are control variables. They were obtained prior to the beginning of the program so that their status as control variables is quite clear.

The use of a single dependent variable is not recommended practice in evaluation work. On the contrary, every writer in the area of evaluation and research design who has discussed the issue has advocated the use of multiple measures of outcomes. This study used a single dependent variable for the sake of simplicity; the next study contains multiple outcome measures.

Study 2: Science Study Units

A high school science teacher wishes to test the efficacy of a series of self-study science units with his ninth-grade students. Each of the twelve units covers a topic that will be studied by the students during

the course of the year. The teacher decides to use the study units with one-half of his students and supplemental material for the remainder of his students.

With the help of a guidance counselor, the teacher randomly assigns one-half of the students in each class section to one group and the other half to another group. The flip of a coin then decides which group will use the study units and which will use the alternate material. Verbal reasoning and numerical ability test scores from Differential Aptitude Tests had been obtained in December of the school year as part of the school's regular testing program. The teacher plans to administer the STEP Science Test and the Roper Science Information Test to all students at the end of the school year, and a locally developed scale of attitudes toward science will also be given to all students at the end of the year.

Exercise 2
Classifying variables according to status

From the above description, list all variables included in the preceding study and indicate whether each variable is independent, dependent, control, or supplemental.

- -

The correct answers are presented below. It is not necessary to have listed the variables in the order shown; inclusion and correct classification are sufficient.

Variable	Status
1. Instructional material (study units or alternate material)	Independent
2. STEP Science Test	Dependent
3. Roper Science Test	Dependent
4. DAT—verbal reasoning	Supplemental
5. DAT—numerical ability	Supplemental
6. Attitudes toward science	Dependent

Study 3: Differentiated Staffing Study

The Aaron Burr Elementary School contains 120 sixth-grade students. Until this past year there were four self-contained classrooms. Two of the sixth-grade teachers had heard about the development of differentiated staffing programs and had become intrigued with the idea. One teacher had deep interests in reading and language arts while the other had taken additional special training in mathematics

and science. The teachers felt that, by moving into a differentiated staffing pattern, they would have more opportunity to teach in their areas of strength and that, as a result, students would benefit more than if they were in self-contained classrooms. They proposed to the principal that they inaugurate a differentiated staffing program. The two teachers would use an available large-group instructional room and be responsible for the education of sixty sixth graders. The principal was a cautious soul who liked to see his teachers show initiative in program development, but he did not want to be put in the position of having to support or defend a program of questionable quality. Accordingly, he encouraged the teachers to go ahead and begin planning the program, but informed them that it would be necessary to carry out a formal evaluation in order to determine how effective it was for the students.

While the teachers began their planning, the principal contacted the director of pupil personnel services for the school district, who agreed to carry out the evaluation of the program.

The director met with the principal and the two teachers a week later and helped them formulate the objectives of the program in the course of several meetings. The director selected the XYZ Reading Comprehension Test, the XYZ Tests of Arithmetic Concepts and Arithmetic Problem Solving, the ABC Social Studies Test, and the DEF Science Test as being suitable measures of student achievement. In addition, the Watt Attitude Scale and the LOX Attitude Inventory were chosen to measure some of the affective objectives of the program.

All students had been routinely tested with the GHI Scholastic Ability Test in the spring of the fourth grade and the entire JKL Achievement Test Battery (vocabulary, reading comprehension, language, work study skills, arithmetic computation, arithmetic concepts, and arithmetic problem solving) in fall of the fifth grade.

The Aaron Burr Elementary School had a long-standing policy of heterogeneous grouping so it was possible to assign all entering fifth graders to one of four groups at random and then to assign two of the groups to the Differentiated Staff Program, also at random. Arrangements were made to present the program to the parents of students destined for the program shortly before they completed the fourth grade. Special planning time was provided during the summer for the two teachers who would be running the program. Also, so as

not to shortchange the other classes, the teachers who would be teaching self-contained classrooms were chosen for summer in-service workshops to augment their teaching proficiency.

The program was initiated in September 1974.

Exercise 3

Classifying variables according to status

From the above description, list all variables included in the preceding study and indicate whether each is independent, dependent, control, or supplemental.

- -

The correct answers are presented below. It is not necessary to have listed the variables in the order shown; inclusion and correct classification are sufficient.

Variable	*Status*
1. Program (differentiated staffing or self-contained classroom)	Independent
2. XYZ Reading Comprehension Test	Dependent
3. XYZ Arithmetic Concepts Test	Dependent
4. XYZ Problem-Solving Test	Dependent
5. ABC Social Studies Test	Dependent
6. DEF Science Test	Dependent
7. Watt Attitude Scale	Dependent
8. LOX Attitude Inventory	Dependent
9. GHI Scholastic Ability Test	Control
10. JKL Vocabulary Test	Supplemental
11. JKL Reading Comprehension Test	Supplemental
12. JKL Language Test	Supplemental
13. JKL Work Study Skills Test	Supplemental
14. JKL Arithmetic Computation Test	Supplemental
15. JKL Arithmetic Concepts Test	Supplemental
16. JKL Arithmetic Problem-Solving Test	Supplemental

Each of the above lists is a compact summarization of an entire evaluation study and will be of assistance in selecting appropriate statistical procedures for analyzing one's data. One important element, however, is missing. It is necessary to know the type of measurement scale for each variable included in a study. The following section presents information on scales of measurement and the classification of variables by their scale of measurement.[2]

2. The following material is reprinted from R. Wolf, "Choosing an Appropriate Statistical Procedure," in R. L. Baker and R. E. Schutz (eds.), *Instructional Product Research* (New York: American Book Co., 1972, pp. 172-175).

"In general, three types of measurement scales are recognized in educational and psychological measurement and evaluation: nominal, ordinal, and interval.

"The *nominal* scale is the lowest level of measurement. This scale or measure assigns numerals, letters, or some other identifying label to each subject or object. Identifying two methods of teaching spelling as *A* and *B, 1* and *2,* or *alpha* and *beta* is an example of using a nominal scale. It should be stressed that no ordering of the various categories of a variable is intended with the use of a nominal scale. Each category is discrete and does not necessarily represent a scale position. When in doubt as to whether the measurement ought to be nominal, merely pose this question: Is there some order inherent in the categorization? If there is no order, the scale involved is nominal.

Exercise 4
Classifying nominal scales

"Place a check beside the number by each variable which involves a nominal scale.

1. ___ Methods of teaching beginning reading
2. ___ Intelligence test scores
3. ___ Type of class organization—graded vs. ungraded
4. ___ Instructional materials—programmed texts vs. conventional texts
5. ___ Scores on the Stanford Reading Test

- -

Answers:

"Items 1, 3, and 4 involve nominal scales, as there is no order inherent in the various categories of each of these variables. In the case of intelligence and reading achievement test scores, on the other hand, an order is inherent in the various score levels. That is, students with higher scores are said to possess greater amounts of the characteristic being tested. These, then, are not nominal scales since there is an ordering inherent in the various categories or score levels.

"An ordinal scale or measure assigns numerals to subjects or objects which are rank ordered with respect to some characteristic. For example, the highest achieving student in a class may be given a rank of 1, the second highest achieving student a rank of 2, and so on. Because the numerals indicate a student's position in the class, this is an ordinal scale. It does not indicate, however, the amount of difference between the individuals. For example, the difference between the

first- and third-ranked students is not necessarily the same as the difference between the seventh- and ninth-ranked students. The ordinal scale shows only that the first-ranked student is higher than the third-, or the seventh-, or the ninth-ranked student. When determining whether a measure is ordinal, ask this question: Is some order inherent in the categorization, but do we nevertheless lack knowledge of the magnitude of the differences? If order is present without specified magnitude, the scale involved will be ordinal.

Exercise 5
Classifying nominal and ordinal scales

"Mark each item as: N (nominal scale) or O (ordinal scale).

1. ____ Rank in class
2. ____ Type of teaching method employed
3. ____ Percentile scores on a standardized test
4. ____ The order of finalists in a Science Fair
5. ____ A list of textbook publishers

- -

Answers:

"Items 2 and 5 are nominal scales, as they involve categories having no inherent order.

"Items 1, 3, and 4 are ordinal scales, as each of the various categories is rank ordered. But we do not know the magnitude of differences between categories. For example, on a percentile scale the difference in performance between the fiftieth and seventieth percentile is not the same as the difference between the seventieth and ninetieth percentile.

"An *interval* scale or measure defines a unit of measurement such that the difference between units is equal. It may be a difference between 4 and 5, 16 and 17, 28 and 30, and so forth. Scores on well-constructed intelligence or achievement tests can be regarded as measures on an interval scale. Thus, an interval scale permits statements not only as to whether one individual ranks higher than another, but also as to the difference between the two in comparison with the difference between another pair of subjects.

Exercise 6
Classifying nominal, ordinal, and interval scales

"Mark each item as: N (nominal scale), O (ordinal scale), or I (interval scale).

1. ___ Aptitude scores on standardized arithmetic tests
2. ___ Responses to the question, "How much do you like your teacher?"
3. ___ Type of school (academic, vocational, comprehensive)
4. ___ Type of classroom organization
5. ___ Scores on the Metropolitan Spelling Test
6. ___ Admittance or rejection by the college of one's choice
7. ___ Scores on the Lorge-Thorndike Intelligence Test
8. ___ Sequence in which students turn in papers after a test
9. ___ Type of textbook used
10. ___ Socioeconomic status of students

- -

Answers:
"The appropriate answers are: 1, I; 2, O; 3, N; 4, N; 5, I; 6, N; 7, I; 8, O; 9, N; 10, O. It should be mentioned that some of the above items could be considered to involve either an ordinal scale or an interval scale. For example, one might consider raw scores on the Metropolitan Spelling Test to imply an ordinal scale, but this might well be considered an interval scale if there is general agreement as to what is going to be meant by the equal unit of measurement, as is the case when one decides on a standard scale of some sort. By the same reasoning, item 10, socioeconomic status, could be considered an interval scale if it were a composite of income and profession which had been numerically developed and standardized.

"A number of variables which are treated as if they were measured on an interval scale are, in fact, measured on an ordinal scale. This is particularly true of many variables included in questionnaires, and rating scales. Consider the following attitudinal item.

"Marriage is the most significant institution in the United States today.

1	2	3	4	5
STRONGLY AGREE	AGREE	UNDECIDED	DISAGREE	STRONGLY DISAGREE

"The numerical values 1 through 5 are assigned to the five response categories. However, this does not imply that the difference between strongly agree and agree is the same as the difference

between undecided and disagree. Thus, since no unit of measurement exists which permits legitimate statements of the differences here, an ordinal scale is involved.

"There exists a fourth scale, the ratio scale, which is the highest level of measurement. This measure is an interval scale having an absolute zero point, so that it is meaningful to speak of one scale value being twice as large as another. Examples of this scale include weights, heights, and lengths of objects. If one object has a measurement value of five feet and other a value of ten feet, one can say that the second object has twice as much length as the first. Because ratio scales are rarely used in educational and psychological measurement, they will not be referred to in classifying the various statistical techniques in this material. The classification scheme used here, so far as type of scale is concerned, will refer only to variables measured on nominal, ordinal, and interval scales.

"The scale of measurement involved in measuring each of the variables under study is an important determiner of the statistical procedures that should be employed when analyzing data."

Exercise 7
Classifying variables according to scale of measurement

Review the variables from Study 1, concerned with the reading program, and their status (see Exercise 1) and identify the scale of measurement for each of the variables.

- -

The correct answers are given below.

Variable	*Status*	*Scale of measurement*
1. Reading program (new or old)	Independent	Nominal
2. Scholastic ability	Control	Interval
3. Gates Reading Comprehension	Control	Interval
4. Metropolitan Reading	Dependent	Interval

Exercise 8
Classifying variables according to scale of measurement

Review the variables from Study 2, concerned with science study units, and their status (see Exercise 2) and identify the scale of measurement for each of the variables.

- -

The correct answers are given below.

Variable	*Status*	*Scale of measurement*
1. Instructional material (study units or alternate)	Independent	Nominal
2. STEP Science Test	Dependent	Interval
3. Roper Science Test	Dependent	Interval
4. DAT—verbal reasoning	Supplemental	Interval
5. DAT—numerical ability	Supplemental	Interval
6. Attitudes toward science	Dependent	Ordinal or interval

Exercise 9
Classifying variables according to scale of measurement

Review the variables from Study 3, concerned with differentiated staffing, and their status (see Exercise 3) and identify the scale of measurement for each of the variables.

- -

The correct answers are given below.

Variable	*Status*	*Scale of measurement*
1. Program (differentiated staffing or self-contained classroom)	Independent	Nominal
2. XYZ Reading Comprehension Test	Dependent	Interval
3. XYZ Arithmetic Concepts Test	Dependent	Interval
4. XYZ Problem-Solving Test	Dependent	Interval
5. ABC Social Studies Test	Dependent	Interval
6. DEF Science Test	Dependent	Interval
7. Watt Attitude Scale	Dependent	Ordinal or interval
8. LOX Attitude Inventory	Dependent	Ordinal or interval
9. GHI Scholastic Ability Test	Control	Interval
10. JKL Vocabulary Test	Supplemental	Interval
11. JKL Reading Comprehension Test	Supplemental	Interval
12. JKL Language Test	Supplemental	Interval
13. JKL Work Study Skills Test	Supplemental	Interval
14. JKL Arithmetic Computation Test	Supplemental	Interval
15. JKL Arithmetic Concepts Test	Supplemental	Interval
16. JKL Arithmetic Problem-Solving Test	Supplemental	Interval

The first variable in each study is measured on a nominal scale since there is no inherent order in the program types. All the achievement and ability tests are measured on an interval scale or can be

regarded as interval in nature insofar as the use of statistical procedures is concerned. The attitude scales have been classified as ordinal or interval. Insufficient information was furnished about these measures to permit an unequivocal classification. Normally, one would and should have more information about the measures one is using. In the present examples, where it is not clear whether a variable is on one scale or another, the evaluator is advised to choose the lower-level scale. This will lead to the employment of statistical procedures which, while less powerful than those used with higher-level scales, will be safer. To be cautious in the present examples, one would classify the attitude scales as ordinal. This does not mean that all attitude scales must be treated this way, just those in the present examples.

ACQUIRING INFORMATION ABOUT THE DATA
TO BE ANALYZED

One might presume that knowledge of the status of the variables of a study and the scale of measurement on which each is based would furnish a sufficient basis on which to make decisions about the kinds of analyses one might perform in order to obtain answers to one's questions. Unfortunately, this is not the case. Knowledge of the status of variables and the scale of measurement of each is a necessary but not a sufficient basis for decisions about data analysis. A certain amount of sniffing and snooping is required. This is directly antithetical to current myths about the ease and rapidity of data analysis because of the availability of computers for statistical processing. While computers can and do carry out highly complex statistical procedures at great speeds, the evaluator or researcher who does not have substantial prior knowledge about the nature of his data risks drawing inappropriate or even incorrect conclusions from the data analysis. How does one obtain the prior knowledge of one's data mentioned above in order to make intelligent decisions about data analysis?

There are essentially two ways of becoming educated about the nature of one's data. The first is to compute basic descriptive statistics for each variable and study them. The mean, standard deviation, and frequency distribution should be computed for each variable that is measured on an interval scale. The median and interquartile or

semi-interquartile range should be computed for each variable measured on an ordinal scale. A count of the number of cases in each category should be obtained for each variable measured on a nominal scale. Such information can be highly instructive in helping to select one of several procedures for analyzing data. The second way of becoming educated about the nature of one's data is to employ graphical procedures. Histograms and bivariate scatterplots can be most instructive in clarifying the nature of the distribution of variables, and, more important, they help to avoid pitfalls in data analysis.

In the era of high-speed electronic computers, an exhortation to return to horse and buggy procedures of data handling may strike the reader as ridiculous, but it is not. The proper use of statistics is predicated on the presumption, unfortunately often false, that the evaluator or researcher understands the nature of his data. Such understanding involves the nature of the distribution of the variables under study. For interval-scale variables, are the distributions roughly symmetrical or skewed? Are they peaked or flat? For pairs of variables where correlations are to be obtained, is the bivariate distribution approximately linear or not? Answers to such questions should be sought before engaging in formal analysis for two reasons. First, the evaluator, if he is more knowledgeable about his data, will be in a better position to select an appropriate statistical procedure. Second, he will be in a better position to wisely interpret the results of his analysis. Consider the example of the evaluator who administered an achievement test and a scale measuring attitude toward the subject to students at the conclusion of an innovative program. As a matter of routine, the evaluator obtained the correlation between the two sets of scores. The resulting correlation coefficient, whether it was Pearson product moment or Spearman rank difference does not matter here, was +.30. What is the evaluator to conclude? It is difficult to draw intelligent conclusions from the correlation coefficient alone without knowing about the nature of the bivariate distribution of the two variables. The bivariate distribution of an achievement and an attitude measure frequently resembles that shown in Figure 4-1.

That is, students who are low in achievement have somewhat unfavorable attitudes toward the subject while students who are average in achievement have more favorable attitudes. Students who are high in achievement do not go around chortling about the subject; their attitudes are not highly favorable. The relationship between the two

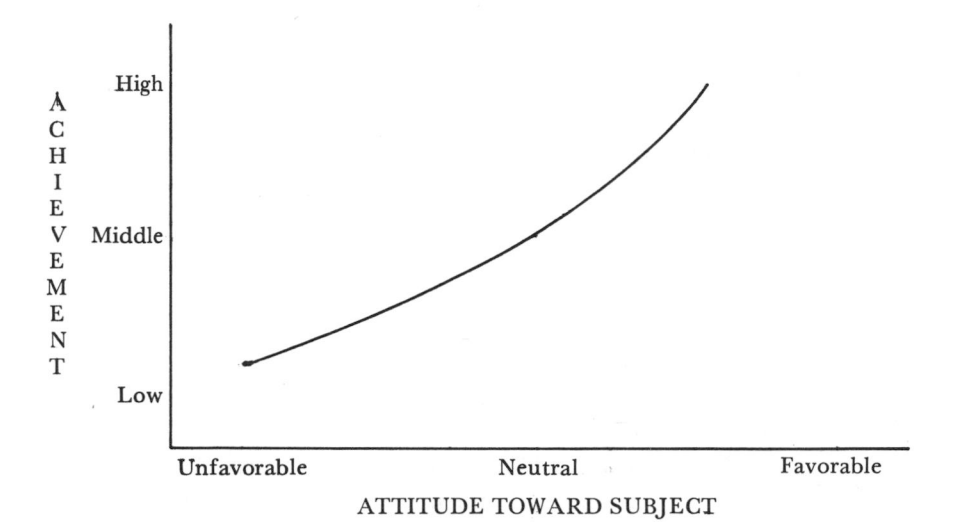

Figure 4-1
Relationship between achievement and attitude toward subject

variables is not linear, and there is no particular reason why it should be.

The evaluator who has knowledge about the shape of a distribution of scores in a bivariate distribution is in a better position to provide an intelligent interpretation of the results of a particular analysis than one who does not have such knowledge. On the other hand, the evaluator who knows only that the correlation between the two variables described above is +.30 is simply not in a position to offer a reasonable interpretation of the results. How often findings are buried in the appendix of a report or go unreported because they could not be readily interpreted can only be guessed at. Thus, the evaluator is strongly encouraged to acquire an understanding of the nature of data to be analyzed before proceeding to formal statistical analysis. Computation of basic descriptive statistics and plotting distributions greatly facilitates gaining such an understanding.

STAGES OF DATA ANALYSIS

The next step for the evaluator is to delineate clearly the three stages in the treatment of the data. The field of statistics is tradition-

ally viewed as being comprised of two stages: descriptive and inferential. Descriptive statistical procedures are concerned with the computation of various measures from a set of scores or observations so as to describe or characterize the sample. Means, medians, variances, standard deviations, and other results calculated from samples are descriptive of a particular sample at a particular time. When, on the other hand, reliable inferences are drawn from a body of data, the results are inferential. They go beyond the actual data in making statements about the efficacy of various educational treatments—programs, instructional materials, teaching procedures, organizational patterns. The distinction often made between descriptive and inferential statistics is that descriptive statistics concern a particular sample while inference statistics concern a larger population or universe to which the sample belongs. More extended definitions and distinctions can be found in almost any statistical text. The difference between these two branches of statistics is important in any analysis of data. There is an additional facet in the handling of such data that is germane to evaluation work, and it does not neatly fit into either of the two classical approaches. This third facet, for want of a better name, is called descriptive-comparative. It involves comparing the performance of students in a particular sample who have taken a standardized test with relevant norms for the test. If students in a certain school district took a standardized test before beginning a new program and were retested at the end of the program, students' performance with relevant beginning of the year norms and end of the year norms can provide a basis for judging the efficacy of the program.

A pretest-posttest situation with a sample group could establish the efficacy of a program if the average score on the pretest fell at the nineteenth percentile using beginning of the year norms while the average score on the posttest fell at the forty-ninth percentile using end of the year norms. Such an increase in performance could not simply be due to maturation because of the shift in norms.

Such a descriptive-comparative approach can be useful in helping to evaluate programs when there is no adequate comparison group of students. In such a case the norm group serves as a comparison or contrast group. (The term *control group* has a special meaning in the nomenclature of research design. The use of a norm group for comparative purposes does not begin to meet the criteria of a control group.)

In a distressingly large number of evaluation enterprises there is no adequate control or contrast group. In such situations a descriptive-comparative approach might furnish the only basis for judging the efficacy of a program. The approach is somewhat hazardous, however, and, while it is obviously not a suitable substitute for well-designed studies, it can serve as a useful supplement to more substantial analyses.

The normal progression in analyzing the data of a study would be to compute descriptive statistics first, inferential statistics next, and, if the situation permits, to use a descriptive-comparative approach, which is not, strictly speaking, statistical in nature, last. These operations will be carried out with treatment control and dependent variables. Supplemental variables will be discussed later. The evaluator or researcher who has sniffed and snooped in his data will have computed the basic descriptive statistics necessary to characterize the treatment and contrast groups under study.[3]

SELECTING AN APPROPRIATE STATISTICAL PROCEDURE

The selection of an appropriate statistical procedure is dependent on three major considerations: the number of independent, control, and dependent variables under study; the type of scale on which each

3. In this presentation of data analysis, the discussion is handled as if the individual student is the basic unit on which the analysis is carried out. For example, in a classical experimental study contrasting two teaching strategies, students would be randomly assigned to one of two class groups and the class groups would be randomly assigned to the treatments. After an appropriate period of instruction, the students would be tested with some outcome measures, and comparisons between the performance of the two groups would be made. The basis of comparison would be the test scores of the individual students. This need not always be so.

It is quite possible that an evaluator begins with a group of intact classes that are randomly assigned to one of two treatments and then tested after a period of instruction. The mean score for each class is computed for each variable, and it is these means which would then be used in subsequent analyses. In this case, the class mean is the unit of analysis. The use of group statistics in analyses is becoming more and more common. In many instances it is the only appropriate way of analyzing one's data. Fortunately, the various formulas one uses do not distinguish between a score for an individual and a mean for a group. They work equally well with either. It is the evaluator's responsibility to decide on the appropriate unit of analysis.

variable is measured; and the nature of the distribution of the variables. Armed with this information, the evaluator is in a position to select an appropriate statistical procedure for analyzing his data. Mastery of the procedure, or assistance from a statistical consultant, is a highly important but independent consideration.

The following section is intended to assist the reader in correctly selecting a statistical procedure.[4] It begins with a form for summarizing a situation, which, in this case, involves the influence of two different approaches on the acquiring of social studies information:

Variable	*Status*	*Scale of measurement*
Instructional approach	Independent	Nominal
Social Studies Information Test	Dependent	Interval

The independent variables are listed vertically in the table according to the number—either "one" or "two or more." These divisions are further broken down into scales of measurement: nominal, ordinal, and interval. Horizontally across the top are the dependent variables, which also are divided first according to number of dependent variables and then subdivided into scales of measurement.

From the summary, one can readily determine that only one independent variable is being studied. Therefore, in Figure 4-2, locate the first set of three rows that appears under the heading "one."

According to the summary chart, the scale of measurement of the independent variable is nominal. Therefore, in Figure 4-2 locate the first row labeled "nominal" in the set of three scales that have been identified. The row is shaded.

Having located the correct row of the table for one independent variable and for the nominal scale of measurement, you need to consult the summary again to determine the dependent variable being studied, which, in the case of the study just presented, is a single dependent variable (achievement score). In Figure 4-2, locate the first set of three columns under the heading "one." Looking at the summary once more, you see that the scale of measurement for the

4. This material is a slightly altered form of a section from R. Wolf, "Choosing an Appropriate Statistical Procedure," in Baker and Schutz (eds.), *Instructional Product Research*, pp. 179-188.

INDEPENDENT VARIABLES							DEPENDENT VARIABLES	
Two or more			**One**					
Interval	Ordinal	Nominal	Interval	Ordinal	Nominal			
Multiple discriminant analysis			Analysis of variance (analysis of covariance)		Chi-Square Test for Independence, Contingency Coefficient, Cochran Q Test, Fisher Extract Probability Test for 2 x 2 Tables	Nominal	One	
Multiple regression analysis		Friedman Two-Way Analysis of Variance	Spearman's Rank Correlation, Kendall's Rank Correlation		Sign Test, Median Test, Mann-Whitney U Test, Kruskal-Wallis One-Way Analysis of Variance	Ordinal		
		Analysis of variance (analysis of covariance), factorial design	Regression analysis (multiple coefficient) correlation	Analysis of variance (analysis of covariance) correlation	Analysis of variance (analysis of covariance)	Interval		
Multiple discriminant analysis			Analysis of variance (analysis of covariance)		Multiple discriminant analysis	Nominal	Two or more	
			Multiple regression analysis			Ordinal		
Canonical correlation			Multiple regression analysis	Analysis of variance (analysis of covariance)	Multiple discriminant analysis	Interval		

Figure 4-2

Statistical techniques classified according to type, number, and measurement scale of variables

dependent variable is interval. This means that the column under the "interval" heading is appropriate. This column has also been shaded.

The box where the two shaded areas intersect indicates the correct statistical procedures to be used with this study. These procedures are analysis of variance (or analysis of covariance).

Selecting which of these two procedures to use depends on whether a control variable is present. If a control variable is present, analysis of variance should be used. As a convention, statistical procedures that are shown in parentheses are for studies in which a control variable is present while those procedures not in parentheses are for use in studies where no control variable is present.

Exercise 10
Determining appropriate statistical procedure

Using the answers to Exercise 7, concerned with the reading program study, select the appropriate statistical procedure.

- -

The answer is analysis of covariance. Be sure of how you obtained this answer. The first consideration is the independent variable. There is only one, so the first set of horizontal rows will be used. Since the independent variable is measured on a nominal scale, the very first horizontal row will be used.

In identifying the appropriate column, note that the study has one dependent variable. It is measured on an interval scale. The intersection of the first horizontal row (one independent variable-nominal scale) with the third vertical column (one dependent variable-interval scale) is at the cell containing analysis of variance and analysis of covariance. The decision as to which of these procedures should be used since both can be used depends on whether there is one or more control variables. In the present example there are two control variables, Scholastic Ability and Gates Reading Comprehension Test scores, so analysis of covariance is the appropriate statistical procedure.

Exercise 11
Determining the appropriate statistical procedure

Using the answers to Exercise 8, concerned with the science study units project, as a summary, select the appropriate statistical procedure. Omit the science attitude scale.

- -

The answer you should have selected was Multiple Discriminant Analysis. The study contains one independent variable measured on a nominal scale—type of

instructional material—and two dependent variables measured on an interval scale—STEP and Roper Science Test scores. The cell containing the appropriate statistical procedure is in the upper right-hand corner of Figure 4-2. Note that the two supplemental variables do not enter into the selection of a statistical procedure. They are not germane to the analysis and should normally be handled separately.

Exercise 12
Determining the appropriate statistical procedure

Using the answers to Exercise 9, concerned with the differentiated staffing study, as a summary, select the appropriate statistical procedure.

- -

The main answer is Multiple Discriminate Analysis. Be sure how you obtained this answer. The first consideration is the independent variable. There is only one, so the first set of horizontal rows will be involved. The independent variable is measured on a nominal scale, which leads one to the first horizontal row.

Turning to the dependent variables, note that there are seven, which means that the last three columns across the top of the table will be involved. To find out which of the three columns to use, one needs to identify the scale of measurement. In this case, five of the variables are measured on an interval scale column labeled "nominal," which pinpoints Multiple Discriminate Analysis as the appropriate procedure for the analysis of the dependent variables measured on an interval scale.

There remains, however, the analysis of the two dependent variables measured on an ordinal scale: the Watt Attitude Scale and the LOX Attitude Inventory. Returning again to Figure 4-2, one locates the row for one independent variable measured on a nominal scale and two dependent variables measured on an ordinal scale. The cell thus located is blank! This indicates that there is no statistical procedure to analyze the two variables simultaneously, but it does not mean that no analysis is possible. Two courses of action are open. First, one could presume that the two attitude scale variables are close enough to being measured on an interval scale to be included in the multiple discriminant analysis with the other dependent variables. Second, one can conduct the analysis on the two attitude scale variables separately. In this latter case, one would use one of the procedures under the column for one dependent variable measured on an ordinal scale.

Neither course of action is particularly desirable. Of the two, though, the latter is preferable because there is greater risk in using a statistical procedure that is inappropriate for one's data than in analyzing data one variable at a time if there are only a few variables to be dealt with. Behind the words "greater risk" in the preceding statement lies a considerable amount of statistical thinking that is beyond the purview of this study. Occasionally, compromise decisions must be made. In the above example, a particular course of action was chosen in a situa-

tion that was ambiguous. The evaluator confronted with a situation in which the course of action is not easily determined is urged to obtain the services of a statistician.

Some additional considerations will be involved in the most effective use of Figure 4-2. First, notice that the figure contains, for the most part, the general title for various statistical procedures. Thus, the term *Analysis of variance* is used in several places, although there are various analysis of variance procedures. A researcher, then, would have to determine which particular analysis of variance procedure to employ by consulting a reference on the topic. In some cases, however, the statistical procedure listed in the table is quite specific. For example, the Kruskal-Wallis One-Way Analysis of Variance is a specific statistical procedure, not a general class of procedures. In such a case, one would simply refer to the appropriate reference to obtain precise details regarding the procedure.

Concerning the hierarchical nature of the scales of measurement, a second point can best be made using Figure 4-2. An interval-scale variable can be analyzed using the statistical procedures appropriate for an ordinal scale or a nominal scale, while an ordinal-scale variable can be analyzed using procedures listed for a nominal scale. Thus a statistical procedure that can be used with a nominal scale can also be used with ordinal- or interval-scale data; a procedure that can be used with ordinal-scale data may also be used with interval-scale data. For example, analysis of variance may be used if there is one independent variable measured on a nominal scale and a criterion measured on an interval scale. However, the criterion variable may also be analyzed with techniques appropriate for an ordinal- or nominal-criterion variable such as the Sign Test, the Median Test, and others.

Although interval-scale data can be analyzed using procedures appropriate for the other scales, the reverse is not true. That is, nominal- or ordinal-scale variables cannot be analyzed using the procedures listed for interval-scale data. The arrows in Figure 4-3 indicate that statistical procedures for lower-order scales may be used with data from higher-order scales. However, this feature applies only to any one subsection of Figure 4-2 (indicated by the heavy intersecting lines).

While it is possible to use a statistical technique intended for data of a lower-order scale, it is usually not advantageous to do so because

			DEPENDENT VARIABLES		
			One		
			Nominal	Ordinal	Interval
INDEPENDENT VARIABLES	One	Nominal	Chi-Square Test for Indepen-dence Contingency Coefficient Cochran Q Test Fisher Exact Probability Test for 2 x 2 Tables	Sign Test Median Test Mann-Whitney U Test Kruskal-Wallis One-Way Analysis of Variance	Analysis of variance (analysis of covariance)
		Ordinal		Spearman's Rank Correlation Kendall's Rank Correlation	Analysis of variance (analysis of covariance)
		Interval	Analysis of variance (analysis of covariance)		Regression analy-sis

Figure 4-3

Modification of Figure 4-2 to show the direction of increasing power
of statistical analysis

statistical procedures for lower-order scales are generally less power-ful than those for higher-order scales. This means that the statistics are more likely to overlook an important difference. Thus a researcher is generally better off using the highest-order procedure available. This will not be possible if the data fails to meet the assumptions required for the use of a particular technique. In these cases an investigator may be forced to resort to the use of a less precise technique.

A further point that should be noted in Figure 4-2 is that the procedure, analysis of covariance, appears in several of the cells. Analysis of covariance is an appropriate procedure when there are one or more control variables. It is preferred to analysis of variance on those occasions since it will result in a more precise analysis of data than analysis of variance. In the example of the differentiated staffing study, the appropriate procedure for analysis of the interval-scale data, multiple discriminant analysis, does not involve the control

variables. Thus, they are not used in the analysis. They should, of course, be used in the descriptive statistics since they will furnish the reader of one's report with evidence on the comparability of the groups at the beginning of the study.

Finally, each statistical technique requires that certain assumptions be made about the data to be analyzed. Some assumptions may be quite simple; others are more complex. Analysis of variance, for example, assumes that the scores for individuals in each treatment group are normally distributed and have equal variances. One can determine the assumptions underlying a particular statistical procedure by checking statistical texts.

The above material on the selection of an appropriate statistical procedure is relatively extensive. In actual practice, the evaluator's course is somewhat more defined. A particular program is to be installed and the evaluator's task is to conduct the evaluation using one or more suitable criterion variable measures. In this case, the statistical procedure most likely to be used, analysis of variance, analysis of covariance, or multiple discriminant analysis would be employed with dependent variables measured on an interval scale. If the dependent variables are measured on a nominal or ordinal scale, the procedures listed in the first two cells of the first row of Figure 4-2 would be used.

After the evaluator has carried out his analysis, he will be in a position to ascertain whether differences between groups are statistically significant or not. That is, are the differences between groups too large to be attributed to chance? If they are not, one can conclude that the new program did not result in a different level of performance on the dependent variable measures under study. (Whether students in the new program would perform differently than students in a conventional program on a different set of dependent variable measures would be a subject for another study.) On the other hand, if the evaluator's analyses resulted in significant differences between groups, much further pondering remains to be done. The detection of a statistically significant difference, in and of itself, is nothing to crow about. The differences between groups must meet two criteria in order to be judged to be educationally important. They must not only be statistically significant, but they must be *meaningfully* different as well. One way of illustrating the importance of determining the meaningfulness of a set of group differences is to describe an apocryphal study.

An aspiring graduate student at a midwestern university obtained ability test score information for a group of veterans and nonveterans shortly after World War II. There were about three thousand students in each group. The average ability test score for the veterans was 117.2, while the average for the nonveterans was 115.6. The difference of 1.6 ability score points was statistically significant beyond the 0.001 level. That is, the difference between the two averages (1.6 ability score points) would occur less than once in a thousand cases by chance. The excited graduate student concluded, "Since veterans and nonveterans differ significantly in ability, colleges and universities should establish separate educational programs for these diverse groups." Fortunately, at this point, a wise professor intervened and persuaded the student to modify his conclusion. Specifically, the professor instructed the student that the detection of a statistically significant difference does not, in and of itself, have policy implications. In the case of a difference of about one and one-half points, there is no basis whatsoever for restructuring the educational program of an institution, especially when one considers the costs involved.

The evaluator has a responsibility to consider the meaningfulness and practical importance of statistically significant differences he finds. To a large extent, this is a matter of judgment. How large must a statistically significant difference be for it to be considered educationally important? Simple inspection of the statistically significant difference can be highly important. For example, if it can be demonstrated that, on an average, students in an innovative program score a half-grade higher than students in a conventional program, then there would seem to be important policy implications. One would also want to examine the score distributions for the two groups. Do students in each quarter of the score group in the innovative program perform better than comparable students in the conventional program?[5]

Beyond the simple inspection of mean differences and score distributions, the evaluator has several procedures available to help him

5. If the answer to this question is, "Sometimes yes and sometimes no," the evaluator may have encountered a phenomenon that has been mistitled Aptitude-Treatment Interaction (ATI). Briefly, the phenomenon denotes the differential effectiveness of instructional treatments with different kinds of individuals, e.g., low ability vs. high ability students, etc. An examination of the literature bearing on ATI is beyond the scope of this chapter. The reader should consult Cronbach and Snow (1969) and Bracht (1969).

evaluate the meaningfulness of significant differences. The intraclass correlation and ω^2 are statistics that describe the degree of association between being a member of a particular treatment group and achieving a particular score level on a dependent variable measure or, as one colleague described it, the extent to which birds of a feather flock together.

The intraclass correlation and ω^2 have the appealing property that they can easily be computed by hand from the summary of the table of the analysis of variance. The formulas are readily obtained in the works of Kerlinger (1973), Hays (1963), and Haggard (1958), and each provides a clear exposition of the notions involved.

An illustration of the importance of these statistics is provided by Schutz (1966) who calculated ω^2 for every study published in the *Journal of Educational Psychology* and the *American Educational Research Journal* during the calendar year 1964 that reported an analysis of variance or a *t* test. Only significant *F* or *t* ratios were included. The results, which are summarized in Table 4-1, below, are

Table 4-1

Distribution of ω^2 for statistical tests reported in *Journal of Educational Psychology* and *American Educational Research Journal* in 1964 (adapted from Schutz, 1966)

ω^2	Percentage of *t* or *F* ratios
0.301 or greater	20
0.201 - 0.300	12
0.101 - 0.200	32
0.001 - 0.100	36
	100

highly sobering. Over one-third of the studies reported statistically significant *t* or *F* ratios, but the value of ω^2 was 0.100 or less. Since ω^2 ranges from 0.000 to 1.000, and is directly interpretable as the percentage of variance in the dependent variable measure that is accounted for by the variance in the independent or treatment variable, the results are notably unimpressive. To say, to cite but one example, that the difference between two groups on a dependent variable measure was significant at the 0.01 level conveys one impression (the treatment was effective in producing measurable differences between

the groups) while saying that four-tenths of a percent of the variance in the dependent variable measure is accounted for by the differences between groups conveys an entirely different impression (the treatment was not effective in producing differences between the groups). Both statements, however, refer to the same study! That is, while the difference between the means of the two groups is statistically significant, the fact that it accounts for only four-tenths of a percent of the variance in the dependent variable measure indicates that it is unimportant.

Inspection of Table 4-1 shows that 36 percent of the studies had a computed ω^2 of 0.10 or less and an additional 32 percent had an ω^2 of 0.101 to 0.200. Less than one-third of the studies had an ω^2 of 0.201 or greater. This last group of studies and only this group contains serious contenders of educationally important effects. The evaluator is urged to reflect upon the results of any of his analyses before rushing to write them up. Inspection of differences between means as well as studies of score distributions for groups can be highly instructive. For those not blessed with calibrated eyeballs, computation of the intraclass correlation or ω^2 can be highly useful in judging the educational importance of statistically significant differences.

Just how instructive these statistics can be is easily demonstrated. The formulas for ω^2 are presented below:

(a) For the t test

$$\text{est. } \omega^2 = \frac{t^2 - 1}{t^2 + N_1 + N_2 - 1}$$

Where: t^2 = square of the computed t value,
N_1 and N_2 = number of individuals in groups 1 and 2

(b) For the one way analysis of variance

$$\text{est. } \omega^2 = \frac{SS_B - (k-1)MS_W}{SS_T + MS_W}$$

Where: SS_B = sum of squares between groups
k = number of levels of the independent variable
MS_W = mean square within groups
SS_T = sum of squares total.

Let us return to the case of the aspiring graduate student who studied the ability test performance of veterans and nonveterans shortly after World War II. The basic statistics are given in Table 4-2, below.

Table 4-2
Ability test performance of veterans and nonveterans
(3,000 in each group)

Group	Mean	Standard deviation
Veterans	117.2	16.1
Nonveterans	115.6	16.0

The computed t value is 3.85. It is significant beyond the 0.001 level. The estimated ω^2 is computed as follows:

$$\text{est. } \omega^2 = \frac{3.85^2 - 1}{3.85^2 + 3,000 + 3,000 - 1} = .002$$

Thus, although the difference between the means of the two groups is highly significant statistically, the estimated ω^2 of 0.002 suggests that two-tenths of a percent of the variation in test performance is due to the difference between groups. Another way of interpreting these results is to view the estimated ω^2 as a measure of the relationship between being a member of a particular group (veteran or nonveteran) and having a particular level of test performance. In this way of interpreting the results, the ω^2 of 0.002 indicates that knowledge of group membership tells virtually nothing about expected level of test performance. Thus, despite the finding of statistical significance, the conclusion of no important difference is upheld.

Now consider the following example where three treatments are compared in Table 4-3:

Table 4-3
Results for three treatments

Group	Mean	Standard deviation	N
A	41.7	6.2	24
B	36.8	5.8	25
C	45.5	6.7	23

Source of variation	SS	df	MS	F
Between groups	915.00	2	457.5	11.8[a]
Within groups	2679.06	69	38.8	
Total	3594.06	71		

[a]$p < .01$

ω^2 is computed as follows:

$$\text{est. } \omega^2 = \frac{915 - (3-1)(38.8)}{3594.06 + 38.8} = 0.23$$

Nearly one-quarter of the variation in the dependent variable is due to the differences between groups. Thus, the differences between groups means can be regarded as being of educational importance as well as being statistically different.

PRESENTATION OF RESULTS

The evaluator who has properly analyzed his data and appropriately interpreted the results is ready to communicate them to others. The problems involved in reporting the results of an evaluation study are often as formidable as those involved in planning and conducting the study. Sometimes they are even more formidable because the audience, apart from other professional evaluators and researchers, is not often technically equipped to understand and appreciate the subtleties and complexities inherent in the results. In simpler terms, most consumers of evaluation reports know little, if anything, about standard errors, F and t ratios, significance levels, and the like. Even standard deviations are beyond the ken of many. The responsibility of the evaluator to communicate results fully and accurately with minimum misunderstanding is enormous.

There are essentially three ways in which results of an evaluation study can be reported in written form: verbal, tabular, and graphic. All three should be used.

An expository presentation of results in language as unadorned with technical terms as possible is necessary to present the objectives, instruments, procedures, and results of the study. The text should flow as naturally as possible and should be as readable as an article in a general news weekly magazine. Technical points should be placed in footnotes, and extended technical discussions should be relegated to an appendix. The reader who wishes more detail can always refer to these parts of the report. The general reader should be able to follow the flow of the report without having to wade through technical impedimenta. One way of checking on the extent to which one is succeeding in this task is to have one's most technically unqualified colleagues review drafts of the text.

It will be necessary to include tables of summary statistics in one's report—means, standard deviations, analysis of variance tables, and the like. As much of this tabular material as possible should be placed in an appendix because some people are fearful of numbers while others are hostile toward the philosophy of quantification and the use of numbers to express educational and psychological qualities. An evaluation report, no matter how carefully and skillfully it is prepared, is not likely to change this state of affairs. All one can do is to try to minimize the effect by keeping tabular presentations as inconspicuous as possible. An appendix is an appropriate place for such material since it is removed from the main body of the text, but it is readily available for the reader who wishes such detail. Another reason for placing tabular material in the appendix is that graphic presentations of results should be emphasized in the main body of the report, the graphs, of course, to be constructed from the tabular material presented in the appendix. The following presentation is intended to suggest several forms such graphic presentations might take, but it is by no means exhaustive. There are a number of standard introductory statistical texts for extended presentations that are not too technical.

The bar graph is one of the most frequently used means of conveying performance levels for groups. In a bar graph, numbers are represented by bars drawn to scale. The bars can be in either horizontal or vertical positions. Consider the set of fictitious results for a fifty-item test presented in Table 4-4.

Table 4-4

Means, standard deviations and P_{25}, P_{75}, and number of
students tested on an achievement test in
innovative and conventional programs

Program group	Mean	Standard deviation	P_{25}	P_{75}	N
Innovative	37.3	8.5	31.6	42.1	48
Conventional	32.4	7.9	27.5	39.4	51

The average performance for the groups can be presented in bar
graph form as shown in either Figure 4-4 or 4-5.

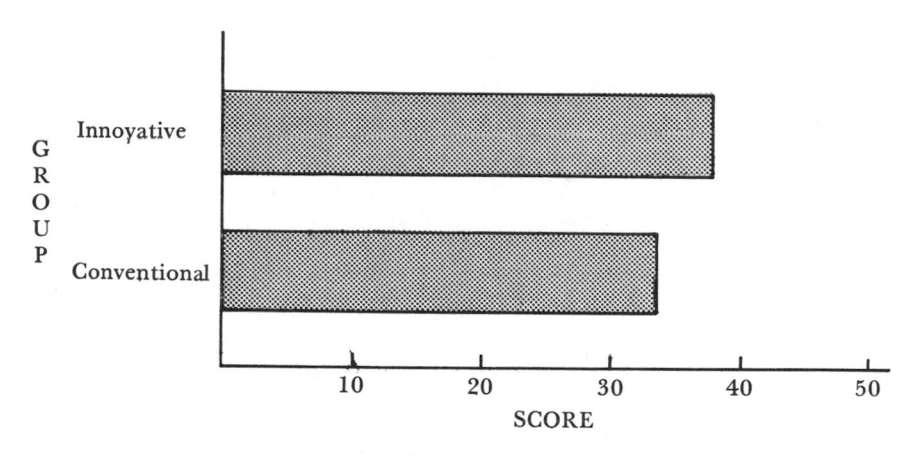

Figure 4-4
Performance of innovative and conventional groups

Either the horizontal or the vertical bar graph is effective in presenting the average performance of the groups. A cursory inspection
of a number of evaluation reports reveals about equal use of the two
forms. Note that in both cases all scale values from zero through fifty
are presented. One might have been tempted to begin the scale at
thirty instead of zero, but such curtailment would have given a misleading picture of the comparative performance of the groups.

If one has pretested students with the same test at the beginning
and end of a treatment period, it is possible to represent the average
performance at both testings in a single bar graph. Figure 4-6
is an example of how such information can be presented in a

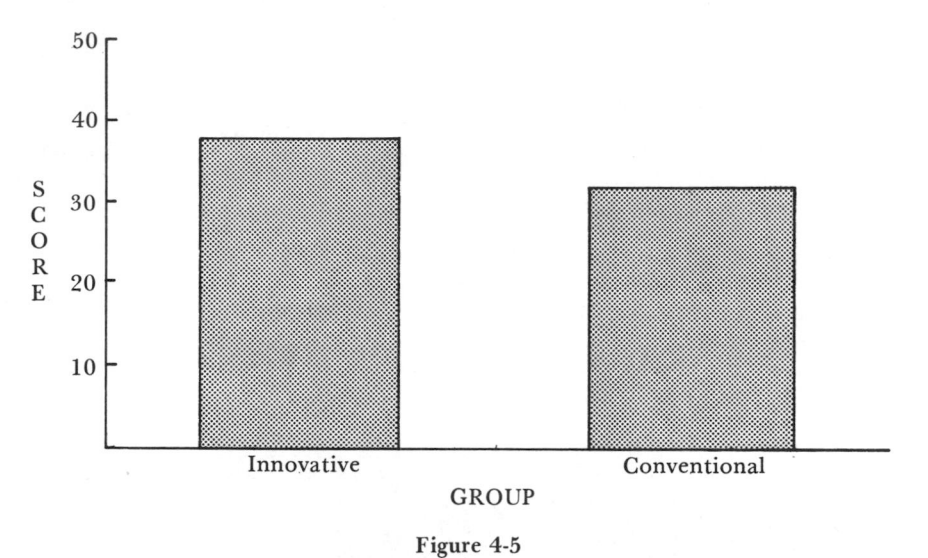

Figure 4-5
Performance of innovative and conventional groups

single figure. Note that pretest and posttest results for four distinct groups of children on a total test as well as eight subtests have been packed into a single figure.[6]

The bar graphs presented above are convenient vehicles for displaying the average performance of groups. They do not, however, convey any information about the extent of variability of performance within a group. To communicate such information, a variant of a bar graph can be used. Again, using the data presented in Table 4-4, the graph in Figure 4-7 can be used to present information on both the level of performance and the variability of performance.

In Figure 4-7, the longer vertical line represents the average performance of each group while the shorter vertical lines represent the score values associated with the twenty-fifth and seventy-fifth percentiles. Approximately one-quarter of each group earned scores in the shaded area between the shorter vertical line $(P_{25}$ or $P_{75})$ and

6. The statistically knowledgeable reader may note that there is a distinct relationship between pretest performance of the groups and the amount of time spent in viewing Sesame Street, the treatment variable. Such correlation between a treatment and control variable makes estimation of the effect of the treatment variable quite difficult.

SESAME STREET:
FIRST YEAR REPORT CARD

Percentage of items answered correctly by all
disadvantaged children at pretest and posttest

Q1 = Children who viewed   Q2 = Children who viewed 2-3
        rarely or never (N=198)*   times a week (N=197)
Q3 = Children who viewed 4-5   Q4 = Children who viewed more
        times a week (N=172)   than 5 times a week (N=164)

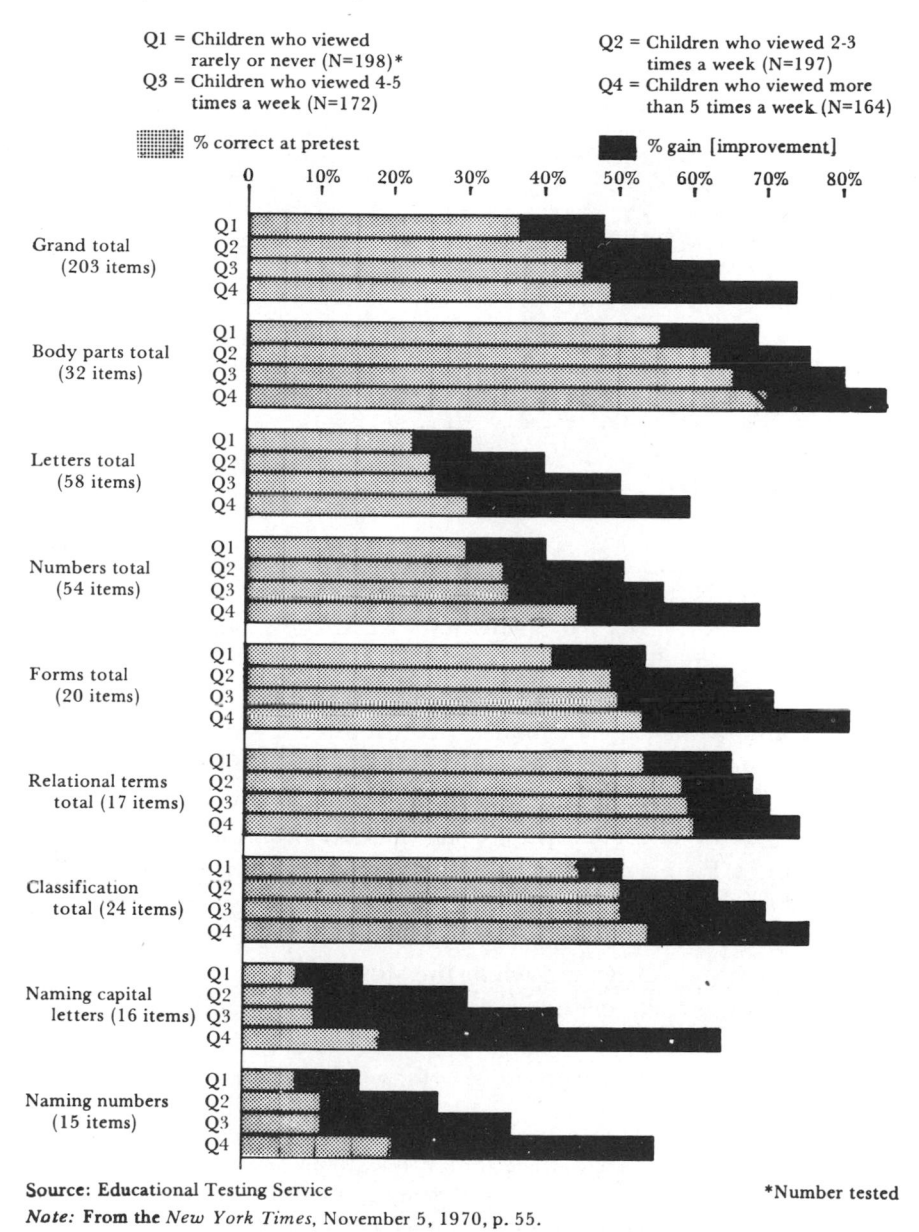

Source: Educational Testing Service   *Number tested
Note: From the New York Times, November 5, 1970, p. 55.

Figure 4-6
Graphic presentation of both pretest and posttest results
(reprinted by permission of Children's Television Workshop)

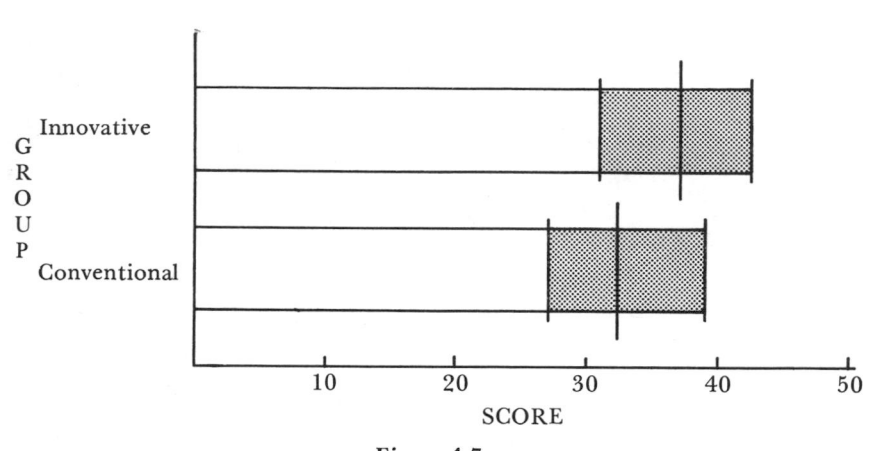

Figure 4-7
Performance levels (mean, P_{25}, and P_{75}) for innovative and
conventional groups

the longer vertical line representing the mean. Had the longer vertical line represented the median instead of the mean, exactly one quarter of the individuals in each group would have obtained scores between the shorter vertical lines and the longer one. The choice of which measure of central tendency to emphasize in a report is important. This decision should have been made at the stage of sniffing and snooping. If there is a marked discrepancy between the two, both will need to be reported and commented on.

Some discussion of the interpretation of the information contained in Figure 4-7 would be needed in the report. The information provided in the figure furnishes several important items of information. First, and obviously, the mean of the innovative group is considerably higher than that of the conventional group. Second, if a test of the significance of the difference between the means had been performed and found to be statistically significant and if the intraclass correlation or ω^2 plus one's judgment had indicated that the difference was of educational importance, then this would be reported in the text. Third, not only does the mean of the innovative group exceed the mean of the conventional group, but so do the twenty-fifth and seventy-fifth percentiles. Thus, at all levels students in the innovative group perform better than students in the conventional group. Fourth, almost three-quarters of the students in the innovative group exceed the mean of the conventional group.

Additional information can be obtained from a graph that displays not only the average level of performance but also information relating to variability, and such information is of considerable importance in describing the effects of an educational program. Graphs can also be useful in communicating information on the level and variability of performance for different groups. They are not, however, suited to conveying information about the significance or importance of differences between groups so an analysis of variance summary table, for example, does not lend itself to graphic presentation.[7] Fortunately, information about the significance and importance of differences between groups can easily be reported in the text of one's results and the interested reader can refer to a tabular presentation in an appendix. Such information should be presented in words only. It is neither necessary nor desirable to report an F or t ratio in the text of a report. Again, the typical reader of an evaluation report is not equipped to judge the numerical value of such test statistics even if the evaluator supplies the associated degrees of freedom.

The above discussion is aimed at reporting information about the results of evaluation studies that primarily employ interval-scale dependent variable measures. This would include standardized achievement tests and many teacher-made tests of academic performance. If a study has used criterion-referenced measures, then the analytic and reporting procedures would be somewhat different. (See Popham, 1973.) Typically, when one uses criterion-referenced tests, one is interested in the proportion of students who meet a criterion level of performance. Thus, a graphic display of the results of a criterion-referenced test would present the percentage of students who reached a criterion level. An example is given in Figure 4-8.

Note that the vertical axis of the graph, unlike the ones previously presented, represents the proportion of students achieving a criterion level rather than the level of test performance. This is consistent with current thinking on the use of criterion referenced measures when one is interested in determining whether students have achieved a particular prespecified level of performance or not, rather than in placing an individual at a particular point along a scale. A statistical

7. This is generally but not wholly true. One can, for example, represent the percentage of variance of a dependent variable accounted for by different courses in a pie chart. Such a chart, however, may result in more confusion than enlightenment.

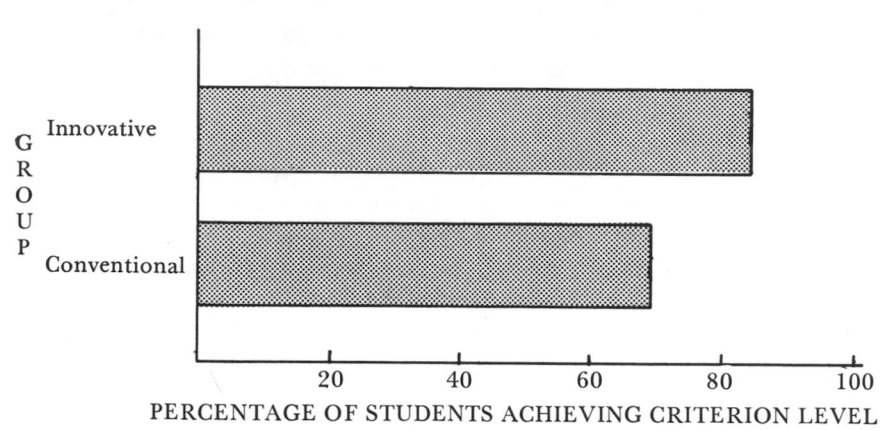

Figure 4-8
Student performance on end-of-unit, criterion-referenced achievement test

test of the proportion of students achieving the criterion level can be easily carried out and reported in the text.

This section has attempted to make two general points. First, reports of the results of evaluation studies should be written as simply as possible since those who read such reports are often not equipped to deal with technical material. If draft copies of the presentation of results were reviewed by members of the intended audience this would test the clarity of presentation. The second general point—that whenever possible tabular material be relegated to appendixes and graphic presentations be used—is intended to aid in communicating results with a minimum of confusion.

One final point needs to be made. The examples presented in this chapter have involved sizable differences between students exposed to an innovative program and students exposed to a conventional program. These examples are fictitious. As Schutz (1966) indicates, most studies show no important treatment differences. If this is the case in one's own evaluation of a particular program, it must, of course, be reported. Negative results do not necessarily mean failure. While some may have an emotional investment in seeing that a program is successful, the detection of no important differences between program effects can be of considerable positive benefit. If two treatments are equally effective in bringing about desired outcomes in student performance, then teachers and administrators are free to decide which should be adopted on bases other than student per-

formance. In such cases, finding no differences of consequence increases the degree of freedom in decision making.

REFERENCES

Bracht, G. H., 1969. *The relationship of treatment tasks, personological variables and dependent variables to aptitude-treatment interaction.* Research Paper No. 30. Boulder: Laboratory of Educational Research, University of Colorado.

Cronbach, L. J., 1963. "Evaluation for course improvement." *Teachers College Record,* 63:672-683.

———— , and Snow, R. E., 1969. *Individual differences in learning ability as a function of instructional variables.* Stanford, Calif.: Stanford University Press.

Ferguson, G. A., 1959. *Statistical analysis in psychology and education.* New York: McGraw-Hill.

Guilford, J. P., and Fruchter, B., 1973. *Fundamental statistics in psychology and education,* 5th ed. New York: McGraw-Hill.

Haggard, E. A., 1958. *Intraclass correlation and the analysis of variance.* New York: Dryden Press.

Hays, W. L., 1963. *Statistics for psychologists.* New York: Holt, Rinehart, and Winston.

Kerlinger, F. N., 1973. *Foundations of behavioral research,* 2nd ed. New York: Holt, Rinehart, and Winston.

Popham, W. J., ed., 1973. *Criterion-referenced measurement.* Englewood Cliffs, N. J.: Educational Technology Publications.

———— , and Sirotnik, K., 1973. *Educational statistics: Use and interpretation.* New York: Harper and Row.

Schutz, R. E., 1966. "The control of 'error' in educational experimentation." *School Review,* 74.2:151-158.

Wolf, R., 1972. "Choosing an appropriate statistical procedure," in R. L. Baker and R. E. Schutz (eds.), *Instructional product research.* New York: American Book Co.

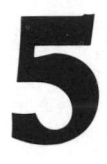

5

The Use of Standardized Tests in Evaluation

Gilbert Sax
University of Washington

The Use of Standardized Tests in Evaluation

Gilbert Sax

Man used principles of measurement to build shelters and tools, to select a mate, to kill prey, and to fashion clothing long before the advent of educational or psychological tests. Noah was commanded to build an ark three hundred cubits long, fifty cubits wide, and thirty cubits high (Genesis 6:15). A cubit, like most physical measurements, was based on the length of familiar and readily available standards of comparison—in this instance, the length of the forearm to the tip of the middle finger, or roughly eighteen to twenty-one inches. A foot was approximately the size of a man's foot; an inch was a twelfth of a foot, or approximately the distance from the joint of the thumb to its tip. Although convenient, these measurements were too arbitrary and unstable for business and scientific purposes, so less variable standards such as the length of the king's forearm (literally, a *ruler*) evolved. As international trade expanded, however, stable measures capable of surviving a specific monarch were needed.

I am indebted to Wadsworth Publishing Company and to its Education Editor, Richard Greenberg, for permitting me to quote freely from my forthcoming text, *Principles of Educational Measurement and Evaluation.* I also appreciate the comments and advice of Robert Branch and Brian Molmen.

Measurement requires a standard by which quantities can be compared. The meter, for example, was originally intended to be a ten-millionth of the distance between the equator and one of the poles measured along one meridian. This measure, so laboriously obtained and so inaccurate, was redefined, for the period from 1889 to 1960, as the distance between two lines of a platinum-iridium bar located at the International Bureau of Weights and Measures near Paris. This definition proved to be too inaccurate for scientific purposes, and the meter is now defined as 1,650,763.73 wavelengths of the orange-red radiation of krypton 86 under specified conditions.

Even where physical measurements are involved, not all countries have agreed to use the same scales. Most European countries have adopted the meter as the standard unit of length, whereas the foot or yard is used for most nonscientific purposes in the United States. The value of both the meter and the yard, however, lies in the fact that virtually every country has agreed to their definitions and to the procedures to be followed in measuring length or distance. In measuring the length of a table, for example, the measurement "rules" seem almost too obvious to mention, but consider the difficulties children face in learning to use such measures. They must learn to (1) determine which terminal points correspond to the two ends of the table; (2) place the meter or yardstick so that the zero point corresponds with one end of the table; (3) "aim" the yardstick in a straight line from the zero position of the table and its agreed-upon terminus; and (4) count the number of units (centimeters, millimeters, inches, half inches, and so forth) by which the length of the table will be defined. Each of these measurement "rules" could be further developed and made more explicit.

Measurement in education and psychology, when compared with measurement in the natural sciences, has had a relatively brief history. Tests of strength appear early in recorded situations (Ramul, 1963), but oral and performance tests, while they are not so well known, have probably also been used in all cultures.

After reading this paper you should be able to:

1. distinguish among the following terms: *tests, measurement,* and *evaluation*;
2. describe the similarities and differences between standardization "rules" in the physical sciences and in education;
3. differentiate between the "rules" required for teacher-made tests and "standardized tests," and describe the consequences of failing to follow these rules;

4. define the terms *internal norms* and *external norms,* and demonstrate how they are related to teacher-made and "standardized" tests;

5. distinguish between *norm-referenced* tests and *criterion-referenced* tests;

6. list procedures used to develop standardized tests and criterion-referenced tests;

7. respond to each of the criticisms leveled against the use of standardized tests (Skager, 1971), which state that they:
   a. are unrelated to instructional goals and objectives,
   b. fail to aid in the planning of instruction,
   c. are unaffected by classroom experiences,
   d. fail to measure the extent of student mastery, and
   e. "lead to corruption and dishonesty among educational professionals";

8. list the conditions and circumstances that call for use of criterion-referenced tests and those that are better served by standardized tests;

9. defend the use of standardized tests for selection purposes by:
   a. defining what is meant by the *composite method* and the *cutoff method* and indicating the advantages and disadvantages of each,
   b. differentiating between a *predictor* and a *criterion,*
   c. developing an *expectancy table* and specifying how the *success ratio* is affected by the *selection ratio,*
   d. providing examples that show how internal and external norms on standardized tests can be used;
   e. indicating the effect of increasing the reliability of the predictor(s) and the criterion, and
   f. indicating the effect of decreasing the correlation among predictors;

10. describe the differences between *selection* and *placement* decisions;

11. describe the difference between *vertical placement* and *horizontal placement* and demonstrate how standardized tests can be used to place children into: optimal grade levels, special classes for the gifted and mentally retarded, and different curricula within a given grade level;

12. describe how placement decisions can be improved by using

standardized test *batteries* and specify the characteristics that such batteries should possess to be most effective;

13. list four different ways of measuring interests and distinguish between *levels of proficiency* and *areas of interest* as related to placement decisions;

14. differentiate and show the similarities between the use of standardized tests for selection or placement and for diagnosis and remediation;

15. distinguish between the use of standardized tests for *screening* and for more detailed diagnoses, and indicate how standardized tests differ with regard to those two functions;

16. list the advantages and disadvantages of using standardized diagnostic tests that provide the reliability and standard error of measurement for each item;

17. provide original and explicit examples of how norms on diagnostic tests can be used to interpret and to help set different levels of competency on teacher-made and criterion-referenced tests;

18. describe how internal norms and external norms can be used to help interpret the meaning of students' raw scores on standardized diagnostic tests;

19. list various criteria used to evaluate a curriculum or other school program;

20. differentiate between the terms *independent variable* and *dependent variable* as they relate to the use of standardized tests in evaluating curricula by experimental methods;

21. describe the advantages of *randomization* over the use of intact groups in curriculum evaluation;

22. describe the disadvantages of using *gain scores* in curriculum evaluation and indicate how standardized tests can be used to reduce their effects;

23. describe how standardized tests can be used most effectively for *matching* students in an experimental program with students in a control group;

24. describe the purpose of the *analysis of covariance* and how standardized tests can be used for this purpose;

25. describe the advantages and limitations of such criteria as absolute standards, cost-benefit analyses, time required for attaining "mastery," and statistical significance as they relate to curriculum evaluation;

26. provide reasons why teachers and administrators have often disagreed on the reasons for using standardized tests and how these "differences" can be resolved;

27. explain why *school norms* (and not *individual norms*) are used in curriculum evaluation;

28. distinguish between *formative* and *summative* curriculum evaluation and demonstrate how standardized tests can be used in each;

29. provide examples of how standardized tests can be used in *product development, demonstrations,* and the *dissemination* of knowledge regarding the effectiveness of a curriculum innovation;

30. list the purposes served by providing the results of standardized tests to students, parents, teachers, and the community;

31. describe the advantages and disadvantages of reporting IQ scores, grade equivalents, percentiles, and standard score norms (z-scores, T-scores, stanines) to parents, indicating what other kinds of *feedback* are possible;

32. provide an example of how standardized tests have contributed to and have benefited from *theoretical* studies of an attribute such as intelligence;

33. list and explain the purposes of various criteria that should be considered in developing a *standardized testing program*;

34. develop a rationale for a school- or district-wide *minimum* standardized testing program by determining, for each grade level, the type of test (intelligence, interest, or other), giving the reasons for using a particular test, and explaining why the test is needed.

These "objectives" may be used as a pretest, posttest, or both. The sequence parallels the presentation of each topic in the chapter.

THE MEANING OF THE TERMS

The purpose of this analysis is not to discuss the procedures to be followed in measuring the length of a table, the characteristics of a meter or a yardstick, or the history of measurement. Each of these topics is, however, relevant to the use of standardized tests in evaluation, at least insofar as an analogy can help clarify the meanings of such terms as *measurement, standardization, test,* and *evaluation.*

Measurement

The assigning of numbers to attributes or characteristics of persons, objects, or events according to explicit formulations or "rules" is involved here. In measuring physical characteristics such as height or weight, the quantification rules have been agreed upon and "standardized" to the point where practically everyone "understands" the procedures to be followed. More complex physical measurements (such as hearing, vision, and so forth), however, require explicit and detailed formulations of rules or procedures to be followed if all observations of the same characteristic are to be quantified the same way.

Educational measurement also requires the quantification of attributes according to specified rules. What is measured are the attributes or characteristics of students, objects, or events, and not the students, objects, or events, themselves. Teachers can measure the height of fifth-grade students, their interests, intelligence, or achievement. Height, interests, intelligence, and achievement are characteristics or attributes of individuals. No one would try to measure a "table"; instead, one measures its length, height, and hardness (that is, its attributes).

As used here, a measurement "rule" is neither a moral imperative nor a prescription to be followed blindly. Indeed, each person can establish his own rules which others are free to follow or not. This does not mean that all rules are equally good. The rules established by one teacher for measuring any given attribute may turn out to be of little empirical value. Other rules, such as allowing students exactly ten minutes to complete a test, must be followed if the teacher wants to know how his pupils performed in comparison with others given that same time limit.

Standardization

Measurements are standardized to the extent that they have been administered and scored under standard (uniform) conditions. These standard rules are as necessary for the proper interpretation of test scores as they are for the interpretation of length by use of a yardstick. In a sense, it is more important to explicitly state the standardization rules in educational measurement than it is to be explicit about many physical measurements which already enjoy a high de-

gree of what may be termed *consensual standardization*—the willingness among individuals in diverse situations and circumstances to accept the meaning of a particular attribute because it has been defined (measured) by a consensus of operations, procedures, or rules.

Teacher-made examinations require standardization of administration and scoring just as much as published tests require such standardization. Within a given class, the standardization rules for teacher-made tests usually include giving all students the same instructions, response format (separate answer sheets or test booklets), time limits, use of supplementary reference materials, and so forth. Scoring, too, will have to be standardized by ensuring that equal degrees of knowledge, interest, or aptitude are awarded the same number of points.

The usual distinction that is made between teacher-made and "standardized" tests is legitimate only if it is understood that *standardized* is a synonym for *published*. Tests are published because they appeal to or have usefulness for a wide range of teachers and students. Test administrators should scrupulously follow standardized administration and scoring rules if they want to compare their students with a norm group that has been tested under the same conditions. If teachers want to measure individual differences only as they exist within the group and not in comparison to any other, it is not necessary to follow the standardization procedures found in the test manual. But even then the standardization rules devised by the teacher must be applied uniformly to all members of the class to provide raw score ranks that correspond to "true" differences in whatever attribute is being measured. Both teacher-made and published tests require standardization. The extent to which teachers can devise their own standardization rules depends on the nature of the comparisons to be made: there can be no revisions or modifications of published or teacher-made tests if intergroup comparisons are desired; if only intragroup comparisons are to be made, the teacher must still make certain that the same uniform procedures are used for all individuals within the group being tested.

Tests that are not standardized serve no purpose since each score will be derived from different procedures and criteria. Even if only one student were given a newly devised test, his score would have meaning only if it were related to some goal, criterion, or the performance of other students, and if it were obtained under uniform or

standardized conditions. This principle is as applicable to teacher-made tests as to "standardized" or published tests.

It is incorrect to think that standardized tests provide norms whereas teacher-made tests do not. A norm is simply a distribution of scores attained by some specified group under uniform or standardized conditions. Most (but not all) published tests do provide *external norms* or distributions of scores obtained by a sample of individuals selected from a population or totality of those individuals. When teachers use tests to compare class results with external norms, these tests must be given under the same rules and conditions that were adhered to by students in the norm or standardization group.

On teacher-made examinations, the distribution of class percentiles, standard scores, or letter grades are *internal norms* used to compare members of the class with one another. Should these internal norms be used by another teacher, or by the same teacher with another class, they become external for these other groups. External norms will have meaning only if the class to be compared against them follows the same set of rules.

To summarize, both teacher-made and published tests require standardized or uniform administration and scoring procedures. If a test yields external norms, the standardization rules must be stated explicitly and in sufficient detail to allow other persons to follow them exactly. Even if only internal norms are needed, the procedures must be kept uniform for all members within the group. Tests or inventories that are not standardized, whether they are teacher-made or not, serve little purpose.

Tests

Any standardized, intrusive procedure or series of tasks used to obtain observations assumed to be representative of some educational or psychological attribute or trait is a test. In a typical test situation students must respond to items or to questions from which the examiner infers something about the attribute being measured. Nothing in the definition implies that tests can only measure cognitive or intellectual attributes or that the student is necessarily aware that he is being tested. It is important that these tasks be standardized and that they do, in fact, measure some specified attribute.

Most teachers think of tests as being limited to true-false, multiple-choice, or essay questions used to measure knowledge in arithmetic,

reading, and other school subjects. This narrow definition fails to include many kinds of tasks that can be devised to observe how a student might behave in a situation that appears uncontrived to him. The purpose might be to observe frustration, anger, protectiveness, or the ability to solve problems without the teacher's help.

Some measurements may be obtained without subjecting the student to any task. Teachers often keep records of student behavior as it occurs in the classroom or on the playground. Since no tasks were devised to elicit behavior, the student was not subjected to a test. Nonetheless, the teacher's observations can still be used to measure or describe important attributes of the child.

Evaluation

Evaluation is a process through which a value judgment or decision is made from a variety of observations and from the background and training of the evaluator. No matter how carefully constructed, administered, and scored a test may be, someone must interpret its results and decide upon the course of action that can best help the student.

An example from the field of medicine may clarify the relationships among the terms measurement, standardization, test, and evaluation. Suppose that a patient complains of such symptoms as a running nose, sneezing, watery eyes, and a cough. These symptoms can reflect a variety of illnesses, each of which requires different treatment. Proper diagnosis requires the physician to prescribe various laboratory and clinical tests. These tests in turn "assign" numbers to different symptoms according to standardized procedures. One test might tell the physician that the patient has a fever of $102°$; another could indicate a white blood count of 10,000 per cubic millimeter. The physician must evaluate the test results to identify the illness and determine the most effective treatment.

Essentially the same process is followed in education. A child who experiences reading difficulties often displays a host of symptoms (such as refusing to read voluntarily, making numerous errors in oral reading, holding the book too far from or too close to his eyes), indicating to the teacher that something is wrong. The teacher may recommend vision and hearing tests to rule out physical causes, an orally administered intelligence test to measure the child's general level of scholastic ability, or a diagnostic reading test to pinpoint possible

areas for treatment. The teacher must evaluate the results (20/20 vision, a 30-decibel loss of hearing, an IQ of 115, two years behind age level in phonetic analysis) to determine the nature and extent of the child's problem and how to help him.

NORM- AND CRITERION-REFERENCED MEASUREMENT

The title of this chapter represents a preliminary comment inasmuch as the introductory pages state that standardization is indispensable to measurement and that the distinction usually made between standardized and teacher-made tests could be improved by contrasting tests that yield internal norms with those that provide external norms. All tests should be administered and scored using uniform or standardized procedures whether they are published or teacher-made or whether norms are internal or external. Because the purpose of this paper is to relate published tests, particularly those that are norm referenced, to their use in evaluation, it is necessary to examine the nature and characteristics of *norm-referenced* tests and *criterion-referenced* measures in some detail.

Norm-referenced measures are designed to determine an individual's relative standing in comparison with an internal or external norm group. The emphasis is on measuring individual differences by demonstrating that a student has more or less knowledge, interest, or ability than other members of one or more reference groups to which he belongs. The student's position in these groups can be ascertained by counting the number of items marked correctly, perhaps converting them to percentiles or to age-, grade-, quotient-, or standard-score norms.

In contrast, criterion-referenced measures compare the student not in relation to others but in relation to the level of performance he will be expected to achieve in a carefully defined domain of behaviors. For example, instead of saying that a student is "average" (a normative judgment), he can be required to perform a given task at some minimum level of proficiency (such as 90 percent or 100 percent) before he is allowed to proceed to the next higher or more complex instructional level.

Because norm-referenced tests attempt to measure individual differences in attributes, much effort is expended by test publishers and teachers to maximize the measurement of such differences. Maximiz-

ing individual differences means that different scores among individuals reflect actual or true differences in the attribute being measured and that differences among scores are as large as possible. Thus, on a 100-item examination, more meaningful and accurate decisions can be made if one person receives a score of 100 and another receives a score of 0. In practice, of course, this ideal is only approximated.

Although some experts in measurement may not agree, there is nothing sinful about measuring individual differences as long as such differences are measured along a true and clearly defined continuum. Body temperature derives its meaning from the fact that most individuals have temperatures of 98.6° in the absence of illness and that temperature correlates positively with seriousness of illness above that level. Indeed, the classical approach to the theory of reliability requires a true continuum of scores underlying a given trait that is approximated as closely as possible by fallible measures.

Those who advocate a criterion-referenced approach to measurement argue that the individual's position within a group does not specify what he is capable (or incapable) of doing. If all students in a particular group are poor spellers, the fact that Johnny is at the 99th percentile still does not speak too highly about his ability to spell. What is more important, they would argue, is the number or percentage of words that Johnny can spell when words are selected from a clearly defined domain or specific universe of words.

The difference between the two approaches may be better understood by a description of how a standardized[1] test is constructed. In developing the Stanford Achievement Test, for example, five steps were followed:

1. Determining test rationale and objectives is the first step in constructing a standardized achievement test. The purpose of the Stanford Achievement Test, for example, is to survey both basic and specialized courses common to most school programs. To determine specific test content, the test authors examined textbooks and courses of study and asked subject matter specialists and teachers what topics should be included. On other standardized tests, detailed lists of topics and objectives are written and distributed to a wide variety of knowledgeable persons who are asked to indicate the

1. To avoid confusion, the term *standardized test* will be used in the remainder of this paper to refer to published tests that provide external norms.

importance of the objective in the school curriculum and the amount of weight each objective should be given.

2. Writing the items is usually the second step in constructing a standardized achievement test. This is usually a cooperative endeavor between subject matter specialists and testing experts. For example, on the Stanford Achievement Test, teams of experts constructed four forms of a test, each with 20 to 50 percent more items than would be used in the final versions. All items were in multiple-choice format, were required to meet specified objectives, and were administered to small groups of school students to estimate difficulty levels, the adequacy of time requirements, and the functional value of each option. Items were reviewed, tried out on new groups, and revised until all appeared clear, unambiguous, and educationally worthwhile.

3. Analyzing items is the third step in constructing a standardized achievement test. In the preceding step, items were analyzed on relatively small numbers of students to obtain a preliminary notion of their effectiveness in measuring individual differences. The full-scale item analysis on the high school level of the Stanford Achievement Test consisted of a national sample of over 26,000 students from nineteen school systems in seventeen different states. Separate analyses were run for each grade level, for students who had continually studied a given subject since entering the ninth grade, and for students who were enrolled in special curriculum programs or projects.

4. Constructing the final test forms is a compromise between item sampling (maximizing content coverage) and administrative requirements. Because many high school classes meet for fifty minutes, it was considered desirable that no subtest take longer than forty minutes.

5. Norming and standardizing the final form is the last step in constructing a standardized achievement test. On the Stanford Achievement Test, almost 23,000 students attending fifty-eight schools in thirty-nine different districts are included in the norm group.

In contrast to standardized tests, criterion-referenced tests are constructed in the following way:

1. Behavioral specifications are written for the test. The specifications describe the universe of behaviors expected of the student. Nothing inherent in criterion-referenced measurement indicates how many domains are to be measured, the scope or breadth of each domain, or even what domains should be included in a single exami-

nation. Ideally, the specifications for criterion-referenced tests should state what the student is to do, under what conditions he is to do it (orally, without references, and so forth), and how well it is to be done (90 percent, 100 percent).

2. Items are written to conform to specification requirements. If possible, all items included in a domain would be written and randomly selected for inclusion on the final form of the test. In practice, of course, this is usually only possible if the universe or domain of items is both finite and accessible (for example, adding all combinations of single digit integers from 1 to 5).

3. Given a choice among items that have all been randomly selected from the same domain, the procedure would be to select those items that have demonstrated the greatest increase in pupil performance over the course of the semester or year.[2] If everyone should miss an item prior to instruction but respond correctly afterward, that item is usually preferred over others.

4. The test is administered under specified conditions. For example, if students are to orally recite the letters of the alphabet, they should not be required to write or print these letters.

5. A comparison is made between the student's performance on the items and the minimum level of competence called for by the objective.

A comparison of the procedures used to construct norm-referenced tests and criterion-referenced tests shows some similarities which can be summarized as follows:

1. Both norm-referenced tests and criterion-referenced tests are concerned with the objectives of instruction.
2. Both types of tests require careful item writing and editing.
3. Both require some form of item analysis to select items.
4. Both require standardization in the administering and scoring of items.
5. Both compare the performance of the student with some criterion.

These similarities should not obscure important differences between norm-referenced tests and criterion-referenced tests. One way of examining these similarities and differences is to examine some of

2. Any comparisons among groups that have been exposed to some instructional sequence and those that have not could also be used to select items.

the usual criticisms of norm-referenced tests as offered by a highly competent critic of these tests (Skager, 1971). Skager lists five "inadequacies" of standardized tests, which will be presented and discussed.

1. "Standardized tests ordinarily have a low degree of overlap with the actual objectives of instruction at any given time or place." As Skager has stated, standardized tests do not measure the unique objectives of any specific program; in fact, they take special care not to do so. That purpose is better served by teacher-made examinations that are designed to measure specific course content.

Nothing inherent in a behavioral objective requires criterion-referenced measurement of that content although this prerequisite relationship is often incorrectly assumed. A behavioral objective must state what the student can do or perform, but feedback can compare the student's performance with that of other students or performance can be compared to the behaviors that define a given domain.

Two other considerations are relevant to the claim that standardized tests "have only a distant, even tenuous, relationship to the outcomes of the real-life instruction in a given situation." The first involves the content validity of standardized achievement tests. As previously noted, they are specifically designed to measure subject-matter content or goals common to most schools and school districts. There is a wide variety of different tests from which to make a selection. Some tests emphasize the measurement of skills, whereas others measure the ability of the student to apply those skills. Because reading, language arts, and arithmetic are taught in essentially the same sequence in most schools, standardized achievement batteries almost always include those three topics. Many batteries also provide subtests that can be substituted for the more "traditional" ones if the school or district has adopted another curriculum such as the "new math." If a teacher or school district selects a test that is invalid for their purposes, the error should not be attributed to the inadequacy of standardized testing but to those who selected a test that was invalid for their purposes.

The second consideration regarding the items found on standardized achievement tests concerns their construct validity. The student's ability to demonstrate knowledge of any skill or subject depends in part on the nature of the items presented to him. A behav-

iorally stated objective might require the item to be in multiple-choice or in essay format, but the specific wording of the item and the selection of alternatives is usually left to the test constructor.[3] No matter how much effort and time is devoted to selecting or writing items that apparently measure the specifications and objectives for a test, there is usually a larger item pool than could be administered in any reasonable time period. This requires that specific items should be selected that empirically measure a given domain.

Factor analysis provides empirical evidence of the extent to which items measure a common domain or universe and can help to construct factorially pure tests and subtests. This is particularly important in measuring complex behaviors where the characteristics of the domain are unknown or where the rules for generating items are not routine.

Many standardized achievement batteries provide the evidence for their factorial validity and demonstrate how each item contributes to the variance of the domain measured by a given subtest. But it is important to remember that all items ultimately selected by item or factor analysis were first selected because they were consensually relevant to commonly held curriculum objectives.

2. *"Standardized tests are not useful as aids in the planning of instruction, particularly the specification of instructional objectives."* This criticism of standardized tests puts the cart before the horse. Standardized achievement tests (or any other achievement tests for that matter) are used to measure how well students have achieved or learned those skills and competencies that are stated by the objectives the tests were designed to measure. One does not scrounge through standardized tests in the hope of discovering what should be included in the curriculum.

A perpetual criticism of standardized tests is that they influence the content taught in schools. This criticism has merit whenever school personnel have used the content on standardized achievement tests as guides on which to build their curriculum. When the test

---

3. This is an essential difference between norm-referenced and criterion-referenced tests. The specifications used to generate items on criterion-referenced tests include their exact wording. Usually, a high degree of specification is possible only if the item-writing rules are applied to the simpler aspects of basic skills, such as those found in arithmetic and reading. This topic will be discussed in greater detail later.

determines what the schools should teach, it becomes the course of study and deprives the school of its right to develop its own objectives and to set priorities among them. No test is a substitute for reason and cannot determine what any given school ought to teach. Considering the fact that the content on standardized achievement tests are derived from surveys of current practices, little change in the educational enterprise could be expected if districts simply taught what was "on the test." The authors and publishers of standardized tests have the obligation to keep abreast of current educational practices and to be cognizant of contemplated changes in the curriculum that require the development of new or revised instruments.

It is true, as Skager has stated, that, "One would hardly examine the Cooperative Reading Test . . . to identify specific skills which might become objectives guiding curriculum development." It is not only true, but one might add that it is fortunate as well. The schools have no obligation to follow the dictates of test publishers or to teach some skills simply because a majority of schools or all schools have done so in the past. If districts propose radical departures from their "traditional" curriculum, the community and state will become the final adjudicating agencies. If teachers and administrators want to modify teaching methods, standardized tests can help measure the effects of these modifications either in relationship to previously obtained test scores in that district or in combination with a different standardized test that more adequately measures the objectives of the new program.

3. *"Standardized tests often require skills or aptitudes that may be influenced to only a limited degree by experiences in the classroom."* Perhaps one might ask whether a standardized achievement test should be sensitive to a specific mode of instruction when its purpose is to measure concepts, principles, and processes common to most if not all curricula. Teacher-made tests can effectively measure the content or effectiveness of a specific lesson.

A second consideration is that all schools devote more time to teaching than to testing. Some activities that go on in a classroom will not be measured by any test; those skills that are deliberately taught are often measured informally (such as by the oral tests). But no matter what skill or knowledge is measured, neither norm-referenced tests nor criterion-referenced tests will reflect instructional

outcomes uninfluenced by aptitude or other skills acquired independently of a given instructional sequence. But it is probably true that teacher-made tests, whether norm-referenced or criterion-referenced, reflect the specific instructional goals of the teacher to a greater extent than do standardized tests. Rather than this being a disadvantage of standardized tests, it merely points out the complementary relationship of both.

4. *"Standardized tests do not indicate the extent to which individuals or groups of students have mastered the spectrum of instructional objectives."* Most manuals that accompany standardized tests warn the user against interpreting raw scores which are usually described as being meaningless or misleading. But they are meaningless only if the attempt is made to compare scores on one subtest with those on another or to compare scores on different tests. Differences in means and standard deviations do make such raw score comparisons unintelligible, but they may be equally uninterpretable on criterion-referenced tests. One advantage to having external norms on a standardized battery of tests is that it allows meaningful comparisons from subtest to subtest should that be desired.

The purpose of criterion-referenced measurement is not to compare one class with another or to compare scores on different tests. Rather, each test is constructed according to rules to yield an independent measure of some specified behavior. The test is constructed to be a stratified-random or random sample from a clearly defined behavioral domain; the student's performance on the test is measured against an explicit level of expected or required performance. Instead of reporting that a student is at the 85th percentile on a particular test in comparison with an external norm group, a criterion-referenced measurement would state what the student can do and what he cannot do.

Whether in fact standardized tests fail to "indicate the extent to which individuals or groups of students have mastered the spectrum of instructional objectives," depends partly on what is meant by a "spectrum of instructional objectives." On criterion-referenced tests, that "spectrum" ideally would refer to a hypothetical universe of tasks that completely describes all elements of the domain as specified by the objectives as well as by the procedures used to generate items. What happens in practice is that either the universe of possible tasks is so narrowly defined and delimited in scope that many other

important behaviors are unmeasured or the universe is so broadly defined that each behavior can be measured by only a few items.

If the hypothetical universe of possible tasks requires the construction of complex items (that is, those that cannot be generated according to explicit rules such as those used to program a computer), the correspondence of items with the hypothetical universe is suspect. Any "score" obtained by a student on the test is most unlikely to reflect equal performance in the universe. And, after all, that is the purpose of criterion-referenced measurement.

This dilemma need not force the teacher into deciding whether it is better to construct items from a highly restricted domain to yield generalizable information regarding student performance in that domain or to construct items that can measure more complex behaviors but which will yield less information regarding performance in those domains. The position taken here is that standardized tests are highly effective, identifying student deficiencies in a relatively broad range of different domains; criterion-referenced tests, in contrast, are more useful for determining proficiency in a rather narrow spectrum of behaviors.

Perhaps one other point should be clarified. The prespecified standards of proficiency required of students on criterion-referenced tests are not only arbitrary at any given level of instruction, but they are often meaningless, unrelated to the purposes of criterion-referencing, and potentially hazardous to students as well. On most criterion-referenced tests, the prespecified standards (such as 90 percent or 100 percent) are entirely arbitrary and not necessarily compatible for all purposes or for all students. If the domain is hierarchically arranged and the attainment of one skill is prerequisite to other, more complex and essential skills, the teacher's goal should always be 100 percent mastery and maximum enjoyment for all students. If the domain is largely unsequenced, the teacher can as easily establish one criterion as another with equally meaningless "justification."

A prespecified standard is psychometrically meaningless except under highly unusual circumstances. A "mastery level of 90 percent" does not necessarily refer to the percentage of elements in the population of behaviors in which the student is proficient. To make that type of inference requires a random or stratified-random sampling plan that will generate items according to rigidly enforced rules. As noted previously, this is usually possible only in limited areas of the

curriculum. If the domain is broad and complex, subjective judgments are likely to enter into the item writing or selection procedures. If that happens, then "90 percent" or any other percentage would have no more meaning on a "criterion-referenced" test than on a standardized or norm-referenced test. The fact that a "standard" has been set does not differentiate criterion-referenced from norm-referenced tests.

The establishment of any criterion or mastery score carries with it an obligation to differentially treat students so that all will be able to reach that level with a minimum of frustration and anxiety. When students fail to reach an arbitrary criterion it is just as indefensible to require that they continuously repeat the same ineffective instruction as it would be to assign a letter grade and do nothing about the quality of instruction. Too many schools have embarked on mastery programs without realizing that such programs assume the availability of a wide range of instructional alternatives to help students attain proficiency.

5. *"The use of standardized achievement tests in the sociopolitical context of 'evaluation' and 'accountability' has and will lead to corruption and dishonesty among educational professionals and to the further erosion of public trust in the schools and the people who run them."* This accusation is more properly a reflection on the honesty and moral turpitude of educational professionals than it is a criticism of standardized tests. Any test, including those that are criterion-referenced, can be improperly and even dishonestly used. When teachers, administrators, or performance contractors are required to meet unreasonable goals or suffer serious consequences, the probability that tests will be misused increases.

This problem will not be resolved by using criterion-referenced tests, no matter how many alternate forms can be generated and kept under secure conditions. Many standardized test batteries have from two to five alternate forms at each grade level, and some even have a "secure" form. But all of these precautions cannot provide any absolute assurance that tests will be used properly.

The purpose of testing is probably a much greater determiner of the likelihood of improper test utilization than whether tests are norm referenced or criterion referenced. Students and teachers exhibit little anxiety if interest inventories are administered to help students better understand their preference for one activity over anoth-

er or if the purpose is to diagnose and remedy a problem. But if the same instrument is used for selecting some students into specialized curricula and denying entrance to others, the anxiety level and the probability of cheating are greatly increased. The dishonesty occurs because punitive decisions are made that are based on the performance of students on tests and not because "standardized achievement tests . . . lead to corruption and dishonesty."

Neither standardized tests nor criterion-referenced tests require justification for their use. Because standardized tests are the major concern in this chapter, only a brief summary of the major uses of criterion-referenced tests can be provided. They are particularly useful in subject areas that are cumulative and progressively more complex, where students might have to reach a high level of proficiency on preceding tasks before being advanced to a higher level. In courses such as mathematics, foreign languages, and reading there is a progression in the sequencing through which students must pass. A student who has not learned the meaning of whole numbers should probably not be taught to work with fractions; the child who is about to learn that a period is placed at the end of a sentence must know what a sentence is. In these examples criterion-referenced measurement provides information about whether or not minimal levels of competence have been reached.

In subject areas that demand competence, criterion-referenced tests can also be of great value. Performing surgery, for example, requires a degree of proficiency and probably should not be entrusted to those who do not meet minimum standards. Auto drivers, airplane pilots, dentists, lawyers, and accountants must demonstrate some stated minimal level of proficiency by passing a licensing examination before being allowed to practice. Here again, interest is not so much in comparing one person against another as in making sure that those who are certified or licensed are capable of performing at a high level. And, in diagnostic work, criterion-referenced feedback can inform the teacher about those particular skills in which the student has demonstrated proficiency and about those in which he needs more assistance. Receiving a C grade in reciting the letters of the alphabet is not as useful in helping the child as knowing that he could only recognize the letters from A to G.

Norm-referenced tests are especially useful in situations where the subject matter is not cumulative and the student does not need to

reach some specified level of competency. The social studies curriculum, for example, is usually not highly sequenced, and it is possible to skip some courses altogether and still do well in a more "advanced" class. In such courses, feedback regarding student performance should be norm referenced since no one defensible criterion exists.

If the objectives are cognitively complex, there may be no source available from which to randomly select items that represent a given domain. It is not by accident that most criterion-referenced tests are restricted to arithmetic and the more elementary skills required in learning to read. The advantage of norm-referencing is that items can be generated to form a universe of tasks or skills demonstrably relevant to the purpose that the test will serve.

If the purpose of testing is for selection, norm-referenced tests can be used to measure individual differences. For example, a university may be forced to accept only the highest-scoring 5 percent of the students from a given high school. Norm-referencing would be important in this case to ensure that the test is particularly capable of discriminating among high-scoring applicants.

Criterion-referenced tests, on the other hand, are not particularly useful if many domains need to be sampled. The measurement of a domain is subject to a large amount of error unless there are enough items administered to students to adequately "represent" that domain. What constitutes "enough" is debatable, but ten items is probably a reasonable minimum. To measure student achievement in most areas of the curriculum with criterion-referenced tests would require more time than most schools would be willing to give.

THE PURPOSES OF EVALUATION IN EDUCATION

Standardized tests are administered with the expectation that measurements derived from them will be helpful in making better decisions than could be made without them. Although every decision involves the element of risk, not all risks lead to serious consequences. Because standardized tests are relatively expensive to purchase, administer, score, and interpret, they derive their greatest benefit when the decision to be made is important and when information is not readily available from other, less expensive sources.

The extent to which tests minimize risk and increase the probabil-

ity of effective decisions is a function of the amount of dependable knowledge the test provides beyond that which is already known. Using a test implies that there is a relationship between the measurements or scores derived from tests and the ability to make effective decisions. Having students take a spelling test presumes a relationship between the students' scores and the decision, for example, to recommend remedial work, additional exercises, or a revision of the curriculum. The use of standardized tests to aid in making effective decisions presumes that measurements derived from those tests can predict a more effective course of action than would be possible without them.

Selection

Standardized tests may be used to help decide who will be accepted or rejected by an institution. Selection decisions demand of tests the ability to predict success and failure with minimum risks both to the institution and to the individuals involved. The risks can be twofold: admitting individuals who later are not successful or failing to admit those who would have been successful. The ideal selection test would admit only those persons who would subsequently prove to be successful while rejecting all applicants who would prove to be unsuccessful. Unfortunately, tests are fallible *predictors* of success, and all selection decisions involve the risks described.

Selection tests are widely used by industry and by colleges and universities, but not ordinarily by the public schools except in counseling students uncertain about their ability to pursue advanced training. For example, high school students are often concerned about their ability to succeed in college, and many are uncertain about their interests in different subjects. Selection decisions are involved even at the prekindergarten level, when many parents insist that their three-year-old children are perfectly able to do first-grade work. Because the usual criterion for admission to kindergarten or the first grade is some minimum chronological age, however, some students who might benefit from attending school earlier if other criteria— "emotional maturity" and scholastic aptitude—were used instead are denied admission. Chronological age is no better predictor for success among less able students than among those preparing to enter school.

The *composite method* and the *cutoff method* are most often used in making selection decisions. A composite selection strategy means

that scores from a number of tests are combined to maximize their correlation with a *criterion*. The test scores are combined by assigning weights that maximize the contribution of each score in predicting the criterion. The procedures for assigning weights are beyond the scope of this paper,[4] but the rationale is straightforward. Tests are included to measure different aspects of the criterion. A battery predicting teaching aptitude, for example, might include tests that measure skills in interpersonal relations, job-related knowledge, intelligence, and other factors hypothesized to correlate with teaching success. Concomitantly, tests that correlate with each other are excluded to prevent duplication. The regression formulas used to assign these weights maximize the correlation between the composite test scores and the criterion measures. Typically, including more than three or four predictors in a battery yields negligible gains in prediction.

If the composite method is used for selection, each individual is given a single value that represents a weighted composite score from all measures included in the battery. These scores are then ranked, and as many individuals as are needed or as can be accommodated are selected.[5]

With the cutoff method, scores for each individual are kept separate for each subtest that correlates with the criterion. Minimum passing scores are determined for each predictor test. Only individuals who pass every test, no matter what their total score is, are eligible for selection.

The decision to use one method of selection over another depends on a number of factors. Less effort and mathematical sophistication is required by the cutoff method. This method assumes, however, that an individual who fails one subtest will not be successful, no matter how well he performs on the remaining subtests. Compensatory behavior is disregarded. This might be justifiable for commercial airline pilots who must have good vision, be relatively immune to air sickness, have good spatial abilities, and be able to fly a plane. A

4. Virtually all statistics texts describe the regression and multiple regression formulas needed for this purpose.

5. The Equal Employment Opportunity Commission (EEOC) and the United States Supreme Court (*Griggs et al.* vs. *Duke Power Company*, March 8, 1971) require the use of selection tests that are demonstrably related to job performance. Factorially pure tests are best suited for this purpose.

serious deficiency in any one of these characteristics should justify the elimination of that person as a pilot.

For many other purposes, however, it is possible to compensate for a deficiency on one subtest by proficiency on another. A school might hire a teacher who is known to encourage lively discussions among students, even though his relationship with his peers might leave something to be desired. If the composite method is used for selection, an individual can be selected if he can compensate for low scores on some variables by high scores on others.

What constitutes minimum performance on an examination is largely a matter of judgment and practical consideration. If the number of applicants is small relative to the number needed, it may be possible to take everyone who applies. If there is a large supply of individuals, a college or employer can afford to be more selective.

The cutoff score is also affected by political, ethical, and social considerations. Setting a high cutting score for admission to a state university might eliminate those most likely to fail and could, therefore, reduce public expenditures for higher education. This monetary saving would, however, be achieved at social cost to the state, at a time when social equality is a major national goal.

Advocates of low cutoff scores propose that everyone should have a chance to succeed regardless of test performance. Since tests are fallible, a low cutoff score would give most individuals the opportunity to surpass their predicted behavior. But this gain for a few individuals must be weighed against the probability that more students will eventually fail.

The effectiveness of a test to predict or distinguish between successful and unsuccessful applicants depends upon the correlation of the test scores with the criterion measure. Predictive and concurrent validity coefficients are useful in describing how well the test scores can predict or can correlate with recently obtained criterion measures. The simplest interpretation of such a correlation can be made by squaring it to yield a coefficient of determination. For example, if scores from an intelligence test administered to high school seniors correlated .50 with their freshmen college grades (this would be a predictive validity coefficient), the coefficient of determination would be $.50^2$ or .25. The coefficient, .25, refers to the proportion of factors that are being measured in common by the intelligence test and by freshmen grades. If the correlation were only .30, the coeffi-

cient of determination would be .09; when a correlation is perfect (1.0), then the two variables being correlated measure exactly the same factors. This might occur, for example, if one should measure height in meters and also in inches.

The correlation between a predictor and a criterion provides a meaningful and useful description of the relationship between the two variables. After all, if there is no relationship, the best one can do is to assign the mean or average value of the criterion measure to everyone, but when the correlation is zero, the predictor test serves no purpose and a more effective one would have to be found. The manual accompanying the standardized test should contain not only the correlations between it and various criteria, but it should also describe in some detail the nature of the group taking the test and the manner in which grades were assigned. This is important because the validity coefficient presented in a manual was obtained under a specific set of circumstances with a specific group of students. Whether the same coefficient would be obtained in a different situation or with a different group of students is an empirical question that the evaluator will have to determine for himself.

Perhaps the simplest and most effective way to evaluate the consequences of a selection strategy is to use an *expectancy table* (see Figure 5-1). These tables show the relationship between scores on a predictor test (or on a composite of predictor tests) and the criterion (for example, subsequent grades obtained by students). In this example, grade-point averages above 2.0 are passing grades; those below

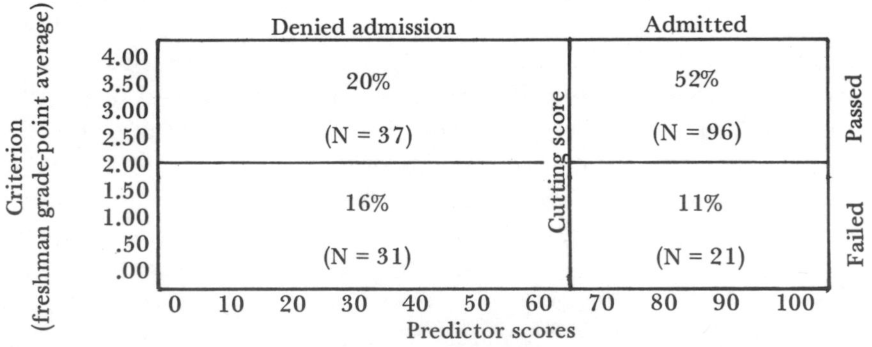

Figure 5-1
Expectancy table relating high school predictor scores
to freshman college grade-point average

2.0 represent failing grades. The total group includes 185 students; 133 of them received passing grades (37+96), and 52 received failing grades (31+21). Of all 185 students admitted, 133 were successful (about 72 percent), and 28 percent failed. If all students with predictor scores of 65 and higher were admitted, 117 students (96+21) would have been admitted, and 96 would have been successful. The ratio of 96 to 117 represents the percentage of successful students admitted and is called the *success ratio*. In Figure 5-1, the success ratio is 96/117 or 82 percent (rounded). The proportion of students accepted is called the *selection ratio*.

The selection strategy that maximizes the success ratio requires that the cutting score (now set at 65 points) be increased. If moved far enough to the right, there is likely to be a point where every student admitted would receive a passing grade, but such a high success ratio would result in selecting fewer students. As the cutting score is lowered, the selection ratio is increased and more applicants will be accepted, but of course a greater number will be expected to fail.

Sometimes the effectiveness of a program is evaluated by comparing the percentage of students who were successful prior to the introduction of an experimental treatment with the percentage after the treatment has been introduced. If the program is effective, the percentage of students who are successful would be expected to increase. It is important to remember that the success ratio can almost always be increased by raising admission requirements, thereby lowering the selection ratio. Instead of attributing a higher success ratio to the effectiveness of some curriculum innovation at the high school level, it may simply be that the college or university raised its standards for entrance.

There are decided advantages to having external norms on tests used for selection. Without external norms it would still be possible to rank each of the applicants on the admissions test and to select the largest number of the highest-scoring persons who could be accepted. If the institution must accept some minimum number of applicants, this procedure will be satisfactory; it may not be adequate, however, if some minimum standard is required for entrance. In that case the highest-scoring person might not be qualified, and some minimum percentile or standard score could be established in relation to previous groups of individuals who were judged to be satisfactory "on the job." The test manual should describe the norm group

clearly enough so that the evaluator knows if students are being compared against other applicants, against a group who were admitted and were all successful, or against a heterogeneous group who demonstrated varying degrees of success. It may be quite satisfactory to be at the 50th percentile compared with a highly successful group; it is quite another matter to be at the 50th percentile in comparison to applicants who later failed the program. The difference is between being an average success, or an average failure.

Criteria, like predictors, are fallible measurements. Whether they are grade-point averages, teacher ratings, or the number of problems solved correctly, they are all subject to random errors or errors of measurement. A student who solves fifty problems correctly today may or may not do as well tomorrow. Because errors of measurement are due to chance conditions, they are as likely to overestimate as they are to underestimate a student's true score,[6] whether on the predictor, the criterion, or both. If the "score" of each student was determined by randomly selecting a number from a hat, chance alone would account for that "score," and the true score would be zero. Any variable that is then correlated against these randomly selected values would result in correlations of zero since the two variables are related only by chance.

If errors of measurement could be eliminated, the resulting correlations would be between true scores. Errors of measurement attenuate, or lower, correlation coefficients. Although criteria themselves are fallible, they should be standards of excellence against which predictor measures are evaluated. Scores on a predictor test may appear to be invalid (that is, they fail to correlate with the criterion) when in fact the criterion is unreliable because it is highly affected by these random errors of measurement. Fortunately, it is possible through statistical techniques to estimate the correlation between the fallible predictor scores with a criterion that is made perfectly reliable. This technique, known as correction for attenuation, can be used to eliminate the effects of random error in the predictor, the criterion, or both.

6. A true score is the difference between the score an individual received and that portion of his score affected by random or chance errors of measurement; it is also defined as the individual's hypothetical mean score on an infinite number of repeated tests that are uninfluenced by practice effects or memory of previous performance. A true score is a theoretical construct.

When tests are used for making selection decisions, a high correlation of the predictor with the criterion is necessary. But when both the predictor and the criterion are corrected for attenuation, the random errors of measurement that are always found in practice are eliminated statistically, and the correlation between predictor and criterion (the predictive validity coefficient) is at its theoretical maximum value.

In reporting validity coefficients, it is important to distinguish between uncorrected and corrected values. The uncorrected coefficients are always empirically determined by correlating a fallible predictor (or combination of predictors) with a fallible criterion. Hence, both contain errors of measurement. In practice, a predictor is not free of error, and its lack of reliability should be reflected in a lowered validity coefficient. Criteria, on the other hand, should be perfectly reliable. When a predictive validity coefficient is low, it could mean that the predictor is unreliable, the criterion is unreliable, both are unreliable, or both are reliable but unrelated to one another. The solution for the first alternative is to improve the reliability of the predictor by adding more items to the test, making a "hard" test easier to reduce the effects of guessing, or replacing the test with a more reliable one. If the criterion is unreliable, it may be possible to improve it by the same procedures, but, if this is not possible, there is considerable doubt whether the measure should be considered a criterion. Should the fourth possibility present itself, a different predictor is needed.

Placement

Once an individual has been selected, he must be placed in a program where he is most likely to be successful. In the public schools, placement decisions determine what curriculum a student will pursue, what reading group he will be assigned to, and which special classes (remedial or advanced) he will take. The placement decision involves both prediction (success) and the risk that predictions will lead to incorrect placements.

A test may be useful for selection but not for placement. A test of general academic aptitude (for example, an intelligence test), may be able to predict who will succeed in college but may not be able to place the student into the best curriculum. The teacher, counselor, or admissions officer usually has many more options for placement than for selection.

The ideal placement test predicts success in one program and discourages or rejects placement in another. Again, as with any decision, risk is involved. The risk becomes greater as placement tests assign individuals incorrectly or as individuals with varying degrees of success in a given program all attain the same predictor test score.

Placement decisions are of two types. The first, which may be called *vertical placement,* is required when it is necessary to estimate the grade level at which the child is best able to function. This might occur, for example, if the child is being placed into a higher or lower grade level than that suggested by his chronological age, or if a child new to the school district transferred from a nongraded program. A second type of placement decision, called *horizontal placement,* is used whenever the student is faced with alternative programs, courses, or curricula, and a choice must be made among them.

Whether to place one child in an advanced class and another child in a program especially designed for slow-learning children can be extremely difficult decisions. Not only are the results of standardized tests taken into account, but numerous subjective factors also enter into the decision. In some states, placement into special classes for the retarded requires evidence from individually administered intelligence tests, along with evidence that the child is not capable of performing in the regular academic program. Typically the school psychologist looks for depressed scores on all, or at least on most, achievement and aptitude subtests. Other conditions being equal, a child is a candidate for special class placement when both the verbal and performance subtests of individually administered intelligence tests are low and when achievement test scores are significantly below his actual grade level.[7]

Although it is not always important that both intelligence and achievement tests be used prior to placing a child in a class for the retarded, it is important that any test be administered individually. The Peabody Individual Achievement Test, for example, could be used to determine which children are in need of special class placement as long as they had been attending school regularly but were not learning at the same rate as most of their classmates or members of the norm group. An individually administered intelligence test

7. If the special class is designed to remedy a specific learning disability, a diagnostic strategy is needed. This will be described in the section on "Diagnosis and Remediation."

would be given to substantiate scores on the achievement measure. This would be particularly important for young children whose test scores tend to be unreliable. The need for individually administered tests is to reduce or eliminate the effects of reading that are present with most group tests as well as to provide the individual motivation and encouragement that younger children may need.

An intelligence test should be administered along with achievement measures if the child's attendance pattern has been irregular. Most achievement tests are constructed to measure subject matter content and skills typically taught at the same grade levels in the majority of schools. Low scores on such tests could mean that the child was not exposed to the same school-related activities as most other children. Conditions that might prevent a child from learning necessary basic skills could include a history of illness or a family pattern of frequent moves. Under such conditions, an intelligence test might be of some advantage because it is less dependent on specific skills learned in school. A relatively high score on an intelligence test coupled with uniformly low scores on the various subtests of an achievement battery often results from atypical attendance patterns. It is not being suggested in any way that intelligence tests are measures of "capacity" or that achievement tests are necessarily independent of heredity. But disregarding errors of measurement, a relatively high score on any subtest of an intelligence or achievement battery means that the child did learn the skills measured by that subtest. The failure to learn other skills measured by those tests is best explained as instructional failure or lack of opportunity rather than any inherent inability to learn.

Special programs designed for gifted children also employ standardized achievement and intelligence test scores for placement purposes. If the program can only accommodate a few children, it will be necessary to select tests yielding sufficiently high score limits capable of making reliable discriminations at the upper end of the distribution. Stanines, for example, may be much too crude for this purpose since a stanine of 9 would be attained by the highest scoring 4 percent of students.[8] Similarly, percentile norms are relatively in-

8. Converting scores to stanines normalizes the distribution whatever its original shape. A normal distribution has no theoretical limits. Stanines 1 and 9, therefore, extend infinitely and there could be quite a difference between the performance of students who are both in stanine 9, for example.

sensitive at the two extremes of the distribution. A more accurate picture of the relative proficiencies of students being considered for a gifted program would be to administer the highest level form of the test capable of making reliable discriminations among students. The students with the highest raw scores would then be placed in the special program.

Vertical placement is also important when children are being considered to "skip" one or more grade levels. For this purpose, an individually administered test is usually recommended—not so much to determine the level of the child's proficiency, although that is important, but to evaluate his potential to handle frustration at a given grade level. For example, a third-grade child might be perfectly capable of doing highly satisfactory work if he were accelerated in school one or two years. On an individual intelligence test such as the Stanford-Binet, it would be possible to observe the child's anxiety or frustration as he attempts items designed for average children one or more years older than he. The optimum level of placement for the child would be at the grade level where he is at least average in comparison to others at that grade level and where he demonstrates few if any signs of anxiety or frustration.

Many new or innovative curriculum programs have eliminated the traditional grade levels based on the child's chronological age. In some of these programs, children are given a great deal of freedom to choose different learning units; in others, there may be less freedom of choice. As long as the child stays within the same school system, there may be few problems transferring from one school to another. But at what grade level should the child be placed if he transfers to a more traditional district? For this purpose, the median grade equivalent attained by the child on the various subtests included on a standardized achievement test battery can be used as a realistic estimate of his current level of performance.

Horizontal placement involves the determination of which of several programs the student should pursue. At the high school level, for example, students often have to select among various curricula such as those that are college preparatory, secretarial-clerical, industrial-technical, and so forth. The decision to select or "major" in one program rather than another is an example of horizontal placement.

Tests used for horizontal placement are most effective if they correlate low with one another and high with the criterion. This is essen-

tially the same procedure used in making selection decisions using the composite method; the major difference is that placement decisions offer a number of criteria whereas selection involves only a dichotomous "admit-deny" judgment. As the number of alternatives increases, placement decisions become more difficult—especially if the skills required in different programs are similar.

The most effective placement decisions are usually made when scores are available from a number of different standardized tests. If the student reports that he is completely uncertain about the type of career or program to pursue, an aptitude battery (such as the Differential Aptitude Tests) can be used to point out his relative strengths on such subtests as verbal reasoning, numerical ability, mechanical reasoning, spelling, language usage, abstract reasoning, clerical speed and accuracy, and space relations; an interest inventory (such as the Kuder General Interest Survey) could also be recommended to measure his relative level of interests in broad areas (such as outdoor, mechanical, scientific, computational, persuasive, artistic, literary, musical, social service, and clerical).

The advantage of using an aptitude *battery* is that all subtests are normed on the same population of individuals. This makes it possible to compare the student's performance on each subtest against the same group of individuals. If he performs at the 95th percentile on one subtest but only at the 40th percentile on another, it is possible to compare these scores since the norms were derived from the same population of individuals.

Because scores on interest scales correlate only moderately with scores on aptitude tests, they can provide additional information in helping the student make the most effective placement decision. Some characteristics of interest inventory scales, however, make it impossible to determine the intensity of interests among different persons. For example, if two students are asked to rank their interest on different activities (the highest interest being given a 1, the next highest a 2, and so on), a rank of 1 assigned by the students on any activity does not mean equally strong interests. This is analogous to ranking students according to height and then trying to determine how much taller one student is in comparison with another.

Another difficulty in interpreting interest inventory scores arises if percentile norms are used. Persons who receive high percentiles have selected a preference for one activity to a greater extent than have

members of the norm group. If members of the norm group generally dislike clerical work, for example, an individual who scores at the 99th percentile in clerical interest would be at the top of a largely disinterested group.

In using interest measures for placement purposes, distinctions should be made between expressed, manifest, inventoried, and tested interests (Super and Crites, 1962). An expressed interest is one in which the student expresses, in writing or orally, a preference or a dislike for various activities; manifest interests are determined by examining those activities in which the student voluntarily engages; inventoried interests are measured by scores on scales that compare the student's interests in one activity in comparison to others; tested interests are measured by cognitive items that require the student to demonstrate his knowledge, for example, of vocabulary related to human relations, commerce, government, the physical sciences, and so on. The assumption is made that students having a relatively high interest in some activity are familiar with the vocabulary related to that activity.

As far as placement is concerned, there is no necessary correspondence among the four ways of measuring interest. An expressed interest, even if given candidly, might not agree with the limited number of scales on an inventory or test. Similarly, the behaviors in which an individual engages (or in which he does not engage) need not necessarily imply interest or dislike.

The use of both interest and aptitude measures for placement decisions is necessitated by the low to moderate correlations between the two, their correlations with various criteria, and the nature of these criteria. When a student states he is interested in medicine as a career, it is all too easy to confuse an *area of interest* with a *level of proficiency*. Medicine is an area that allows for many different levels of ability from those that require specialized degrees to those that require virtually no training. Some areas of interest differentiate among levels of proficiency by the use of titles such as physician, registered nurse, laboratory technician, and orderly. Some interest inventories only describe areas of interest (such as the Kuder General Interest Survey), while others (such as the Strong Vocational Interest Blank) compare the individual's responses with men or women who are successful in specific occupations. A student with a high score on the physician scale only means that he displays the same pattern of inter-

ests (reads the same magazines, enjoys the same school subjects, and so forth) as do successful physicians. Although interest is necessary to help students make effective placement decisions, it alone is not sufficient. They also need the knowledge, skills, and proficiencies required for a particular program. Aptitude and achievement measures can be used for this purpose.

The title of a scale may be highly deceptive when interpreting normative data. For example, the "farmer" scale on the Strong Vocational Interest Blank was normed largely on a group of graduates from agricultural colleges; on the Kuder General Interest Survey, only half the men in the norm group had completed college programs. Obviously, a scale derives normative meaning by providing knowledge of the background and training of those who are in the standardization group. The evaluator has to know what these characteristics are so as not to misinterpret the meaning of any given scale.

Other kinds of tests and inventories can help to make effective placement decisions. Many personality inventories contain subtest scores that are useful in this regard. A quiet, reserved, and introverted individual is likely to find some programs more to his liking than others. More extroverted students may prefer activities in which they can be surrounded by many people. Certain phobias might limit the choices available to the student.

All of these various tests and inventories yield information that can help evaluate the advantages and disadvantages different programs offer the students. As previously noted, placement decisions require independent predictor tests and subtests (that is, low intercorrelations) and high correlations with success in one program but low or negative correlations with success in another. For example, the Differential Aptitude Tests provides information regarding the intercorrelations on the eight subtests. These intercorrelations range from .16 (Clerical Speed and Accuracy and Mechanical Reasoning) to .74 (Verbal Reasoning and Grammar).[9] The median battery intercorrelation is .54. The Clerical Speed and Accuracy subtest, which correlates low with all other subtests, meets the criterion of independence. But, unfortunately, it does not meet the second requirement—the ability to differentiate among programs. For example, one might

9. The 1973 revision of the DAT has substituted a Language Usage subtest for Grammar.

expect clerks to obtain high scores on Clerical Speed and Accuracy, but they perform no better on this subtest than do other workers. It would not be too useful, therefore, in placing clerks or clerical workers.

The manual for the Differential Aptitude Tests is unusually complete in reporting validity studies. Perhaps the most important finding is that the composite of the Verbal Reasoning and Numerical Ability subtests is best able to predict course grades in virtually all subjects in the curriculum. Even in the so-called nonacademic courses, the Verbal Reasoning and Numerical Ability combination is the best predictor of course grades. In art, for example, the highest predictive validity coefficient for Verbal Reasoning + Numerical Ability was .62; the next best predictor for art was Abstract Reasoning.

Because verbal and number ability are measured by most intelligence tests, it apparently makes little difference which type of test is used. Virtually all programs and courses of students are dependent upon verbal and numerical skills. For vertical placement, either aptitude or intelligence tests could be used (along with measures of achievement).

The effectiveness of horizontally placing individuals with the same level of overall ability into different programs will not be improved by using aptitude or intelligence tests unless a battery of factorially pure subtests can be found or developed that is empirically capable of differential placement.[10] Even without that aptitude battery, however, the evaluation can still benefit from the use of various interest and personality inventories and from consideration of those economic and social factors that may affect the student's chances for success.

Diagnosis and Remediation

A test used to determine a student's strengths and weaknesses in order to improve performance serves a diagnostic function. Before

10. Many test batteries claim differential placement properties, but few provide "hard" evidence to support their assertions. It is one thing to speculate on relationships but quite a different thing to verify empirically that successful completion of one program requires high scores on tests A, B, and C but low scores on tests D, E, and F and that a different pattern is required in an alternative program.

teachers or counselors can recommend a remedial program, they need to know in what specific topics an individual is having difficulty. The type of decision made on the basis of test results differs for diagnosis, selection, and placement. In diagnostic testing, the individual usually has already been selected into a school or industrial setting. The type of program that will be recommended to him is a matter of placement. In neither selection nor placement does the school necessarily provide remedial services.

The use of tests for placement and for remedial decisions overlaps to some degree, however. As a result of diagnostic testing, for example, the teacher may recommend that the child be placed in an easier or more advanced reading group or in a different program entirely. Some diagnoses suggest continuing a current program or proposing some other treatment not involving placement, such as hiring a tutor or using a simpler textbook.

Diagnosing a problem is prerequisite to its treatment. Diagnosis serves no end in itself, but it is needed if reasonable treatment decisions are to be made. The teacher will be better able to recommend specific types of remediation if he knows the specific skills in which the child is deficient.

Diagnostic tests can be used in different ways. First, they can help identify which students have problems. Since students can have numerous problems, tests can usually contain only a limited number of items designed to measure each of the most likely sources of difficulty. For example, the Sequential Tests of Educational Progress (STEP) consists of six subtests: Reading Comprehension, Writing, Mathematics, Science, Social Studies, and Listening Comprehension. Students with low scores on any of these subtests can be identified as having a problem, but the specific nature of that problem is not likely to be discovered without further diagnostic testing. The subtest scores on most standardized achievement batteries can be used for *screening* or identifying general areas of weakness.

Suppose the teacher has been able to identify a student as being weak in mathematics. He might next administer the Stanford Diagnostic Arithmetic Test (Level II) which measures Concepts (number systems and operations), Computation (addition, subtraction, multiplication, and division), Common Fractions (understanding and computation), Decimal Fractions and Percent, and Number Facts (addi-

tion, subtraction, multiplication, division, and carrying). The administration of this test requires seven testing periods, each taking fifteen to fifty-three minutes, making it impractical to administer the entire battery to all students without first identifying those who need this much testing.

The two most important criteria for diagnostic tests are highly specific objectives and a relatively large number of items measuring each objective. Specific objectives are needed to define the knowledge, skills, and proficiencies required to perform more complex tasks such as reading and arithmetic. The large number of items (perhaps ten to twenty for each objective) is required to adequately sample the child's performance on any given objective. The failure to respond correctly on a single item does not necessarily mean that the child is deficient or weak on the objective measured by that item; he might have misunderstood the directions, accidentally marked the answer sheet incorrectly, or simply been unable to answer that particular item. Similarly, a student might respond correctly to a single item but not be able to perform equally well if a larger sample of items were presented.

It would certainly be possible and advantageous to use criterion-referenced tests for diagnostic purposes. Specific objectives and a reasonable number of items for each are exactly the same criteria desired for criterion-referenced measurement. But criterion-referenced tests might be less efficient for screening since too many tests and items would be involved.

Sometimes it is argued that standardized tests fail to describe the explicit nature of the domain being measured. Such terms as "Language" or "Reading Comprehension" are too broad for diagnostic purposes (except perhaps for rough screening). If subtests are described more explicitly (for example, addition of fractions, use of commas), no norms are usually provided. This general practice discourages test users from making unwarranted claims based on a limited sampling of items; it no doubt also saves the test publishers the embarrassment of having to print low reliability coefficients that might discourage potential test purchasers. Nonetheless, there are advantages in providing norms for more discrete portions of subtests, including the individual item response norms. Although a student's response to any given item is likely to be unreliable, there is no good

reason why test publishers should not report item reliabilities and their errors of measurement.[11] A perfectly reliable item (that is, one that correlates 1.0 with a parallel or equivalent item) would measure its domain without error. A student responding correctly to that item would also respond correctly to other perfectly parallel items. But as the reliability of a single item decreases, errors of measurement increase (assuming item difficulty remains constant). In that case, either more items will have to be administered or the tentative nature of the student's performance must be kept in mind.

Because diagnostic testing is usually concerned with the performance of students who are failing to make normal progress, the teacher requires an operational definition of such terms as *weak, normal,* and *proficient.* On criterion-referenced tests, a distinction is usually made only between mastery and nonmastery. The level established for proficiency may or may not take errors of measurement into account, but, even if they did, the cutoff point is usually decided by fiat or by arbitrary consensus. If the skill is so basic that 100 percent mastery is required of everyone, it would be meaningful to establish that high a level of proficiency, but, when testing is for diagnosis and remediation, those students in greatest need of assistance will be unlikely to attain that level of proficiency. The teacher has the option of lowering standards or of devoting even greater effort, time, and expense with no assurance that all students will be able to reach 100 percent mastery within reasonable time constraints and without producing undesirable anxiety. In those areas of the curriculum that do not suggest any predetermined level of competence, there is no reason for not using the norms on standardized tests to indicate to teachers the kinds of skills and knowledge that average children are able to perform at different age or grade levels. This in no way violates the previously described position that standardized tests that meet the objectives of a school or district should be selected and that it is inappropriate to develop a curriculum by surveying the content found on standardized tests. But when a student misses four out of eight items

11. For the usual test that has more than one item, the standard error of measurement is $s\sqrt{1 - \text{reliability}}$ where s is the standard deviation of the distribution of scores. The standard deviation of an item is $\sqrt{pq}$ where p is the proportion of individuals who responded correctly and q is the proportion responding incorrectly. If $\sqrt{pq}$ is substituted for s, the standard error of measurement would be $\sqrt{pq}\,(1-r)$, and p is an estimate of item difficulty.

on a given subtest, the adequacy of his performance has to be compared against some criterion. If mastery is required at 100 percent, any lower performance will not do, but if a score of four corresponds to the 80th percentile on a national sample of his peers, the teacher can reasonably believe that remediation in that particular skill is not required.

For diagnostic purposes, both external and internal norms can help provide meaning to a student's score, even if the test was initially constructed solely for criterion-referenced interpretation. For example, suppose a student received a score of 9 on a ten-item criterion-referenced test; suppose also that he will be allowed to proceed to the next higher level in a sequenced curriculum since he attained mastery. Knowing the number of other children in the class (or in a national sample) who also reached that level of proficiency in the same time period can give the student's score greater meaning. For example, if only one other student in the class was able to reach mastery, it is possible that the teacher's standards were set too high, that instruction was ineffective, or both. Furthermore, national norms might suggest that students in the class are below average on most scales but above average on the skill under consideration. Rather than detracting from criterion-referenced interpretations related to diagnosis, the presence of norms can help teachers estimate reasonable levels of expected performance.

Even if there are no norms provided on standardized tests, the fact that items are sequentially ordered in difficulty can be of assistance in diagnosing student problems and strengths. A child who has failed to respond correctly to any of the items on a criterion-referenced test might require a good deal of similar testing to discover the reasons for his failure. Because items on most standardized tests are arranged in ascending order of difficulty, the failure to respond correctly to items at a given level provides the teacher with information related to performance on prerequisite tasks. The fact that there may be few items at each level can easily be compensated for by constructing similar types of items to improve item sampling and to reduce errors of measurement.

Two other advantages of standardized diagnostic tests should be mentioned. Although diagnosis usually refers to, and is more relevant for, those objectives that students have failed to master, diagnostic instruments should also be capable of describing strengths and

possible areas in which students can be assigned more advanced topics. The different levels of complexity on standardized tests allow the teacher to estimate which topics at a more advanced level the student might attempt. When diagnostic tests provide a range of difficulty levels, they can serve both a diagnostic as well as a vertical placement function.

Another advantage of standardized tests is that they can suggest whether or not mastery or a high level of achievement in one subject was attained at the expense of an equally important area of the curriculum. High scores in language could have been attained by disregarding instruction in mathematics, or a high level of proficiency in spelling might be the result of failing to teach any number of different topics within the language arts curriculum. Standardized achievement batteries are especially useful in the comparison of student competencies in different subject areas.

Diagnostic tests differ widely in the specific areas they attempt to measure and in the kind and amount of information they provide. As is true for criterion-referenced tests, standardized tests that provide detailed information about specific student difficulties and proficiencies are found only in arithmetic and reading, probably because of the sequential nature of those skills. But *item responses* on any standardized achievement test can be used for diagnosis as long as the teacher is mindful of the limitations of relatively high standard errors of measurement and constructs additional items to provide more accurate diagnostic information.

Numerous tests exist to help diagnose problems in arithmetic. Some tests, such as the Buswell-John Diagnostic Test for Fundamental Processes in Arithmetic, are administered orally, and the teacher carefully notes the process used as the student attempts each item. This test not only provides information regarding the level of competence, but it also helps the teacher to understand the thinking process of the child as he works a given problem. The oral nature of the test also makes it possible to prevent poor reading skills from contaminating performance in arithmetic.

One of the most ambitious attempts to measure various aspects of arithmetic is the Diagnostic Tests and Self-Helps in Arithmetic, published by the California Test Bureau for students in grades three through twelve. Three screening tests help discover which students need help in fractions, decimals, and whole numbers. Another test

contains more difficult items used to screen more advanced pupils in need of remediation. Based on the results of these screening tests, any or all of the twenty-three diagnostic tests can then be administered.

These tests are also cross-referenced. In performing any complex mathematical operation, errors can be made on division facts, multiplication facts, subtraction of whole numbers, and division of decimals. Each of these processes is represented by a separate subtest that can help locate the child's specific problem.

Once a student is screened, exercises show him how to solve each type of problem. In addition to pointing out student errors, the materials also encourage the child to solve his own problems. It is this combination of screening, detailed diagnosis, and instructional materials that make the Diagnostic Tests and Self-Helps in Arithmetic unique. Many other test publishers have excellent diagnostic tests that may be better suited for different purposes. Before selecting any standardized test, the specific objectives of the school's curriculum need to be compared with the content and technical information reported in test manuals and technical reports. The *Mental Measurements Yearbooks,* edited by Oscar K. Buros, will prove to be invaluable sources of information on the quality of most standardized tests.

Diagnostic tests in reading are also available. Some are designed to be administered individually while others can be used for class or group administration. For example, the Gilmore Oral Reading Test is administered individually. It consists of ten paragraphs, each accompanied by five comprehension questions. The test measures accuracy (substitutions, omissions, and disregard of punctuation), reading rate, and comprehension. Another individually administered test is the Gates-McKillop Reading Diagnostic Test. Designed for children in grades two and higher, its two forms contain the following subtests: Oral Reading (paragraphs), Word Pronunciation (flash and untimed), Phrases (flash), knowledge of Word Parts (word attack, recognizing and blending common word parts, giving letter sounds, naming capital letters, naming lowercase letters), Recognizing the Visual Form or Word Equivalents of Sounds (nonsense words, initial letters, final letters, vowels), Auditory Blending, and Supplementary Tests (spelling, oral vocabulary, syllabification, auditory discrimination). Unlike the Gilmore test, the Gates-McKillop contains no measures of comprehension or reading rate.

Many of the diagnostic reading tests for older children are of the pencil-and-paper variety. Most assume that the child is capable of word-attack skills and emphasize such abilities as reading for different purposes, comprehension, word meaning, study skills, and reading rate.

Program or Curriculum Evaluation

Standardized tests can be of great value in making evaluative decisions about programs and curricula. Programs can involve innovative projects instituted by a school, a district, or by individual teachers who want to evaluate the effectiveness of their teaching methods. In these instances, standardized tests can help administrators and teachers decide whether the innovation or method is effective and therefore worth retaining.

A curriculum involves the complex interaction of students, teachers, methods, and materials (texts, syllabi, work sheets, programmed instructional "packages," films, filmstrips, audiotapes, and so forth). The evaluation of a curriculum could include any or all of these various components.

Evaluative criteria are also highly varied. Although student achievement most readily comes to mind, the schools do not (or at least should not) act within an intellectual vacuum unrelated to the affective goals that educators claim to be important. A child who, although proficient, greatly fears or dislikes a given subject or program may have lost the desire to learn and to attempt new skills not only in that area but in related ones as well. No matter what the subject matter may be, schools should not separate the acquisition of cognitive skills from students' interests and attitudes. When curriculum evaluation neglects to measure these affective components of learning, an important source of information relevant to evaluation is lost.

Curriculum evaluation depends not only on student achievement and attitudes; it also relates to the attitudes and values within the community. Most hours of the child's day are not spent in school, and an administrator or teacher who implements or abolishes a program without being cognizant of community desires and aspirations is only asking for trouble. Furthermore, any element of a curriculum being evaluated has to be weighed against possible losses in other areas. Little purpose is served by recommending the continuance of a

project because it produced a high level of learning when that increase was accompanied by substantial losses in other equally important subjects.

In developing the objectives for a curriculum, it is probably as important to specify what the child is not to learn as it is to be unambiguous in stating what goals he is to acquire. Years ago E. L. Thorndike found that arithmetic books were heavily loaded with content related to banking, computing interest charges, and other topics that middle-class textbook writers might have been expected to include. Many currently used texts in the social studies (and in most other areas of the curriculum as well) inadvertently teach or reinforce racial, ethnic, and religious stereotypes. These by-products should not only be measured for evaluation purposes, but their measurement may point out attitudes, beliefs, stereotypes, and prejudices that schools cannot afford to disregard. Similarly, there is no good reason for not including a measure of school morale and of interest in various aspects of the curriculum in the minimum school testing program. An important caveat is that the administration of such tests carries with it both legal and ethical considerations related to those published guidelines of the Department of Health, Education, and Welfare that relate to practices which may place students "at risk." Unless the test can be justified as having direct benefit to the student, parental permission is probably necessary.

In evaluating the effectiveness of a curriculum, standardized and teacher-made norm-referenced tests can be used in experiments and surveys.

The Experiment in Curriculum Evaluation

The purpose of an experiment is to study the effects of one or more variables (called *independent variables*) upon a criterion measure (called a *dependent variable*). A program designed, for example, to reduce the dropout rate among inner-city students by improving skills in reading might use standardized tests for a number of different purposes. First, of course, those students who have the greatest need for remediation and will gain the greatest benefit from it need to be placed into that program. Standardized aptitude and achievement tests, along with such factors as prior grades, records of absenteeism, and teacher recommendations, can be used for this purpose. Second, standardized tests could be used to diagnose specific areas of

difficulty. An individually administered diagnostic reading test would probably be most useful for this purpose and would serve as a check on the results of the placement test. And third, a standardized reading test could be used as the dependent variable to measure improvement in reading.

The most effective procedure for conducting an experiment is to randomly assign students to different groups. One (or more) of these groups is called the experimental group, and its performance is to be compared to that of a control group. The experimental and control groups should be as similar as possible except that the experimental treatment is withheld from the students placed in the control program. In the previous example, all of the names of students who met the criteria for admission to an experimental program could be placed on slips of paper and put in a box, and half of the slips would be drawn on a completely blind or random basis to form the experimental group,[12] for example, in reading. The other half of the students would be taught the usual program by equally competent teachers and for an equal amount of time. In practice the difficulty arises when ethical considerations or social pressures do not permit the formation of control groups or if students cannot be drawn randomly and placed in separate groups.

If no control group can be formed, the progress of the students could be compared against their previous annual gains as measured by a standardized reading test. Standard scores will be most satisfactory for this purpose because percentile gains are unequal at different portions of the scale (the difference between a percentile of 1 and 5 is roughly equivalent to a gain of 20 percentile points near the center of the scale) and because age and grade norms are too inexact, especially at the extremes of a distribution.

Although *gain scores* tend to be unreliable (that is, they contain the combined errors of measurement of both the pretest and posttest), reliability can be improved by administering two or more parallel forms and combining the standard scores. This should be done for both the pretest and posttest.

Two other problems are involved if pre-post comparisons are re-

12. A table of random numbers can be used if the number of students to be assigned is relatively large.

quired: regression effects and threats to the internal validity of the experiment. The regression effect occurs because test scores are not perfectly reliable. If students are placed into a program on the basis of a low score, a portion of that score contains the effects of chance. When students are retested, these chance effects are unlikely to be present again, and scores are more apt to increase; the same effect can be noted at the upper extremes where students are likely to decrease in performance. The solution is to develop tests with high reliabilities and small errors of measurement, particularly at the extremes of the distribution. Administering two parallel forms for the pretest and the same two forms for the posttest, assuming that practice effects are unlikely, can improve reliability and reduce the effects of regression.

Overcoming the threats to internal validity is a more difficult problem if only a pretest and posttest are available. Internal validity is the extent to which extraneous variables have been eliminated so that a clear and unambiguous interpretation of the relationship between the independent and dependent variables can be made. How, for example, can one tell if the new reading program was responsible for student gains or if extraneous variables were responsible (maturation, effects of instruction in other classes, and so forth)? Unfortunately there is no ideal solution to this problem. One suggestion, however, is to examine the average gains on standardized tests made by eligible students for as many years prior to the initiation of the experimental program as possible and to follow their progress afterward. Standard or scale scores that span various grade levels are especially useful for this comparison.

Sometimes it is possible to increase the power or sensitivity of an experiment to detect the effects of an experimental treatment by *matching* or equating individuals on a variable that correlates highly with the dependent variable. For example, the names of all students in need of remediation could be ranked with respect to intelligence or to whatever standardized tests were used for placement. If an experimental and control treatment are to be compared, the two highest individuals would be paired, then the next two, and so on. One member of the pair would then be assigned randomly (the toss of a coin does nicely) to the experimental group and the other to the control group. The value of using standardized tests for "matching" is

that groups are formed using tests that are known to correlate highly with each other.[13]

When experimental and control subjects have been assigned randomly, standardized achievement test scores can be used effectively to measure differences in achievement levels between the groups at the end of the experiment. If this matching procedure is followed, the difference in achievement between experimental and control groups at the end of the program should be compared, not the difference between the pretest and posttest scores for each group. When only the posttest scores are compared following randomization, differences between experimental and control groups, if statistically significant, reflect the gains or improvement of one program over another. The differences between pretest and posttest gains for each group do not necessarily mean that comparisons are valid between the two groups.[14] In addition, the pretest may affect the external validity of the experiment (that is, the extent to which valid generalizations may be made to other groups not normally pretested).

When randomization is not possible, standardized tests and demographic data may be used to equate the groups statistically through a procedure known as *analysis of covariance*. Suppose, for example, that all students in need of a remedial reading program have been placed into two groups but not randomly. One group might be slightly brighter than the other, perhaps somewhat younger, and possibly be better readers. The analysis of covariance permits the evaluator to "adjust" the posttest scores to account for some of the initial differences between them. Variables that correlate with the dependent variable are used for this purpose. Such variables are called covariates or adjusting variables.

When nonrandom groups have to be compared, there is no way to eliminate all initial differences that might affect the dependent vari-

13. The appropriate statistic to use for measuring whether the difference found between the means of an experimental and a control group is statistically significant is the t-test, which is described in all elementary statistics books. Because individuals were paired, a "t-test for matched or correlated groups" is needed. Pairing, as described above, is only advantageous if the scores used to form the pairs correlate highly with the scores used as the dependent variable. Alternate forms of a test are ideal for this purpose.

14. Some standardized tests provide standard score norms that span a number of grade levels and can provide meaningful comparisons of gain scores.

able. Although cumulative records of students often contain information other than test scores that can be used as covariates, it is not always easy to determine which covariates will most effectively reduce or eliminate the effects of the initial differences between groups.[15] The variables to select for this purpose can be determined by using a stepwise multiple regression equation available in most "canned" computer programs. The computer searches for the three or four variables that correlate most highly with the criterion or dependent measure but least with each other. Generally, no more than three or four covariates are used since additional ones contribute inconsequential increments in equating groups. Although the analysis of covariance is useful in reducing differences among intact groups, it is not a substitute for randomization. Used with randomization, however, the analysis of covariance can be a powerful statistical tool.

Numerous criteria are available for evaluating the effectiveness of a curriculum or program. Certainly standardized tests are commonly used to compare experimental and control groups. Raw scores may be compared, or these scores may be converted to standard score norms. In addition, the evaluator may want to consider the advantages and limitations of other types of criteria that are based on standardized test scores.

Absolute standards. When an external agency is employed as a performance contractor, the school often specifies an absolute standard to be reached by a given proportion of the students, or it gives some minimum absolute standard for all students to reach. Because raw score values are difficult to interpret as an absolute standard, the district and contractor might agree on an increase of 1.0 grade equivalents or some number of scale score units comparable to 1.0 grade equivalents. To prevent the contractor from teaching students specific test content, an external evaluator could be employed to make the actual test selection based on the goals agreed upon by the district and contractor. When districts evaluate their own programs, the administrator or project evaluator can specify an absolute level of performance as a criterion without informing the teachers about the specific test to be used.

15. The analysis of covariance may be applied to any number of groups. The previous references to a single experimental group and a single control group were made to simplify the discussion.

Cost-benefit analyses. The evaluation of any given program often assumes some form of cost-benefit analysis. Costs not only include the expenditure of funds for books, salaries, equipment, and materials; they also include the amount of time required for students to reach a given criterion level. Benefits can be measured by student performance on standardized tests, public support in the form of money voted for the operation of schools, or the extent to which a school is capable of reducing dropout rates. A program may be considered effective if it can accomplish its objectives at a specified cost or if it involves lower costs for an equal (or higher) unit of gain.

All programs involve both costs and benefits (or losses). The teacher who insists on working individually with students will incur higher costs than if he lectures to a class of fifty students. The assumption, rarely verified, is that the benefits of a proposed curriculum modification outweigh the costs. The teacher who recommends new textbooks is increasing the cost per pupil, and he should be able to demonstrate that the benefits (student achievement and enjoyment) are worth the additional expense.

Time. The amount of time it takes students to reach a given criterion level should be included as a cost. Programs increase in effectiveness as the student learns more in a given period of time or as equal performance is attained within a reduced time period.

Most curriculum innovations are measured by the relative amount of knowledge students possess with time held constant. For example, students in experimental and control groups may be compared at the end of a school semester or year, or the amount of time required to reach a specified level of proficiency could be used as the dependent variable (see Figure 5-2).

Figure 5-2 shows two hypothetical learning curves that depict the performance of two groups, A and B, at four different time periods. If student performance is measured at time 1 or 3, there will be no differences in the test performance of the two groups. If performance is measured at time 2 (for example, the end of a semester), group B will have outperformed students in group A. If proficiency is measured at time 4 (for example, the end of the school year), group A has the advantage over group B. Obviously, different results can occur depending upon when students are compared.

Even if mastery is specified as the criterion, the required level of performance could determine which of two groups was superior. If

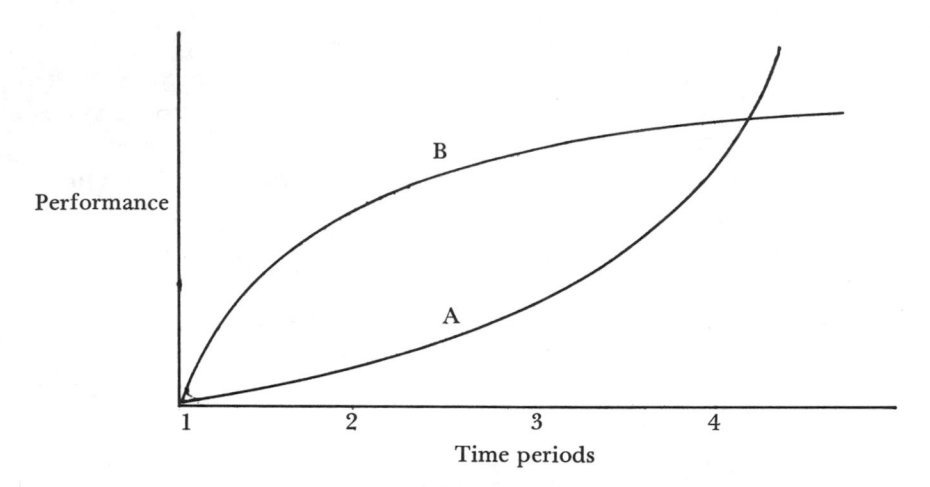

Figure 5-2
Two hypothetical learning curves (A and B) measured
in relationship to different time periods

mastery were set at the point where curves A and B intersect (time 3), the evaluator would conclude that these groups were equally effective, but if mastery is defined as that performance reached at time 2, then group B's performance is superior to that attained by group A.

Statistical significance. Sometimes a statistically significant difference is stated to be the criterion for judging that one program is more effective than another. A statistically significant difference simply indicates that the difference between two means is larger than would be expected by chance. Both programs, of course, would be ineffective, but one might be even worse than the other. Norms on standardized tests can be used as a basis for interpreting the instructional meaning of statistically significant differences. While it might be difficult to state that a statistically significant difference of five points had any educational significance, the fact that five points corresponds to an increase of so many standard score units or to the average amount of time expended by the highest performing 10 percent of school districts to reach this level gives additional meaning to statistical results.

The Use of Surveys in Curriculum Evaluation

Schools regularly use standardized tests to survey student achievement, sometimes to satisfy an inquisitive school board or sometimes to respond to allegations made by members of the business community as to the "incompetence" of district graduates. School administrators and teachers are also concerned about the general level of student achievement at all grade levels as a means of determining which schools and which areas of the curriculum need additional resources.

In the past, the use of standardized achievement tests for surveying student achievement has led to misunderstandings among teachers, students, and administrators who see the purpose of testing from their own perspective. The teacher is usually most concerned with diagnosis and placement, and the student, if interested at all, probably expects tests to tell him about the kinds of programs for which he is best suited and his chance for success in each. Administrators, being more immediately concerned with problems that affect all students, have not always been sensitive to the needs of teachers and students who, in turn, too often and correctly, perceive standardized tests to be administrative requirements unrelated to their own purposes.

Another misunderstanding in using tests is that administrators want test results at the end of the school year, whereas teachers want these results as early in the school year as possible. It does seem meaningless to diagnose a student's problem or to place him in an appropriate program when the school year is almost over; it may seem equally meaningless to the administrator to attempt to describe the effects of instruction at the beginning of the year. Sometimes this apparent dilemma is resolved by unnecessarily testing students twice to satisfy the needs of both groups or by acceding to the demands of the more influential group.

Part of this misunderstanding is due to the confusion of both teachers and administrators concerning the difference between the beginning and ending of an academic school year and the beginning or ending of the student's education. Even if tests were administered early in the school year and returned to teachers promptly, those scores are not necessarily more valid for diagnosis and placement purposes than scores obtained by the student in previous years. If tests are administered in June, scores will be available for diagnosis, place-

ment, and evaluation of the previous year's curriculum when school resumes in September. Similarly, if testing is carried out at the beginning of the school year, those results, along with previously attained standardized test scores, can be used by the teacher for diagnosis and placement and by the administrator to evaluate the district's curriculum at the end of the summer months. Whether testing should be scheduled early in the school year or at the end can probably best be decided after considering the amount of time it will take for tests to be scored, entered into cumulative records, and returned to teachers; the pressure of other activities that might interfere with or invalidate standardized test results (the scheduling of College Boards or other "external" test programs, final examinations, the instability of classes at the beginning of the year, and so forth); and the availability of school or district norms on standardized tests and the time of year in which students in the norm group took the test.

The most important feature of a standardized achievement test is that its items should closely match the objectives of the school or district. An invalid test, no matter what other desirable characteristics it may have, serves no purpose and should not be used. For curriculum or school evaluation, not only must the test be valid but it must also provide *school norms*. Most manuals accompanying standardized achievement tests provide norms useful for comparing *individual* students. The scores of individuals, however, are more variable than school norms based on the average performance of students in different schools or districts. Figure 5-3 shows the relationship between individual and school average performance ranges (the numbers correspond to percentiles) in hypothetical national samples. The top line refers to the variability of scores attained by a group of individuals (fifth graders); the shorter line refers to the variability or

1	50	99	Individual performance range
1	50	99	School average performance range

Figure 5-3
Relationship between individual and school
performance ranges

spread of scores in fifth-grade classes. The lowest-scoring individuals will score much lower than will the lowest-scoring class; similarly, the brightest individual will score at a higher level than the brightest class.

Meaningless results will occur if the wrong norms are used. For example, suppose that an administrator discovered that the average raw score of his fifth-grade students was 62.7 points. In the test manual he finds a table of norms in which a raw score of 63 corresponds to the "70th percentile." Generally, this would be considered as reasonably good performance, but in this case the hypothetical administrator will have to explain how it happened that achievement was at the 70th percentile when he had already boasted that the average IQ of the students was at the 90th percentile!

One possible explanation is that the achievement and IQ tests were normed on different groups, but assume that this is not the problem. Another explanation is that the wrong table of norms was used. Find the point on the top line of Figure 5-3 that corresponds (at least roughly) to the 70th percentile. The 70th percentile in this case refers to the achievement of individual students in the national sample. A raw score of 63, in comparison with the average performance of schools, would put the fifth graders near the top of this distribution. Similarly, the use of the wrong norms can place a student at the first percentile (if he should incorrectly be compared to schools) when he is closer to the 30th percentile relative to other students.

Not only is it important to use school norms for curriculum evaluation; it is also important to be able to describe the schools in the norm group. Many test publishers can provide norms for both schools and individuals that more closely approximate the demographic characteristics of a particular district than do the norms published in the test manual. A school district's fifth graders might be at the 30th percentile in comparison to a randomly selected national group of fifth-grade classrooms, but in comparison with other schools in the same geographic area whose expenditures per child are approximately equal and where the mean IQ's are more comparable, these fifth graders might be average or above average. The point is that more than one norm group can be used for comparison. Future evaluations of the school, of course, should be based on the same norm group(s).

Three other suggestions might be useful in surveying the achievement of students to evaluate schools or curricula. The first is to include a measure of scholastic aptitude (that is, intelligence) along with the achievement battery. A practical example can demonstrate the value of doing so. In one state that decided to evaluate the performance of its twelfth-grade students, the average achievement level turned out to be far below national norms. When these data were made public, the responsibility for this poor achievement was placed solely on the schools. An examination of the achievement test scores of students who had remained in the state from grades K through 12 showed a marked decrease relative to national norms at the beginning of the high school years. Although there are numerous possible interpretations of these data, there was a considerable amount of evidence that many of the brightest students in that state attended private high schools and were not included in the survey. Intelligence testing would have allowed school administrators to present additional evidence to the public that there had been changes in the school population that accounted for a drop in achievement.[16]

Second, junior and senior high school surveys should include affective measures regarding the quality of instruction, the variety of courses available, the appropriateness of school rules regarding student conduct or personal behavior (dress codes, smoking regulations, and the like), and perhaps the future goals of students (to compare school offerings with students' level of aspiration).[17] Some attitude

16. Intelligence and achievement test scores correlate highly with one another, particularly in the upper grades. If the public had been more willing to compare the junior high school achievement test scores of those who had transferred into private schools with those who remained in public high schools, there would be less need to use intelligence tests. But assuming that the norms of intelligence and achievement measures were established on the same population, the decrease in mean scores on both tests would have simplified the explanation (e.g., "Students at all grade levels are achieving at the level predicted by scholastic aptitude tests. In the elementary and junior high schools, the overall achievement and aptitude scores corresponded closely to national averages, but at the twelfth grade, achievement and aptitude scores were both lower than national norms").

17. The 1973 revision of the Differential Aptitude Tests includes a Career Planning Questionnaire that can be used for this purpose. The reference to any test in this paper is to illustrate a point and should not necessarily be interpreted as a recommendation.

scales have been standardized and can provide important information regarding student perceptions of the school. If administrators or school boards are interested in interschool comparisons within a given district, either standardized measures can be used or such tests can be constructed by district personnel, perhaps with the advice of consultants. Curriculum surveys at the elementary grades should also include affective measures, but they will probably have to be constructed by local school personnel since few standardized instruments are available for younger children. Local norms can be developed for these tests.

Third, curriculum surveys do not always have to involve all students or all subtests. For example, rather than having to test large numbers of students, there is no reason that students could not be selected randomly and in proportion to the number of students enrolled at each grade level. The crucial element is *randomization* or the "blind" selection and subsequent testing of students who are to comprise the sample. The number of students to be tested depends partially on the amount of tolerable "error" in generalizing from a sample of students to the totality or population of students. Assuming randomization, greater precision is obtained by increasing the number of students tested. This increase, however, has to be weighed against the added costs of conducting the survey.

Similarly, it is not necessary to administer all subtests of an achievement battery. Instead, only those subtests that meet the school's objectives and that provide meaningful normative data should be considered.

Formative and Summative Curriculum Evaluation

Sometimes a distinction is made between formative and summative program evaluations. Formative evaluation is designed to help the teacher or administrator make effective decisions throughout the project's duration and to provide continuous information to improve program effectiveness and efficiency. Short unit tests, measures of interest and attitude, and frequent interviews or conferences with students and their parents contribute to formative evaluation. Teacher-made examinations (whether norm-referenced or criterion-referenced) would probably be more effective for this purpose than standardized tests.

Summative evaluation occurs at the end of a program or course and is used to determine its overall effectiveness. The term *summa-*

tive means the summing up of all available information regarding a program at its "terminal point," defined by a point in time (for example, the end of a school year) or by some stated level of competence or mastery. When mastery is used as a criterion in summative evaluation, standardized tests can be used to make sure that gains in one area were not made at the expense of other, equally important, subjects.

Administrators and teachers need not decide between using tests exclusively for formative or for summative evaluation. Both are needed in any well-developed program evaluation. Formative evaluation not only can help to improve a continuing program, but it can also be of value to future groups of students by affecting the ultimate decision to continue, modify, or eliminate a given program. Cost-benefit analyses should be considered at each decision point in the evaluation of a program beginning with the needs assessment and analysis of the current and previous costs that have been expended to bring students up to their present level of performance in each area of the curriculum. The needs assessment might also include surveys of the attitudes and beliefs of the community, the school administration, teachers, and students as to what the schools ought to be teaching and what priorities should be established among competing goals. The responsibility of the evaluator is to design and conduct this assessment and to describe the current status of the school program as it relates to the goals and priorities of the school and the community.

Unfortunately, it is all too common for school districts to request the services of an evaluation consultant only to conduct the summative evaluation of a project or to conduct the needs assessment. Rarely does a school district involve the consultant in all phases of decision making related to program evaluation. Competent evaluation is more than helping to write behavioral objectives, selecting a test, and using some esoteric statistic that, even if it does nothing else, is likely to impress the granting agency or school board.

Standardized tests can be used to compare current levels of student proficiency with surveys of school-community goals and priorities. The evaluator or consultant should know, or should be able to ascertain, which tests are valid for this purpose.

The evaluation also requires knowledge of the various instructional alternatives used by other districts or suggested in the literature that might be applicable to the district's unique problems. Admittedly,

this is one of the most difficult decisions or suggestions the evaluation consultant will face.

Prior to recommending the widespread implementation of any drastic, expensive, or relatively unexplored program, the school and the evaluator have the responsibility of implementing the innovation with a small number of students who are closely monitored to discover unanticipated difficulties as they occur and to remedy these situations as soon as possible. Perhaps this could best be accomplished in a quasi-laboratory setting where each step of the program could be carefully examined, starting with just a few students and expanding the scope as evidence is accumulated on the effectiveness of the program and its effect on other areas of the curriculum. A comparison of student gains on standardized achievement tests can suggest what effects the innovation is having in different subject areas.

In the early formative stages of program evaluation, *product development*[18] is the primary goal. Its purpose is to develop lessons, materials, and methods that are feasible, economical, and demonstrably effective. It may be described as an attempt to "build a better mousetrap." The student must be fed on some solid substance that will improve his academic health. The summative evaluation carried out with a larger sample of students should provide evidence of the overall effectiveness of the intervention in relationship to other areas of the curriculum and in comparison with achievement in similar school districts.

If the summative evaluation is favorable, product development would be continued, and two additional phases of curriculum evaluation would need to be implemented.[19] The first may be called *dem-*

18. "Product development" should be broadly defined to include tangible evidence that students have met an objective and the specific materials and methods that have led to student achievement.

19. Product development is a continuing process that should probably be terminated when the product is no longer worth retaining or when some other product has been shown to be more effective. If all phases of the formative evaluation provide positive feedback to the evaluator, but summative evaluation is negative, either the program can be modified at its least effective point, or it can be scrapped in favor of a new program. Whether it is better to modify or scrap depends on the nature of the criteria used in the summative evaluation, on the extent to which the program failed to meet its objectives, on the availability of alternative programs, and on estimates of costs.

onstration, and the second, *dissemination.* The purpose of demonstration is to provide teachers and administrators with concrete and practical experiences showing how the program can be implemented in the classroom. Ideally, teachers in the school who have worked with the program should perform this function. The role of the evaluator is to provide these teachers with the evidence of program effectiveness, the reasons for its development as established by the needs assessment, the steps taken to make it practical, and the steps that will be taken to ensure that the program remains effective. The evaluator should also be prepared to answer whatever questions teachers, parents, and the school board might have regarding the program's evaluation. The evidence from standardized tests can be used to back up claims regarding the program and its effectiveness.

The final phase of curriculum evaluation is dissemination. A description of a program that has been carefully evaluated deserves to be disseminated to other evaluators in professional journals, at research conventions, or as an Educational Research Information Center report. More important than whether or not the program was successful in the sense that expected gains were made is the dissemination of the unique and valuable features of the program and its evaluation.

Feedback

Most school districts devote considerable time, funds, and effort to purchasing, administering, and scoring standardized tests and recording their results. Because of the widespread use of tests in education, efficient methods of disseminating and reporting test results must be developed. Disseminating test results is important. Decision making should be a cooperative endeavor involving teachers, parents, students, and administrators. If members of these groups lack valid information, then the decisions made are likely to be ineffective. Also, in order for tests to provide valid information about pupils, the students must see them as important, relevant, and beneficial. Providing them with their test scores will keep them informed of their progress and will motivate them to improve skills in which they are weak. Then there are the taxpayers, who face many conflicting pressures for public funds and who increasingly demand that the schools hold themselves accountable for the progress and achievement of the pupils. They must be kept informed about educational needs and stu-

dent progress. Finally, both students and parents need specific information to plan effectively for the future. Unless feedback is effective, students may set inappropriate goals. Knowing what not to report can also help to avoid misinterpreting test scores.

Reporting IQ Scores

In general, IQ scores should not be reported to parents or students unless their meaning and interpretation is also made clear. The problem is that IQ scores are easily misinterpreted as capacities for learning.

Today the tendency is to replace the term intelligence with a less semantically loaded term such as *academic aptitude*. Rather than saying that a student has an IQ of 115, the teacher can tell his parents that he is performing as well as or better than about 85 percent of other students his age who have taken the same test. The general principle to follow is to provide parents with as much information as they are able to understand and use for the benefit of the student.

Reporting Grade Equivalent Scores

Grade equivalent norms are too easily misinterpreted to be given to parents indiscriminately. These norms are often extrapolated, making scores at the extremes of a distribution difficult to explain and interpret properly. The amount of error in any grade equivalent norm usually varies from half a year to a year and a half—a fact not easily appreciated by most parents. Differences of four or five months between scores on different subtests may reflect random error rather than differences in achievement. Because the means and standard deviations of grade equivalent norms are not equal, a 4.7 in spelling may not have the same meaning as a score of 4.7 on another subtest.

Two other problems occur when interpreting grade equivalent norms. The first is that these norms are developed by testing all students at different grade levels at the same time (the fifth month of the sixth grade, that is, 6.5; the fifth month of the seventh grade, or 7.5; and so on). All values between 6.5 and 7.4 are determined by assuming that students make equal progress from one month to the next. Because these norms are constructed by interpolating values between successive grade levels, grade equivalents only approximate the values that might have been obtained if students were actually tested one month apart.

Grade norms are also difficult to use in counseling with parents. A parent of a tenth-grade student who is told that his son is functioning at the seventh-grade level is likely to greet this disclosure with hostility; furthermore, the student will not appreciate being compared with those at a lower grade level.

Reporting Percentile Scores

Percentiles are probably the simplest to explain to parents and students. The teacher should, however, clarify the group with whom the child is being compared and remind parents that differences in percentiles at the extremes of a distribution have greater significance than differences of equal numerical value near the center of the distribution. Parents should also be cautioned to avoid confusing percentiles with the percentage of items answered correctly. The use of percentile bands that are drawn from a point that is one standard error of measurement above and below the student's obtained percentile helps parents remember the fallible nature of these measurements.

Reporting Standard Score Norms[20]

Standard scores (such as z-scores, T-scores, and stanines) are useful because they yield equal means and equal standard deviations. For example, z-scores always have a mean of 0 and a standard deviation of 1.0; T-scores have means of 50 and standard deviations of 10. As a matter of fact, multiplying all z-scores in a distribution by a constant will change the standard deviation by that constant; adding a constant to the product will convert the mean to whatever the value of the constant may be. Thus, it is relatively easy to convert from one standard score to another. What many teachers and administrators fail to realize is that these converted standard score distributions retain the shape of the original raw score distribution (the exceptions are normalized standard scores and stanines). Standard scores are the most meaningful norms for teachers and administrators; they are, in most instances, too difficult to explain to parents.

Reporting standard score norms to parents can be simplified by using stanines which divide the normal curve into nine equal portions except that stanines 1 and 9 extend to infinity. For example, stanines 1, 2, and 3 (the lowest-scoring 4, 7, and 12 percent of individ-

---

20. The reader is referred to any basic textbook in measurement or statistics for a more detailed description of standard scores than can be provided here.

uals, respectively) may be described as being below average; stanines 4, 5, and 6 (the next highest-scoring 17 percent, 20 percent, and 17 percent) as average; and stanines 7, 8, and 9 (the highest scoring 12, 7, and 4 percent, respectively) as above average. Sympathetic and understanding parents can be given additional information such as "In comparison with children who represent a random national sample (boys of similar age in this state and so forth), Albert was among the lowest 4 percent on a given subtest." Parents might also be told that their child was "below average" in spelling when compared with the performance of students nationally but that he is average within his class.

Another possibility is to report evaluative decisions and recommendations. For example, parents can be told that their child's current spelling program will be continued, that further diagnostic testing is being recommended, that additional help with initial blends will be given, or perhaps that he will be placed at a more appropriate spelling level. The various placement and diagnostic decisions and recommendations can form the basis of a reporting system.

Standardized achievement tests are not substitutes for teacher-made norm- and criterion-referenced tests. A child who is average in relation to national norms may be at a different position compared to his classmates or to levels of mastery specified by his teacher. Information derived from each of these sources can give additional meaning to the child's progress and can aid in making more effective decisions.

Standardized and teacher-made tests serve complementary roles, each acting as a check on the other. For example, obtaining mastery or receiving an A in spelling could have a different meaning depending on the student's performance on a valid standardized spelling test. When these scores are related to a norm group, the teacher may discover that his standards were set too low, that the instructional materials were too simple, that progress in spelling was attained at the cost of deficiencies in other subjects, or that students might have had difficulty in spelling if they transferred to a different school or district. On the other hand, standardized test norms depend on the average performance of students at each grade level. If an absolute criterion was specified, the average performance of students on a standardized test might simply reflect the generally low (or high) spelling ability found in the population. Because the average level of

proficiency in different school subjects does change, test publishers need to develop revised norms periodically.

Theory Development

In addition to the many practical uses of standardized tests, they have also contributed to the understanding of human behavior. For example, the understanding of child growth and development has been increased as a result of testing children's intelligence, achievement, attitudes, interests, and personalities at different phases of their development. Many commonly accepted beliefs have had to be modified because testing demonstrated that they could not be verified empirically (for example, attempts to judge intelligence by appearance, the belief that intelligent individuals are more neurotic than average persons).

The ability to measure human attributes has made it possible to study these attributes. Different theoretical positions have resulted from testing and, in turn, have contributed to the improvement of standardized tests. Controversy among theoreticians has led to long, and sometimes bitter, debates that have often raised more important questions than they were able to resolve.

The effects of operationalism have been felt in both education and psychology. The operationalist believes that concepts derive their meanings from the operations or procedures used to measure them. For example, length has no meaning independent of its measurement. Similarly, human attributes have meaning to the extent that their measurement is possible. The development of factor analysis and other statistical procedures has made it possible to operationally define attributes and to show the interrelationships among them. When educators speak of *creativity, self-concept,* or *capacity for learning,* these terms may have different meanings, or none, depending on how or if they are measured.

Not only have tests helped to develop theoretical positions and concepts, but they have also contributed to psychometric theory or the study of educational and psychological measurement to better understand measurement theory and its assumptions and implications.

Criteria for Developing a School or District
Standardized Testing Program

No standardized testing program is ideal for all purposes or for all districts, but the following suggestions may be of value in developing and evaluating testing programs for schools and districts:

1. Testing programs should be developed cooperatively with teachers, administrators, parents, and measurement and evaluation specialists. If possible, participation should be from all grade levels and subject fields. The reason for this broad participation is that objectives and priorities will require consensus from those persons who will use or be affected by test results.

2. The standardized testing program should consist of a *minimum program,* required of all students, and a supplemental program to meet the needs of more limited numbers of students and teachers. The minimum program should be designed to serve a wide variety of purposes, such as placement, initial diagnosis, and curriculum evaluation. The supplemental testing program should be used for more detailed diagnoses and to enrich the minimum testing program in specific subjects not commonly taken by all students (algebra, chemistry, and others).

3. Tests selected for the minimum program should provide individual and school norms. Because results of the minimum testing program will, or at least should, be communicated to parents, percentiles, percentile bands, or stanine norms should be available. Standard score norms should also be available for use by the professional staff.

4. Although practical considerations (time limits, costs, and so on) may prevent a particular test from being used, no test should be selected unless its validity for given purposes has been evaluated.

5. If possible, different levels of the same battery of tests should be used at all grades to ensure comparability of norms.

6. The availability of separate answer sheets and the use of electronic machine scoring services can reduce testing costs and reduce clerical errors made by teachers in correcting or scoring standardized tests. Consumable test booklets are advisable for students below the fourth grade.

7. Tests should be administered no oftener than necessary to provide reliable data on student progress or when important decisions are required.

8. Tests should be most reliable in the range of ability in which the most accurate decisions need to be made.[21] Otherwise, additional testing may be required.

9. The emphasis should be placed on testing achievement. If interest inventories are used, some measure of aptitude should also be administered. Other noncognitive tests, such as personality measures, should probably be reserved for the supplemental testing program and parent permission obtained before the test is given.

10. Because of the importance of reading in all areas of the curriculum, it may be desirable to administer alternate forms of reading tests annually at the elementary grades, especially in schools where student performance in reading is low.

11. Testing programs should be evaluated periodically and revised if necessary to meet new demands or major changes in school philosophy. The minimum testing program, however, should be revised only after considerable deliberation because comparability of norms and subtests will be forfeited when a school or district switches from one battery of tests to another.

A Final Word

In attempting to describe the use of standardized tests, it was not intended, either by the title of this paper or by its emphasis on standardized tests, to disregard the importance of teacher-made tests in evaluation or to imply that criterion-referenced interpretations have less value. On the contrary, measurement is not at the point where it can afford to disregard valid data no matter how a test might have been constructed or the nature of the comparisons that are to be made.

It is important, however, to dispel the notion (which, unfortunately, seems to be increasing both in breadth and intensity) that there is some inherent psychometric principle that rules out the measurement of individual differences or that these differences would disappear if criterion-referenced tests only were used. Indeed, there is accumulating evidence that criterion-referenced tests do, in fact, also yield norms that measure individual differences and that standard-

21. To select or to place the highest scoring students, a difficult test that has enough "top" is needed. Relatively easy tests are needed for lower-ability students. Such tests would probably be a part of the supplemental program.

ized tests can be used to estimate the amount of knowledge students possess.

It is also important not to confuse evaluation as a decision-making function with subjective rigidity. Decisions are not made by setting arbitrary standards but by the empirical evidence that the student can, in fact, proceed to the next higher or more complex unit of instruction. This evidence need not (and should not!) be restricted solely to scores on tests. Rather than either subjective rigidity or capriciousness, evaluative decisions should be made on the basis of the best evidence available and modified if the consequences are adverse, ineffective, or inadequate.

REFERENCES

Ramul, Konstanin, 1963. "Some early measurements and ratings in psychology." *American Psychologist,* 18.10(October):653-659.

Skager, Rodney, 1971. "The system for objectives-based evaluation—Reading." *Evaluation Comment,* 3.1(September):6-11.

Super, Donald E., and Crites, John O., 1962. *Appraising vocational fitness by means of psychological tests.* New York: Harper and Brothers.

6

Criterion-Referenced Measurement

Jason Millman
Cornell University

Criterion-Referenced Measurement

Jason Millman

A CONCEPT OF CRITERION-REFERENCED TESTS

Criterion-referenced (CR) measurement has been popular for a relatively short time, but the literature is voluminous and growing at a seemingly exponential rate. This study is rooted in that literature, and it should not only acquaint the reader with the present state of the art but also suggest profitable directions for further inquiry and future literature. Concepts and terms in any newly discovered area of inquiry are far from standardized, and the goal of the first part of the study is to deal with the definitional dilemma by proceeding from the more traditional view of CR measurement to one that, if it is not more productive, at least provides a unifying theme for the entire study.

A Traditional Definition

A number of definitions of CR tests have been proposed. Perhaps the most popular is the notion that such tests provide information about the specific knowledge and skills of examinees and yield scores

I wish to acknowledge the helpful comments of W. James Popham, Melvin Novick, and Richard Darlington. In addition, my students, participants at workshops on criterion-referenced measurement, and other colleagues have helped contribute to the development of this work.

interpretable in terms of tasks or performances. The term *criterion* in CR measurement is confusing. The CR test score does not refer to a criterion in the sense of a normative standard, but, rather, to "specific tasks a student must be capable of performing before he achieves one of (the established) knowledge levels. It is in this sense that measures of proficiency can be criterion-referenced" (Glaser, 1963, page 519). Criterion in the traditional definition of a CR test means more than a performance standard; it indicates that performance on tasks can be interpreted for the individual without reference to the performance of others.

Criterion-referenced and norm-referenced measures are often compared. Scores for the latter are assessed by relating them to the test results achieved by some external reference group. It is difficult, if not impossible, to interpret a raw score on a typical standardized achievement test in terms of the knowledge or skill possessed by the examinee. Desired outcomes are seldom specified in performance terms prior to test construction, and the score is meaningful only in comparison with the scores of others taking the same test. Norm tables are used for this purpose; hence, the term *norm-referenced*. Because the scores on any test could be compared with the results achieved by some external group, any test could yield norm-referenced interpretations.

A norm-referenced statement about a student's spelling ability based on the score he obtained on a 20-item spelling subtest of a standardized, survey achievement test might be:

The examinee's score fell at the 15th percentile; thus, his performance was better than 15 percent of those in the norm group.

A CR inference made from a different test might be:

The examinee correctly spelled eight out of ten words selected from a basic sixth-grade vocabulary list. His spelling ability is satisfactory.

The performance of other students is a factor in the first example. The score is low because it exceeds only 15 percent of the norm group. The second example makes no reference to other examinees; the test user determines that eight words correct out of a total of ten signifies satisfactory spelling ability.

A frequently stated limitation of CR measurement is that it is a delusion because all meaning comes from relative assessments; performance cannot be interpreted unless a person has some idea what

the score values should be. There is, of course, merit in this position. A typing score of thirty-five words per minute achieves added meaning when compared with how fast people similar to the examinee can type, but the thirty-five words per minute has a meaning of its own.

Apart from this consideration, the CR movement has undoubtedly proved beneficial. It prompted educators to focus on what students can and cannot do and on what ways instruction has and has not been effective. *The concept has gained greater acceptance as a type of general interpretation, however, than it has as a testing procedure.* A part of the confusion originates with traditional definitions of CR tests, such as that just offered, which allow for dramatically different notions of how such tests should be developed and validated. Two distinct approaches are provided in the next section.

A Refined View

The nature and validity of a CR interpretation depends upon the degree to which the content, format, and selection of the items potentially available for the test have been specified. (Throughout this chapter the word *items* will be used in the broadest sense possible.) If an item writer has merely been told to construct 10 items measuring a student's military knowledge of the U.S. Civil War, the resulting test score would not be well suited for a CR interpretation. A student answering none of the items correctly might, nevertheless, know much about the Civil War had the set of items measured obscure battles, men, and dates.

Now suppose that the item writer was told to construct 10 items to match the objective: Given the name of a major battle of one of the U.S. wars, the student will write the name of the war, the year of the battle, the name of one of the leading figures of the battle, and the name of the victorious army. A score on such a test permits a CR interpretation because the content of the tasks being sampled by the items is specified. There is still uncertainty about the content, format, and selection of the items, however, that prevents a satisfying CR interpretation. What criteria make a battle major? What constitutes a U.S. war? Must the answers be spelled correctly? How did the item writer select the specific battles used on the test? (The difficulties of making CR interpretations from such objectives-based tests are discussed again later.)

For many instructional objectives it is possible to describe, with a

high degree of specificity, the content of a population of items from which the items appearing on the test are drawn in a random or stratified random fashion. A test thus formed is called a domain-referenced test (DRT). DRT's permit the most satisfactory CR interpretations because test scores can be interpreted most directly in terms of performance tasks and, also, the percent of the population of tasks the student would answer correctly or in a given direction can be estimated.

Note that "specificity" of content and "homogeneity" of content are different concepts. Although a more detailed specification of the items permitted to appear on a test usually leads to a more restricted content than a vague specification does, this relationship need not necessarily follow. In at least one sense, specific questions about the battles of *all* major U.S. wars are less limited than undefined questions about the military facts of only the Civil War. *The domain being referenced by a DRT may be extensive or a single, narrow objective, but it must be well defined, which means that content and format limits must be well specified.* The reader is cautioned against thinking of a domain as a large, conceptual territory like the affective domain or the domain of reading skills. A much more limited concept is intended.

Tests differ not only in the completeness with which the item population or domain is specified, but also in terms of how they are constructed. In contrast with DRT's, some tests are developed with heavy reliance on empirical procedures for item selection and test validation as the test is designed to differentiate groups of individuals believed to differ on the attribute purportedly measured by the test. Such instruments are referred to in this monograph as differential assessment devices (DAD's). Most DAD's lack even an implied formulation of a population of performance tasks. Because of their empirical test construction procedures, however, they are well suited for norm-referenced interpretations. Some DAD's, however, do reference a particular objective or skill with sufficient specification that a CR interpretation, as well as a norm-referenced one, is reasonable. When this is the case, the differential assessment device will be labeled CRDAD. The example of a CR inference involving spelling ability given earlier illustrates a CR interpretation possible from a CRDAD.

Two broad differences, then, of a domain-referenced test (DRT) and a differential assessment device capable of a CR interpretation

(CRDAD) are the specificity with which the item population is stated, and, thus, the quality and nature of the CR interpretation; and the reliance on empirical methods of test development, and, thus, the discrimination power of the test results. There is a trade-off between the ability to interpret and the ability to discriminate. DRT's maximize the former; DAD's, the latter. Differential assessment devices which permit a criterion-referenced interpretation, CRDAD's, constitute the middle ground.

Domain-Referenced Tests [1]

Any test consisting of a random or stratified random sample of items selected from a well-defined set or class of tasks (a domain) shall be referred to here as a DRT. As will be explained more fully later, "well-defined" refers to an explicitly stated domain of items or tasks or to an item-generating procedure. Items are eliminated only if they do not conform to the domain definition; they are not dropped because all students answer them correctly. Indeed, if instruction is effective, such results are to be expected. Thus, item and test variance are not required.

The major advantage of the DRT is that it permits the user to make a special kind of CR interpretation, namely, an estimation of an examinee's domain score or level of functioning, defined as the percent of the population of items the examinee could answer correctly or in a given direction. Reliability of DRT's can reasonably be thought of as the consistency of estimates regarding an examinee's level of functioning. The validity of a DRT can best be assessed by logical analysis of the domain definition, the item generation scheme, and the individual test items. This analysis is similar to content validity, except that content validity has historically tolerated much looser definitions of the content domain than is permitted with DRT's, and it has been limited to cognitive achievement tests.

An interpretation made from a DRT score might be:

The examinee correctly spelled 8 out of 10 words randomly selected from a basic sixth-grade vocabulary list. It is estimated that he knows how to spell 80 percent of the words on the list.

Unlike other examples of spelling test score interpretations given earlier, this one describes the student's status in terms of a class of

1. For another discussion of DRT's, read Hively (1974) and the other articles in *Educational Technology*, 14(June 1974).

performance (behavioral) tasks. It specifies how well a student can perform in terms of the tasks rather than in terms of general descriptors (for example, satisfactory) or percentile ranks.

A limitation of DRT's is that they

> may be practical (only) in those few areas of achievement which focus on culti vation of a high degree of skill in the exercise of a limited number of activities. In areas where the emphasis is on knowledge and understanding, the effective use of criterion-referenced measures seems less likely [Ebel, 1970, page 5].

The concern is that we shall be unable to construct tests permitting CR interpretations for the assessment of important educational achievements. The task is undoubtedly very difficult, but we have just not had enough experience constructing tests, such as DRT's, using methods described later in this chapter, to know the validity of this criticism.

A DRT is distinctly different from the types of instruments used by social scientists during this century. Its roots go back at least to Ebel's (1962) notion of content standard test scores and to the idea of items as a random variable found in the generalizability theory of Cronbach *et al.* (1963). Hively (1962) and Osburn (1968) were the leading, early advocates of DRT's.

Differential Assessment Devices

Designed to measure individual or group differences and to yield norm-referenced interpretations, DAD's go back much further in psychometric history and persist as the dominant testing approach. The CRDAD's are of this type, except that the items must refer to a specified objective or skill, which is why CRDAD's also permit a criterion-referenced interpretation. Some individual difference measures are constructed to allow most any item to be included in the test if it improves prediction or the selection process. The items of a CRDAD must, however, be congruent with the objectives so that it makes at least some sense to say that the score has meaning regardless of the performance of others.

No population of ways that the objective could be measured is conceptualized with a CRDAD as it is in the development of a DRT. The items selected are expected to maximize the conventional measures of reliability and the discrimination of those criterion groups chosen because they are considered relevant to the purpose of the

specific test in question. Items all students can answer correctly are deleted from the test because they do not increase its discriminating power. *It is not meaningful to convert a raw score on a CRDAD to an estimate of the examinee's level of functioning because some of the items in the item pool (the poor discriminators) are intentionally excluded from the test.* It is *not* reasonable to expect the items retained in a CRDAD to be either a random or a representative sample of a defined class of performance tasks. The capability being measured by a CRDAD depends on the choice of criterion groups and on which items happened to be constructed and placed in the original item pool. These distinctions between DRT's and CRDAD's are summarized in Table 6-1.

Some test experts have argued that there is little that is distinctive about CR test development methodology. This position is easy to understand, especially if they equate CR tests with CRDAD's. Because a CRDAD is an individual or group difference measure having items which reference a specified objective or skill, it is not surprising that the test construction and evaluation procedures which have served testers well in the past will, for the most part, be applicable for CRDAD's.

At the present time most test experts turn to CRDAD's to measure a person's capability. In spite of his concept of content standard tests, Ebel (1973) holds to the traditional view that:

the job of any test is to test. This means that it must distinguish between those who have and those who lack a particular capability. It must distinguish between one who has more and one who has less capability. . . . Test reliability and item discrimination are just as important for criterion- as for norm-referenced tests [page 278].

A reviewer of an earlier draft of this monograph responded similarly. For him "accurate prediction of whether a person can or cannot perform a task *means exactly* accurate discrimination between groups of people who can and cannot perform the task." Again, a CRDAD is recommended for ascertaining status.

The claim that accurate measurement of a person's capability requires discrimination is debatable. One legitimate way to describe a person's capability on a class of tasks is to administer a random sample of these tasks. For such a test, the items need not discriminate. (All examinee's might, in truth, be equally capable with respect to

Table 6-1

Characteristics of two types of tests used to make criterion-referenced inferences

Characteristic	Domain-referenced test (DRT)	Differential assessment device capable of criterion-referenced inferences (CRDAD)
Content limitations of the items	Generated from the domain's definition; maximum specification of content limits	Made to "match" an instructional objective; content limits only partially specified
Item selection procedures	Random selection from the item pool	Empirically selected to maximize desired discriminations
Item and test variance required?	No	Yes
Types of reliability	Consistency of level-of-functioning estimates	Conventional procedures
Primary type of validity	Content	Criterion-related
Nature of the criterion groups[a]	None used in test development	Groups treated differently or individuals believed to differ in the capability being assessed
Inference most appropriate about . . .	Examinees' levels of functioning	Examinees' differential capabilities

[a] Criterion groups are the standards of categorization against which the test is compared. The test constructor and user hope that members of the two or more criterion groups will score differently on the test. For a test designed to measure an adolescent's interest in school, for example, school dropouts and graduates are reasonable, but not perfect, criterion groups.

the domain being referenced.) Further, for many important kinds of educational applications, a domain-referenced description of a person's capability is more appropriate. Practice in matching test type and educational application is the primary focus of the next section.

Relation of Test Uses to Desirable Test Characteristics

Recall that a particular feature of a DRT is that it permits estimation of an examinee's domain score or level of functioning, which describes a test taker's status in a most direct way as being the percent of tasks of a specified type he is expected to pass or answer in a given direction. In contrast, a distinguishing attribute of a CRDAD is that it is optimal for differentiating students who have more or less of a given capability as defined by the choice of criterion groups and the particular items constructed to match an instructional objective or measure a skill.

Given the above considerations, it follows that DRT's are advisable when the test user wishes to assess status relative to the performance tasks. This is in contrast to CRDAD's which are best suited for comparing examinees in order to determine their relative capability or predict group membership. *In general, a test cannot provide scores directly interpretable in terms of a set of performance tasks (that is, interpretable as an estimate of a domain score) and, at the same time, be optimal for differential assessment.* Items randomly chosen from a specified population of items will not be the same items optimal for discriminating criterion groups.

Because of the differences in the development and validation of domain-referenced and differential assessment instruments and their relative utility for a variety of educational purposes, it is important that the reader be able to distinguish which test type is more appropriate for a given educational application.

Three uses made of test scores are identified below. Following each one is a discussion about whether a DRT or a differential assessment instrument is the more appropriate one to use.

Example 1: To maximize preinstruction, postinstruction differences. As this first example is worded, a DAD is more appropriate because the test user wishes the test scores to differentiate the preinstruction and postinstruction criterion groups. (Although the same students may be in the two groups, their performance can be expected to differ the two times they are tested and are considered as separate criterion groups.)

Why would an educator wish to make such a discrimination? Glaser (1963) wrote that:

achievement tests used primarily to provide information about differences in treatments need to be constructed so as to maximize the discriminations made between *groups* treated differently and to minimize the differences between individuals in any one group. Such a test will be sensitive to the differences produced by instructional conditions. For example, a test designed to demonstrate the effectiveness of instruction would be constructed so that it was generally difficult for those taking it before training and generally easy after training. The content of the test used to differentiate treatments should be maximally sensitive to the performance changes anticipated from the instructional treatments. In essence, the distinction between achievement tests used to maximize individual differences and tests used to maximize treatment or group differences is established during the selection of test items [page 520].

Glaser was reacting against the use of individual difference measures, such as survey achievement tests, that contain items not well matched to the instructional objectives and thus not likely to reveal a treatment effect. Glaser's stance was quite reasonable. The solution offered in the above quote, however, is still a DAD. In spite of the critical remarks that follow—observations made with the benefit of a dozen years of hindsight—the pioneering contributions of people like Robert Glaser were indeed significant.

Proponents of DAD's for assessing treatment effectiveness could argue that DRT's are inefficient. DRT's could contain items that fail to relate preinstruction to postinstruction gains or, in the case of two programs being compared, fail to produce large between-treatment differences.

The wisdom of selecting items to maximize the gains or differences identified above is questioned. Such items are likely to measure more general skills or to refer to only a fraction of the instructional content. The goals that were not achieved, that were already mastered prior to instruction, or that are common to the two treatments will be underrepresented. Magnifying molehills to look like mountains may be important in politics, but the educator dedicated to program improvement requires a glass that does not distort. DRT's that can provide a realistic picture of student capabilities relative to all the domains of interest afford a sounder basis for program modification than is possible with DAD's.

The limitations of DAD's for program evaluation can be lessened if items measuring all the instructional goals are required to appear in the test, even though all the items referring to certain goals have meager discriminating power. Even then, however, the items that are selected may differ from those that are not because of unintentional item format or content congruences with an instructional treatment. Why not go all the way and define the classes of learner behaviors to be included in the assessment and randomly sample from such domains?

Example 2: To determine whether a student can solve percentage profit-and-loss word problems. Taken on face value, ascertaining this student's ability on such tasks is desired, and it is reasonable to conclude that a DRT would be the more effective way to achieve this. There is no implication in the stated application that the test user wishes to discriminate among students. Why would an educator want to determine the student's ability? The answer that comes to mind is to decide whether remediation is needed. For such a purpose, a DRT that contains items from a carefully defined domain is preferred. It would provide the educator with evidence of the student's ability on a representative sample of percentage profit-and-loss problems, and, thus, on whether further instruction were needed.

Example 3: To select students who can succeed on the next unit of instruction. A test able to determine whether two student groups can or cannot succeed on the next unit is desired. The purpose of the testing is not to describe how well the students can do on items like those on the test but to differentiate one group from another. A DAD is recommended for this, and to build such a test, criterion groups must exist. In the present example, two groups differing in their ability to succeed on the next unit of instruction need to be identified.

If such differentiated groups do not yet exist, the practitioner has a choice. He can make certain assumptions about data associated with such groups, an option discussed later in the section on "Criterion Groups Unobserved." Or, he can offer the next unit to an unselected group of students, note which students fall into the "succeed" and "cannot succeed" groups, and build a test following procedures listed in the section on "Criterion Groups Observed." Such a test can then be used to select students in other classes or in future

years. The practitioner can also select students based on scores on a test covering either the content in the unit just completed or the material in the next unit. Such tests designed to describe a student's status with respect to some content area may not be valid for predicting their success in learning new material.

The first problem set contains other test uses. The discriminations called for in these examples are important if the remaining material in this chapter is to be used most effectively. The reader is encouraged to attempt the examples in Problem Set 1 and read the commentary that follows.

Problem Set 1
Matching Test Type to Test Use

Directions:

For each application, discuss whether a domain-referenced test (DRT) or a differential assessment device (DAD) is more appropriate.

_____ 1. To assign letter grades on a curve: A to the highest achieving students, B to the next highest, etc.

_____ 2. To determine for which kinds of electrical circuits a student can compute the value of its total resistance.

_____ 3. To place the top twenty-four of the tenth graders in Honors English.

_____ 4. To ensure quality control by requiring each student to meet a minimum standard in assigned work.

_____ 5. To measure whether an objective has been mastered by a student so that remedial work can be assigned if needed.

_____ 6. To improve an instructional program by ascertaining those objectives that have and have not been met.

_____ 7. To correctly sort students into "levels of instruction," that is, according to how much instruction they received on the relevant content.

- -

Answers:

1. *DAD.* Curve grading means that some percentage of students will receive A's, some B's, etc. Since the allocation of the letter grades to the students depends upon one student's performance relative to another, a test that discriminates among the students yet references course objectives is required. In general, DAD's are preferred for classification, selection, or placement situations having a fixed quota, that is, having a predetermined number of examinees who will be classified or treated in a given way. The criterion variable in an example such as this is often the total score on the test. Items are retained which correlate highly with total test score, i.e., which discriminate the high from the low test scorers.

2. *DRT.* Diagnostic tests describe the status of the examinee with respect to several sets of tasks. A test which provides a random sample of items selected

from each set of tasks is appropriate. One question which helps in choosing between a DRT and a DAD is: If most students can answer a proposed test item correctly, do I still want it in my test? A "yes" answer implies that a DRT is preferred.

3. *DAD*. Since only twenty-four students can be selected for Honors English, it is important that the test results be able to differentiate the most deserving from the least deserving. Another fixed quota situation is being illustrated. As in problem 1, above, the criterion variable could be total score on the (English) test. Alternatively, the test user might wish to employ a criterion variable that is independent of the test, such as teacher ratings or previous grades in English.

4. *DRT*. The test user seeks to determine whether the student can achieve minimum performance on assigned tasks. In general, certification tests in a quota-free situation (that is, any examinee can qualify regardless of the performance of others taking the test), are more appropriately domain referenced.

5. *DRT*. Again, primary interest is on the student's performance relative to a set of tasks and not on differentiating among examinees.

6. *DRT*. This example is an extension of problem 5. For the reasons given when discussing the first example of the use of test scores, I believe that proficiency on the skills described by instructional objectives can best be assessed by a DRT.

7. *DAD*. This is essentially the same problem presented in the first example of the use of test scores. A test that is measuring the instructional objectives should yield different scores for students exposed to varying degrees of instruction. The criterion groups are defined by the several levels of instruction.

Other Terminology for Tests

Several terms have been employed to identify tests alleged to provide information about the specific knowledges and skills of examinees. In practice, such tests differ among themselves with respect to the explicitness with which this set of knowledges and skills is defined.

Content-Standard Tests

Ebel (1962) suggested the term *content-standard* for tests having scores that indicate "the per cent of a systematic sample from a defined domain of tasks which an individual has performed successfully" (page 15). The score "is based directly on the tasks which make up or provide the content of the test" (page 15). A key feature of the definition is that "the processes by which the scores are obtained—test construction, administration, and scoring—are explicit and objective enough so that independent investigators would obtain substantially the same scores for the same persons" (page 16). Ebel illustrated his concept with a test of word meanings.

Universe-Defined Tests

Osburn (1968) used the term *universe-defined* to describe "a test constructed and administered in such a way that an examinee's score on the test provides an unbiased estimate of his score on some explicitly defined universe of item content" (page 96). Like the case with content-standard tests, the criteria by which items are or are not included in the domain are made explicit, and those items that appear on the test are selected in some systematic way from the universe.

The difference between content-standard tests and universe-defined tests is primarily in Osburn's use of formalized schemes originated by Hively (1962), called *item forms,* to help generate the universe of test items and to describe the items' salient characteristics. (An item form is illustrated in Figure 6-1.) It appears that Osburn had in mind a more heterogeneous collection of test items in his universe than Ebel was considering, but this is really a matter of degree and not of kind.

Hively (personal communication) has used the term "domain-referenced" to refer to universe-defined tests because, for him, " 'universe' tends to suggest an attempt to specify *all* of the knowledge in a given field of subject matter in terms of an enormous set of test items. This turns out to be impossible: one can only define certain central or 'nuclear' portions from which other behavior is expected to generalize. The term 'domain' has therefore been chosen because of its less ambitious connotations."

Objective-based Tests

This term is much more nebulous than the others mentioned above. No test construction or validation procedures have been agreed upon. For some test users, any test constructed on the basis of a behaviorally stated (that is, performance) objective is objective-based. Such tests do not, however, guarantee that a satisfying criterion-referenced interpretation will be possible.

Consider the following reading comprehension (subcategory, inferences) objective taken from Borg Warner's System80 program on Reading Words in Context: "Given a picture and a printed question which refers to it, the student will select a conclusion which may be inferred from the material." One item on an objective-based test shows a picture of a very young boy and the printed question, "Was

the boy once a man?" The possible conclusions from which the student is to select are "yes" and "no." Note how the test item follows directly from the behaviorally stated objective.

A characteristic of such objective-based tests is that the nature of the final test depends largely on the idiosyncracies of the item writers. There is no reason to believe, for example, that two sets of item writers given the same behaviorally stated objective would construct tests that either looked alike or provided comparable scores if the same examinees took both. There are more ways to match an objective than are presented in the test. Too much slippage is possible in the item format used, choice of options, selection of stimulus material, resulting level of difficulty, and other areas for such congruence to occur. As an extreme example, a test writer could legitimately test for achievement on the objective cited in the paragraph above using an item containing a picture of a musical score and the question, "With which of the following five categories of music is the score most consonant?"

The problem with the likely lack of congruence between the efforts of different item writers is that objective-based tests are much less effective in satisfying the description function of tests than, say, a DRT. This is because an examinee's score depends upon the test constructor and is consequently hard to interpret in terms of absolute performance standards.

The objective-based tests of the National Assessment of Education Progress provide a good example of this difficulty. Although project workers attempt to cluster items to improve comprehension, meaningful interpretation of test results requires an inspection of actual test items. The objectives used as a basis for test construction do not result in a clear definition of a class of examinee performances which has meaning independent of the items employed in the assessment. Baker (1972) expressed this concern somewhat differently. To her, objective-based tests "contract for more than they deliver. . . . Tests which appear precise but are not can seriously mislead teachers and administrators" (page 4).

There is a significant practical problem here. On the one hand, scores on objective-based tests are less than optimum for communicating what the examinee knows or can do. On the other hand, generation of well-defined domains of test items as required in DRT's is often not feasible or, at the least, extremely difficult and time con-

suming. Further, they are susceptible to restrictive domain defini-tions because, in the attempt to be very precise about the content and format of the items in the population, the natural tendency is to delimit and reduce the magnitude of the domain being defined. Com-promise schemes are described later, in the section devoted to "De-fining the Item Population."

Mastery Tests

Mastery tests have been defined as "criterion referenced tests that are administered at the end of an educational treatment to determine whether the persons can perform all of the tasks specified in the ob-jectives of the program" (Cleary, 1971, page 7). Mayo (1970) used the term in the same way. In his description of mastery learning theory, Bloom (1968, 1973) distinguishes between "formative" and "summative" achievement instruments to measure mastery. The for-mer corresponds to the definition given above; the latter to the tradi-tional concept of a survey achievement test.

Nothing in the definition presented above prevents mastery tests from being either DRT's or CRDAD's. It describes primarily the function of such tests rather than their nature. The impact of mas-tery learning has not been, nor is it claimed to be, in stimulating a new kind of test development. Rather, it is in encouraging educators to set as their goal the surpassing by practically all students of per-formance standards set prior to instruction, and in offering advice on how such a goal can be realized.

An exception to the lack of specification of the nature of a mas-tery test is Harris' (1974) work. He offers a definition consistent with that above, namely, "an objectives-based test that is restricted to one or more specific objectives" (page 99) and designed for "mak-ing a 'mastery'–'non-mastery' decision for a given student" (page 99). For Harris, the ideal mastery test is a DRT with the further re-striction that, for an appropriate sample of students, the test items have both conceptual homogeneity "in the sense that the individual tasks are interchangeable *for the purpose of determining mastery*" (page 100) and response homogeneity, "a constant conditional prob-ability of answering an item correctly, given that the student has answered another item correctly" (page 102).

Other Expressions

In a worthwhile paper, Donlon (1974) states that, "We must aban-don our effort to get by with one term, criterion referenced, for it

simply cannot carry all of this semantic freight" (page 7). He proposes ten terms; namely, behavior referenced, decision referenced, distribution referenced, scale referenced, standard referenced, treatment referenced, and four others already mentioned in this chapter. Donlon's distinctions are consistent with the central thesis of his work that the defining aspect of a test is the interpretation one wishes to make from it.

The position taken here is that the several kinds of interpretations require one of only two general test development strategies leading to DRT's and DAD's. Test construction and evaluation guidelines for each of these tests will be offered in turn.

DOMAIN-REFERENCED TESTS

The focus of this part of the chapter is on tests intended to describe the current status of an examinee with respect to a well-explicated set of performance tasks called a domain. A random, or stratified random, sample of items from a domain will be called a domain-referenced test (DRT). Specific topics include defining the item population, selecting test items, establishing a passing score, estimating a domain score, determining test length, and evaluating the DRT.

Defining the Item Population

Discussion begins with the assumption that at least a general statement of the knowledges, skills, or attitudes to be measured exists. Whether emphasis should be placed on the importance of transfer tasks, useful knowledge, or humanistic objectives is not important here.

Traditional item-writing approaches use test plans that often list subject matter topics as row headings and constructs like knowledge and application as column headings. The cells are filled with numbers that designate how many items will measure a certain cognitive skill employing the designed subject matter topic. A test plan, for example, may specify inclusion of two items about Shakespeare's plays that measure the student's comprehension of main ideas. "These labels (constructs like comprehension) refer to mental processes, not to observable events. When the test writer selects such a label, he is using it to refer to something which occurs only in his private mental life" (Bormuth, 1970, page 11).

Test plans provide little guidance to the item writer in the sense

that the specific items he produces will largely reflect his own background and writing style. Two item writers given the same test plan and working independently would produce tests likely to correlate only moderately with each other and to have different difficulty levels.

Production of DRT's usually begins with behaviorally stated objectives, although at least one project (Rahmlow, 1972) began with a group of items that typified the abilities to be measured. "Unfortunately, it is almost impossible to state important objectives in behavioral terms that can be directly and unambiguously translated into measures that give explicit information about what an examinee can or cannot do" (Cleary, 1971). Good objectives are not item specific, which means there is usually a multitude of possible items that reference a given objective. Good objectives are referenced by a host of learner behaviors. More than behaviorally stated objectives are needed to define the domain.

The goal is to build meaning into the test so that when it is reported that a student answered 95 percent of the items correctly, such a score can be interpreted in terms of a set of tasks on which the student has demonstrated high proficiency. Such interpretation is not possible unless the population of items is clearly identified. Thus, we now consider the task of generating such an item population.

In another context, Popham (in press, a) states well the dilemma confronting a DRT constructor who

> must achieve that delicate balance between the twin criteria of clarity and practicality. The trick, it would appear, is to devise a scheme for isolating the important dimensions of a *class* of learner behaviors we are attempting to promote, then to describe those dimensions with a degree of detail such that the description is sufficiently circumscribing for clear communication, yet not so lengthy that educators will avoid employing it. That is a nontrivial trick.

Linguistics-based Schemes

At one extreme of clarity stands Bormuth's (1970) approach of deriving items using operational definitions:

> [These] operations should be capable of being systematically applied to an instructional program in such a way that all the items of the type derivable by those operations will be produced. When this requirement is met by a set of operations, not only does it insure the definability of item populations but it also insures that tests made by these operations will be independently reproduci-

ble given only a knowledge of what operations were used to derive the items and their responses [Bormuth, 1970, page 35].

By "operations" Bormuth means item transformations. Suppose the sentence, "The older sister put out the fire," was part of an instructional sequence. Some item transformations applicable to this sentence are provided below:

Transformation Name	Question
Echo	The older sister put out the fire?
Tag	The older sister put out the fire, didn't she?
Yes-No	Did the older sister put out the fire?
Noun deletion	Who put out the fire?
	What did the older sister put out?
Noun modifier deletion	Which sister put out the fire?

Using these examples of item transformation, supply answers for Problem Set 2.

Problem Set 2
Item Transformations

The following statement appears as part of a paragraph in a science unit on balance scales: The heavier object is closer to the ground. Only items formed by the "yes-no" and "noun modifier deletion" transformations are to be used in a test to measure comprehension of this statement. What questions can be used?
    1. Yes-No: _____
    2. Noun modifier deletion: _____

- -

Answers:
    1. Is the heavier object closer to the ground?
    2. Which object is closer to the ground?

This problem set demonstrates that it is possible to structure the rules by which test items can be generated such that any two test item writers will produce essentially the same questions and that the nature of the test domain is clearly understood. Bormuth (1970) and Anderson (1972) provide many more transformations that can be used to generate questions from written discourse.

Item Forms

Item forms is another technique used to define domains of test items very precisely.

An item form has the following characteristics: (1) it generates items with a fixed syntactical structure; (2) it contains one or more variable elements; and (3) it defines a class of item sentences by specifying the replacement sets for the variable elements [Osburn, 1968, page 97].

Figure 6-1 is an example of an item form. Other examples appear in Osburn (1968) and in Hively *et al.* (1973). The latter reference also provides a detailed accounting of DRT construction and use in the evaluation of a large curriculum development project.

The use of item forms permits an accurate description of the population of items in a DRT. The item form shell specifies the structure of the question (including materials, directions, script of the question), and the replacement sets contain the permitted variations in questions. For example, cell 7 in the cell matrix shown in Figure 6-1 denotes a situation in which the weights placed on the two sides of a beam balance are equal but they differ in size. (The weight on the left is greater in size than the weight on the right.) The replacement scheme for cell 7 indicates that appropriate items may be formed using replacement set 16.15. Replacement set 16.15 consists of ordered pairs (b,a) and (o,m) which translate to large and small size 23-gram weights and large and small 25-gram weights, respectively. (See the description of materials matrix.) Not all item forms are, or need be, this complex.

The payoff of such an elaborate scheme is that the population of items is known and can be precisely described. Further, if a student is administered a random or representative sample of these items, it makes sense to estimate the proportion of the domain of content he knows.

One pays for this clarity either in terms of time and effort required to specify the domain precisely or in terms of restrictiveness in setting domain bounds. Implementing the approaches suggested by Osburn (1968), Bormuth (1970), Anderson (1972), and Hively *et al.* (1973) either requires a lot of work or it forces the test writer to settle for a very homogeneous set of tasks that define the content domain. Sentence transformations and item forms may not adequate-

ITEM FORM 16.14*

Comparing two objects on equal-arm balance and choosing a symbol to complete a statement of the weight relation.

GENERAL DESCRIPTION

The child is asked to compare the weights of two objects that may be (1) indistinguishable by hefting but easily distinguished on the balance, (2) indistinguishable even on the balance. In each of these situations, size varies as an irrelevant dimension. An equal-arm balance is available but instructions for its use are non-directive. The child is asked to select one of the three symbols (>, <, and =) and place it in the blank space provided between the two weight symbols.

STIMULUS AND RESPONSE CHARACTERISTICS

Constant for All Cells

The equal-arm balance is of similar construction to that used in MINNEMAST Unit 16, made of Tinkertoys, cardboard, string, a metal weight, and foot ruler.

The objects are opaque, cylindrical bottles, identical except for weight (either 23 gm, or 25 gm) and size (either 2" × ⅜" or 2½" × 1¾"). Each is identified by a lower-case letter assigned at random.

The child is asked to complete a symbolic statement, corresponding to the weight relation, by choosing the correct relation symbol.

Distinguishing among Cells

Three weight relations (detectable by balance only, not by hefting or "feel") defined in terms of the location of the objects when placed in front of the child:

left > right; left < right; left = right.

Three size relations:

left > right; left < right; left = right.

CELL MATRIX

| Size | Weight Relations (Detectable by Balance Only) |||
	$W_l > W_r$	$W_l < W_r$	$W_l = W_r$
Relations			
$S_l > S_r$	(1)	(4)	(7)
$S_l < S_r$	(2)	(5)	(8)
$S_l = S_r$	(3)	(6)	(9)

* Originally developed by Wells Hively.

ITEM FORM SHELL

MATERIALS

Beam Balance
Objects 1 and r
from T.O. 16.14.0
Stimulus-Response sheet
(attached)
Pencil

DIRECTIONS TO E

Place materials in front of child. (Keep order of objects given above.)

	SCRIPT
+ → objects □ → S-R sheet	Here are two objects. They have symbols attached to them. Compare them by weight, and write one of these three signs (point) in the blank space to form the comparison sentence.
Balance Subject	You may use this balance if you need to.

RECORDING

Attach Stimulus-Response sheet to this page. Describe what child did.

If balance was used, insert object symbols in schematic drawing of the balance given below, and mark the position of the plumb-line at the time of child's judgment.

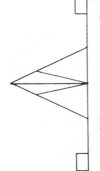

DESCRIPTION OF MATERIALS

Pencil (T.O. 16.1.1): Equal-arm beam balance made from tinker-toy materials as described in MINNEMAST Unit 16.

Beam Balance (T.O. 16.13.1): Equal-arm beam balance made from tinker-toy materials as described in MINNEMAST Unit 16.

Set of Weight Comparison objects (T.O. 16.14.0): Set of opaque plastic cylindrical bottles with firmly fitting lids. Two sizes of bottles have been chosen. The small bottle has a length of 2" and a diameter of ⅜". The large bottle has a length of 2½" and a diameter of 1¾". Two weight values have been chosen so that the objects cannot typically be distinguished by hefting but can be distinguished on the balance. Each object is designated by a randomly chosen, lower-case letter.

Size		Weight	
		23 gm	25 gm
small	a	m	
large	b	o	n

Stimulus-Response sheet (attached to item) (T.O. 16.14.1): a sheet of paper approximately 6" × 4" with the following display:

Write >, <, or = in the blank

$$W_l \_\_\_\_\_ W_r$$

where 1 and r are the appropriate subscripts (from Replacement Scheme).

REPLACEMENT SCHEME

(l,r) Objects		
Cell 1:	(o,a)	
Cell 2:	(m,b)	
Cell 3:	Choose	from R.S. 16.13
Cell 4:	(a,o)	
Cell 5:	(b,m)	
Cell 6:	Choose	from R.S. 16.13
Cell 7:	Choose	from R.S. 16.14
Cell 8:	Choose	from R.S. 16.15
Cell 9:	Choose	from R.S. 16.16

REPLACEMENTS SETS

R.S. 16.13	Ordered pairs	(m,a);	(o,b)
R.S. 16.14	Ordered pairs	(a,m);	(o,o)
R.S. 16.15	Ordered pairs	(b,a);	(o,m)
R.S. 16.16	Ordered pairs	(b,b);	(o,n)
R.S. 16.17	Ordered pairs	(m,k);	(o,n)

SCORING SPECIFICATIONS

A correct response is made by writing the correct symbol (>, <, or =) in the blank space to complete the comparison sentence. This should be the > in Cells 1, 2, and 3; < in Cells 4, 5, and 6; = in Cells 7, 8, and 9.

Figure 6-1

Example of an item form (from Hively *et al.*, 1973; reprinted with permission of the Center for the Study of Evaluation, University of California, Los Angeles)

ly capture the variety of test tasks an item writer may wish to employ in measuring a knowledge, skill, or attitude.[2]

Facet Analysis

Facet design was conceived by Louis Guttman as a way of laying out a domain for research. An excellent introduction to facet analysis is provided by Runkel (1965). See also Humphreys (1962) and Guttman (1969). Like the other approaches considered thus far, facet analysis can also be used to describe the boundaries and structure of a domain of testing conditions.

Facets are dimensions of a situation believed relevant in the measurement effort. In the domain-referenced application, facets can be thought of as the dimensions or characteristics on which the items in the domain are to differ. Facets are chosen before an item domain is described, and, thus, they differ from factors that emerge after data are collected and analyzed, which occurs with factor analysis.

Facets are often linked semantically in a "mapping sentence." Figure 6-2 illustrates a mapping sentence representing a combination, plus my corruption, of two noteworthy applications of facet analysis to attitude measurement (Jordan, 1971; Tunks, 1973).

The lettered facets illustrated in Figure 6-2 are referent, referent's commitment, level, and so on. The numbered aspects listed below each facet are called "elements." Items are formed from the mapping sentence by specifying the combinations of elements (one from each facet) to be included in the question. For example, use of A_1, B_1, C_1, D_2, E_2, F_3 would produce a question like, Do you believe that the elementary school music curriculum is taught by specialists for the purpose of giving students a break from academics? Using this pattern, work out Problem Set 3.

---

2. Durnin and Scandura (1973) have criticized the item forms approach because it is "based primarily on extensional analyses of item domains (i.e., analyses in terms of observable properties of items) . . . There appears to be little basis other than (possible) sound intuitive judgment as to how items should be categorized" (p. 263). Durnin and Scandura suggest an algorithmic approach based on an intuitive analysis of intension (i.e., analysis in terms of underlying rules or procedures). The algorithmic approach would appear to be most useful in the field of mathematics. Durnin and Scandura's criticism seems to be directed not so much at the item form concept as it is toward the manner in which the technology is implemented.

	A. REFERENT		B. REFERENT'S COMMITMENT
The subject attributes to the	1 self 2 music educators 3 general public 4 students	the	1 belief 2 feeling

	C. LEVEL		D. ACTOR'S (i.e., music curriculum's) BEHAVIOR	
that the	1 elementary 2 secondary	school music curriculum	1 should be 2 is	taught by

E. TEACHER		F. GENERAL STUDENT NEEDS
1 classroom 2 specialist	for the purpose of fulfilling	1 relaxation 2 means of expression 3 break from academics 4 emotional stimulation 5 self-discipline 6 fun time 7 contact with a human 8 group activity 9 uncover unknown talents 10 public performance 11 creative outlet 12 success 13 bring out shy students

Figure 6-2
A mapping sequence

Problem Set 3
Facet Analysis

1. Using the mapping sentence in Figure 6-2, write a question to measure attitude toward music curricula which employs the following elements: A_2, B_2, C_2, D_1, E_1, and F_{13}.

2. Suppose that the mapping sentence in Figure 6-2 ended as follows: for the purpose of developing F. SPECIFIC ABILITIES. List at least five possible elements which could reasonably be associated with the facet, specific abilities.

- -

Answers:

1. Do music educators feel that secondary school music curriculum should be taught by classroom teachers for the purpose of bringing out shy students?

2. The elements listed by Tunks (1973) are: sense of pitch, sense of timbre, sense of loudness, enjoyment of skills, awareness of instruments, awareness of various kinds of music, aesthetic capacities, understanding of music in cultures,

appreciation of musical organization, critical listening, listening concentration, group cooperation, word rhyming, and coordination through rhythm. This list is obviously not exhaustive.

At this point it may seem that there is a close parallel between an item form and a mapping sentence and between a replacement set and elements of a facet. Indeed, inspection of Figure 6-2 might well lead one to that opinion.

When one examines other mapping sentences, including those constructed by Guttman, himself, it becomes obvious that the nature of the possible test items is left very vague. This is especially true of Tidhar and Guttman's complex mapping sentence for the design of observations on the effectiveness of teaching methods (Guttman, 1969, page 57) and in the following sentence:

The performance of student (X) on an item presented in

verbal
digital   language and requiring   inference   of a rule
figural   application

exactly like
similar to   one taught within one of his school courses ⟶
unlike

high
low   performance   (Guttman, 1969, page 54).

It should be pointed out that Guttman and many of his followers do not use facet analysis to produce tests that can yield information concerned with percent of mastery. They seek to identify the dimensions important in accounting for test item responses and the structure of these dimensions. Nevertheless, it does appear that some of the ideas of facet analysis have utility for the construction of DRT's. An approach to test development that uses such ideas follows.

Amplified Objectives

Popham (in press, a) has suggested the need for a balance between clarity and practicality. The "amplified objective," a term originating

with Popham and illustrated in Figure 6-3, provides this balance. An amplified objective is an expanded statement of an educational goal which provides boundary specifications regarding testing situations, response alternatives, and criteria of correctness.

Notice that the amplified objective in Figure 6-3 gives the item writers a much clearer notion of the kinds of items they are to write than the unadorned objective would provide. There is still uncertainty, however, about what the complete class of learner tasks looks like. What are simple sentences? What constitutes familiar vocabulary? How are abstract and concrete nouns distinguished? Yet these ambiguities and others may be a small price to pay for the relative ease with which some domains can be described.

Popham (in press, b) offers a general, but lengthy discussion of the elements of an amplified objective. According to Popham, an exemplary amplified objective must possess a thorough description of what situations or stimuli can constitute an item, including the potential content from which items can be generated. This can be accomplished either by constructing content generation rules (algorithms) or by listing entire topics, novels, principles, years, authors, or other areas about which the items can deal.

Popham cites the need to detail not only what constitutes the correct or preferred answer (as in some affective tests) but also the incorrect or less acceptable answers. This need is great for selected response items like multiple-choice and true-false questions. The description of domains containing constructed response items like essay questions must, Popham argues, set forth a clearly delimited set of criteria by which to judge the adequacy of the answers.

Baker (1974) has also provided discussion of the components of a domain definition. Her list of aspects includes: (1) response description, that is, a behaviorally stated objective; (2) content limits, that is, a set of rules or a list of contents eligible for inclusion in the test items; (3) criteria for judging the adequacy of constructed responses or specification of the nature of the incorrect options for items requiring selected responses; (4) the format in which the items will be presented to the students; and (5) test directions.

Domain Size and the Defining Facets

All the item generation schemes discussed in this chapter leave unspecified the question of how to decide which of the possible tasks

Objective: Given a sentence with a noun or verb omitted, the student will select from two alternatives the word which most specifically or concretely completes the sentence.

Sample Item

Directions: Mark an "X" through one of the words in parentheses which makes the sentence describe a clearer picture.

Example: The racer (tumbled, went) down the hill.

Amplified Objective

Testing Situation

1. The student will be given simple sentences with the noun or verb omitted and will be asked to mark an "X" through the one word of a given pair of alternative words which more specifically or concretely completes the sentence.

2. Each test will omit nouns and verbs in approximately equal numbers.

3. Vocabulary will be familiar to a third- or fourth-grade pupil.

Response Alternatives

1. The student will be given pairs of nouns or pairs of verbs with distinctly varied degrees of descriptive power.

2. In pairs of verbs, one verb will either be a linking verb or an action verb descriptive of general action (e.g., is, goes), and one verb will be an action verb descriptive of the manner of movement involved (e.g., scrambled, skipped).

3. In pairs of nouns, one noun will be abstract or vague (e.g., man, thing), and one noun will be concrete or specific (e.g., carpenter, computer).

Criterion of Correctness

The correct answer will be an "X" marked through the more concrete, specific noun or through the more descriptive action verb in each given pair.

Figure 6-3
Amplified objective (reproduced with permission of the
Instructional Objectives Exchange, Post Office Box 24095, Los Angeles, 90024)

should be included in the domain. Rather, they provide rules for generating an item pool once the facets or dimensions of the domain are identified. There appear to be two related problems here: The first involves the domain size or how large a population of tasks should be conceptualized; the second concerns specific facets and elements that should be selected to define the domain.

Regarding the question of domain size, a trade-off is operating. A test user wishes to assess a broadly defined domain whose coverage matches program or instructional goals. Yet a test user also wishes to know what a student can or cannot do, and broadly defined domains (with their corresponding item heterogeneity) are apt to yield a test interpretation that the student can do some things but not others. Understanding new math is too broad; understanding elementary notions of set theory is better; understanding elementary operations on sets is manageable; discriminating between equal and equivalent sets *may* be too narrow. Test constructors fearful of defining domains too broadly would be well advised to consider dividing the domain into subdomains and assessing status separately for each. Optimum domain size depends on the test's purpose. A larger domain size can be tolerated in tests used for making major decisions or in gross score reporting. For remedial instruction in which information about specific skills is needed, smaller domain sizes are recommended.

Popham (in press, b) identifies three practical considerations in determining domain size. First, he suggests the test maker estimate the amount of instructional time it would take to acquire the skills in the domain. Domains that can be mastered in one instructional session are too small; those requiring an entire semester are too large. Second, he suggests that the test user estimate domain size by dividing the total number of high-priority skills and behaviors the test maker wishes to measure by the number of tests he is willing to give. A third consideration is to make the domain as large as one can and still maintain content homogeneity.

Once the knowledge, skill, or attitude to be assessed is determined, then, subject to practical constraints, the test developer should choose facets and elements within those facets that are believed to maximize item variance. As Lloyd Humphreys stated back in 1962: "The implication for practice in test construction is deliberately to make the test as heterogeneous as possible within the limits of the definition of what you are trying to measure" (page 481).

The general objective referenced by the domain presented in Figure 6-1 is that the examinee will be able to compare "two objects on equal-arm balance and (choose) a symbol to complete a statement of weight relation." The test constructor decided to vary the size-weight relationship between the two objects being compared, feeling perhaps as we do that such comparisons will be the ones on which an examinee is most likely to show varied performance. The test constructor also manipulated which side of the balance had the heavier weight and yet ignored number-weight comparisons, other magnitudes of weights, and other shapes of objects. The test constructor chose not to compare, for example, two objects totaling 28 grams with three objects weighing only 26 grams. We are not arguing that he should have, but merely call attention to the fact that decisions have to be made regarding which attributes of the testing situation are to be treated as variables in developing the domain definition.

We suggest that a domain be defined by those facets and elements that make a difference in how the examinee responds. Thus, for example, if the color the beam balance is painted does not affect how the student answers a weight comparison question, then color can be held constant or ignored. We know of no reason why facets of a domain need to be hierarchically arranged.

What facets make a difference? Our intuition can help. For some knowledge areas there is some empirical evidence on this question. More research is needed on the content and method variables that affect test performance. Two potentially useful procedures for research on this problem are the multiple regression approach as used by Smith and Shaw (1969) and the components of variance scheme proposed by Cronbach *et al.* (1972) to conduct generalizability studies.

Generating and Selecting Test Items

Defining the domain is not a simple task, as the preceding section has shown. A well-defined domain will, however, facilitate item construction. The task of the item writer is to produce items that adhere to the restrictions imposed by the domain definition. This task is almost mechanical for some situations; intelligence, rather than creativity, is needed for others.

In the attempt to write items, many questions about the domain's definition arise. Which testing formats are acceptable? Are transfer

tasks relevant? How bound to the instructional content and methods should the items be? Domain definition and item writing are reciprocal activities.

The test constructor is advised to submit the items to independent reviewers in order to evaluate item-domain congruence. This step is especially important when less precise domain-defining approaches, like amplified objectives, are used. It is preferable that the judges should not previously have been involved in either the creation of the domain or the writing of the items. A review of techniques for ascertaining agreement among judges is provided by Light (1973).

Assuming that there are more items written or conceptualized than will be used, the test should be constructed by taking a random or stratified random sample of items from the domain. This task has been accomplished by a computer so that different samples of items, that is, tests, are administered to different students. As long as students are not being compared with each other, they need not respond to the same tasks. Indeed, there is some advantage in their not doing so. This point will be amplified in the section "Educational Applications."

Should item difficulty and item discrimination indexes be used to choose items? No! Selection of items on these criteria can result in a test where the items are not representative of the domain in difficulty level or in the underlying attributes being measured. An examinee's status relative to a well-defined domain can best be gleaned from the examinee's responses to a representative sample of items from the item population. Items chosen by empirical means are likely to be average in difficulty and more homogeneous than is true of all the items. The use of item statistics destroys the random selection process, a defining characteristic of DRT's. Unless items are selected randomly, the estimate of a person's level of functioning loses meaning and the interpretability of the test score is reduced.

Item statistics can, however, be used to detect flawed items. For example, if it is believed that pairs of items matched on content should yield similar responses, or that all items should be about equally difficult, or that all items should all have high correlations with a composite score, then any item having statistics that do not conform to these expectations can be singled out for further scrutiny. Such examination could consist of interviewing students as they respond to the item. Such an encounter might reveal, for example,

that a sentence was unintentionally worded ambiguously, that a picture was not interpreted as the artist intended, or that students were ignorant of facts or vocabulary assumed known. If the item with aberrant data passes this examination, however, then it should be retained.

These same item statistics can help detect desirable modifications in the domain definition. For example, a subset of items having low correlations with other items may suggest the advisability of dividing the domain.

Empirical work has been encouraged as a means of identifying which of a multitude of potential facts and elements should be included in the definition of a domain. It will be shown later that test statistics can also supplement logical analysis when evaluating both the domain's definition and the test. Although empirical data are relevant for defining and evaluating a domain and the test, they should not be used as the basis for selecting the items on a DRT. This lack of a requirement for the usual large-scale empirical tryouts of items does not mean that DRT development is less rigorous than that of other tests. It simply means that the rigor has largely been transferred to defining the domain. Unfortunately, well-specified domain descriptions are almost nonexistent.

Establishing a Passing Standard

Why have a passing score? If the purpose of a DRT is to assess the present status of the examinee, then why is a passing score or standard needed? Unless some decision is to hinge on the score, then why set a passing one? An educator may wish to set a passing score, not necessarily because any decision rests on which side of the passing score the examinee is, but, rather, because he wishes to identify and communicate to others what performance is deemed acceptable.

If a test is to function as the basis for decision making, then a passing score can be established in accord with empirical relationships between DRT scores and outcomes experienced when the several decision alternatives are implemented. Data on what happens when students with different degrees of proficiency are subjected to alternative courses of action are very helpful in setting a passing score.

Whether or not to pass a student should depend not only on his test score in comparison with the standard, but also on the loss values associated with false positives and false negatives. For example,

the test user may want to promote a low-scoring student if the loss associated with holding back a person who should go ahead is high. This idea is formalized later when "Evaluating the Domain Definition and Test" is discussed.

Millman (1973) has described five sources of information helpful in setting standards on DRT's. One source identified is the test items themselves. Each test item or group of items can be inspected and a judgment made about how important it is that it be answered correctly. Millman (1973) has detailed a few of the procedures for translating these judgments to a passing score, but such procedures are of limited use for tests with content-homogeneous items.

Estimating Domain Scores

Assume that a test consisting of items randomly sampled from a domain has been administered to one or more individuals. In this section, two approaches will be described for estimating an examinee's domain score, that is, his level of functioning or the percentage of items likely to be answered correctly if the entire set of items in the domain were administered.

The two approaches are the binomial model and a Bayesian procedure described by Novick, Lewis, and Jackson (1973) and by Lewis, Wang, and Novick (1973). Both formulations limit generalizations about a person's domain score to a large population of items, a random sample of which is contained in the test. No assumptions are made about the homogeneity of item content or of item difficulty. Both approaches require that each item be scored either correct or incorrect. Both procedures assume independence of the responses, or, in effect, an examinee's expected performance is not likely to change as the items are completed. Contrary to the last named assumption, it is quite possible that learning or interference will take place during the conduct of an examination even without feedback to the examinee. If this were to happen, both of the following procedures would inappropriately estimate a person's domain score.

Binomial Model

In this conceptualization no group measures are considered, only the performance of the individual in question. The examinee's ability to pass or fail each of the items in the domain is likened to mixing two colors of marbles in a jar. Based on the examinee's performance

Table 6-2

Percentage of students expected to be misclassified

Passing score		Number of test items	Student's true level of functioning[a]						
			40	50	60	65	75	80	90
1	out of	1	40	50	60	65	25	20	10
2	out of	2	16	25	36	42	44	36	19
3	out of	3	6	13	22	27	58	49	27
3	out of	4	18	31	48	56	26	18	5
4	out of	5	9	19	34	43	37	26	8
5	out of	6	4	11	23	32	47	34	11
5	out of	7	10	23	42	53	24	15	3
6	out of	8	5	14	32	43	32	20	4
7	out of	9	3	9	23	34	40	26	5
7	out of	10	5	17	38	51	22	12	1
9	out of	12	2	7	23	35	35	21	3
11	out of	15	1	6	22	35	31	16	1
14	out of	20	1	6	25	42	21	9	—
18	out of	25	—	2	15	31	27	11	—
21	out of	30	—	2	18	36	20	6	—
28	out of	40	—	1	13	31	18	4	—
35	out of	50	—	—	10	28	16	3	—
42	out of	60	—	—	7	25	15	2	—
53	out of	75	—	—	4	18	16	2	—
70	out of	100	—	—	2	17	10	1	—

Note: Minimum passing score is 70 percent.

[a]The true level of functioning is the percentage of items a student would be able to answer correctly if he were given the entire universe of items. Students having true level-of-functioning values less than the minimum passing score of 70 should fail a test composed of items from this universe. However, on any given test of finite length, some of these students will get over 70 percent of the items correct and be considered "passers." The expected percentage of such misclassifications are given in the body of the table to the left of the broken line. Students having true level-of-functioning values greater than the passing percent of 70 should pass such a test. The percentage of these students who will be misclassified as "failures" are shown in the table to the right of the broken line.

on items in the test, an inference is made concerning the domain score in the same way that a statistician would infer the likely mix of the marbles given the proportion of each in a random sample. If instruction of a student has been particularly effective, most of the marbles should be the color designating "pass."

The percentage of items answered correctly on the test is taken as a point estimate of the examinee's domain score. If the examinee answers 6 out of 8 questions correctly, then, according to the model, the best guess for this individual is that, were all the items in the domain administered, the examinee's percentage correct score would be 6/8 or 75 percent.

The proportion of items on a particular test an examinee will answer correctly depends upon which items from the domain are sampled for that test. Tables like Table 6-2 are helpful in assessing sampling variations, and a collection of such tables appears in Millman (1972). Shown in Table 6-2 is the percentage of students likely to be misclassified, that is, the percentage of students whose test and domain percentages lie on opposite sides of the passing standard, or of any test score of interest. Practice in interpreting the table is provided in Problem Set 4.

Problem Set 4
Interpreting Table 6-2

1. What is the passing percent standard for which Table 6-2 is constructed?
2. How many items out of 40 must a student pass in order to meet the standard?
3. Assume a student could only answer 60 percent of the items in the entire domain if they were all administered. How likely is it that the student will meet the standard when given a 40-item test?
4. How likely is it for a person whose domain score (i.e., level of functioning) is 80 percent to pass a 40-item test?

- -

Answers:

1. The minimum passing percent for Table 6-2 is 70.
2. In order to meet this minimum, a student must answer correctly at least 70 percent of the 40 items or 28 items.
3. The student described in question 3 has a true level of functioning of 60. The intersect of the 60 column and the 28 out of 40 row yields a misclassification error rate of 13 percent. That is, there is a 13 percent chance that a student who can only answer 60 percent of all the items in the domain correctly will,

Jason Millman

nevertheless, be able to answer 28 or more of a sample of 40 items correctly and thus equal or exceed the 70 percent passing score.

4. The table entries represent percentages of misclassifications. Only 4 percent of students functioning at the 80 percent level will, on a 40-item test, be expected to dip below the passing score of 70 percent. Thus, the other 96 percent are expected to pass the 40-item test.

Table 6-2 can be of some value even if no passing percentage has been established. Assume an examinee scores 14 on a 20-item test, that is, 70 percent. (Other tables are available for other percents in Millman, 1972.) From Table 6-2, it can be seen that if this examinee's domain score were 50 percent, the chances would only be 6 percent that this examinee could have answered correctly 14 or more items out of 20. Thus, it is reasonable to conclude that this examinee most likely knows how to answer correctly at least 50 percent of the items in the domain. The binomial model, however, does not provide a numerical estimate of this likelihood; the Bayesian model discussed below does.

The binomial model can be used to provide estimates for other situations, such as when items are sampled in a stratified manner (say by facets), when a mean domain score for a group of individuals is desired and item-examinee sampling plans have been employed, or when changes in domain scores are of interest. These extensions have been discussed briefly by Millman (1974).

A Bayesian Model

The binomial model described above treats each examinee separately, as though data on other examinees taking the test do not exist. In contrast, the infrequently used Model II Bayesian approach described here considers the collateral information available on other students and on beliefs of the investigator as *prior* information. That is combined with the DRT results to provide refined, *posterior* estimates of domain scores.

More precise estimates are available using the Bayesian model or, if preferred, the same precision achieved through the binomial model is possible using shorter tests. The greater precision of the Bayesian model is "bought" at the "cost" of requiring more restrictive assumptions than the binomial formulation requires. Not only do the methods differ in precision; they also differ as to the estimated val-

ues for the domain scores. If the assumptions seem reasonable to the investigator, then the Bayesian model is to be preferred.

Before examining the nature of these assumptions and working a numerical problem, some notation will be helpful. Each of m students is administered the same test of n items. The jth student answers x_j questions correctly, and thus the student's score, expressed as a proportion, is $x_j/n = p_j$. The student's domain score, the proportion of all the items in the population which the student would answer correctly and the parameter being estimated, is π_j. In order to facilitate the analysis, p_j and π_j are transformed (using an inverse sin transformation) into two new variables, g_j and γ_j respectively. Following the analysis γ_j is transformed back to π_j, the parameter of interest.

One assumption of the model being described is that upon repeated administrations of n-item tests to person j, the distribution of g_j would be normal with mean γ_j and variance $= 1/(4n+2)$. This assumption will not be met for small n, but the approximation is seen as good enough for $n \geqslant 8$ and for values of π_j in the interval .15-.85 (Lewis, Wang, and Novick, 1973).

A second distribution is assumed, and this is the distribution of the transformed domain scores γ_j. Recall that m students are tested and, in theory, each has a γ_j. The m γ_j's are assumed to be a random sample from a normal distribution having mean μ_Γ and variance ϕ_Γ. The transformation from π_j to γ_j is to effect this normalization for a broad class of distributions for the π_j. This transformation will not be successful if the distribution of domain scores is U-shaped, as would occur if the test measured a unitary skill that does not admit to partial mastery.

Next, investigators are required to state their belief about the values of μ_Γ and ϕ_Γ as prior Bayes distributions, and must do so without regard to the particular sample of m students who were tested. It must be true that the investigator's prior beliefs about μ_Γ and ϕ_Γ are independent. This implies that the kind of thinking the investigators go through to state their belief about μ_Γ is not related to the determination of the prior values for ϕ_Γ.

This model also requires that the investigator set a uniform density function on his prior belief about μ_Γ, and set an inverse chi-square function for ϕ_Γ. According to Lewis *et al.* (1973), "The assumption of a uniform distribution for μ_Γ is more convenient than realistic but

does not significantly affect the analysis, provided m is reasonably large" (page 3). Reasonably large is later defined as fifteen or more people. A later formulation of the model permits the investigator to avoid the use of a uniform prior distribution on μ_Γ (Novick, personal communication). The inverse chi-square distribution, besides being mathematically tractable, is seen by Lewis *et al.* as a reasonable choice of a prior distribution. The investigator must still decide on appropriate values for ν and λ, two parameters of the inverse chi-square distribution. A method will be described for making this evaluation.

This model also makes an assumption that prior information is exchangeable. This means that the students should be considered part of a specifiable population and within that population prior information is identical about all students. This is a particularly important assumption because, if a given student is not seen as belonging to the group about which there are collateral data, inappropriate estimates of the student's domain score will be made if he is included in the analysis for that group.

Procedures for using the Bayesian model follow. These procedures are sufficiently detailed that they may seem out of place in this otherwise general treatment of CR measurement. They are included because a good expository treatment of them does not exist elsewhere at the present time. If the reader does not need the computational details of the Bayesian procedure, the text resumes following Table 6-5.

To begin, the reader is advised to note the summary of symbols for the Bayesian model found in Table 6-3. Listed in Figure 6-4 are the steps used in deriving both an estimated domain score for a student and the probability that the student's domain score exceeds some minimum passing standard or other score of interest. Alternatively, a computer program called MARPRO, written in the conversational mode, is available to perform these calculations (Lewis *et al.*, 1973).

Table 6-3

Symbols used in the Bayesian procedure to
estimate a person's domain score and the probability
that it exceeds a specified standard

Symbol	Identification
m	Number of individuals taking the test
j	Index identifying a particular examinee
x_j	Number of test items person j answers correctly
n	Number of items on the test
p_j	Proportion of test items person j answers correctly
π_j	True (but unobserved) domain score for person j (p_j is taken as the best estimate of π_j in the classical binomial model but not in the Bayesian one)
π_o	Minimum passing percentage score or other score of interest
g_j	Arc sin transformation of p_j
γ_j	Different arc sin transformation of π_j
γ_o	Arc sin transformation of π_o
μ_j	Mean estimate of γ_j which, when transformed back to units of proportions, is the estimate of π_j written $\hat{\pi}_j$
$\mu_\Gamma;\ \phi_\Gamma$	Mean and variance of a distribution of which the m γ_j's are considered a random sample
$\lambda;\ \nu$	Parameters of the inverse chi square distribution which must be set by the investigator based on subjective prior judgments
t	Measure of the strength of the investigator's prior knowledge about π_j which is then used to specify λ
$\rho^*; \phi^*; \omega^*$	Indexes used for intermediate calculations
z_o	Normal deviate; the area under the unit normal curve to the right of z_o is the probability that a person's domain score exceeds the passing score or other score of interest

1. For each person, compute the proportion of items answered correctly.

$$p_j = x_j/n$$

2. Convert π_o to γ_o units using the formula:

$$\gamma_o = \text{arc sin}\sqrt{\pi_o}$$

and Table 6-4. This value will not be used until Steps 13 and 14, which yield the probability that a person scoring p_j will have a domain score that exceeds π_o, any specific score of interest such as a passing score.

3. Convert each p_j to a g_j using the formula:

$$g_j = \text{arc sin}\sqrt{(x_j+3/8) / (n+3/4)} \ .$$

4. Compute the mean of all m g_j's.

$$g. = \Sigma g_j / m$$

5. Compute the sample variance of the g_j's.

$$s_g^2 = \Sigma(g_j-g.)^2 / m$$

6. Set a value for ν. Lewis et al. (1973) suggest $\nu=8$.

7. Set a value for t. One way to do this is the following. On the basis of your knowledge about the group of examinees, guess what the domain percent score will be for a single examinee randomly picked from the group. (You do not know who this examinee will be, however, at the time you make your estimate.) Now pretend the chosen examinee is given a test consisting of t items randomly sampled from the domain. How many items must there be on the test before you would accept the results of the testing as a better estimate of π_j than your own prior expectations? This number is t.

8. Compute

$$\lambda = \frac{\nu - 2}{4(t+1)}$$

9. Using the values of s_g^2, ν, and λ (Steps 5, 6, and 8), as well as the values of n and m for your situation, look up the values of $\rho*$ and $\omega*^2$ in tables provided by Wang (1973).

10. Calculate

$$\sigma*^2= \omega*^2 - \rho*^2.$$

11. Calculate

$$\mu_j = \rho*g_j + (1-\rho*)g. \ .$$

Each test score, x_j, will have associated with it a μ_j.

12. Estimate the domain score corresponding to an observed score by converting the μ_j's back into percentage units. Specifically, locate the value of μ_j in the θ column of Table 6-4 and read the corresponding estimated domain score given in the Y column.

13. Compute, for each value of g_j,

$$z_o = \frac{\gamma_o - \rho^*(g_j - g.) - g.}{\sqrt{\dfrac{1 + (m-1)\rho^*}{m(4n+2)} + (g_j - g.)^2 \sigma^{*2}}}$$

14. Look z_o up in a table of areas of the unit normal distribution. The area to the right of z_o is the probability that a person scoring p_j will have a domain score that exceeds the score of π_o. Note: The entire posterior distribution for a π_j (i.e., a distribution showing the probability of the jth person's domain score for all values of π from 0 to 1) can be estimated using formula 2 in Wang (1973).

Figure 6-4

Bayesian procedure for estimating domain scores

Table 6-4

Arc sin transformation ($\theta = $ arc sin $\sqrt{Y}$)

Y	θ	Y	θ	Y	θ	Y	θ
.00	.0000	.25	.5236	.50	.7854	.75	1.0472
.01	.1002	.26	.5350	.51	.7954	.76	1.0588
.02	.1419	.27	.5464	.52	.8054	.77	1.0706
.03	.1741	.28	.5576	.53	.8154	.78	1.0826
.04	.2014	.29	.5687	.54	.8254	.79	1.0948
.05	.2255	.30	.5796	.55	.8355	.80	1.1072
.06	.2474	.31	.5905	.56	.8456	.81	1.1198
.07	.2678	.32	.6012	.57	.8557	.82	1.1326
.08	.2868	.33	.6120	.58	.8658	.83	1.1458
.09	.3047	.34	.6226	.59	.8759	.84	1.1593
.10	.3218	.35	.6330	.60	.8861	.85	1.1731
.11	.3380	.36	.6435	.61	.8963	.86	1.1873
.12	.3538	.37	.6539	.62	.9066	.87	1.2020
.13	.3688	.38	.6642	.63	.9169	.88	1.2170
.14	.3835	.39	.6745	.64	.9273	.89	1.2328
.15	.3977	.40	.6847	.65	.9378	.90	1.2490
.16	.4115	.41	.6949	.66	.9482	.91	1.2661
.17	.4250	.42	.7050	.67	.9588	.92	1.2840
.18	.4382	.43	.7152	.68	.9696	.93	1.3031
.19	.4510	.44	.7252	.69	.9803	.94	1.3234
.20	.4636	.45	.7353	.70	.9911	.95	1.3453
.21	.4760	.46	.7454	.71	1.0021	.96	1.3694
.22	.4882	.47	.7554	.72	1.0132	.97	1.3967
.23	.5002	.48	.7654	.73	1.0244	.98	1.4289
.24	.5120	.49	.7754	.74	1.0358	.99	1.4706
						1.00	1.5708

Problem Set 5
A Numerical Example of the Bayesian Procedure

x	f	p_j	$(x+3/8)/(n+3/4)$	g
5	1	____	____	____
7	2	____	____	____
8	4	____	____	____
9	8	____	____	____
10	5	____	____	____
	20			

1. How many students took the test, and what symbol is used to express this number?

2. Although not possible to know for sure from the data presented above, $n=10$. What does that mean? Could $n=6$?

3. Fill in the blanks in the p_j column (Step 1).

4. Complete Step 2. Assume 70 percent is the score of interest.

5. Complete the remaining blanks (Step 3).

6. Complete Steps 4 and 5.

7. Set $\nu=8$. Assume you felt you had very little idea how students would do on the test and set $t = 2.75$. Calculate λ (Step 8).

8. Complete Step 9. The appropriate excerpt from Wang (1973) is reproduced in Table 6-5. It will be necessary to perform a linear interpolation to estimate values for $s_g^2 = .0244$.

9. Calculate $\sigma*^2$ (Step 10).

10. Calculate μ_1, the estimate of the first person's domain score in transformed units (Step 11). Compute μ_j for the other examinees.

11. Calculate the Bayesian estimate of person one's domain score. Recall his test score was 50 percent. Repeat for students receiving scores of 7, 8, 9, and 10.

12. What is the probability that π_1 (person one's actual domain score) is above 70 percent, the score of interest?

- -

Answers:

1. Twenty students ($m = 20$) took the test.

2. There were 10 items on the test. Since the test score, x, is the number of items answered correctly, n cannot equal 6. All but one student had scores over 6.

3. For the student scoring 5, say the first student, $p_1 = 5/10 = .50$. The p_j's associated with the other scores are .7, .8, .9, and 1.0.

4. $\pi_0 = .70$. From Table 6-4 one reads that arc $\sin\sqrt{.70} = .991$ (rounding).

5. For p_1, $(x_1+3/8) / (n+3/4) = 5.375/10.75 = .500$. For the other scores, the values are .686, .779, .872, and .965. When these five values are transformed, the g values are .785, .976, 1.081, 1.205, and 1.383. (See Table 6-4.)

6. $g. = 1.181$. Note that the values in the g column must be weighted by the number of examinees receiving the corresponding score. Use 20 in the denominator of the formulas for mean and variance. $s_g^2 = .0244$.

7. (Step 8) $\quad \lambda = \dfrac{8-2}{4(2.75+1)} = .4$

8. The top value in each set is for $\rho*$; the bottom one for $\omega*^2$. $\lambda/\nu = .4/8 = .05$.

For $m = 20$, $n = 10$, $\lambda/\nu = .05$, and $s_g^2 = .02$: $\rho* = .5500$
$$\omega*^2 = .3086$$
For $m = 20$, $n = 10$, $\lambda/\nu = .05$, and $s_g^2 = .03$: $\rho* = .5760$
$$\omega*^2 = .3380$$
For $s_g^2 = .0244$, $\rho* = .5500 + .44(.5760-.5500) = .561$
$$\omega*^2 = .3086 + .44(.3380-.3086) = .322$$

9. $\sigma*^2 = \omega*^2 - (\rho*)^2 = .322 - (.561)^2 = .0063$.

10. $\mu_1 = \rho* g_1 + (1-\rho*)g. = .561(.785) + (1-.561)1.181 = .959$. For students scoring 7, 8, 9, and 10, their μ_j's are, respectively, 1.066, 1.125, 1.195, and 1.294.

11. $\mu_1 = .959 = \arcsin \sqrt{\hat{\pi}_1}$. $\hat{\pi}_1 = 67$ percent. The estimated domain scores for students scoring 7, 8, 9 and 10 are, respectively, 77 percent, 81 percent, 86 percent, and 93 percent.

12. Substituting into the formula given in Step 13, $z_o = .265$. The area under the unit normal curve to the right of .265 is 40 percent. Thus, the probability is .40 that the first student's domain score exceeds 70 percent, the score value of interest.

Table 6-5

Excerpt from "Tables of Constants for the Posterior Marginal Estimates of Proportions in m Groups" (Wang, 1973)

Table of $\rho*$ and $\omega*^2$ for $m=20$, $n=10$

λ/ν	s_g^2				
	.01	.02	.03	.04	.05
.01	.2500	.2746	.3058	.3452	.3933
	.0677	.0820	.1018	.1296	.1671
.02	.3591	.3877	.4207	.4577	.4978
	.1353	.1576	.1854	.2187	.2576
.03	.4305	.4588	.4897	.5226	.5565
	.1917	.2176	.2474	.2811	.3178
.04	.4833	.5102	.5385	.5678	.5972
	.2398	.2669	.2969	.3294	.3635
.05	.5248	.5500	.5760	.6022	.6282
	.2813	.3086	.3380	.3688	.4007

Consideration of the results of the numerical example provides some interesting insights about this Bayesian procedure. Note that a person in this population scoring only 50 percent on this 10-item test is predicted to have a score of 67 percent on the universe of items. In general, students scoring below the mean of their group will be predicted to have higher domain scores than test scores and students scoring above the mean of their group on the test will be predicted to have lower domain scores. These adjustments operate very much like regression-toward-the-mean effects. Further, note that the adjustment is quite sizable for the person who has a somewhat extreme score. In fact, for a score of 50 percent on the short 10-item test, the Bayesian method estimates that there is a 40 percent probability that the person's domain score exceeds 70 percent.

Compare these results with those from the binomial model. According to that model, a person who had a domain score of 70 percent would be expected to score 5 or less on a 10-item test only 15 percent of the time whereas, according to the Bayesian model, a person who scored 5 on a 10-item test would be expected, 40 percent of the time, to have a domain score of 70 percent or more. *These statements must be read carefully as they are not directly comparable.*

When the investigator's confidence about prior beliefs increase from $t = 2.75$ (that is, $\lambda/\nu = .05$) to $t = 17.75$ (that is, $\lambda/\nu = .01$), the estimated domain score for the first person changes from 67 percent to 77 percent and the probability that the person's domain score exceeds 70 percent increases from 40 percent to 79 percent. That is, a person scoring 50 percent on a short test is thought to have about 4 chances in 5 of achieving a 70 percent or better domain score. In this case we are introducing very strong prior beliefs that the γ_j's are very tightly distributed about μ_Γ.

I believe the Bayesian approach holds much promise. More work is needed, however, regarding the robustness of the model against violations in its assumptions. Until such data are in, estimations lying somewhere between those generated from the conservative binomial model and the Bayesian model do not seem unreasonable.

Determining Test Length

A trade-off operates when a decision is made about the number of items for a DRT. Practical constraints, often in terms of available testing time, suggest that only a few items be used; desire for precise

information suggests a longer test. The trade-off is particularly evident when the test user wishes to measure status on a large number of domains simultaneously. For many applications, this situation either does not occur or a matrix sampling plan that reduces the testing time for any one student can be employed.

Some test publishers have employed very short tests. The Prescriptive Mathematics Inventory of the California Test Bureau has only single-item tests to measure each skill; the Individualized Criterion-Referenced Testing Program of the Educational Development Corporation uses 2-item tests. Besides being of questionable precision, such tests can only provide information about how a student can do on the particular test item and not on a more generalized class of tasks. Knowledge of ability to answer a specific item correctly has limited value, and almost invariably test publishers, the National Assessment of Educational Progress, and other developers of single-item indicators have found it necessary to attempt some kind of profile analysis in which responses to additional test items are employed. Rather than present student assessment data on a miscellaneous array of specific items, it would appear to be more profitable if the actual collection of items was carefully chosen from a well-defined domain.

Binomial Model

Tables like Table 6-2, above, can be of help in determining test length. They provide information on how precision of estimation varies as a function of test length. For example, suppose that 15 percent of the time the test constructor is willing for a student whose true domain score (level of functioning) is 60 percent to receive a test score as high as 70 percent. By going down the column labeled 60, we read that a test of 25 items would provide this accuracy. That is, there is only a 15 percent chance that a student whose domain score is 60 percent would receive a 70 percent or higher score on a 25-item test.

Question: How many items are needed if the test constructor wants roughly a 10 percent chance that a student whose domain score is 90 percent will receive less than 70 percent on the test?

Answer: An 11 percent error will occur if 6 items are used—that is, 11 percent of the time a person whose level of functioning is 90 percent will answer correctly only 4 or fewer questions on a 6-item DRT.

A Bayesian Model

Novick and Lewis (1974) have proposed a Bayesian solution to the problem of test length. Application of their procedures usually results in recommendations of shorter tests than obtained under the binomial model. The greater precision is achieved, in part, at the expense of requiring the educator to make many additional assumptions.

Some recommended test lengths are shown in Table 6-6. More extensive tables are being prepared (Novick, personal communication).

Table 6-6
Recommended domain-referenced test lengths[a]

π_o[b]	$\epsilon(\pi)$[c]	\multicolumn{4}{c}{Loss Ratio[d]}
		1.5	2.0	2.5	3.0
70%	70%	6/8 (75%)[e]	10/13 (77%)	11/14 (79%)	12/15 (80%)
75%	75%	8/10 (80%)	16/20 (80%)	17/21 (81%)	18/22 (82%)
80%	80%	6/7 (86%)	7/8 (88%)	17/20 (85%)	19/22 (86%)
80%	85%	8/10 (80%)	9/11 (82%)	10/12 (83%)	11/13 (85%)
85%	85%	7/8 (87½%)	9/10 (90%)	17/19 (89%)	19/21 (90%)

[a]Adapted from Novick and Lewis (1974). Assumes prior Beta distributions in which the amount of prior information contained in these distributions is equivalent to what would be gained from a test having 8-15 items.

[b]π_o is the criterion level or level of functioning that is sufficient to evidence mastery. Typically, these values have ranged from 70 percent to 85 percent.

[c]$\epsilon(\pi)$ is the expected mean level of functioning (for the group of examinees being tested) which is estimated *prior to* observing the actual test results. It is probably reasonable for an educator to expect that students who have completed a unit of instruction for which there was a 70 percent mastery criterion, for example, to have a mean true level of functioning value of 70 percent or higher. The values in the two rows for which π_o = 80 percent illustrate how sensitive test length recommendations are to $\epsilon(\pi)$.

[d]Loss ratio = $\dfrac{\text{loss associated with advancing a student whose } \pi \text{ is} < \pi_o}{\text{loss associated with retaining a student whose } \pi \text{ is} > \pi_o}$.

A loss ratio of 2, for example, means that it is judged twice as serious to advance a student erroneously (true level of functioning, π, is below the criterion level of π_o) than it is to retain a student erroneously. Note the sensitivity of the test length recommendations to the loss ratio chosen.

[e]Is read: An 8-item domain-referenced test and a passing score of 6 (75%) is recommended when the mastery criterion is 70 percent, the group's expected mean level of functioning is 70 percent, and the loss ratio is 1.5.

In addition to the usual binomial assumptions of independent observations on a random sample of pass-fail-type items, the values given in the table result from an assumption of the educator's prior belief that an examinee's level of functioning has a Beta distribution. This assumption may not be appropriate if the test's domain spans a single, specific skill that examinees either do not have at all (observed scores close to 0 percent) or have mastered completely (100 percent performance).

The technique also requires the educator to state his confidence in his prior information. The confidence or amount of information used to construct Table 6-6 is equivalent to what would be gained from a test having 8 to 15 items. Further, the educator must specify the criterion level, the mean level of functioning, and the loss ratio as defined in the footnotes to Table 6-6.

The reader should note that the suggested passing percents (shown in parentheses in Table 6-6) almost always exceed the criterion level, π_o, judged sufficient to evidence mastery. This difference is necessitated, in part, because a loss ratio greater than one is used. The reason for this will be explained in the following section of this chapter.

Not evident in the table is the fact that a trade-off is operating. The educator could make the passing score closer to the criterion level by having a longer test or, conversely, could employ shorter tests having very high passing percent scores. The test lengths shown in the table represent to Novick and Lewis a reasonable balance between having passing percents close to the mastery criterion and having efficient test lengths. Such tables, then, give advice on how much mastery the educator should aim for as well as on the length of the domain-referenced assessment instrument. The Novick and Lewis tables thus provide a resource for studying the effects on the instructional decision making process of four variables: average group attainment, loss ratio, specified criterion level, and test length.[3]

3. There is another approach to the problem of test length and to the question of test reliability than that presented here and in the next section. Some writers (for example, Emrick, 1971; Roudabush, 1974) have developed models in which they assume that an examinee occupies only one status with respect to the skill being tested, complete mastery or complete ignorance. Because these models assume that partial knowledge or skill does not exist, they are considered unrealistic and are not discussed further here.

Evaluating the Domain Definition and Test

Two characteristics by which tests are most often evaluated are reliability and validity. As explained by Hambleton and Novick (1973), the traditional ways of assessing these characteristics are probably inappropriate for tests which have "a well-specified content domain and the development of procedures for generating appropriate samples of test items" (page 161). Hambleton and Novick write:

> Because the designer of a criterion-referenced test has little interest in discriminating among examinees, no attempt is made to select items to produce a test of maximum test score variability, and thus, that variance will typically be small if instruction is effective. Also, criterion-referenced tests are usually administered either immediately before or after small units of instruction. Thus, it is not surprising that we frequently observe homogeneous distributions of test scores on pre- and post-tests, but centered at the low and high ends of the achievement scales, respectively. It is well known from the study of classical test theory . . . that when the variances of test scores is restricted, correlational estimates of reliability and validity will be low. Thus, it seems clear that the classical approaches to reliability and validity estimation will need to be interpreted more cautiously (or discarded) in the analysis of criterion-referenced tests [page 167].

Reliability

Reliability means consistency, but consistency does not require variability. It is suggested, therefore, that the reliability of DRT's be assessed by measuring the consistency of test performance (or of decisions based on test performance) for examinees administered two sets of items drawn from the same domain. It is recommended that the items from the two tests be intermingled during a single administration rather than giving all the items of one test after all the items of the other test were completed. Three specific data analysis approaches are provided below.[4]

Consistency of scores on parallel tests. For each examinee, compute his total score on each of two sets of items drawn from the same domain (that is, on randomly parallel tests). The smaller the discrepancy, the greater the reliability. This reliability can be displayed using a table or graph which indicates the percent of exam-

---

4. For an extensive summary of reliability and validity indexes for CR measures, see Brennan (1974).

inees having each possible difference score. (The direction of the difference, positive or negative, may be ignored.)

Because parallel tests with more items are expected to have greater differences in raw scores, it is recommended that such differences be expressed as differences in *percent* of items correct on the two tests. Further, it should be noted that this index is influenced by the difficulty of the tests. Thus, as is true of any empirical measure of goodness, the mean test scores should be stated, and the test group should be appropriate and described.

Consistency of decisions made from parallel test. For those situations in which the DRT will be used to make a decision (for example, pass or fail), it is recommended that the test be evaluated by computing the agreement of decisions suggested by the scores on the two parallel tests.

The decision whether to pass or fail a student need not be made solely on the basis of whether his estimated domain score exceeds, or fails to exceed, π_o, the criterion level judged sufficient to evidence mastery. Because the domain scores must be estimated, students may be incorrectly classified on the basis of their test performance. If the loss associated with the error of passing a student whose actual domain score is below the criterion level is very high, for example, the test user may wish to require a score higher than the criterion level before making the decision to pass. More specifically, one should choose this score, π, such that

$$a/b = \frac{\text{Probability } (\pi \geqslant \pi_o | \text{data})}{1 - \text{Probability } (\pi \geqslant \pi_o | \text{data})} \quad \text{where}$$

a/b is the ratio of the loss associated with incorrectly passing a student with an actual domain score below the criterion level to the loss associated with the error of failing to pass a student whose domain score is above the criterion level. π_o is the criterion level or original passing standard. π is the modified passing score, adjusted up or down to take into consideration the differential loss values associated with the two errors of misclassification, false positives (a) and false negatives (b). The probability values can be calculated using the Bayesian procedures described in Figure 6-4. The effect of the loss ratio on the modified passing percent is illustrated in Table 6-6.

Once a decision rule has been implemented, the consistency of the decisions made on parallel tests can be calculated. A simple index is the percentage of agreements, that is, the proportion of examinees placed into the same decision categories by both tests.

If a very low passing score is used and all examinees easily surpass this value, the test will be considered very reliable—even though there may be considerable variation in scores on the parallel forms of the test. The reliability of the decisions is high, of course, and it is the consistency of decisions that the index references. The passing score affects the size of the reliability index. Since this percentage of agreements depends on the decision rule (and the ability of the examinees relative to the critical test values), this information should accompany the reliability index.

Swaminathan *et al.* (in press) recommend that the index of agreement of decisions be adjusted to correct for chance agreements as follows:

$$p'_o = \frac{(p_o - p_e)}{(1 - p_e)}, \text{ where}$$

p'_o and p_o are the adjusted and observed proportion of consistent decisions, and p_e is the expected (by chance) proportion of agreements. The expected value is computed by multiplying and then summing the marginal proportions of the same decision categories for the two tests, as done in a chi-square test of association and as illustrated in Problem Set 6.

The numerator of the above formula is the difference between observed and chance proportions of agreements; the denominator is the maximum value this difference can take. Thus, p'_o may be interpreted as the proportion of the total number of possible agreements above the chance level that was actually achieved. The values of p_o and p'_o can be very different because they measure different notions of decision-making consistency. For this reason, it is recommended that both values be reported.

Consistency of item scores. Several authors have suggested that the reliability of a DRT be assessed by noting the consistency of responses to matched items on parallel tests. A typical index is the proportion of all the times the test users passed both or failed both of each pair of matched items.

This index provides more information about the properties of the items than it does about the reliability of the test. Like the other indexes mentioned, it is influenced by item difficulty. Lengthening the test will not increase this so-called reliability coefficient, a property we come to expect of such indexes. It is recommended that this third approach not be used. (Lengthening the test will increase the other indexes of consistency mentioned above, however.)

Because the index based on item-by-item comparisons is not influenced by item length, a test user need not have parallel tests. He can merely divide his items into matched pairs and let the consistency measure calculated on these pairs be the "reliability" index for the entire test.

Such a procedure will not work for the first two approaches recommended. The reliability computed on a half test will underestimate the agreements which would be expected to occur if the double-length test were used. Nor can the Spearman-Brown correction be used since the indicators in these approaches are not correlation coefficients.

Practice in computing the several indicators described above is provided in Problem Set 6.

Problem Set 6
Reliability Indicators for Domain-Referenced Tests

Consider the following data:

Person	Test A (4 items) 1	2	3	4	Score	Randomly Parallel Test A' 1	2	3	4	Score
A	1	0	1	1	3	1	1	0	1	3
B	1	1	0	1	3	1	0	0	1	2
C	1	1	1	1	4	1	1	1	0	3
D	0	1	0	0	1	1	1	0	1	3
E	1	1	1	0	3	1	1	1	1	4

Exercises:

1. Construct a table showing the consistency of test scores (in percent) on the randomly parallel DRT's.

2a. Indicate the consistency of pass-fail decisions made from the parallel tests and correct this value for chance agreements. Assume that a passing score of 75 percent is employed, that the test score is used as a direct estimate of the domain score, and that losses associated with false positives and false negatives are considered equal.

2b. In reference to exercise 2a, would the score used to decide if the person should be passed be (i) greater than 75 percent, (ii) equal to 75 percent, or (iii) less than 75 percent if the test user wished especially to avoid "failing" a student whose actual domain score might be greater than 75 percent?

3. Compute the proportion of times matched items are both passed or both failed.

- -

Answers:

1.

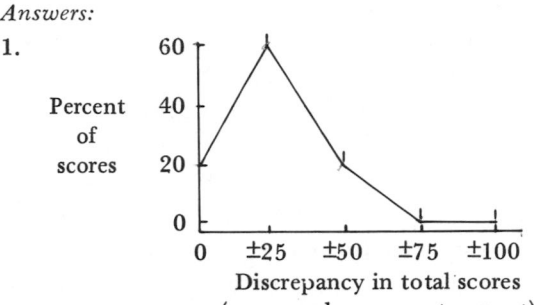

Discrepancy in total scores
(expressed as percent correct)

2a.   Test A$'$

		P	F	
Test A	P	.6	.2	.8
	F	.2	0	.2
		.8	.2	1.0

$p_o = .6 + 0 = .6$ (i.e., 3/5)

$p_e = (.8 \times .8) + (.2 \times .2) = .64 + .04 = .68$

$$p'_o = \frac{.6 - .68}{1 - .68} = \frac{-.08}{.32} = -.25$$

The negative value indicates that the agreement rate was less than that expected by chance.

2b. iii (less than 75 percent).

3. Number of times each person passed both or failed both matched items:
A(2), B(3), C(3), D(2), E(3).

Total = 13/20 = .65.

Validity

Validity can best be thought of as the accuracy of inferences made from test scores. What are the inferences most appropriate for a DRT? As was indicated in Table 6-1, the inference most appropriate for a DRT is about an examinee's level of functioning. This inference concerns the student's status relative to a previously defined domain and, in our view, can most effectively be evaluated by a logical analysis of the domain definition, item generation scheme, and individual test items.

If a very large number of items in the domain could be adminis- tered to several individuals, then a measure of validity for an n-item test would be the similarity of each person's percentage score on the very large set of items to the score on the smaller set of n items. If correlations were computed between the smaller and larger sets of items, then the above view of validity of a DRT would correspond to the classic test theory notion of the index of reliability (the correla- tion between observed and true scores) which, in turn, is the upper bound for test validity. That is, except for sampling variability, in theory the correlation between the DRT and a very large number of items taken from the same domain must exceed the correlation be- tween the DRT and any other observable criterion measure.

There are other, more feasible, empirical procedures of some use in evaluating a DRT. In each case, a psychometric property of the DRT is hypothesized. The test user has a theory (or wish) about how the scores should behave. The validation procedure is to note the cor- respondence between the predicted and actual empirical relationship.

One such predicted relationship "is that all items are of equal diffi- culty for that student and the conditional probability of his passing a randomly chosen item, given that he has passed another item in the item form, is unity" (Harris, 1974, page 101). Some test constructors may, on the other hand, choose to define their domain more broadly than Harris so that the above requirement of item response homo- geneity is neither reasonable nor likely.

Another prediction might be that the items in the test reference a hierarchically arranged set of skills such that, for given pairs of items, students who pass one item should pass an item measuring a sup- posedly prerequisite skill, but the reverse need not occur. For this prediction, the test user might compute Yule's Q, a coefficient which, unlike the phi coefficient, is independent of the difficulty lev- els of the two items. The formula for Yule's Q is:

$$\frac{ad - bc}{ad + bc} \text{ where}$$

a, b, c, and d are defined in Problem Set 7, where test results and criterion group are changed to items 1 and 2, respectively, and in- structed and uninstructed become pass and fail.

Predictions can be made between the relationship between the test

scores and criterion variables such as score differences prior to and after instruction, teacher ratings, and so forth. Such predictions are a central part of the construction and validation process of differential assessment devices and are discussed in greater detail in the next part of this chapter.

All such empirical evidence is useful for validating a DRT only to the extent that the hypothesized relationships are reasonable because the evidence is a measure of both the quality of the test and of the theory on which the predictions are based. One's ideas may be in error about how items should relate, about how successful the instruction is (in the preinstruction-postinstruction example), or about hypothesized correlates of the test scores. Failure to find empirical confirmation for the validity of a DRT should not be taken as conclusive evidence that the DRT is invalid.

DIFFERENTIAL ASSESSMENT DEVICES

One use of tests mentioned at the beginning of this chapter is to discriminate between individuals or groups of individuals believed to differ on the attribute purportedly measured by the test. Tests having this function were referred to earlier as differential assessment devices (DAD's). Some DAD's reference a particular objective or skill with sufficient specification that a criterion-referenced interpretation is reasonable. The development and evaluation of such tests, labeled CRDAD's, follows. A review of Table 6-1, where the distinctions between domain-referenced tests (DRT's) and differential assessment devices capable of a criterion-referenced interpretation (CRDAD's) are made and the definition of criterion groups is supplied, might prove helpful.

One difficulty encountered in constructing DAD's is that the attribute on which the individuals or groups of individuals are to be differentiated is a construct. These attributes are described in terms of knowledges, skills, or attitudes that are unobserved. The test constructor does not know the true status of the examinees. He does not have available, for example, criterion groups of examinees who have mastered and examinees who have not mastered a particular skill because mastery cannot be seen, only inferred.

The educator has at least three ways out of this dilemma: (1) He can avoid the need for criterion groups and estimate the examinee's

status using the domain-referenced test construction procedures described earlier. Such tests are not optimum for differential assessment because DRT's may contain nondiscriminating items. (2) He can substitute known groups for the unobservable criterion variable. Thus, the criterion groups are now observable and can be employed in the test construction process in ways described in "Criterion Groups Observed." (3) He can make assumptions about the relationship between performance on the test items and the unobserved criterion variable or group memberships, as explained in "Criterion Groups Unobserved."

Criterion Groups Observed

Choosing the Criterion Variable

Two of the most popular substitute groups to serve as an observable criterion variable are preinstruction and postinstruction groups (the same individuals tested twice), and instructed and uninstructed groups (different individuals in the two groups). The rationale for using such groups is that, when examinees have not been instructed, they may be expected to have relatively less of the skills or abilities being measured; instructed groups should have more. The groups should differ in their mastery of the objective referenced by the test items.

The use of these substitute groups permits the test constructor to develop an instrument sensitive to instruction. "There are problems with such methods, however: they assume that the instruction was indeed effective; they tend to produce instructionally dependent measures; and they are biased by maturation and other irrelevant systematic factors that might tend to improve scores over time" (Klein and Kosecoff, 1973, page 6). Selecting items on the basis of how well they discriminate groups differing in level of instruction, then, can produce tests that give too much weight to general skills and certain aspects of the instructional content.

Another popular observable criterion is the total score on the test. The rationale is that examinees having most of the attribute are the ones who will score highest, and the most valid items are those having the greatest correlation with the total score. This criterion is also useful in the construction of affective measures. It is not as effective as the levels of instruction criteria for building a test that is both sensitive to instruction and optimum for documenting changes

produced by an instructional program. Further, total score as a criterion tends to lead to the selection of items more homogeneous in content and difficulty than would appear warranted by the nature of the underlying skill or attitude being measured.

There is another basis for grouping which, although rarely found in the literature, appears to have greater utility. If the classification variable is the degree to which an examinee has profited from instruction provided under specified conditions, then a test which predicted success in later instruction could be most helpful in making instructional decisions for that individual. This discrimination problem resembles the situation for which aptitude tests were originally constructed. An illustration of the use of this criterion within an instructional management context is provided by Moncrief (1974).

The degree to which an individual has profited from instruction differs from other observable criterion variables in one important respect. This variable is not necessarily a substitute for an underlying construct. The indicators of success in an advanced stage in the instructional sequence may be considered to be the real criterion of interest and not a proxy. It is for this reason that DAD's constructed using this criterion variable are seen as particularly well suited when the resulting test is to be used to make an instructional decision for each learner.

It is important to note that the items chosen for a CRDAD will not be the same when different criterion variables are used. (See, for example, Cox and Vargas, 1966; Gorth and Hambleton, 1972.) A test constructed to perform one set of discriminations will not be optimum to predict a different criterion.

Developing an Item Pool

The view was expressed earlier that a trade-off existed between tests that maximize interpretability (DRT's) and those that maximize differential assessment (DAD's). Those DAD's that required the items to match an instructional objective (CRDAD's) are less discriminating, but more interpretable (in a criterion-referenced sense), than DAD's in general. The reason that CRDAD's do not maximize differential assessment is because the items best able to discriminate between the criterion groups may not be those which reference specific objectives.

Schriber (1973) presented some data that bear on this issue for the criterion variable, success in future instruction as measured by semes-

ter course grade. Three tests were available as predictors. One consisted of a 40-item unit test that measured how well the examinee could learn an initial aspect of the course. The second was an aptitude test, the School and College Ability Test (SCAT). The third test contained 34 items randomly chosen from the domain of test items covering the course content. A second set of 34 randomly chosen test items administered one month later was also available.

The unit test correlated highest with the criterion variable ($r = .69$); the SCAT test followed ($r = .49$); the test of randomly chosen items was last ($r = .36$, one set; $R = .44$, both sets).[5] Thus, identifying whether an examinee would do well in a course was predicted better both from an achievement test over a short section of the course and from an ability test than from a test consisting of items randomly sampled from the domain of content for the course.

It is not my purpose to offer, on the basis of this one set of data, any generalization about which items best predict the criterion—the degree to which learners profited from future instruction as measured by the semester course grade. The point that is clear is that a test composed of items referencing the terminal course content may not be best for differentiating learners on this variable.

Similarly, the best predictors of the criterion, level of instruction, or even total test score may not be items which match instructional objectives. Nevertheless, the loss in discriminability may be slight, and the gain in face validity and CR interpretability may warrant restricting the predictors to items that do match an instructional objective.

If the decision is to produce a CRDAD, then many of the same considerations as discussed in reference to DRT items apply here. The test constructor must decide on the variety of testing formats desirable, the degree to which transfer tasks are relevant, and, in general, how closely bound the items should be to the particular instructional content and methods used.

Once a pool of items judged to match an instructional objective has been produced, the next task in the CRDAD construction

---

5. It is not clear how the semester course grade was arrived at. Three unit tests and a final semester test (consisting of a fourth unit test and another set of 34 items randomly chosen from the same content domain) were available. It appears unlikely that the semester course grade depended sufficiently on only the first unit test to explain its markedly higher predictive validity.

process is to select the specific items to appear on the test. It is at this stage that DRT and CRDAD development procedures are most diverse. For DRT's, the selection of items is random. For CRDAD's (or DAD's, in general) the selection is empirically based and criterion related. Some of these techniques are discussed in the next section.

Selecting the Specific Test Items

Several procedures have been suggested for choosing from a larger pool of items those that would be best for use in a CRDAD. The goal is to develop for future use a shorter test of designated length that will maintain, perhaps surpass, the validity of the test composed of all the items in the pool.

The techniques mentioned below are described as though each examinee in the test development group responded to each item in the item pool. Such data may be difficult to obtain, especially if a large number of items are being considered. Spreading the testing over several days may alleviate the problem. Since all the techniques merely require certain data about the items and their relation to the classification variable, it is possible to obtain such data by matrix sampling techniques. (See the section on "Program Evaluation.")[6]

It should be noted that the techniques described below for selecting items do not mention a further content analysis of the items per se. This is because the task is now viewed as one of maximizing discriminations using the items already included in the pool. The focus is on the usefulness of the item in this regard and not its content. Of course, the test constructor is free to make further compromises with discriminability to achieve increased interpretability and require that a certain number of items from each subset of items be chosen, even though they would not have been selected using only an empirical criterion.

Finally, it would seem advisable that the test construction group be as similar as possible to future groups using the test. The data serv-

6. Because item intercorrelations are needed for the Step-Wise Multiple Regression technique, each examinee must take two or more subtests, and all pairs of subtests must be administered. The difficulty with such a plan besides some added administrative complexity is that the item intercorrelations will be based on only a fraction of the number of cases as they would be had all items been given to all examinees. This can be particularly serious for the Step-Wise Multiple Regression technique, which requires a large number of cases when the number of items in the pool is large.

ing as the input to all the methods of item selection described below should be obtained in a situation closely resembling the conditions under which the test will be employed.

Item Discrimination Method. Perhaps the easiest item selection method to employ is picking those items demonstrating the largest differences in difficulty levels between the criterion groups. For each criterion group (for example, students instructed, students not instructed; preinstruction group, postinstruction group), the proportion of examinees answering each item correctly is calculated. Those items for which the discrepancy in difficulty levels is largest (in the predicted direction) are chosen for the test.

This method amounts to saying: pick the items having the highest validity coefficients with the criterion classification. This is because difference in means can be thought of in correlational terms—the greater the difference, all things being equal, the higher the correlation. Should the criterion be a continuous variable, like profits from instruction as measured by semester grade, for example, this method amounts to computing the validity correlations directly.

Variations in this procedure are possible. Kosecoff and Klein (1974) provide a review of several indexes of item goodness and offer two of their own. See also Brennan (1974). The difficulty with all these statistics is that knowledge of the discriminability of the individual items does not provide the best guidance for selecting the group of items to be included in the test. The correlations among the items (predictors) are ignored, and it is well known that discrimination can be improved when item intercorrelations are employed in the selection process. For example, it may be better to use two items, each having moderate validity but measuring different aspects of the criterion (low intercorrelation), than to use two items, each having high validity but with a high correlation between them. The two procedures suggested next both consider interitem correlations.

Step-Wise Multiple Regression. This analysis procedure is advocated when two conditions are met: first, the number of items in the item pool is not too large (say fifty or less); second, the ratio of the number of examinees for whom complete data are available to the number of items is high (say 15 to 1).[7] If these conditions are not

7. This ratio can be relaxed somewhat if the multiple correlation between the items and the criterion is high (say greater than .7) and the pool of items represents a somewhat heterogeneous collection having fairly low interitem correlations relative to item validities.

met, a procedure is recommended which uses partial correlations as a screening device.

The step-wise multiple regression procedure involves the computation and utilization of all the interitem correlations. When the number of items is large, the number of interitem correlations is very large, and the resulting pattern of such correlations is particularly susceptible to sampling variability unless the number of examinees is also very large. This sampling variability can result in marked validity shrinkage when the test is employed with a group of examinees different from the test construction groups, and this is why the procedure is not recommended unless the two conditions mentioned above are met.

Question: Is the step-wise multiple regression procedure recommended if you wish to pick 10 of 30 items and you have data on 200 students?

Answer: Although the size of the item pool (30) is not considered too large, the second condition above is not met. Given 30 predictors, a sample size of over 400 is recommended. Thus, the step-wise multiple regression procedure should be dropped in favor of the partial correlation one in this situation. Note that the fact that the final test is to have only ten items is not taken into account in choosing between the two contending item selection procedures.

Multiple regression is a standard statistical procedure which yields a system for weighting a set of predictors (test items) to maximize their correlation with a criterion. Step-wise procedures attempt to choose a smaller set of predictors which have maximum validity (for their number) in the sample of examinees on which the data were analyzed.

The procedure consists simply of feeding into any one of the canned step-wise computer programs the scores on all the items and the criterion group for each examinee. Zero-one coding can be used for dichotomous variables. (If the criterion consists of three or more unordered groups, discriminant analysis discussed in standard multivariate statistical texts is to be used.) The output of the computer program includes a number of prediction equations, each containing one more predictor (test item) than the previous one. That prediction equation which employs the number of items desired on the test should be used to determine not only which items are to be selected

but also how the item scores are to be weighted. Using integer values roughly proportional to the regression coefficients should not seriously affect the test's validity.

Partial Correlations as Item Selection Criteria. Although this procedure suggested by Darlington and Bishop (1966) indirectly makes use of interitem correlations in the selection of test items, these correlations are not so heavily involved as they are in the step-wise multiple regression technique. Consequently, when the number of items is large or the ratio of the number of examinees to the number of items is low, the partial correlation method can be expected to yield higher validity values with a replication sample than can regression techniques or simple validity coefficients. This has repeatedly been found to be true (Richard Darlington, personal communication).

Three types of data about each examinee are employed when the partial correlation technique is used. First, there are responses to each item. If the items are scored right or wrong, the responses are usually coded 0 (wrong) and 1 (right). The letter i will be used to designate the item score variable. There will be as many i variables as there are items in the item pool.

Second, there is exactly one criterion score, c, for each examinee. If the classification basis is uninstructed-instructed, then the criterion score of 0 is given to examinees in the uninstructed group and a score of 1 is given to examinees in the instructed group. If the classification basis is preinstruction-postinstruction, then the test constructor has three options at least for assigning a criterion score to each examinee. The preferred option to be chosen depends upon the nature of the discrimination which the test user wishes and this, in turn, depends upon the intended use of the test results.

1. Randomly divide the sample into two groups and let $c = 0$ for examinees being considered the preinstruction group and $c = 1$ for examinees considered the postinstruction group. Let the coded preinstruction item responses be the i values for the preinstruction group and the coded postinstruction item responses be the i values for the postinstruction group. A test measuring sensitivity to instruction will be formed.

2. Let the criterion variable be the difference in total score on all the items between the preinstruction and postinstruction administrations. The i values are the coded responses to the items on the *pre*instruction administration. A test predicting gain will be formed.

3. Let c be the *post*instruction total score and i be the coded item responses on the *pre*instruction administration. A test predicting postinstruction test performance will be formed.

The third kind of data needed for each examinee is his scores on the several trial versions of the CR test being developed by this iteration procedure. The symbols t_1 and t_2 represent such scores.

Correlations between the i, c, and t variables will be computed. The i variables and possibly the c variable will likely be coded 0-1. A Pearson product-moment correlation, r, can be computed to represent the correlations involving such dichotomous variables and is numerically equivalent to the phi coefficient (when both variables being correlated are dichotomies) or the point-biserial coefficient (when only one of the two variables is a dichotomy). The steps to be followed in this item selection procedure are shown in Figure 6-5.

---

1. Compute r_{ic} for each item.
2. Select the n items having the highest values of r_{ic} where n is roughly 70 percent of the total number of items desired on the final test. (For example, if a 25-item CRDAD test is planned, select 17 or 18 items.) These n items represent the first version of the CRDAD test being developed.
3. Compute for each examinee his total score, t_1, on this first version test.
4. For each item in the entire pool compute

$$r_{ic} - (r_{it_1} \times r_{ct_1}). \quad (1)$$

Expression (1) is the numerator of a partial correlation. Alternatively, the partial correlation coefficient itself can be employed in place of expression (1) if the test constructor finds it more convenient to do so.
5. Select the roughly one-third n items having the highest values for expression (1). Add these items to the original n items to form the second version of the CRDAD test being developed. If the same item is selected in both steps 2 and 5, note the algebraic sign of r_{ic} and expression (1) for that item. If the signs are the same, retain the item in the test and, if you like, give it a double weight in determining an examinee's test score. If the signs are different, eliminate the item from this version of the test.
6. Repeat steps 4 and 5 with these changes. In expression (1), replace t_1 by t_2 and select only enough new items to insure that the third (and final) version of the test will have the preferred number of test items.

Figure 6-5
Item selection procedure based on partial correlations
(from Darlington and Bishop, 1966)

Choosing Procedures for Validation

Test scores and criterion status are the basic observed information needed to validate tests designed to discriminate groups. These data should preferably be collected on a replication sample, that is, obtained from a different group of examinees than the test development group.

There are two possible focuses of validation for tests intended for use in group differentiation. One is criterion group-oriented and is concerned with the relationship between test scores and criterion status. A second is decision-oriented and concerned with incremental utility, the difference in utility achievable using the test compared to not using the test. As will be illustrated, a test able to discriminate among criterion groups may not have the utility in a specific context.

Evaluating test score and criterion status correspondence. Correlational techniques are one way to demonstrate test score and criterion status correspondence. When both the test scores and the indicator of criterion status are continuous, a Pearson product-moment correlation, r, can be used to index the test's validity. When the criterion status is a dichotomy, then a point-biserial correlation between the test score (continuous variable) and the criterion score (dichotomy) is appropriate. When more than three criterion groups are employed, the correlation ratio eta can be used. The phi coefficient is appropriate when both the criterion and the test scores are dichotomies. Several other indexes have been proposed for evaluating tests designed to differentiate groups and some of these methods are referenced and briefly described in Marshall (1973). Problem Set 7 provides practice in evaluating the criterion-related validity of tests using a correlational approach.

Problem Set 7
Criterion-related Validity for Differential
Assessment Devices Using a Correlational Procedure

Assume the following data:

Test results	Criterion group	
	Instructed	Uninstructed
Pass	a (42)	b (3)
Fail	c (6)	d (9)

Questions:

1. If students who pass the test are predicted to be classified as instructed and those who fail the test are not, what is the "hit rate" (percent of correct differentiations) for the test?

2. Using the correlation index, phi, what is the correlation between the test results and the criterion classifications? The formula for phi is:

$$\text{phi} = \frac{(a \times d) - (b \times c)}{\sqrt{(a+b)(c+d)(a+c)(b+d)}}.$$

3. (a) How many students were classified as instructed?
   (b) How many students passed the test?
   (c) If the passing score on the test were lowered so that three more students were able to pass it, how would the values of the correct answers to questions 1 and 2 be affected?

- -

Answers:

1. (42+9) / 60 = 85%

2. $\text{phi} = \dfrac{(42 \times 9) - (6 \times 3)}{\sqrt{45 \times 15 \times 48 \times 12}} = .58$

3. (a) 48
   (b) 45
   (c) The answers to questions 1 and 2 would probably change but with the information available it is impossible to know whether or not the validity values would increase or decrease.

A set of techniques called analysis of variance offers another way to assess the ability of test scores to differentiate criterion groups. Figure 6-6 displays the layout of data for subsequent analysis when the same students are in each criterion group. This situation most often occurs when a test's sensitivity to preinstruction, postinstruction changes is being judged. When instructed and uninstructed groups contain different students or, more generally, when a test's sensitivity to different treatments is being evaluated, the data layout shown in Figure 6-7 is more appropriate.

It is recommended that the data be analyzed using one of the several available analysis of variance computer programs. The output of such programs contains the values for the mean squares (MS's) needed in the formula for validity. The validity coefficient can be interpreted as the proportion of variance due to criterion groups to

	Occasion 1,					Occasion o,				
	students					same students				
Items	1	2	. . .	s		1	2	. . .	s	
1	x	x	. . .	x		x	x	. . .	x	
2	x	x	. . .	x		x	x	. . .	x	
3	x	x	. . .	x		x	x	. . .	x	
.	.	.	. . .	.		.	.	. . .	.	
.	.	.	. . .	.		.	.	. . .	.	
.	.	.	. . .	.		.	.	. . .	.	
i	.	.	. . .	.		.	.	. . .	.	

x: score on an item, usually has the value of 0 or 1.

o: number of occasions. For example, $o = 2$ if one occasion is pretest and the other occasion is posttest.

s: number of students. Each student must be tested on each occasion.

i: number of items on the test.

$$\text{Validity} = \frac{\sigma^2_{occasion}}{\sigma^2_{occasion} + \sigma^2_{item \ by \ occasion \ by \ student \ interaction}}$$

$$= \frac{\sigma^2_{occasion}}{\frac{MS_{occasion} - MS_{student \ by \ occasion \ interaction} - MS_{item \ by \ occasion \ interaction} + MS_{item \ by \ occasion \ by \ student \ interaction}}{MS_{student \ by \ occasion \ interaction} - MS_{item \ by \ occasion \ interaction} + (1 + is)MS_{item \ by \ occasion \ by \ student \ interaction}}}$$

MS: mean square, computed during an analysis of variance.

Figure 6-6

Validity of a test to discriminate between two or more occasions (each student must be tested on each occasion)

Treatment 1,   · · ·   Treatment t,
different students   different students

Items	\multicolumn{4}{c}{students}				\multicolumn{4}{c}{students}			
	1	2	...	s	1	2	...	s
1	x	x	...	x	x	x	...	x
2	x	x	...	x	x	x	...	x
3	x	x	...	x	x	x	...	x
.	.	.	...	.	.	.	...	.
.	.	.	...	.	.	.	...	.
.	.	.	...	.	.	.	...	.
i	x	x	...	x	x	x	...	x

x: score on an item. Usually has the value of 0 or 1.

t: number of treatments. For example, $t = 2$ if one treatment is instructed and the other is not instructed.

s: number of students in each group.

i: number of items on the test.

$$\text{Validity} = \frac{\sigma^2_{treatment}}{\sigma^2_{treatment} + \sigma^2_{item\ by\ student\ interaction\ within\ treatments\ (error)}}$$

$$= \frac{MS_{treatment} - MS_{item\ by\ treatment\ interaction} - MS_{students\ within\ treatments} + MS_{item\ by\ student\ interaction\ within\ treatments}}{MS_{treatment} - MS_{item\ by\ treatment\ interaction} - MS_{students\ within\ treatments} + (1 + si)MS_{item\ by\ student\ interaction\ within\ treatments}}$$

MS: mean square, computed during an analysis of variance.

Figure 6-7
Validity of a test to discriminate between two or more treatments
(different, but equal number of students in each treatment)

the sum of the variance attributed to criterion groups and to "error." All things being equal, the larger the differences in test performance between criterion groups, the greater the variance due to criterion groups, and the higher the validity index.

Ozenne (1971) has presented different formulas derived from analysis of variance models that I feel are less applicable to the evaluation tasks considered in this chapter. Millman and Glass (1967) provide rules of thumb for hand calculation of the analysis of variance and for computation of other sources of variation the test user may wish to consider as error. The most comprehensive treatment of the use of analysis of variance in test evaluation is contained in Cronbach *et al.* (1972). Problem Set 8 provides practice in evaluating the criterion-related validity of tests using analysis of variance.

Problem Set 8
Criterion-Related Validity for Differential Assessment Devices
Using Analysis of Variance

Assume the following data:

Item	Pretest S_1	S_2	S_3	S_4		Posttest S_1	S_2	S_3	S_4
1	1	1	0	0		1	1	1	1
2	0	0	0	0		1	1	0	1
3	0	0	0	1		0	1	0	1

Note: Application of this procedure in practice should involve many more students than shown here.

$MS_{occasion} = 1.5$

$MS_{student \ by \ occasion \ interaction} = .05556$

$MS_{item \ by \ occasion \ interaction} = .125$

$MS_{item \ by \ occasion \ by \ student \ interaction} = .18056$

Questions:

1. Which set-up is more appropriate for this problem, that shown in Figure 6-6 or that shown in Figure 6-7?
2. What is the posttest score for the first student?
3. What are the values of i and s?
4. What is the validity coefficient for this test for discriminating between pretest and posttest scores?
5. Give a verbal interpretation of your answer to question 4.

- -

Answers:

1. If the same four students took the pretest and the posttest, then Figure 6-6 is the more appropriate.

2. Two. Item three was missed.

3. $i = 3; s = 4$.

4. $1.50/3.67 = .41$.

5. The variance due to differences between the pretest and posttest scores is 41 percent of the total variance attributed to the two testing times and to error.

There have been objections to using correlational and analysis of variance procedures because they depend upon score variability. A typical argument is:

Since the meaningfulness of a norm-referenced score is basically dependent on the relative position of the score in comparison with other scores, the more variability in the scores the better . . . . With criterion-referenced tests, variability is irrelevant. The meaning of the score is not dependent on comparison with other scores; it flows directly from the connection between the items and the criterion [Popham and Husek, 1969, page 3].

It has been pointed out that descriptive interpretations and group differentiation are two uses to which test information is put. Writers who argue that correlational and related techniques have no place in evaluating CR tests undoubtedly are thinking of the descriptive functions of these tests and, more specifically, of domain-referenced or objectives-based measures. Nevertheless, when the purpose of the test is group differentiation, then variability of test scores is not only relevant, but it is essential. This is because the criterion has variability, and only a test yielding scores having variability can have predictive validity. (If the criterion classification had no variability—that is, all examinees are in the same group—then no discrimination task remains and a test is of no value.) For a further discussion of whether item and test variance is needed for CRT's, see Woodson (1974) and Millman and Popham's (1974) reply to Woodson.

There is frequently a desire to establish a cutoff or passing score when the criterion is a dichotomy (for example, preinstruction-postinstruction scores). Two simple ways such a cutoff score might be determined are: (*a*) in the test development group consider successive cutoff scores and choose the one producing the greatest differentiation index (validity coefficient) for the test, or (*b*) select as the cutoff score that value which divides the test scores of the test development group in the same proportion as there are members in each of the criterion classifications. In both cases, the test developer hopes that the data for a replication group are similar to that for the test

development group on which the cutoff scores were based. (A technical treatment of procedures for establishing cutoff scores and measuring classification error rates may be found in Hockersmith, 1969.)

Evaluating the incremental utility of the test.[8] In the example provided in problem set 6, the hit rate was 51 out of 60. If the test were not used at all and all the examinees were classified as instructed, the hit rate would be almost as high: 48 out of 60. One limitation of the techniques referenced in the previous section, then, is that they do not describe the value of the test in comparison with a competing alternative such as not using the test at all. In general, the value of a test is less as the base rate (proportion of cases in a criterion group) approaches zero or one.

A second limitation of the correlational- and analysis of variance-based techniques is that they do not weight the seriousness of the two kinds of misclassifications (false positives, false negatives) nor the benefits of the correct classifications. Although the setting of relative utility values for these kinds of hits and errors is admittedly subjective, it is better to try to estimate them than to assume them equal by default.

The approach presented in Figure 6-8 meets these limitations head on. Four elements in the applied setting are considered. Like before, there are the test results and independently arrived at criterion classifications. These classifications might utilize teacher judgments or past performance of the student and represent a basis for making instructional decisions which the test is attempting to improve. The third element is the educational treatments, dealing with the choices available next in the instructional program of a student. Finally, there are the utilities associated with employing each instructional treatment with each type of student. The procedure presented in Figure 6-8 is appropriate when there are two treatments and two criterion classifications. The formulas can be generalized readily, however, for situations having more treatments or categories.

To illustrate a situation in which the procedure is applicable, suppose that some students are permitted to take an instructional unit (t_1). Students not exposed to t_1 continue with a remedial lesson, t_2. The basis for the decision as to whether a student would be allowed to take the new unit is the teacher's judgment, that is, the teacher classifies the students into "take" (g_1) and "not take" (g_2) cate-

---

8. For another expository treatment of the material presented in this section, see Darlington and Stauffer (1966).

Symbols

P_p	: Proportion of the entire sample who passed the test
P_{g_1}	: Proportion of the entire sample in group 1
$P_{g_1\|p}$	: Proportion of those who passed the test who are in group 1
$P_{g_1\|f}$	: Proportion of those who failed the test who are in group 1
$U_{t_1g_1}(U_{t_1g_2},$ $U_{t_2g_1}, U_{t_2g_2})$	: Mean utility of treatment 1 (1, 2, 2) for students in group 1 (2, 1, 2)
$A(B, C, D)$	: Mean utility when students who passed (passed, failed, failed) the test are given treatment 1 (2, 1, 2)
E	: Mean utility when test results are used to assign treatments
$F(G)$	: Mean utility when treatment 1 (2) is given to all students
V	: Incremental value of the test

Formulas

$$A = (P_{g_1|p})(U_{t_1g_1}) + (1-P_{g_1|p})(U_{t_1g_2})$$
$$B = (P_{g_1|p})(U_{t_2g_1}) + (1-P_{g_1|p})(U_{t_2g_2})$$
$$C = (P_{g_1|f})(U_{t_1g_1}) + (1-P_{g_1|f})(U_{t_1g_2})$$
$$D = (P_{g_1|f})(U_{t_2g_1}) + (1-P_{g_1|f})(U_{t_2g_2})$$
$$E = P_p(\text{higher of } A \text{ and } B) + (1-P_p)(\text{higher of } C \text{ and } D)$$
$$F = P_{g_1}(U_{t_1g_1}) + (1-P_{g_1})(U_{t_1g_2})$$
$$G = P_{g_1}(U_{t_2g_1}) + (1-P_{g_1})(U_{t_2g_2})$$
$$V = E - (\text{higher of } F \text{ and } G)$$

Figure 6-8
Symbols and formulas for determining the incremental value
of a differential assessment device

gories. The question is, what value does a test covering, say, the content of the old unit have in this context?

To continue the example, suppose it was felt that the benefit (utility) of the new instructional unit to the g_1 students is twice the benefit that the g_2 students get from the remedial lesson, and this benefit in turn is only slightly more than these same g_2 students are expected to receive were they to get the new lesson instead. Thus, relative utility values of 6, 3, and 2 seem reasonable for $U_{t_1g_1}$, $U_{t_2g_2}$,

and $U_{t_1 g_2}$, respectively. Finally, the benefit expected for students classified as g_1, were they made to continue with the remedial lesson, is to be very slight, and $U_{t_2 g_1}$ was set equal to one.

These utility values are used in Problem Set 9. For the example in this problem set, the test had a zero relative utility. That is, the educator would be as well off by not giving the test and letting everyone take the new lesson. However, when the benefit of g_2 students taking remedial work is seen to be substantial ($U_{t_2 g_2}$ = 8), then the test's value was positive, although relatively small. (See questions 3 and 5, Problem Set 9.)

Problem Set 9
Determining the Incremental Value of a Test

Frequency of students

Test results	Group (classification determined without reference to the test results)	
	1. Take (new unit)	2. Not take (remedial)
Pass	42	3
Fail	6	9

Utility values

Treatments	Group (classification determined without reference to the test results)	
	Take	Not take
1. Study new unit	6	2
2. Remedial study	1	3

Questions:

1. Compute the incremental value of the test (see Figure 6-8).
2. How should the test be used in assigning students to the instructional alternatives?

3. If $U_{t_2 g_2}$ were 8, what would the incremental value of the test now be?
4. If $U_{t_2 g_2}$ = 8, how should the test be used in assigning students to the two treatments?

5. What meaning does the numerical value which is the answer to question 3 have? Is it a big number in terms of V units?

Answers:

1. $A = (.933)(6) + (.067)(2) = 5.73$
   $B = (.933)(1) + (.067)(3) = 1.13$
   $C = (.40)(6) + (.60)(2) = 3.60$
   $D = (.40)(1) + (.60)(3) = 2.20$
   $E = .75(5.73) + .25(3.60) = 5.20$
   $F = .80(6) + .20(2) = 5.20$
   $G = .80(1) + .20(3) = 1.40$
   $V = 5.20 - 5.20 = -.00$

2. The test should not be used. The fact that F and E are numerically equal indicates that the mean utility obtained by permitting everyone to study the new unit is no higher than if treatments were assigned on the basis of test score.

3. The values for A, C, and F would remain unchanged.
   $B = (.933)(1) + (.067)(8) = 1.47$
   $D = (.40)(1) + (.60)(8) = 5.20$
   $E = (.75)(5.73) + (.25)(5.20) = 5.60$
   $G = (.80)(1) + (.20)(8) = 2.40$
   $V = 5.60 - 5.20 = .40$

4. Since A = 5.73 is greater than B = 1.47, students who passed the test should be given treatment 1 (study new unit). Since D = 5.20 is greater than C = 3.60, students who failed the test should be given treatment 2 (remedial study).

5. The incremental value, given the utilities specified in Question 3, is four-tenths of a utility unit. The interpretation of this magnitude can best be made in light of the four values chosen for U_{tg}. In the present example, the incremental value of .4 is equivalent to one-fifteenth of the estimated benefit derived when a student in group 1 elects the new unit ($U_{t_1 g_1}$ = 6) and somewhat less than half the benefit when a group 1 student is assigned the remedial work. This may seem a small increment in per student utility. Still, given that V is a positive value and assuming the various costs associated with the testings can be ignored, the test should be used in allocating students to the two educational programs.

Criterion Groups Unobserved

The technique described here is particularly appropriate when the test constructor wishes to build an instrument which will have maximum validity for classifying examinees into unobserved criterion groups. A likely situation is one in which the test user wishes to discriminate masters from nonmasters but has no independent way of

knowing which examinees are masters and which are nonmasters. The test user does not know the value of the criterion, c, and so cannot employ the techniques just discussed.

When the test constructor establishes criterion groups, as was done in the procedures described above, it is assumed, which means that the test constructor acts as though, such groups are formed without error and that less than perfect classification represents a weakness of the test. An alternative is for the test constructor to make assumptions not about the infallibility of the group memberships but about his accuracy in judging the relative magnitudes of the relationship between an unobserved criterion group membership (or an unobserved continuous criterion variable) and potential test items or other observed data about the examinees. These assumed relationships can then be used to develop a classification system that uses the available predictors and will maximize the percentage of correct classifications on the unobserved criterion. The test constructor still must decide on the nature of the true criterion variable on which he wishes to maximize predictive accuracy, but in this procedure the scores or classification of examinees on this variable need not be available.

In addition to the unobserved criterion variable, two other classes of variables are employed: (1) validating variables and (2) predictor variables (usually test items in the application we are considering). A validating variable is one for which the test constructor can estimate the relative validity (correlation) with the unobserved criterion, but it will not be part of the test. A predictor variable can be used as part of the prediction system with samples of examinees other than the test construction group. The relative validity of a predictor variable may or may not be estimated. These classes of variables need not be mutually exclusive; a variable may be either a validating or a predictor variable or it may be both.

For purposes of illustration, suppose the test constructor has the following information on the test construction sample:

(a) scores on 25 items, 10 of which will be selected for a test to differentiate masters from nonmasters;

(b) teacher's rating of the student's mastery level;

(c) student's sex.

The 25 items are clearly predictor variables because it is anticipated that the 10 best will be used in future samples. Assuming the test constructor is unwilling to have variables (b) and (c) be part of

his test (regardless of how useful they turn out to be for differentiating masters from nonmasters), these variables are not predictor variables. The requirement for variables to be validating variables, however, is that the test constructors can estimate their relative validities.

Let us pretend that the test constructor believes that all 25 items are equally valid predictors of mastery or nonmastery. He might then assign a validity weight of 1 to each item as his estimate of these variables' relative validities. It is not necessary that every item be estimated to have the same validity or even that the relative validity of all the items be estimated.

Further, let us suppose that the test constructor feels the teachers' ratings are not that accurate and would have the same weight as 4 test items. That is, teachers' ratings are estimated to have as much validity as a 4-item test. In this case, the relative validity (V) for teachers' ratings can be estimated by:

$$V = v \sqrt{\frac{K(1 - r + r/n)}{(1 - r + Kr/n)}} \quad \text{where} \quad (2)$$

v is the average relative validity estimate given to each test item

K is the number of items in the test which is believed to have the same validity as the variable whose relative validity (V) is being estimated

r is the reliability of the test estimated by the Kuder-Richardson Formula 20 or a split-half technique

n is the number of test items on which the reliability value was calculated

Question: What are the values of v, K, and n in the present example?

Answer: $v = 1$, $K = 4$, and $n = 25$. If $r = .50$ and these values are substituted into equation (2), then $V = 1.9$. That is, the relative validity for teachers' ratings should be estimated to be 1.9 if the validity of each test item is estimated to be 1. Note that a 4-item test does not have four times the validity of a single-item test.

Continuing our example, assume that the test constructor believes there is a difference between the sexes in their mastery level, but he cannot estimate the relative validity coefficient between mastery-nonmastery and sex. In this case, sex would not be a validating variable. Since previously it was determined that sex would not be a pre-

dictor variable either, the sex data would be ignored in the test construction process.

Thus, in our example, the 25 items are both validating and predictor variables, teachers' ratings are a validating variable, and sex is neither class of variable. Given both validating and predictor variables, Darlington (1970) has provided a series of techniques for maximizing the validity of a set of predictors for an unobserved criterion. The techniques involve substituting the correlations among observed variables and the estimated relative validities into a multiple regression computer program. The details depend on the mix of validating and predictor variables and are straightforward and well described in Darlington (1970).

The last regression analysis to be run using the Darlington techniques should be stepwise. In that way the test constructor can decide which items to retain in his test and an appropriate weighting of the items for purposes of determining total score on the test. Because the Darlington techniques use regression analysis, they are thus most appropriate when the number of variables is moderate and the ratio of the number of examinees to the number of variables is high.

Darlington provides the details for estimating the correlation between the test and the unobserved criterion (validity coefficient). Since the calculations are somewhat involved, yet clearly discussed in an available reference, they will not be provided here. To obtain limits on this validity coefficient, Darlington suggests that different test developers make the estimates required by his method and note the range of the resulting validity coefficients.

Finally, the reader may object to having to estimate validities in order to use this technique. Darlington (1970, pages 5-6) makes compelling arguments which should reduce the anxieties of even the most zealous skeptic.

EDUCATIONAL APPLICATIONS OF DOMAIN-REFERENCED TESTS AND DIFFERENTIAL ASSESSMENT DEVICES

Very early in this chapter DRT's and DAD's were distinguished. DRT's require a highly specified description of a population of performance tasks from which the test items can be sampled randomly, and they provide the most precise description of a learner's status. In contrast, DAD's are constructed to maximize discriminations among

individuals or groups. Discussed below are selected areas of application in education which call for measuring status or differentiating individuals or groups.

Needs Assessment

Schools, frequently aided by community input, have been attending to the task of setting priorities. Need is one criterion by which instructional goals that are to receive additional attention can be selected. A need can be defined as the difference between expected and actual status. Thus, we can speak of a need for improved or expanded instruction in critical thinking when a discrepancy exists between desired and observed performance on measures of critical thinking behavior. To determine present status, DRT's are most appropriate.

Individualized Instruction

One way to individualize instruction is to permit students to proceed through a set curriculum at their own pace. Scores on tests covering the content of the unit serve as the criterion for determining whether or not students are allowed to proceed. Figure 6-9 is a flow chart depicting such a management-by-test scheme. Other systems include Individually Prescribed Instruction associated with the University of Pittsburgh and the Individualized Mathematics Program associated with the University of Wisconsin. Hambleton (in press) has reviewed the testing and decision-making procedures for selected individualized instructional programs.

Domain-Referenced Tests

Such individualized, instructional programs require mastery of content of each unit, regardless of whether this achievement is truly a prerequisite for acquiring proficiency on the terminal objectives of the program. Consequently, DRT's are appropriate for determining if the student has mastered the instructional unit or if remedial work is required.

Specific item results on a DRT can provide diagnostic information which may be of value in planning remedial instruction. Diagnostic scoring of tests is facilitated when distractors are systematically formed. Self-correcting tests, such as those of Science Research Associates and Zweig Associates, help reduce logistical problems. Further,

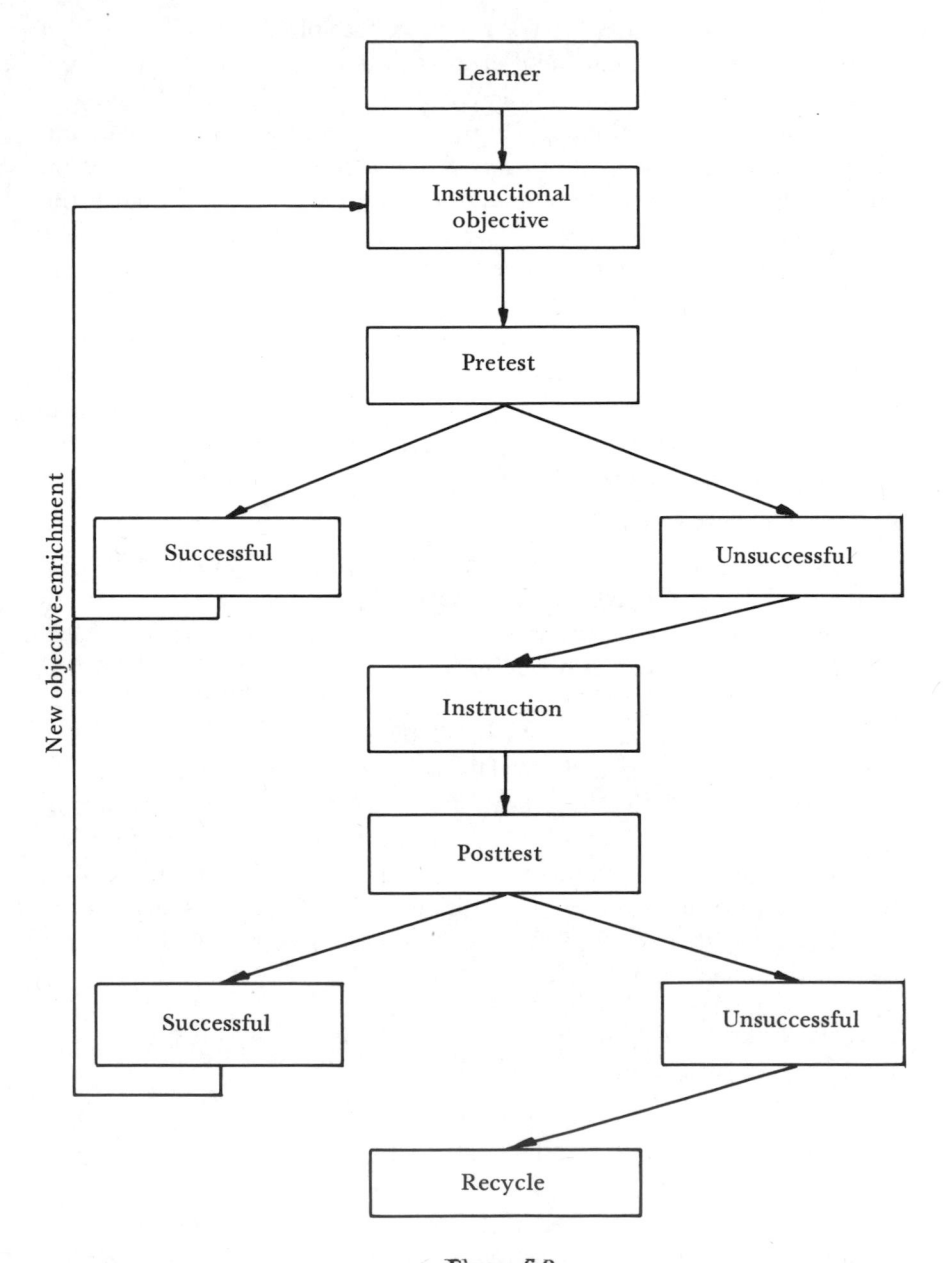

Figure 6-9
Read system of the American Book Company: A management-by-test scheme

item generation schemes for DRT's make feasible the construction of large numbers of content parallel tests that are desirable for repeated testing of students or when students are tested at different times.

Several authors (Millman, 1970; Airasian and Madaus, 1972; and others) have proposed marking and reporting schemes that rely on DRT's. Instead of norm-referenced grading (A, B, and so forth), the suggestion is made to report a student's status relative to the course's objectives. Figure 6-10 illustrates a record form; Figure 6-11, a report form.

An advantage of such domain-referenced reporting systems is that emphasis is placed on a student's achievement relative to his own past performance. Progress is more evident than under traditional systems in which improvement in grades can only be acquired at the detriment of one's peers.

Differential Assessment Devices

When the *goals* of instruction are individualized (not all students study the same things), DAD'S have an obvious role to play in matching instructional treatments to the interests and abilities of students. This use of tests has a long history, and no more will be said here.

When instruction is individualized by varying the *pace* at which common goals are learned, DAD's would appear to be particularly useful to differentiate those who are likely to succeed in future instruction from those who are not likely to succeed. The criterion groups should be two groups that differ in their ability to succeed on the next unit of instruction. The utility of DAD's in this specific context has been discussed in Example 3, which appeared in the first part of this chapter.

Program Evaluation

Domain-Referenced Tests

One consideration in the evaluation of instructional programs is the degree to which the objectives of the program have been met. DRT's are designed to present such information. Further, in contrast to national, norm-referenced tests, tests referencing the specific domains of learner behavior to which the instructional effort is directed have a much better chance of detecting areas in which the program has been successful or is in need of modification. It is not necessary

to throw out an entire program. Improvements can be targeted to those program goals which were not met.

Some writers (Cox and Sterrett, 1970; Heuer, no date) have recommended rating each item on a standardized, norm-referenced achievement test as to its relevance to the school's curriculum and then comparing student performance on those items rated as referencing objectives considered part of the instructional system with the performance on items not so rated. Interesting as such comparisons might be, they fail to provide the educator with knowledge about what objectives have or have not been successfully taught. The difficulties inherent in attempting to tease out criterion-referenced interpretations from objectives-based tests, discussed in the first part of this chapter, are also pertinent here.

When the purpose of the testing is to make decisions about an instructional program, it is not necessary that every student receive the same test items or even that every student be tested. Much economy can be realized by sampling both students and items and making estimates of total domain proficiency for an entire population of students on the basis of such sampling.

Examples of such assignment plans are provided in Figure 6-12. Plan A illustrates an assignment plan in which a random sample of four students are tested on the same 3 items, themselves a random sample of items from the entire domain. The mean domain score is estimated by the percentage of the 12 answers that are correct. Formula 11.11.6 in Lord and Novick (1968) provides the sampling variance for such domain scores. Plan A' is meant to illustrate the same plan as A, namely that a random sample of examinees is each given the same random sample of items. The four examinees and three items, however, have been placed first for convenience and cover the shaded area. The advantage of Plans A and A' over the others shown in the figure is primarily convenience of administering and scoring. Only a single test needs to be constructed.

Plans B and C illustrate multiple matrix sampling schemes in which nonoverlapping random samples of items are formed, and each is administered to a different, random group of examinees. Plan C is a special case of Plan B in which all items and all examinees in the domain are randomly divided into nonoverlapping subgroups.

The domain score for the sample is an unbiased estimate of the domain score for the population. Assuming an equal number of items

DIRECTIONS TO THE TEACHER: These profiles are to be used as a continuous record of the pupil's progress in Mathematics. In recording the results of each test, make sure you are using the correct skill profile. Each one indicates the objectives on individual tests. Based on the scoring instructions, write the date of the test beside the skill in the "Proceed" or "Reteach" column. Count the number of incorrect responses for each behavioral objective.

Pupil's Name: _____

NUMBERS AND OPERATIONS

		Reteach	Proceed			Reteach	Proceed
BLUE PART 1	5-1-1. add.: whole numbers w/o renaming			**PURPLE PART 3**	6-1-10. fractional parts		
	5-1-2. add.: whole numbers w renaming				6-1-11. equivalent fractions		
	5-1-3. sub.: whole numbers w/o renaming				6-1-12. reducing fractions		
	5-1-4. sub.: whole numbers w renaming				6-1-13. fractional numbers > 1		
BLUE PART 2	5-1-5. mult.: whole nos. w/o renaming (1 digit)				6-1-14. fractions: indicated division		
	5-1-6. mult.: whole nos. w renaming (1 digit)			**PURPLE PART 4**	6-1-15. improper fractions as mixed numerals		
	5-1-7. mult.: whole nos. w/o renaming (2 digit)				6-1-16. mixed numerals as improper fractions		
	5-1-8. mult.: whole nos. w renaming (2 digit)				6-1-17. order relations, fractional numbers		
BLUE PART 3	5-1-9. div.: whole nos. w/o remainders (1 digit)				6-1-18. add.: fractional numbers w like denom.		
	5-1-10. div.: whole nos. w/o remainders (2 digit)				6-1-19. add.: fractional numbers w unlike denom.		
	5-1-11. div.: whole nos. w remainders (1 digit)			**PURPLE PART 5**	6-1-20. add.: fractional nos. w like denom., = or > one		
	5-1-12. div.: whole nos. w remainders (2 digit)				6-1-21. add.: fractional nos. w unlike denom., = or > one		
BLUE PART 4	5-1-13. equivalent fractions				6-1-22. add.: fractional nos. > one, like denom.		
	5-1-14. reducing fractions				6-1-23. add.: fractional nos. > one, unlike denom.		
	5-1-15. improper fractions as mixed numerals				6-1-24. sub.: fractional nos. w like denom.		
	5-1-16. mixed numerals as improper fractions			**PURPLE PART 6**	6-1-25. sub.: fractional nos. w unlike denom.		
	5-1-17. order relations w fractional numbers				6-1-26. sub.: fractional nos. = or > one, no renaming		
BLUE PART 5	5-1-18. add.: fractional numbers, like denom.				6-1-27. sub.: fractional nos. > one; w renaming		
	5-1-19. add.: fractional numbers, unlike denom.				6-1-28. sub.: fractional nos. > one; unlike denom.; renam.		
	5-1-20. sub.: fractional numbers, like denom.				6-1-29. mult.: fractional nos., whole nos. & proper frac.		
	5-1-21. sub.: fractional numbers, unlike denom.			**PURPLE PART 7**	6-1-30. mult.: fractional nos., proper fractions		
BLUE PART 6	5-1-22. mult.: fractional numbers				6-1-31. mult.: fractional nos., improper fractions		
	5-1-23. div.: fractional numbers				6-1-32. mult.: fractional nos., mixed numerals		
	5-1-24. reciprocals and applications				6-1-33. reciprocals		
	5-1-25. ratios				6-1-34. div.: equivalent reciprocal		
BLUE PART 7	5-1-26. decimal fractions			**PURPLE PART 8**	6-1-35. div.: by a fractional number		
	5-1-27. decimal fractions, hundredths				6-1-36. div.: of a fractional number		
	5-1-28. add.: decimal fractions				6-1-37. div.: fractional numbers w like denom.		
	5-1-29. sub.: decimal fractions				6-1-38. div.: fractional numbers w unlike denom.		

PURPLE PART 2 / PURPLE PART 1 / BLUE PART 12 / BLUE 11 / BLUE 10 / BLUE PART 9 / BLUE PART 8

5-1-30. order relations (>, <, =, ≠)	6-1-39. div. of fractional nos., mixed numerals
5-1-31. number patterns	6-1-40. fractional numbers as decimal fractions
5-1-32. literal variables in number sentences	6-1-41. decimals as proper fractions
5-1-33. commutative property: add., mult.	6-1-42. renaming decimal fractions
5-1-34. associative property: add., mult.	6-1-43. add.: decimal fractions
5-1-35. identity element: add., mult.	6-1-44. sub.: decimal fractions
5-1-36. distributive property: mult. over add.	6-1-45. mult.: decimal fractions
5-1-37. add., sub.: inverse operations	6-1-46. mult., decimal frac.: both fact. in decimal frac. form
5-1-38. mult., div.: inverse operations	6-1-47. div.: decimal fractions
5-1-39. base five (numeration)	6-1-48. percent: geometric model
5-1-40. meaning of exponents	6-1-49. fractional numbers as percents
5-1-41. use of exponents	6-1-50. add.: percent notation
5-1-42. prime numbers	6-1-51. sub.: percent notation
5-1-43. prime factorization	6-1-52. non-decimal numeration: "base two"
5-1-44. sets of multiples	6-1-53. number sentences: second power (squaring)
5-1-45. least common multiples	6-1-54. number sentences: radicals (square root)
5-1-46. sets of factors	6-1-55. computing square roots of perfect squares
5-1-47. greatest common factors	6-1-56. rounding nos. to tenths and hundredths
6-1-1. add.: whole numbers, w renaming	6-1-57. estimating products
6-1-2. sub.: whole numbers, w renaming	6-1-58. solving function equations
6-1-3. mult.: whole nos. w renaming, 3-digit factors	6-1-59. clock arithmetic (mod 7): add. & sub.
6-1-4. mult.: whole nos., w renaming, (more than 3 dig.)	6-1-60. clock arithmetic (mod 7): mult.
6-1-5. div.: whole nos., 1-digit divisors, w/o remainders	6-1-61. commutative property: add. & mult.
6-1-6. div.: whole nos., 1-digit divisors, w remainders	6-1-62. associative property: add. & mult.
6-1-7. div.: whole nos., 2-digit divisors, w/o remainders	6-1-63. distributive property
6-1-8. div.: whole nos., 2-digit divisors, w remainders	6-1-64. add. & sub. as inverse operations
6-1-9. order relations: whole numbers	6-1-65. additive property of zero
	6-1-66. multiplicative property of one

PURPLE PART 9 / PURPLE PART 10 / PURPLE PART 11 / PURPLE PART 12 / PURPLE PART 13 / PURPLE PART 14

Age: _____ Year in School: 5 6 7 8

STK No. MPP-2

Figure 6-10

Pupil record form (reproduced with permission of Richard L. Zweig, Associates, 20800 Beach Boulevard, Huntington Beach, California)

STUDENT SUMMARY

MATHEMATICS

TULSA SCHOOL DISTRICT
SEPTEMBER 23, 1973
MARY SMITH
PRO. NO. · 1234-567

WILLIAMS, KEVIN
ROBERT FROST SCHOOL

YOU WERE ABLE TO:

TELL IF TWO SETS HAVE THE SAME NUMBER OF OBJECTS
TELL IF ONE SET WAS A SUBSET OF ANOTHER SET
TELL HOW MANY TENS AND ONES ARE IN A NUMBER
WRITE THE TOTAL VALUE OF A SET OF COINS
TELL TIME TO THE HOUR

	CPL NO.	OBJ NO.	DRILL TAPES
YOU NEED TO REVIEW HOW TO:			
TELL WHICH NUMBERS ARE ODD AND EVEN	115	2	NN 1-2 NN 2-1
USE A RULER TO MEASURE LENGTH IN INCHES	115	4	
WRITE EQUIVALENT MEASURES FOR CUPS, PINTS AND QUARTS	117	3	
COUNT BY FIVES OR TENS TO COMPLETE NUMBER PATTERNS	117	1	NN 4-2
YOU NEED TO LEARN HOW TO:			
TELL WHICH FIGURES ARE TRIANGLES, SQUARES OR CIRCLES	127	3	
ADD ONE-DIGIT NUMBERS USING THREE ADDENDS	129	2	AD 3-2 SU 3-2
SUBTRACT ONE-DIGIT NUMBERS	131	1	SU 2-1 SU 4-1
SUBTRACT TWO-DIGIT NUMBERS (NO REGROUPING)	131	2	SU 2-2 SU 4-2
USE ADDITION TO SOLVE WORD PROBLEMS	133	2	PS 2-1 PS 4-2
ADD TWO-DIGIT NUMBERS WITH FOUR ADDENDS	133	3	AD 5-2 AD 6-1

Figure 6-11

Student summary report form (reproduced with permission of the Educational Development Corporation, Post Office Box 45663, Tulsa, Oklahoma)

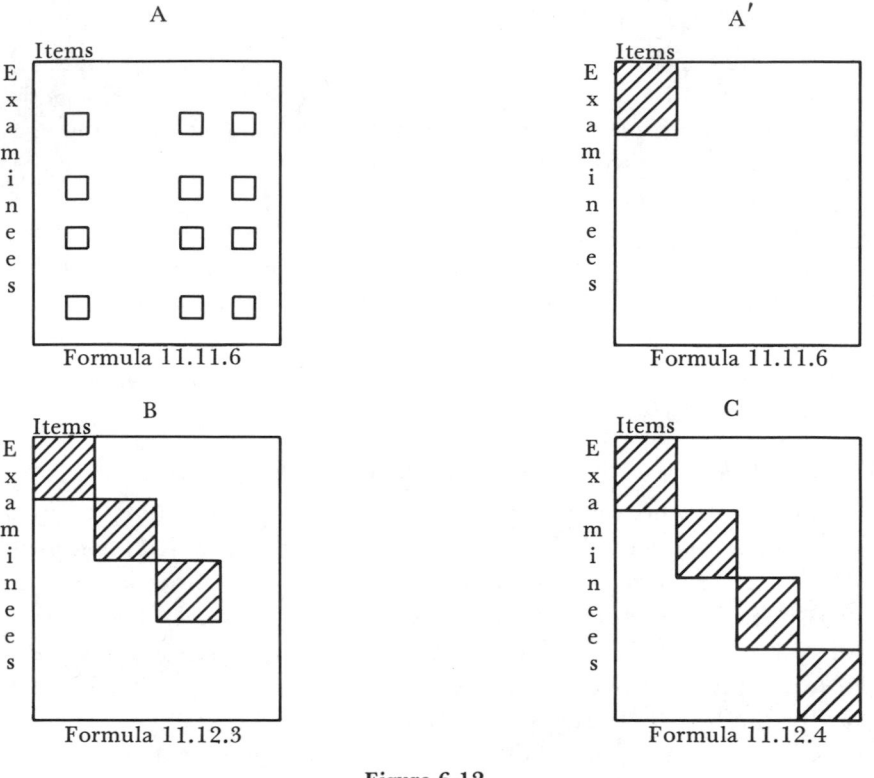

Figure 6-12
Assignment plans for domain-referenced tests

on each test and an equal number of examinees in each administration group, then the formulas in Lord and Novick (1968) referenced under the plans in the figure can be used to compute the sampling variance of the estimates of the domain scores. The advantage of Plans B and C over A (and A′) is greater precision in estimating the domain score. This added precision comes about primarily because a greater proportion of the items in the domain is being sampled.

In a school setting it is advisable that the several tests (that is, random samplings of items) be administered simultaneously in a single setting. This is not possible if the specific items must be read aloud, a common situation when young children are tested. Further discussion of matrix sampling schemes can be found in Chapter 8.

Differential Assessment Devices

Two questions an evaluator of an instructional program might ask are: How well have the program's objectives been mastered? Has the program made some kind of difference? It was argued in Example 1, earlier in the chapter, that DRT's are best suited to answer the first of these questions.

When, perhaps for political purposes, the effort is directed toward documenting that some kind of difference has taken place, then a DAD is appropriate. That is because there is less need for a test of items randomly selected from a well-defined domain than there is for a test that will discriminate treatment groups or display preinstruction to postinstruction changes.

Teaching Improvement and Personnel Evaluation

Perhaps the most important skill of a teacher is the ability to bring about changes in the behavior of students on prespecified objectives. When student performance is measured by DRT's, the desired student behavior becomes explicit. The precise boundaries of the behavior to be assessed are defined, and criteria for judging the adequacy of learner responses are identified. Such information makes it possible for the teacher to devise more relevant instructional materials and provides for a fairer evaluation of the teacher's performance.

One serious criticism of behavioral objectives is the contention that they cause instruction to be focused narrowly. DRT's can provide a safeguard against this problem as they index a clearly laid out class of behavior. This specification helps teachers to expand their concept of the instructional requirements.

Does all this mean that teaching to the test is condoned? No! However, Hively (personal correspondence) has remarked that the degree of secrecy surrounding a test program is an index of the ignorance surrounding its objectives. A well-defined domain should be made public, and only the specific items to be used on a given occasion need be kept secret.

Whenever test uses have been discussed in this monograph, DAD's permitting criterion-referenced interpretations (CRDAD's) have rarely been mentioned. The reader might ask: Why must a test be either domain-referenced or one which maximizes group differences? Why

not construct a CRDAD using empirical methods of item selection that maximize differential assessment while restricting the original item pool to those having content validity?

When the compromise CRDAD is employed, it is no longer reasonable to convert test scores to domain scores (because the random or stratified item selection process has been destroyed), and there is a risk that a reduced criterion-related validity will result. Thus, although some compromises permit the recipient to have the best of two worlds, this compromise may leave the user up in the air without a planet to stand on.

REFERENCES

Airasian, Peter W., and Madaus, George F., 1972. "Criterion-referenced testing in the classroom." *Measurement in Education*, 3:1-8.

Anderson, Richard C., 1972. "How to construct achievement tests to assess comprehension." *Review of Educational Research*, 42:145-170.

Baker, Eva L., 1974. "Beyond objectives: Domain-referenced tests for evaluation and instructional improvement." *Educational Technology*, 14:10-16.

———, 1972. "Using measurement to improve instruction." Paper presented at the annual meeting of the American Psychological Association, 8 pp.

Bloom, Benjamin S., 1968. "Learning for mastery." *Evaluation Comment*, 1.2:1-12.

———, 1973. "An introduction to mastery learning theory." Paper presented at the annual meeting of the American Educational Research Association, 9 pp.

Bormuth, John R., 1970. *On the theory of achievement test items*. Chicago: University of Chicago Press.

Brennan, Robert L., 1974. "The evaluation of mastery test items." U.S. Office of Education, Project No. 2B118, 227 pp.

Cleary, Anne T., 1971. "Strategies for criterion-referenced test construction using classical procedures." Paper presented at the annual meeting of the American Educational Research Association, 10 pp.

Cox, Richard C., and Sterrett, Barbara G., 1970. "A model for increasing the meaning of standardized test scores." *Journal of Educational Measurement*, 7:227-228.

———, and Vargas, Julie C., 1966. "A comparison of item selection techniques for norm-referenced and criterion-referenced tests." Paper presented at the annual meeting of the American Educational Research Association, 12 pp.

Cronbach, Lee J., *et al.*, 1963. "Theory of generalizability: A liberalization of reliability theory." *British Journal of Statistical Psychology*, 16:137-163.

———, et al., 1972. *The dependability of behavioral measurements: Theory of generalizability for scores and profiles.* New York: John Wiley.

Darlington, Richard B., 1970. "Some techniques for maximizing a test's validity when the criterion variable is unobserved." *Journal of Educational Measurement,* 7:1-14.

———, and Bishop, Carol H., 1966. "Increasing test validity by considering interitem correlations." *Journal of Applied Psychology,* 50:322-330.

———, and Stauffer, Glenn F., 1966. "Use and evaluation of discrete test information in decision making." *Journal of Applied Psychology,* 50:125-129.

Donlon, Thomas F., 1974. "Some needs for clearer terminology in criterion referenced testing." Paper presented at the annual meeting of the American Educational Research Association, 16 pp.

Durnin, John, and Scandura, Joseph M., 1973. "An algorithmic approach to assessing behavior potential." *Journal of Educational Psychology,* 65:262-272.

Ebel, Robert, 1962. "Content standard test scores." *Educational and Psychological Measurement,* 22:15-25.

———, 1970. "Some limitations of criterion-referenced measurement." Paper presented at the annual meeting of the American Educational Research Association, 9 pp.

———, 1973. "Evaluation and educational objectives." *Journal of Educational Measurement,* 10:273-279.

Emrick, John A., 1971. "An evaluation model for mastery testing." *Journal of Educational Measurement,* 8:321-326.

Glaser, Robert, 1963. "Instructional technology and the measurement of learning outcomes: Some questions." *American Psychologist,* 18:519-521.

Gorth, William P., and Hambleton, Ronald K., 1972. "Measurement considerations for criterion-referenced testing and special education." *Journal of Special Education,* 6:303-314.

Guttman, Louis, 1969. "Integration of test design and analysis," in *Proceedings of the 1969 Invitational Conference on Testing Problems.* Princeton, N.J.: Educational Testing Service.

Hambleton, Ronald K., in process. "A review of testing and decision-making procedures for selected individualized instructional programs." *Review of Educational Research.*

———, and Novick, Melvin R., 1973. "Toward an integration of theory and method for criterion-referenced tests." *Journal of Educational Measurement,* 10:159-170.

Harris, Chester W., 1974. "Some technical characteristics of mastery tests," in Chester W. Harris, Marvin C. Alkin, and W. James Popham (eds.), *Problems in Criterion-Referenced Measurement.* Monograph Series in Evaluation, No. 3. Los Angeles: Center for the Study of Evaluation, University of California.

Heuer, Edwin, no date. *Making standardized tests work for your IGE School.* Madison: Wisconsin Research and Development Center, University of Wisconsin, 6 pp.

Hively, Wells, 1962. "Specifying 'terminal behavior' in mathematics." Harvard Committee on Programmed Instruction, unpublished.

———— , 1974. "Introduction to domain-referenced testing." *Educational Technology*, 14:5-10.

———— , *et al.*, 1973. *Domain-referenced curriculum evaluation: A technical handbook and a case study from the Minnemast Project.* Monograph Series in Evaluation, No. 1. Los Angeles: Center for the Study of Evaluation, University of California.

Hockersmith, Fred B., 1969. "Evaluation of new approaches to classification error rates." U.S. Office of Education Special Report, Project 6-2151.

Humphreys, Lloyd G., 1962. "The organization of human abilities." *American Psychologist*, 17:475-483.

Jordan, John E., 1971. "Attitude-behavior research on physical-mental-social disability and racial-ethnic differences." *Psychological Aspects of Disability*, 18:5-26.

Klein, Stephen P., and Kosecoff, Jacqueline, 1973. *Issues and procedures in the development of criterion-referenced tests.* ERIC Clearinghouse on Tests, Measurement, & Evaluation, TM Report 26. Princeton, N.J.: Educational Testing Service.

Kosecoff, Jacqueline B., and Klein, Stephen P., 1974. *Instructional sensitivity statistics appropriate for objectives-based test items.* Report No. 91. Los Angeles: Center for the Study of Evaluation, University of California, 26 pp.

Lewis, Charles, Wang, Ming-Mei, and Novick, Melvin R., 1973. *Marginal distributions for the estimation of proportions in m groups.* Technical Bulletin, No. 13. Iowa City: American College Testing Program, 40 pp.

Light, Richard J., 1973. "Issues in the analysis of qualitative data," in Robert Travers (ed.), *Second Handbook of Research on Teaching.* Chicago: Rand McNally.

Lord, Frederic M., and Novick, Melvin R., 1968. *Statistical Theories of Mental Test Scores.* Reading, Mass.: Addison-Wesley.

Marshall, J. Laird, 1973. "Reliability indices for criterion-referenced tests: A study based on simulated data." Paper presented at the annual meeting of the American Educational Research Association, New Orleans, 18 pp.

Mayo, Samuel T., 1970. "Mastery learning and mastery testing." *Measurement in Education*, 1.3:1-4.

Millman, Jason, 1970. "Reporting student progress: A case for a criterion-referenced marking system." *Phi Delta Kappan*, 52:226-230.

———— , 1972. *Determining test length: Passing scores and test lengths for objectives-based tests.* Los Angeles: Instructional Objectives Exchange, 33 pp.

———— , 1973. "Passing scores and test lengths for domain-referenced tests." *Review of Educational Research*, 43:205-216.

———— , 1974. "Sampling plans for domain-referenced tests." *Educational Technology*, 14:17-21.

———, and Glass, Gene V, 1967. "Rules of thumb for writing the anova table." *Journal of Educational Measurement,* 4:41-51.

———, and Popham, W. James, 1974. "The issue of item and test variance for criterion-referenced tests: A clarification. *Journal of Educational Measurement,* 11:137-138.

Moncrief, Michael H., 1974. "Procedures for empirical determination of en-route criterion levels." Paper presented at the annual meeting of the American Educational Research Association, 44 pp.

Novick, Melvin R., Lewis, Charles, and Jackson, Paul H., 1973. "The estimation of proportions in *m* groups." *Psychometrika,* 38:19-46.

———, and Lewis, Charles, 1974. "Prescribing test length for criterion-referenced measurements," in Chester W. Harris, Marvin C. Alkin, and W. James Popham (eds.), *Problems in Criterion-Referenced Measurement.* Monograph Series in Evaluation, No. 3. Los Angeles: Center for the Study of Evaluation, University of California.

Osborn, H. G., 1968. "Item sampling for achievement testing." *Educational and Psychological Measurement,* 28:95-104.

Ozenne, Dan G., 1971. *Toward an evaluative methodology for criterion-referenced measures: Test sensitivity.* Report No. 72. Los Angeles: Center for the Study of Evaluation, University of California, 91 pp.

Popham, W. James, in press (a). "Curriculum design—The problem of specifying intended learning outcomes," in J. Blaney, I. Housego, and G. McIntosh (eds.), *Program Development in Education.* Vancouver: Centre for Continuing Education, University of British Columbia.

———, in press(b). *Educational evaluation* (tentative). Englewood Cliffs, N.J.: Prentice-Hall.

———, and Husek, T. R., 1969. "Implications of criterion-referenced measurement." *Journal of Educational Measurement,* 6:1-9.

Rahmlow, Harold F., 1972. "Implementing a mixed program of criterion- and noncriterion-referenced measurement." Paper presented at the annual meeting of the American Educational Research Association, 7 pp.

Roudabush, Glenn E., 1974. "Models for a beginning theory of criterion-referenced tests." Paper presented at the annual meeting of the American Educational Research Association, 19 pp.

Runkel, Philip J., 1965. *Some recent ideas in research methodology.* Eugene: Center for the Advanced Study of Educational Administration, University of Oregon, 1965.

Schriber, Peter E., 1973. "An empirical comparison of criterion-referenced data collected by mastery testing versus repeated item-examinee sampling." Paper presented at the annual meeting of the American Educational Research Association, 40 pp.

Smith, Timothy A., and Shaw, Carl N., 1969. "Structural analysis as an aid in designing an instructional system." *Journal of Educational Measurement,* 6:137-143.

Swaminathan, H., *et al.* (in press). "A decision-theoretic approach to issues in criterion-referenced assessment." *Journal of Educational Measurement.*

Tunks, Thomas W., 1973. "An application of Guttman facet theory to attitude scale construction in music." *Council for Research in Music Bulletin*, No. 33:47-53.

Wang, Ming-Mei, 1973. *Tables of constants for the posterior marginal estimates of proportions in* m *groups.* Technical Bulletin, No. 14. Iowa City: American College Testing Program, 31 pp.

Woodson, M. I. Charles E., 1974. "The issue of item and test variance for criterion-referenced tests." *Journal of Educational Measurement*, 11:63-64.

7

Cost Analysis for Educational Program Evaluation

Emil J. Haller
Cornell University

Cost Analysis for Educational Program Evaluation

Emil J. Haller

This chapter, concerned with the problem of determining program costs as part of the evaluation process, is intended to help you arrive at useful conceptions of the term *cost* and procedures for assessing the costs of an educational program. This statement of purpose implies several things. It suggests that cost may be conceived in alternative ways, that there are alternative methods by which costs may be assessed, and that choices among both conceptions and methods are conditioned in some way by the activity called educational program evaluation. It most certainly implies that the usual conception and measurement of program costs, that is, dollars expended, may not be adequate for all evaluation purposes.

Before turning to the issues involved in the notion of cost, it is necessary to set those issues in the evaluation context. Readers familiar with the burgeoning evaluation literature are already aware that the term *program evaluation* has been variously defined. The Phi Delta Kappa (PDK) National Study Committee on Evaluation (1971,

I would like to thank Steven J. Klees and Jason Millman for their helpful comments on an earlier version of this chapter.

401

pages 9-16) notes that three definitions have gained particular prominence. They have termed these the measurement, congruence, and judgment definitions, and suggest that each carries with it certain advantages and disadvantages and that each affects the manner in which the evaluators carry out their tasks. Each, in addition, conditions the evaluator's conception of costs and the manner in which he attempts to assess program costs. It is important that our own choice of definitions be made explicit, for that choice has exerted a strong influence on the contents of this chapter.

For Daniel Stufflebeam and his colleagues on the committee, educational evaluation is "the process of delineating, obtaining and providing useful information for judging decision alternatives" (page 40). For the moment it is only necessary to note that, by this definition, the purpose of conducting an evaluation is to improve decision making. The decision maker and his alternatives are of central concern to the evaluator, and the evaluator is often viewed as an extension of the program administrator's thought process. The evaluator's task is to provide reliable, relevant, and timely information in order to improve the administrator's decisions. One class of relevant information is most certainly information about costs, for all decisions involve costs. The evaluator who does not have a clear and defensible conception of cost appropriate to each of his evaluational tasks, or who does not specifically address the issue of costs when reporting to a decision maker, has performed less than a completely adequate service.

Perhaps an example of the relationships among the concepts of evaluation, decisions, and costs will help to illustrate these points. The example, deliberately chosen, is perhaps the paradigmatic program evaluation problem, and, on the surface, neither decisions nor costs seem to be involved.

Suppose a school superintendent asks you to conduct an evaluation and poses his problem as: "Is our foreign-language (or reading or math) program meeting its objectives?" You might conceivably carry out your study and respond with a one-word memorandum—"Yes" or "No"—though it is unlikely that the superintendent would consider such a response adequate. It is almost certain that he had something more in mind. (This assumption is usually a safe one since the conduct of even a cursory evaluation requires the expenditure of school resources. Often these resources may not involve simply, or

even principally, the evaluator's time, but, more importantly, they involve the time of students and staff from whom the evaluator must obtain the requisite data.) If substantial resource expenditures are involved in this evaluation, you may assume that the superintendent is not motivated by idle curiosity in seeking an evaluation of his district's foreign-language program. Rather, you can assume that he strongly suspects that the answer to his own question is "no," and, further, that he already has some ideas about why goals are not being met and what needs to be done to improve the situation. In such circumstances, your original charge would be more accurately phrased as: "What is going wrong with this program and what can I do about it?" Even in a case where the administrator believes that his foreign-language program is meeting its objectives, however, he normally has other questions on his mind. Such questions might include: "How can I expand the program to reach a larger number of students?" "How can the program be even further improved?" "Is there some way to reduce the cost of the program without impairing its effectiveness?"

The obvious characteristic that all of these implicit questions have in common is that they represent potential decisions. An important preliminary requirement of the role of an evaluator is to help a program administrator make such decisions explicit. Then, since all decisions imply the existence of at least one alternative course of action, the essential task is to assist in specifying the alternatives and to provide information necessary to evaluate them, that is, to choose. In order to choose rationally among competing alternative courses of action, a decision maker must not only know the potential benefits accruing to each; he must also be able to assess their potential costs. The client will, therefore, need pertinent information about costs and benefits associated with the alternatives.

In summary, then, evaluation problems concern decisions. Decisions presume the existence of alternatives, and so the purpose of evaluation is to help delineate alternatives and to provide information to help decision makers arrive at more rational choices. Such information, at least in part, necessarily concerns the likely costs of each alternative, which means that evaluators must also have a clear and appropriate conception of the term cost and reasonable procedures for determining costs.

Although many readers might agree with the conclusions just set

forth, it may not be obvious to some that the notion of cost in program evaluations is complex enough to require extensive treatment. If one is talking about dollars, for example, he might consider the determination of a program's costs relatively simple for, while reasonable men might differ on the total dollar cost of a program, it might well be felt that such differences would be relatively small. Unfortunately, that is not the case. In a recent evaluation, for example, three competent evaluators looking at the same existing program, with no cost projections involved, individually concluded that the program was costless, that it cost approximately $1,200, and that it cost well over $100,000. Differences of such magnitude are not trivial. They arise not from varying interpretations of the program's budget but from fundamentally different conceptions of cost.[1] Additional evidence that the notion of cost is not simple can be inferred from the fact that professional cost accountants, the General Accounting Office of the federal government, and the U.S. Congress have been concerned with the various meanings of the term, but have not yet arrived at an entirely satisfactory conception (Anthony, 1970). If one is concerned with estimating future dollar costs (as in the case of a program evaluation), the problem becomes more complex. Finally, if one is willing to admit the possibility that educational programs might carry nonmonetary costs (for example, psychological or social costs), the complexity of the term is further increased. In short, the meaning of the term *cost,* as used in the phrase, "the cost of an educational program," is by no means clear.

If program cost is important in educational evaluation, and if it is a complex concept, we might expect that it would have received extensive treatment in evaluation literature. It is a minor irony that such is not the case. A check of frequently used textbooks shows that cost, when treated at all, is treated almost tangentially. A comment by Robert Stake (1973, page 312), coming as it does from one of the country's leading authorities on evaluation, is both refreshingly candid and seemingly typical of the attitude of many evaluation specialists. He writes: "It embarrasses me to admit that I do not know anything about the measurement of costs. I will have to leave that to somebody else." Perhaps the "somebody else" Stake refers to

---

1. Specifically, the differences arose from a confusion as to whether average marginal or total cost was the appropriate conception of cost to be used.

is the industrial accountant. Michael Scriven (1973, page 102) suggests that accountants can provide most of the appropriate analysis. Unfortunately for the working evaluator, Scriven proves himself wrong as he goes on to list numerous and important types of program costs that cannot be assessed by standard accounting procedures. And, what is even more important, cost accountants tend to be concerned with financial accounting—the analysis of *past* expenditures. In educational evaluation designed to serve decision making, the evaluator's primary concern is the estimation and analysis of *future* costs, which include, but are not limited to, expenditures. Evaluators cannot "leave it to somebody else." Most particularly, they cannot leave it to cost accountants. They will need to develop their own procedures for assessing program costs, procedures appropriate both to educational program evaluation and to the specific evaluation at hand.

Finally, a word needs to be said about what is not treated here. We shall not be concerned with the problems of measuring program outcomes, nor, more importantly, with specific techniques for relating these outcomes to program costs. Such techniques, which generally fall under the rubrics of cost-benefit or cost-effectiveness analyses are beyond the scope of this effort.[2] We are, in effect, ignoring one-half of the cost-benefit relation in order to concentrate attention on determining a program's costs.

The purpose of this chapter, then, is to help design costing procedures for evaluation situations that are commonly encountered. Unfortunately, a standard set of procedures appropriate to all evaluation problems simply is not possible. Hence, this cannot be a "cookbook." Instead, I will attempt to develop, first, a set of general conceptions to encourage thoughts about program costs, and, second, a set of more specific procedures to apply to decision-oriented evaluation. The procedures depend, however, upon the conceptualization of the relationship between decisions and costs.

2. Readers are referred to the list of references for a listing of some works that deal specifically with these topics.

COSTS: GENERAL CONSIDERATIONS

What is a Cost?

If the purpose of program evaluation is to help decision makers choose among alternative courses of action, the concept of cost is useful because it provides a criterion for choosing among available alternatives. If two events are equally possible and desirable, we should choose the one with the lower cost. This means that one should compare the costs and benefits of doing something before a choice is made. Often, however, costs tend to be equated with the undesirable consequences of an event—a step that robs the concept of its usefulness (Alchian, 1968, page 404). For example, suppose you have recently purchased a home with an extensive backyard. Being an avid tennis player you are considering building a court in that area. Because you are also a rational decision maker, you decide to compare the undesirable and the desirable consequences (the costs and benefits) of doing so. The costs include several thousand dollars outlay for materials and several hundred hours of hard labor on your part to put the court in. Further reflection produces other possible costs: having unwanted guests stopping by to play, and potential liability for accidents on the court. As for the benefits of court ownership, there is the exercise it will provide and the consequent improvement in your health, the enjoyment you obtain from playing, and an increase in the value of your property. What you have done is to assemble an amalgam of undesirable attributes of building and having the court and another amalgam of desirable attributes.

The usefulness of the concept of cost is that it provides a criterion for choice. If you have in fact established the costs and benefits of having the court, are you now in a position to decide? You might say "no," because you cannot really compare its costs with its benefits; the amalgams are in qualitatively different units—money, hours of labor, enjoyment, and so forth. If, however, you could manage, through some ingenious procedure, to convert both amalgams to a common unit of value, they could be compared. If, say, having the court is equivalent to a loss of 40 units of value (disadvantages) and a gain of 70 units of value (advantages), would you decide to build it?

The appropriate answer is, of course, "I don't know." Even if you have correctly enumerated and measured the advantages and disad-

vantages of owning a tennis court, you have not established its cost. What you have established is its *net value*—70 minus 40, or 30 units of value. Only if you possessed unlimited resources so that (for you) all goods were free or if you had no alternative but to build the court would you now be in a position to decide. Such conditions rarely obtain. It is much more common that your decision would be from among several alternative uses for your principal resources—in this case, yard space, money, and labor. For example, you might seriously want to consider a swimming pool, a handball court, or a vegetable garden, instead. Because your resources are limited, when you choose one alternative you necessarily give up the others. Each of these possible events has a pair of associated amalgams of desirable and undesirable attributes. Suppose that you calculate that the next best alternative (that is, the next highest valued) is a pool with measured undesirable attributes of 70, desirable attributes of 90, and a net value of 20. If you choose to build a court, its cost is the loss of the value you would have obtained from a pool. Thus its cost is 20 units of value and not 40. Similarly, the cost of choosing the pool is the 30 units you give up by not having the court, not 70. In short, the cost of an event is the highest valued opportunity necessarily forsaken.

Now, let us consider program costs in an educational context. Just as your resources relevant to a tennis court are scarce, so are the resources of a school district. The time of students, teachers, and administrators, the space required to house educational programs, equipment, and supplies—all are in short supply. If some of these resources are used to develop and maintain one program, those same resources are obviously not available for use in some other, perhaps better, way. If it is decided to use them to produce one set of desired outcomes, another set must be sacrificed. As in the case of the tennis court, this idea, which links the act of choosing among desired alternatives with the notion of sacrifice, provides the meaning of cost. A cost is a sacrifice of one benefit in order to attain another. Costs occur when a choice is made among several desired benefits. In short, costs are benefits—benefits given up by choosing to do one thing rather than another. For example, the only reason to hesitate in spending $3,000 for new equipment in a chemistry laboratory is a reluctance to give up the benefit that those dollars would provide when used in some other way, say, new textbooks for a reading program or the hiring of a teacher aide. It is this simple notion, the

notion of costs as benefits forgone—*opportunity costs*—that provides an appropriate starting point for anyone concerned with costs in educational program evaluation.[3]

The concept of opportunity costs gives meaning to the term as it is used in program evaluation. When, for example, pupils are assigned to study halls for several hours each week, that time is not available for classroom instruction in mathematics, woodworking, or some other subject. The cost of such a decision, therefore, is the forgone benefits that would derive from alternate uses of student time.[4] Thus, an estimate of the costs of any choice is an estimate of benefits forgone as a consequence of that choice. *Costs are benefits lost.*

There are some immediate implications of such a conception. One implication is that, from the evaluator's perspective, costs are inextricably tied to decisions. In a sense, school buildings, textbooks, and the services of teachers do not have costs. Instead, the decision to build a school rather than adopt a double-shift schedule has a cost, and the decision to utilize teachers in one way rather than another has a cost. This distinction is not merely a nicety of language. It serves as a reminder that it is the job of the program evaluator to analyze decisions, that every decision has alternatives, that the value of alternatives not chosen is the cost of a decision, and that, therefore, the meaning of cost in any evaluation depends upon the alternatives involved.

A second implication is that an evaluator cannot accurately estimate the cost of one decision without carefully defining the consequences of at least one alternative. Obviously, if there are no alternatives, no choice exists; hence, no costs. This much is trite, not to say tautological. The point is, however, that the accuracy of the evaluator's cost estimates depends directly on the accuracy of his description of the consequences of at least one alternative to the decision. In effect, the evaluator's cost analysis task is to accurately portray two or more alternative futures so that the decision maker can choose among them.

3. Those who are interested in an excellent treatment of the concept of opportunity costs from a theoretical and historical perspective might read Buchanan (1969).

4. The example is deliberately chosen. Perhaps the greatest waste in educational organizations results from the tendency of teachers, administrators, and evaluators to treat the time of students as a "free good" rather than as a scarce resource. We shall return to this point later.

A third implication is that costs typically lie in the future (though they may be estimated from past experience), and, since they are measured by an alternative not chosen, they can seldom, if ever, be assessed with absolute accuracy. For evaluators concerned with a pending decision, program costs normally lie in the future. They will be incurred over a period of time that is sometimes quite lengthy. Because the costs of deciding to implement a reading program may be felt for many years, these costs must normally be estimated, and the evaluator usually strives for relative, not absolute, accuracy.

Measuring Costs

If costs are alternatives lost, why are they normally measured in dollars? Would it not be more appropriate to describe carefully a set of alternative futures to an administrator who wants to know the cost of a proposed program? For example, if he wants to know the cost of a reading program that he is considering, why not respond to his question with the value of the best alternative program (say, in science) that must be forgone if the reading program is implemented? Why is it typical to respond with some dollar figure? Perhaps it will be helpful to try to clarify the relationship between costs as measured by lost opportunities and costs as measured by dollars.

Cost analysis consists essentially of identifying, measuring, and evaluating alternatives, but not necessarily in dollars (Bickner, 1971). The three steps can often be accomplished almost simultaneously, however, when dollars are used as a measure of cost. This becomes clear, for example, when the measurement process itself is considered, where essentially four options are available to the evaluator.

Consider the following situation. You are asked to help a school superintendent decide whether or not to implement a new reading program. As part of this job you are also requested to determine the cost of the proposed program, which could be measured in any of the following four ways:

1. You could develop a list of the resources required to operate the program. Such a list might include the number of teachers or aides needed, the space necessary, books and other materials that need to be acquired, and other relevant information. This list, which could be quite lengthy, is one measure of the costs of the new reading program. That is, you might respond to the superintendent's request by saying that, if he adopts the program, it will cost his dis-

trict the time of 6 reading specialists, 7 classrooms, 520 books, and other resources.

2. On the basis of the list above, you might go one step further and describe some alternative uses for the same resources. If the resources are not highly specific to the proposed program, many quite different alternatives might be set forth for the superintendent's consideration, and those alternatives are the programs he must give up (for example, an augmented basic mathematics program, or a career education program, among others) if he chooses to implement the reading program. These alternatives forgone also represent the cost of the proposed innovation. If the resources required are highly specific to the proposed program, and some of them almost always are, few alternative programs will be possible. It is difficult to teach high school physics, for example, with reading specialists and first-grade primers.

3. Carrying your cost analysis still further, you might attempt to estimate the value of the alternatives you have listed under the second measurement procedure. That is, since each alternative program is itself represented by one amalgam of advantages and one of disadvantages, you might establish the net value of each alternative. The cost of the reading program, then, is the value of the next best alternative to it. This procedure would produce a measure of the program's opportunity costs since it would provide the best assessment of the program benefits forgone.

4. Finally, you could attach a dollar expenditure figure to the inputs listed under the first procedure and call this figure the cost of the reading program.

Several points should be made in regard to these alternative procedures for measuring costs. First, no matter which is selected, the results should be useful to the decision maker. The first (listing resources) is an essential prerequisite to the remaining three, but, in itself, it is probably the easiest to accomplish and the least useful to a client. The third procedure (valuing the alternatives) is the most difficult to perform, and it is dependent upon the second procedure (prior specification of alternative programs). The fourth procedure (estimating dollar costs) is, of course, the most common. The important thing to note in regard to the last of the procedures is that, when dollars are used as a measure of costs, they simultaneously serve as a measure of the results of the other three procedures and as

a substitute for them. If you choose to answer the superintendent's question about the cost of the proposed reading program with a dollar figure, you are assuming that that figure will serve as an adequate measure and description of the resources required, the programs forgone, and the value of forgone programs.

How can dollars serve in these various ways, especially as measures of the value of alternatives forgone, that is, measures of opportunity costs? Briefly, it can be assumed that voluntary market exchanges among individuals will reveal the highest values of the options available to them (Alchian, 1968). Hypothetically, for example, in a barter economy the rate of exchange for two objects, A and B, might be 2 for 1. That is, numerous individuals freely exchanging the objects might create an exchange rate wherein the possession of two A's would equal one B in value. The cost of possessing the second is two of the first. In highly developed societies, of course, barter economies do not exist. Instead, money is the medium of exchange. It is a convenient, generalizable, and comparable measure of the exchange value of goods and services. In our hypothetical situation for these developed societies, A might cost one dollar, and B, two dollars. Since goods are substitutable sources of utility and since substitution is made easier when money is utilized as a medium of exchange, we can say that the dollar cost of an option is a reasonable measure of the next highest valued forsaken option. Having B costs two dollars, which is a measure of the forsaken option of having two A's. Similarly, when goods or services are used in the production of a product, as when the services of teachers and school facilities are used to produce changes in children, the costs of these goods and services in dollars is assumed to be an approximation of the value of options forsaken, those other changes that could have been produced using different resources.

When can dollars serve as an adequate measure of a program's total cost? There is simply no set answer to this question. It must be kept in mind that the dollar, as a unit of measure, is not equivalent to the same dollar you spend in a grocery store. Ultimately, its adequacy as a measuring device is dependent upon the existence of alternative uses for the resources involved. The evaluator must be alert to the possibility that some of the resources required for a program may not be subject to alternative uses; hence, measuring them with dollars might prove misleading. At the same time, however, the absence of

such a market (and, hence, the absence of a meaningful dollar figure) should not make one ignore a real program cost.

This is what happens, for example, when evaluators do not take into account the expenditure of student time as a program cost. Since there is not a free market economy to place a dollar value on the time of students, especially elementary school students, evaluators and decision makers typically do not consider that time as a resource and its expenditure is not accounted as a program cost. Perhaps the best way to avoid such mistakes is to develop very carefully the list of resources required to operate the proposed program, paying particular attention to the time of all personnel involved, including students.[5] After such a list has been developed, a decision can be made as to which items are adequately measured in dollars and which must be measured in such other terms as square feet of space and pupil instructional hours.

Some program costs can be measured in dollars, and others cannot. When costs can be reasonably measured in dollars, which sometimes requires a little ingenuity, it is usually desirable to do so because dollars, as measuring devices, provide a convenient, generalizable, and comparable estimate of the opportunity costs of a program. If a decision maker knows the dollar cost of a proposed program, he is in a position to make a reasonable estimate of opportunities forgone as a consequence of implementing a program. That is, he can reasonably infer what other programs he will have to forgo because dollars are merely means for attaining something valued. To the extent that money can do this, it is a proxy for what is valued and a meaningful measure of real costs. If, however, some program costs must be measured in another way, it is necessary to measure them in whatever way is appropriate to the cost analysis.

These, then, are major concerns in any consideration of program costs:

1. Costs are the consequences of decisions. A cost of a decision is a benefit forgone.
2. From a decision-making perspective, costs normally lie in the future; hence, they must usually be estimated.
3. Costs need not necessarily be measured in dollars. Measurement may be accomplished by:

---

5. The classic work on the value of student time is probably Theodore Schultz (1963).

    a. listing the resources required for a program;

    b. developing a description of alternative uses for those resources;

    c. estimating the value of these alternative uses;

    d. ascertaining the dollar value of required resources.

4. All of these procedures are useful. Which is to be used in a particular evaluation will depend on the decision alternatives and the needs of the decision maker.

5. The dollar cost of a program's resources may provide a reasonable estimate of the opportunity costs of that program. Dollars, as units of measurement, are helpful in this regard because they are convenient, generalizable, and comparable.

COSTING PROCEDURES

Now it is time to turn our attention toward the development of a set of guidelines for program evaluators concerned with determining the cost of a program. It should already be clear that the cost of a program is entirely dependent upon the decision at hand. The program evaluator must always remember that it is the decision to be made that is crucial, and any time spent clarifying that decision prior to beginning cost analysis is time well spent. The procedures an evaluator utilizes to determine costs—deciding what is to be included and how it is to be measured—must be specific to the particular problem. The following pages contain a series of procedural steps intended to be general enough to cover most evaluational problems but specific enough to help in working through an individual case. It will be necessary to describe the decision alternatives and develop an activities list, develop an input structure, determine relevant costs, measure and project costs, and compare costs.

Some Suggestions[6]

There is a strong temptation in any evaluation study to begin considering what are essentially methodological questions almost immediately. When, for example, the decision maker is concerned about the level of student satisfaction with a program, there is often a tendency to press the evaluator with questions about satisfaction and its measurement. If the evaluator succumbs to such pressure, he

6. This discussion derives from Coombs and Hallak (1972, p. 131).

may rapidly find himself discussing the relative merits of alternative instruments or scaling procedures well before the specific purpose for the evaluation is clear—before the decision that hangs on student satisfaction is explicated.

A similar temptation exists in regard to program costing. That is, if the decision maker is concerned about the cost of a program, discussions with an evaluator may often be reduced to specific questions about measuring costs. This threat is perhaps even stronger than that present in the case of student satisfaction because student satisfaction, or its lack, is often only dimly sensed, whereas the administrator deals with cost questions daily and may have some preconceived notions about how costs should be tabulated. Specifically, costs are often equated with dollar expenditures. Data about educational costs are extensive and "hard." Current and past budgets, cost projections, and revenue source information are often available in abundance, and you may find yourself immersed in budget figures before you have any clear idea of their relevance to the particular problem. This tendency may be further exacerbated because, while most educational systems do not have experts on student satisfaction on their payroll, nearly all have one or more business managers who are very knowledgeable about the financial affairs of the district. (As we shall see, however, they may have no knowledge of the costs of a particular program.)

It is important to consult extensively with a client, not only at the initial stage of the cost analysis but throughout its course. As the analysis unfolds, additional alternatives may occur to the evaluator or the decision maker. Further, an alternative considered plausible at the initial stages of the analysis may subsequently appear quite implausible as a viable choice, and there is no point in continuing to develop a comprehensive and detailed costing of an alternative if its resource requirements clearly exceed any possibility of implementation. By consulting with the client as the evaluation proceeds, however, modification of the alternative might make it feasible. The decision maker is in the best position to suggest such modification, and consulting regularly with him could save the evaluator considerable effort.

Relationships with people both inside and outside the organization whose skills and knowledge regarding the decision are complementary are also often useful. For example, if the decision to be

serviced concerns the adoption of a new program involving the hiring of additional teachers, it is necessary to estimate the costs of paying those teachers for some years hence. Such estimates are aided by information concerning the expected future state of the economy, the supply of teachers with the desired qualifications, and impending changes in salary structures. Such information may be available from economists, state education department officials, and representatives of state and local teachers' associations. A cost analysis frequently requires information about demographic trends, construction costs, or statistical estimation techniques—information an evaluator may not possess. In such cases, assistance from knowledgeable persons familiar with the problem can save considerable time.

Describing Decision Alternatives and Developing an Activities List

The starting point for the cost analysis aspect of an evaluation is normally the development of accurate preliminary descriptions of the major alternatives facing a decision maker. This involves three distinct but interrelated phases: describing the decision to be made in terms of alternative courses of action, ascertaining the objectives to be attained from each alternative, and developing as accurate and complete a description as possible of the activities necessary to attain each objective.

Since decisions and the decision maker are at the core of most evaluation efforts, the first task is to describe as precisely as possible the decision problem at hand. This can often be accomplished by phrasing the decision in the form of a question concerning alternative courses of action. Examples of such questions are: Should we adopt the ABC Reading Program or stay with our present one? Should we choose textbook series A or B? Should we expand our new science program to the entire district or not? Often you will need to spend a considerable amount of time working with an administrator to accomplish this, since evaluation problems are not often posed in a form that identifies explicit alternatives. The common evaluation question—"Is the program meeting its objectives?"—is an example of a question that does not contain explicit choice among competing courses of action, even though, as was noted earlier, decision makers usually have implicit choices in mind when posing an evaluation task in this guise. The first job of the evaluator, therefore, is to describe

the decision situation in terms of a choice among alternative courses of action. Preliminary discussions with the decision maker should work toward phrasing a question that embodies a choice among the relevant alternatives as *he* sees them. Obviously he must be satisfied that the question guiding evaluative work is appropriate. (One reason why evaluation reports have had little impact on decision making is that evaluators persist in answering questions that decision makers did not ask!)

Concurrent with the process of describing alternatives, it is necessary to ascertain the goals that an administrator can expect to attain by choosing an alternative. Essentially, the evaluator's objective will be to describe the outcomes or benefits that might derive from each of the available alternatives. This step is crucial to any analysis, not only because it is necessary to complete the cost phase but also because it focuses the decision maker's attention on the relationship between costs and benefits. That is, in a world of scarce resources, it focuses his attention on the benefits that he will forgo as a consequence of his choice. It is also important to note that the person who will make the decision is not necessarily the one most knowledgeable about the objectives and benefits attached to each alternative. Very often, the professional staff actually operating the program is more informative in this regard than the decision maker.

When objectives have been determined, it is necessary to describe carefully the activities that will be undertaken if those objectives are to be attained. The evaluator and the decision maker must begin to develop a precise description of the actions that program staff will initiate in order to reach the objectives. Again, while decisions about activities constitute the administrator's "output," suitably precise descriptions of the activities required to begin a program must often be obtained from the professional staff most familiar with the program area, and that staff should be consulted extensively. This description of the activities necessary to mount and maintain a program forms the basis of the remaining aspects of cost analysis—listing resources and ascertaining dollar costs.[7]

Although I have defined costs as opportunities forgone and have said that they are consequences of decisions, there has been no men-

7. It might also be noted that a comparison of intended activities with intended objectives provides an opportunity for what has been called "input evaluation." See PDK, National Study Committee on Evaluation (1971).

tion of *how* they occur. Costs do not miraculously appear when a decision is made. The superintendent who opts to implement a new science program in his district does not thereby incur any costs. The costs are incurred as a consequence of activities engendered by the decision: a curriculum coordinator may begin to spend some of his time planning implementation strategies, science teachers may attend workshops designed to acquaint them with the new program, a consultant may be hired and textbooks purchased, teachers and students will use the new program in their classrooms. All of these activities engender costs. For example, the time of staff and students will be utilized, and money will be spent for materials. In short, decisions result in activities that in turn bear costs. Costs do not exist; they happen.

Note especially that any description of activities necessary to attain an objective is not equivalent to a description of the activities that will constitute the program in full operation. Rather, it is necessary to list activities needed to set up or change a program as well as those necessary to sustain it. For example, if a new textbook is to be selected, and textbook selections are normally made by a committee of teachers, setting up and operating such a committee is an activity that should be included in the list as well as the purchase of the books themselves. The list should be as comprehensive as possible. The accuracy of cost estimates is directly related to this comprehensiveness, and the input structure described next is intended to help achieve it.

Developing an Input Structure

The cost of a given educational program cannot be estimated per se. All such programs, even the simplest, are made up of many different resource elements—teachers, books, students, classrooms, and so forth. In order to estimate the cost of a program, you first need to break it into its constituent parts, that is, its resource components and their respective functional categories. A set of these components and categories will be referred to as an *input structure*, which is based upon the activity list described above.

One example of a kind of input structure is a school district budget. This example is mentioned because budgets are familiar to most evaluators, and it is natural to turn to them when considering cost analysis. They may appear to be a ready-made input structure, but using them in this way will almost invariably prove to be a mistake.

All school budgets contain extensive categories for the resources required to operate a district's schools. Typically, these resources are grouped under such functional headings as "administration" and "instruction." The U.S. Office of Education has recommended a uniform budget structure that is now commonly in use (Reason and White, 1957). The basic categories of this structure are as follows (instruction is further broken down to illustrate its component parts):

Administration
Instruction
   Salaries
      Principals
      Consultants or supervisors
      Teachers
      Other instructional staff
      Secretarial and clerical assistants
      Other salaries for instruction
   Textbooks
   School libraries and audiovisual materials
   Teaching supplies
Other expenses
   Attendance and health services
   Pupil transportation services
   Operation of plant
   Maintenance of plant
   Fixed charges
   Food services and student body activities
   Community services
   Capital outlay
   Debt service from current funds
   Outgoing transfer accounts

You will undoubtedly encounter minor variations on the above scheme (for example, budgeting by school building) when you begin the process of costing an educational program. Regardless of the variations, there is one point you must remember: this type of budget is virtually useless for evaluative purposes.[8] It is almost impossible to

8. This statement is a slight exaggeration. The typical budget might usefully serve as a kind of checklist in setting up an input structure. For example, it might be used to ascertain whether or not transportation or plant maintenance activities are involved in the proposed program.

determine the current cost of a particular program in order to decide whether to replace it with an alternative using the budget as a data source. There is simply no way of relating the inputs listed in any category to a particular program. (Every superintendent knows the cost of his district's total program, but not the cost of any specific program, and this budget structure is the reason. Its categories do not allow him to ascertain the cost of teaching high school biology or first-grade reading, for example.) Put another way, the purpose of an input structure is to facilitate the analysis of decision alternatives. The school budget document obfuscates rather than facilitates such an analysis; hence, an evaluator must develop his own input structure. Further, budgets are short-range documents that typically contain cost information for the current or the next fiscal year, and an evaluator normally needs to project costs considerably further into the future than that.

As a starting point in developing an input structure, it is best to consult the activity list prepared earlier. Consider each activity and, in consultation with knowledgeable personnel, determine what resources will be utilized in carrying it out. That is, each activity requires the organization to utilize some of its available resources. The input structure you develop is simply a categorization of resources or "inputs" according to the set of activities associated with each program alternative.

It will be useful if you keep in mind the basic types of resources that any administrator has available for allocation. These are the "building blocks" that he utilizes in providing a service. The four major types are:

1. time (his own, his staff's, his students', volunteers', and others');
2. space (classrooms, offices, playgrounds, and so forth);
3. equipment (school busses, desks, and microscopes, for example);
4. supplies (paper, workbooks, and pencils, as well as other materials).[9]

A program administrator uses each of these four resources in various combinations or packages to achieve a program's objectives. Through the authority vested in him, he is able to allocate or assign specific

9. The distinction between equipment and supplies generally turns on whether or not the item in question can be expected to be consumed in a single budget period. Equipment is expected to last longer than one year.

resources representative of each of these to the accomplishment of some organizational goal.

Time, space, equipment, and supplies provide only one dimension of an adequate input structure. A second dimension is based on the function that the resources are to serve. That is, a second set of categories needs to be defined that would relate resource expenditures to their purpose in the program under consideration. One useful conception to meet this need is the notion of a program life cycle (Bickner, 1971, page 66). Most proposed new educational programs, or proposed changes in existing programs, involve a stream of costs over a period of time, usually years, in one or more of the following categories:

> *Research and development costs*—resources required to develop the program to the stage where it can be introduced into the system. For example, the time a science coordinator spends investigating a possible program, money used to hire consultants, and evaluation effort are appropriately classified as research and development (R&D) costs.
>
> *Investment costs*—costs necessary to implement the program. Equipment purchases and the costs of running a workshop to train staff are examples of investment costs.
>
> *Operating costs*—recurring costs required to operate the program over time. Maintenance of equipment, salaries of personnel, and the cost of supplies are examples.[10]

Considering costs in terms of a proposed program's life cycle is useful because it helps to make certain that the full cost impact of a proposal is considered. This is important because decision makers often become overly concerned with the investment costs of a program and neglect to consider that a decision to implement a new program, or to change an existing one, involves a stream of operating costs over a potentially long period of time. R&D and investment costs, however, may have a generally brief impact. In short, considering costs in terms of their function—R&D, investment, and operating —brings the very important dimension of time into an analysis.

10. Note that it is possible to classify some costs in more than one category. For example, the cost of a workshop to train personnel to operate a program might be considered as either R&D or investment. Where you place such costs is not usually important. What is important is that you not omit them.

Figure 7-1 illustrates a hypothetical relationship between these types of costs and the life cycle of a program. Notice that each type of cost typically behaves somewhat differently over time and is incurred at different points. It is extremely important that the evaluator, in consultation with the decision maker, identify the time span or horizon of the decision under consideration for it is impossible to determine a program's cost without specifying the time span of the analysis, that is, knowing how far into the future costs will be projected. A common error in educational cost analyses is the failure to consider time and to act as if the only costs of a new program that are important are those that occur in the first year of operation. The importance of this will be obvious when it is considered that organizations seldom have more than 5 percent of their current budget available as discretionary funds; the rest is already committed as a result of decisions made in the past. Decisions made now will incur costs over several years and, hence, will place additional constraints on decisions made years from now.

The notion of a program's life cycle is also useful because it facilitates cost analyses when decisions about program size and duration are considered. R&D costs, for example, are typically unaffected by either program size or duration. That is, the cost of developing the capability to implement a new science program (for example, the cost of researching alternative programs and field testing them) is

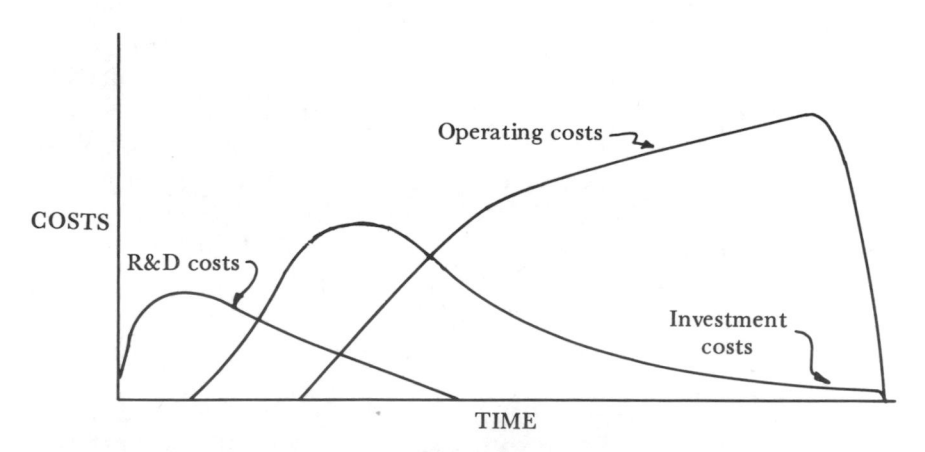

Figure 7-1
Relationship between costs and the life cycle of a program
(adapted from Fisher, 1971)

roughly the same whether the program is eventually implemented throughout the school district or only in a single school and regardless of how long it is operated. Many investment costs in education, on the other hand, are closely related to the scope of implementation but less affected by length of operation. Operating costs vary directly with both the size of the program and its duration.

A useful basic input structure for costing in program evaluations, therefore, can be represented as:

R&D costs	Investment costs	Operating costs
1.1 Time	2.1 Time	3.1 Time
1.2 Space	2.2 Space	3.2 Space
1.3 Equipment	2.3 Equipment	3.3 Equipment
1.4 Supplies	2.4 Supplies	3.4 Supplies

Several points need to be made in regard to this structure. First, and most important, the categories are merely suggested ones; an evaluator needs to choose resource and functional groupings that are both analytically useful and satisfactory to the decision maker. For example, despite the difficulties presented, a client may wish to include functional groupings that correspond to his expenditure budget system.[11] Second, regardless of the input structure used, it will have to be developed in considerably more detail than the skeleton outlined above. Under 3.1, for example, all categories of personnel affected by the decision at hand should be entered. Thus, the estimated time expenditures of administrators, consultants, paraprofessionals, students, custodians, bus drivers, and others would need to be separately noted if their time were implicated in the decision. Note also, however, that an input structure can be made too detailed, particularly when a relatively long time horizon is being considered. Since future costs will need to be estimated for each category, a fine-grained structure can require considerably greater effort in the estimation phase of the costing procedure than it is worth. In effect, the coarse structure noted above is designed primarily to serve as a kind of checklist to help ascertain which category of resources would be

11. In this case, however, it is probably better to first use a system such as the one described and, when the cost analysis is complete, assign dollar costs to budget categories. Note, however, that only expected dollar expenditures can be categorized in existing budgets; many program costs will remain outside the budget, e.g., student time.

affected by a decision. (In any particular instance it is likely that all of these general categories will be implicated.) Once a category is implicated, subcategories appropriate to the particular evaluation can be developed.

Finally, note that separate input structures must be developed for each alternative course of action for a given decision. Hence, any structure must be designed to facilitate comparisons. The structure suggested above has been deliberately designed to allow for this. The structures for competing alternatives will differ from each other. Perhaps this becomes clear if one considers the four decision types proposed by Stufflebeam *et al.* (PDK, National Study Committee on Evaluation, 1971): (1) planning decisions, or, "Should the program's goals be changed?" (2) structuring decisions, or, "How should the proposed program be designed?" (3) implementing decisions, or, "Should new procedures be instituted?" (4) recycling decisions, or, "Should the program be continued?" In the first case, the alternatives being considered might be initiating an entirely new program and maintaining an existing one. The input structure for the first of these alternatives would probably involve substantial costs (hence, entries) under R&D and investment, while the competing alternative, maintaining an existing program, would presumably contain few such costs. In the second case, comparing two alternative intended procedures, there would probably be costs in all major categories for each alternative, though differing subcategories would be likely. Implementing decisions, perhaps involving a choice between a proposed procedure and an existing one, might require input structures with fairly detailed operating cost subcategories, but differ substantially in the elaboration required under R&D and investment. In the case of a recycling decision regarding program termination, only one input structure might be required (primarily involving operating costs), which would allow the evaluator to determine the cost consequences of continuing the program.

To develop an input structure specifically for an evaluation, there are really only three criteria to keep in mind. First, it should be comprehensive, including every significant resource affected by the decision. Second, categories should be carefully defined and related in some fashion to the format of the data—past, present, and future— which the decision requires. Finally, the structures should facilitate the comparison of the alternatives over time. After an input structure

has been developed, the types of costs to be entered into it must be considered.

Determining the Types of Costs to be Considered: Relevant versus Irrelevant Costs

In general, determining the types of costs to be included in an analysis will be a matter of distinguishing relevant from irrelevant costs. Relevant costs, that is, those affected by the decision being considered, are the only ones that should be entered into an input structure. Making this distinction is a very important aspect of a program-costing job. If the distinction becomes muddled, the final output of the cost analysis may seriously mislead a client.

Since costs are consequences of decisions, distinguishing relevant ones from irrelevant ones requires a careful examination of the particular decision at hand, its alternatives, and the particular position of the decision maker himself. This implies that, from the evaluator's perspective, there is no such thing as *the* cost of an educational program; rather, a program has many costs, depending upon the decision alternatives and the decision maker. In brief, only relevant costs should be considered in a program evaluation. A judgment regarding relevance is decision and context specific, and making such judgments is an important task of the evaluator.

Costs come in an almost endless array. The jargon of economists, cost accountants, and cost analysts is replete with a wide variety of adjectives commonly prefixed to the word *cost*. Marginal costs, sunk costs, and indirect costs are examples. A few of these can be used to help us distinguish between relevant and irrelevant costs.

The first distinction is between *sunk* and *incremental* costs. For example, what are the costs of a school building? If costs are seen solely as resources expended, the cost of the building lies in the past. If, however, we are deciding whether or not to utilize the building in some particular way, its costs appear to lie in the future. Where should one look to determine the cost of the building? By now the answer should be obvious. Relevant costs lie in the future. The cost of a building already constructed is irrelevant to any present decision regarding its future use. Costs that have already been incurred result from past decisions, and they are sunk costs. Such costs, representing past alternatives, are irrelevant to an evaluation since those alternatives no longer exist. Deciding to use a school plant in one way rather

than another, however, involves incremental costs. These are costs that will be incurred if some change is instituted in a program. In program evaluations designed to inform decision makers, only incremental costs are normally important. The evaluator, therefore, in deciding which costs are to be entered in his input structure, must ensure that no sunk costs creep into his accounting, for they will only confuse the issue.

Although the need to exclude sunk costs from a current decision analysis may seem obvious, the principle is often violated. Recently, for example, I witnessed a board of education debating the merits of remaining affiliated with a national organization concerned with promoting a set of experimental practices in high schools. The particular district, after several years of working with the national organization, was deeply involved in the change process and had gone a considerable distance in reorganizing its high school program along the lines advocated by the organization. Teachers had been hired who were familiar with the new practices, the administrative procedures of the school had been extensively changed, and much effort had gone into devising new curricula that had been partially implemented. Because problems arose, a decision to discontinue was being considered. Opponents of a decision to end the experiment based much of their case on the argument that a great deal of money and effort had already gone into the new program, which was true, and that all of this would be "wasted" if it were ended. Clearly, however, such costs were irrelevant to the decision at hand. The only costs relevant to the decision to continue were those that lay in the future.

A second distinction, that between *fixed* and *variable* costs, is particularly useful when a decision about expanding or contracting a program is to be made. Fixed costs are essentially those costs that remain the same regardless of expansion or contraction of the program; variable costs change with program output. Within fairly broad limits, fixed costs include, typically, administrative salaries, maintenance, "overhead," and so forth. For example, expanding a science program to a higher grade, thereby enlarging its enrollment, does not usually involve additional administrative salaries. Variable costs, on the other hand, are tied more directly to the size of the program and vary closely with it. The costs of books and supplies are typical of the latter type. Thus, in the above example, expanding the science program might mean the purchase of additional books. Obviously, at

the extreme, no costs are truly fixed. Given a large enough change in program size, normally fixed costs become variable. Similarly, very small changes in program size may have little effect, and costs that are usually variable become fixed.[12] The evaluator must be certain to accurately determine which costs are fixed and which vary for a particular decision. When program expansion is under consideration, fixed costs—those unaffected by the size of the program—should not be included in the input structure.

Again, fixed costs must normally be excluded from an evaluation, but, as with sunk costs, this principle is often ignored. Perhaps this occurs most frequently when dealing with the indirect costs of a program, for example, "administrative overhead." Oftentimes, when programs are costed, some pro rata share of administrative expenses is charged to the program. When a decision to expand or contract an existing program is being considered, however, no such charges should be considered, unless, of course, administrative salaries (or time) are, in fact, affected. This particular example also illustrates what is often called a *joint cost.* Joint costs are those shared among programs—the salaries of administrators, guidance counselors, and school secretaries, for example.

A third distinction is drawn between *recurring* and *nonrecurring* costs. This distinction is particularly relevant to a decision to continue a program for some specified time. An example of nonrecurring investment costs might be those involved in an in-service program to train teachers prior to implementing a new curriculum. Nonrecurring costs, as the name implies, are those met only once within a specified period. Recurring costs, those to be met repeatedly, might include such items as salaries and wages and equipment repair. When the time period under consideration spans only a few years, R&D and investment costs are often nonrecurring. As with incremental and sunk costs and fixed and variable costs, the distinction between recurring and nonrecurring costs is not hard and fast. Whether a cost is classified as one or the other depends on the time frame of the decision. Thus, in the example above, the cost of in-service training for teachers is probably nonrecurring if the extension time of the program is

12. Cost analysts sometimes utilize the notion of a "semivariable" cost—i.e., one that is fixed over some range of output and then becomes variable, producing a "step function" cost curve. We shall have more to say about these later.

only one year since most trained members of the staff can be expected to remain for the coming year. If it is decided to extend the program for five years, these costs might well become recurring as a consequence of teacher attrition. Again, the point is obvious: only costs that will be incurred within the time frame of the decision should be counted in the input structure.

Bickner (1971, page 36) notes that these distinctions are related to what he terms the time, the scope, and the horizon of the decision being analyzed. Thus, the costs of continuing an educational program (and the distinction between sunk and incremental costs) depends upon the point in time of the decision. The costs of expanding or contracting a program (and the distinction between fixed and variable costs) depends upon the proposed change in the scope of the program. Finally, the cost of extending a program, as well as the distinction between recurring and nonrecurring costs, depends upon the initial and revised termination dates or the horizon of the program.

There are still other distinctions among costs that the evaluator must consider. One of these has to do with determining who bears a given cost and whether or not that person or organization is of concern to the decision maker. For example, nearly all states reimburse local school districts for most of the expenses resulting from the operation of school buses. Similarly, most states provide some sort of "incentive grants" for certain educational innovations under which the state matches the money that districts invest in a new program. We shall call these program costs *external* because they are borne by someone or some organization other than the evaluator's client. Conversely, *internal* costs are borne directly by the decision maker's organization.

Whether a cost is external or internal is directly dependent upon the decision maker's position in the organizational hierarchy. A principal considering whether or not to implement a particular program can usually consider the salaries of teachers (but not their time) as external; their salaries are borne by the school district. The superintendent, however, would certainly consider the same salaries as internal costs. For him, the dollar expenditure cost of program implementation is considerably higher than it is for the principal.[13]

13. This assumes, of course, that most principals do not control their own budgets in regard to staff salaries, a generally safe assumption. Note also that, for the principal, teachers' time might be appropriately measured in dollars, but not

This again illustrates the fact that the same program can have different costs, that the cost of a program is dependent upon factors other than the resources that go into it.

An evaluator must be careful to include all of the internal costs of a program in his analysis. These are the costs that are of direct concern to a program administrator since they change as a result of his decision and those changes will be reflected in his budget. Whether or not external costs should be included depends upon whether they, too, are of concern to the decision maker. The evaluator will need to identify such costs and determine his client's desires in this regard. If these costs are included, however, they are generally reported separately from internal costs.

This discussion of internal and external costs illustrates a rather paradoxical feature of cost analysis that may occur as a consequence of viewing costs as alternatives forgone: the higher the position of the decision maker, the higher the cost of a given choice. In another case, however, the higher the position of the decision maker, the lower the cost (Bickner, 1971, page 46). Consider this example. Suppose that a decision concerning the allocation of paraprofessionals is to be made. Often, the higher the decision maker, the higher the cost of using these individuals in some particular way because higher decision makers have more alternative uses for personnel. The chairman of the English department has fewer alternative uses than the school principal, who in turn has fewer than the superintendent. While the chairman might use the paraprofessionals as graders or monitors, the school principal can, among other things, use them to supervise the lunchroom or assign them to other departments. If some of these alternatives have higher values than the alternatives available to the department chairman, the costs of using them in any particular way are higher for the principal—the value of the opportunities forgone is greater. On the other hand, if the decision is whether or not to provide paraprofessional graders to overworked English teachers in a certain school, there may be an inverse relationship between cost and hierarchical level since there are more alternative resources available at higher levels to meet this purpose. Thus, while the department

---

as dollar expenditures. The latter, however, would be appropriate for the superintendent. The distinction between dollars and dollar expenditures is discussed below.

chairman might have only the alternative of hiring a group of para-professionals to relieve his overworked staff, the principal might be able to reallocate existing aides already available in the school, while the superintendent might also have the alternative of reallocating English teachers among schools in order to reduce class size in the particular building. In general, then, we may find that, in analyzing the cost of alternative ends for a given means, the higher the decision maker, the higher the cost because more alternative ends exist. If, however, the analysis concerns the cost of a choice among means to reach a given end, the cost may go down as the decision-making level rises because more means are available.

Finally a word needs to be said about "indirect costs." These are incurred as a result of a decision, though they are typically not reflected in any record of expenditures. These costs include depreciation of buildings and equipment, property and sales tax exemptions, and, in the case of older students, forgone earnings. In many program evaluations these costs (with the possible exception of the last) are relatively minor and can probably be ignored. In some cases, however, they are substantial, especially when large capital expenditures are involved. For example, if a school district purchases an existing building for some use, the cost of that building to the district may include not only the dollars expended for it, but also the loss of the income it produced for the district when it was on the property tax rolls. You should be particularly alert for "hidden" costs in such instances. Thomas (1971, page 38), for example, estimated that the imputed value of depreciation, interest, and forgone property taxes was almost 25 percent of the total cost of education in the state of Michigan.

Measuring and Projecting Costs

After having prepared an appropriate input structure and having determined which resources are relevant to the decision alternatives, an evaluator is ready to measure the current cost of the resources and to project the costs into the future. When procedures for doing this are considered, the costing of time and space are treated more extensively than equipment and supplies, since time and space, particularly time, are relatively more important.

The challenge to the evaluator concerned with costs is to be com-

prehensive. Typically you will find that there are four kinds of costs in an evaluation (Bickner, 1971, page 41):

1. costs that can be measured in dollar expenditures;
2. costs that can be reasonably measured in dollars, though they are not reflected in expenditures;
3. costs that are quantifiable;
4. costs that are not quantifiable.

A comprehensive analysis of the costs of an educational program commonly involves all four of these. The first is most familiar; teachers' salaries and the purchase of equipment are examples of costs that are reflected in actual dollar expenditures resulting from program operation. The second includes such things as depreciation and property tax exemptions. These are real costs of running a program, and they are appropriately measured in dollars. Further, they are frequently overlooked in cost analysis. The third category, other quantifiable costs, consists principally of the time of students and volunteers, and the cost of space. The latter, usually measured in square feet, can often be measured in terms of dollars (a procedure to be discussed shortly) and, hence, can be transfered to the second category. Finally, the last category, nonquantifiable costs, includes those opportunity costs of a choice that cannot be easily measured in any useful way. Effects on staff morale, public reaction, or effects on other programs as a consequence of implementing the one under consideration are examples. Although these are not dollar costs and they are not quantifiable, they are still important to decision makers, and they should be included in a cost analysis if it is to be comprehensive.

The important point for you to note from the foregoing is that the usual definition of program cost—dollar expenditure—can be quite misleading. Merely to total the expected expenditures for teachers, administrators, equipment, and supplies should a particular alternative be chosen would be to ignore potentially important cost considerations. In sum, dollar expenditures do not equal a program's costs.

In considering the problem of measuring and projecting program costs, the general input structure suggested earlier will be used, and the types of costs noted above will guide the discussion. Suppose, as a result of developing an input structure for an evaluation problem, an evaluator finds that the time of teachers, administrators, and stu-

dents are all involved in the program decision. How should the costs be measured and projected?

Since the magnitude of many program costs is directly tied to the size of the client population, a good starting point for cost analysis is student time. Unless the upper grades, the college level, or adult education is involved, student time typically falls in the third category of types of costs—those quantifiable, but not in terms of dollars. Measuring these requires a knowledge of how many students will be involved now and each year of the program through to the selected time horizon. The resulting figures represent the program's current and projected client population. Next, the extent of the time commitment demanded of students by the program must be determined. Many academic school programs (for example, a high school algebra course) require approximately 180 hours of instructional time per student per year, which constitutes the common five classes per week over a school year of 180 days. The product of the number of students involved and the time commitment required yields the number of student instructional hours, an important component of a program's costs.

Two points should be made in regard to student instructional hours. First, while student time may be measured in a number of time units—weeks, years, and so forth—it is generally preferable to utilize hours as the unit of measurement. Comparing the costs of programs that vary in length requires a comparable unit of time. It is also frequently desirable to determine the unit costs of a program and its alternatives—the dollar cost of the provision of some unit of service. Again, the instructional hour is quite useful. Second, total instructional hours may seriously underestimate the amount of student time a program requires. Time spent on homework, in resource centers, and in language laboratories may represent a substantial additional resource expenditure required by a program. It may be necessary to distinguish between student instructional hours—typically time spent in a classroom with an instructor—and total student time, which includes instructional hours and the time students are expected to spend outside of a classroom as part of the program.

In your costing of student time, you might want to consider what Bowman (in Thomas, 1971, page 32) has termed "forgone learning." That is, when decision makers decide to implement a new educational program, they may neglect to consider the consequences that

decision will have on existing programs. Since student time is limited, it usually happens that a new program "steals" time from an existing one—either by eliminating it entirely or, more commonly, by reducing the amount of student time currently allocated to it. Unless there is sufficient "slack" in the existing program, other desired student outcomes may be adversely affected. A decision to implement a new unit on interpersonal relations in a health course may have, as one of its costs, a decrease in student knowledge about the care of teeth or eyes or some other aspect of health covered in other units. While it would be difficult to measure these costs when a decision is to be made, their possible existence should be noted in your analysis.

Next, the time of paid personnel, typically teachers and administrators, must be considered. These costs can often, though not always, be measured as dollar expenditures. In order to assign a dollar cost to the time of teachers and administrators, the current and projected number of personnel involved and the amount of their time being allocated by the decision must be determined. In addition, the composition of the program's personnel force and the components of their salary costs are usually needed before future dollar expenditures can be estimated. Note also that, as with students, teachers' time is not confined to the classroom. A program may require substantial out-of-class time commitments from the instructional staff for training, preparation, or some other facet. This time must also be taken into account.

The effect of the composition of the program's personnel force on the dollar cost of an educational program is obvious. Teachers' salaries are commonly determined almost entirely by two variables—experience in years and level of education. These variables, operating through a salary schedule, are sufficient to make the time of one teacher in a district cost twice that of another. Hence, whether a personnel force is composed primarily of a staff close to the bottom of the salary schedule, or of a staff that is experienced and highly trained makes a considerable difference in the dollar cost of a program. The salary schedule is also important in projecting future program costs; it is necessary to estimate both movement of staff through the schedule to the program's horizon and changes in the schedule itself. These steps involve ascertaining personnel attrition, likely characteristics of replacements, and the probability of significant changes in the schedule. Information relating to these issues can

often be obtained from district personnel offices and from representatives of state and local teachers' associations.

In addition to the composition of the work force, it is necessary to examine the component parts of professional salaries. That is, a significant proportion of the dollar cost of teacher and administrative time is not shown in salary schedules, which reflect only expenditures paid directly to these personnel. "Fringe benefits"—retirement, medical and dental insurance, accident insurance—typically constitute a substantial additional cost borne by a district, sometimes as much as 25 percent of direct salaries. These "hidden" costs cannot be ignored. Also, they tend to behave differently than salaries themselves in that their cost may rise considerably faster than direct salary payments. Likely changes must be estimated and considered when projecting future dollar expenditures. Again, personnel officers and representatives of teacher organizations can be helpful.

Space requirements are commonly ignored in evaluating a program's costs. Yet, space, like the time of students, is not free. Classrooms allocated to one program cannot be simultaneously used for another. The cost of space may constitute a significant part of the total costs of a program. Because space does not usually represent a dollar expenditure (a program does not usually require the construction of new facilities), decision makers sometimes neglect these costs.

Costing of space should begin with determining the number of classrooms involved in a program and the amount of time they will be used. In many cases this part of the cost analysis need be carried no further, or a conventional measure of space requirements, such as square feet, can be adopted. That is, these costs may be left in the third category—those that are quantifiable. The procedure for measuring the cost of space in dollars (in order to arrive at a total dollar cost of a program, for example) is relatively straightforward.

The five components of the dollar cost of space (Thomas, 1971, page 44) are:
1. the interest on any unpaid debt;
2. the forgone interest on equity;
3. depreciation or annual decrease in value;
4. overhead—heat, light—associated with the space;
5. maintenance.

Suppose that one of the alternatives to a decision involves the allocation of five classrooms, each encompassing approximately 1,000

square feet. To assess the dollar cost of the space, you will need to know its construction cost (say, $20.00 per square foot); its expected life, hence, its present value after depreciation (say, $80,000); the remaining amount owed (say, $60,000), the interest rate on this debt (say, 4 percent), maintenance costs, which are usually recorded on a square-foot basis (say, $.10 per square foot), and overhead, which is also typically computed on the same basis (say, $.15 per square foot). The yearly cost of allocating the five classrooms to the program under consideration is:

Interest on debt (4 percent of $60,000)	$2,400
Foregone interest on equity (say, 5 percent of $20,000)	1,000
Depreciation (assuming an additional life of twenty years)	4,000
Overhead	750
Maintenance ($.10 × 5,000 square feet)	500
	$8,650

If the classrooms are to be used only part of the time for the program, only the appropriate fractional part of $8,600 would be charged to it.

The cost of equipment and supplies for a program can be provided by district personnel or suppliers. If substantial equipment costs are involved, these should be prorated over their expected life. In this case, the components of imputed interest, maintenance, and depreciation may need to be taken into account. Because of the nature of educational programs, however, the cost of supplies and equipment is a relatively minor consideration in most evaluations, and rule-of-thumb estimates are appropriate. For example, the total cost of supplies can often be reasonably estimated by dividing current budget figures for supplies by the number of pupils to determine an average cost per pupil and applying this figure to the number of pupils served by the program under consideration.

In regard to estimating the future costs of a program, some general comments may be helpful. First, it is usually unprofitable to spend a great deal of time carefully estimating the future costs of all the resources contained in an input structure. If the program being considered is extensive, the number and diversity of these resources may be quite large. They do not, however, all contribute equally to total program costs. As noted above, for example, supply and equipment costs are often relatively small. Hence, to spend a great deal of time

carefully estimating the cost of these over, say, the next five years is often not worth the effort. On the other hand, since education is highly "labor intensive," very carefully estimating the cost of time is often crucial. Put another way, relatively small mistakes in estimating future salary costs can be disastrous, while small errors in regard to supplies are rarely so. Therefore, it is usually a good idea to allocate cost analysis time in rough proportion to the contribution of each category of costs to the total. Typically this means spending the greatest effort on time, followed by space, equipment, and supplies, in that order.

Second, uncertainty must be explicitly accounted for in any analysis. This means that it is often not desirable to develop a single cost projection for a program but several projections. This recommendation follows from the fact that you are attempting to estimate costs that are dependent on future (and, hence, unknown) "states of the world." Point estimates, that is, single estimates of a decision's costs five years from now, may turn out to be grossly in error because of a failure to take into account some reasonable alternative assumptions about the state of the world at that time. Consider a simple example of the consequences of this failure. During the teacher shortage in the late 1950's and early 1960's many school districts, in an effort to attract and retain staff, adopted salary schedules with very high ceilings, providing large salaries for experienced and highly trained teachers. Similarly, they adopted policies that tied the entire schedule to starting salaries, such that, as salaries for beginning teachers went up, the entire schedule was increased proportionately. Such decisions were relatively harmless during a period of teacher shortage and high teacher mobility, when the majority of a staff were "at the bottom" of the schedule. Both of these conditions have now changed, and some districts find themselves with an increasingly large proportion of their staff in the top salary ranges, resulting in a higher total personnel cost, both absolute and proportionate, than they had expected. This situation could have been avoided had the cost consequences of alternative schedule decisions been examined under varying assumptions about the future composition of the teaching force.

Two important aspects of an evaluation help to avoid such situations. The first is to identify the sensitivity of a cost to each of its resource components. That is, large variations in the cost of some resources required for a program will have relatively little impact on

the program's total cost, for the program is insensitive to such variations. For example, a 100 percent increase in the cost of supplies or of custodial salaries may have little effect on total costs. On the other hand, total program cost may be closely tied to relatively small variations in the cost of other resources. Again, because education is labor intensive, time costs are typically of the latter type; a 10 percent increase in teacher salaries will usually make a large difference in the total cost of a program. Note also that the absolute or relative magnitude of the cost of some resource is not necessarily an indication that the program will be sensitive to it. It is sensitivity to *variations* in cost that is important. Also, it may be necessary to make alternative assumptions about the amount of a particular resource a program will require in the future since increases or decreases in such requirements also will affect total costs. For example, salary costs are closely tied to the size of the client population. If variation in the population is expected, or if substantial variations in the demand for a course are likely, the effect of such variations needs to be taken into account.

A second aspect of this sensitivity analysis is to make alternative assumptions about the future behavior of the costs of key resources through to the program's horizon. Often this means making at least three different sets of assumptions and deriving three corresponding estimates of a resource's cost—a "best guess," an "optimistic guess," and a "pessimistic guess"—noting the effects of these estimates on the cost of a program. In effect, if substantial uncertainties exist in regard to the quantity or cost of key resource components, these uncertainties must be taken into account through a sensitivity analysis. Any report to the decision maker, therefore, should alert him to these by providing several estimates of the cost of a particular decision alternative. Finally, the assumptions that generated each estimate must be made explicit since the quality of a decision depends upon the decision maker's understanding and judgment regarding which of these assumptions about the future is most likely to be valid.

A third general comment in regard to estimating costs concerns the problem of accuracy, which is related to the problem of uncertainty. Absolute accuracy in cost projections is neither possible nor necessary. It is not possible, normally, since these costs all lie in the

future. Since evaluations designed to serve decision making are most often concerned with providing cost estimates of alternative courses of action, the decision maker is typically concerned with the relative costs of two or more alternatives. It is most important that an analysis be accurate in the sense that the cost of each alternative stand in its correct relative relationship to the others. Although it is unnecessary, therefore, to spend a great deal of time trying to get a correct estimate of costs in an absolute sense, the procedures used to assess the costs of alternatives should be comparable. The same assumptions and techniques used to estimate future dollar expenditures for salaries under one alternative must be used when estimating salary expenditures under another.

We noted in discussing input structures that greater accuracy is not necessarily attained by breaking down a resource category into the finest possible detail. Similarly, when projecting cost estimates it is not always efficient to break down the components of the cost of a resource into great detail since such a fine breakdown may simply require more time without a corresponding increase in accuracy. Consider the case of teachers' salaries. One method of estimating future cost would involve merely ascertaining the current costs of direct salaries and fringe benefits and projecting these ahead with a suitable adjustment for expected increases in each. One might choose, alternatively, to identify the components of fringe benefits (for example, health insurance) and estimate the cost of each of these separately in order to arrive at a total. While the latter procedure would seem to be more accurate, this is not always the case, particularly when the needed projections go far into the future. In that situation uncertainties abound, and more global estimates may be satisfactory.

A fourth suggestion also concerns accuracy. It will sometimes be necessary to estimate the relative costs of a substantial number of alternatives to a particular decision. Even if there are only two to begin with, it frequently occurs that, in the process of analysis, other alternatives come to mind. In the initial stages, it is often more efficient to use "quick and dirty" procedures aimed at narrowing the number of alternatives to a few. You can then cost these in finer detail, attempting to achieve a relative degree of accuracy suitable to the decision maker's needs.

Comparing the Cost of Alternatives

In this section we will examine a few of the common procedures involved in comparing the cost of alternative courses of action—the last step in your analysis of program costs. When you have described the decision alternatives, developed appropriate input structures, determined the relevant costs, and developed estimates of those costs, you are in a position to structure the results of your work in such a way as to allow the decision maker to make the pertinent comparisons of his alternatives. Usually this procedure will involve a comparison of alternatives in terms of their total, average, or marginal costs. The choice of which of these is appropriate depends upon the decision at hand.

Total Costs. A determination of total costs is commonly required when a decision involves the question of adopting a new program. For example, suppose a superintendent is considering implementing an intramural athletic program for girls as part of his district's physical education offerings. He will normally want to know the total cost of doing so over some period of years. The relevant alternative to this course of action might be to reject the program, retaining the present physical education offerings intact. Hence, the cost analysis problem will be to determine the total cost of altering the present program so as to offer girls an opportunity to participate in intramural sports.

A convenient and useful way of thinking about this task is to utilize the concept of a *base case*. Essentially, a base case is a projection (or a "spendout") of the costs of decisions made to date. That is, assuming no new decisions, it is a statement of the cost implications of decisions already made as they unfold out to some chosen point of time in the future. In this particular situation, retaining the present program provides the relevant base case, and cost analysis consists of examining the total cost implications of adopting an alternative to this base case. Utilizing the input structure and cost projections prepared for retaining the present program, a spendout of the existing offerings out to the decision horizon under the assumption of no change can be prepared. Graphically, this spendout can be shown as in Figure 7-2, where the area under the curve AB represents the cost of retaining the present program.

Next, the input structure and cost projections prepared for the intramural program that allows for girls' participation can be used

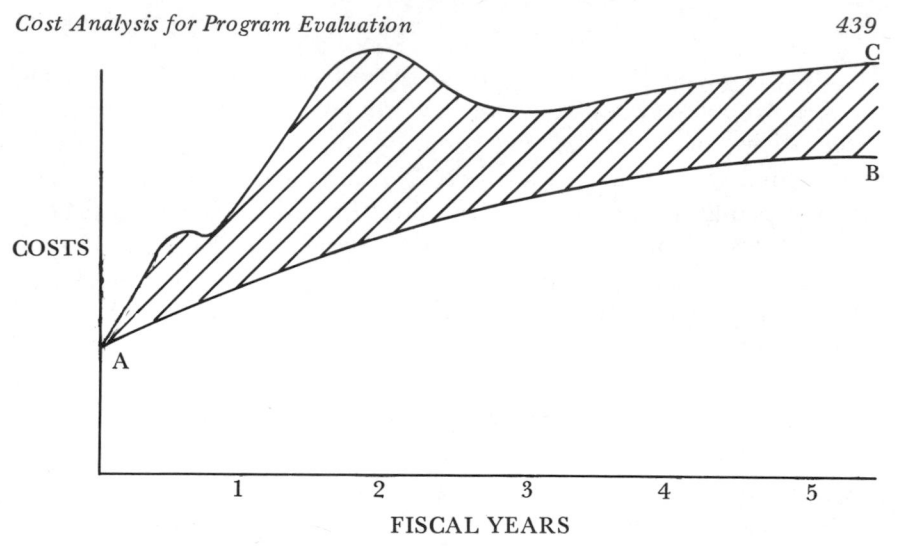

COSTS

FISCAL YEARS

1   2   3   4   5

Figure 7-2
A projection or "spendout" of the costs of decisions made to date
(adapted from Fisher, 1971)

because it represents the costs of the present program plus those of the proposed alternative. This particular situation would probably show significant R&D costs (for example, the cost of planning the program), investment costs (for example, additional equipment and facilities), and operating costs (for example, salaries for coaches) spread out over the same time period. Graphically, the total cost of adding the girls' program is represented by the shaded area under curve AC. That is, it represents the total incremental cost of this alternative, while the total area under AC represents the projected total cost of the entire intramural program, should the alternative be adopted. Both of these figures, of course, will be important to the superintendent's decision.

This example also illustrates an important advantage of explicitly taking time into account in an analysis. Note that adopting the girls' program results in a substantial increment in costs during the second fiscal year. That probably represents the relatively large investment costs likely to be incurred as a result of the purchase of necessary equipment and facilities. Upon examining the results, the superintendent may decide that this peak in costs is unacceptably high. That is, since he is able to compare projected program costs to projected revenues, he might conclude that the proposed program is not

feasible as planned because of its high costs during a particular time period. Knowing this, however, it is possible to examine additional alternatives that might spread some of the investment costs over a longer period of time without causing an unacceptable loss in program capability. For example, the implementation of a particularly costly sport as part of the intramural program might be delayed until the third or fourth year in order to reduce the budgetary impact of investment costs in the second fiscal year. In brief, a careful projection of the time phasing of total costs often results in a reconsideration of alternatives and one or more iterations in the cost analysis.

An issue that occurs when one considers cost projections such as this one is that of discounting. This problem arises because dollars are not all alike. Put simply, a dollar today is worth more than a dollar tomorrow.[14] For example, if your local bank will give you $1.05 next year for each $1.00 you deposit now, you may reasonably conclude that a dollar available now is worth more than one available next year. Implementing an educational program, such as the girls' intramural program being considered, results in a stream of costs over a period of years, and those dollars are not all of equal value. Hence, they should not all be added as if they were equal when arriving at a total dollar cost for the program. It may be important, therefore, to discount future dollar expenditures back to their present value when considering the total cost of an educational program. Unfortunately, this is seldom done, even though the procedure for doing it is relatively simple.[15] The choice of an appropriate discount rate is not simple, however, since this rate depends on such factors as the subjective time preference of the decision maker and his alternative uses for resources. The subject of choosing a correct rate is beyond the scope of this chapter.[16] It is usually not worthwhile initially to spend a great deal of time trying to arrive at *the* appropriate rate. Instead, several rates—5, 10, 15 percent—might be tried, and the results studied to determine whether or not variations are of sufficient magnitude to warrant closer study and an attempt to choose a relatively accurate rate. This particular problem should be

14. This problem of discounting is *not* the problem of inflation, which is the decline in the purchasing power of money.

15. Thomas (1971, p. 3) provides a general formula for discounting.

16. See Fisher (1971, p. 227) for a discussion of this matter.

treated in a manner similar to those suggested for attaining accurate cost projections: spend time on those costing procedures that are potentially important in their impact on the decision.

Average Costs. The computation of average costs often arises in an evaluation when comparing the costs of two alternative procedures to reach the same end. For example, suppose you are asked to evaluate the cost implications of two proposed procedures for teaching a foreign language in a district's junior high school. Let us say that one of these consists of adding a series of "listening stations" to the school learning center. These stations consist of small portable carrels equipped with tape recorders, headsets, and tapes of native speakers using the target language in a series of guided lessons. Students utilize the carrels on an individual basis to improve their speaking and listening skills. The second alternative being considered is to hire teacher aides from the community, who speak the language, to assist the school's foreign-language teachers by working with small groups of students or with individuals in conversational settings. The superintendent needs to know the relative costs of each of these alternatives.

Utilizing the input structures and cost projections prepared for each of these, the costs can be compared. A problem such as this presents the typical situation in which the two alternatives "overlap." That is, fully developed input structures for each alternative would contain many resources common to both alternatives, such as the time of teachers. When such resources are common to each alternative and expended equally under each, they may be eliminated from the input structure and cost projections since they make no difference in the decision at hand. To include them amounts to adding a constant to both sides of an equation. The major task in constructing the input structures will have been to identify those resource expenditures that differ between the alternatives. (However, in certain cases there may be some interest in knowing the total cost of each alternative. In these instances identical costs would be retained.) In this particular example, each input structure would contain teacher time, but the amount of time needed to mount each program would probably differ. For example, some proportion of teacher salaries would probably have to be added to the aide alternative since some teacher time would have to be utilized in supervising and coordinating their work. Similarly, a different, and probably smaller, proportion of

teacher salary costs might need to be charged to the listening station alternative for the time expended in developing the lessons to be taped. In addition, some of the salary costs of personnel assigned to the learning center might need to be included.

In comparing these alternatives, a good procedure would be to determine their unit costs per student instructional hour. (Such costs are useful for many purposes, such as comparing costs across time as well as in situations such as that described here.) Unit costs are simply the total dollar expenditure, the total dollar costs, or the total of other measurable nondollar costs in a given period divided by some measure derived from the students involved. One such measure might be simply the number of students enrolled in a particular period, for example, the common expenditure-per-pupil figure used by many districts. For many evaluation problems, however, such a figure is too gross to be useful since it would hide important differences between alternative programs. Often, as in this case, cost per student instructional hour can be used as the unit for comparison. The choice of what unit to utilize is important, and it should be made while planning the cost analysis so that the input structure can easily provide the information needed in the last stage of the work. It is sometimes useful to utilize the number of students who complete a program rather than the number enrolled if attrition rates are expected to vary significantly between alternative programs. That is, two programs with the same cost per student enrolled might differ widely in cost per student completion if one program were likely to result in a significant number of dropouts.

Cost can, of course, be determined for a variety of units—teachers, classrooms, schools, and so forth. Choose the unit with the particular decision in mind and keep that unit clearly in mind throughout an evaluation project. Remember that unit costs represent average costs, not the cost for, say, any particular student. In general, choose a unit that is tied most directly to the major variable costs of the input structure. For example, if the cost of supplies bulks large among alternatives, choose some measure based on students since supply costs normally vary quite closely with the number of students served. On the other hand, equipment costs—for example, audiovisual equipment—are sometimes more closely tied to the number of classrooms involved in the program than the number of students, and cost per classroom might be a more appropriate unit cost for your analysis.

Another problem that may have to be dealt with in an evaluation such as the one described arises from the generally higher initial costs of a program and the consequent effect of these on a cost-per-student figure. For example, one of the alternatives in this particular decision involves rather large investment costs in the form of listening stations. Since such costs will probably occur in a restricted time period, say one fiscal year, the cost per student hour during that year will be considerably higher than those for the alternative program. In general, equipment and facilities costs will need to be amortized over their expected life span in order to arrive at useful cost figures.[17]

Utilizing unit cost figures usually produces a "fixed effectiveness" analysis. That is, average cost comparisons are of greatest value for decision making when it is possible to assume that each of the alternative courses of action is equally effective; hence, choices between those alternatives are rationally made on the basis of their respective costs. Ideally, then, in an evaluation such as the one we have been describing, the alternatives of listening stations versus aides should be designed so that, on the basis of the first stage of the analysis—descriptions of the alternative courses of action—the superintendent is indifferent to the choice on educational grounds—that is, he believes that they will be equally effective. In practice this usually requires working closely with the operational program staff (in this case, the foreign-language teachers) to develop a description of the alternatives since they are most likely to possess the requisite professional knowledge to judge the potential effectiveness of alternative procedures.

Finally, we note that, as before, the time phasing of costs yields potentially important information for decision-oriented evaluation. In the present example, average costs per student hour should be computed for each year out to the program's horizon. Figure 7-3 illustrates the hypothetical results of such a procedure. Note that the equipment costs have not been amortized in one case so that their point of greatest fiscal impact can be shown. It is evident that, while both programs have relatively substantial initial costs resulting from R&D and investment, the listening station alternative would result in considerably higher costs per student hour prior to the third year of

17. See Coombs and Hallack (1972, ch. 9) for a useful discussion of this topic.

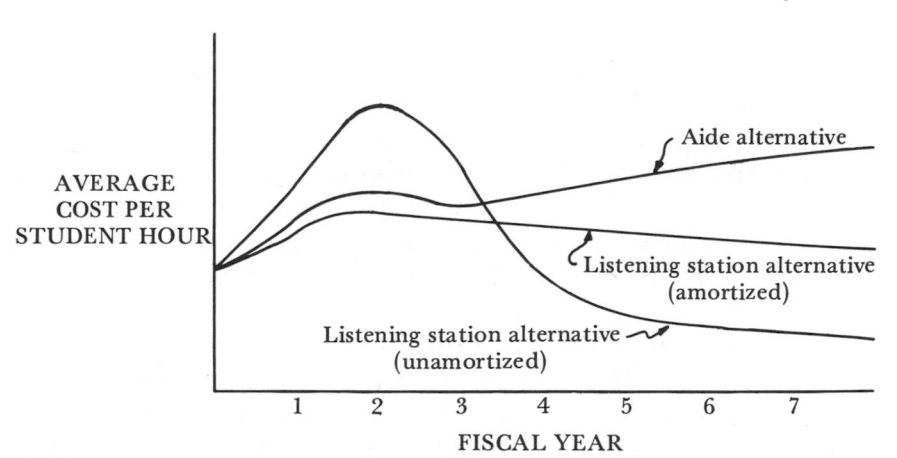

AVERAGE
COST PER
STUDENT HOUR

Aide alternative

Listening station alternative
(amortized)

Listening station alternative
(unamortized)

1   2   3   4   5   6   7

FISCAL YEAR

Figure 7-3
Hypothetical results of computing average cost per student hour
for each fiscal year of the program

the program. However, after amortization, the aide alternative results
in greater average costs per student.

Marginal Costs. A consideration of the notion of average cost leads
directly to the concept of marginal costs. A marginal cost is simply
the additional or incremental cost of producing one additional unit
of some good or service. The concept of marginal cost is especially
useful in evaluation studies concerned with questions of expanding
or contracting an educational program.

Earlier we noted the important distinction between fixed and variable costs. Ascertaining the presence of fixed costs in providing an
educational service is important for some evaluations because, whenever these costs are involved, the possibility of substantially significant variations in average and marginal costs exists. An obvious
example illustrating this is to imagine a completely equipped but
empty classroom. The costs of constructing and maintaining it are
typical fixed costs, incurred regardless of whether or not the room is
even used. As soon as one student enrolls, however, additional costs
are incurred for a teacher, supplies, and other needs. Subsequent enrollments incur additional costs for supplies, but the cost of the
teacher has become fixed. As enrollment increases, the average cost
per student declines up to the point where the classroom approaches
its capacity. At that time, a decision must be made as to whether or

not another classroom should be added. In such a situation, the fixed costs of both space and teacher time become variable, the average cost per student will rise, and the marginal cost of adding additional students will also rise, often precipitously. Thomas (1971, pages 45-50), in analyzing the cost of adding a biology class to a high school program, provides useful hypothetical examples of these phenomena. In his illustration, it is assumed that a single classroom and teacher can serve 120 students at normal capacity (24 per period for 5 periods), and that up to 80 additional students can be served if some overcrowding is permitted. Figure 7-4 illustrates the movement of average costs as enrollment changes.

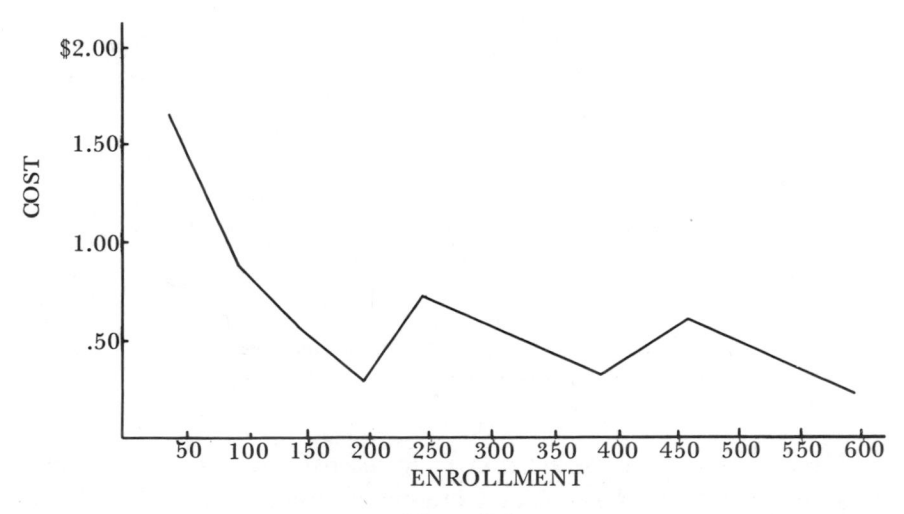

Figure 7-4
Average cost per student per hour of instruction in biology 1
(from Thomas, 1971, p. 48)

Note that average costs per student hour fall at a rapid but decreasing rate as additional students are enrolled up to the maximum capacity of the available classrooms. At those points the curve shifts direction. (Theoretically, the curve "breaks" at these points, since, for example, enrolling the 201st student presumably requires that an additional classroom and teacher be provided.) These points of inflection are critically important in an evaluation concerned with a decision to expand an educational program. Typically, programs may

be expanded at a relatively small additional cost per each new enrollment until these points are reached, at which time costs increase
dramatically. Figure 7-5 illustrates this. Notice that the marginal cost
of each additional student is quite small until capacity is reached, at
which point costs jump dramatically.

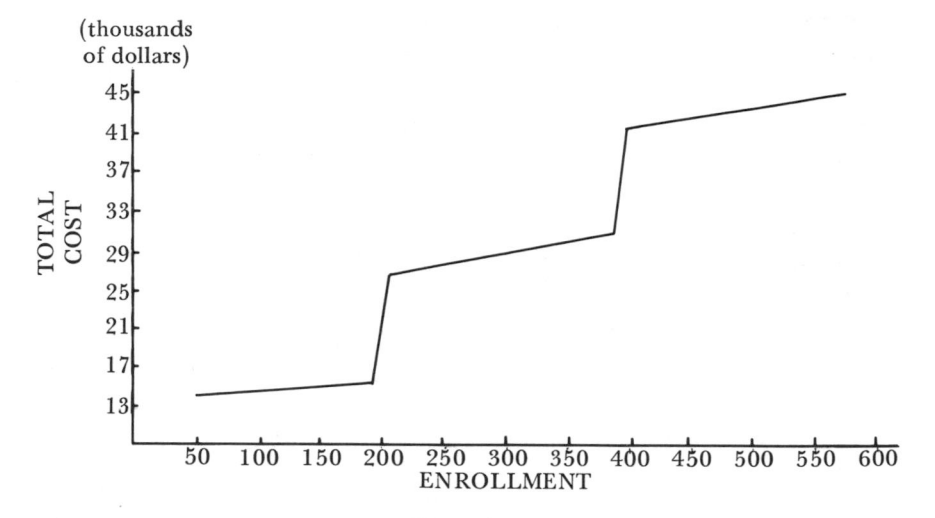

Figure 7-5
Cost per student as enrollment increases
(based on Thomas, 1971)

These dramatic discontinuities in total costs are commonly found
in educational programs. They are the consequence of two facts:
first, the major resource inputs to the educational process are the
time of teachers and space; second, both inputs are commonly
thought of as indivisibilities. This term means simply that, as program enrollment expands (or contracts), additional staff and space
cannot be added (or removed) continuously; rather, these resources
must usually be bought in discrete "chunks." If enrollment goes up
10 percent, administrators cannot always add a fraction of a classroom, nor a part of a teacher (except, of course, when it is possible
to hire teachers part-time).

Earlier I distinguished between fixed and variable costs, noting
that the distinction is never hard and fast but that it depends on the
decision at hand. In considering the costs of expanding a program,

resource inputs such as teachers and space may shift back and forth between being fixed or variable, depending upon the magnitude of the planned enrollment change. The presence of these types of costs indicates that economies of scale may be available, that is, the marginal or incremental cost of expanding a program's enrollment may be less than the existing average cost per student. It is critical to determine whether those resources should be treated as fixed or variable for the particular decision at hand. Depending upon their treatment, "bargains at the margin" may be available—a program may be expanded to reach a considerably larger number of students at a very low additional cost.

Obviously, such bargains are not always available. Whether or not they are depends upon the administrator's and the evaluator's ingenuity in developing alternative courses of action that allow a more intensive use of existing resources (keeping as many costs as possible fixed as enrollment increases), in devising alternatives that involve securing fractional increments in a resource that is normally secured in whole units, or in substituting less expensive resources for more expensive ones. An example of the first strategy is the movement toward year-round schools. Space and, in some plans, teacher time are maintained as fixed costs while total enrollments are increased by spreading a larger number of students through the course of the year. The second strategy is exemplified by the hiring of part-time teachers to meet enrollment increases which, though small, would otherwise exceed present staff capacities. Hiring teacher aides to carry out some of the work presently done by professionals is an example of the third.

SUMMARY

In this chapter I have briefly discussed some major areas of concern in a cost analysis for educational program evaluation, and I have suggested several procedures for conducting such an analysis. When investigating the potential costs of a decision, consider the following:

1. Be prepared to work closely with the decision maker throughout the course of your work, and beware of the common tendency to become involved in essentially methodological questions before the decision is clearly specified. Remember, a cost problem is always a decision problem. It is often useful to establish a working relation-

ship with other individuals whose knowledge about the future behavior of factors influencing program costs will supplement your own.

2. As a starting point, try to get the decision stated clearly in the form of two or more alternative courses of action from which a choice is to be made. In addition, develop a description that is as accurate as possible of the objectives and benefits that are presumed to derive from each choice. Finally, prepare a list of activities that will be necessary to develop and maintain the organization's capacity to attain these objectives.

3. Develop an input structure that will serve as a comprehensive description of the resources necessary to carry out the activities listed. These resources are specific instances of time, space, equipment, and supplies. The input structure should specifically take time into account; it should allow you to project resource use into the future. A useful way to do this is to consider resource costs in terms of functional categories—research and development, investment, and operating costs. A horizon, some future point in time that defines the boundary of projections, must be set. Standard budgets usually do not serve your purpose.

4. Only relevant costs should be considered. Relevant costs are those affected by the decision under consideration. In general, your decisions concerning relevance often turn on a determination of whether a cost is incremental or sunk, variable or fixed, and recurring or nonrecurring. Note also that costs may be external or internal and that, while the latter should always be included in your analysis, the former need not be. Finally, you should remember that the cost of a program is dependent upon the organizational position of the decision maker.

5. Costs may be measured in dollar expenditures, dollars, other quantifiable units, or in nonquantifiable subjective judgments concerning the consequences of a decision. Normally all four types will be of concern. Using the input structure developed, measure the cost of each activity using whatever procedure is most appropriate. In dealing with student time, instructional hours are most often useful. Salaries of paid personnel must usually be considered in terms of their component parts—direct payments and fringe benefits—and any projections of these costs must take into account the salary schedule and possible changes in it, and the composition of the work force. Space requirements are normally measured as square feet or as dollar

costs. Equipment and supplies typically present the least problem to your analysis and can be measured in dollar expenditures.

6. In projecting future costs, a rough rule of thumb is to allocate your time in proportion to the magnitude of the impact of a given category of costs on the total program. Take explicit account of uncertainty in your analysis. Often this requires positing alternative assumptions about the future state of the world and providing the decision maker with several cost estimates. Strive to attain relative accuracy; absolute accuracy in a cost projection is virtually impossible.

7. Alternatives are usually compared in terms of their total, average, or marginal costs. Total costs are typically involved in decisions about implementing a new program. In this situation, the costs of implementing a new program are compared to a base case. Total costs and total incremental costs are normally of interest.

Average (or unit) costs are often involved when comparing two or more alternative procedures for attaining some goal. The choice of the unit to be used is important, and its selection must be done with some care. An implicit assumption in many average cost comparisons is that the alternatives being compared are equally effective.

Marginal costs are the incremental costs of producing one additional unit of some good or service. A determination of marginal costs is usually involved in deciding whether or not to expand or contract a program. When determining marginal costs, be especially alert to those costs that are "semivariable," producing large jumps in marginal costs at specific points. Often you will want to try to develop alternatives that allow program expansion without causing a fixed cost to become a variable one.

Knowledge of the concepts and procedures summarized above does not equip you to carry out all cost analyses that you might encounter. I hope, however, that this chapter has provided you with some understanding of the concept of cost and the process of cost analysis in educational program evaluation.

REFERENCES

Alchian, Armen A., 1968. "Cost," in David Sills (ed.), *International encyclopedia of social science.* New York: Macmillan Co. and the Free Press, III, 404-415.

Alexander, Mood (ed.), 1970. *Do teachers make a difference?* Washington, D.C.: U.S. Government Printing Office.

Anthony, Robert N., 1970. "What should cost mean?" *Harvard Business Review*, 48.3 (May):121-131.

Bickner, R. E., 1971. "Concepts of economic cost," in Fisher, *Cost considerations in systems analysis.*

Bowman, Mary Jean, 1966. "The costing of human resource development," in E. A. G. Robinson and J. E. Vaizey (eds.), *The economics of education.* New York: St. Martin's Press.

Buchanan, James, 1969. *Cost and choice.* Chicago: Markham Publishing Co.

Coombs, P. H., and Hallak, J., 1972. *Managing educational costs.* New York: Oxford University Press.

Fisher, Gene, 1971. *Cost considerations in systems analysis.* New York: American Elsevier Co.

Hallak, J., 1962. *The analysis of educational costs and expenditures.* Paris: UNESCO International Institute for Educational Planning.

Hartley, Harry J., 1968. *Educational planning-programming-budgeting.* Englewood Cliffs, N.J.: Prentice-Hall, Inc.

Jameson, Dean, 1971. *Alternative strategies for primary education in Indonesia: A cost effectiveness analysis.* Palo Alto, Calif.: Stanford University Graduate School of Business Research.

Levin, Henry M., 1974. "Cost effectiveness analysis in evaluation research." Palo Alto, Calif.: Stanford University (mimeo).

Phi Delta Kappa (PDK) National Study Committee on Evaluation, 1971. *Educational evaluations and decision making.* Bloomington, Ind.: Phi Delta Kappa.

Reason, Paul F., and White, Alpheus L., 1957. *Financial accounting for local and state school systems.* Washington, D.C.: U.S. Office of Health, Education, and Welfare.

Schultz, Theodore, 1963. *The economic value of education.* New York: Columbia University.

Scriven, Michael, 1973. "The methodology of education," in Worthen and Sanders (eds.), *Educational evaluation.*

Stake, Robert E., 1973. "Evaluation design, instrumentation, data collection and analysis of data," in Worthen and Sanders (eds.), *Educational evaluation.*

Thomas, J. Alan, 1971. *The productive school.* New York: John Wiley and Sons, Inc.

Vaizey, J., and Chesswas, J. P., 1967. *The costing of educational plans.* Paris: UNESCO International Institute for Educational Planning.

Worthen, Blaine, and Sanders, James (eds.), 1973. *Educational evaluation: Theory and practice.* Worthington, Ohio: Charles A. Jones.

8

Introduction to Matrix Sampling for the Practitioner

Kenneth A. Sirotnik
Beverly Hills, California

Introduction to Matrix Sampling
for the Practitioner

Kenneth A. Sirotnik

Evaluators' cries for new approaches to data collection are almost as loud as their pleas for new tests. If the multiple outcomes of educational programs are to be assessed, then techniques for measuring such outcomes are essential. However, having tests does not solve this problem if there is no practical way of obtaining scores on the tests. A basically simple technique called *matrix sampling* constitutes at least one solution. Matrix sampling is a very general topic. The basic terminology, uses, and guidelines associated with the technique are presented in this chapter, which was written expressly for the practitioner of matrix sampling methodology. There is a technical appendix, but the body of the text has been kept at a level commensurate with a one-semester course in elementary descriptive and inferential statistics. The statistical procedures employed focus on a rather simple and specific (but widely employed) matrix sampling design; however, the concepts generalize quite readily to more complex applications.

A number of individuals have contributed valuable comments, suggestions, and corrections to earlier drafts of this manuscript, many of which have been incorporated into this final version. In particular, I wish to thank James Popham, Roger Wellington, Frederic Lord, Thomas Knapp, and David Shoemaker.

Educators and evaluators have traditionally thought of a test as a collection of items that you give to every examinee in a group. In order to study the achievement of students in a new program, a test is constructed and given to every student in the program, and a separate test is needed for each potential outcome of the program, cognitive or affective. Each test, to be reliable, must usually contain many items. If such tests must indeed be administered to each examinee in the program, the practical problems involved in such an approach become overwhelming.

Fortunately, however, the basic assumption underlying such an approach is often inappropriate to the evaluation of educational programs. If an evaluator wants to examine the effects of an instructional program, there is no reason why every student in the program must answer every item in every test related to the outcomes of the program. In fact, obtaining data from every examinee on every item is often a waste. To make decisions about programs, one needs data on the programs. If a population of examinees is exposed to an instructional program and a population of items is developed to assess the effects of that program, then the evaluator needs to know how well the population of examinees does on the population of items. The individual student is important to himself, to his teacher, to his parents, and even to the evaluator, but he is not, in this case, the object of evaluation—the program is.

Before launching into other important but abstract concepts associated with matrix sampling (and inference, generally), it is necessary to lay out the specific fundamentals of the matrix sampling process, including the needed terminology, notations, and types of sampling designs. This discussion will then be followed by sections on potential uses and limitations of matrix sampling methodology, specific computational procedures associated with the estimation of selected population parameters, and statistical as well as practical guidelines in the development of useful matrix sampling designs. Throughout these discussions, "real-life" examples will be used to illustrate the concepts and procedures involved.

MATRIX SAMPLING FUNDAMENTALS: TERMINOLOGY, NOTATION, AND SAMPLING DESIGN

Suppose, for example, that in a large high school with 250 examinees (students) in the eleventh grade the school administration de-

cides for one reason or another to learn how proficient (defined in terms of the mean and standard deviation) the eleventh grade is in fundamentals of arithmetic. Some test having sixty arithmetic fundamental items is to be the means of measuring this proficiency.

One approach would be to give all 250 examinees (the *population* of examinees) the arithmetic test, with each examinee answering all sixty items (the *population* of items). This would amount to 15,000 (250 X 60) *examinee-item* responses. Depending upon how many examinees could take the test at one time and how long it would take to respond to each of the items, such a test would require more time than would perhaps be feasible given the schedules of students, personnel, and the school in general. Since evaluative interests often involve more than one content area, more than one test is required, which compounds the administrative problems.

A second approach, one traditionally used in establishing norms for standardized tests, would be to *randomly* select a *sample* of examinees, say 125, and give them the entire sixty-item test. This procedure, referred to here as *examinee sampling,* requires collecting only half the number of examinee-item responses involved in the first procedure. The sample of examinees' scores can be used to *estimate* what the mean and standard deviation of examinee scores would have been had all 250 examinees taken the test. Note that in the first procedure no estimation would be necessary; since all 250 examinees' scores on all 60 items would be available, and the mean and standard deviation could be calculated directly.

A third approach, the logical (although not usually the statistical) equivalent of the second approach, would be to randomly select a sample of items, say thirty, and administer them to the entire population of examinees. This procedure is referred to here as *item sampling.* Again, this amounts to collecting only half of the examinee-item responses of the first procedure, and the mean and standard deviation must be estimated from the data obtained. Since individual item data is relatively more important in test construction than individual examinee data, this approach is rarely, if ever, used in the development of standardized test norms. It does, however, constitute the theoretical basis for a generalized approach to test theory (see Cronbach, Gleser, Nanda, and Rajaratnam, 1972) as opposed to the "classical" approach presented, for example, by Gulliksen (1950).

A fourth approach, known as *matrix sampling,* is due primarily to

the work of Frederic Lord.[1] It combines the item and the examinee sampling approaches by drawing random samples from each of the populations. For example, the sample of 125 examinees might each be given a sample of thirty items, which would again reduce by half the number of examinee-item responses required by the examinee sampling procedure (which would be only a quarter of the responses required by the first procedure). Again, the resultant sample data would be used to obtain estimates of what the mean and standard deviation of the arithmetic fundamentals scores would have been had the population of examinees responded to the population of items.

Frequent reference has been made to *examinee-item* responses; a convenient way to graphically represent these responses is through the use of the data *matrix* (see Figure 8-1). A data matrix is simply a two-dimensional box of numbers representing the score any given examinee got on any given item. These scores may be one's and zero's, as in the case of many achievement-type (cognitive) test data (1 = correct; 0 = incorrect), or one's, two's, three's, etc., as in the case of many attitude-type (affective) test data (1 = "always," 2 = "sometimes," 3 = "never"). The example in Figure 8-1 portrays a 5-item spelling test taken by 10 examinees. The rows correspond to the examinees, and the columns correspond to the items. If we wish to know what score the seventh examinee received on the third item, we simply go down to the seventh row and across to the third column—in this example, the student received a score of 1, which means that he spelled the third word correctly.

We can now portray the various approaches to handling the proposed evaluation problem discussed above. Consider Figure 8-2, in which box A represents the examinee-item data matrix for the entire population of responses, box B represents these responses in the case of examinee sampling, box C represents the responses in the case of item sampling, and box D illustrates the data collected in the case of matrix sampling. It should be clear that in examinee (or item) sam-

---

1. A rather large body of matrix sampling literature has evolved since the initial theoretical papers of Lord (1955, 1959a, 1959b, 1960, 1965) and Hooke (1956a, 1956b). (Chapter 11 in Lord and Novick's *Statistical Theories of Mental Test Scores* is essentially Lord's 1965 paper.) It is not the purpose of this chapter to provide the reader with an extensive review of the matrix sampling literature; the interested reader is advised to consult the up-to-date annotated bibliography compiled by Knapp (1973).

ITEMS

		1	2	3	4	5
	1	1	0	0	1	1
	2	0	1	1	1	1
	3	1	0	1	1	0
E X A M I N E E S	4	1	1	0	0	0
	5	0	0	0	0	0
	6	1	1	1	1	1
	7	0	0	1	1	0
	8	0	0	0	0	0
	9	1	0	1	0	1
	10	0	1	0	1	0

Figure 8-1
Data matrix

pling, only *one* "dimension" of the population matrix A is being sampled, namely, the examinee (or item) dimension. In matrix sampling, however, *both* examinee and item dimensions are being sampled. Two-dimensional arrays of numbers are known in the field of mathematics as matrices—hence, the term matrix sampling. It should be emphasized that the entire set or population of examinee-item responses (box A) is never available when matrix or any other type of sampling is used. Instead, the numbers of box D are used to *infer* or *estimate* characteristics of the numbers in box A—numbers that would have been obtained had all of the examinees responded to all of the items.

The first procedure, that of collecting complete data on everybody, is most desirable for we would not have to estimate the mean score of all 250 students. The actual mean could, in fact, be computed. It is assumed here, however, that the collection of complete

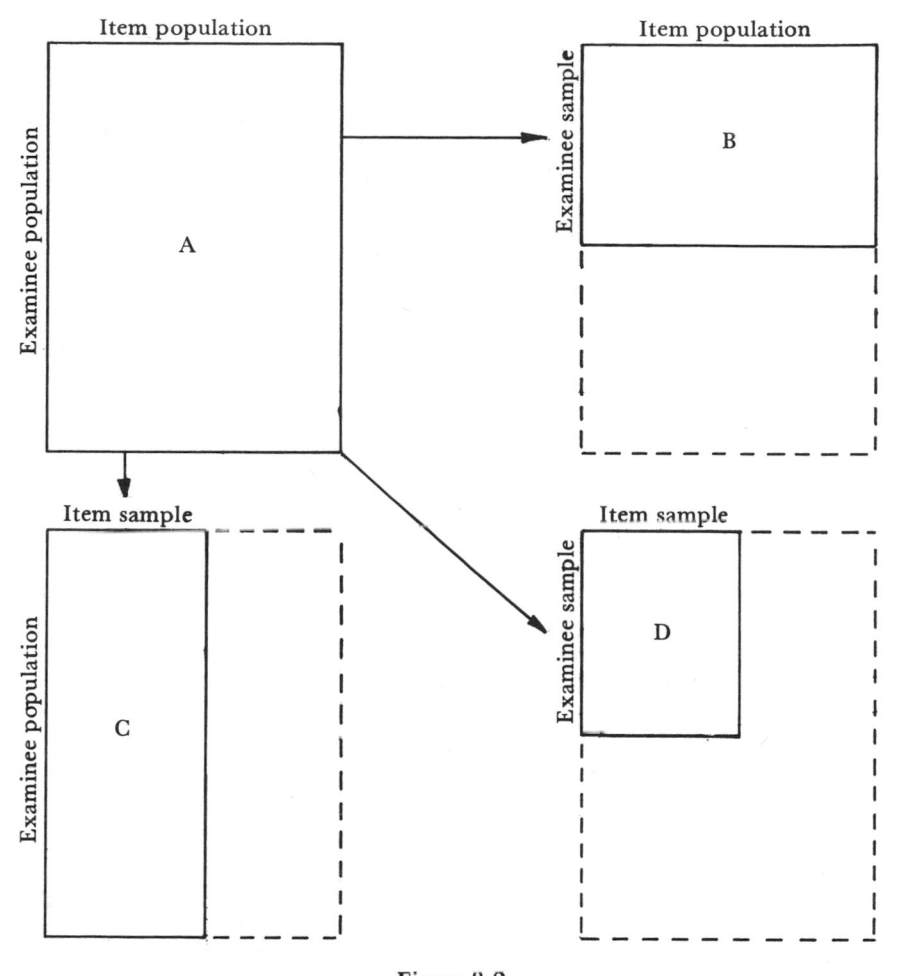

Figure 8-2
Matrix population (A); an examinee sample (B); item sample (C);
and matrix sample (D)

data is not feasible for some reason, such as lack of time, money, or
personnel. If complete data are not obtained, then it would be desirable that as many items and examinees be sampled as possible. Examinee (or item) sampling (as illustrated in Figure 8-2) would appear,
therefore, to be preferable to matrix sampling. If, however, more
than one matrix sample is strategically extracted from the population
matrix, a procedure called *multiple* matrix sampling, then matrix

sampling can be more representative of the population than any other sampling procedure. Figure 8-3 illustrates this point. The large rectangle represents the examinee-item *matrix population* of responses for a population of 25 randomly arranged examinees and 15 randomly arranged "right-wrong" items. The smaller rectangles, arranged diagonally, represent 5 random matrix samples having 5 examinees and 3 items each; thus, each matrix sample has 5 x 3, or 15, examinee-item responses. The shaded rectangle represents one possible random examinee sample of 5 students responding to all 15 items—a total of 75 examinee-item responses. Clearly, both the combined matrix samples and the single examinee sample require the same number of examinee-item responses. It should be clear from an intuitive standpoint, however, that the matrix samples are more representative of the entire 25 x 15, or 375, possible examinee-item responses than the examinee sample. Not only is each item responded to by some examinees, but each examinee responds to some items.

Although computational procedures will be considered in more detail later, the estimate of the mean will be computed here in order to "operationalize" the concepts presented thus far. Since the items are dichotomously scored (0, 1), the mean examinee score is simply the examinee's proportion correct score. Thus, the mean examinee score for the entire population matrix is 190/375 or .507; for the examinee sample it is 32/75 or .427; and for the combined matrix samples it is 40/75 or .533. Both the examinee sampling and multiple (combined) matrix sampling means (.427 and .533, respectively), are estimates of the population mean,[2] which we know, in fact, to be .507. In actual practice, of course, the evaluator would not know this population mean; had multiple matrix sampling been used to estimate this mean, only the examinee-item responses included in the diagonal boxes in Figure 8-3 would have been available. In other words, five separate subtests of 3 items each would be prepared and administered, respectively, to five separate subgroups of 5 examinees each.

It is instructive, however, to start with a complete population of data, to extract data post hoc in accordance with various sampling designs, and then to compare the relative efficiency of these sampling plans in estimating the known population parameters. In the above

2. Population "statistics" such as the mean are referred to as *parameters*; corresponding sample statistics are estimates of these parameters.

EXAMINEES

ITEMS

	1	2	3	4	5	6	7	8	9	10	11	12	13	14	15
1	0	0	0	0	0	0	1	1	1	0	0	0	1	1	0
2	1	0	0	0	1	0	0	1	1	1	0	0	1	1	1
3	1	0	1	0	0	0	1	1	0	0	0	0	1	1	1
4	1	0	0	0	0	0	1	1	1	0	1	1	1	1	1
5	1	1	1	0	0	1	1	1	1	1	1	1	1	1	1
6	0	0	0	0	1	0	1	0	0	0	0	0	1	1	0
7	0	0	0	1	0	0	1	1	1	1	1	1	1	1	1
8	1	0	0	0	1	1	1	0	1	1	0	0	1	0	1
9	0	1	1	1	1	1	1	0	0	1	1	1	1	1	1
10	0	0	0	0	0	0	1	1	1	1	1	1	1	1	1
11	1	1	1	1	1	1	1	1	1	1	1	1	1	1	1
12	0	0	0	1	0	0	0	1	1	1	0	0	1	1	1
13	1	1	1	1	1	1	1	1	0	1	1	1	1	1	1
14	1	0	0	0	0	0	1	0	0	1	0	0	1	0	1
15	1	0	0	0	1	0	1	0	0	0	0	0	1	1	1
16	0	0	0	0	0	0	0	0	0	0	1	1	1	0	1
17	1	0	0	0	1	0	1	1	0	1	0	0	0	0	0
18	1	1	0	1	1	1	0	0	1	1	1	1	0	1	1
19	1	0	1	1	1	1	1	0	0	0	1	0	1	0	1
20	0	0	0	0	0	0	0	1	0	0	0	1	0	1	1
21	0	0	1	1	1	1	0	1	0	0	0	0	0	1	1
22	0	0	0	0	1	1	1	1	1	1	1	1	0	1	1
23	1	1	1	1	1	1	0	1	1	0	1	0	1	0	0
24	1	1	1	1	1	0	0	0	0	1	1	1	1	1	1
25	1	0	0	0	1	0	0	0	0	0	0	1	0	1	0

Matrix population

One of 5 matrix samples

One possible examinee

Figure 8-3
Nonoverlapping multiple matrix sampling
compared with examinee sampling

example of this process it is clear that the multiple matrix sampling estimate of the mean is closer to the actual population mean than the "traditional" examinee sampling estimate. Yet both are based upon the same number of randomly sampled examinee-item responses. This single comparison is "unfair," however, insofar as it represents only one of many possible post hoc samplings of the given matrix population. In Figure 8-4, the rows (examinees) and columns (items) of Figure 8-3 have been randomly and independently rearranged so that new multiple matrix sampling and examinee sampling estimates (.440 and .453, respectively) of the mean can be computed. Yet the response of any given examinee to any given item has remained unchanged, and the population mean is still .507. Repeating this process several more times, we obtain five multiple matrix sampling and five examinee sampling estimates of the population mean; these data are presented in Table 8-1. In four out of the five times, multiple matrix sampling estimates the mean better than examinee sampling.

The important result to note, however, is that the multiple matrix sampling estimates are closer together (less variable) than those of examinee sampling. In the long run, over all possible post hoc sampling extractions, the variability of the multiple matrix sampling mean estimates will never be greater, and it will usually be substantially less, than that of the examinee sampling estimates. This variability can be statistically measured by simply computing the standard deviation (or variance) of the set of mean estimates. In statistical terminology, the standard deviation of all possible mean estimates is called the *standard error* of the mean; the set of all mean estimates could be graphically portrayed and would be referred to as the *sampling distribution* of the mean. The data in Table 8-1, then, are members of the sampling distributions of the mean using both matrix and examinee sampling. Even with only five members (estimates) of these distributions, we can see the general principle illustrated; namely, that the multiple matrix sample mean estimates tend to be closer to the actual population mean, and closer to each other, than are those of the examinee sampling process.

Although admittedly abstract, this discussion should provide some intuitive feeling for the statistical advantages inherent in the multiple matrix sampling procedure. There are, of course, many nonstatistical advantages in being able to "get away with" gathering only a fraction

ITEMS

	07	15	12	08	14	11	04	10	02	13	01	05	09	03	06
04	1	1	1	0	1	1	1	0	1	1	1	1	1	1	1
16	0	1	1	0	0	0	0	0	0	1	0	0	1	0	1
24	0	0	0	1	1	0	0	0	0	1	0	1	1	0	1
06	1	1	1	1	1	1	1	1	1	0	1	1	1	1	1
13	0	0	0	0	0	0	0	1	0	1	0	0	0	0	0
01	0	0	0	0	0	0	0	0	1	0	0	0	1	0	0
05	0	1	0	1	1	1	1	1	0	1	1	1	0	1	1
20	0	0	0	1	0	0	0	0	0	1	0	0	0	0	0
18	0	1	0	0	1	1	0	0	0	0	1	1	1	1	1
10	1	1	0	0	0	0	1	1	1	0	1	0	0	1	0
15	1	1	1	1	1	1	0	0	0	0	0	0	0	0	0
07	1	0	0	0	0	0	0	0	0	1	1	1	0	0	1
14	0	0	0	1	0	1	1	1	1	1	1	0	0	0	0
09	1	1	1	1	1	0	0	0	1	1	0	1	0	1	0
25	0	0	0	0	0	0	1	1	1	1	1	0	0	0	0
22	1	0	1	1	1	1	0	0	0	0	0	1	0	1	1
11	0	0	0	0	0	0	1	1	1	1	1	0	1	0	0
23	1	1	1	1	1	1	0	0	0	1	0	0	1	1	1
02	0	0	0	0	0	0	1	1	0	0	1	0	1	0	1
17	1	1	1	1	1	1	1	1	1	1	1	0	0	1	1
03	0	0	0	0	0	0	0	1	0	0	0	1	0	1	1
21	0	1	1	1	0	0	1	0	0	0	0	0	1	1	1
19	1	1	0	0	1	1	0	0	0	0	0	0	1	0	1
12	0	1	1	1	0	0	0	0	0	1	1	1	1	1	1
08	1	1	0	0	1	1	1	0	1	1	1	1	0	0	0

Figure 8-4
Rerandomization of the population matrix
depicted in Figure 8-3

Table 8-1
Comparison of five, post hoc multiple matrix and examinee samples
of the hypothetical matrix population

Post hoc sampling	Estimates of the mean	
	Matrix sampling	Examinee sampling
1	.533	.427
2	.440	.453
3	.480	.427
4	.507	.666
5	.533	.440
Mean of mean estimates	.499	.483
Standard deviation of mean estimates	.076	.092

of the potential matrix population of data, and these advantages, as well as associated problems, will be discussed later.

The increasing abundance of matrix sampling literature and the increasing tendency to interchange various matrix sampling terminologies make it necessary to introduce one final set of abstractions—the number of ways in which more than one matrix sample may be selected. Additionally, depending on the way in which the matrix samples are selected, the resultant data may be more or less appropriate for the estimation of certain population parameters. Thus, it is necessary to develop a semantic framework for the various multiple matrix sampling designs that is both consistent with most of the literature and descriptive of the actual sampling process involved.

Consider once again Figure 8-3, which illustrates one possible type of multiple matrix sampling design. Random samples of examinees and items are matched in such a way that any given examinee or item appears once, and only once, in any given matrix sample. The result is a set of *nonoverlapping* matrix samples. More technically, a set of nonoverlapping matrix samples results whenever examinees and items are sampled *without replacement* from their respective populations. Operationally, the practitioner who might have created the new set of nonoverlapping matrix samples pictured in Figure 8-4 could have arranged two sacks of marbles: one containing 25 marbles (numbered

1 to 25) representing the examinee population, and one containing 15 marbles (numbered 1 to 15) representing the item population. Three marbles would then be randomly selected from the item sack, and, once drawn, they would never be replaced in the sack and thus would never again be eligible for resampling. In the case represented by Figure 8-4, the first three marbles would have been numbered 7, 15, and 12. Examinee marbles would also be randomly selected, without replacement; in this case marbles 4, 16, 24, 6, and 13 identify the first examinee subgroup. These examinees and the above subtest of items are matched up to form the first matrix sample. Remaining matrix samples are similarly constructed except that fewer examinees and items from which to sample remain in their populations.

Thus far, then, we have been discussing and describing examples utilizing nonoverlapping multiple matrix sampling, where it is understood that examinees and items are sampled randomly and without replacement from their corresponding populations. This constitutes just one class of potential matrix sampling designs. The remaining class of designs can be succinctly defined as multiple matrix sampling *with replacement*, where it is understood that items are sampled randomly, *with replacement* from the item population.[3] Returning to the practitioner's sack of marbles, had the marbles (representing items) been replaced in the sack after they were drawn, all marbles (items) would be eligible for resampling at all times. One possible set of results for 5 consecutive samplings with replacement from the item sack are presented in Table 8-2; the items are arranged in groups of three to correspond with the item subtests to be matched up with five examinee subgroups, forming five matrix samples. Clearly, items can and do appear in more than one matrix sample. For example, matrix samples one and two overlap on item 5; matrix samples three and five happen to be nonoverlapping, although, in matrix sample three, item 4 happened to be selected twice.

3. Examinees are rarely (if ever) sampled with replacement since it would require administering more than one item subtest to some examinees (those who happened to be sampled again). This is operationally unsound from a practical standpoint and not of any particular statistical benefit from a psychometric standpoint. Thus, the overlapping-nonoverlapping terminology will apply to the item dimension with it being understood that examinees are always sampled without replacement.

Table 8-2
Hypothetical set of five overlapping matrix samples

Matrix sample	Item numbers
1	3, 2, 5
2	5, 12, 15
3	4, 4, 6
4	3, 10, 14
5	7, 8, 15

The difference, therefore, between the two major classes of multiple matrix sampling designs rests upon whether the items are sampled with or without replacement (assuming examinees are always sampled without replacement). It should also be noted that the above example of multiple matrix sampling with replacement did not result in the sampling of all items in the population. When this occurs, either by chance or design, the sampling is termed *nonexhaustive* (of the population). If, however, all the items and/or examinees are eventually sampled, the sampling process would be termed *exhaustive.* Thus, various sampling designs can be exhaustive and/or nonexhaustive of the examinee and/or item populations. The design illustrated in Figure 8-3 would be termed *"exhaustive, multiple matrix sampling without replacement on both examinee and item dimensions."*

Figure 8-5 portrays a number of design variations for multiple matrix sampling without replacement, including the additional design factor of equal- or unequal-sized matrix samples. The intent is not to provide all possible and potentially useful designs; rather, it is to indicate the generality of sampling matrices without replacement from a fixed population. Perhaps the most common applications of multiple matrix sampling to date are those of the form pictured in Figure 8-5A. This form is generally applicable when the practitioner wants to estimate the mean and standard deviation of a fixed population of examinees' scores on a fixed population of items but lacks the resources to obtain the entire population matrix of data. In this case, the practitioner will often end up with matrix samples like those pictured in Figure 8-5E since the practical administration of the item subtests invariably results in unequal examinee subgroups. Designs wherein the sampling of items is nonexhaustive are rarely used, espe-

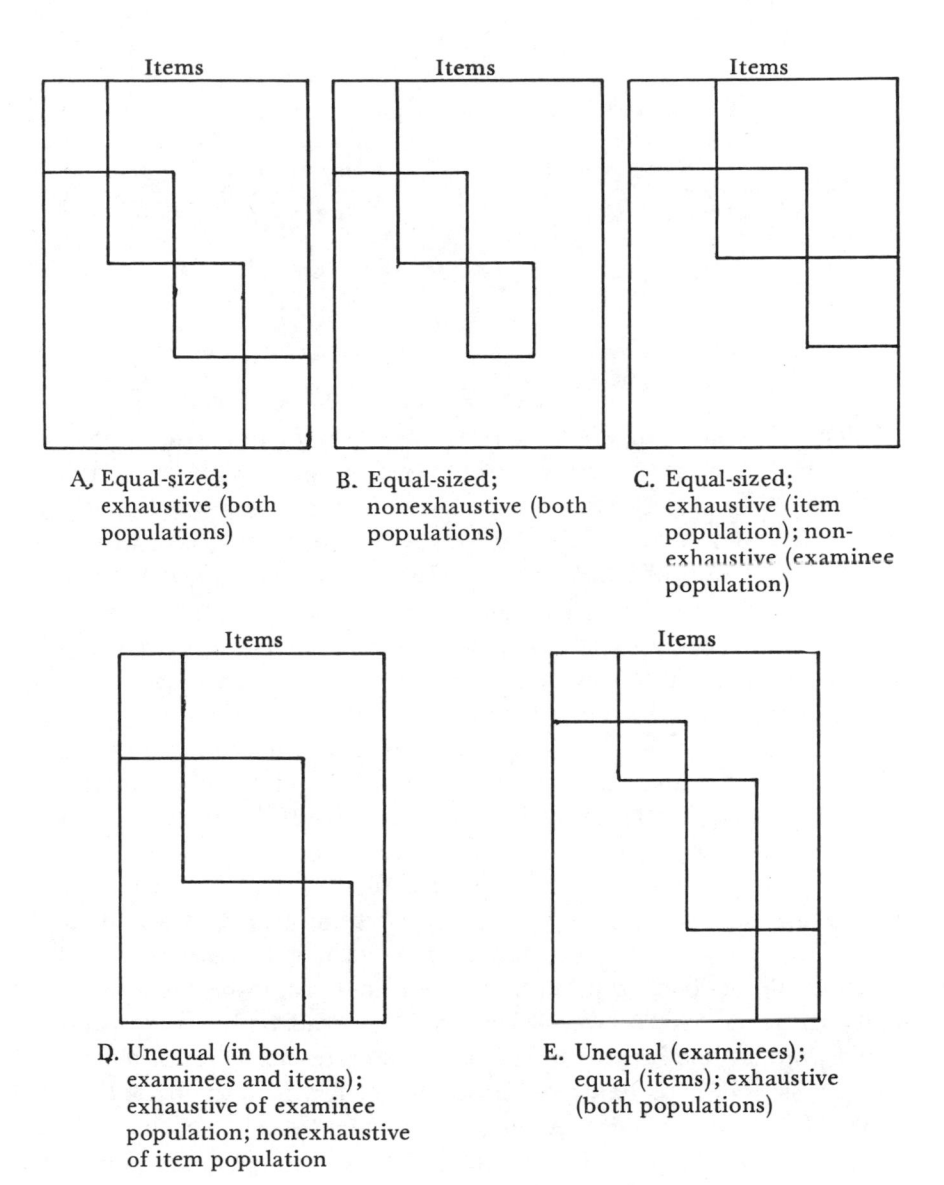

A. Equal-sized;
   exhaustive (both
   populations)

B. Equal-sized;
   nonexhaustive (both
   populations)

C. Equal-sized;
   exhaustive (item
   population); non-
   exhaustive (examinee
   population)

D. Unequal (in both
   examinees and items);
   exhaustive of examinee
   population; nonexhaustive
   of item population

E. Unequal (examinees);
   equal (items); exhaustive
   (both populations)

Figure 8-5
Design variations in multiple matrix sampling without replacement

cially since the estimation errors due to sampling can be quite large when even one item is left out (see Lord and Novick, 1968, pp. 256-257).[4] Designs wherein the sampling of examinees is nonexhaustive are more common since the population of examinees is usually much larger relative to the population of items (see Figure 8-5C). Finally, it should be noted that the design shown in Figure 8-5A can be reduced to a special and simplified case, when the practitioner desires only to estimate the mean score. Given an M-item test of interest, the practitioner can randomly subdivide his examinee population into M subgroups and administer only *one* item to each subgroup. The average of all the resulting item responses will provide a remarkably precise estimate of the population mean.

Regardless of the design employed, practitioners must not lose sight of the fact that they are making a "two-dimensional" inference from partial examinee-item data to the whole population examinee-item matrix. In statistical jargon, this matrix sampling inferential process can be labeled *statistical-psychometric* inference (Husek and Sirotnik, 1967) in contrast to the unidimensional *statistical* inferences made in examinee sampling and the *psychometric* inferences made in item sampling. Statistical-psychometric inferences are made whenever examinee-item matrices are sampled, whether with or without replacement. We have concentrated here on matrix sampling without replacement because it represents a commonly employed family of designs with great economic advantages, and the computational procedures used later in this chapter will generally be applicable to only this family of designs. It is important, however, that the reader not be deterred from considering "with replacement" designs and, accordingly, they will be briefly discussed here.

---

4. This consideration loses much of its importance when the population of items is quite large. Given the recent trend toward building criterion-referenced item pools, designs such as those in Figure 8-5B and 8-5D may become more frequently employed. In this case, the practitioner will be making inferences regarding examinee "true scores," *i.e.*, cognitive or affective abilities as defined by some large domain (population) of items (for example, the ability to add and subtract all numbers containing from one to three digits). The term *true score* is placed in quotes because, theoretically, this concept is defined as the examinee score on a conceptually *infinite* item population. Computationally, the difference between infinite and finite item population estimates are negligible for sufficiently large (say 500 or more) item populations.

With the exception of the population mean, most typically employed population parameters are functions of the variability due to the interrelationships among items (statistically, the interitem covariances). Such parameters, for example, are the standard deviation or variance of the examinee scores and the Kuder-Richardson formula 20 (K-R 20) measure of internal consistency among items (more generally, coefficient alpha). In order that efficient estimates of these parameters be obtained from sampled data, it is important that the data can reflect interitem relationships.[5] To measure the relationship between any two items, it is necessary that a group of examinees respond to both items. In multiple matrix sampling without replacement, interitem data is available for those items *within* any given matrix sample, but not for items *between* matrix samples. What is needed is a sampling design wherein every possible pair of items is responded to by some subgroup of examinees. This is possible only when matrices are sampled with replacement. Given the inordinate number of possible item pairs for even small item populations, completely random matrix sampling with replacement would not guarantee efficient item subgroups. Designs can be worked out, however, which strategically sample items with replacement forming item subgroups wherein all possible item pairs are represented; the item subtests are administered to examinees so that all items and all item pairs are responded to a fixed number of times.

The intent here is not to provide a working knowledge of matrix sampling with replacement; rather, it is to indicate that such designs may be the best designs given the needs and resources of the practitioner. Knapp (1968) is the major proponent of these "with replacement" designs (commonly referred to as balanced incomplete block designs (BIBD) in analysis of variance terminology), and his recent monograph (1973) on matrix sampling is recommended. Although no specific guidelines are yet available for computing the relative trade-offs between with and without replacement designs, the practitioner might well consider BIBD designs when the population of examinees is relatively small and the population of items is relatively heterogeneous; that is, when there is relatively great diversity in mag-

5. Although matrix sampling has not yet been used to estimate correlations between tests of different content, it can be so employed, and sampling designs based on systematic pairings of items between contents would be more efficient for these purposes.

nitudes of interitem covariances. For many applications in educational evaluation, however, the practitioner works with large examinee
populations (at least 30 examinees assigned to each matrix sample)
and fairly homogeneous populations of items, defining specific abilities or attitudes. In these cases, multiple matrix sampling without replacement can prove to be an efficient procedure for estimating most
commonly desired population parameters (such as the mean, standard deviation, standard error of the mean, K-R 20, and examinee
score percentiles).[6] In the final analysis, the practitioner should attempt to locate others who have employed various matrix sampling
designs using similar examinees or items in order to obtain some empirical feeling for the relative advantages, both practical and statistical, involved. Knapp's annotated bibliography (1973) is most helpful
in this regard.

SOME USES OF MATRIX SAMPLING:
ADVANTAGES AND LIMITATIONS

The central idea of matrix sampling is quite simple. It is not necessary to give every item to every student if one desires to estimate the
performance of a group of students on a group of items. The initial
example in the previous section—that of the administrator interested
in the proficiency of the eleventh grade in fundamentals of arithmetic—is typical of the many uses of matrix sampling where economy (of time, money, personnel, and so forth) is an important consideration. Had the administrator been able to collect, say, at least
three-quarters of the entire 250 students' responses to all 60 items,
the usual procedures of examinee sampling would probably have provided estimates as good as or better than matrix sampling. Matrix
sampling becomes extremely useful when it is not feasible to administer the entire test (or battery of tests) to each member of the

---

6. A number of post hoc studies have demonstrated the efficiency of multiple matrix sampling in estimating certain population parameters (primarily the
mean and variance). These studies have started off with the actual population
matrix of data, and, thus, the actual (or known) values of the parameters in
question; multiple matrix samples are then drawn and estimates are computed
and compared to the known population values. The interested reader should review, for example, Lord (1962), Plumlee (1964), Cook and Stufflebeam (1967),
Husek and Sirotnik (1968), Shoemaker (1970a), and Pugh (1971).

group. After all, if the administrator wished to know the mean level of arithmetic fundamental achievement for the eleventh grade for a particular school, there would be no better way than to administer the arithmetic test to all eleventh-grade pupils in the school and compute the mean. Usually, however, economic constraints are such that the practitioner cannot follow this procedure, and matrix sampling or some other kind of estimation procedure becomes an important alternative consideration. Perhaps the best way to indicate the use of matrix sampling in these situations is by quoting the following statement by Lord (Lord and Novick, 1968):

[Matrix] sampling can be used not only to provide a theoretical basis for mental test theory; sometimes it also may be introduced advantageously into the design of a research study. There are at least three obvious considerations:

1. If only a limited amount of time can be demanded of each research subject, the total amount of information obtained from a given number of subjects may be greatly increased by [matrix] sampling.

2. If a test can be administered to only one examinee at a time, the examiner's time may be the limiting factor; more information about a group of examinees may be obtained by giving a few items to each examinee than by giving the entire test to just a few examinees.

3. With certain tests, scoring costs may be the limiting factor; in this case, it would be better to score a few items from the answer sheets of every examinee than to score every item on the answer sheets of a few examinees [p. 252].

Thus, for reasons of time, money, and economical considerations in general, matrix sampling becomes an important technology in large-scale group evaluation.

However, the issue of economy should not be allowed to obscure the fact that for many educational problems, especially in the field of educational evaluation, matrix sampling provides the only viable method for collecting adequate data. The practical problems of educational research and evaluation often prohibit the use of students for more than a short time, yet do not seriously interfere with the testing of *many* students. In these frequent cases the issue is not whether matrix sampling will provide better population estimates than other procedures. The point is that, in many situations, matrix sampling not only permits more efficient data collection, but allows the educational researcher and/or evaluator to perform some research which might not otherwise be possible. Several examples will serve to illuminate some of these points.

Consider a large class of 100 students and an examination of 40 items. The 40 items are used to judge the *individual* students for grading purposes. Matrix sampling, however, could be a useful technique for obtaining evaluative data on class performance, not individual performance, without consuming extensive testing time and without doing much damage to the general goal of differentiating among students. In other words, little damage would be done by shortening the "regular" part of the test to 35 items and using the remaining 5 items per examinee in a multiple matrix sampling design for course evaluation purposes. Five items per examinee and 100 examinees permits 500 examinee-item observations to be made. Since the course, rather than the individual student, is to be examined through these observations, this number of observations is sufficient to obtain additional (and often overlooked) information on the meeting of course objectives, instructor performance, and even student reactions to the course. The 500 observations can be subdivided in many different ways depending on the desires and needs of the instructor.

Matrix sampling becomes particularly useful in large-scale evaluation programs. In studying a school or a school system, the following procedure might be used: For certain tests, perhaps some achievement tests, all of the examinees might receive the entire test. For other tests, matrix sampling might be used, but with relatively large item samples. With still other tests, far fewer examinee-item observations would be obtained. In this fashion, data on a large number of evaluation instruments can be obtained, with the amount of information obtained for a test dependent on the known or suspected value of the test. In this situation, matrix sampling permits the exploration of a number of new and potentially important variables related to the outcomes of educational programs. It magnifies the potential for obtaining a wide band of generalizability that accrues from the facility to sample large numbers of content domains, which is so important to large-scale evaluation studies.

A third simple, but valuable, use of matrix sampling is with change or growth studies. If the researcher or evaluator is interested in obtaining some index of growth for a group of examinees with respect to a measure containing 100 items, it is possible, using matrix sampling, to obtain data on all of these items at several times during the term without any student necessarily taking any item twice. Although the ability to test the same examinees at various points in

time with different random item samples from the same item population of interest does not eliminate all of the problems of change studies, it does alleviate some of the more serious difficulties, such as practice effects and other problems related to the comparability of measures during the study.

In any research or evaluation situation where there are large numbers of examinees or items, matrix sampling can be of great assistance. The technique is not limited to estimating parameters for a single examinee (or item) population. Matrix sampling procedures can be generalized to estimating the *differences* between parameters for two or more populations of interest. For example, evaluative research designs typically involve the comparison of two or more competing instructional programs (experimental designs) or two or more groups (classes, schools, districts) in the same curriculum (ex post facto designs). In either case, multiple matrix sampling designs can, for example, be worked out to estimate, and test for statistical significance, the mean differences between groups on a variety of cognitive, affective, and even psychomotor variables.

The statistical advantages of matrix sampling (versus other methods of sampling, for example, examinee sampling) have already been mentioned previously, namely, the reduction in errors necessarily associated with having to estimate parameters from partial data. In particular, exhaustive multiple matrix sampling without replacement generally results in smaller standard errors of the mean than any other sampling method extracting the same amount of data (examinee-item responses).

Aside from these more technical statistical considerations, however, the reader should be aware of the more general implications of matrix sampling as a statistical concept. We have been dealing thus far with examinee-by-item matrices of data where examinees have constituted the *rows* of the matrix and items the *columns* of the matrix (see Figure 8-1). From a more general perspective, we have been considering any row-by-column matrix of data where the rows represent *units* of observation, the columns represent *variables* upon which the units are observed, and the *unit-variable* data within the matrix are the observations themselves. This framework lends itself particularly well to analysis of variance concepts, terminology, and computations (see Sirotnik, 1970a) insofar as a matrix is a two-factor design, with the rows (or units) and the columns (or variables) constituting the levels of the respective factors. In our particular applica-

tion of the two-factor design, examinees constitute the levels of the "examinee factor," and items constitute the levels of the "item factor." Furthermore, in matrix sampling the levels (examinees and items) are randomly sampled from their respective populations creating what is termed a *random* model; this contrasts with a *fixed* model where levels are not sampled at all (the population examinee-item matrix) and the *mixed* model where one factor is fixed and the other is random (examinee and item sampling, discussed earlier).

The point, again, is the generality of matrix sampling. Instead of examinees and items, the units and variables sampled might be schools and organizational climate characteristics; the unit-variable "responses" might be a rater's ratings of the schools on the climate variable. Finally, the number of factors can be extended beyond two; that is, three-, four-, and generally, multidimensional matrices can be sampled. For example, raters might be added as a third factor to the school-climate characteristic design above. Although such extensions of the examinee-item matrix sampling design have yet to appear in the literature, they undoubtedly will, and the specifics of the computational process will follow as needed.

The advantages, then, of matrix sampling are many—substantive, statistical, and conceptual. Although not as proliferous, there are limitations and disadvantages in the use of the technique. The most salient of these is the clear orientation, historically and methodologically, of matrix sampling as a technique for estimating *group* parameters. From the description of matrix sampling discussed here, it should be clear that it is not an individual- or examinee-centered approach. That is, if decisions have to be made at the examinee level (counseling, diagnosis, cognitive or affective standing, and so forth), then the ordinary use of matrix sampling is not the way to go about collecting the data. The response of an individual to a relatively small number of items is generally not reliable enough to serve as a basis for decision making. The practitioner, then, is faced with a dilemma when the evaluational purposes are two-fold (individual and group) and the economic advantages inherent in sampling techniques are required.[7]

7. From a logical standpoint, this problem would present itself in terms of gathering reliable data about individual items, that is, *item difficulties* in the case of achievement-type tests. Generally, however, there are relatively larger numbers of examinees responding to any given item than there are items to which any examinee responds; matrix sampling, especially in large-scale evaluation studies, can provide fairly reliable estimates of item "scores."

Having imposed this somewhat severe restriction on the utility of matrix sampling, the reader should be advised that some researchers have begun to extend the matrix sampling methodology to include procedures whereby individual examinee scores are estimated. Such procedures are essentially based upon estimating the interitem covariances and using linear multiple regression methods to predict examinees' scores from the estimated, weighted combination of items. (See, for example, Kleinke, 1972, and Bunda, 1973.) Caution must be exercised, however, since these procedures are highly dependent on the particular item and examinee populations involved; the practitioner may well need to conduct cross-validation studies for each application. The practitioner is also faced with certain ethical considerations when making decisions about individuals (versus groups) on the basis of only partial data. Although equal levels of probability error (for example, 5 percent) may be associated with predicting a remedial versus a normal reading class for a junior high school student and also with predicting the superior performance of one school district using a "modern" algebra text versus a "traditional" text as compared with another district, the "levels" of value judgment associated with each decision are probably not equal. Although admittedly extreme, this example should serve to illustrate that the practitioner's decision to use matrix sampling to estimate individual scores will ultimately depend on the balance between the nature of the decision to be made and the value of reordering economic priorities.

A second problem area not to be ignored is that matrix sampling is based on the assumption that the response of an examinee to an item is independent of the context in which the item is presented. That is, it is assumed that the examinee would respond to the items in a sample the same way the examinee would had they been *embedded* in the population of items. This assumption is made whenever one works with tests and test theory, but it is probably more important in matrix sampling since each examinee receives only a few items. The research which has been conducted to test this assumption has generally resulted in favorable conclusions, that is, estimates of population parameters are nearly the same whether or not items are responded to as part of the total test. (See Owens and Stufflebeam, 1969; Sirotnik, 1970b; and Cahen, Romberg, and Zwirner, 1970.) Additional context effects are created by ordering items according to their difficulties and mixing items with respect to different content.

Again, research to date (for example, French and Greer, 1964; Sax and Cromack, 1966; Marso, 1970; Huck and Bowers, 1972; Sirotnik and Wellington, 1974) suggests that these effects are minimal. Finally, the use of speeded tests (versus tests of power) introduces a context effect dependent on the examinee's ability to reach items toward the end of the test. Although certain commonsense procedures (for example, proportional item timing plus random item arrangements) can be employed, it has been recommended that matrix sampling not be applied to speeded ability tests. Research is lacking on this particular aspect of context effect.

A third problematic area relates to the nonexistence of theoretical guidelines with which the practitioner can determine the most efficient matrix sampling design for a particular application. In other words, given the practitioner's examinee and item population characteristics and economic constraints, what are the optimum number of matrices to be sampled, the optimum number of examinees and items in each matrix, and the relative advantages of sampling exhaustively or nonexhaustively and with or without replacement? A sufficient amount of empirical evidence based upon practical experience and Monte Carlo simulation studies is available to establish general working guidelines for the practitioner,[8] and these will be summarized later.

A fourth problematic area centers around the complexity of multiple matrix sampling mechanics, statistical as well as procedural. Although the theoretical formulas needed for most applications are now available, they are fairly complicated beyond the mean, standard deviation, and standard error of the mean estimates. Although selected computational procedures will be given here primarily to provide a greater feeling for the principles and uses of matrix sampling, the practitioner may ultimately wish to use any of a number of computer programs already available for performing most of the arithmetic needed (see, for example, Shoemaker, 1973b).

Procedurally, the logistics of creating and administering item subtests to examinee subgroups in accordance with the selected multiple matrix sampling design can become quite complex, especially when different item contents are included in a single "package" or certain

8. See, for example, Barcikowski, 1972; Cook and Stufflebeam, 1967; Shoemaker, 1970a,b, 1971.

items require specialized instructions or response formats. These problems, and others already mentioned, certainly pose problems for those using the matrix sampling technique, but they generally do not prevent using it effectively. Again, guidelines will be offered for dealing with these and other issues based on the research to date and practical experiences.

SELECTED STATISTICAL PROCEDURES
IN MATRIX SAMPLING[9]

Only a selected subset of the possible statistics and statistical procedures associated with matrix sampling methodology will be presented here. This subset resulted from an attempt to represent both the more elementary matrix sampling concepts and the most commonly applied procedures. Specifically, the parameters to be estimated, for which computational procedures will be illustrated, are as follows:

1. mean of the examinee score distribution;
2. variance (or standard deviation) of the examinee score distribution;
3. standard error of the estimated mean of the examinee score distribution;
4. standard error of the estimated difference between means of two examinee score distributions;
5. median (50th percentile) and interquartile range (25th and 75th percentiles) of the examinee score distribution;
6. coefficient alpha index of internal consistency among items.

Procedures for computing confidence intervals about the estimated mean for a single examinee population, and the estimated mean difference between two examinee populations will also be illustrated.

All of these procedures will be discussed in terms of multiple matrix sampling *without replacement*.[10] The formulas presented will be

9. The concepts to be discussed in this section require no more than an elementary knowledge of descriptive and inferential statistics. Although practitioners without this background may still profit from reading this section, they are strongly advised to obtain the assistance of a data analyst when attempting to implement matrix sampling methodology.

10. As discussed previously, multiple matrix sampling with replacement may often present a better alternative to the practitioner. Many of the computational

general, applying to nonbinary (polychotomous) items scored 1, 2, 3, . . . , etc., as well as binary (dichotomous) items scored 1-0. (The appendix contains proofs for all the formulas included herein.)

In order to provide a context in which the computational procedures presented below can be illustrated, consider the following evaluation setting, which, although realistic, is admittedly oversimplified for this presentation. An evaluator is faced with the task of establishing a "viable interface" for communication between the principals and superintendent of a given school district such that there exists a basis for decision making (budget, curriculum, community attitude, and so forth) relative to certain cognitive and affective goal areas deemed appropriate (arithmetic fundamentals, reading comprehension, studying skills, tolerance, self concept, and so forth). Suppose, and herein lies perhaps the greatest leap in simplification, the content and objectives are sufficiently understood and under control so that good, objective, paper-and-pencil tests in each of the desired goal areas are available and appropriate criterion levels of performance are known. The district staff decides that the evaluation will be beneficially augmented by quantitative data obtained in each goal area for every grade level both within and across the individual schools in the district. For example, certain curriculum decisions regarding ninth-grade vocabulary proficiency in some schools might be facilitated, in part, by inspecting the mean levels of achievement on the appropriate vocabulary tests over two or more semesters for the school. Certain budgetary decisions regarding the arithmetic reasoning programs at the seventh-grade level for two different schools might be facilitated, in part, by inspecting the difference in mean scores on the appropriate arithmetic test for the schools for some time period. Suppose the entire test battery requires 10 hours of supervised testing time per student. If economic restraints are such that this time is not available, then the above data are not collectible (and perhaps the evaluation system is not feasible) unless some kind of sampling and estimation procedure can be reliably employed. If such an estimation procedure were available, the evaluator would want some assurance that differences between estimated means or an estimated

---

procedures for BIBD matrix sampling with replacement designs can be found in Knapp (1973), as well as a good discussion of their advantages and applications; the basic computational procedures for completely random matrix sampling with replacement can be found in Sirotnik (1973a).

mean and some criterion value were not artifacts of the sampling process. Implicit in this illustration is the need for the evaluator to estimate the mean, variance (or standard deviation), and standard error of the mean of each examinee score distribution for each item population (test) of interest. Additionally, the evaluator may desire to estimate the cumulative frequency distribution so that percentiles (such as the median) can be approximated, or estimate the internal consistency coefficient among the items in order to investigate the unidimensionality of the construct (such as arithmetic reasoning) represented by the test.

Matrix sampling, of course, can meet the evaluator's needs. Introducing some new notation by way of summary, the matrix sampling technique can be employed in educational research or evaluation in order to estimate parameters (for example, mean and variance) of any given examinee (or item) score distribution for a population of N examinees responding to a population of M items. The estimates are computed using the data matrix resulting from the responses of n examinees to m items, each randomly and independently sampled from the corresponding populations of examinees and items. Usually, the more efficient procedure of *multiple* matrix sampling is employed, where the final estimates are the averages of the estimates obtained from k matrix samples, each sample being formed by randomly sampling n examinees and m items from their corresponding populations without replacement.

For purposes of illustration, suppose we (and the evaluator) have a population of 90 students (or examinees) in the sixth grade of a given school. We are interested in finding out, for example, what the mean and standard deviation are for the *relative* scores of these students on a power test of reading fundamentals containing 30 multiple choice, dichotomously scored (right-wrong) items. An examinee's relative score is equal to his total item score divided by the number of items. If an examinee answers 24 of the 30 items correctly, then his total score is 24 and his relative score is 24/30 or .80. When the items are scored polychotomously, the relative score indicates the examinee's mean location on the item scoring scale. For example, if the 30 items were scored on a 1- to 6-point scale, total scores would range from 30 to 180, whereas relative scores would range from 1 to 6. Both scoring methods provide identical information; relative scores may be preferable from a descriptive standpoint insofar as

they immediately locate the examinee's standing on the test construct as operationally defined by the item measurement scale. Since the matrix sampling formulas are somewhat simplified when relative scores are used, all the formulas to follow will be based on relative scoring.

We are starting, then, with a potential matrix population of 90 examinees and 30 items; using the notation introduced above, $N = 90$ and $M = 30$. Instead of giving all examinees (or a sample of examinees) all 30 items, however, we decide to use multiple matrix sampling. Therefore, we randomly divide the examinees into, say, ten samples of 9 examinees each, and we randomly divide the items into ten samples of 3 items each. If we then pair up samples of examinees and items, we have 10 matrix samples, 9 examinees-by-3 items each.[11] Using the above notation, $n = 9$, $m = 3$, and $k = 10$.

Figure 8-7 (see below) illustrates what any one of these matrix samples of data might look like. The numbers inside the matrix (or box) are the item scores of the examinees—that is, a 1 if the question was answered correctly and a 0 if it was answered incorrectly. Figure 8-6 illustrates the situation in general for any matrix sample having n examinees and m items, respectively. The columns at the right of the matrix contain each examinee's total score (sum of the numbers in the *row* corresponding to the examinee) and the square of this total score (the total score multiplied by itself). The rows at the bottom of the matrix contain exactly the same information, but for items. That is, each item's total score is the sum of the numbers in the *column* corresponding to the item. Then, the numbers in each of these additional columns and rows to the right and bottom of the matrix are themselves summed, yielding sums ΣE, ΣE^2, ΣI, ΣI^2. The squares of all the numbers inside the matrix are summed yielding sum ΣX^2. (The numbers inside the matrix are identified by the letter X, the number of the examinee, and the number of the item; it is not important to understand this notation. Simply remember that the sum ΣX^2 is obtained by adding up the squares of each examinee's

11. Concealed in this small paragraph are a great number of procedural logistics, including the selection of 1/10 as the sampling fraction. These issues will be treated in more detail in the next section. Suffice it to say here that the evaluator has managed to save 9/10 of the testing time by obtaining the responses of 10 different subgroups of 9 examinees each to 10 different subtests of 3 items each, respectively.

EXAMINEES / ITEMS

	1	2	3	.	.	.	m	Examinee total scores	Examinee total scores squared
1	X_{11}	X_{12}	X_{13}	.	.	.	X_{1m}	E_1	$E_1{}^2$
2	X_{21}	X_{22}	X_{23}	.	.	.	X_{2m}	E_2	$E_2{}^2$
3	X_{31}	X_{32}	X_{33}	.	.	.	X_{3m}	E_3	$E_3{}^2$
.								.	.
.								.	.
.								.	.
n	X_{n1}	X_{n2}	X_{n3}	.	.	.	X_{nm}	E_n	$E_n{}^2$
								ΣE	ΣE^2

Item total scores: I_1 I_2 I_3 . . . I_m : ΣI

Item total scores squared: $I_1{}^2$ $I_2{}^2$ $I_3{}^2$ . . . $I_m{}^2$: ΣI^2

ΣE = Sum of examinee total scores
= $E_1 + E_2 + E_3 + \ldots + E_n$

ΣE^2 = Sum of examinee squared total scores
= $E_1{}^2 + E_2{}^2 + E_3{}^2 + \ldots + E_n{}^2$

ΣI = Sum of item total scores
= $I_1 + I_2 + I_3 + \ldots + I_m$

ΣI^2 = Sum of item squared total scores
= $I_1{}^2 + I_2{}^2 + I_3{}^2 + \ldots + I_m{}^2$

ΣX^2 = Sum of all X's squared in matrix
= $X_{11}{}^2 + X_{12}{}^2 + X_{13}{}^2 + \ldots + X_{nm}{}^1$

$$A = \left[\Sigma E^2/m - (\Sigma E)^2/nm \right] /(n-1)$$

$$B = \left[\Sigma I^2/n - (\Sigma I)^2/nm \right] /(m-1)$$

$$C = \left[\Sigma X^2 - \Sigma E^2/m - \Sigma I^2/n + (\Sigma E)^2/nm \right] /(n-1)(m-1)$$

NOTE: ΣE must always equal ΣI.

Figure 8-6

Computations for the general matrix sample containing
n students and m items sampled from a population of N students and M items
(usual summation notation is used here employing the operator Σ.)

response or score on each item.) Three additional quantities, *A, B,* and *C* must also be computed from the values already calculated; their formulas are given in Figure 8-6.

At this point, we have all the necessary quantities to enter into formulas for estimating a number of parameters associated with the examinee and item relative score distributions in the population. Parameters are merely "statistics" computed for the population data, if, in fact, the data were available. Parameters are usually symbolized by lowercase Greek letters. Suppose all 90 examinees responded to all 30 items and the 90 examinee relative scores were computed. The mean of these 90 scores will be denoted by the symbol μ (Greek letter mu), and the variance of these scores will be denoted by the symbol σ_E^2 (Greek letter sigma). (The standard deviation, being the square root of the variance, will be denoted by the symbol σ_E.) The same parameters can be computed for the population of item relative scores. (These scores are more commonly referred to as item difficulties when the items are dichotomously scored.) Since the mean of the item relative scores is algebraically identical to that of the examinee relative scores, it is also symbolized by μ. The variance of the item relative score distribution is symbolized by σ_I^2 and the standard deviation by σ_I.

Since the populations of data are really not available, however, *estimates* of these parameters must be computed from the sample data. These estimates are commonly referred to as *statistics* and are symbolized by placing a caret above the appropriate parameter symbol. Estimates of all the parameters discussed above would be symbolized as follows: $\hat{\mu}$, $\hat{\sigma}_E^2$, $\hat{\sigma}_E$, $\hat{\sigma}_I^2$, and $\hat{\sigma}_I$.

With this notation in mind, and the computation of the quantities (*A, B,* and *C*) indicated in Figure 8-6 completed, formulas can now be written for these parameter estimates as follows:

$$(1)\ \hat{\mu} = \frac{\Sigma E}{nm}\ (= \frac{\Sigma I}{nm})$$

$\quad\quad\quad\quad$ = estimated mean of examinee (and item) relative score distribution

$$(2)\ \hat{\sigma}_E^2 = \frac{N-1}{N}\ [\ \frac{A - (1-m/M)C}{m}\ ]$$

= estimated variance of examinee relative score distribution

$$(3)\ \ \hat{\sigma}_I^2 = \frac{M-1}{M}\ [\ \frac{B-(1-n/N)C}{n}\ ]$$

= estimated variance of item relative score distribution

(Standard deviation estimates are simply obtained by taking the square root of the computed variances.)

Again, it should be noted that these formulas apply to relative scores only. It is easy, however, to convert the estimates so that they apply to total scores by "undoing" the effect of dividing by the number of items, M (in the case of examinee relative scores), or by the number of examinees, N (in the case of item relative scores). Thus, the mean and variance estimates for examinee total scores would be $M\hat{\mu}$ and $M^2\hat{\sigma}_E^2$, respectively; these estimates for item total scores would be $N\hat{\mu}$ and $N^2\hat{\sigma}_I^2$, respectively.

Using the results in Figure 8-7, a hypothetical matrix sample of the reading test data, we can see how the procedures outlined above and illustrated in general in Figure 8-6 are applied to actual numbers. The application of the estimation formulas for the examinee relative score distribution follows:

$$\hat{\mu}\ \ =\frac{12}{(9)\ (3)}=.444$$

$$\hat{\sigma}_E^2 = \frac{90-1}{90}\ [\ \frac{.167-(1-3/30)(.153)}{3}\ ] = .00965$$

$$\hat{\sigma}_E =\sqrt{.00965}\ = .0982$$

If estimates based on examinee total scores are desired, they are obtained as follows: $30(.444) = 13.32 =$ estimated mean; $(30)^2 (.00965) = 8.69 =$ estimated variance; and $(30)\ (.0982) = 2.95 =$ estimated standard deviation.

Now, returning to our original *multiple* matrix sampling design, the hypothetical data matrix in Figure 8-7 is only one of the ten matrices sampled by the evaluator. That is, according to the sampling

EXAMINEES	ITEMS 1	ITEMS 2	ITEMS 3		Examinee total score	Examinee total scores squared
1	0	0	1		1	1
2	0	0	0		0	0
3	0	1	0		1	1
4	0	0	1		1	1
5	0	0	1		1	1
6	0	1	1		2	4
7	0	1	1		2	4
8	0	1	1		2	4
9	0	1	1		2	4
					12	20
Item total scores	0	5	7	:	12	
Item total scores squared	0	25	49	:	74	

$$\Sigma E = 1+0+1+1+1+2+2+2+2 = 12$$
$$\Sigma E^2 = 1+0+1+1+1+4+4+4+4 = 20$$
$$\Sigma I = 0+5+7 = 12$$
$$\Sigma I^2 = 0+25+49 = 74$$
$$\Sigma X^2 = 0+0+1+0+0+0+0+1+0+0+0+1+0+0+1+0+1+1+0+1+1+0+1+1+0+1+1 = 12$$

$$A = [20/3 - (12)^2/(9)(3)] \;/(9-1) = .167$$
$$B = [74/9 - (12)^2/(9)(3)] \;/(3-1) = 1.444$$
$$C = [12 - 74/9 - 20/3 + (12)^2/(9)(3)] \;/(9-1)(3-1) = .153$$

Figure 8-7
Computations for a hypothetical matrix sample of data
(9 students and 3 items sampled from a population of 90 students and 30 items)

design, nine matrices of data remain to be analyzed, each composed of the responses of 9 sixth-grade examinees to 3 reading fundamental items. Now, suppose we have completed these computations for the remaining 9 matrix samples and have obtained the results indicated in Table 8-3 (for examinee relative scores). To get a final and more

Table 8-3
Estimates of the mean and variance for ten hypothetical matrix samples

Matrix sample	Mean $(\hat{\mu})$	Estimates of variance (σ_E^2)
1	.444	.00965
2	.409	.05776
3	.434	.00001
4	.366	.08843
5	.467	.12215
6	.326	.00030
7	.308	.09052
8	.424	.00138
9	.334	.26337
10	.531	.00260
Arithmetic averages	.404	.06362

stable estimate for both the mean and variance, the arithmetic averages (or means) of the 10 estimates for each parameter are taken.[12] Thus, in the final analysis, we can say that the *multiple matrix sampling estimated mean score for all 90 students taking all 30 items is .404 and the estimated variance of these scores is .06362*; the estimated standard deviation would be $\sqrt{.06362}$ or .252. (In terms of examinee total scores, the multiple matrix sampling estimates $\hat{\mu}$, $\hat{\sigma}_E^2$, $\hat{\sigma}_E$ would be, respectively, 12.1, 57.3, 7.6.)

In this illustration, thus far, we have assumed *equal-sized* matrices or matrix samples with the same number of examinees and the same number of items. In practice, however, some matrix samples end up with more or less examinees than others, and sometimes the practi-

12. In some instances, especially when matrix populations (and consequently examinee subgroups and item subtests are quite small), it is possible to obtain *negative* variance estimates. It is recommended that such estimates be averaged in *as they are, i.e.,* with their negative sign. (See Sirotnik, 1970a.)

tioner may have to design item subtests with different numbers of items. In any case, the computational procedures illustrated above are exactly the same for each individual matrix sample, so long as the values of n and m are changed accordingly. To obtain the multiple matrix sampling estimates, however, the simple unweighted averaging procedure would be incorrect. Instead, each matrix sampling estimate must be weighted (multiplied) by the total number of examinee-item observations (or responses) upon which it is based; these weighted estimates are then summed, and the result is divided by the total examinee-item responses over all matrix samples. This weighted averaging procedure can be illustrated with the data in Table 8-3. Suppose, for example, that matrix sample one contained the responses of only 5 examinees to the 3 items; matrix sample nine contained the responses of 13 examinees to only 2 items; and matrix sample ten contained the responses of 9 examinees to 4 items. The total number of examinee-item responses for each of these matrix samples would then be: 5 x 3 = 15; 13 x 2 = 26; and 9 x 4 = 36, respectively. The remaining matrix samples two through eight still contain the same number of examinee-item responses, namely, 9 x 3, or 27. The total number of examinee-item responses across all matrix samples would then be 15 + 26 + 36 + 7(27) or 266. The weighted average of the mean estimates would be computed as follows:

$$[15(.444) + 27(.409 + .434 + .366 + .467 + .326 + .308 + .424) + 26(.334) + 36(.531)]/266$$

or .407. The weighted average of the variance estimates would be computed in like fashion as follows:

$$[15(.00965) + 27(.05776 + .00001 + .08843 + .12215 + .0030 + .09052 + .00138) + 26(.26337) + 36(.00260)]/266$$

or .06324. Clearly, the difference between weighted averages and unweighted averages will not be great unless substantial differences exist in examinee or item dimensions from matrix to matrix.

We have thus far assumed in the illustration that all the examinees and all the items in the populations are sampled, that is, that the sampling design was exhaustive. Suppose the sampling of examinees was nonexhaustive and the 90 examinees were themselves a sample from a population of, say, 1,000 examinees. Computationally, the above procedures would proceed identically, except that $N = 1,000$,

instead of 90. Likewise, if the 30 items were but a sample from a population of, say, 500 items, the computational procedures would simply require $M = 500$, instead of 30.

For those readers familiar with analysis of variance procedures, the above analyses can be carried out straightforwardly using an examinee-by-item, random model, factorial design. Each matrix sample is an $n \times m$ design; the estimated mean is merely the sample mean or arithmetic average of all the cell entries (examinee-item responses); and the estimated variance is merely $(N-1)/N$ times the estimated component of variance associated with the examinee effect. (See Sirotnik, 1970a.) (The quantities A, B, and C in Figure 8-6 are the mean squares for examinees, items, and the examinee-by-item interaction, respectively.) In fact, the single matrix sample design can be extended to a multiple matrix sample design with the addition of a fixed k-level factor associated with the k matrix samples. Any good analysis of variance computer program which permits flexibility in design specification and estimation of variance components can be used to carry out mean and variance estimation when multiple matrix sampling designs are employed with equal-sized matrices.[13] Complete details for this analysis of variance approach are given by Sirotnik (1973a).

Summarizing the computations carried out so far, we have an evaluator, who, by sampling only 1/10 of his potential matrix population of data, has an estimate of the mean and standard deviation of the distribution of examinee scores that would have been available had all 90 examinees responded to all 30 items. Whenever estimation becomes necessary, it behooves the practitioner to be concerned about the *errors* being made or, more specifically, the sampling variance of the estimators. The practitioner may very well want answers to such questions as:

1. What numerical interval would be expected to include the actual population mean if the matrix sampling estimation procedure were repeated a large number of times? (Confidence interval estimation for a single mean.)

2. Is the matrix sampling estimate of the mean a reasonable expectation from a population with some specified mean? (Testing the null hypothesis $H_o : \mu = $ constant c.)

13. See, for example, BMD 08V in the Biomedical Computer Program series (Dixon, 1968).

Similar questions could be raised regarding the estimation of the means, and the differences between them, for two or more populations. These questions are not unusual; they are basic topics in elementary statistical inference. But here they are not necessarily linked to any substantive research hypothesis. They can arise only out of the fact that complete data could not practically be collected for all examinees' responses to all items. (If all data could have been collected, the answer to the first question above would be that the "interval" would have a width of zero; the answer to the second question could be determined upon a simple inspection of the obtained and hypothesized means.)

The key statistic to be computed so that these questions can be answered is the standard error of the estimated mean, which will be denoted here as $\sigma_{\hat{\mu}}$. (The concepts of the standard error and sampling distribution of the estimated mean were discussed earlier.) In order to compute the estimate of the standard error, denoted $\hat{\sigma}_{\hat{\mu}}$, we must first compute the estimate of another kind of variance associated with the matrix population, namely, the variance due to the "interaction" between examinees and items and denoted by the symbol σ_{EI}^2. Readers familiar with analysis of variance will recognize this as one of the four components of variance associated with the examinee-by-item population matrix, the remaining three being those already discussed: the mean (μ), the examinee variance (σ_E^2), and the item variance ($\hat{\sigma}_I^2$). It is not necessary to understand these analysis of variance concepts in order to proceed computationally, however, and the formula for the estimate of this interaction variance, denoted by the symbol $\hat{\sigma}_{EI}^2$, is as follows:

(4) $\hat{\sigma}_{EI}^2 = \dfrac{(N-1)(M-1)}{NM} C$ (C is defined in Figure 8-6, above.)

For example, with respect to the data in Figure 8-7 (the first matrix sample),

$$\hat{\sigma}_{EI}^2 = \frac{(90-1)(30-1)}{(90)(30)} (.153) = .146$$

Again, as in the procedures illustrated above, $\hat{\sigma}_{EI}^2$ estimates would be computed for all ten matrix samples; these estimates would then be averaged to produce the final, multiple matrix sampling estimate of

σ_{EI}^2. For purposes of illustration, suppose all ten estimates were computed and the average was .158.

We now have the necessary quantity to enter into the formula for the standard error of the mean, when the mean is estimated using multiple matrix sampling without replacement. When the sampling of matrices is exhaustive (of both the examinee and item populations), this formula can be written as follows:[14]

$$(5) \quad \hat{\sigma}_{\hat{\mu}} = \sqrt{\frac{k-1}{(N-1)(M-1)}} \, (\hat{\sigma}_{EI}^2)$$

where it is understood that $\hat{\sigma}_{EI}^2$ is the averaged, multiple matrix sampling estimate. For the exemplary data above, the standard error of the multiple matrix sampling estimate of the mean is

$$\hat{\sigma}_{\hat{\mu}} = \sqrt{\frac{10-1}{(90-1)(30-1)}} \, (.158) = .024$$

(If we wish to compute the standard error in terms of examinee total scores, then we simply multiply this quantity by M, the number of items in the population, that is, $30 \times .024 = .72$.)

This standard error estimate can be used in exactly the same manner as it is employed in the traditional, examinee sampling designs upon which most elementary statistical inference tests are based. For example, in examinee sampling we know that, due to the central limit theorem, the sampling distribution of the estimated mean is given by the normal, bell-shaped curve, with a mean equal to μ and standard error equal to $\hat{\sigma}^2 / \sqrt{n}$.[15] Thus, we are able to construct, say, the 95 percent confidence interval boundary points as follows:

---

14. For the case in which sampling is not exhaustive, the formula is somewhat more formidable, requiring the estimates of all three variance components:

$$\hat{\sigma}_{\hat{\mu}} = \sqrt{\frac{1}{knm(N-1)(M-1)} \left[m(M-1)(N-nk)\,\hat{\sigma}_E^2 + n(N-1)(M-mk)\hat{\sigma}_I^2 \right.}$$
$$\left. + \left[(N-n)(M-m) + nm(k-1)\right]\hat{\sigma}_{EI}^2 \right]$$

15. Technically, this is *approximately* the case when the number of examinees (n) sampled is greater than thirty. More rigorously, the sampling distribution is Student's t with $n-1$ degrees of freedom.

$$(6) \quad \hat{\mu} \pm 1.96 \, \hat{\sigma}_{\hat{\mu}}$$

(Any confidence interval can be constructed in this fashion by substituting the appropriate standard normal deviate value for 1.96; for example, the values 1.65 and 2.58 for the 90 percent and 99 percent confidence intervals, respectively.) Also, we are able to test null hypotheses of the form H_o: $\mu = c$ through the use of the standard normal deviate

$$(7) \quad z = \frac{\hat{\mu} - c}{\sigma_{\hat{\mu}}}$$

Now, suppose that in multiple matrix sampling, the same kind of central limit theorem applied—namely, that the sampling distribution of the multiple matrix sampling estimate of the mean was normal with a mean equal to the population μ and a standard error equal to that given by formula (5), above. In this case, formulas (6) and (7) would apply to multiple matrix sampling as well. Unfortunately, the theoretical developments in matrix sampling thus far have stopped short of deriving the nature of the sampling distributions of multiple matrix sampling estimates. Nevertheless, it has been empirically demonstrated (Sirotnik, 1973b; Shoemaker, 1973a) using simulation techniques that, whatever the theoretical shape of the sampling distribution of the mean, it is closely approximated by the normal distribution. Therefore, the practitioner can, in fact, construct confidence intervals and test hypotheses regarding the population examinee score mean (μ) using formulas (6) and (7), above.

To illustrate these points, we continue with the evaluator, the matrix populations of 90 sixth-grade examinees and 30 reading fundamental items, and the ten, 9-examinee-by-3-item matrix samples, from which we have computed the estimates $\hat{\mu} = .404$ and $\hat{\sigma}_{\hat{\mu}} = .024$. Applying formula (6), we have lower and upper boundary points of the 95 percent confidence interval given by $.404 - (1.96)(.024) = .357$ and $.404 + (1.96)(.024) = .451$. Now, the evaluator is able to report not only that the best guess of the population mean is .404; but that if the above multiple matrix sampling process and confidence interval construction process were repeated indefinitely (using the same matrix population of data), the true mean would be

contained in 95 percent of the constructed intervals. Thus the probability would be .95 that the interval .357 to .451 contains the true mean. Since we are working with dichotomous items and examinee relative (proportion correct) scores, we can easily translate the above conclusions into percentage scores by multiplying by 100. In other words, we estimate the examinee percentage correct mean score to be 40.4 percent; in so doing, we make a standard error of 2.4 percentage points. In repeating the estimation process, 95 percent of the time we can make errors as great as 4.7 percentage points above or below our estimate of 40.4 percent; that is, the "true" population will be somewhere between 35.7 percent and 45.1 percent, a confidence interval having a *width* of 9.4 percentage points.

Depending upon the nature of the decisions for which our evaluator has estimated the mean, a 95 percent confidence interval as large as 9.4 percentage points may or may not be adequate. The interval can be tightened by lowering the confidence level, say, to 90 percent or sampling more data (for example, 1/5 as opposed to 1/10). In fact, the practitioner should decide beforehand what confidence level and what standard error (or confidence interval width) should be tolerated. In the last part of this chapter procedures will be illustrated whereby practitioners can use these prerequisites in order to estimate, beforehand, how many matrix samples (k), or, reciprocally, what sampling fraction ($1/k$), is necessary to meet their requirements.

A functionally equivalent procedure to confidence interval construction is the testing of null hypotheses of the form $H_o : \mu = c$. Suppose, for example, the evaluator wished to determine whether or not the population of ninety examinees reached a criterion level performance of, say, 50 percent, or a mean proportion correct score of .5. Using formula (5), above,

$$z = \frac{.404 - .5}{.024} = -4.01$$

which, when referred to a table of standard normal deviates, is significant beyond the .001 level. Thus, the evaluator can report that the population of examinees did not reach the expected criterion level of performance. Had c been equal to any value within the 95 percent confidence interval .357 to .451, the evaluator would not have rejected his H_o (at the 5 percent level of significance) and would have

concluded that the criterion level of performance was met within the bounds of error stated by the confidence interval.

Recapping, the evaluator now has estimates of the mean of examinee scores ($\hat{\mu}$), the standard error of this mean ($\hat{\sigma}_{\hat{\mu}}$), the estimated confidence interval for the mean, and the estimated variance of examinee scores ($\hat{\sigma}_E^2$). There are, of course, many other estimates to be computed: for example, the standard error of the estimated variance and associated confidence interval and the estimated third and fourth moments, their standard errors, and their confidence intervals.[16] The computations involved in these procedures become exceedingly complex. (See Pandey and Shoemaker, 1973.) Furthermore, the sampling distributions of the variance, third, and fourth moments are unknown, theoretically; an empirical investigation has provided some evidence that they are normally distributed (except for the fourth moment), provided that the population score distribution is normal (Shoemaker, 1973). Certainly, these issues can, and should, be settled theoretically, with procedures for the practitioner to follow.

All the parameters which have been estimated thus far have been associated with the examinee score distribution, that is, the distribution of scores which would have resulted if all 90 examinees would have responded to all 30 items. The procedures of matrix sampling can, in fact, be extended to estimate this distribution itself; that is, for any given score value, we can estimate the percentage of examinees in the population that we would expect to obtain that score. (This is quite different from estimating any single examinee's score.) Although somewhat tedious, the computational procedures are very straightforward, and the practitioner is referred to Shoemaker (1973b) for a detailed presentation for the case in which test items are scored dichotomously (1-0). It is instructive, however, to consider the end product of the computations involved in estimating the examinee score distribution. In our example, the evaluator is dealing with a population of 30 "right-wrong" items; thus, there is a possibility of thirty-one score values ranging from 0 to 30. The estimation process results in a list such as that in Table 8-4, wherein, for each

16. The third and fourth moments are more commonly associated with the measures of skewness and kurtosis, respectively, of the examinee score distribution.

Table 8-4
Hypothetical estimated examinee score distribution

Score value	Estimated proportion	Cumulative percentage
0	.0207	2.07
1	.0205	4.12
2	.0214	6.26
3	.0239	8.65
4	.0254	11.19
5	.0318	14.37
6	.0362	17.99
7	.0306	21.05
8	.0393	24.98
9	.0369	28.67
10	.0412	32.79
11	.0507	37.86
12	.0416	42.02
13	.0516	47.18
14	.0519	52.37
15	.0436	56.73
16	.0408	60.81
17	.0427	65.08
18	.0401	69.09
19	.0386	72.95
20	.0352	76.47
21	.0383	80.30
22	.0397	84.27
23	.0351	87.78
24	.0336	91.14
25	.0271	93.85
26	.0224	96.09
27	.0201	98.10
28	.0139	99.49
29	.0028	99.77
30	.0023	100.00

possible score value, the proportion of the examinee population expected to achieve the score is indicated. These proportions can be multiplied by 100 and summed to form a cumulative percentage distribution; from this, we can read off various estimated percentiles (or percentile ranks) of interest. For example, the estimated 25th, 50th (median), and 75th percentiles are the approximate score values 8,

14, and 20, respectively; the estimated interquartile range is thus 20 − 8, or 12. It should be noted that the procedures used to estimate the examinee score distribution were originally developed for (and empirically tested on) large norm groups (1,000 or more examinees). The theory has not been extended to include formulas and procedures for standard errors, sampling distributions, and associated confidence intervals for percentile estimates. The practitioner can expect the precision of these estimates to drop markedly when small examinee populations are employed.[17]

With the exception of the mean, all estimates and procedures which have been described thus far, although explicitly relating to the examinee score distribution, have been functionally dependent upon the interrelationships (specifically, covariances) among the items in the item population. (In fact, all above formulas can be rewritten analogously to apply to the item score distribution, and, as such, they would be functionally dependent upon the covariances among examinees.) A parameter explicitly associated with the interrelationships among items and of particular interest to the practitioner is coefficient alpha (a), the generalized measure of internal consistency (Cronbach, 1951). Coefficient alpha is basically equivalent to the proportion (ranging between 0 and 1) of the interitem covariance relative to the total test score variance. As such, it reflects the degree to which items are highly correlated (positively) with each other, or, alternatively, the degree to which each item is highly correlated (positively) with the total test score. (When items are scored dichotomously, $1 - 0$, a reduces to the Kuder-Richardson coefficient 20.) Coefficient a can be estimated for the M-item population using the following formula:

$$(8) \quad \hat{a} = \frac{(M-1)\hat{\sigma}_E^2 - \hat{\sigma}_{EI}^2}{(M-1)\hat{\sigma}_E^2}$$

where it is understood that the $\hat{\sigma}_E^2$ and $\hat{\sigma}_{EI}^2$ are the averaged, multiple matrix sampling estimates of the examinee and interaction variance

17. Computer-simulated investigations are clearly needed to develop sampling error guidelines for the practitioner when estimating the examinee score distribution. In the absence of these studies or theoretical developments, standard errors can be approximated using the "jackknife" procedure as developed by Quenouille (1956) and as applied to multiple matrix sampling estimates by Shoemaker (1973b).

estimates. Returning to our illustration, these estimates have been calculated and are, respectively, .064 and .158; the evaluator can then compute the estimate of a as follows:

$$\hat{a} = \frac{(30-1)(.064) - .158}{(30-1)(.064)} = .92$$

Again, theoretical procedures for estimating the standard error and confidence interval for the multiple matrix sampling estimate of alpha are lacking. (See preceding note.)

We now have an evaluator, who, for a *single* population of examinees, has estimated the mean, variance, standard error of the mean, selected percentiles of the examinee score distribution, and coefficient alpha for the population of items. The evaluator has obtained this information not by testing each of the 90 examinees on all of the 30 items, but by strategically sampling 1/10 of the data, that is, forming 10 random matrix samples by repeatedly sampling the responses of 9 different examinees to 3 different items without replacement from the matrix population. As was pointed out in the beginning of this chapter, meaningful evaluations often necessarily involve the comparison of at least two different examinee populations in either ex post facto (sixth grade in school A versus sixth grade in school B) or experimental (group A, treatment 1, versus group B, treatment 2) designs. Had our evaluator been interested in the performance of a second population of examinees on the same item population, the multiple matrix sampling design could have been repeated and the same set of parameters estimated. Just as there was sampling error associated with each estimate when dealing with a single examinee population, there is sampling error associated with the *difference* between estimates when dealing with two examinee populations. For example, if the evaluator wished to construct the confidence interval for the difference between the examinee score means, he would need to know the estimation formula for the standard error of the mean difference and the theoretical (or approximate) nature of the sampling distribution of the mean difference.

Once again, however, the theory has left the practitioner groping. Matrix sampling has been extended only as far as estimating the mean for two populations when only a single matrix sample is extracted in each case (Lord and Novick, 1968, pp. 257-259). No theory is available for the case of multiple matrix sampling without

replacement using two (or more) examinee populations.[18] It is not difficult, however, to extend the procedures of multiple matrix sampling to estimate mean differences, and the practical consequences of this extension are considered now.

In order to illustrate the procedures to follow, we offer the reader a new evaluator, with some slight changes in the dimensions of the multiple matrix sampling design. Our evaluator is interested in the sixth-grade levels of two schools and their proficiency on a number of standardized power tests of ability (reading fundamentals, arithmetic reasoning, and social studies, among others). Specifically, we will relate our computational procedures to the reading test, which contains 40 dichotomously scored (right-wrong) items; each school contains 55 students at the sixth-grade level. The entire test battery, including the test of reading fundamentals requires approximately 10 hours of testing time per examinee, but only two hours of testing time are available. The battery, and thus the reading test, must be cut by 80 percent. For the purposes of analysis, then, the examinee population size is $N = 55$; the item population size is $M = 40$; the number k of the multiple matrix samples to be drawn for each school is 5 (the sampling fraction, $1/k$, is $1/5$), and, for each of these matrix samples, the number of examinees is $n = 11$ and the number of items is $m = 8$. In other words, five subtests are formed by successively sampling eight items at random and without replacement; within each school, five subgroups are formed by successively sampling 11 examinees at random and without replacement; within each school, the five item subtests are paired with the five examinee subgroups. In actuality, the resulting matrix samples of data would be obtained by administering the appropriate item subtest to each examinee. For the present illustration, the entire populations of data are actually available—that is, all 55 × 40, or 2,200 examinee-item responses are available for each school, and the matrix sampling data is extracted on a post hoc basis.[19]

18. With respect to mean differences, the theory is a direct consequence of adding an independent group factor to the $k \times n \times m$ mixed model analysis of variance design referred to above, when matrices are randomly sampled *with* replacement. (See Sirotnik, 1973a.)

19. I wish to thank Fred Wellington and the Applied Technology Center for Education (Anaheim, California) for supplying the context and data used for purposes of illustration here.

We know, therefore, exactly what the mean and standard deviation are for this population, and we know what the estimates of these parameters would be for a random, multiple matrix sampling of the data. Table 8-5 presents the actual population values and matrix

Table 8-5

Multiple matrix sample estimates and population values
of the mean and standard deviation for schools 1 and 2

	Mean	Standard deviation	Standard error of the mean
School 1			
Multiple matrix sampling estimates	.777	.158	.0158
Actual population values	.778	.155	—
School 2			
Multiple matrix sampling estimates	.689	.216	.0163
Actual population values	.711	.216	—

sampling estimates of the mean, standard deviation, and standard error of the mean for both schools. These data should afford the reader an opportunity to appreciate the precision with which multiple matrix sampling can estimate population parameters, even for relatively small matrix populations. As discussed above, we can assume that the sampling distributions of the estimated mean for each school are approximated by the normal distribution and construct, say, 90 percent confidence intervals for the mean for each school as follows:

School 1: .777 ± (1.64)(.0158) or .751 to .803
School 2: .689 ± (1.64)(.0163) or .662 to .716

Given the tightness of these intervals, the evaluator would feel fairly secure in using matrix sampling to estimate the means.

Now, suppose the evaluator was interested in assessing the *differences* in test performance between the two schools. Since the sampling distributions of the mean for both schools are nearly normal, it can be assumed that the sampling distribution of the difference between estimated means is nearly normal, or at least normally distributed for all practical intents and purposes. All the evaluator needs is the formula for estimating the standard error of the difference between means when using multiple matrix sampling without replacement.

Denoting the mean of the first school, μ_1, and the mean of the second school, μ_2, we can symbolize the standard error of the estimated mean difference by $\sigma_{\hat{\mu}_1 - \hat{\mu}_2}$ and its estimate by $\hat{\sigma}_{\hat{\mu}_1 - \hat{\mu}_2}$, and write the required formula as follows:[20]

$$(9) \quad \hat{\sigma}_{\hat{\mu}_1 - \hat{\mu}_2} = \sqrt{\frac{2(k-1)}{(N-1)(M-1)}} \, (\hat{\sigma}^2_{EI})$$

where it is understood that the quantity $\hat{\sigma}^2_{EI}$ is now the *pooled* multiple matrix sampling estimate *across both schools* for the examinee-item interaction variance.

We can illustrate the application of this formula with the data available in Table 8-5. First, the estimates of the examinee-item interaction variance $(\hat{\sigma}^2_{EI})$ must be computed for each school. Although these values were not supplied in Table 8-5, they could have been computed and are, in fact, .131 and .140 for schools 1 and 2, respectively. The pooled estimate $\hat{\sigma}^2_{EI}$ is then $(.131 + .140)/2 = 1.36$. Entering this pooled estimate into formula (9), we obtain

$$\hat{\sigma}_{\hat{\mu}_1 - \hat{\mu}_2} = \sqrt{\frac{2(5-1)}{(55-1)(40-1)}} (.136) = .023$$

The estimated standard error of the difference between the estimated means for schools 1 and 2 is .023, a value typically larger than the standard error of the estimated mean for either school separately. Our evaluator can now construct the 95 percent confidence interval for the mean difference in analogous form to that given by formula (6) above, namely,

$$(10) \quad (\hat{\mu}_1 - \hat{\mu}_2) \pm 1.96 \, \hat{\sigma}_{\hat{\mu}_1 - \hat{\mu}_2}$$

(90 percent and 99 percent confidence intervals would be constructed using, respectively, 1.65 and 2.58 instead of 1.96.) Applying

20. In the event that the multiple matrix sampling design is nonexhaustive of the item population, the formula can be written more generally as follows:

$$\hat{\sigma}_{\hat{\mu}_1 - \hat{\mu}_2} = \sqrt{\frac{2}{knm(N-1)(M-1)} \left[m(M-1)(N-nk)\hat{\sigma}^2_E + [(N-n)(M-m) + nm(k-1)] \, \hat{\sigma}^2_{EI} \right]}$$

this formula to our data, we have lower and upper boundary points of the 95 percent confidence interval given by $(.777 - .689) - (1.96)(.023) = .043$ and $(.777 - .689) + (1.96)(.023) = .133$.

The evaluator is now able to report that the two schools are estimated to differ in their reading fundamental mean scores by $.777 - .689$ or $.088$, that is, 8.8 percentage points; and that the probability is .95 (given infinite repetitions of the sampling process) that the "true" mean difference is contained in the interval .043 to .133. We can also approach these data from the standpoint of testing null hypotheses of the form $H_o : \mu_1 - \mu_2 = c$. The usual normal deviate can be computed and tested for significance. It is typically of interest to let the constant c equal 0

$$(11) \quad z = \frac{(\hat{\mu}_1 - \hat{\mu}_2) - c}{\hat{\sigma}_{\hat{\mu}_1 - \hat{\mu}_2}}$$

and thus test the $H_o : \mu_1 = \mu_2$, or that, in our example, the mean of school 1 equals the mean of school 2. It is evident that a mean difference of zero does not fall within our 95 percent confidence interval, and so we can conclude that the two schools are, indeed, different in mean performance. Alternatively, we can approach the significance test directly:

$$z = \frac{(.777 - .689) - 0}{.023} = 3.83,$$

a z value significant beyond the .05 level. (Since our matrix sampling data was extracted on a post hoc basis, we know for a fact that the true population means are .778 and .711 and are, of course, unequal.)

The above example is typical of a class of comparative research models referred to as ex post facto designs, where the examinee membership in the two groups (schools) is predetermined. In contrast, experimental designs are such that examinee membership in the two groups is determined at random, and the two groups usually represent two different treatments (as, for example, two different teaching methods for a given set of history objectives). Given the current trend toward large-scale evaluative research designs, wherein large pools of examinees can be considered to constitute randomly formed treatment groups, multiple matrix sampling can be employed to test

the null hypothesis of no treatment effect. The evaluator would use exactly the same computational procedures illustrated above, with one exception—the following formula for $\hat{\sigma}_{\hat{\mu}_1 - \hat{\mu}_2}$ would be used instead of formula (9), above:

$$(12) \quad \hat{\sigma}_{\hat{\mu}_1 - \hat{\mu}_2} = \sqrt{\frac{2}{knm(M-1)} \left[m(M-1)\hat{\sigma}_E^2 + (M-m)\hat{\sigma}_{EI}^2 \right]}$$

Regardless of the total number (population) of examinees N in each treatment group, the appropriate statistical inference in an experimental design is to the population of all possible randomizations of the examinees that could have occurred. (See Edgington, 1969.) The best approximation for this model is to assume the examinee population sizes to be *infinite*; in fact, formula (12) is merely the formula in the preceding note, when N approaches infinity. Otherwise all computational procedures remain the same. Applications of multiple matrix sampling designs in the comparison of two groups have rarely been used, judging from the literature. The reader is referred to Sirotnik and Wellington (1974) for an actual application of matrix sampling in the comparison of two experimental groups.

GUIDELINES IN THE DESIGN OF MATRIX SAMPLING STUDIES

Suppose we are faced with designing a multiple matrix sampling (without replacement) study with relatively large examinee and item populations, say, 5,000 and 500, respectively, wherein not all examinees or items would be sampled. In this case, we would have great flexibility in choosing values for all three basic design parameters, including the number of examinees (n), the number of items (m), and the number of matrix samples (k).[21] For example, we can choose $n = 100$ and $m = 25$ and then randomly sample anywhere from one to twenty $(k = 1$ to $20)$ matrix samples without replacement. If we choose $k = 10$, we could, in fact, sample as many as $n = 500$ examinees per matrix. Clearly, a large number of possible values are available for n, m, and k.

---

21. There does not appear to be any advantage to purposely designing matrix samples with unequal examinee and item dimensions; therefore, it will be assumed that each matrix sample will be of $n \times m$ dimensions.

It is often the case that interest centers on a smaller population of items, usually defined by some standardized or specially constructed test, long enough to cover the objectives and short enough to be compatible with the attention span of the intended examinee population. Such a test, instead of 500 items, might be, say, 60 items in length. It is important in this case that every item be sampled in the matrix sampling design and thus, we have flexibility in only two of the three design parameters. For example, if we choose $m = 15$, then k must be 60/15 or 4. The number of examinees per matrix sample can vary, but can be no more than 5,000/4 or 1,250.

In smaller studies—at the school or even district level, for example —it is often desirable to test all the examinees of interest. In a given district we might have 500 fifth graders and a standardized arithmetic test having 60 items. In this case, we have flexibility in choosing only one design parameter, which is essentially the sampling fraction $1/k$. If we choose $m = 15$, then $k = 60/15 = 4$ and $n = 500/4 = 125$; that is, $1/k$ or 1/4 of the total 500 X 60 matrix population will be sampled.

The questions with which this final section is concerned are twofold: (1) How does the practitioner decide on the values for n, m, and k? (2) Once these values are selected, what are some of the practical concerns in constructing and administering the matrix sampling packages? The first and second sets of questions can be informally labeled statistical and procedural considerations, respectively, in the design of matrix sampling studies. We will discuss the statistical considerations first.

At the outset, the reader must be informed that there are no hard and fast statistical guidelines to fit any and all applications of matrix sampling. Even in the best of circumstances, when formulas are available to estimate $1/k$, the practitioner must have enough knowledge regarding the characteristics of the particular examinee and item populations such that "guestimates" can be supplied for the parameters to be estimated. In many cases, the best available guidelines often contain phrases such as "relatively greater" or "sufficiently large" with no actual numbers attached to the "greatness" or the "largeness." In other words, no table exists whereby for every given matrix sampling problem, practitioners can input a specified set of parameters, and receive as output the necessary n, m, and k for their sampling designs. In fact, it may often be the case that statistical

guidelines will be of little help to the practitioner, who is faced with strict, economic restraints. Consider the above case with the 500 fifth graders and 60 arithmetic items. Suppose the test is part of an extensive achievement battery which requires a total of 10 hours of testing per examinee. Suppose only 2 hours of testing time per student are available. Matrix sampling, perhaps the only viable method of obtaining evaluative information in this case, could be employed sampling no more than 1/5 of the potentially available data. The evaluator may have no choice but to select $k = 1/5$ and construct 5 subbatteries of achievement tests accordingly.

Thus, it is a truism with matrix sampling, as with all other estimation techniques relying upon partial data, that the more data (examinee-item responses) obtained, the better the estimates. The "better" a matrix sampling estimate of a given parameter is, the smaller is the standard error of the estimated parameter. (Other criteria, such as cost-benefit considerations, could be used to define "better"; for our purposes, the simpler statistical definition will suffice.) Ideally, then, the practitioner would want to state the parameters of interest (for example, μ and σ_E) and "guestimates" of their values, the examinee population size N, the item population sizes M for all item populations of interest, and the maximum tolerable standard errors for each parameter of interest. In return, the practitioner would want the optimal balancing of the design parameters n, m, and k.

Unfortunately, even if the theory were sufficiently advanced to provide this type of output, the optimal n, m, and k design for estimating one parameter is not usually optimal for estimating another parameter. An extreme case in point is estimating the mean. It can be shown (Lord and Novick, 1968) that, for a fixed number of examinee-item responses, the multiple matrix sampling design resulting in the smallest standard error of the mean is that accomplished by administering a different item to each subgroup of examinees. For example, in the illustration above, $N = 500$ and $M = 60$. The best design for estimating the mean would be to choose $k = M = 60$ and thus $m = 60/60 = 1$ and $n = 500/60 \doteq 8$. That is, 60 matrix samples would be formed, each containing the responses to 1 item by approximately 8 examinees. With this design, however, it is impossible to estimate any other parameters; to estimate the variance, for example, each examinee must respond to at least two items.

The point here is not to demoralize the practitioner, but simply to

indicate that no universal rules exist presently. There are, however, a number of general guidelines derived from empirical and computer-simulated matrix sampling studies that can help the practitioner. It cannot be too strongly emphasized that perhaps the best guideline for the practitioner to follow is to contact other practitioners who have used matrix sampling in similar situations and to obtain some ideas of the likely standard errors to result, given specified sampling fractions and examinee and item score distribution characteristics. For large (and expensive) matrix sampling studies, it may be well worth the cost of simulating various designs with a range of parameter values most likely to include those to be encountered in the particular study. Shoemaker (1973b) has prepared and documented a computer program designed to accomplish this kind of pilot investigation.

We will now proceed to outline how the practitioner can compute the required sampling fraction $(1/k)$ for a specific application of matrix sampling, namely, the case when exhaustive, multiple matrix sampling without replacement is employed to estimate the examinee mean score. Although this application represents a rather special case of matrix sampling, it is instructive to pursue on three accounts: it is one of the more common and basic applications of matrix sampling; it is illustrative of what the practitioner can expect once the "legwork" is done with respect to the theoretical developments for other matrix sampling designs and parameters; and it results in guidelines similar to those developed empirically for more general situations.

We have already seen how the standard error of the mean is employed to construct confidence intervals, giving the evaluator some notion of the precision of the mean estimate. Thus, for decision-making purposes the practitioner can set the probability level and width of the desired confidence interval at the outset, thereby determining the maximum standard error to be tolerated. For example, in the case of achievement testing using binary (right-wrong) items, a standard error of 0.01 would result in a 95 percent confidence interval having a width of 4 percentage points or two standard errors on either side of the estimated mean. Alternatively phrased, the practitioner requiring a 95 percent confidence interval with a maximum width of 4 percentage points (a maximum error in estimating the mean of ± .02), requires a standard error of no more than .01.

Once the standard error is fixed, we can simply work "backwards" using formula (5) for $\hat{\sigma}_{\hat{\mu}}$ to solve for the value of k, estimating the remaining population parameters when necessary. (This procedure is basically analogous to that for determining sample sizes in simple experimental designs for given levels of design sensitivity.) It will be instructive to follow this procedure through for the special case where items are scored dichotomously (1-0), and then indicate the general solution for all item scoring procedures.

First, it can be shown that formula (5), when written more specifically to apply only to binary (dichotomous) items, takes the following form in terms of population parameters:[22]

$$\sigma_{\hat{\mu}} = \sqrt{\frac{k-1}{(n-1)(m-1)} \left[\mu(1-\mu) - \sigma_E^2 - \sigma_I^2 \right]}$$

Working in terms of the *variance* error $\sigma_{\hat{\mu}}^2$ (instead of the standard error $\sigma_{\hat{\mu}}$), this formula can be rewritten as follows:

$$(13) \quad k = 1 + \frac{(N-1)(M-1)\,\sigma_{\hat{\mu}}^2}{\left[\mu(1-\mu) - \sigma_E^2 - \sigma_I^2 \right]}$$

Clearly, for a fixed value of the standard error, the number of multiple matrix samples k is dependent upon the estimated population mean and the estimated population variances of both item and examinee scores. Computationally, the practitioner would need to supply the desired value for $\sigma_{\hat{\mu}}^2$ as well as guesses of the values for μ, σ_E^2, and σ_I^2, and substitute them into formula (13). (The computed value for k would always be rounded *up* to the nearest integer.) Given the use of standardized tests or objective-based tests with pilot test data, the practitioner often has available sufficient information on which to

---

22. The reader interested in theoretical derivations can note that the variance of all the examinee-item responses in the population matrix is equivalent to $\sigma_E^2 + \sigma_I^2 + \sigma_{EI}^2$ which, when items are scored 1-0, is equivalent to $\mu(1-\mu)$. Thus, all the formulas in Lord and Novick (1968, ch. 11) containing the term $\mu(1-\mu)$ can be written generally, to apply to any polychotomous item scoring system, by substituting the above equivalency. Proofs for the formulas to follow can be found in Sirotnik (1973c). (See also the Technical Appendix.)

base reasonable guesses for both σ_E^2 and σ_I^2. This may not be the case for μ, however, especially since estimating the mean motivated the use of matrix sampling in the first place. Since these three estimates are not independent of one another, several alternative approaches are available.

One approach results from noting that the maximum value of the bracketed denominator in formula (13) is .25, assuming positive internal consistency (coefficient a) among the population of binary items. Therefore, when no reasonable estimates of the three parameters exist, this constant can be substituted into formula (13) yielding a *conservative* estimate of k:

$$(14) \quad k = 1 + 4(N{-}1)(M{-}1)\ \sigma_{\hat{\mu}}^2$$

For example, with as small a matrix population as 200 examinees and 50 items and as stringent a confidence interval as 95 percent with a width of 4 percentage points ($\sigma_{\hat{\mu}}$ = .01), k = 1 + 4(199)(49)(.01)^2 $\doteq$ 5. In other words, the sampling fraction (1/k) is 1/5 and the practitioner can cut the testing time by 4/5 by using multiple matrix sampling with five 40-examinee-by-10-item, random nonoverlapping matrix samples.

It would be preferable, however, to have a more accurate estimate of the bracketed denominator in formula (13), above. To this end, the formula can once again be rewritten in terms of only two parameters which require "guestimates" by the practitioner:

$$(15) \quad k = 1 + \frac{(N{-}1)\sigma_{\hat{\mu}}^2}{\sigma_E^2\ (1{-}a)}$$

(This formula is general, applying to all item scoring systems.)

Thus, practitioners have available a simple equation whereby they can estimate the number of matrix samples (or alternatively the sampling fraction 1/k) needed to realize a given standard error and confidence interval in estimating the mean, provided they can supply "educated" guesses for the internal consistency (coefficient a) among items and the variance of examinee scores in the matrix population. These expectations are not particularly limiting, especially when tests have some backlog of experience on similar examinee

populations. To illustrate the computation of k as well as the economic power of multiple matrix sampling, consider the following hypothetical situation: A relatively small school district wishes to estimate the mean performance of its 200 sixth graders on a standardized test of vocabulary containing 50 items. Previous testing on similar populations has resulted in a rather unimpressive alpha of 0.77 and a rather large examinee standard deviation of 10 percentage points ($\hat{\sigma}_E = .1$). The district does not have the time to test all examinees on all items, yet wishes to be 95 percent confident in the mean value obtained using some estimation procedure such that no more than ± .02 error will be made ($\hat{\sigma}_{\hat{\mu}} = .01$). Substituting these parameters into formula (15), the district will find that employing a multiple matrix sampling design with $k = 1 + (200-1)(.01)^2 / (.1)^2 (1-.77)$ ≐ 10 will meet these tolerance requirements assuming the parameter estimates were realistic. In other words, only 1/10 of the potential examinee-item responses in the rather heterogeneous matrix population need be sampled, using ten randomly sampled (without replacement), 20-examinee-by-5-item matrices.

The reader familiar with the elementary principles of classical test theory may have noted that the denominator in formula (15) is equivalent to the square of the *standard error of measurement* (for examinee relative scores). A third estimation approach arises for binary items due to the empirical finding of Lord (1959c) that this standard error of measurement is usually equal to the constant .432 divided by the square root of the test length (number of items, M) for most achievement tests in common use. Thus, we can assume a typical value $(.432/\sqrt{M})^2$ or $.187/M$ for the denominator in formula (15), resulting in a third approximation formula:

$$(16) \quad k = 1 + \frac{M(N-1)}{.187}\sigma_{\hat{\mu}}^2$$

Now the practitioner need only provide his tolerance specifications and the number of examinees and items in the population matrix. For example, continuing with the illustration above, $k = 1 + (50)(200-1)(.01)^2 / .187 ≐ 7$.

By inspecting these formulas, it is possible to come up with some general statements regarding the number of examinee-item observations which must be sampled to meet any specified standard error

level. It must be remembered that for our particular design, exhaustive, multiple matrix sampling without replacement, the larger the number of examinee-item responses sampled, the larger the sampling fraction $1/k$, requiring fewer (but larger) matrix samples; conversely, the fewer examinee-item responses sampled, the smaller the sampling fraction, requiring more (but smaller) matrix samples. Inspecting formula (15), we see that:

a. for fixed levels of internal consistencies (a), more examinee-item observations are required when the examinee score variance is larger;

b. for fixed values of examinee score variance, fewer examinee-item observations are required when the test has a higher coefficient a.

Inspecting formula (13), we see that:

c. for fixed values of examinee and item score variances, fewer examinee-item observations are required when the test is either easy or difficult (when μ tends to be closer to 1 or 0, respectively).

Although not necessarily the case mathematically, it is often true that the examinees' score distribution for easy or difficult tests tends to be skewed (negatively and positively, respectively), whereas the distribution for tests having μ near .5 tends to be more normally distributed; consequently,

d. for fixed values of examinee and item score variances, fewer examinee-item observations are required when the examinee score distribution is skewed; more observations are required when it is normal.

Inspecting any of the formulas, it is clear that:

e. the fewer examinee-item observations are required, the larger the standard error the practitioner is willing to tolerate.

Although these five statements were deduced from the simplest and most restrictive case of multiple matrix sampling, interpreted in more general terms they are surprisingly compatible with guidelines derived from empirical and computer-simulated studies with greater variety in design specifications and estimated parameters. (See Shoemaker, 1973b.) A major exception occurs with statement b, which is highly dependent upon the fact that the formulas are concerned only with estimating the mean. In fact, the reverse of statement b is more likely true for parameters beyond the mean (for example, variance, third and fourth moments), that is, more examinee-item observations are required when the test has a higher coefficient a.

In a manner completely analogous to the procedures illustrated thus far, it is possible to estimate the required number of matrix samples k in designing a comparative study, that is, an evaluative research design wherein two groups of differentially treated examinees are observed on the same test(s). Rather than solving formula (12) directly for the value of k, however, it can be rewritten in terms of the parameters σ_E^2 and a as follows:

$$(17) \quad \sigma_{\hat{\mu}_1 - \hat{\mu}_2}^2 = \frac{2\sigma_E^2}{knm} [M - (M-m)a]$$

Since both k and n are unknowns, the practitioner must use "trial and error" methods, substituting various trial values of k and n (and $m = M/k$) and "guestimates" of σ_E^2 and a into formula (17), until the desired level of σ_μ^2 is reached. An example of this procedure will be included in the case study at the end of this section.

The final portion of this chapter will be concerned with practical aspects of implementing a multiple matrix sampling design. Basically the following sequence of events transpires in conducting any matrix sampling study:

1. *Determine the examinee and item populations of interest.* In typical evaluation studies, more than one item population (test) is of interest; all tests must be specifically defined in terms of their item composition. Also, more than one examinee population may be of interest; for example, two different schools, or, within a given school, different examinee strata such as male-female or advanced-regular-remedial. The identification, and incorporation into the design, of examinee and item strata cannot be overemphasized. Suppose an evaluator has a population of items covering the following areas: arithmetic fundamentals, spelling, arithmetic reasoning, and vocabulary. Suppose, further, that the population of interest is a particular elementary school. Now suppose the evaluator employs the methodology discussed heretofore and comes up with an estimated mean and standard deviation. What does, for example, the mean *mean*? Obviously, it is impossible to evaluate the meaning of such summary statistics when the items represent different skills and the examinees are at different academic levels. The point is that matrix sampling should have been employed for at least six different examinee populations (the six elementary grades) and for four different

item populations (the four content areas above)—a total of twenty-four separate applications of multiple matrix sampling. This is not to say that physically the data cannot all be collected at once. But theoretically and computationally, the data must be separated.

2. *Determine the population parameters of interest.* In making this determination, it is well to specify priorities (of need) for each parameter and sampling error tolerances in terms of confidence level and magnitude of standard error.

3. *Determine the economic constraints imposed by the selection of examinee and item populations.* For example, it is possible to determine the testing time per examinee for the population battery of tests. This must be compared to the available testing time per examinee. The result is the sampling fraction as determined on the basis of economic considerations. For example, an evaluator, with a total test package (battery) requiring 10 hours of testing time per examinee and having only 2 hours available per examinee, must choose a sampling design approximating a sampling fraction no greater than 2/10 or 1/5.

4. *Determine the sampling fraction required to conform with statistical criteria stated in step 2.* If primary interest centered upon estimating the mean (or difference between means), then the procedures illustrated above could be employed. Typically, the practitioner deals with more than one test and, thus, more than one set of "guestimates" for μ, σ_E^2, σ_I^2, and a. The required number of matrix samples k (or sampling fraction $1/k$) can be computed for each test. In this way the practitioner will meet or surpass the tolerance requirements for each test. (An approximate procedure is simply to compute k for the test containing the smallest number of items.)

5. *Compare statistical results for 1/k obtained in step 4 with economic considerations in step 3 and determine "practical" 1/k accordingly.* For example, suppose economic considerations led to a required sampling fraction of 1/5. If statistical considerations dictate a sampling fraction of less than 1/5, then the practitioner can save even more testing time than required or add additional tests to the total test battery of interest. If statistical considerations dictate a sampling fraction greater than 1/5, then the practitioner must either attempt to procure more testing time, decrease the size of the test battery of interest, and/or lower the statistical requirements for sampling error.

6. *Assuming the number of multiple matrix samples* (k) *has been determined, construct and assemble* k *subtests for each item population (test) of interest.* For any item population of size *M*, each of the *k* subtests will contain *m* = *M/k* items, sampled randomly and without replacement. As such, several procedural difficulties arise:

a. M *is not an integral multiple of* k. In this case, the quotient *M/k* can be represented algebraically as *s* + *t/k* where *s* is the number of integral multiples of *k* contained in *M* and *t* is the remainder. For example, if *M* = 68 and *k* = 5, then *M/k* = 13 + 3/5 and *s* = 13 and *t* = 3. When the practitioner does not wish to alter the item population (such as using a standardized test), (*k*−*t*) items can be randomly selected from the *M* item population and added to the item population. This slightly larger population, when divided by *k*, will result in an integral number equal to *s* + 1, and we can set the number of items (*m*) in each subtest equal to *s* + 1. In the above example, *k* − *t* = 5 − 3 = 2, adding 2 randomly selected items out of the 68-item pool back into the item pool results in 70 items; 70/5 = 14 = (13+1). Computationally the 5 subtests of 14 items each are treated as though they came from a 68-item population; in effect, 2 random items are sampled *with* replacement, only one time, doing little (if any) harm to the theoretical formulas. The practitioner who can, in fact, alter his item population, can either delete *t* items or add *k* − *t* items (changing *M* to *M* − *t* or *M* + *k* − *t*, respectively) and conduct the computations accordingly. Alternatively, the practitioner can simply deal with unequal subtest sizes such that *t* of the subtests contain *s* + 1 items and the remaining *k* − *t* subtests contain *s* items.

b. *Assembling subtest batteries.* Although fairly tedious for large item populations, especially when several or more populations are of interest, each of the *k* subtest batteries can be defined using a random numbers table to select the items and reproducing the items into separate subtest booklets. Suppose *k* = 5 and item populations *A*, *B*, and *C* contain 35, 60, and 75 items, respectively. The first subtest battery would contain 7, 12, and 15 items (randomly sampled without replacement) from tests *A*, *B*, and *C*, respectively; the remaining 4 subtest batteries would be similarly formed. One random permutation of *A*, *B*, and *C* (for example, *CAB*) is usually selected, and the items are arranged by content

accordingly in the five subtest packages. Alternatively, a random order of the 34 items within each subtest package can be determined and items arranged accordingly. The advantage to scrambling items across content in this fashion is to prevent any systematic incompletion of items of a given content for those individuals unable to complete the subtest batteries in the allotted time.[23] This alternative assumes no separate timing problems for specific groups of items and no context effects due to scrambling test content. (See Sirotnik and Wellington, 1974, for supporting evidence on the latter assumption.) Several computerized systems have been developed to form random subtest batteries given the matrix sampling design parameters. (See Gorth and Grayson, 1969, and Barcikowski and Patterson, 1972.) One organization[24] has developed a system whereby the "skeletons" of the random set of items for each subtest battery are generated on 8 1/2 x 11-inch paper, numbered consecutively, and coded so that the "meat" of the item can be added (cut and paste methods); the results are the actual test booklet pages, suitable for photographing and reproduction.

c. *Intact item groups.* It is often the case, for example, in reading comprehension, graph, and map interpretation, and other areas that a group of items are to be answered in relation to a preceding written paragraph or figure. Assuming context effects are minimal, it is recommended that each item and its associated paragraph (or figure) should be reproduced for each associated item when that item appears at random in a particular subtest.

d. *Stratifying on item difficulties.* Just as it is important to stratify the item population in terms of content, it is important that, for a particular item content, no one subtest happens to contain a disproportionate number of difficult (or easy) items—or, in the case of attitudinal items, "favorable" (or "unfavorable") items. If the logistics are not prohibitive, items within each content population should be arranged into several difficulty strata, and stratified random sampling of the items should be used in forming the k subtests. If this stratification is not performed, the practitioner should at least inspect the random subtests for dispro-

---

23. Timing of subtests is proportional to the timing of the total test on a per item basis. In all cases, timing should be generous, as for a power (vs. speeded) test.

24. Applied Technology Center for Education (see note 19, above).

portionate allocation of item difficulties; should this occur, it would be well to randomly rearrange the items among subtests to reflect a more equal distribution of item difficulties upon inspection.

7. *Administer subtest batteries to examinee subgroups.* When the entire population of N examinees are to be tested, we conceptualize k examinee subgroups, each subgroup containing $n = N/k$ examinees randomly sampled without replacement. If $N = 1,000$ and $k = 5$, then five random examinee subgroups having $1,000/5 = 200$ examinees each would be formed, and each subgroup would respond to a different subtest battery. In actual practice, however, the examinee subgroups are rarely formed in advance; instead, the subtest booklets are administered to the N examinees in random order such that there will be nearly equal numbers of examinees randomly receiving and responding to each of the k subtest batteries. To ensure this kind of randomness, subtest booklets can be arranged consecutively (1, 2, 3, 4, 5, 1, 2, 3, 4, 5, 1, 2, . . . , etc.) and passed out to examinees in that order. Or, if administered in more than one examinee group (perhaps by classroom), subtest booklets should be arranged for each group in a different cyclical order (Group 1: 1, 2, 3, 4, 5, 1, 2, 3, . . . ; Group 2: 4, 5, 1, 2, 3, 4, 5, 1, 2, . . . ; Group 3: 2, 3, 4, 5, 1, 2, . . . , etc.) and passed out consecutively. In this way, there will be no systematic tendency for more or less examinees to respond to a given subtest booklet. The procedure increases in complexity if the examinee population is stratified on some important variable (school, sex, achievement level, for example). The easiest procedure is to make sure that strata are physically separated into different examinee groups and subtests are administered as suggested above. In this way, the multiple matrix sampling design is essentially replicated for each examinee stratum.

8. *Compute required parameter estimates and confidence intervals.* Regardless of whether the computational phase is done manually or by computer, the data are essentially rearranged by test content, item subtests, and examinee subgroups so that matrices of the form illustrated in Figure 8-7 can be analyzed and pooled with similar matrices for each specified examinee and item population of interest. Scoring test booklets can be most easily accomplished using coded (by item subtest and examinee subgroup) electrographic or optical scanning scoring sheets on which examinees respond to the subtest

items.[25] Using an item scoring code (generated at the time items were organized into subtests) specifying the test content and the correct response, the data can be reorganized into the required examinec-item response matrices. These in turn are analyzed following the procedures outlined earlier. Again, computer programs are available for accomplishing this entire sequence of events. (See Gorth *et al.,* 1971; Shoemaker, 1973b; and note 24, above.)

In an attempt to summarize the entire matrix sampling process as discussed in this chapter, the following actual case study will be detailed point by point in line with the eight procedural steps indicated above. Once again, it is acknowledged that many of the guidelines and computational procedures presented here have dealt with a rather specific application of matrix sampling—namely, exhaustive, multiple matrix sampling without replacement, where primary interest centers upon the estimation of the mean and its associated confidence intervals. Although specific, this design is representative of a great number of applications of matrix sampling studies in educational evaluation to date. Furthermore, the procedures and guidelines generalize quite readily to parameters beyond the mean, such as variance, and third and fourth moments, assuming the appropriate theory and formulas comparable to that presented herc are available in a form suitable for the practitioner. With this in mind, the following case study[26] can be viewed as a prototype for those possible in more general situations.

1. *Determination of examinee and item populations.* The examinee population consisted of 2,463 eighth-grade students spread among six elementary (K-8) schools comprising a single, rather large district. Although the matrix sampling design was replicated within each school, so that parameter estimates could be obtained for each

25. An alternative and quite flexible procedure is to use prescored (cut) IBM cards in similar fashion to the machine tabulation system now in practice for absentee balloting in large elections. Examinees can punch their responses into one (or more) IBM cards keyed to an accompanying subtest booklet. This method can be particularly useful in large-scale survey studies employing matrix sampling methodology.

26. Gratitude is again expressed to the Applied Technology Center for Education for supplying the data used in this case study and many of the practical procedures recommended herein.

school separately, primary interest centered upon obtaining parameters estimated for the district as a whole. Five different item populations were of interest, each constructed by combining items from several different sources (primarily teachers, curriculum specialists, and standardized tests). These tests (item populations) consisted of the following content and number of items: mathematics (88), science (52), social studies (64), reading (52), and language arts (56). All items were multiple choice and dichotomously scored (1 = correct; 0 = incorrect). The items within each population were considered to be homogeneous and representative of specified sets of curriculum objectives (that is, content valid), such that a summary score over all the items would be a meaningful index of achievement in the particular content area. Thus, $N = 2,463$ and $M = 88, 52, 64, 52,$ and 56 for the five item populations, respectively.

2. *Determination of population parameters of interest.* Primary interest centered on estimating the mean examinee proportion correct score for each item population and the standard error of these means such that, for each test, the district could be 90 percent confident that the true means fell within an interval no wider than 4 percentage points. Of secondary interest was the estimated standard deviation of these examinee scores for each item population. Additionally, it was of interest to estimate the internal consistency for each item population—coefficient alpha, or, in this case, K-R 20).

3. *Determination of sampling fraction dictated by economic constraints.* Previous experience with similar test items indicated an approximate testing time per item of 45 seconds for any given examinee. This estimate was fairly liberal so that the items would constitute power tests of ability, containing no factors related to speed of performance. Thus, given a total of 312 items, total testing time for the combined populations of items would be estimated at $(312)(.75)/60$ or about 4 hours. In fact, no more than 1 hour of testing time was available for any given examinee. (Each class period was 40 minutes long and the schools' staff was willing to extend testing through nutrition (20 minutes), but not eager to tie up more than one class period.) Thus, practical considerations indicated that at least four matrix samples could be drawn, that is, the sampling fraction could be no greater than 1/4.

4. *Determination of sampling fraction required by statistical criteria.* As indicated above, the district required a 90 percent confi-

514 Kenneth A. Sirotnik

dence interval for the mean no wider than 4 percentage points. Translated into standard error units, the district wished to estimate the mean such that the standard error would be no more than .0122. This can be deduced from consideration of formula (6) for the 90 percent confidence interval, namely, $\hat{\mu} \pm 1.64 \hat{\sigma}_{\hat{\mu}}$. Since no more than 2 percentage points of error can be tolerated on either side of the estimated mean, $1.64 \hat{\sigma}_{\hat{\mu}}$ must equal .02 or $\hat{\sigma}_{\hat{\mu}} = .02/1.64 = .0122$. Also, previous experience with item and examinee populations like those used here indicated that the population parameters behaved much like those commonly found in standardized test results. Instead of "guestimating" likely values of μ, σ_E^2, and σ_I^2, it was therefore decided that the empirically justified formula (16) would be sufficient to estimate the number of matrix samples needed to meet the statistical criteria. Thus, k was calculated for the smallest of the item populations (the reading and science tests) containing 52 items as follows:

$$k = 1 + \frac{(52)(2463-1)(.0122)^2}{.187} \doteq 103$$

The enormity of this result indicates that the district can achieve virtually any level of precision, primarily due to the fact that the population of examinees is large and every examinee is destined to be tested on some items. In point of fact, the district also wished to estimate the parameters for each school. Since the schools were approximately equal in size, they each contained approximately 410 examinees. To gain the required precision in each school, k would be recalculated as follows:

$$k = 1 + \frac{(52)(410)(.0122)^2}{.187} = 18$$

Thus, only 1/18 of the data could be collected to achieve the desired σ_μ whether estimating the mean for the entire district or for a single school.

5. *Determination of the "practical" sampling fraction.* Clearly, the district was in good shape; it could reduce the testing time by 17/18 by constructing 18 different subtest batteries requiring only (4)(60)/18 or roughly 14 minutes of testing time for any examinee. However, with this design, item subtests as small as 3 items each would be formed for the smaller item populations. Although this was

sufficient for estimating the mean, estimating the standard deviation was also of importance. Since the standard deviation is a function of the systematic variation among all items, the more items included in each subtest, the better (smaller standard error) the estimate of the standard deviation. In view of the time leeway possessed by the district, it was decided to increase the sampling fraction, adding more items to each subtest and more precision to the standard deviation estimates (as well as the K-R 20 estimates to be computed).

An experimental variable was also included in the study: a random half of the examinee population was to receive the subtest batteries arranged in scrambled item content (items randomly arranged regardless of content), and the remaining random half of the examinee population was to receive the subtest batteries arranged in fixed item content (items organized in sections according to context). This would test the hypothesis that there is no difference in mean test performance whether items are segregated or mixed in terms of their content. In other words, the multiple matrix sampling design would be replicated twice: once using the scrambled subtest forms and once using the fixed subtest forms, each replication being conducted on groups of approximately 1,230 examinees. The district wished to be 95 percent confident that the true mean difference between the treatment groups (for each test content) was also contained in an interval no greater than 4 percentage points. In other words, the district was willing to reject the null hypothesis $H_o : \mu_1 = \mu_2$ at the .05 level of significance if the absolute value of the difference $\hat{\mu}_1 - \hat{\mu}_2$ was equal to or greater than 2 percentage points. Thus, the maximum tolerable standard error of the estimated mean difference was computed as follows: $.02 = 1.96\sigma_{\hat{\mu}_1 - \hat{\mu}_2}$ or $\sigma_{\hat{\mu}_1 - \hat{\mu}_2} = .01$. Making a rather conservative "guestimate" of .7 for the expected value of a, the empirical relationship $\sigma_E^2(1-a) = .187/M$ provides a "guestimate" for the expected value of σ_E^2, namely $.187/(52)(1-.7) = .012$. The reader can verify that the equality given by formula (17) is approximately satisfied by trial values of $k = 15$, $n = 1230/15$, and $m \doteq 52/15$ as follows:

$$(.01)^2 \doteq \frac{2(.012)}{(15)(82)(4)} [52 - (52-4)(.7)]$$

By sampling fifteen matrices within each treatment group, therefore, the district could probably attain its desired sampling precision.

Recall, now, that the total test battery required 4 hours of testing time; the maximum time available was 1 hour, making the largest sampling fraction possible 1/4. The district was clearly in the pleasant situation of having more time available than was required for achieving the statistical precision in all analyses it desired to undertake. In fact, the district could consider shortening the testing period, adding additional tests (contents), increasing its tolerance levels, or some combination of all three. In the final analysis, however, it was decided to make use of all available testing time without adding any additional tests. In other words, 4 matrix samples would be constructed ($k = 4$), with the sampling fraction $1/k = 1/4$. With this decision, the district figured it could possibly achieve even more estimation precision and, at the same time, obtain more items in each matrix sample thus improving the estimation of the standard deviation and other parameters of interest beyond the mean.

6. *Construction of subtest batteries.* Since $k = 4$, four equal-sized subtests were formed from each item population by randomly sampling $m = M/4$ items without replacement, four times, for each item population. Table 8-6 presents the actual values of m and M for each

Table 8-6
Subtest design for $K = 4$ for five item populations

Item population	Population size (M)	Subtest size ($M/4$)
Mathematics	88	22
Science	52	13
Social studies	64	16
Reading	52	13
Language arts	56	14

item population or test. After the subtests were formed, they were randomly combined across contents forming four subtest batteries, each containing $(22 + 13 + 16 + 13 + 14) = 78$ items. In view of the experimental variable included by the district, each subtest battery was organized in two different formats, scrambled and fixed item content arrangements. Thus, eight different booklets were printed and coded as follows: 11, 12, 13, 14, representing the four subtest batteries with the fixed format; and 21, 22, 23, 24, representing the

same subtest batteries with the scrambled format. No stratification on item difficulties was attempted; inspection of the data below shows relatively little variability in the estimates of the mean by each matrix sample for each test, indicating a fairly proportionate representation of item difficulties in each subtest.

7. *Administration of subtest batteries.* Testing was conducted separately at each of the six schools in the district and, within each school, separately within the eight to twelve classrooms containing students (examinees) at the eighth-grade testing level. In packaging the booklets for delivery to the district, the total enrollment for each class at each school was ascertained. A separate package was then prepared for each class with the maximum number of subtest booklets required, ordered consecutively (11, 12, 13, 14, 21, 22, 23, 24, 11, 12, 13, . . . , etc.) and beginning at a different cycle for each classroom (13, 14, 21, 22, 23, 24, 11, 12, 13, 14, . . . , etc.). Each booklet contained a precoded optical scanning scoring sheet, coded in terms of treatment group (1-2), subtest number (1-4), and school (1-6). At the time of administration, the booklets were handed out in each classroom row-by-row (or column-by-column) in the order packaged. In this way, the total district examinee population was randomly, and near equally, divided into four subgroups responding, respectively, to the four subtest batteries; in addition, each of these subgroups was randomly, and almost equally, divided into two treatment groups, responding, respectively, to the fixed and scrambled item content formats. (This distribution of examinees would be expected to prevail at the eighth-grade level within each school, as well, so that all analyses could be conducted separately by school if desired.)

8. *Computations of required parameter estimates and confidence intervals.* Ignoring the experimental variable, and focusing upon the estimation of parameters for the entire district, the examinee-item responses for each test were arranged into four matrices, of the form illustrated in Figure 8-7, and computations, illustrated earlier in this chapter, were conducted accordingly. For each item population, results were obtained such as those illustrated in Table 8-7 for the mathematics test. This table presents the parameter estimates for the individual matrix samples, the final, multiple matrix sampling estimates, and the construction of the confidence interval for the mean. The district, then, reported that the estimated mean proportion

Table 8-7
Multiple matrix sampling analysis for the mathematics test

Matrix sample	Sample dimensions		Examinee-item responses($n \times m$)	Parameter estimates			
	Examinees(n)	Items(m)		$\hat{\mu}$	$\hat{\sigma}^2_E$	$\hat{\sigma}^2_I$	$\hat{\sigma}^2_{EI}$
1	615	22	13530	.75203	.03502	.01306	.12195
2	619	22	13618	.80643	.03109	.00705	.10755
3	612	21[a]	12852	.74946	.02519	.02443	.11035
4	617	22	13574	.74864	.03037	.01544	.12391
Totals:	2463 = N	87 = M	53574				
Weighted averages:				.76438	.03048	.01486	.11600

[a]Item was discovered to have more than one correct answer and was eliminated for scoring purposes.

$$\hat{\sigma}_{\hat{\mu}} = \sqrt{\frac{4-1}{(2463-1)(87-1)}} \, (.11600) = \sqrt{.0000016429} = .00128$$

90 percent confidence interval:

.76438 ± (1.64)(.00128) or .762 to .766

$$\hat{a} = \frac{(87-1)(.03048) - .11600}{(87-1)(.03048)} = .956$$

correct score for its eighth-grade students on the mathematics test was .764 or (76.4 percent) with a standard error of .00128 and 90 percent confidence that the true mean was no less than .762 and no greater than .766.[27] The estimated standard deviation of the proportion correct scores was $\sqrt{.03048}$ or .175. The estimated internal consistency coefficient (a, or in this case, K-R 20) among the mathematics test items was .956. (Confidence intervals could be constructed for the standard deviation and K-R 20 assuming the standard errors of these estimates and sampling distributions were known. With respect to the variance, there is empirical evidence that the sampling distribution is approximately normal; a formula for the standard error is available, provided the examinee population is sufficiently large [theoretically infinite], and could be used by the district in this example. Standard errors can also be empirically approximated using the "jackknife" technique for those parameters, such as KR-20 and percentiles, for which no formulas are available. See Shoemaker, 1973b, for computational details.)

Finally, the district reorganized and analyzed the data in terms of the experimental variable included in the study. Reconsider Table 8-7; approximately 616 examinees were included in each matrix sample. Because of the administration procedures and subtest battery formats, these subgroups of 616 examinees really were composed of two treatment subgroups of approximately 308 examinees each. In essence, two tables of results analogous to Table 8-7 would be formed: one table presenting the results for the four 308-examinee-by-22-item matrix samples under the fixed format condition and one table presenting the results for the other four 308-examinee-by-22-item matrix samples under the scrambled format condition. Instead of including these tables here, the summary in Table 8-8 is given showing the weighted average estimates of the needed parameters for each treatment group. Using the pooled estimates across treatment groups, the standard error of the mean difference was calculated according to formula (12) and the confidence interval constructed. Thus, the district also reported that the mean difference was estimated at .002 with the fixed group scoring less than half a percentage point above the scrambled group. The standard error of this

27. Estimates can be transformed to apply to total correct scores by multiplying by the number of math items: the estimated mean = 87(.764) = 66.5; the estimated standard error = 87(.00128) = .111; the estimated confidence interval = 66.3 to 66.6; the estimated standard deviation = 87(.175) = 15.2.

Table 8-8

Multiple matrix sampling estimates for the fixed and scrambled treatment groups

| Treatment group | Approximate matrix sample dimensions | | | Parameter estimates | | |
	n	m	$\hat{\mu}$	$\hat{\sigma}^2_E$	$\hat{\sigma}^2_I$	$\hat{\sigma}^2_{EI}$
Fixed	312	22	.76531	.03104	.02953	.11874
Scrambled	304	22	.76343	.03003	.02936	.11726
Pooled estimates	308	22	.76437	.03054	.02945	.11800

$$\hat{\sigma}_{\hat{\mu}_1 - \hat{\mu}_2} = \sqrt{\frac{2}{(4)(308)(22)(87-1)} \, [22(87-1)(.03054) + (87-22)(.11800)]}$$

$$= \sqrt{.00056158} = .00749$$

95 percent confidence interval:

$(.76531 - .76343) \pm 1.96 \, (.00749)$ or $.00188 \pm .01468$ or $-.013$ to $+.017$

difference was under one percentage point (.0075); the 95 percent confidence interval was no wider than three percentage points and included the value of zero difference. Alternatively, the district could have reported the highly nonsignificant test of $H_o : \mu_1 = \mu_2$ as follows:

$$z = \frac{.00188 - 0}{.00749} = .251.$$

The district concluded that the difference between fixed and scrambled formats was, for all practical intents and purposes, negligible with respect to the mathematics test. (Although not reported here, similar conclusions were drawn for the remaining four test contents. See Sirotnik and Wellington, 1974.)

TECHNICAL APPENDIX

Formulas (1) through (4)

Any n x m matrix sample of examinee-item responses X_{ij} can be viewed as a random model analysis of variance design, the n examinees representing a random sample from a population of N examinees and the m items representing a random sample from a population of M examinees. The usual linear model can be written as follows: $X_{ij} = \mu + \epsilon_i + \iota_j + \epsilon\iota_{ij}$ where μ is the overall "level" effect equivalent to the population mean, ϵ_i is the random effect for examinee i (his relative score over the population of items), ι_j is the random effect for item j (its relative score over the population of examinees), and $\epsilon\iota_{ij}$ is the random effect for the interaction between examinee i and item j in the population. Each random effect has a corresponding variance component denoted σ_ϵ^2, σ_ι^2, and $\sigma_{\epsilon\iota}^2$, respectively. (These components correspond to the σ_E^2, σ_I^2, and σ_{EI}^2 variance terms, which appear in the chapter under less rigorous notational conventions.)

Exhibit 1 presents the expected mean squares $(E[MS])$ and source table for this single matrix sampling design. Formulas (1) through (4) are a direct consequence of estimating the corresponding variance components of this design. The sample mean is always the best estimate of the population, hence

$$(1) \quad \hat{\mu} = \Sigma E/nm.$$

EXHIBIT 1

Source	df	MS	$E[MS]$
Examinees (E)	$n-1$	MS_E	$(1-m/M)\sigma_{\epsilon\iota}^2 + m\sigma_\epsilon^2$
Items (I)	$m-1$	MS_I	$(1-n/N)\sigma_{\epsilon\iota}^2 + n\sigma_\iota^2$
EI	$(n-1)(m-1)$	MS_{EI}	$\sigma_{\epsilon\iota}^2$

NOTE: In the chapter, MS_E, MS_I, and MS_{EI} are denoted by the quantities A, B, and C, respectively.

To derive the variance component estimates, it must first be noted that, σ_ϵ^2, σ_ι^2, and $\sigma_{\epsilon\iota}^2$ are defined as:

$$\frac{\Sigma\epsilon_j^2}{N-1}, \quad \frac{\Sigma\iota_j^2}{M-1}, \quad \text{and} \quad \frac{\Sigma\Sigma\epsilon_{ij}^2}{(N-1)(M-1)}.$$

Since we wish to estimate the actual variance quantities

$$\frac{\Sigma\epsilon_i^2}{N}, \quad \frac{\Sigma\iota_j^2}{M}, \quad \frac{\Sigma\Sigma\epsilon_{ij}^2}{NM},$$

the usual variance components must be multiplied by the "correction" factors $(N-1)/N$, $(M-1)/M$, and $(N-1)(M-1)/NM$, respectively. Making these corrections, and allowing the use of the same variance component symbols, the estimation formulas are derived by equating MS estimates with their corresponding $E[MS]$ and solving for the desired component:

$$(2) \quad \hat{\sigma}_\epsilon^2 = \frac{N-1}{N} \left[\frac{MS_E - (1-m/M)MS_{EI}}{m} \right]$$

$$(3) \quad \hat{\sigma}_\iota^2 = \frac{M-1}{M} \left[\frac{MS_I - (1-n/N)MS_{EI}}{n} \right]$$

$$(4) \quad \hat{\sigma}_{\epsilon\iota}^2 = \frac{(N-1)(M-1)}{NM} (MS_{EI}).$$

Formula (5)

The formula for the standard error of the mean in multiple matrix sampling without replacement has been given by Lord (Lord and Novick, 1968, ch. 11, formulas 11.12.3 and 11.12.4) for the special case in which items are dichotomously scored (1-0). Note, however, that the variance of all X_{ij} *in the population matrix* can be partitioned into sources corresponding with the above variance components ("corrected" definitions):

$$\sum_{ij}^{NM} (X_{ij}-\mu)^2 = M\sum_i^N (\bar{X}_{i.}-\mu)^2 + N\sum_j^M (\bar{X}_{.j}-\mu)^2 + \sum_{ij}^{NM} (X_{ij}-\bar{X}_{i.}-\bar{X}_{.j}+\mu)^2$$

$$NM \text{ Var } (X_{ij}) = NM\sigma_\epsilon^2 + NM\sigma_\iota^2 + NM\sigma_{\epsilon\iota}^2$$

Since Var (X_{ij}) is well known to be $\mu(1-\mu)$ when the X_{ij} are binary, we have

$$\mu(1-\mu) = \sigma_\epsilon^2 + \sigma_\iota^2 + \sigma_{\epsilon\iota}^2.$$

Substituting this relationship in, for example, Lord's formula 11.12.4, we obtain

$$(5) \quad \sigma_{\mu}^2 = \frac{k-1}{(N-1)(M-1)} \left[\mu(1-\mu) - \sigma_{\epsilon}^2 - \sigma_{\iota}^2 \right]$$

$$= \frac{k-1}{(N-1)(M-1)} \left[(\sigma_{\epsilon}^2 + \sigma_{\iota}^2 + \sigma_{\epsilon\iota}^2) - \sigma_{\epsilon}^2 - \sigma_{\iota}^2 \right]$$

$$= \frac{k-1}{(N-1)(M-1)} (\sigma_{\epsilon\iota}^2) .$$

Formulas (6) and (7)

These are standard formulas to be found in any elementary textbook on statistical inference.

Formula (8)

Following the Hoyt analysis of variance formulation for the general case of coefficient alpha for the M item population, we obtain

$$a = (MS_E - MS_{EI})/MS_E$$

For the $N \times M$ population matrix, we have, by definition,

$$\sigma_{\epsilon}^2 = \frac{N-1}{NM} MS_E \quad \text{and} \quad \sigma_{\epsilon\iota}^2 = \frac{(N-1)(M-1)}{NM} MS_{EI}$$

Substituting parameters for mean squares,

$$(8) \quad a = \frac{NM \, \sigma_{\epsilon}^2/(N-1) - NM \, \sigma_{\epsilon\iota}^2/(N-1)(M-1)}{NM \, \sigma_{\epsilon}^2/(N-1)}$$

$$= \left[(M-1)\sigma_{\epsilon}^2 - \sigma_{\epsilon\iota}^2 \right]/(M-1)\sigma_{\epsilon}^2 .$$

Formula (9)

Following Lord's derivation for the single multiple matrix sampling design (Lord and Novick, 1968, p. 255), we have, for the case of two populations,

$$\hat{\mu}' = \frac{1}{k}\sum_p^k \bar{X}_p' \quad \text{and} \quad \hat{\mu}'' = \frac{1}{k}\sum_p^k \bar{X}_p''$$

where $\hat{\mu}'$ and $\hat{\mu}''$ are the multiple matrix sampling estimates for populations 1 and 2, respectively, and $\bar{X}_p'$ and $\bar{X}_p''$ are the pth (of k) single matrix sampling estimates of the two populations, respectively. Then

$$\text{Var}(\hat{\mu}' - \hat{\mu}'') = \text{Var}(\hat{\mu}') + \text{Var}(\hat{\mu}'') - 2\,\text{Cov}(\hat{\mu}', \hat{\mu}'').$$

Under the null hypothesis, that is, the equality of all parameters across both populations, we have from formula (5)

$$\text{Var}(\hat{\mu}') + \text{Var}(\hat{\mu}'') = \frac{2(k-1)}{(N-1)(M-1)} (\sigma_{\epsilon\iota}^2)$$

for the case of exhaustive sampling, and

$$\mathrm{Var}(\hat{\mu}') + \mathrm{Var}(\hat{\mu}'') = \frac{2}{knm(N-1)(M-1)}\Big[m(M-1)(N-nk)\sigma_\epsilon^2 + n(N-1)(M-mk)\sigma_\iota^2 \\ + [(N-n)(M-m)+nm(k-1)]\sigma_{\epsilon\iota}^2 \Big]$$

for the case of nonexhaustive sampling (see note 14, above). Substituting above definition of the $\hat{\mu}$,

$$\mathrm{Cov}(\hat{\mu}', \hat{\mu}'') = \frac{1}{k^2}\,\mathrm{Cov}(\Sigma\overline{X}_p', \Sigma\overline{X}_p'')$$

$$= \frac{1}{k^2}\,[\Sigma\,\mathrm{Cov}(\overline{X}_p', \overline{X}_p'') + \underset{p\neq q}{\Sigma\,\Sigma}\,\mathrm{Cov}(\overline{X}_p', \overline{X}_q'')]$$

Referring to Chapter 11 in Lord and Novick (1968),

$$\Sigma\,\mathrm{Cov}(\overline{X}_p', \overline{X}_p'') = \frac{k(M-m)}{m(M-1)}\sigma_\iota^2$$

(See equation 11.13.2, on page 258.) To obtain the necessary formula for Cov $(\overline{X}_p', \overline{X}_q'')$, that is, the covariance between matrix sampling mean estimates for different item subtests across populations, we first note the formula for $\mathrm{Cov}(\overline{X}_p, \overline{X}_q)$, that is, the corresponding covariance within a given population, given by equation 11.12.2 on page 255 of Lord and Novick (1968), and written generally for polychotomous items as follows:[28]

$$\mathrm{Cov}(\overline{X}_p, \overline{X}_q) = -\frac{1}{(N-1)(M-1)}\,[(M-1)\sigma_\epsilon^2 + (N-1)\sigma_\iota^2 + \sigma_{\epsilon\iota}^2]$$

The negative sign is due to sampling without replacement from finite examinee and item populations—sampling a relatively bright examinee subgroup for one matrix sample increases the probability of sampling a relatively dull examinee subgroup for another matrix sample; likewise, a relatively difficult item subtest sampled for one matrix sample increases the probability of sampling a relatively easy item subtest for another matrix sample. However, when comparing estimated parameters across populations (for the same item subgroup sampling plan), the restriction due to the finite examinee population is no longer apparent—that is, sampling (without replacement) a particularly bright (or dull) examinee subgroup from one population does not affect the probability of sampling (without replacement) a particularly bright (or dull) subgroup from another population. Conceptually, the problem is reduced to multiple matrix sampling from a single, infinite population. It follows, then, that[29]

28. The reader attempting to follow the derivations in Lord and Novick, page 255, should note that, due to a typographical error, a *negative* sign was omitted following the equal sign in equation 11.12.2; however, the subsequent formulas there derived from 11.12.2 were not affected.

29. This formula has been proved directly by Roger Wellington, Applied Technology Center for Education (Anaheim, California), TM 73-10-01, 1973.

$$\text{Cov}(\bar{X}_p', \bar{X}_q'') = \text{Cov}(\bar{X}_p, \bar{X}_q) \text{ as } N \to \infty$$
$$= -\sigma_\iota^2 / (M-1)$$

Therefore,

$$\sum_{p \neq q} \sum \text{Cov}(\bar{X}_p', \bar{X}_q'') = -\frac{k(k-1)}{(M-1)} \sigma_\iota^2$$

and

$$\text{Cov}(\hat{\mu}', \hat{\mu}'') = \frac{1}{k^2} \left[\frac{k(M-m)}{m(M-1)} \sigma_\iota^2 - \frac{k(k-1)}{M-1} \sigma_\iota^2 \right]$$

$$= \frac{M-mk}{mk(M-1)} \sigma_\iota^2$$

In the case of exhaustive, multiple matrix sampling, $M = mk$ and $\text{Cov}(\hat{\mu}', \hat{\mu}'') = 0$. Thus, the error variance of the estimated difference between means is simply the sum of the error variances of the two estimated means, *i.e.*,

$$(9) \quad \sigma_{\hat{\mu}'-\hat{\mu}''}^2 = \frac{2(k-1)}{(N-1)(M-1)} (\sigma_{\epsilon\iota}^2).$$

However, when multiple matrix sampling is not exhaustive of the item population, $\text{Cov}(\mu' - \mu'') \neq 0$ and the more complicated formula in note 20 results as follows:

$$\sigma_{\hat{\mu}'-\hat{\mu}''}^2 = \frac{2}{knm(N-1)(M-1)} \left[m(M-1)(N-nk)\sigma_\epsilon^2 + n(N-1)(M-mk)\sigma_\iota^2 + \right.$$
$$\left. [(N-n)(M-m) + nm(k-1)]\sigma_{\epsilon\iota}^2 \right] - \frac{2(M-mk)}{mk(M-1)} \sigma_\iota^2$$

$$= \frac{2}{knm(N-1)(M-1)} \left[m(M-1)(N-nk)\sigma_\epsilon^2 + n(N-1)(M-mk)\sigma_\iota^2 \right.$$
$$\left. - n(N-1)(M-mk)\sigma_\iota^2 + [(N-n)(M-m) + nm(k-1)]\sigma_{\epsilon\iota}^2 \right]$$

$$= \frac{2}{knm(N-1)(M-1)} \left[m(M-1)(N-nk)\sigma_\epsilon^2 + [(N-n)(M-m) + nm(k-1)]\sigma_{\epsilon\iota}^2 \right]$$

If $N \to \infty$, as appropriate for randomized experimental designs, then

$$(12) \quad \sigma_{\hat{\mu}'-\hat{\mu}''}^2 = \frac{2}{knm(M-1)} [m(M-1)\sigma_\epsilon^2 + (M-m)\sigma_{\epsilon\iota}^2].$$

Formulas (10) and (11)

These are standard, inference formulas.

Formulas (13), (14), and (16)

These are the result of simple algebraic manipulations.

Formulas (15) and (17)

These formulas are the algebraic result of substituting the following relationship between $\sigma^2_{\epsilon l}$, σ^2_{ϵ}, and a:

$$\sigma^2_{\epsilon l} = \sigma^2_{\epsilon}(M-1)(1-a).$$

This relationship is simply derived by solving formula (8) for $\sigma^2_{\epsilon l}$.

REFERENCES

Barcikowski, R. S., 1972. "A Monte Carlo study of item sampling (versus traditional sampling) for norm construction." *Journal of Educational Measurement*, 9:209-214.

——, and Patterson, J. L., 1972. "A computer program for randomly selecting test items from an item population." *Educational and Psychological Measurement*, 32:795-798.

Bunda, M. A., 1973. "An investigation of an extension of item sampling which yields individual scores." *Journal of Educational Measurement*, 10:117-130.

Cahen, L. S., Romberg, T. A., and Zwirner, W., 1970. "The estimate of mean achievement scores for schools by the item-sampling technique." *Educational and Psychological Measurement*, 30:41-60.

Cook, D. L., and Stufflebeam, D. L., 1967. "Estimating test norms from variable size item and examinee samples." *Journal of Educational Measurement*, 4:27-33.

Cronbach, L. J., 1951. "Coefficient alpha and the internal structure of tests." *Psychometrika*, 16:297-334.

——, Gleser, G. C., Nanda, H., and Rajaratnam, N., 1972. *The dependability of behavioral measurements: Theory of generalizability for scores and profiles.* New York: John Wiley and Sons.

Dixon, W. J., 1973. *BMD Biomedical Computer Programs.* University of California Publications in Automatic Computation, No. 2. Berkeley, Calif.: University of California Press.

Edgington, E. S., 1969. *Statistical inference: The distribution-free approach.* New York: McGraw-Hill.

French, J. L., and Greer, D., 1964. "Effect of test-item arrangement on physiological and psychological behavior in primary-school children." *Journal of Educational Measurement*, 1:151-153.

Gorth, W. P., Allen, D. W., and Grayson, A., 1971. "Computer programs for test objective and item banking." *Educational and Psychological Measurement*, 31:245-250.

——, and Grayson, A., 1969. "A program to compose and print tests for instructional testing using item sampling." *Educational and Psychological Measurement*, 29:173-174.

Gulliksen, H., 1950. *Theory of mental tests.* New York: Wiley.

Hooke, R., 1956a. "Symmetric functions of a two-way array." *Annals of Mathematical Statistics,* 27:55-79.

―――― , 1956b. "Some applications of bipolykays to the estimation of variance components and their moments." *Annals of Mathematical Statistics,* 27:80-98.

Huck, S. W., and Bowers, N. D., 1972. "Item difficulty level and sequence effects in multiple-choice achievement tests." *Journal of Educational Measurement,* 9:105-111.

Husek, T. R., and Sirotnik, K., 1967. "Item sampling in educational research." Center for the Study of Evaluation, Occasional Report No. 2. Los Angeles, University of California.

―――― , and Sirotnik, K., 1968. "Matrix sampling in educational research: An empirical investigation." Paper presented at the 1968 convention of the American Educational Research Association.

Kleinke, D. J., 1972. "A linear-prediction approach to developing test norms based on matrix sampling." *Educational and Psychological Measurement,* 32:75-84.

Knapp, T. R., 1968. "An application of balanced incomplete block designs to the estimation of test norms." *Educational and Psychological Measurement,* 28:265-272.

―――― , 1973. "Item-Examinee Sampling." University of Rochester, unpublished monograph.

Lord, F. M., 1955. "Sampling fluctuations resulting from the sampling of test items." *Psychometrika,* 20:1-22.

―――― , 1959a. "Statistical inferences about true scores." *Psychometrika,* 24:1-17.

―――― , 1959b. "An approach to mental test theory." *Psychometrika,* 24:283-302.

―――― , 1959c. "Tests of the same length do have the same standard error of measurement." *Educational and Psychological Measurement,* 2:233-239.

―――― , 1960. "Use of true-score theory to predict moments of univariate and bivariate observed-score distributions." *Psychometrika,* 25:325-342.

―――― , 1962. "Estimating norms by item-sampling." *Educational and Psychological Measurement,* 22:259-267.

―――― , 1965. "Item sampling in test theory and research design." Princeton, N.J.: Educational Testing Service, RB-65-22.

―――― , and Novick, M. R., 1968. *Statistical theories of mental test scores.* Reading, Mass.: Addison-Wesley.

Marso, R., 1970. "Test item arrangement, testing-time, and performance." *Journal of Educational Measurement,* 7:113-118.

Owens, T. R., and Stufflebeam, D. L., 1969. "An experimental comparison of

item sampling and examinee sampling for estimating test scores." *Journal of Educational Measurement,* 6:75-83.

Pandey, T. N., and Shoemaker, D. M., 1973. "Estimating moments of universe scores and associated standard errors in multiple matrix sampling for all item-scoring procedures." Southwest Regional Laboratory, Technical Memorandum, 3-73-01.

Plumlee, L. B., 1964. "Estimating means and standard deviations from partial data—An empirical check on Lord's item sampling technique." *Educational and Psychological Measurement,* 24:623-630.

Pugh, R. C., 1971. "Empirical evidence on the application of Lord's sampling technique to Likert items." *Journal of Experimental Education,* 39:54-56.

Quenouille, M. H., 1956. "Notes on bias in estimation." *Biometrika,* 43: 353-360.

Sax, G., and Cromack, T. R., 1966. "The effects of various forms of item arrangements on test performance." *Journal of Educational Measurement,* 3:309-311.

Shoemaker, D. M., 1970a. "Allocation of items and examinees in estimating a norm distribution by item sampling." *Journal of Educational Measurement,* 7:123-128.

———— , 1970b. "Item-examinee sampling procedures and associated standard errors in estimating test parameters." *Journal of Educational Measurement,* 7:255-262.

———— , 1971. "Further results on the standard errors of estimate associated with item-examinee sampling procedures." *Journal of Educational Measurement,* 8:215-220.

———— , 1973a. "A preliminary investigation of the theoretical sampling distribution of pooled estimates of moments in multiple matrix sampling." Southwest Regional Laboratory, Technical Memorandum 2-73-03.

———— , 1973b. *Principles and procedures of multiple matrix sampling.* Cambridge, Mass.: Ballinger.

Sirotnik, K., 1970a. "An analysis of variance framework for matrix sampling." *Educational and Psychological Measurement,* 30:891-908.

———— , 1970b. "An investigation of the context effect in matrix sampling." *Journal of Educational Measurement,* 7:199-208.

———— , 1973a. "Some notes on the estimation formulas in matrix sampling." The Instructional Objectives Exchange, Los Angeles, California, Technical Paper No. 9.

———— , 1973b. "Matrix sampling in educational evaluation: Using the standard error of the mean." The Instructional Objectives Exchange, Los Angeles, California, Technical Paper No. 10.

———— , 1973c. "Determining the sampling fraction in estimating the mean using multiple matrix sampling." The Instructional Objectives Exchange, Los Angeles, California, Technical Paper No. 11.

——— , and Wellington, R., 1974. "Scrambling content in achievement testing: An application of multiple matrix sampling in experimental design." *Journal of Educational Measurement* (in press).

9

Formative Evaluation of Instruction

Eva L. Baker
University of California, Los Angeles

Formative Evaluation of Instruction

Eva L. Baker

I suffer attacks of self-recrimination at the end of lengthy exposi-
tions. I feel a little better this time because a minimum length was
suggested. Nonetheless, it has taken a long time to write and requires
somewhat less, but still considerable, time to read. Maybe we all
could have been doing something more productive. My introspective
stance derives not only from the sheer volume of words on the topic
but also from concern regarding the varied audiences that will pore
over or skim the material. Some readers will receive this with moderate appreciation. Others, usually in my same business, will wish
they had done it, totally self-assured that their effort would present
better ideas more gracefully. I assume reader reaction will be normally distributed from positive to negative. My concern is more for
those who will think that they have found a good idea or two. Is
writing about a process as complex as formative evaluation a way to
improve practice in the area of instruction? Writing, although time
consuming, seems a weak and somewhat casual way to effect change,
particularly when elaborate procedures are to be applied. So, for
once, I am constrained from ending a work with a flag-waving, snap-
py salute to education, aimed at improving the lot of all children in
schools. I have also refrained from promising to make the world of

teachers a happier place. At the very least, I must make the prediction that formative evaluation, as rendered by me, could revolutionize instruction substantially if numbers of educators were to take the idea seriously. Taking things seriously, especially ideas, is hard to do.

I fear that formative evaluation has become a jingle reverberating around schools and other places responsible for instructional planning. People quickly tire of jingles. Their messages get lost. And it may be too late already for formative evaluation. Since education is superjingleland, practitioners probably learn and discard more slogans more rapidly than they do in any other field. Very few of the ideas behind even the most exciting educational terms have survived to grow at all. To put it another way:

> Will formative evaluation be yet another soundless wave in the tide of superficial innovation?
>
> Can formative evaluation, unlike chewing gum, keep its flavor long enough to do some good?

This chapter will ignore such metaphorically burdened questions and instead broach the topic of formative evaluation as practically as possible. Formative evaluation will be described as evaluation for the purpose of improving instructional programs. Certainly other sorts of formative evaluation are possible, but the discussion here will be limited to the use of such procedures in the improvement of instruction. This chapter will attempt to provide some discussion about what formative evaluation is, what it is for, and some guidelines regarding how to go about the evaluation of instruction. Many of the points made will be subject to dispute by other, more cantankerous evaluators. A broad purpose of this writing is to stimulate the consideration of alternatives rather than to disseminate a particular set of rules or truths. The use of the term "instruction" will be construed very broadly to encompass classroom activities at all levels, including elementary, secondary, and college programs as well as programs of instruction designed for implementation in nonschool settings.

The organization of the chapter will reflect a variety of purposes. An underlying theme is my skepticism regarding the ways formative evaluation has been employed in the recent past, and, as a result, I shall encourage the consideration of alternative principles for the conduct of formative evaluation. The "principles" espoused, of course, do not rightly deserve that designation. They represent ideas and tried procedures synthesized into guidelines for formative evalua-

tion activities. You will have to assess their use in your own evaluation setting. The chapter will be organized to treat concerns related to the following broad questions: What is formative evaluation for? How does one use formative evaluation at different stages of development? What are the data sources appropriate to such evaluations? Brief treatment of topics related to data analysis, the evaluator, and evaluating the effects of evaluation also appear. And, there are optional exercises to clarify some of the guidelines proposed. These exercises may be treated as tasks for the reader to complete, or they may be read through, serving as unelaborated examples. Segments of this chapter have been subject to formative evaluation, but the entire chapter has not.

WHAT IS FORMATIVE EVALUATION FOR?

The Problem of Orientation

Years of experiments with color and number patterns have led us to the not so startling conclusion that set, or orientation to a process, is extraordinarily linked with our tendencies to understand, perceive, and accept what we are doing. If we do not have a "set" to learn colors of printed cards, we do not see the colors and concentrate on recalling only the printed symbols. Although apparently tenuous, this psychological phenomenon is particularly important for the study of innovation. Time and time again, participants go through the motions of innovation, whether writing objectives, forming teams for teaching, or developing practice materials; yet they end up with nothing real or useful. Beyond the training session itself, the in-service workshop, the lecture by a famous person, no real sense of change emerges in the day-to-day activities of educators. Things proceed pretty much as before. The primary explanation for the lack of success in implanting innovation is that educators have not perceived the usefulness of the innovation to be sufficient to warrant a change in their habits or routines. Thus, educational life goes on as usual, and the innovation is implicitly, if not otherwise, discredited.

The introduction of a concept like formative evaluation is likely to suffer from an educator's previous experience with evaluation, and any response is likely to be tinted or tainted by history. This does not bode well for formative evaluation, for evaluation is not new to educators. We have all observed testing programs that were labeled

"evaluation" in operation in our schools. While these programs were often administered with meticulous attention to the conventions of appropriate data collection, decisions based upon interpretation of the data followed only sporadically. Because people did not observe many changes attributable to the testing programs, evaluation activity was sometimes regarded as exercises rather than as an integral part of program development and improvement. Evaluation came to be seen as a burden to be borne by school people in grudging compliance with directives from above.

Some viewed institutionalized school evaluation as activity that hovered approximately four feet above real decisions about instructional programs made by administrators, curriculum specialists, and teachers. Like smog, one knows what causes the evaluation cloud, but it apparently was an evil to which school people have decided to adapt.

Press the unwholesome analogy one degree further: suppose unimpeachable sources claimed that a variant of smog had positive effects rather than the more usual sorts of outcomes. Our incredulity would be aroused, and repeated, dramatic demonstrations would be required before skeptics would come to accept felicitous claims. In the same way, I would posit that formative evaluation will not be easily accepted as a process to assist in the schools since prior experience has been that evaluation exists as a response to administrative mandates and has no immediate utility at the instructional level. Evaluation as a concept interacts with the classroom in only one narrow sense: students are often evaluated and assigned grades or categorical labels. To suggest that the main purposes of evaluation are to improve programs, to identify successful and deficient instructional activities, and to provide information that might permit the advancement of teachers and students in the act of instruction represents a drastically different picture of evaluation. Those of us committed to the prospect of evaluation for instructional improvement must find ways to elevate the debased image that routine and irrelevant formal evaluation has created. We might all be further ahead if we promulgated a new term, excising the word "evaluation" and calling the activity something else, so old ghosts would be less visible. Unfortunately, education is already suffocating in its own terminology, so much so that it is unseemly to propagate another term, despite the need.

What is Formative Evaluation?

After blithely implying that formative evaluation represents a quantum leap in potential usefulness from previous evaluation charades, let us not defer unveiling its definition. *Formative evaluation* is information and judgments to assist in the revision and improvement of instructional programs, and it will be treated as evaluation for the purpose of improving instruction. The distinction between formative and summative evaluation was well made by Michael Scriven (1967) in his original formulation of the terms. Essentially, formative evaluation demands a feedback phenomenon, where the data collected and the judgments made are used to improve instruction as it is undergoing development. The clearest sort of example of formative evaluation comes from the field of instructional development, where instructional systems or packages are consciously planned, developed, and implemented. Formative evaluation of such products requires the collection of data at many stages in the development process. The information collected has a direct purpose in that it should subsequently help one to improve the system or product so that it works better the next time.

A more common and also more complex situation, regular classroom instruction, can be conceived of as appropriate for formative evaluation. Teachers are presumably seeking to increase their effectiveness with students, and they *should* (read: "if they knew the meaning of life") welcome the use of systematically collected data to help them diagnose areas of ineffectiveness in their teaching. The availability of such information could help them find ways to improve the learning of their students.

Formative Evaluation for What Kinds of Programs?

One of the singular tasks of formative evaluation is to provide a basis against which to assess the quality of different kinds of instructional sequences. Instruction, once again, is conceived broadly to include teacher-mediated instruction, teaching through media, self-instructional materials in any form, or the provision of an environment in which each student actively plans his own activities. Ideally, in any form of extensive program development, the instruction should conform to the requirement of replicability, or repeatability. There is little sense, for instance, in mounting a full-scale formative

evaluation activity to improve teaching that is mutable and evanescent. There must be substance enough to the program to support the cost of trial and revision. If a program is not describable and repeatable, serious questions about developing it should be raised.

There is a similar analogy in the sad history of educational research. Great sums of money and enormous hopes, not to say ambitions, have been exhausted in the quest for reasonable research findings in almost every subspecialization of education. Unfortunately, most of the expended resources were wasted. Treatments were compared—for example, mathematics programs B and Z—that were not clearly described in the research reports. The researchers only rarely bothered to verify that treatment B differed from treatment Z in the planned manner. Thus, research "evidence" generated from such comparisons was meaningless (and there have been hundreds of such studies).

The situation is similar concerning the development of instruction. Programs not expected to operate in a describable manner should be regarded as unsuited to formative evaluation because data interpretation and revision suggestions will be difficult, if not impossible, to apply. In the morass of "programs" developed each year, there is great latitude in program structure. Some only suggest loose guidelines for teachers to follow in selecting content and in ordering activities. The type of program that evolves, however, depends largely upon the teacher's unique interpretation and implementation of the "curriculum." At the other end of the continuum of instructional structure is what some still call "programmed instruction." The teacher's discretion regarding activities, sequence, or purposes is subordinated to the program designer's ideas of what instruction should be. The students are given instruction in a carefully designed (and sometimes tested) format. The teacher is essentially exempted from instructional responsibility, and the role of teacher has been changed from that of instructor to that of sidelines observer. Within these extremes obviously lay a range of instructional programs, many of which tend more toward being the indescribable, nonrepeatable sort. (By the way, this continuum should not be assumed to be identical with formulations of traditional versus open structure curricula. Some open structure classroom developments can be clearly described and replicated in terms of the types of opportunities available for learners. Revisions based on formative evaluation are possible in

these cases.) Programs that are intended to provide total teacher option over program content and instructional opportunities may profit little from data-oriented formative evaluation since any program effects will be only indirectly attributable to the central design of the curriculum.

More importantly, what implications for decisions will formative evaluation of such programs have? If the premise of teacher option is not to be challenged, then the answer is straightforward: formative evaluation of such program effects will not be useful for revisions in program sequence, or content will likely make little difference in the way the program operates. Thus, at best, the data of interest in this situation are how the teacher feels about the program and whether the teacher wishes to continue to use it or to see it adapted. Notice that pupil performance data are not particularly germane since there is little reason to suspect that program revisions will have any particular effect in that arena. The manner in which publishers typically evaluate textbooks follows a similar pattern. Teachers are queried regarding their appraisal of text material, and they may suggest revisions. Because texts are essentially tools to be used at the complete discretion of the teacher, the assembling of performance data on students is close to meaningless in the sense of serious formative evaluation.

To remind you, the uselessness of the data stems from the fact that we cannot say how the materials were used in the first place. Formative evaluation implies change, and there is no initial concrete set of events from which to depart. It is certainly possible, however, to test textbooks, curricular guidelines, and almost anything else using student performance as a dependent measure. One could tell if a program, curriculum, text, or random innovation, however it happened to be used, was having any effect on student performance. If testing is done, however, one should use control groups and do it right. The data help us understand the use of the program produced. The data assist in the *formative* evaluation of instruction itself only when one has an idea of what actually happened in the program or when one can make changes in program design that will be reflected in the next tryout.

One could draw at least two disparate conclusions from the above discussion. Either formative evaluation is not important for school programs since the repeatable or replicable character is not a strong

characteristic of most classroom-based development efforts, or some
school-based programs should attend to the development of more
replicable instruction, recalling, of course, that a program can be
replicable without being either "programmed" or homogenized
through use of mimeographed lesson plans.

Remember, formative evaluation implies evaluation for the improvement of instruction. Programs that do not have the intent to be
responsible in describable ways for producing learning growth are
"unrevisable" and should not be subjected to formative evaluation. It
would be a waste of time and resources. It could build expectations
that never materialize, further discrediting evaluation activity. Save
formative evaluation for programs where there is a commitment for
the program to bear responsibility for student performance, and
some likelihood that changes in program operation will be impli-
mented.

Contexts for Formative Evaluation

Formative evaluation of instruction can be considered in a context
of grace and purity, apart from the requirements of the schools,
teachers' strikes, parent conferences, and bussing concerns. Anointed
agencies devoted to instructional development activities provide a
source of examples through which the contribution of formative
evaluation can be assessed. The situations are valuable to consider,
and, even though the problems faced by developers and their institutions are as complex and troublesome as those of the schools, the
concentration of development agencies on formative evaluation
allows one to see what is happening without becoming lost in larger
school-district-type concerns that impinge only indirectly on instructional effectiveness.

As a final aside, instructional development people in research and
development (R&D) settings often contend that they operate on a
high empirical plateau, and, in some ways, they are correct. Their
decisions are presumably informed by data describing program
strengths and weaknesses. Staff in instructional program development settings, such as regional laboratories, have had a longer history
than school people in looking at specific program effects in terms of
obtained outcomes. Therefore, the R&D situation provides a model
both for many of our subsequent illustrations and for modified emu-
lation by practitioners in the schools.

Broad Concerns of Formative Evaluation

In considering newly hatched instruction and attempting to determine if the chick is acceptable, we, as formative evaluators, must attend to certain basic matters. First, we must determine what the results of the program were. Second, we must be prepared to diagnose areas of weakness in order to improve instruction through subsequent revision. Third, we are obliged to limit the number of subjects exposed to an initial or early rendering of a program because the number of students exposed must be minimized in programs where confidence is low. Fourth, any formative evaluator should limit costs of early program versions because the instruction may need to be substantially reworked.

Categories of Formative Evaluation Data

When acting in our role as evaluator or developer, we must also consider some of the broad classes of data most pertinent to the formative evaluation of instruction. First, some product or outcome data is needed. We also need information that tells us what the program is doing and how students performed. We can label this category as *program effects.* These effects may be related only to the goals announced by the progenitors of the program, or they may also include an analysis of the unanticipated results that use of the program produced, whether positive or negative. Assembling data on effects is essential to provide a basis for determining whether the program needs improvement.

Besides data to determine program effects, a second important focus of formative evaluation data is derived from analyses of the instructional process itself. How the program is operating, adequacy of presentation, of sequence and format are concerns of *instructional process* evaluation. The main purpose of such evaluation, in a formative context, is to diagnose points of inadequacy in the program and indicate where program revision might be needed.

Formative evaluation mainly relies on data about program effects and the instructional process. These categories of data collection help us determine what is working in the program and what aspects might be improved.

The trick in formative evaluation is to correlate the data on program effects with the information on the instructional process so

that revisions instituted will have a high probability of success. Given the wobbly state of the art in instructional design, with imperfect or nonexistent evidence, successful interpretation of data is many times an unfulfilled desire.

Another important concern in formative evaluation is the manner in which data are collected. Information should be gathered in a way that does not wreak undue violence on the students who are program participants. Finally, formative evaluation should be conducted so that it does not interfere with important scheduling requirements of instructional program development. Procedurally, we should try to find ways to collect information about both the effects and processes of instructional programs and do so in a manner that is economical of all the resources in our instructional setting, including time, money, and psychic energy.

Since formative evaluation is always conducted in a decision context in order to collect enough information to help decide what and what not to change, the first rule of formative evaluation is pretty straightforward. *We must collect information on areas that we can do something about.* This pithy, if colloquial, mandate may seem to belong to that ever-expanding pile of educational platitudes. Why, a reader might conjecture, would anyone collect data about an area that would not be germane to improving a program? A look at formative evaluation documents should convince any skeptic that data are often collected when an evaluator's brain is on automatic pilot, showing little concern for whether the data are useful.

There are, for example, numerous reports of data collection in formative evaluation situations where standardized test information is being recorded. There is absolutely no intention of using the information to improve the program, and, even if there were, there are no well-known ways to improve instruction based on tests of the standardized achievement sort. Because standardized tests have been frequent accouterments in evaluation situations, however, the formative evaluator decided to give such a test again.

Someone might benignly counter with, "Why not? How can more data hurt us?" I would argue that collecting such information uses up valuable time and money. It also exhausts the patience of individuals close to the testing process, namely, teachers and students. Subsequent analytical routines conducted on the data have very little bearing on any reasonable sets of interpretation, reducing the hope for

program revision. To paraphrase a tenet of Eastern philosophy, in the case of formative evaluation data, less is usually more.

When collecting the kind of information useful to program revision, one might easily suppose that it would be useful for the evaluator to know or have some understanding of the range of decision alternatives that exist for the administrator of a program. For instance, if an evaluator determined that children exposed to instruction consisting of 75 percent film liked school better than control group children, the data would be interesting but not particularly useful, especially if the program administrator had no discretionary power to fire teachers and replace them with Bell and Howell automatic projectors. The usual formative evaluation effort should be directed to collect information that can assist in the range of decision alternatives open to the program administrator or developer. Collecting extra information usually is costly both in terms of aggregation and in the inherent wastefulness and negativism of polishing something not useful or admired by anyone.

How Many People Do We Need?

A second general guideline for formative evaluation is related to the first. Just as data sources need to be selected on the basis of how well the information relates to the range of available decisions, the number of subjects selected to try out a program must be regulated by the purpose of the trial. For instance, it makes sense that, when a new set of materials is undergoing development, very few students be used to try out first drafts. We restrict the number of students in this case because we do not know as yet if the program is any good and thus want to limit the potential damage it might do. Also, a more detailed analysis of students' responses is possible if students are fewer in number. Some developers recommend that one student be involved as a learner-informant, talking through difficulties with the program as they are encountered. Other developers recommend using just a few students at first and then, if the instructional sequence seems to be gaining effectiveness, increasing the size of the groups. The process starts all over again when considering how well teachers are implementing materials or programs. First, perhaps, it would be wise to look at just one or two classrooms. Assuming success and no major disaster, more classrooms would eventually be involved. I belabor this point because it is written somewhere that one needs a

number of 30 to approximate normal distribution, so many formative evaluators try to involve that number at any field trial. Large amounts of data may encourage some of us to feel like true scientists, but I discourage such desires for enormous numbers of students because of the inevitable delays caused in development activity. Waiting for data from formative evaluators with the clock running out on the development schedule has proved a sad experience for many of us. We wait for data knowing well that we should be preparing for field tests. None of the alternatives are satisfactory. Either we can wait and then do a rush job once the data analysis arrives, or we can forge ahead without the data, hoping that we made good choices. This action renders the idea of empirical development irrelevant, for the data come at a time when they can be used only to confirm or refute decisions already made.

Since most development agencies run on thin resources and tight schedules, expanding the number of subjects usually increases exponentially the delay in projects. When programs are well underway and there have been a few successes in limited tryout settings, then using more students in field tests might be justified. Certainly, the focus at this latter point of program testing would be on how to use the materials in more usual classroom settings. It also wastes paper to produce a thousand copies of one's first draft. The instruction probably will not be perfect, and revision will almost certainly be needed. So, along with the guideline to gather data that can help you make improvements, there is a second: use very few subjects for early versions of new programs and expand the numbers of subjects only as there is evidence that the program is working.

Consideration of formative evaluation might proceed best from an analysis of what decisions are available to program developers at various points in the process of generating or improving an instructional program. Zealots might claim the applicability of formative evaluation to all points in curriculum development. For instance, needs assessment activities may be construed to be formative evaluation of goals; tryouts of instruments may be portrayed as formative evaluation of measures; taking photographs of your children might be interpreted as formative evaluation of growth and life. In this document, I constrain my own tendencies to fit the world's major activities somewhere in the context of formative evaluation and limit direct concern to the area of instruction. It is true that sometimes the goals of pro-

grams are changed as a consequence of instructional tryouts. Similarly, measures and instruments often change as a result of the evaluation of a program. There is enough to say about the peculiar problems of formative evaluation for instruction in such a short work as this. The virtues and processes of formative evaluation in disparate arenas must be left to others.

In a brave act of simplification, instructional development activity can be divided into *instructional prototypes* and *operational programs*. Richard E. Schutz (1970), in his now classic article on the process of instructional development, points out that the development of the prototype proceeds until uncertainty about instructional effectiveness is resolved. Resources in the development process are concentrated on getting the program to meet its goals (in a goal-oriented development context). Even beyond the limits of goal-oriented instructional development, the prototype evaluation should attend to results produced by use of the program, results that are planned, dreamed of, or surprising, both good and bad. A prototype is obviously judged to be satisfactory when the consequences it produces are viewed as "good" by the developers and their publics, and then negative outcomes are minimized or totally avoided. A successful operational version of a program has more characteristics than just instructional effectiveness. It must be able to be implanted in settings of interest, its parts must fit together properly, and, despite the "noise" of the environment, it should maintain its effectiveness.

These different sorts of development outcomes have, expectedly, different kinds of formative evaluation data requirements. Guidelines to be presented regarding formative evaluation will vary, therefore, with the stage of development of the program, and vary most directly with the kinds of decisions that program developers need to make.

FORMATIVE EVALUATION OF INSTRUCTIONAL PROTOTYPES

In this discussion of formative evaluation, the emphasis has been on data collection of a rather formal sort. That is, data on program effects and instructional process may seem to suggest that student responses serve as the only legitimate basis of information. Another data requirement needs to be met. The segment or total instructional prototype needs to pass a prior set of criteria. These criteria, for

want of more eloquent descriptors, can be grouped together to tell us if the program looks the way it is supposed to look. We can determine that using either hard or soft edges to our measures. Probably both should be used.

The Way the Prototype Is "Supposed" to Be: Internal Review

The awkwardness of this subhead is engendered by my hesitancy to talk about the plans that the program developer has made. If planning and specification activities have characterized the development process, then, by inspection of the materials of the program, one might be able to ascertain the extent to which the program appears to be in satisfactory condition. Such review is conducted with respect to the written specifications of desired outcomes and constraints of setting that the developers have evolved in their formulation of their task. On the other hand, as any number of individuals suggest, not all projects have engaged in "prespecification" in any overt way. Instead, the staff operates in an "evolutionary" model (Wardrop, 1974) when goals emerge as a consequence of trials of materials, rethinking by developers, remarks by friendly critics, and so on. It is still possible to review material without clear goals or measures prior to the actual tryout of the program in a laboratory or school setting. The types of criteria one uses were long ago described as "internal" by the Joint Committee on Programmed Instruction and Teaching Machines (1963). A partial listing of dimensions for emphasis during reviews of materials follows.

Content-based Review

Are the materials accurate? Content experts can look at curriculum materials, instructors' guides, and learner activities to determine if the concepts are presented properly and reflect the most accurate information within the field. A very simple example of content review might require that someone check mathematics materials to ensure that information regarding set theory and diagrams illustrating sets are free of error.

Does the content reflect an "appropriate" range? Again, depending upon project intents, there is often a concern that materials contain a representative set of concepts, rather than being unintentionally restricted to a narrow set. For instance, if a course were named "Introductory Psychology," the content reviewer might be interested

in determining whether the chosen content represented major legitimate forms of psychological inquiry—such topics as development and maturation, learning, clinical, social, and experimental psychology. If the course, as designed, heavily overrepresented a learning approach, the content reviewer should so inform the staff. Although such overemphasis might have been deliberate, unconscious prejudices are often reflected in instructional plans, and this might be remedied prior to tryout of the instruction.

Instructional Review

Is the product well designed instructionally? The character of the instructional review is *in part* determined by the extent to which the project staff pursued conscious goals during development. For instance, if instructional specifications were fairly clear, a reviewer could estimate the extent to which the instruction reflected adequate practice for acquisition of the skills intended by the program. Similarly, materials or plans could be critiqued from a viewpoint of research in organization and memory to determine whether adequate structuring of conceptual material had been incorporated into the design. In "hard-line" instructional development, this task is partially guided by the design specifications themselves. For example, developers may have planned to use certain principles of learning. In a good technical review of instruction, the reviewer's task is twofold: to determine the extent to which the developer's materials adhere to what was intended, and to find out whether other instructional design principles might be suggested for use.

Does instruction account for all planned outcomes? When goals are specified, this aspect of review is not difficult. Sometimes, however, the development staff fails to include all goals deemed important. The most frequent omissions are effective goals. Probably the best indication of the usefulness of the instructional reviewer's role occurs when one considers the importance for most programs of developing positive attitudes in learners. Many projects have been reviewed with an eye to assessing the extent to which materials incorporated "principles" of learning. Yet, if the reviewer had understood the importance of affect and had attended to all the issues of motivation, maintenance of interest, and other affective strategies, certain instructional procedures would have required radical transformation.

In situations where those in charge of program development have

(either willfully or otherwise) imprecise ideas of their product's outcomes, then the instructional reviewer has a more dangerous course
to chart. Gentle inquiries must be made to find out the sorts of
things that the project development staff might like to have happen.
One can approach this delicate task by asking, "Would X outcome be
all right? Would Z outcome be so bad?" This represents an attempt
to determine the extent of interest in cognitive vis-à-vis affective outcomes (or the ideal coordinate pairing of both). My favorite instance
of this fragile inquiry strategy involved talking with a friend who was
developing an "open," "humanistic" program for training teachers.
My friend contended that any outcome was all right as long as the
teacher candidate was satisfied with his or her own performance and
could explain it. I asked, "Would you consider your program successful, if, after two years, many former students adopted highly authori-
tarian styles in the classroom and attributed their decisions to their
reactions against too much ambiguity and freedom?" He answered he
would not consider that a satisfactory outcome. (So, the moral goes,
even he had some sense of goals.) In any case, a program can be better assessed when the instructional reviewer has at least some broad
guidelines about what might be considered satisfactory.

What is the instruction's level of quality? Instructional process reviewers might also make judgmental comments about the quality of
planned instructional activities, operating from the general viewpoint
of a concerned person rather than a technically oriented instructional
psychologist. Sometimes another person's impression of an activity
that seems to us to be stimulating and delightful can be a sobering
event. Some of my best exercises have been reviewed by others, who
have unhesitatingly suggested deletion of what I considered my most
whimsical lines. Obviously, instructional reviewers are not always
right, and, as in my own case, their comments are not necessarily
always followed. They do provide a useful basis for analysis of the
"insides" of instructional products.

Accuracy and Coordination Review

Do things fit together? The remembrance to take away from this
brief section is that the simplest things ruin our plans. References to
pages that are not there or are numbered something else, a subtle
shift in labeling a concept from section to section, portions of text
omitted in typing, printing, or some other reproduction process—

these are but a short list of the sort of problems careful inspection of materials might uncover in time to be fixed. Obviously, "proofing" materials is part of it, but this practice also involves "proofing" for sense. Frustration and annoyance are generated quicker (I would guess) by materials that snipe at the learner with mispagination, omitted paragraphs, and typographical errors, than by materials that proceed smoothly but illogically. People involved in development often deal with conceptual and higher-level technical problems. They assume that when the issues of content, instructional approach, and style are resolved, the rest follows like the night the day, or the day the night, depending upon where you start. I have been personally punished by trivial errors in coordination between instructors' guides and materials, pages, labels, and other infantile disturbances—errors so small yet so important that they destroyed the validity of subsequent prototype test data.

Inferences from Internal Review

What does one wish to do with information obtained from review of content, instruction, and coordination of instructional materials? If the responses obtained from reviewers are consistent with what the project staff already knows, then implications depend upon the case. For example, when a reviewer says that a psychology course ignores issues of child development and is greeted with the reaction—"Well, of course. That was our intention."—no remedy is instituted. On the other hand, when reviewers' comments take staff by surprise— "You're right, we did ignore that area and didn't intend to."—then the staff may need to plan alternative remedies. The message here is that the staff is under no compulsion to adapt or modify materials based on internal review of the materials. They should be prepared to explain why they did not, but there should be no implications that a suggestion, once uttered, must be incorporated.

A last word about reviewing. There are people in this world who have difficulty letting go of anything. Perhaps Erik Erikson would say they never made it through one of the critical phases of growth and maturity. Skinner would suggest they have had different reinforcement histories. Whatever the epidemiology, such people, unfettered too long, can bring grief to instructional development and formative evaluation. A time to look out for them, and to identify who is and who is not afflicted, is during internal review activities.

Carriers of such tendencies may be revealed by the unwholesome pleasures they obtain by poring over materials, by their penchant for re-editing, changing roman numerals to arabic, and outlines to tables. They fuss over materials until some staff members cease to care whether the blasted things work at all. While these tendencies might be more happily portrayed as exhibits of highly developed moral conscience, too much playing around with materials looks to me suspiciously like the individual is reluctant to find out whether the program works or not. The lurking concern, of course, is that unnecessary time is spent refining instruction, on the wrong track entirely. To suggest the alternative viewpoint, keep internal reviews small and limited and, as soon as possible, verify assumptions with the learners at whom you are directing the program. Your ego investment will be small enough so you can absorb the blow of poor results, should these unhappily come crashing your way.

EXTERNAL DATA GATHERING: PROTOTYPE TRYOUTS

After the internal review process, the program or segment needs to be tried out on a sample of learners. The purpose of this trial, again, is to determine if adequate instructional attributes have been incorporated within the program as planned. There are a number of patterns in which data may be collected to provide usable information. Some of these involve pretests, others look more like experiments, and some are highly informal in implementation. In all patterns of data collection, however, certain information requirements must be met. Different sources of data for instructional improvement will be described in the following sections.

Data Sources for Prototype Tryouts

A table of useful information for formative evaluation has been constructed below.

	Effects	Instruction	Process
Student performance			
Student reactions			
Observers' evaluations			

We can look at student performance, student reactions, and observer evaluations as they pertain to whether the program was successful,

whether it generated unanticipated outcomes, or, in other words, its *effects*. We can also examine data to determine which parts of the program were probable areas for revision to find out about its *process*. In order to obtain such data, we need to employ instruments like questionnaires, observer records, and tests. The kinds of data needed and some of the problems inherent in obtaining such information are considered next.

Postinstructional Student Performance: Learning

The first source of data for the formative evaluation of an instructional program is the postinstructional performance of students on the range of outcomes anticipated for the program. One way to determine program effects is to fall back upon data from a posttest situation related to the goals of the program. Usually the way to measure these outcomes involves the use of some end-of-product task or test that samples the desired response class. Posttest performance should be considered broadly either in terms of learner behavior (doing something, like giving a speech) or product orientation (making an artifact or completing an examination). When program goals themselves are primarily affective, "posttests" may be records of observed behavior or interviews or perhaps the results of self-report instruments.

The shaky edifice upon which formative evaluation totters is based upon the skill with which the measures are prepared, the extent to which they provide a reasonable sample of the outcomes desired, and the appropriateness of the conditions under which the data are obtained. Without going into great detail, it is especially important that test situations employed to assess the effects of programs be properly constructed and that criteria used to evaluate student performance be clearly articulated.

Simply writing items that look like the objectives is no longer satisfactory. It is no particular feat, for instance, to demonstrate that after x number of trials and revisions of a program, students can be taught to "master" a certain set of items that "measure" an objective. That finding falls in the same class as significance tests on pre- to posttest performance. What assurance does anyone have that the items that happened to be generated are good measures of the objective? Behavioral objectives enthusiasts (a group from which I am only partially repatriated) are particularly attentive to the matching of

items and objectives in terms of the observable activity of the students. For example, if the objective calls for a student to select an answer from a set of four by circling the letter in front of the correct answer, the minimum requirement for a good item is that the student make circles in front of letters. Other examples could be given.

Comparing student overt behavior in the test situation with the behavior called for in the objective is obviously an insufficient, imprecise basis for validating suitability of the measure. Unfortunately, repeated seductive glances in the direction of the statisticians have produced very little in the way of empirical procedures to deal with the objectives-based test validity question. It may be, of course, that the quality of the glance is at fault. Sometimes evaluators forget that program goals must usually go beyond the particular set of test items prepared for use in formative evaluation. Performance on idiosyncratic items that are not carefully designed will certainly lead us to draw the wrong inferences from our data. The goals of the program should be tested in a way that reflects generalization of the learning. For most instructional programs, there should be a way to generate testing situations of great range. The description of test specifications should enable individuals, *other than the writer of items,* to produce replaceable sets of items appropriate to the goals. One should be suspicious if there are claims that the test used is the only possible measure of the set of program objectives.

The use of domain-referenced models of test development would surely increase the confidence we have in objectives-based measurement. Domain-referenced testing has been described by Wells Hively and others (1968) and by Millman in Chapter 6 of this volume. These models are gaining increased emphasis in the activities of evaluation. Let the point rest here that the confidence that one places in data from formative evaluation is directly proportional to the confidence engendered by the test. Seventy-eight trial and revision cycles and 100-100 performance levels mean little when there is lack of belief in the validity of the measures used to generate the ball of data.

It is ironic; data-based development is trumpeted as critical, and yet decisions about whether costly revision cycles will be required are very often made on the basis of student performance on hastily contrived tests. The caveat of careful test construction must tag along with the primary data source for formative evaluation: student performance on posttests is a crucial factor in any formative evalua-

tion activity—provided the test has been carefully constructed and is well justified. Student performance on the goals of the program is a critical data source, one that should be included in any stage of formative evaluation, from the most informal tryout of primitive materials to the grandest, most elaborate field test.

Postinstructional data may also be collected on the subobjectives as well as the criterion objectives of a program. Poor performance on subobjectives might lead one to speculate on a variety of revisions depending upon the criterion performance. For example, if posttest performance is high on program objectives, and subobjective performance is low, then one would reconsider the relevance of the subobjective to the goal. Perhaps the subobjective should be retained for its own sake, without regard to its contribution to the criterion objective. In that case, the instruction on the deficient subobjective would certainly require modification. On the other hand, poor performance on both subobjective and criterion objectives on the posttest should send one scurrying to inspect the process data on both dimensions in order to determine whether failure on the tasks was consistently mirrored in practice exercises as well. Although process data are treated in the next section, this discussion should provide you with a preview of a fact of life in formative evaluation: data sources are interrelated, and sensible interpretation will require looking at results from multiple sources concurrently. Choosing one over any other may ultimately be inefficient.

Student Performance during Instruction: Process

A second sort of student performance data is important in formative evaluation. We want to find out how the student performed during the process of instruction. The most common way of determining student performance is by collecting practice exercises or work sheets that the students completed during the instructional program. By relating performance on these exercises to posttest successes and failures on the objectives and subobjectives under consideration, the formative evaluator can determine possible errors in sequence or weaknesses in instruction for potential revisions. Sometimes records of student work are not as readily available as paper-and-pencil practice exercises. In-process work samples may be collected and rated so that points of difficulty in performance can be identified. Further, the use of an observer during the instructional process can help

pinpoint consistent problems students experience during instruction. Obviously, observation data are particularly important if the learner will be engaged in manipulative activities as part of the instruction. As with all process data, the purpose of observation is essentially diagnostic and should help in the identification of revision requirements. Student performance data during the process instruction is most useful at this prototype tryout stage of development, when instructional sequences are fluid enough for massive revision. Thus, the diagnostic function of the process data can actually be served.

Student Reactions toward the Program: Affect

Beyond obtaining estimates of student performance during and following instruction, the evaluator must also be sensitive to the attitudes and feelings the program has consciously or unwittingly developed in the student. Thus, in addition to performance, program effects and need for revision can be evaluated by assembling the affective responses of the student to the instructional program. Student attitudes can be assessed following instruction serving a post-test-like function or during instruction itself. Students can and should be asked to assess the value of the program as it affects them and to identify strengths and weaknesses in it. Different techniques can be used to acquire such attitudinal information. During the early stages of program development, when very few students are going through instruction, the lessons and activities may be observed to ascertain student reaction as the program progresses. An interview session may be arranged following the tryout to get direct reports of student reaction. Interviews must, of course, follow a careful plan so that students are not overly sensitized to the desired responses. The interview can begin in a very unstructured way and move toward structure and completeness. This pattern may also permit the identification of unplanned outcomes of a program. The simplest way to gain some rough idea of students' postinstructional attitudes toward a program may be through responses to questionnaires. A few minor rules of questionnaire giving might be in order since they are often violated in many formative evaluation situations. A simple guideline is to arrange the questionnaire and posttest in random order so that performance on the examination will not systematically bias responses to the attitude questionnaire. Second, some sort of coding procedure should be used so that students feel free to answer honestly, which preserves a means of correlating students' performance

scores with attitudes. Finally, questionnaires should be short. A few well-constructed items can provide about the same amount of useful information as detailed, elaborate batteries. Short questionnaires avoid the problem of instrument disintegration. As students respond to unending questions about instructional nuance, their tolerance for the whole enterprise is likely to deteriorate and may result in lower scores on the attitude instrument itself. In gathering attitude information, recall the first precept of formative evaluation. Acquire information that you can use in program revision.

Students can greatly assist in revision when they serve in the role of coevaluators. They may be asked to mark X's in a written program by unclear passages or examples. They may be asked to list questions that occur to them as they proceed through a set of materials. Through participation of this type, even young learners may develop the understanding that instruction can and should be improved and that their own performance and feelings are critical to its success.

PROTOTYPE DATA SOURCES: SUMMARY

To summarize the role of data in prototype tryouts, the developer at once tries to determine if the program is successful, and, if it is not, what aspects need revision. Developers are assisted in this task if good measures are available for assessing postinstructional performance of students. Following instruction, the developer attempts to obtain information regarding the reactions of students to the instruction and to detect unplanned outcomes the program produced. To assist in the task of revision, the developer-evaluator uses data derived from the instructional process. Obtaining samples of student performance, observing student behavior, and looking at suggestions students provide on written material may combine to permit the detection of program strength and weakness.

The alternative decisions for the developer who assembles such a data pool are many, but center on the main purpose of prototype tryouts: the implementation of an effective instructional sequence.

ISSUES IN PROTOTYPE TRYOUTS

Design for the Collection of Criterion Data

Suppose you are engaged in a prototype tryout of a newly developed program. You have written some items that you think (we will

not specify why) are appropriate measures of your goals. What do you do? Some people will instantly, automatically respond "pretest-instruction-posttest." Is that the right answer? Sometimes. Why might one not want to pretest? A pretest:

—emphasizes the "I-am-a-subject-in-an-experiment response,"

—may unduly intimidate respondents and result in reactive effects with the program,

—may overcue respondents to program intents and result in positive reactive effects that will disappear during regular implementation.

People continue to like pretest-posttest designs because they provide a commodity that can be displayed, analyzed, and otherwise interpreted: student gain in achievement. Without attempting a proper treatment of the statistical questions associated with raw gain scores, let me adominish those with a predisposition toward data of this sort to be wary. Tests consisting of improperly sampled items will inevitably supply results that are subject to question when gain scores are used. Regression techniques may appear to be a solution, but, given the restricted number of subjects usually appropriate for participation in formative tests, elaborate statistical treatments are not suggested. What alternative is there to a pretest-posttest design? One simple procedure is to use data gathered on another sample of subjects as base line information for the product being tried out. Such information should be available if the product was appropriately planned. There should be some ready source of performance information on the target group, information that was used to establish the need for the product and to justify development in the first place. The use of performance data in needs assessment activities has been recommended (Baker, 1973), and certainly the learners' deficiencies ought to be established in some manner before program development progresses to the stage of instructional prototype.

Experimental Comparison of Prototypes

As most instructional psychologists plainly admit, the state of the art in instructional design is relatively weak. We cannot make surefire assertions that using particular instructional techniques or strategies will produce effective products. If we could, all this formative evaluation business would be unnecessary, for we would know that certain design attributes consistently produce predictable results. How does one decide to select one or another method, format, or instructional

sequence? One little-used, but potentially important, tactic is to employ controlled experimentation during the formative evaluation phases of instruction. When one does not know whether one sequence of instructional subobjectives is better than any other, a nice solution may be obtained through a controlled experiment where two samples of individuals received alternative treatments. The cost of such experiments is relatively low, and the results might save a development staff from pursuing an arbitrarily selected strategy of instruction to ultimate defeat. Experiments are also reinforcing for developers and evaluators with research training, and they may be assigned (on intermittent schedules) by benevolent project directors as small tokens for good service.

Sampling for Prototype Tryouts

As already noted, parsimonious use of subjects is a desired characteristic of instructional prototype tests. We want to use students to get an initial idea of the utility of our instructional strategies, but, since we may be wrong, we should not involve a cast of thousands and unnecessarily expose many students to poor instructional experiences. A short-term rotten instructional experience is not, however, permanently damaging. Students only complain a little more heartily about how dumb school is. We must recognize, on the other hand, that careless involvement of students in poorly conceived instructional sequences uses up goodwill fast, and, unless your development enterprise is situated on the fringe of a megalopolis, the graciousness with which one is allowed access to students diminishes quickly.

In a recent paper, Quellmalz and Hanson (1974) argue for involving larger numbers of students in prototype tryouts. They contend that data from only a few students may be randomly sampled for analysis even though the entire class participates fully in the activity. Their argument is based cogently, I think, on the notion of generalizability. They contend that, in the case of instruction ultimately planned for classroom implementation, the classroom should be involved *at the start* of any formative evaluation activity, thereby eliminating the need for laboratory trials of prototypes. The only limit I see to their point involves the extent to which teachers are important to the instruction process. Poor results in cases where teachers play a heavy part may be uninterpretable. Instructional planning on the part of the developer might be faulty (a poor sequence of activities,

for example), or a teacher's idiosyncratic execution of instruction might destroy performance levels. In any case, the Quellmalz-Hanson notion of sampling students properly is an important one, whether or not tryouts occur in classroom or laboratory settings.

While on the topic of sample size, the question of economics comes up a number of times. Once having selected a small sample of subjects, evaluators should extract as much good information as possible from that sample. They should talk to participants, watch them, and have searching discussions with them, when feasible, in order to find out what is really going on in the program. When evaluators move to larger-scale field testing, their commitments to their programs have had time to mature, and it may be more difficult to hear and to use information of this sort. Normally, field tests themselves do not have the intimate exciting character of prototype tests performed early in the development process, when the staff has close to total control of instructional design. One might easily argue that such intimacy with the development staff can markedly enhance the subjects' reactions to the program, resulting in bias in all directions. I think that is a fair exchange for carefully exploring student reactions to programs. In any case, the program can be retested without the serious staff-student interaction.

Bank, Eu, and Mann (1974) take the position that formative evaluation is an especially collaborative effort for development staff and participants. They seem to contend that the more talking one does with participants in a tryout, the better sense one has of the adequacy of instructional plans for the target group's needs. The situation that they described in their paper was special, in that they were dealing with adult learners who were displaying resistance to the product being developed. Bank *et al.* interpret the utility of such formative evaluation sessions as providing a better check on the needs of a client group for a product than we usually obtain.

Magnitude of Prototype Products

How much of a program should be developed in order to conduct an efficient prototype tryout? How long should it be? When developers have had a history of successful experience with similar successful programs, then the prototype developed for tryout may be limited in scope and serve only a confirming role for the developers' plans. When the program being developed represents a very different prob-

lem for the development staff to solve, then the prototype program should be of a magnitude to permit ready inferences and the scope of the program should be large enough to permit data acquisition on all significant aspects. Such guidelines for program scope are obviously very general. Formative evaluation technology has produced few recipes. Certain ingredients should, however, be avoided at all costs. (No cook would put talcum in chocolate cake!)

A prototype program should represent a modest investment of time. It probably should not include essential duplications of the same instructional process. As little as possible in the way of resources should be expended in order to arrive at a decision. Conducting prototype tests on skeletal segments runs a risk, of course, that the responses will not generalize to the endomorphic form of the program. The strategy does, however, permit repetition of prototype tryouts with successively improved, larger-scale versions.

Economics of prototype tests also involve decisions about the physical design of materials. The extent of expenditure on graphic design for early versions of products is a serious concern. On the one hand, materials should not be illegible or unusually ugly, for that might produce unnaturally negative reactions. On the other hand, it is foolish to spend too much on design, fancy paper, art work, and so on, when the results of the tryout are by no means certain. Although different procedures are followed by different development agencies, largely influenced, I think, by the amount of funding available, a minimum design strategy might be recommended. Materials for initial tryouts should be in formats that do not put undue pressure on participants. Print size should be right for young children, and the iridescent purple of spirit master reproduction might be avoided. But the development staff should expect that many aspects of the materials will be radically changed as a consequence of external tryouts. Too great an investment of resources in early drafts of materials could inhibit the decision to eliminate the program, even when the data warrants it. It is hard enough to relinquish something earlier perceived as a "good idea"; it is even more difficult when the idea has handsome, expensive clothes.

To review, prototype revision involves both internal and external tryouts of materials. The use of good measures, small numbers of properly sampled subjects, a variety of data types, and carefully chosen but not overly elaborate materials are recommended.

Coordination of the results of such tests should enable the development staff to become ultimately more sanguine about its instructional sequence. Beware! It may take many prototype tests to reach that point.

OPERATIONAL TESTING

After the prototype has been successfully tested and most lingering doubts about the efficacy of the instructional sequence have been removed, the next development task requires that the prototype be expanded, combined with other components, and placed in a format that is suited to the real conditions for which it was planned. Formative evaluation comes into play when these development activities are complete. Unlike the prototype stage, where instructional effectiveness was the major concern, the operational or field test is conducted to determine the feasibility of the product under relatively natural conditions. Potential revisions from such data collection activities relate to making the product "fit" better rather than revising the instruction itself. Thus, attention in a field test is directed toward issues of program utility, access, and integration. Because instructional effectiveness is not the sole interest in field testing, data will be required from other sets of participants beyond the students themselves.

Operational Field Testings: Internal Review

Prior to distribution at field test sites, materials of a program may well need another cycle of internal review. Internal reviews at the prototype stage may be insufficient at this point for a variety of reasons. First, prototypes may be very short sequences, designed to reassure developers that they are on the right instructional tracks. Thus, a prototype for a phonics program might last only two or three instructional hours, even when the entire program was planned for a semester's use. Second, there are different requirements largely engendered by the staff's increasing remoteness from the actual instructional administration itself.

Content Review

An internal reviewer will wish to ascertain whether the program, expanded to the length of actual use, properly retains the instruc-

tional design specifications embodied in the prototype. In other words, does the content conform to what was successfully tested in the prototype? If not, do the developers know, and have they explanations? A second area of concern for content review is to determine whether all content described in objectives (if there are some) or intended by the developers is included. The same rules for determining accuracy of information certainly apply during the review preparatory to the operational field test. Mistakes in content can discredit newly developed materials more easily than almost any other class of error. A simple error in content raises suspicions that the development staff did not know much about instruction and measurement as well.

Instructional Review

In the same fashion as during the prototype test, the instructional reviewer must determine whether design requirements have been suitably incorporated into the desired program. When looking at a prototype, the reviewer may be focusing on the efficiency with which a particular strategy was employed. At this point the reviewer may also attend to the variety of experience provided for the students across program components to reduce the chance of boredom.

Format Coordination Review

Both within and among program components, the reviewer must give careful attention to the format of the program, attempting to simulate use of the program to determine if it is possible to negotiate from one component to another, given the directions provided. Clarity of directions may be the single most important new element incorporated in operationally ready materials. The program will not be tested by anyone who has special information or particular insight into the history of the development process. Instead, the directions will need to stand alone in communicating program intents. Even with nominally skilled developers, a repeated failure is their tendency to assume that directions are understood, and disasters have sometimes ensued. Thus, the reviewer can serve an invaluable service. This may be the place where there is a premium on naïveté. The less format reviewers know about the history of the program, the better reaction they can provide regarding the probable utility of the program for other novices.

Sample Size

Field tests, by their very nature, are activities that usually involve many people. Many different classrooms are used, and sometimes different schools, or even school districts, are sampled. By the time a field test is appropriate, the development staff should have more confidence in the program, and extending the number of students involved in operational program tests should not require any great lapse of conscience.

Field Test Settings

A program designed for classroom use, with a teacher guiding students through exercises and simulations, should be tried out in exactly such a setting. Only under those conditions can the formative evaluators determine whether the "great ideas" developed and honed during prototype have any chance of success in the world at large.

Decision Range for Operational Testing

In planning for any formative evaluation activity, one must determine what decisions are possible, given our stage in the development process. While any aspect of the program can legitimately be modified at any point, by the time a program is at the field test stage one can attach a broad range of probabilities to decisions:

It is not very likely that the program will be scrapped.

It is somewhat unlikely that major changes within instructional sequences will be made.

It is probable that changes in format and coordination of program components will be required.

It is highly likely that roles planned for teachers or program administrators will be modified.

Thus, in general, we might expect to prepare materials to facilitate teacher use of the program, including teacher training, and we will attend to program attributes that seem to inhibit easy access and use of materials by students and teachers. During the prototype stage, the form of the program might have been very rough, primarily because interest was directed to the innards of the instructional sequence. In operational testing, the program should be rendered in versions that closely approximate the developer's view of the "final" format of the program. One can justify the expense associated with

such renderings in the same manner as using an expanded set of participants. One has developed confidence in materials as the result of successful prototype trials. Instead of a question mark with respect to program effectiveness, the development staff now has reason to believe that the materials will be successful. Thus, an expenditure of resources on physical design of the materials represents a much smaller risk than it would in the case of an untried program.

Data Sources for Operational Field Tests

As usual, the data collected should relate to the sorts of decisions available to the developer.

Student Postperformance Data: Learning

In most program development ventures, student performance is an essential category for scrutiny. At the field test level, one wishes to determine if the quality of performance achieved in the more controlled prototype tests can be maintained under the regular conditions into which the program was placed. The standards for development of criterion-testing instruments are the same as those identified during the prototype test. It is important that performance on measures related to program goals be assessed during the field testing. Sometimes developers, for whatever reasons, like to include measures other than those designed for the evaluation of program goals, perhaps to establish something as vague as "parity" with other programs or perhaps to find unplanned consequences of the program. In general, the data obtained from use of these measures will contribute very little to the actual revision and improvement of the program being developed. Other measures can be employed, but they are not likely to assist in the formative evaluation process.

Given the large number of subjects involved in field tests, sometimes developers are tempted to modify test procedures to accommodate their administrative burdens rather than their evaluative ones. For example, many times the criterion task of interest is whether a student can actually make something, pronounce something, or do something that can be observed. We might wish to see whether the student can write compositions with different expository patterns, pronounce new words in a reading program, or improvise a speech given a topic. Some formative evaluators shudder when they think of the enormous problems generated by the examination

and scoring of so many specific instances of constructed behavior. As a substitute, they may base student performance data on responses that are more easily summarized, preferably scorable with the use of an optical scanner. Likely substitutions are discrimination measures where learners select the right answer from a list of alternatives, where the responses are easily scored with an answer key. Unless the evaluator has evidence to support the contention that performance on the discrimination and construction tasks under consideration are of equal difficulty and highly correlated, the data obtained from such trials is clearly suspect.

An alternative procedure would suggest that all students be asked to produce or prepare the criterion performance activity. A compromise in the direction of the feasibility of data processing might permit the evaluator to sample only a percentage of student work for actual evaluation. Such a sampling plan would necessarily make allowances for different teachers, school settings, or entry skills of learners. If data appeared aberrant in the sample, the evaluator would usually have the option of selecting a wider sample of responses to include in his evaluation.

Student Reactions

In the same way the posttest information tells the developer whether the objectives have continued to be met during the field test, some source for knowing what students' attitudes and interests are positively affected should be identified. A questionnaire, like that in the prototype test, should be administered to ascertain how important the students consider the program. The questionnaire can also be a means of determining if the program components have been properly integrated. For instance, it would be possible for a mathematics program to consist of workbooks, practice kits, and readings. Each of the components may have been tested in prototype form. It would be important to discover whether the components work together, whether they confuse students, whether shifting from one to another presents any problems. Questions attending to these sorts of concerns can provide the program developer with information that may be significant in revising the sequence or the manner in which program elements are related to each other. As in the prototype test, the questionnaire used in field tests should be brief, should employ a checklist or other simple-to-tabulate format, and should provide

space for comments. While questionnaires may be sufficient data sources for determining attitude toward the program, the conscientious formative evaluator might wish to interview students who participated in the program. Such interviews might follow the limited sampling plan discussed previously. Or the interviews might be conducted on a follow-up basis, with students being selected to participate in them on the basis of their data pattern during the field test. For example, students who do very well and very poorly in programs might be sampled to determine what factors might be the hypothesized causes of the performance difference. If consistent differences emerged, the program might be modified by adding a segment designed, perhaps, to remedy an entry skill.

Student Performance within the Program: Process Data

Student responses to within-program activities such as practice exercises should be collected. It is a hedge against the unpalatable likelihood that criterion performance turns out to be poor. In such an event, the developer-evaluator can inspect performance during the program in an attempt to isolate factors contributing to poor post-instructional performance. Such responses should be saved for just such a contingency, but they probably will have no other use. Remember, at this point in the development cycle there is only a small chance that the internal aspects of any learning sequence will be modified. There is a better chance that coordination across program components will be the likely culprit. It is best to learn to live with a set of data, unanalyzed, than compulsively to check each and every student response. Even if the field test were very small, with only five classrooms, there would still be somewhat over 150 students included, and each of them probably makes many responses during the program. The formative evaluation staff should avoid getting seriously involved with data-recording tasks that have little likelihood of making important contributions to the formative evaluation of the program.

Within the field test context, however, students can again be encouraged to act as coevaluators, pointing out inconsistencies that they discern among program components. A simple scheme like asking them to write question marks or X's by passages of difficulty or ambiguity may seriously assist in instructional improvement. All that is required of the staff is some scanning, again on a sampling basis, of

the program materials through which the learners worked. Areas of deficiency will be those that jump out at the evaluator because of repeated identification by different students.

Teacher and Administrator Data Sources

In data collection described so far, the student is the primary source. Student performance during and following instruction, students' attitudes determined by either interview or questionnaires, and students used as coevaluators to isolate consistent problems in program operation have been discussed.

The second major category of data collection depends upon the administrator or teacher involved in activating the program. When a program is developed specifically for use by a leader, trainer, or teacher, not only must student responses be carefully assessed, but the responses of the teachers must also be recorded.

Observation of Instructor Behavior: Process

Teacher performance in properly implementing a program must be observed during an operational field test. Areas for observation should include not only indications of adherence to specific sequence and procedure, but also anecdotal records to explore for possible program revision.

The purpose of teacher observation is, of course, partly to determine if poor student performance can be attributed to specific misdeeds by the instructor, partly to find if the teacher has discovered some better ways of using the materials or program, and partly to determine requirements, if any, for teacher training, either in the concepts or the procedures of the program.

An on-site observer who attends to critical aspects of teacher-administrator activity and prepares a report describing potential sources of weakness as well as success can record necessary information. During the first field tests, where the format decisions represent only hypotheses about what will work, an on-site recorder may be particularly useful. The record made should consist at least of a checklist of critical points: For example, was the teacher able to find materials quickly? Did the teacher follow instructional guidelines? In addition, an anecdotal record of interesting, useful, or problem-solving events should be kept, for it may provide a rich store for possible format revisions.

The one simple recommendation I would make regarding teacher observation would be to make sure the observers get an estimate of the flavor of what is happening, either good or bad, rather than only attending to elaborate coding schemes for specific teacher behaviors. Recommendations for program redesign are often made at general, rather than minutely detailed, levels anyway, so that the data assembled need not be microscopic in focus.

After the program has been reasonably successful in field-testing situations, the record of events may be kept on a periodic basis by the teacher-administrator, with no on-site development staff member present. This shift reflects the additional confidence with which the development staff comes to view the program as a consequence of periods of successful data collection activities and the desire to get some notion of how the program works without the constraining influence of the presence of a staff observer.

Reactions of Teachers and Program Administrators: Affect

Teachers' satisfaction with the instruction should also be determined through interview or questionnaire proceedings during the program to determine how the program might be made more suitable. It is one of the world's well-known facts that lack of teacher enthusiasm can wipe out program effectiveness. Perhaps it is one of the few undisputed generalizations in education. Sources of dissatisfaction may be discerned and remedied before they destroy the field test entirely.

On a regular basis, some assessment of program progress should be sought from individuals administering the program. A short questionnaire asking about major requirements of the program would be suitable. Questions or rating scales designed to assess the user's satisfaction with program design should also appear on the questionnaire. Finally, as usual, a space for open-ended comments should be provided.

Of extreme importance is the role expectation of the teacher as to what is expected of him or her during the operational field test. A research study, which shall remain unattributed, might underscore this point. A researcher gave a sample of teachers a lesson to teach. The researcher told the teachers that they could augment the lesson and that he was going to tape-record their lessons. The researcher was then properly horrified when the teachers did not depart from the

lesson as planned. If I had been a teacher asked to participate in such a study, I would have done my best to conform to the expectations that I felt were appropriate. Thus, some teachers in a field test might infer that their "goodness" depends upon how closely they adhere to particular guidelines and formats. And in some field test situations, they would be right. Yet, I have participated in other field tests where teacher deviation from procedures was encouraged, carefully observed, and correlated with the results. In some cases dramatic improvements were made in programs by watching how effective teachers reorganized and presented the materials.

The on-site observer has a delicate task. No impressions should be given that observers consider it their role to serve as arbiters of good instructional practice. To the extent that the observer can facilitate the perception of collaboration with the teachers involved in the field test, the information obtained is useful. When teachers assume, however, that observers are there to make personal judgments, teacher reactions can range from ungeneralizable submissiveness to open hostility. Fostering the perception of collaboration represents no moral hiatus on the part of the field tester since field testing requires extensive collaboration and mutual learning by all participants—students, teachers, administrators, and development and evaluation staff.

Interviews or Debriefings of Teachers and Administrators: Affect

Since the person of primary interest in a field test is the teacher or program administrator (assuming, of course, that student learning is maintained at expected levels), then the most complete sort of data should be obtained by the staff regarding how the teacher felt the program operated. Although face-to-face contacts are relatively expensive, the quality of data potentially extractable from them certainly justifies the cost. A procedure similar to that recommended in the interview of students in the prototype test stage should be followed. The interview should begin with uncued questions, the sorts of questions that attempt to elicit free responses about the program. Obviously, interviewers must try to remain relaxed and should not attempt to provide explanations or excuses for program malfunctions or teacher or administrator dissatisfaction. Data from the range of field-tested teachers can be aggregated, and indications of desirable program modifications can be inferred.

Consequences of Field Tests

One of the most likely outcomes from operational tests is the staff's realization that teacher training is required. The fact that "they" fouled up, or did not understand procedures can shock complacent staff. Teacher training will be implied when data indicate teacher dissatisfaction with materials, poor performance by students on those portions of the instruction under a teacher's direction, or observer reports of confusion when order and beauty were intended. Despite fond hopes of development personnel, teacher training cannot be decreed and assumed to work. The training should be carefully developed and should be subjected to rigorous prototype tryout, using the teacher's subsequent behavior in the classroom as the dependent measure of program effectiveness.

When is Formative Evaluation Over?

Just as with prototype tests, there is no rule limiting the number of operational field tests that might be necessary for a given program. The number of tests will be determined by how well the program is working, how much improvement successive revisions have been able to produce, and the resources and interests of the developer. In addition, if the program must be adapted to meet the needs of subgroups within the learner population, subgroups which differ on entry skills, motivational attributes, or any other significant characteristic, then the program will have to be retested until satisfactory performance is obtained in all settings and with all users of interest.

This process might not be unbroken in time. A program might be developed, field tested to a satisfactory level, and then disseminated. During the time the program is being implemented in schools (on a cash and carry plan), the development staff might be working on a revision for release two or three years later. Unlike the planned obsolescence that automobile manufacturers have been accused of, the revisions would bring serious and useful modifications to the program. The decision to release a program before it is perfect can be justified. Such a pattern of development is appropriate when one considers the level of common practice in the area being developed. In some areas that have been identified as high priority by schools, parents, and the general public, a working program would be welcome, even if not at the level or as comprehensive as ultimately

planned. Furthermore, the boundaries of what is possible for a program expand in the very act of trying to develop it. At the outset, the view may be limited, but, as the program develops, the staff's vision of the program's long-term dimension grows.

Not all programs, however, stimulate us to our highest level of thought. Many times we are relieved when the thing works and we can be done with it. That happens when we were bored, when there was no real need for the program, and when the entire venture was uphill. In cases where the program does not fill the earliest visions of implementation, it should probably not be started.

Thus, formative evaluation, in the penultimate triteness, may be viewed as a continuing process, constrained by real time and money limits, but not by the ability to do it right.

POTPOURRI

The following section includes a menu of topics too important to overlook: data analysis, who is a formative evaluator, and evaluating evaluation. They have been given the proverbial lick-and-promise treatment.

Data Analysis for Formative Evaluation

If one is reasonably compulsive about observing the appropriate protocols of data collection and, at the same time, moderately circumspect in sampling information from a variety of sources using a range of instruments, no one should be startled to discover that a considerable data analysis and interpretation task remains. This segment of formative evaluation provides the greatest challenge for the staff since it combines the most ordinary routines with the highest risk and speculation. The regularized aspects of data analysis are easily accessible to most. Typical statistics obtained for use in formative evaluation include measures of central tendency (usually averages) and measures of dispersion (often standard deviations). There have been reported instances, best left unspecified, of comparisons between pretest and posttest performance, with unabashed pride displayed in the case of significant findings. Where is the justification for such activity, except for communicating with the public, and only then in those instances where the staff has an unusually low estimate of the public's ability?

Such summaries of results are inadequate because they provide

only the grossest idea of how a program is working. Other suggestions are available for alternative data analysis procedures (Baker and Soloutos, 1974). In general, the data analysis should provide a clear picture of what happened during tryout. The best way to get a picture of anything is in visual display. Graphing data, using simplified frequency polygons from all sources, is recommended. In fact, overlays of data sources (provided, of course, that the same scale is used) can give the formative evaluation staff a sharp image of the patterns of effect that various sources of data produce. Process data can be correlated with outcome information dealing with both cognitive and affective dimensions of the program. Observer ratings can be compared with self-reports of students to obtain a finer resolution. Dividing graphs in terms of student entry skills or characteristics can provide another dimension for interpretation of results. Similarly, performance that can be attributed to discrete program elements may be graphed separately. Such displays may suggest to the formative evaluation staff that particular formats of program elements are, on the whole, less or more successful than others. The major benefit from subdividing data in terms of program elements or learner characteristics is that decisions relating to revision may be less costly to implement. When a program's performance is described only by a summary percentage, for example, 64 percent success, the staff has very little guidance for economic program revision. They can operate on their intuition, of course, and make some guesses. If data were presented in a way that indicated a particular component was not succeeding or that performance of an identifiable subgroup was artificially elevating or depressing scores, the formative evaluation would be somewhat more useful.

Even with fine graphs recorded according to program elements and learner characteristics, ideal courses of action are sometimes obscure. Data sources often do not agree with one another, no pattern in program effectiveness emerges, and the only positive data source left is cosmic energy unleashed by staff meditation. In other instances, when program revisions costs are considerably reduced, analysis of data by subdivision pays off.

Who is a Formative Evaluator?

Are there people on this planet for whom the designation "formative evaluator" is a source of pride? Is there a genus formative evaluators? Should there be? People who train evaluators seem to think

such people exist. Scriven (see chapter 1 in this volume) has recommended goal-free evaluators who come and study programs without regard to the rhetoric of goals. Stake (1973) has called for collaborative, responsive evaluation conducted in a client-centered environment. For projects staffed by skilled individuals experienced in R&D, external evaluation may be accomplished by nonstaff members through review of materials, goals, and measures, augmented by appropriate discussions with staff following such reviews. The kind of formative evaluation discussed in this paper, however, relates more to the kinds of decisions necessary to modify the insides of programs. Program insides, at the prototype stage, consist of instructional sequences. Program insides, at the operational stage, consist of program coordination and teacher-training requirements. In both instances, the persons most qualified to conduct formative evaluation are the development staff themselves. Blasphemy? They will be biased and self-serving? Even if they were, and even if such biases were not detected and made public at the next review of materials, I would choose the staff anytime. They can perform the *function of evaluation* without being named evaluators. The immediate benefit of such a role first relates to the mundane, but critical, concerns of scheduling. The staff's turn-around time is bound to be quicker. The more important consequence is that they have a specific interest in instruction itself. They should know what options are available. They have an idea of what kinds of information they really need. So, for reasons of practicality rather than elegance, I would opt for using staff as primary actors in formative evaluation activity.

Evaluating Formative Evaluation

I have always been taken with redundant titles, like research on research, innovating innovation, and, in this case, evaluating evaluation. Even if the meaning is dubious, repetition provides a sense of comfort. In the case of writing on evaluation, many authors feel obligated to step back a bit and view their pronouncements.

How does one evaluate the utility of formative evaluation? Research studies have been conducted to determine if formative evaluation is a useful activity. These have been more recently reviewed by Baker and Alkin (1973). The findings are encouraging if you want them to be. Evaluation and revision seem to improve instruction. Unfortunately, most of these controlled studies were conducted within

short-term or artificial environments, and so the general applicability of their findings is suspect. Instead of rushing to the research literature for support, instead, I would suggest that one observe the activities of the most successful projects in the most successful instructional research and development agencies. Most of the guidelines involved in this paper could be observed in such sites. One could obtain additional verification by involving instruction and evaluation people and asking for independent corroboration. Obviously, the sternest test is whether you can apply the ideas in your own settings, and whether adaptations required because of the reality of your own situation modify the ideas beyond recognition. What survives is probably what is worth something.

OPTIONAL EXERCISES

A series of six brief exercises is presented for your use. Three exercises pertain to data requirements for formative evaluation at the prototype tryout phase, and three relate to operational field tests. Cues are provided at the beginning of each set in order to facilitate success. Confirmation for each exercise is provided, although, of course, there is plenty of room for disagreement. The exercises have several purposes. First, they can clarify, by example, some of the guidelines presented in the expository section. Second, they can provide an opportunity for self-testing to determine if your understanding of the guidelines parallels my intentions. Last, they serve as a training mechanism to use with students or staff members who need a fast introduction to formative evaluation. Certainly these problems will not be sufficient to develop high-level skills, yet they might serve as a point of departure for more elaborate treatments.

PRACTICE EXERCISES FOR PROTOTYPE TESTING

In the problems that follow, you will be given a description of instructional materials, their objectives, the setting and purpose of their use. For each set of materials, a prototype test plan will be described. This plan may or may not be well designed. It will be your job to pinpoint weaknesses in the prototype test plan and to suggest ways to remedy those weaknesses.

Remember,

1. READ each problem.
2. DECIDE which aspects of the test plan are weak.
3. WRITE alternative test plan procedures to modify deficiencies.

After you have completed a problem,

COMPARE your answers with the confirming ones to verify the adequacy of your responses.

The following cues should help you with your modifications.

Directions:

1. Mark an X in the appropriate column.
2. If some aspect of the test plan is unsatisfactory, write a suggestion to remedy the plan on the lines provided.
3. Be brief and specific in your recommendations. For example, some revisions of a test plan might include adding practice exercises to student workbook, or changing the level of student subjects to third grade.

Satisfactory   Unsatisfactory

_____   _____   1. Number/type of participants
                              Suggestions: _____
                              _____
                              _____

_____   _____   2. Degree of readiness of materials
                              Suggestions: _____
                              _____
                              _____

_____   _____   3. Criterion test data collection
                              Suggestions: _____
                              _____
                              _____

_____   _____   4. Process data collection
                              Suggestions: _____
                              _____
                              _____

_____ _____ 5. Interview data collection

Suggestions: _____

_____

_____

_____ _____ 6. Attitude questionnaire data collection

Suggestions: _____

_____

_____

Problem 1

Description of Materials

Sound film: "Consider Yourself Invisible"

—presents 20 common dangers to cyclists and appropriate avoidance strategies for each hazard situation.

Written exercises to accompany the film

—require viewers to recommend in writing an avoidance strategy for each of 20 potential accident situations shown at the conclusion of the film.

Police-designed obstacle course

—replicates 20 hazard situations introduced in the film.

—requires participants to reproduce appropriate avoidance behaviors as each potential accident situation occurs.

Objective

When presented with 20 bicycle hazard situations, participants in the class will replicate avoidance strategies recommended in the instructional sequence.

Setting

YWCA adult bicycle safety class

Purpose

YWCA instructors and local police officials are considering the use of this class on a statewide basis. It is hoped that the results of this and subsequent field tests will result in affirmative action toward the institution of similar classes in police and other "Y" facilities.

Test Plan

Forty students in two bicycle safety classes will view the film, then complete and return the written exercises. The following week, each student will cycle through the obstacle course while police officers tally the number and type of errors committed by each participant. A YWCA instructor will question the participants about their perceptions of the film, exercises, and obstacle course. As a follow-up procedure, local police authorities will notify the "Y" of participants' cycle-related traffic violations during a six-month period following the class.
WHAT ASPECTS OF THIS TEST PLAN ARE UNSATISFACTORY?

Directions

Use the cues given earlier to indicate which aspects of the test plan are inadequate. For each weakness, *suggest a specific method of remediation.*

- -

Confirming answers

Satisfactory	Unsatisfactory	
_____	X	1. Number/type of participants Suggestions: drastically reduce number of students. No more than ten would be satisfactory.
_____	X	2. Degree of readiness of materials Suggestions: use film scripts or printed replica of film rather than completed movie—cost
X	_____	3. Criterion test data collection Suggestions: _____
X	_____	4. Process data collection Suggestions: _____
X	_____	5. Interview data collection Suggestions: _____
_____	X	6. Attitude questionnaire data collection Suggestions: _____

Problem 2

Description of Materials

Self-instructional illustrated technical handbook
—describes and illustrates each step of the three processes necessary to complete the objectives.
Teacher's guide to accompany the handbook
—suggests specific methods for students' use of handbook.
—provides additional activities intended to clarify each of the three procedures treated in the handbook.
Practice observation forms (three types)
—list errors of commission and omission possible during each of the required procedures.

Objectives

Upon finishing the instructional sequence, students will successfully complete each of the following tasks:
1. adjust the timing of an engine,
2. gap spark plugs according to specifications,
3. change a battery.

Setting

Junior college vocational education course in automotive repair

Purpose

Teachers in the vocational education department are considering the adoption of this handbook as a supplement to their old "lecture style" presentation. A prototype test is necessary to determine the effectiveness of the materials before they are tried out in all six automotive repair classes at the college.

Test Plan

One teacher and six vocational education students will participate in the test. The students will complete the dittoed technical handbook exactly as suggested in the teacher's guide. In addition, the teacher will include in the instruction all of the supplementary activities suggested in the teacher's guide. Each student will be required to complete each of the three tasks while being observed and rated by classmates using the practice observation forms. At the conclusion of the course, students will complete a questionnaire assessing their feelings about the instruction. Subsequently, the instructor will lead a round table discussion of the materials.
WHAT ASPECTS OF THIS TEST PLAN ARE UNSATISFACTORY?

Directions

Use the cues given earlier to indicate which aspects of the test plan are inadequate. For each weakness, *suggest a specific method of remediation.*
- -

Confirming answer

In your recommendations, you should have included the following information:
1. Criterion test data collection procedures were inadequate. This problem could be solved by an additional observation and rating of criterion tasks by an evaluator, in addition to the practice observations done by the students.
2. Process data collection procedures were not provided in the test plan. To alleviate this weakness, practice exercises for each important step in the three procedures could be added to the written material contained in the handbook.

The number and type of participants, degree of readiness of the materials, interview data collection and attitude questionnaire data collection procedures were adequately provided for in the test plan.

Problem 3

Description of Materials

Programmed instruction booklets (6)
—explain the balance of a single color and its complement.
Photographs to accompany each booklet (15 for each, 90 total)
—demonstrate acceptable and unacceptable levels of color in a photograph.
Written exercises to be used with each booklet
—require trainee to lable photographs from least to most amount of a given color.
—require trainee to differentiate "acceptable" from "unacceptable" levels of color.

Objective

Trainees will judge as acceptable or unacceptable the amount of red, green, blue, magenta, yellow, or cyan in color prints. Judgment of the trainees will coincide with standard presented in the instructional sequence.

Setting

Independent color processing laboratory

Purpose

Five graduate students in education have been asked as a part of their field studies to determine whether a commercially developed programmed instruction kit needs to be adapted for use with a group of bilingual employees. The kit is designed to train individuals as professional color print inspectors in laboratories where color printing is done by machine. A large laboratory wishes to purchase the kits if they prove to be "cost effective" (the instruction must prove to be extremely successful in a short amount of time to compensate for the high price of the kits). The developers of the materials are willing to comply with minor revisions indicated by the results of the prototype test.

Test Plan

Each bilingual trainee will first be tested for partial color-blindness prior to beginning the instruction. Three newly-hired employees will then use the programmed instruction kit exactly as suggested in the instruction booklet, completing the exercises included in each. After the entire sequence has been finished, the employees will apply the skills they have learned by beginning their jobs as professional print inspectors.
WHAT ASPECTS OF THIS TEST PLAN ARE UNSATISFACTORY?

Directions

Use the cues given earlier to indicate which aspects of the test plan are inadequate. For each weakness, *suggest a specific method of remediation.*
- -

Confirming answer

In your recommendations, you should have included information similar to that given below:

1. Criterion test data collection procedures were not present. You might have suggested adding a criterion task such as mixing up the photos that accompany each booklet and requiring the trainees to label them as "acceptable" or "unacceptable" according to the standards given in the booklet.
2. There were no provisions for acquiring interview data from the employees. It would be necessary, therefore, to design an interview form and collect attitudinal data included on that form after the instructional sequence had been completed.
3. There was no opportunity for the trainees to express feelings about the instruction in an anonymous fashion. An open-ended questionnaire could be filled out by the trainees before they begin their jobs in the laboratory to remove this deficiency in the plan.

The number and type of participants, degree of readiness of the materials (the developers indicated a willingness to revise, if necessary), and within-program data collection procedures were adequately provided for in the test plan.

PRACTICE EXERCISES FOR FIELD TESTING

In the problems that follow, you will be given descriptions of several field test plans which may or may not be well designed. It will be your job to pinpoint weaknesses in the test plan and to write modifications that could remediate those weaknesses.

Remember,

1. READ each problem.
2. DECIDE which aspects of the test plan are weak.
3. WRITE alternative test plan procedures to modify deficiencies.

After you have completed a problem,

COMPARE your answers with the confirming ones to verify the adequacy of your responses.

The following cues should help you with your modifications.

Directions:

1. Mark an X in the appropriate column.
2. If some aspect of the test plan is unsatisfactory, write a suggestion to correct the deficiency on the lines provided.
3. Be brief and specific in your recommendations. An example of appropriate test plan revisions is: Change testing situation to replicate class setting.

Test Plan Status

Satisfactory	Unsatisfactory	
		Data sources (student)
_____	_____	1. Performance on criterion test
		Suggestions: _____
		_____
		_____
_____	_____	2. Process responses
		Suggestions: _____
		_____
		_____
_____	_____	3. Reactions to attitude/satisfaction questionnaire
		Suggestions: _____
		_____
		_____
		Data sources (instructor)
_____	_____	4. Record of performance
		Suggestions: _____
		_____
		_____

_____   _____   5. Responses to questionnaire
                         Suggestions: _____
                         _____
                         _____

_____   _____   6. Interview or debriefing
                         Suggestions: _____
                         _____
                         _____

                              Field test principles
_____   _____   7. Program components to be integrated
                         Suggestions: _____
                         _____
                         _____

_____   _____   8. Program use in intended setting
                         Suggestions: _____
                         _____
                         _____

Problem 4

Test Plan Description

A major university is developing a set of materials to train families of kidney patients to operate a dialysis machine which enables patients to receive home treatment. Successful prototype testing has already taken place. The developers wish to ensure the practicality of the training program in a hospital setting, using medical personnel as instructors. Eighty nurses in 20 hospitals have agreed to participate in the field test. The training materials include:

  an instructor's guide,
  an introductory film,
  self-instructional booklets for trainees (2),
  simulation exercise outlines (5).

All materials will be used within the hospital. Family members will participate in the instruction under the direct supervision of a doctor or nurse. At the conclusion of instruction, the instructors will administer both a written and practical test of proficiency in machine use. Finally, completed exercises within the booklets will be returned to the developers.

WHAT ASPECTS OF THIS TEST PLAN ARE UNSATISFACTORY?

Directions

Use the cues given earlier to indicate which aspects of the test plan are inadequate. For each weakness, *suggest a specific method of remediation.*

- -

Confirming answers

Test plan status		
Satisfactory	Unsatisfactory	**Data sources** (student)

Satisfactory	Unsatisfactory	
X	___	1. Performance on criterion test Suggestions: _____ _____ _____
___	X	2. Process responses Suggestions: observer could attend to learn-er reactions
X	___	3. Reactions to attitude/satisfaction question-naire Suggestions: have students complete ques-tionnaire after instruction is completed

Data sources (instructor)

Satisfactory	Unsatisfactory	
___	X	4. Record of performance Suggestions: trained observer could monitor instruction, note difficulties, strong points, etc.
___	X	5. Responses to questionnaire Suggestions: teachers should complete ques-tionnaire after instructional sequence is over
___	X	6. Interview or debriefing Suggestions: observer could also act as in-terviewer at conclusion of training sessions

Field test principles

Satisfactory	Unsatisfactory	
X	___	7. Program components to be integrated Suggestions: _____ _____ _____
X	___	8. Program use in intended setting Suggestions: _____ _____ _____ _____

Problem 5

Test Plan Description

A free-lance photographer has designed a looseleaf binder for high school students which teaches the fundamentals of composition and lighting through the

use of text, photographs, and written exercises. In addition, the materials include slides and an extensive teacher guide. Several prototype tests have rendered the materials instructionally valuable. Now, the package is to be operationally tested by five photography classes at the junior college level. Each of 150 students will complete the activities and exercises suggested in the binder and will return both written responses and actual photographs which exhibit knowledge of the principles and techniques expounded in the materials. Trained assistants will act as independent observers during each of the classes, making note of teacher activities, periods of difficulty and success. The assistants will also interview the instructors at the conclusion of each session to obtain further information regarding instructor satisfaction and/or difficulties in using the materials.
WHAT ASPECTS OF THIS TEST PLAN ARE UNSATISFACTORY?

Directions

Use the cues given earlier to indicate which aspects of the test plan are inadequate. For each weakness, *suggest a specific method of remediation.*

- -

Confirming answers

The test plan was inadequate in the following areas:
1. Students were not given an opportunity to respond anonymously to the instructional sequence. A questionnaire could be provided for this purpose at the conclusion of instruction.
2. Teachers need a similar opportunity to air their views of the materials without revealing their identity. Again, a questionnaire would effectively fill this gap.
3. The program plan does not test the program in the setting for which it is intended. The subjects in the test plan are junior college students, while the intended user group consists of high school students. To ensure the validity of the field test, the materials should be tested in a high school classroom situation.

Problem 6

The history department of a large university is developing a college-level series of short texts and tape recordings which teach fifteen concepts related to 19th-century U.S. immigration. An instructor's guide provides four alternative methods of presenting the instruction. These methods are based upon the following instructional techniques *a)* lecture, *b)* discussion, *c)* simulation, and *d)* independent study. The tape scripts and rough versions of the text and instructor's guide already have been tested. The department now needs to analyze the effectiveness of what they hope will be their final version of the components. One hundred and ten undergraduate history students will complete pre- and posttest items for each of 15 objectives. Five professors will select the method of instruction they wish to use. Each has agreed to be observed and interviewed by per-

sons associated with the development project, and to complete a questionnaire concerning the effectiveness and usability of the materials.
WHAT ASPECTS OF THIS TEST PLAN ARE UNSATISFACTORY?

Directions

Use the cues given earlier to indicate which aspects of the test plan are inadequate. For each weakness, *suggest a specific method of remediation.*

- -

Confirming answer

The test plan in this problem was deficient in the following respects:

1. There is currently no provision for within-program student response. If student performance levels were to drop during the field test, the present plan would not provide sufficient information for effective location and removal of the instructional problem. Such provisions could be made by written exercises, or a recording of the discussions or simulations to see if students were acquiring specific concepts.
2. Students should be given the opportunity to complete an anonymous questionnaire assessing the instruction.
3. Although the program components are to be integrated (texts and tapes will presumably be used in conjunction with one another), plans for the professors' selection of an instructional technique should probably be changed. At present, it is quite possible that not all the methods would be selected. In addition, the number of professors in any treatment might be expanded. The record of teacher performance data would not reflect the full range of possibilities for the instruction.

REFERENCES

Baker, Eva L., 1973. "The technology of instructional development," in R. M. W. Travers (ed.), *Second handbook of research on teaching.* Chicago: Rand McNally.

———, and Alkin, Marvin C., 1973. "Formative evaluation of instructional development," *AV Communication Review,* 21.4(Winter):389-418.

Bank, Adrianne, Eu, Laurel, and Mann, Thomas, 1974. "Communication processes and formative evaluation." Paper presented at the annual meeting of the American Educational Research Association, Chicago, 25 pp.

Hively, W., Maxwell, G., Rabehl, G., Sension, D., and Lundin, S., 1973. *Domain-referenced curriculum evaluation: A technical handbook and a case study from the MINNEMAST project.* CSE Monograph Series in Evaluation, No. 1. Los Angeles: Center for the Study of Evaluation.

———, Patterson, H. L., and Page, S. H., 1968. "A 'universe-defined' system of arithmetic achievement tests." *Journal of Educational Measurement,* 5.4:275-290.

Joint Committee on Programmed Instruction and Teaching Machines (American Educational Research Association, American Psychological Association, Department of Audio-Visual Instruction, National Education Association), 1963. "Criteria for assessing programmed instructional material." *Audiovisual Instruction,* 8(February):84-89.

Quellmalz, Edys, and Hanson, Ralph, 1974. "Expanding the formative evaluation data base." Paper presented at the annual meeting of the American Educational Research Association, Chicago.

Schutz, R. E., 1970. "The nature of educational development." *Journal of Research and Development in Education,* 3.2:39-64.

Scriven, M., 1967. *The methodology of evaluation.* AERA Monograph Series on Curriculum Evaluation, No. 1. Chicago: Rand McNally.

Stake, R. E., 1972. "Responsive evaluation." University of Illinois, unpublished manuscript.

Wardrop, James, 1974. "An evolutionary model of instructional development." Paper presented at the annual meeting of the American Educational Research Association, Chicago.